ENCYCLOPEDIA OF COMPUTER SCIENCE AND TECHNOLOGY

VOLUME 39

ENCYCLOPEDIA OF COMPUTER SCIENCE AND TECHNOLOGY

EXECUTIVE EDITORS

Allen Kent   *James G. Williams*

UNIVERSITY OF PITTSBURGH
PITTSBURGH, PENNSYLVANIA

ADMINISTRATIVE EDITOR

Carolyn M. Hall

ARLINGTON, TEXAS

VOLUME 39
SUPPLEMENT 24

CRC Press
Taylor & Francis Group
Boca Raton London New York

CRC Press is an imprint of the
Taylor & Francis Group, an **informa** business

CRC Press
Taylor & Francis Group
6000 Broken Sound Parkway NW, Suite 300
Boca Raton, FL 33487-2742

First issued in paperback 2019

ISBN-13: 978-0-8247-2292-0 (hbk)
ISBN-13: 978-0-367-40034-7 (pbk)

LIBRARY OF CONGRESS CATALOG CARD NUMBER: 74-29436

**Visit the Taylor & Francis Web site at
http://www.taylorandfrancis.com**

**and the CRC Press Web site at
http://www.crcpress.com**

CONTENTS OF VOLUME 39

CONTRIBUTORS TO VOLUME 39

CESARE ALIPPI, Ph.D. CESTIA, CNR, Milan, Italy: *Neural Networks for Identification, Control, Robotics, and Signal and Image Processing*

HAMID R. ARABNIA, Ph.D. Associate Professor, Department of Computer Science, The University of Georgia, Athens, Georgia: *The Transputer Family of Products and Their Applications in Building a High-Performance Computer*

SALVADOR BAYARRI, Ph.D. Institute of Traffic and Road Safety (INTRAS), Universidad de Valencia, Valencia, Spain: *Virtual Reality in Driving Simulation*

HELMUT BECKER, Ph.D. Aachen, Germany: *A Semantic Justification of the Fuzzy Control Method*

JAMES E. BOWEN Compengserv Ltd., Ottawa, Ontario, Canada: *Real-Time Situation Management: A Java Application*

COLIN BOYD, Ph.D. Lecturer, School of Data Communication, Queensland University of Technology, Brisbane, Queensland, Australia: *Measuring the Strength of Cryptosystems*

INMACULADA COMA Department of Computer Science, Universidad de Valencia, Valencia, Spain: *Virtual Reality in Driving Simulation*

ED P. DAWSON Director, Information Security Research Centre, Queensland University of Technology, Brisbane, Queensland, Australia: *Measuring the Strength of Cryptosystems*

LEO EGGHE Professor, Limburgs Universitair Centrum, Diepenbeek, Belgium: *Sensitivity Aspects of Inequality Measures*

IOANNIS Z. EMIRIS, Ph.D. Institut National de Recherche en Informatique et Automatique, Sophia-Antipolis, France: *Symbolic–Numeric Algebra for Polynomials*

MARCOS FERNÁNDEZ Institute of Robotics, Universidad de Valencia, Valencia, Spain: *Virtual Reality in Driving Simulation*

ASHISH GUPTA, Ph.D.   Vice President of Engineering, Junglee, Sunnyvale, California: *Maintenance of Materialized Views: Problems, Techniques, and Applications*

HELEN M. GUSTAFSON, Ph.D.   Lecturer, School of Mathematics, Queensland University of Technology, Brisbane, Queensland, Australia: *Measuring the Strength of Cryptosystems*

RONALD P. HIGUERA   Director Acquisition Risk Management, Software Engineering Institute, Carnegie Mellon University, Pittsburgh, Pennsylvania: *Risk Management*

JOHN R. KOZA   Consulting Professor, Computer Science Department, Stanford University, Stanford, Connecticut: *Genetic Programming*

PIERRE L'ECUYER   Professor, Département d'Informatique et de Recherche Opérationelle, Université de Montréal: *Uniform Random Number Generation*

EE-PENG LIM, Ph.D.   Lecturer and Director, Center for Advanced Information Systems, School of Applied Science, Nanyang Technological University, Singapore: *Entity Identification*

HUAN LIU, Ph.D.   Information Systems and Computer Science, National University of Singapore, Singapore: *A Family of Efficient Rule Generators*

JIEPING LU, Ph.D. Candidate   Department of Industrial and Manufacturing Systems Engineering, Louisiana State University, Baton Rouge, Louisiana: *Knowledge Acquisition Problem in Monotone Boolean Systems*

RAMI MELHEM   Department of Computer Science, University of Pittsburgh, Pittsburgh, Pennsylvania: *Massively Parallel Processing Using Optical Interconnections*

JOHN N. MORDESON   Professor, Department of Mathematics and Computer Science, Creighton University, Omaha, Nebraska: *Trees, Cycles, and Cocycles of Fuzzy Graphs*

INDERPAL SINGH MUMICK, Ph.D.   President and Chief Technology Officer, Savera Systems, Summit, New Jersey: *Maintenance of Materialized Views: Problems, Techniques, and Applications*

PREMCHAND S. NAIR   Associate Professor, Department of Mathematics and Computer Science, Creighton University, Omaha, Nebraska: *Trees, Cycles, and Cocycles of Fuzzy Graphs*

VINCENZO PIURI, Ph.D.   Associate Professor, Department of Electronics and Information, Politecnico di Milano, Milan, Italy: *Neural Networks for Identification, Control, Robotics, and Signal and Image Processing*

CHARLES SALISBURY   Department of Computer Science, University of Pittsburgh, Pittsburgh, Pennsylvania: *Massively Parallel Processing Using Optical Interconnections*

VALERY SOLOVIEV, Ph.D.   Assistant Professor, Computer Science Department, North Dakota State University, Fargo, North Dakota: *An Incremental Memory Allocation Method for Mixed Workloads*

BOLESLAW K. SZYMANSKI   Professor, Computer Science Department, Rensselaer Polytechnic Institute, Troy, New York: *Scalable Computers*

EVANGELOS TRIANTAPHYLLOU   Associate Professor, Department of Industrial and Manufacturing Systems Engineering, Louisiana State University, Baton Rouge, Louisiana: *Knowledge Acquisition Problem in Monotone Boolean Systems*

MANSOUR K. ZAND   Associate Professor, Computer Science Department, College of Information Science and Technology, University of Nebraska at Omaha, Omaha, Nebraska: *An Introduction to Software Reuse*

ENCYCLOPEDIA OF COMPUTER SCIENCE AND TECHNOLOGY

VOLUME 39

ENTITY IDENTIFICATION

INTRODUCTION

In modern organizations, one can often find databases developed independently at different times by different people to satisfy different application requirements. As the organizations evolve to cope with new challenges, new applications emerge and they may require information consolidated or integrated from multiple legacy databases. To realize these new applications, one may have to derive an integrated database from the legacy databases. This process is known as *database integration*. Database integration is performed only once when the resultant integrated database is materialized with all applications migrated to or developed on the materialized integrated database. However, when the integrated database is defined as a virtual view on top of legacy databases, part of the database integration (i.e., integration of instances) can only be carried out when instances of the integrated database are required during query processing. A distributed database system that supports queries on such a virtual integrated view is known as a *multidatabase system* (1–3).

As part of the database integration process, one has to compare records from different legacy databases in order to decide whether they represent the same real-world entities; this process is known as *entity identification* (4). Entity identification is necessary because independent databases often contain overlapping information about entities in the real world. These overlapping but possibly inconsistent information have to be resolved before they can be used by the new global application.

Database Integration Process

As shown in Figure 1, the database integration process consists of *schema integration* (5) and *instance integration*. The former resolves the differences between the meta-description of legacy databases, whereas the latter resolves the difference between the database instances. The schema integration process examines the elements of the schemas of different databases and derives the schema of the integrated database. The instance integration consists of two subprocesses: entity identification and attribute-value conflict resolution. Attribute-value conflict resolution refers to the merging of attribute values from different instances representing the same property of a real-world entity. Hence, it can only be performed after entity identification. As there is only a schema for every database and the schema is usually fixed at database creation, schema integration is done only once for the databases involved. In contrast, instance integration involves all instances in the databases. Effective and efficient techniques to perform entity identification and attribute-value conflict resolution are, therefore, important.

In this article, entity identification in database integration is described in detail. The remainder of the article is organized as follows. A formal definition of the entity identification problem and a motivating example are given in the second section. The

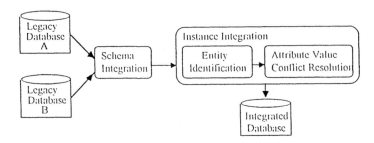

FIGURE 1   Database integration process.

knowledge required for entity identification and a taxonomy of entity identification techniques will be introduced in the third and fourth sections, respectively. Based on the
taxonomy, one can evaluate and compare the various entity identification techniques.
Conclusions and the future research directions of entity identification will be discussed
in the fifth section.

ENTITY IDENTIFICATION PROBLEM AND MOTIVATING EXAMPLE

The objective of entity identification is to determine the correspondence between object
instances from multiple databases. In the case of a relational data model, real-world
entities can be represented as tuples in relations from different preexisting databases.
Each relation is expected to have one or more candidate keys to uniquely identify its
tuples. Each candidate key may consist of one or more attributes. In this article, we
assume that schema integration has been performed and real-world entities of the same
type can be represented by at most one relation in each database. If two tuples from
different relations model the same real-world entity, they are said to *match*. Let *e1* and
e2 be two entities modeled by two tuples. We write ($e1 \equiv e2$) when *e1* and *e2* refer to
the same real-world entity.

In the following, we show an example of the entity identification problem. It serves
to illustrate the complexity of the entity identification problem as well as to illustrate the
various proposed entity identification techniques. Consider the relations *R* and *S* from
databases *DB1* and *DB2*, respectively. Both relations contain tuples that describe computer companies in the real-world. The content of *R* and *S* are shown in Table 1. Relation
R has (**Cname, Street**) as its candidate key, whereas relation *S* has (**Cname, District**)
as its candidate key. The key attributes are underlined in Table 1. To integrate relations
R and *S*, we first have to determine which tuples in *R* and *S*, respectively, describe the
same company entity in the integrated world.

In the above example, it is clear that the simple approach of matching the common
candidate key of the two tables does not work since both tables do not share a common
candidate key. Although the tables share a common key attribute **Cname**, one may not
conveniently conclude that Cybersoft in *R* and Cybersoft in *S* refer to the same company.
If a tuple (Cybersoft, Hillview Ave, Databases) is inserted into *R*, we will have a situation
where one tuple in *S* matches two tuples in *R*. It is not clear which of them is the correct

TABLE 1   Content of Relations *R* and *S*

Relation *R*

Cname	**Street**	**Product**
Cybersoft	Ford Road	Internet
Neurowave	Queens Street	Expert Systems
Webcorp	Pioneer Ave	Databases

Relation *S*

Cname	**District**	**Manager**
Cybersoft	Downtown	John
Digitech	East	Michael
Webcorp	North	Smith

match. With this example, we illustrate that entity identification in general can be a complex problem. Extra semantic information about the real world and databases will be required to carry out the entity identification.

KNOWLEDGE REQUIRED FOR ENTITY IDENTIFICATION

Entity identification is essentially a matching problem. However, unlike other matching problems, entity identification does not usually have a straightforward set of matching criteria. To match tuples from different databases, one has to understand not only the domains of real-world entities represented by the legacy databases but also the integrated domain. Entity identification can further be complicated by possible erroneous data in the legacy databases. In the following, we describe identity rules and instance-level attribute knowledge as the two important classes of knowledge required by entity identification methods.

Identity Rules

Identity rules define the matching criteria to be satisfied by a pair of records, from different databases, in order for them to be considered as modeling the same real-world entity. Clearly, every entity identification method must adopt some matching criteria to match records from different databases although their matching criteria may not be the same.

Example 1

For example, if *Cname* is only key in both relations *R* and *S*, an identity rule that could possibly be used is that, as long as two records share a common *Cname* value, they are considered to be representing the same real-world entity. An informal representation of this identity rule is given below. This type of identity rules is also known to be *key based*.

(*r1* & *r2* have identical *Cname* values) *implies r1* & *r2* represent the same real-world entity, where *r1* & *r2* are records from *R* and *S*, respectively.   □

The above identity rule is generic, as it can be applied to multiple database records in *R* and *S*. Identity rules can also be specific if they are only applicable to specific database records.

Example 2

If it is known that Smith manages only one company on Pioneer Ave. that sells database products and there is only one company on Pioneer Ave., the following identity rule can be formulated:

(r1.Street = "Pioneer Ave." and r1.Product = "Databases" and r2.Manager = "Smith") *implies* r1 & r2 represent the same company entity where r1 and r2 are records from *R* and *S*, respectively.

Unlike the previous example, the above identity rule can only be applied to specific database instances in *R* and *S*.   □

Typically, identity rules are determined by the users who can be legacy database administrators or database integrators.* Hence, the correctness of these rules has to be verified by the users. In the fourth section, we will describe different types of identity rule in detail.

Instance-Level Attribute Knowledge

Instance-level attribute knowledge refers to knowledge about attribute values within the domain of real-world entities modeled by a legacy database. This attribute knowledge allows one to infer attribute values which can be used to match database instances from a legacy database with database instances from another legacy database. Instance-level attribute knowledge is particularly useful when a given identity rule requires attribute values which cannot be found directly in the original database content.

An example is if there is an identity rule that states the matching criteria

(*r1* & *r2* have the same *Cname* and *District* values) *implies r1* & *r2* represent the same real-world entity.

In this case, without *District* values, it is not impossible to match records in *R* with records in *S*. However, if it is known that Pioneer Ave is located in the North district, the company Webcorp in *R* can be matched with the company Webcorp in *S*. This instance-level attribute knowledge can be expressed as.

r.Street is "Pioneer Ave" *implies* r.District is "North"

Unlike identity rules, instance level attribute knowledge may not always be used in an entity identification method. It is only used in entity identification methods that adopt identity rules which require attribute values not found in some legacy databases.

---

*Henceforth, the word user refers to legacy database administrator or database integrator.

A TAXONOMY OF ENTITY IDENTIFICATION METHODS

Although entity identification is a relatively new research problem, there has been a number of different solution methods proposed by database integration researchers. Most of these entity identification methods have been discussed in isolation and they are proposed under different integration assumptions. A taxonomy of entity identification methods is therefore necessary to determine the appropriate entity identification method to be adopted for any given integration scenario. In this article, we derive a taxonomy of entity identification methods based on the different categories of identity rules adopted by the methods. Identity rules can be classified based on their *matching criteria* and *precision*.

The matching criteria of identity rules can be one of the following:

1. Key based: This refers to the use of common candidate key(s) to match tuples from different relations. Key-based matching criteria are based on the assumption that tuples sharing a common candidate key value represent the same real-world entity. However, key-based matching criteria only apply to relations sharing common candidate keys.

2. Attribute based: This refers to the use of common attributes to match tuples from different relations. Attribute-based matching criteria is based on the assumption that tuples sharing a lot of similar attribute values represent the same real-world entity. This matching criteria does not rely on common candidate keys. Instead, it requires relations to be integrated together share a number of common attributes which can be used to characterize the real-world entities represented by the tuples. Hence, these attributes are required to be highly *discriminatory*.

3. User Specified: User-specified matching criteria provide the flexibility for users to determine matching tuples by specifying one or more identity rules that are customized for the domains of entities represented by the relations to be integrated. Subsuming both key-based and attribute-based matching criteria, user-specified matching criteria require users to have a good understanding of the integration domain. Furthermore, entity identification methods adopting user-specified matching criteria usually require more processing overhead then those adopting the other matching criteria.

The precision of an identity rule determines how accurately the rule can be used to determine matching tuples representing the same real-world entities. In terms of precision, identity rules can be classified to be one of the following:

1. Precise: A precise identity rule provides full accuracy in determining whether two tuples represent the same real-world entity. No probabilistic or uncertain element exists in such a identity rule. So far, the identity rule examples given in the previous subsections are precise. Ideally, all identity rules should be precise. However, in reality, not all identity rules could be precise because legacy databases may contain inaccurate or incorrect information. Moreover, by relying on precise identity rules alone, an entity identification method may not be able to suggest to the users the tuples that are *likely* to represent the same real-world entities.

2. Imprecise: To cater to integration scenarios in which imprecise matching tuples are useful and legacy databases can be inaccurate, imprecise identity rules can be used. For example, an international bank officer may wish to determine if

bank records from different branch office databases belong to the same persons. In this entity identification process, it would be desirable to utilize imprecise knowledge to derive those possibly matching banking records. As there are different ways of modeling imprecise information, different approaches of accommodating imprecise identity rules have been introduced by different proposed entity identification methods. For example, identity rules can be formulated based on probability theory (6), fuzzy theory (7), evidential reasoning theory (8), and so forth.

Based on the above classification of identity rules, a taxonomy for entity identification methods has been derived and used to classify a number of previously proposed entity identification methods as shown in Figure 2. Each class of entity identification methods will be further described in the following subsections.

Entity Identification Using Key-Based Precise Identity Rules

Entity identification methods using key-based, precise identity rules are the simplest to adopt in database integration. They are based on the assumption that common key(s) can be found between relations to be integrated together, and the key(s) adequately identifies the real-world entities modeled by tuples in the relations. Examples of such entity identification methods have been used in the Multibase project (9,10) and other database integration research (11–13).

In Refs. 9 and 10, a functional data model known as Daplex is used to represent local views and integrated views. Each local view is defined for each local database in order to homogenize the local databases. Each integrated view is defined by merging multiple related local views. A Daplex schema consists of entities and their functions. These functions correspond to the attribute and foreign key concepts, respectively, in the relational model. To perform entity identification on records from two related local views, a *merge condition* that compares the keys of the local views has to be specified. This merge condition is essentially a key-based, precise identity rule.

In Ref. 11, an instance integration approach that employs *partial values* to resolve attribute-value conflicts has been introduced. A partial value is considered as a finite set of possible values such that exactly one of the values in the set is the true value. To determine if two tuples represent the same real-world entity, a common candidate key is

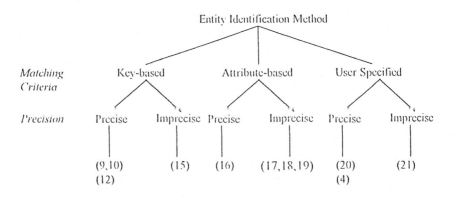

FIGURE 2   Taxonomy of entity identification methods.

used. Further extensions of this approach (12,13) continue to use common candidate key to perform entity identification.

As the entity identification methods using key-based, precise identity rules are relatively simple to implement, it has been widely used in multidatabase systems which support queries on virtual views defined on legacy databases (9,14). In this case, local instances are integrated during query processing. Hence, a simple entity identification method will facilitate the implementation of multidatabase query processors.

Entity Identification Using Key-Based Imprecise Identity Rules

Entity identification methods using key-based, imprecise identity rules, liked its precise counterpart, are based on the assumption that the key values of tuples can uniquely identify the real-world entities the tuples represent. However, due to inaccuracies in the content of legacy databases, it is sometime necessary to allow some imprecision when the key-based identity rules are used in matching tuples. In the following, we describe a probabilistic approach to introduce imprecision into key-based entity identification.

Example 3

Let **EmpA(<u>Name, Dept</u>, Salary)** and **EmpB(<u>Name, Dept</u>, Salary)** be relations from databases A and B, respectively. Because *Name* and *Dept* together form the common candidate key of *EmpA* and *EmpB*, a conventional entity identification method using key-based precise identity rule would require two tuples having the same values for their *Name* and *Dept* attributes before they can be determined to represent the same real-world entity. An entity identification method using a key-based, imprecise identity rule may instead assign different weights [i.e., $w(Name)$ and $w(Dept)$] to attributes in the common key (i.e., *Name* and *Dept*) such that sum of the weights is 1 [i.e., $w(Name + w(Dept) = 1$]. These weights indicate the differences in discriminatory power among key attributes. Given tuples $ta = (John, Sales, 10000)$ and $tb = (John, Marketing, 12000)$ from *EmpA* and *EmpB*, respectively, their differences can be represented by a binary comparison vector of two components for *Name* and *Dept* attributes. A vector component is assigned a unit value if there is no difference between the corresponding attribute values in the two tuples being compared. Otherwise, a zero is assigned. In the case of *ta* and *tb*, the comparison vector is $(1, 0)$. By multiplying the comparison vector with the attribute weights [i.e., $1*w(Name) + 0*w(Dept)$], a final value between 0 and 1 is obtained and it represents how likely the two tuples represent the same real-world entity. □

In Ref. 15, a simple method of using imprecise identity rules for entity identification was described. The proposed method only considers person name to be the only common candidate key between two relations to be integrated. In other words, there is only one component in the comparison vector and the weight assigned to the name attribute is 1. However, in this proposed method, the comparison between two different name values does not simply yield a binary value. By breaking down the name attribute value into first, middle, and last names, and by comparing them separately, the method attempts to quantify the name value difference by some numeric value. Unfortunately, the exact formula used to compare two name values was not given in Ref. 15.

Entity Identification Using Attribute-Based Precise Identity Rules

This category of entity identification methods make use of common attributes between two relations to determine if their tuples represent the same real-world entities. Although these methods do not require the common key assumption, they rely on the assumption that tuples representing the same real-world entities should have identical values for their common attributes. When common key exists between two relations, the key attributes will be compared in these methods. As other common attributes will also be compared, entity identification methods using attribute-based precise identity rules impose matching criteria stricter than their key-based counterparts. In other words, tuples determined to represent the same real-world entities by key comparison may be determined otherwise by common attribute comparison.

In Ref. 16, Wang and Madnick proposed an entity identification method that compares common attributes between two relations in order to determine tuple pairs that represent the same real-world entities. In cases where there are too few common attributes between two relations for tuple comparisons, some heuristic rules can be introduced to increase the accuracy of entity identification.

Example 4

Let **EmpA(Ename, Age, Qualification, Dept)** and **EmpB(Eid, Ename, Age, Position, JobDesc)** be relations from two different legacy databases. Their tuples are shown in Table 2.

By comparing the common attributes (i.e., *Ename* and *Age*) between *EmpA* and *EmpB*, the tuple (*John, 24, M.Sc., R&D*) in *EmpA* can be matched with three tuples in *EmpB*. To improve the matching accuracy, the following heuristic rules can be applied to the three tuple pairs that share common *Ename* = John and *Age* = 24 attribute values.

Heuristic rule 1: Business planning is not one of the R&D activities.
Heuristic rule 2: A researcher must have a Ph.D. degree.

Heuristic rule 1 determines that (*1, John, 24, Manager, Business planning*) cannot match with (*John, 24, M.Sc., R&D*). Heuristic rule 2 determines that (*3, John, 24, Researcher, Proposal writing*) cannot match with (*John, 24, M.Sc., R&D*). By removing the inaccurate matching pairs, only the second tuple from *EmpB* is determined to match with the John tuple in *EmpA*.   □

TABLE 2   Content of EmpA and EmpB

EmpA			
Ename	**Age**	**Qualification**	**Dept**
John	24	M.Sc.	R&D
Mary	30	M.B.A.	Marketing

EmpB				
Eid	**Ename**	**Age**	**Position**	**JobDesc**
1	John	24	Manager	Business planning
2	John	24	Engineer	Project design
3	John	24	Researcher	Proposal writing
4	Mary	30	Salesperson	Product advertisement

Entity Identification Using Attribute-Based Imprecise Identity Rules

To model the uncertainty associated with the entity identification process, a probabilistic framework of comparing attributes of tuples from different legacy databases has been proposed by Chatterjee (17–19). Similar to the probabilistic entity identification method described in the subsection Entity Identification Using Key-Based Imprecise Identity Rules Chatterjee's method derives a comparison vector involving all common attributes between tuples. The major assumption behind this method is that tuples representing the same real-world entity should have identical values for *most* of their common attributes.

Let M be all pairs of tuples such that each pair of tuples represents a real-world entity. Let t be a pair of tuples $(t1, t2)$. The comparison vector constructed for t is denoted by $v(t)$. Let $v–i(t)$ be the ith component (the ith common attribute) of the $v(t)$. The precision of the matching tuple pair t is measured by *tuple probability* denoted by *Ptuple(t)*. Formally,

$$Ptuple(t) = Pr\{t \in M \mid v(t)\}$$

Using Bayes' Theorem,

$$Ptuple(t) = Pr\{t \in M \mid v(t)\} = \frac{Pr\{v(t) \mid t \in M\} \cdot Pr\{t \in M\}}{Pr\{v(t)\}}.$$

To evaluate *Ptuple(t)*, $Pr\{v(t)\}$, $Pr\{t \in M\}$, and $Pr\{v(t) \mid t \in M\}$ have to be estimated accordingly. In Ref. 18, algorithms to estimate these probabilities using the distribution information of comparison vectors are given.

Entity Identification Using User-Specified Precise Identity Rules

In general, entity identification methods using key-based and attribute-based identity rules are not difficult to implement. However, their applicability is sometime quite restricted because they can only be used in situations where common keys or attributes are able to determine matching tuples. To overcome this drawback, entity identification methods using user-specified identity rules are introduced (4,20). In this category of entity identification methods, users are allowed to freely specify which tuple pairs represent the same real-world entities. Users do not need to identify the common attributes or keys to compare *all* tuples. Moreover, the methods can accommodate multiple identity rules that apply to different subsets of tuples.

In Ref. 4, an entity identification method based on *logical formulation* of user-specified identity rules was introduced. In this method, users can define identity rules according to their understanding about the integrated domain of legacy databases. Being expressed in logical formulas, the user-specified identity rules can be readily used in the entity identification which can now be implemented as a theorem-proving system. Using identity rules examples in Examples 1 and 2, we illustrate how they can be formulated as logical formulas using the entity identification method proposed in Ref. 4.

Example 5

The key-based identity rule (assuming that *Cname* is a common key in relations R and S) in Example 1 is written as

$\forall e1, e2 \in E, (e1.Cname = e2.Cname) \rightarrow (e1 \equiv e2)$ where E represents the set of real-world entities in the integrated domain.

The identity rule in Example 2 applies to only some subsets of tuples in relations R and S. It is written as

$\forall e1,e2 \in E,$ $e1.Street =$ "*Pioneer   Ave*" $\wedge$ $e1.Product =$ "*Databases*" $\wedge e2.$
$Manager =$ "*Smith*" $\rightarrow (e1 \equiv e2)$ □

To provide more flexibility to entity identification, the method proposed in Ref. 4 further allows instance-level attribute knowledge to be formulated as logical formulae known as *instance-level functional dependencies* (ILFDs). ILFDs are a special kind of rule useful for deriving the missing identifying attribute values of some database instances.

Example 6
The example in the section Instance-Level Attribute Knowledge can be expressed as the ILFD below:

$\forall e \in E(R),e.Street =$ "*Pioneer Ave*" $\rightarrow e.District =$ "*North*" where
$E(R)$ denotes the entities represented by tuples from R.   □

By performing reasoning on the user-specified identity rules and ILFDs, a matching table listing all matching tuple pairs as matching key values is constructed.

Unlike the method proposed in Ref. 4, the entity identification method proposed in Ref. 20 allows users to explicitly specify matching tuple pairs directly as pairs of local object identifiers in the matching table. Here, users can freely decide to use any appropriate approach to generate the matching object identifier pairs. To facilitate global query processing, unique universal object identifiers are assigned to matching local object identifier pairs.

Entity Identification Using User-Specified Imprecise Identity Rules

Although user-specified identity rules in the previous subsection provide great flexibility in specifying the matching criteria for entity identification, they require the matching criteria to be precise and accurate. This is sometimes very difficult because a major bulk of human knowledge is inherently imprecise and uncertain. To generalize entity identification methods to handle imprecision and uncertainties in the users' knowledge, the standard logic formalism is not sufficient.

In Ref. 21, a formalism of logic with supports known as *evidential support logic* has been used to represent imprecise identity rules and instance-level attribute knowledge. Extending the entity identification method proposed in Ref. 4, this evidential reasoning approach to entity identification requires each identity rule/instance-level functional dependency to be quantified with a support pair denoted by (sn,sp). sn and sp denotes the *necessary support* and *possible support*, respectively, for the identity rule/ instance-level functional dependency being *true*. $(sp\text{-}sn)$ represents the uncertainty in support. sn and sp must also satisfy the following constraints:

sn is less than or equal to sp, and
$sn + (1\text{-}sp)$ is less than or equal to 1

The necessary and possible supports of identity rules/instance-level functional dependencies are specified by users to indicate their precision levels. A *voting model* can be used to derive these support values. Given an assertion that can be an identity rule or instance-level functional dependency, one assigns votes to the following three possibilities:

Possibility 1: The assertion is true.
Possibility 2: The assertion is false.
Possibility 3: The truth of assertion is unknown.

Let the votes for possibilities 1, 2, and 3 be denoted by *vote(true)*, *vote(false)*, and *vote(unknown)*, respectively. The necessary support of the assertion defined by the proportion of votes assigned to possibility 1. The possible support of the assertion is defined by the proportion of votes assigned to possibilities 1 and 2. Formally,

$$sn = \frac{vote(true)}{vote(true) + vote(false) + vote(unknown)},$$
$$sp = \frac{vote(true) + vote(unknown)}{vote(true) + vote(false) + vote(unknown)}.$$

Example 7
The imprecise versions of the two identity rule examples in Example 5 are as follows:

$$\forall e1,e2 \in E,(e1.Cname = e2.Cname) \rightarrow (e1 \equiv e2) : (0.8, 1)$$
$$\forall e1,e2 \in E, e1.Street = \text{``Pioneer Ave''} \wedge e1.Product = \text{``Databases''} \wedge$$
$$e2.Manager = \text{``Smith''} \rightarrow (e1 \equiv e2): (0.7, 0.9)$$

The first imprecise identity rule has a necessary support of 0.8 and a possible support of 1. The latter has a necessary support of 0.7 and a possible support of 0.9. □

Example 8
By extending the ILFD example in Example 6 with evidential information, we derive the following evidential ILFD:

$$\forall e \in F(R), e.Street = \text{``Pioneer Ave''} \rightarrow e.District = \text{`North''}: (0.5, 0.9) \quad □$$

Nevertheless, reasoning with evidential identity rules and ILFDs is quite different than that of logic programming. The major differences include the following:

• Determining the degree to which the antecedent conditions are supported and deriving the degree to which the consequent conditions are supported after applying the rules
• Merging the results of evidential reasoning because there may be different supports given to the same conclusion that can be derived by different proof paths

In Ref. 21, an evidential support logic programming proposed by Baldwin (8) has been adopted to handle reasoning over identity rules and ILFDs with supports.

CONCLUSIONS

In this article, the problem of entity identification during database integration has been defined and different solution approaches to the problem have been presented. Although entity identification is an indispensable task during database integration, entity identification methods must rely on knowledge or semantic information about the source databases and the integrated domain. Two important classes of knowledge required are identity rules and instance-level attribute knowledge. By systematically categorizing the identity rules, a taxonomy of entity identification methods is developed. The taxonomy facilitates database integrators and administrators to select the appropriate entity identification methods for different integration scenarios.

Although a number of entity identification methods have been developed so far, a complete database integration solution is yet to arrive. As part of future database research, entity identification methods will be integrated with solution methods for other database integration subproblems (e.g., schema integration and attribute-value conflict resolution). With a fully or semiautomatic and comprehensive database integration tool, it is envisaged that increasing the number of legacy databases can be seamlessly integrated without difficulty.

REFERENCES

1. W. Kim and J. Seo, "Classifying Schematic and Data Heterogeneity in Multidatabase Systems," *IEEE Computer*, 24(12), 12–17 (1991).
2. A. Sheth and J. A. Larson, "Federated Database Systems for Managing Distributed, Heterogeneous, and Autonomous Databases," *ACM Comput. Surv.*, 22(3), 183–235 (1990).
3. M. W. Bright, A. R. Hurson, and S. H. Pakzad, "A Taxonomy and Current Issues in Multidatabase Systems," *IEEE Computer*, 25(3), 50–60 (1992).
4. E.-P. Lim, J. Srivastava, S. Prabhakar, and J. Richardson, "Entity Identification Problem in Database Integration," in *International Conference on Data Engineering*, Vienna, 1993.
5. C. Batini, M. Lenzerini, and S. B. Navathe, "A Comparative Analysis of Methodologies for Database Schema Integration," *ACM Comput. Surv.*, 18(4), 323–364 (1986).
6. R. E. Walpole, *Probability and Statistics for Engineers and Scientists*, Macmillan, New York, 1993.
7. L. A. Zadeh, *Fuzzy Sets and Applications: Selected Papers*, John Wiley & Sons, New York, 1987.
8. J. F. Baldwin, "Evidential Support Logic Programming," *Fuzzy Sets Syst.*, 24, 1–26 (1987).
9. U. Dayal, "Processing Queries over Generalized Hierarchies in a Multidatabase Systems," in *Proceedings of the 9th Very Large Data Bases Conference*, 1983.
10. U. Dayal and H-Y. Hwang, "View Definition and Generalization for Database Integration in Multibase: A System for Heterogeneous Distributed Databases," *IEEE Trans. Software Eng.*, *SE-10*(6) (1984).
11. L. G. DeMichiel, "Resolving Database Incompatibility: An Approach to Performing Relational Operations over Mismatched Domains," *IEEE Trans. Knowledge Data Eng.*, *KDE-1*(4), 485–493 (1989).
12. F. S. C. Tseng, A. L. P. Chen, and W-P. Yang, "Answering Heterogeneous Database Queries with Degrees of Uncertainty," *Distrib. Parallel Databases*, V *1*, 281–302 (1993).
13. E-P. Lim, J. Srivastava, and S. Shekhar, "Resolving Attribute Incompatibility in Database Integration: An Evidential Reasoning Approach," in *Proceedings of the Tenth International Conference on Data Engineering*, Houston, 1994.
14. S. Y. Hwang, E. P. Lim, H. R. Yang, S. Musukula, K. Mediratta, M. Ganesh, D. Clemente, J. Stenoien, and J. Srivastava, "The Myriad Federated Database Prototype," *ACM SIGMOD International Conference on Management of Data*. Minneapolis, MN, May 1994.
15. C. Pu, "Key Equivalence in Heterogeneous Databases," *International Workshop on Interoperability in Multidatabase Systems*, 1991.
16. Y. R. Wang and S. E. Madnick, "The Inter-database Instance Identification Problem in Integrating Autonomous Systems," *International Conference on Database Engineering*, 1989.

17. A. Chatterjee and A. Segev, "Data Manipulation in Heterogeneous Databases," *SIGMOD Rec.*, *20*(4), 64–68 (1991).

18. A. Chatterjee and A. Segev, "A Probabilistic Approach to Information Retrieval in Heterogeneous Databases," *Workshop on Information Technologies & Systems*, December 1991.

19. A. Chatterjee and A. Segev, "Resolving Data Heterogeneity in Scientific and Statistical Databases," *International Working Conference on Scientific and Statistical Database Management*, Switzerland, June 1992.

20. R. Ahmed, P. DeSmedt, W. Du, B. Kent, M. Ketabchi, W. Litwin, A. Rafii, and M-C. Shan, "The Pegasus Heterogeneous Multidatabase System," *IEEE Computer*, *24*(12), 19–27 (December 1991).

21. E.-P. Lim and J. Srivastava, "Entity Identification in Database Integration: An Evidential Reasoning Approach," *International Symposium on Next Generation Database Applications*, Fukuoka Japan, 1993.

BIBLIOGRAPHY

Schema Integration

Garcia-Solaco, M., F. Saltor, and M. Castellanos, "A Structure Based Schema Integration Methodology," in *Proceedings of the Eleventh International Conference on Data Engineering*, Taipei, Taiwan, March 1995.

Garcia-Solaco, M., F. Saltor, and M. Castellanos, "Semantic Heterogeneity in Multidatabase Systems," in *Object-Oriented Multidatabase Systems*, O. A. Bukhres and A. K. Elmagarmid (eds.), Prentice-Hall, Englewood Cliffs, NJ, 1996, pp. 129–195.

Haynes and S. Ram, "Multi User View Integration System (MUVIS): An Expert System for View Integration," in *Proceedings 6th International Conference on Data Engineering*, 1990.

Johannesson, P., "A Logic Based Approach to Schema Integration," in *Proceedings of the 10th International Conference on Entity Relationship Approach*, Amsterdam, 1991.

Kaul, M., K. Drosten, and E. J. Neuhold, "ViewSystem: Integrating Heterogeneous Information Bases by Object-Oriented Views," in *Proceedings of the Data Engineering Conference*, 1990.

Kent, W., "Solving Domain Mismatch and Schema Mismatch Problems with an Object-Oriented Database Programming Language," in *Proceedings of the 17th International Conference on Very Large Data Bases*, San Mateo, CA, 1991, pp. 147–1160.

Larson, J., S. Navathe, and R. Elmasri, "A Theory of Attribute Equivalence in Databases with Applications to Schema Integration," *IEEE Trans. Software Eng.*, *15*(4), 449–463 (1989).

Li, W-S. and C. Clifton, "Semantic Integration in Heterogeneous Databases Using Neural Networks," in *Proceedings of Twentieth International Conference on Very Large Data Bases*, Chile, September 1994.

Mannino, M., S. Navathe, and W. Effelsberg, "A Rule-Based Approach for Merging Generalization Hierarchies," *Inform. Syst.*, *13*(3), 257–272 (1988).

Navathe, S., R. Elmasri, and J. Larson, "Integrating User Views in Database Design," *IEEE Computer*, *19*(1), 50–62 (January 1986).

Sheth, A. (ed.), *ACM SIGMOD Rec.*, *20*(4) (1991); special issue on Semantic Heterogeneity.

Sheth, A., J. Larson, A. Cornelio, and S. Navathe, "A Tool of Integrating Conceptual Schemas and User Views," in *Proceedings of the Fourth International Conference on Data Engineering*. Los Angeles, 1988.

Spaccapietra, S., C. Parent, and Y. Dupont, "Model Independent Assertions for Integration of Heterogeneous Schemas," *VLDB J.*, *1*(1), 81–126 (1992).

Spaccapietra, S. and C. Parent, "View Integration: A Step Forward in Solving Structural Conflicts," *IEEE Trans. Knowledge Data Eng.*, *KDE-6*(2), 258–274 (1994).

Instance Integration

Kent, W., "The Entity Join," in *Proceedings of the International Conference on Very Large Data Bases*, 1979.

Kent, W., "The Breakdown of the Information Model in MDBSs," *SIGMOD Rec.*, *20*(4), 10–15 (1991).

Kent, W., R. Ahmed, J. Albert, M. Ketabchi, and M-C. Shan, "Object Identification in Multidatabase Systems," in *IFIP Interoperable Database Systems (DS-5)*, Australia, November 1992.

Lim, E-P., J. Srivastava, and S. Shekhar, "An Evidential Reasoning Approach to Attribute Value Conflict Resolution in Database Integration," *IEEE Trans. Knowledge Data Eng.*, *8*(5), 707–723 (1996).

Sheth, A. and V. Kashyap, "So Far (Schematically) Yet So Near (Semantically)," in *IFIP Interoperable Database Systems (DS-5)*, Australia, November 1992.

Tseng, F. S-C., A. L. P. Chen, and W-P. Yang, "A Probabilistic Approach to Query Processing in Heterogeneous Database Systems," in *Proceedings of the Workshop on Research Issues in Data Engineering: Transaction and Query Processing*, 1992.

Vermeer, M. W. W. and P. M. G. Apers, "On the Applicability of Schema Integration Techniques to Database Interoperation," in *Proceedings of the Entity Relationship Conference*. Cottbus, Germany, 1996.

Multidatabase Systems

Busse, R., P. Fankhauser, G. Huck, and W. Klas, "IRO–DB: An Object-Oriented Approach Towards Federated and Interoperable DBMS," in *Proceedings of the International Workshop on Advances in Databases and Information Systems ADIS94*, Moscow, 1994.

Goh, C. H., S. E. Madnick, and M. D. Siegel, "Context Interchange: Overcoming the Challenges of Large-Scale Interoperable Database Systems in a Dynamic Environment," in *Proceedings of the Third International Conference on Information and Knowledge Management (CIKM)*, Gaithersburg, MD, 1994.

Litwin, W. and A. Abdellatif, "Multidatabase Interoperability," *IEEE Computer*, *19*(12), 10–18 (December 1986).

Litwin, W., A. Abdellatif, A. Zeroual, and B. Nicolas, "MSQL: A Multidatabase Language," *Inform. Sci.*, *49*, 59–101 (1989).

Liu, L. and C. Pu, "The Distributed Interoperable Object Model and Its Application to Large-Scale Interoperable Database Systems," in *Proceedings of the Fourth International Conference on Information and Knowledge Management (CIKM)*, Baltimore, MD, 1995.

Papakonstantinou, Y., H. Garcia-Molina, and J. Widom, "Object Exchange Across Heterogeneous Information Sources," in *Proceedings of the Eleventh International Conference on Data Engineering*, Taipei, Taiwan, March 1995.

Templeton, M., D. Brill, A. Chen, S. Dao, E. Lund, R. MGregor, and P. Ward, "Mermaid: A Front End to Distributed Heterogeneous Databases," in *Proc. IEEE*, *75*(5), 695–708 (1987).

Thomas, G., G. Thompson, C-W. Chung, E. Barkmeyer, F. Carter, M. Templeton, S. Fox, and B. Hartman, "Heterogeneous Distributed Databases for Production Use," *ACM Comput. Surv.*, *22*(4), 237–266 (1990).

EE-PENG LIM

A FAMILY OF EFFICIENT RULE GENERATORS

INTRODUCTION

Classification rules are sought in many areas from automatic knowledge acquisition (1,2) to data mining (3,4) neural network rule extraction (5–7). This is because classification rules possess some attractive features. They are explicit, understandable, and verifiable by domain experts, and can be modified, extended, and passed on as modular knowledge.

Although many different models of induction, such as decision trees, neural networks, and linear discriminants, have been used for classification, they share a common goal: prediction accuracy. Model complexity and prediction accuracy are highly related. Learning from sample data can be described as estimating a model's parameters from a view point of statistics. There are strong theoretical reasons for developing learning methods that cover patterns in the most efficient and compact manner (8,9). This article describes our efforts toward finding simple classification rules with high prediction accuracy.

This work stems from practical needs in knowledge acquisition, neural network rule extraction, and data mining. To cater for different needs, variations of rule generators are implemented centering around a base algorithm. This work can find its relevance in decision-tree rule induction (1), but is more related to single-best-rule covering (4,10) that expands only one rule at a time and add conditions one by one until the rule set covers all the training patterns. The distinction of this work from related work mainly lies in how to efficiently add these conditions in a rule plus some special considerations for particular applications. Details will be given later. Another line of related work is of AQ11 and its variations (11). However, AQ11 (12) is a candidate-elimination algorithm that requires a generalization hierarchy in the search of learned concepts. This is an advantage when domain knowledge is available. Here, we assume no domain knowledge.

In the following section, we describe the base algorithm. The third section, we explain how different family members are constructed by modifying the base algorithm. In the fourth section, we introduce two evaluation measures for prediction accuracy and compactness. In the fifth section, we account for the experiment method and present empirical results for comparative study with a discussion on issues as efficiency, and so on. In the last section, we conclude this project and propose some future work.

BASE ALGORITHM

The aim of this work is to search for simple rules with a high prediction accuracy. The basic idea of the proposed algorithm is simple: using first-order* information in the data

---

*The degree of order is determined by the number of attributes involved in a search. If one attribute is used, the search only makes use of the first-order information.

to determine shortest sufficient conditions in a pattern (i.e., the rule under consideration) that can differentiate the pattern from patterns belonging to other classes. The sole use of first-order information avoids the combinatorial complexity in computation, although it is well known that using higher-order information may provide better results.

The pseudocode of the base algorithm for rule generation is given in Figure 1. The technical details are given to the extent that a reimplementation of the algorithm can be done without much difficulty. The variations of the rule generator are produced by modifying, adding/deleting, some key components of the base algorithm. Each variation is discussed in the next section.

The base algorithm is composed of three major functions:

Base Algorithm

```
Rule Generation:

    i=0;

    while (Data is NOT empty/marked) {

        generate shortest R_i to

            cover the current pattern and

            differentiate it from patterns in other categories;

        remove/mark all the patterns covered by R_i;

        i++;

    }

Rule Clustering:

    cluster rules according to their class labels;

Rule Pruning:

    eliminate redundant rules;

    determine a default rule.
```

FIGURE 1   The pseudocode of the base algorithm.

1. Rule generation: This function iteratively generates shortest rules* and removes/marks the patterns covered by each rule until all patterns are covered by the rules.
2. Rule clustering: Rules are clustered in terms of their class labels.
3. Rule pruning: Redundant or more specific rules in each cluster are removed.

A default rule should be chosen to accommodate possible unclassifiable patterns. If rules are clustered, the choice of the default rule is based on clusters of rules.

In addition to the three functions, one of the key concepts of the algorithm is *generating the **shortest** rule R_i* at each iteration *i*. The method of finding the shortest rule determines the efficiency of the algorithm. Our method is straightforward and makes use of first-order information only. It finds the shortest sufficient conditions for each rule of a class. *x/y* means choosing either *x* or *y*. The pseudocode of this algorithm is given in Figure 2.

FAMILY OF RULE GENERATORS

Centering around the base algorithm, we describe four rule generators in turn.

Order-Dependent Version

By being order dependent we mean that the order of the rules cannot be changed. In other words, the first rule is always tested first. An order-dependent (OD) rule generator produces OD rules by removing all patterns covered by each new rule until the data set is empty. In the base algorithm, if *empty* and *remove* remain in the while loop, an OD rule generator is obtained. Because the rules are ordered, Rule Clustering and Rule Pruning components cannot apply and should be deleted from the base algorithm.

Order-Independent Version

By being order independent we mean that the firing order of the rules can be changed without affecting the result of classification. An order-independent (OI) rule generator forms OI rules by keeping all the patterns for generating each new rule. In effect, an OI rule generator results from keeping *marked* and *mark* in the while loop of the base algorithm. To *mark* a pattern is to register the pattern as having been considered. When all patterns are considered (*marked*) for rule generation, the algorithm stops.

Binary Version—Perfect Rules

By and large, rule generators (1,13,14) and other versions of this work focus on generalization, avoiding overfit of the training data. This version is to generate perfect rules, as it is required in neural network rule extraction applications (7,15). By perfect rules we mean that rules can cover the patterns with a 0% error rate. In some cases such as neural network rule extraction, the training data for rule induction is noise-free and all patterns are equally important. The two features that distinguish this version from others are (1)

---

*A shortest rule is a rule with a minimum number of conditions.

Generating the Shortest Rule R_j

```
for each attribute value v of the current pattern p of class c_i,

    count v's occurrence in the patterns

        belonging to other classes (≠ c_i),

order the attributes according to their value occurrences

    in an increasing sequence A_freq[ ] and its sister

    sequence A_order[ ] storing the indexes of attributes,

if A_freq[1] = 0

    (value v alone can differentiate pattern p from others)

    obtain R_j as: if A_k = v then c_i,

        k is determined by A_order[1];     ---- (1)

else

    find A_freq[1 − n] that can uniquely represent pattern p

        by increasing n from 2 to the maximum number of attributes,

    obtain R_j as in ---- (1) by ANDing all the chosen attributes.
```

FIGURE 2   The pseudocode of finding the shortest rules.

that only binary data is used and (2) that patterns are grouped in terms of class labels before learning begins. Apart from these two features, this version per se is an order-independent rule generator with a special treatment for binary data. Because this version is specifically designed for neural network rule extraction based on the base algorithm, no further discussion will be given.

Noise-Handling Version

In choosing which pattern to start with, the base algorithm is data-order sensitive in the sense that the rule set could be different if the order of patterns is changed, or patterns are shuffled. There would be no problem if no patterns are corrupted. In the presence of noise (or corrupted patterns), however, it is important to start with a noise-free pattern.

Therefore, in order to handle noise, some additional information is required. One piece of information is the frequency of each distinct pattern in the training data. Under the assumption that there are only a small number of corrupted patterns, if we begin with a pattern that occurs most frequently, it is then remotely likely that it is a corrupted pattern. In order to handle noise, the base algorithm is modified by adding the following at the very beginning of the algorithm.

```
sort-on-freq(Data-without-Duplicates);
```

The frequency of each pattern can be obtained by counting each distinct pattern's occurrence and removing duplicates. The output of Chi2 (16), which is a program that does discretization and feature selection for numeric data, also provides such information. More on handling noise in various cases can be found in Ref. 17.

EVALUATION MEASURES

The evaluation of rules is performed in two ways. One is the estimation of error rates (18). In a sense, it measures how well the rules generalize from data, because usually the data is split into two sets: one for training, and the other for testing. The lower the error rate for the test set is, the better the rules generalize from the data. Rules that do not generalize are of minimum use. However, if there are two sets of rules and their estimated error rates are similar, the comparison of the two should be done in terms of the compactness of a rule set. As was mentioned in Introduction, a simpler set is preferred.

- **Error rates.** The training data is used to learn rules. What we would like to know is the proportion of errors made by this set of rules, and classifying new observations (the test data in experiments) without the benefit of knowing the true classifications. The true classifications of test data are known but are not told to the rule generator. The most common evaluation method is called "one-shot" train-and-test, which applies rules to the data, counts the errors made, and calculates the error rate as the number of errors divided by the number of data. When the test data are not available, this evaluation is done on the training data. As we know, it is very biased. The more sophisticated methods are cross-validation (*m*-fold, leave-one-out, etc.) and bootstrap (18).
- **Compactness measure.** An ideal rule set has a minimum number of rules and each rule is as short as possible. In practice, it is quite often that a rule set contains fewer rules but some of which have more conditions. Therefore, the concept of compactness is multidimensional. The dimensions that need be considered are (1) the number of rules in a set, (2) the number of conditions in a rule, and (3) the number of patterns covered and correctly classified by a rule. The following compactness measure was proposed in Ref. 4:

$$E = \frac{1}{r} \sum_{i=1}^{r} \frac{t_i}{n} \frac{1}{c_i}, \tag{1}$$

where r is the cardinality of the rule set, n is the number of patterns, t_i is the number of patterns correctly classified by rule, i, $1 \le i \le r$, and c_i is the number of conditions in rule i.

One problem with this compactness formula is that it cannot handle the default rule, because $c = 0$ for the default rule, which is often very useful for accommodating those patterns that cannot be covered by any other rules. An adjustment is to let its c be 1 for the default rule. Another problem will be discussed in the end of the next section about the use of the formula for comparison.

EXPERIMENTS

Equipped with the above two evaluation measures, we can conduct some experiments to empirically compare the four versions of rule generators with other known methods (4,10).

Method

One data set—CAR—will be used to show the differences between the versions of our rule generator, as compared with the results reported in Ref. 4 because they have done some comparisons with other methods such as ID3 (13) and the one by Han et al. (19).

Then, we show the results for another two data sets: Golf-Playing (10) and Iris (20). The authors of Refs. 4 and 10 did not provide test data. Only the Iris data are divided evenly into two sets (75 patterns each) for training and testing. Datasets CAR and Golf-Playing are given in Tables 1 and 2. Iris data can be obtained from the University of California, Irvine (21).

In the presence of numeric attributes (e.g., in Golf-Playing and Iris data), Chi2 (15) is applied to discretizing these attributes. The resulting data contain discrete values only and are guaranteed that they can keep the original discriminating power of the data, shown in Tables 3 and 4.

Detailed Results

In the following comparative studies, three data sets (CAR, Golf-Playing, Iris) are used, respectively. Noise handling is shown in Comparison 3 because the first two data sets do not have any noise. Some notations are "0" means a wild card and "–" means *not*. The noise in Iris data was purposefully introduced in data discretization.

Comparison 1 (CAR)

Given below are the rules and relevant information for calculating the compactness of each rule set.

---A complete set of rules (order independent) ---
Rule0: 0 0 3 0 0 -> 3
Hit: 1 and Miss: 0

Rule1: 3 0 0 0 0 -> 3
Hit: 3 and Miss: 0

Rule6: 0 3 0 3 0 -> 3
Hit: 2 and Miss: 0

TABLE 1   CAR Data Set

Displace[a]	Fuelcap[b]	Mass[c]	Speed[d]	Cyl	Cost[e]
3	3	2	2	6	3
3	1	3	3	6	3
2	2	1	3	6	2
1	1	1	1	6	1
3	2	2	2	6	3
3	2	1	2	6	3
1	1	1	2	6	1
1	2	1	1	4	1
2	1	2	2	6	2
2	3	2	3	6	3
2	3	1	3	6	3
1	3	3	2	4	3
1	3	1	2	4	1
2	1	3	2	4	3
2	2	2	2	4	2
2	3	2	2	4	2
1	2	2	3	4	2
2	2	3	1	4	3

[a]Displace: 1—small; 2—medium; 3—large.
[b]Fuelcap: 1—low; 2—medium; 3—heavy.
[c]Mass: 1—light; 2—medium; 3—heavy.
[d]Speed: 1—slow; 2—medium; 3—fast.
[e]Cost: 1—cheap; 2—medium; 3—expensive.

TABLE 2   Golf-Playing Data Set

Outlook[a]	Temp.	Humid.	Wind[b]	Decision[c]
1	21	96	1	0
1	17	70	1	0
2	21	90	1	1
2	29	78	2	1
1	23	80	2	1
2	16	66	1	1
3	23	70	1	1
3	27	90	1	0
3	30	85	2	0
2	27	75	2	1
1	18	80	2	1
1	20	96	2	1
3	21	95	2	0
3	19	70	2	1

[a]Outlook: 1—rainy; 2—overcast; 3—sunny.
[b]Wind: 1—strong; 2—light.
[c]Decision: 0—do not play; 1—play.

TABLE 3   Discretized Golf-Playing Data

Outlook	Temp.	Humid.	Wind	Decision	Freq.
1	0	2	1	0	1
1	0	1	1	0	1
3	0	2	1	0	1
3	0	2	2	0	2
2	0	1	1	1	1
3	0	1	2	1	1
3	0	1	1	1	1
2	0	1	2	1	2
1	0	1	2	1	2
2	0	2	1	1	1
1	0	2	2	1	1

Rule7: 1 0 1 0 0 -> 1
Hit: 4 and Miss: 0

Default: 2
Hit: 5 and Miss: 0

---Testing rules for training data: ---
Total #Item: 18; Hit: 18; Miss: 0; Acc: 1.00

$E = 15/18/5 = 0.166$ according to formula (1).

TABLE 4   Discretized Iris Data Obtained by Chi2

S-len[a]	S-wid	P-len	P-wid	Class	Freq
		(a) Training Data			
0	0	1	1	0	25
0	0	2	2	1	24
0	0	2	3	1	1
0	0	3	3	2	21
0	0	2	3	2	3
0	0	3	2	2	1
		(b) Testing Data			
0	0	1	1	0	25
0	0	2	2	1	23
0	0	3	3	1	1
0	0	3	2	1	1
0	0	3	3	2	19
0	0	3	2	2	3
0	0	2	3	2	3

[a]S—sepal; P—petal; len–length; wid—width; freq—frequency.

---A complete set of rules (order dependent) ---
Rule0: 0 0 3 0 0 -> 3
Hit: 4 and Miss: 0

Rule1: 3 0 0 0 0 -> 3
Hit: 3 and Miss: 0

Rule2: 2 2 0 0 0 -> 2
Hit: 2 and Miss: 0

Rule3: 0 0 0 1 0 -> 1
Hit: 2 and Miss: 0

Rule4: 1 1 0 0 0 -> 1
Hit: 1 and Miss: 0

Rule5: 0 1 0 0 0 -> 2
Hit: 1 and Miss: 0

Rule6: 0 0 0 0 6 -> 3
Hit: 2 and Miss: 0

Rule7: 0 0 1 0 0 -> 1
Hit: 1 and Miss: 0

Default: 2
Hit: 2 and Miss: 0

---Testing rules for training data: ---
Total #Item: 18; Hit: 18; Miss: 0; Acc: 1.00

E = 16.5/18/8 = 0.115 according to formula (1).

The compactness values for the three systems reported in Ref 4 are 0.12, 0.062, and 0.014 for LCR of Ref. 4, ID3 and Han et al.'s algorithm, respectively. It seems obvious that the order-independent (OI) rule set is more compact than the order-dependent (OD) one since the former has much fewer rules. When comparing the latter to the rule set generated by LCR, although LCR generates six rules only, the difference between the two (0.115 versus 0.12) is rather insignificant. This may be due to the OD rules having fewer conditions. ID3 generates nine rules, four of which contain three conditions each.

Comparison 2 (Golf-Playing)
The discretized data are shown in Table 3. Here, we continue to see the difference between the rule sets generated by the OI and OD versions. A rule (Rule 6) is pruned in the OI version because there is another rule (Rule 3) that is more general.

---A complete set of rules (order independent) ---
Rule1: 3 0 2 0 -> 0
Hit: 3 and Miss: 0

Rule3: 1 0 0 1 -> 0
Hit: 2 and Miss: 0

*Rule6: 1 0 2 1 -> 0 (pruned)

Default: 1
Hit: 9 and Miss: 0

---Testing rules: ---
Total Item: 14; Hit: 14; Miss: 0; Acc: 1.00

---A complete set of rules (order dependent) ---
Rule1: 3 0 2 0 -> 0
Hit: 3 and Miss: 0

Rule4: 1 0 0 –2 -> 0
Hit: 2 and Miss: 0

Default: 1
Hit: 9 and Miss: 0

---Testing rules: ---
Total Item: 14; Hit: 14; Miss: 0; Acc: 1.00

The two sets generated by the OI and OD versions are not exactly the same but their compactness values are because both sets of rules have the same number of rules, number of conditions, and number of Hits and Misses. In this case, we prefer the OI rule set because it can be understood without concern of ordering. The results reported in Ref. 10 are that RULES-2 produced 8 and 14 rules for options 1 and 2. Under the normal circumstances, we prefer a rule set with fewer and shorter rules.

Comparison 3 (Iris)

The discretized training and test data sets are shown in Table 4. The noise-handling version is applied to get the results as follows. Both OI and OD versions produce the same rule set.

---A complete set of rules ---
Rule0: 0 0 1 0 -> 0
Hit: 25 and Miss: 0

Rule1: 0 0 2 2 -> 1
Hit: 24 and Miss: 0

Default: 2
Hit: 25 and Miss: 1

---Testing rules for training data: ---
Total #Item: 75; Hit: 74; Miss: 1; Acc: 0.99

---Testing rules for testing data: ---
Total #Item: 75; Hit: 73; Miss: 2; Acc: 0.97

Translating the discretized data back to their original meanings, we obtain the following rules:

Rule 1: If Petal-length ≤1.9, then *Iris setosa*.
Rule 2: If Petal-length ≤4.9 and Petal-width ≤1.6, then *Iris versicolor*.
Default Rule: *Iris virginica*.

For reference, the rule set (DT Rules) generated by C4.5rules (1) (which is based on a decision-tree method but generates more concise rules than the tree itself) is included here:

Rule 1: If Petal-length ≤1.9, then *Iris setosa.*
Rule 2: If Petal-length >1.9 and Petal-width ≤1.6, then *Iris versicolor.*
Rule 3: If Petal-width >1.6, then *Iris virginica.*
Default Rule: *Iris setosa.*

Results on Real-World Data Sets

In the above, the detailed results are reported on the several data sets used in the cited references. All these data sets are relatively small. Here, two relatively large data sets are chosen for further experiments from the machine learning databases at the University of California, Irvine (21). They are as follows:

- **Mushroom.** The training and test data sets contains 7124 and 1000 instances, respectively. The 1000 instances in the test set are randomly selected. The rest are used for training. The data has 22 discrete attributes. Each attribute can have 2–10 values.
- **Wisconsin Breast Cancer.** The training and test data sets contains 350 and 349 instances, respectively. The 350 instances are randomly selected for training; the other half is for testing. There are nine discrete attributes. Each attribute has 10 values.

The results of running the order-dependent (OD) and order-independent (OI) rule generators are summarized below, following the style in Ref. 22, to provide the accuracy (Acc) and number of rules (# Rules). The accuracy for the training data sets is 100% in all cases. The reported accuracy in Table 5 is for testing data only.

Due to the relatively large number of rules, the rules are omitted here but are available upon request. Some extra information about rules may be helpful to the readers who are familiar with the two data sets. For the mushroom data sets, the rules only contain up to four attributes—attributes 4, 5, 12, and 22; for the breast cancer data set, the rules only need a maximum number of three attributes—attributes 1, 2, and 6. The above reported accuracy rates are comparable to the best ones reported in the literature.

Discussion

- *Efficiency issue.* Given in Ref. 10, the computational complexity of RULES-2 in its worst cast is

TABLE 5   Reported Accuracy for Test Data

Dataset	OC Acc.	OI Acc.	OD # Rules	OI # Rules
Mushroom	100%	99%	12	11
Breast cancer	93%	92%	20	12

$$N_{\text{RULES-2}} = O\left(n^2 \sum_{i=1}^{m} \frac{m!}{(m-i)!i!} i \right) \geq O(n^2 2^m),$$

where n is the number of patterns, m (>1) is the number of attributes for the given problem. Suppose the average number of distinct values in each attribute is h, LCR's computational complexity given in Ref. 4 in its worst case is

$$N_{\text{LCR}} = O\left(\sum_{i=1}^{m} \frac{h^i m!}{(m-i)!i!} n * i \right).$$

In addition, the LCR algorithm requires a lot of memory to store tables for calculating Semantic Association Degrees.

The computational complexity of the base algorithm in its worst case is

$$N = O(n^2 m^2).$$

It is clear that N is smaller than $N_{\text{RULES-2}}$. A comparison of N to N_{LCR} is not straightforward due to N_{LCR}'s complex representation as well as its reliance on massive memory usage. Consider only the complexity of its last term $i = m$ (the smallest in the factorial); its complexity is $O(n_{\text{max}} n m)$. Hence, it is conjectured that N and N_{LCR} are similar. For a reference of the scale of thee complexities, the worst-case computational complexity of a decision-tree method is $n^2 m C$, where C is the cost to calculate a split function (e.g., information gain in ID3). All these worst-case computational complexities are approximate. For example, N is approximate since at any time only k (approximated by n divided by the number of classes) patterns are checked and, on average, $m \simeq 2$.

- *Order dependent* versus *order independent*. The two versions have their pros and cons. It is natural to have OI rules because all matched rules will have a chance to get fired. However, a conflict resolution mechanism is normally required to choose which is the best rule to be fired. The disadvantage of OD rules is that the ordering hinders our understanding of the rules. As was suggested in Comparison 1, the OD rules tend to have fewer conditions.
- *Compactness measure*. From the experiments, especially Comparison 1, it is clear that the measure favors rules with a smaller number of conditions. If each rule has only one condition, even if the number of rules is equal to the number of patterns, the measure would become $1/r$. In the example of CAR, it is $1/18 = 0.055$, which is still more compact, according to formula (1), than the rules produced by Han et al.'s algorithm. This does not seem reasonable.

CONCLUSION AND FURTHER WORK

This article introduces a basic rule generation algorithm and its variations for different applications. In essence, the algorithm exploits the first-order information in the data and finds shortest sufficient conditions for a rule of a class that can differentiate it from patterns of other classes. Two evaluation measures (accuracy and compactness) are used in comparative studies. Although the rules produced by the versions of our rule generator are different, they are compact and accurate. Noise handling of the algorithm is effective. It is best used in conjunction with Chi2 (15) because Chi2 provides the frequency information. Rule pruning removes redundant rules.

Four rule generators can be used in different circumstances, as their names suggest. In summary, if the induced rules are not employed in sequence, the order-dependent rule generator should not be considered, although it may produce shorter rules than other versions. If the frequency information is not available, the noise-handling rule generator should not be considered. If the comprehensibility of rules is the top concern, the order-independent rule generator should be used. In the case of binary data, the binary version is strongly suggested because it takes into account the special features of binary data.

The future work includes the following: (1) searching for a better compactness formula to deal with the factors that are not well expressed in the current formula (1); (2) handling noise data without the frequency information, as this information may not always be available, and (3) improving the base algorithm by making the conditions of a rule not only sufficient but also necessary while keeping the scale of the current computational complexity.

REFERENCES

1. J. R. Quinlan, *C4.5*: *Programs for Machine Learning*. Morgan Kaufmann, San Mateo, CA, 1993.
2. S. Russell and P. Norvig, *Artificial Intelligence*: *A Modern Approach*. Prentice-Hall, Englewood Cliffs, NJ, 1995.
3. R. Agrawal, T. Imielinski, and A. Swami, "Database Mining: A Performance Perspective," *IEEE Trans. Knowledge Data Eng.*, 5(6), 914–925 (1993).
4. S-J Yen and A. L. P. Chen, "An Efficient Algorithm for Deriving Compact Rules from Databases," in *Proceedings of the Fourth International Conference on Database Systems for Advanced Applications*, 1995.
5. G. G. Towell and J. W. Shavlik, "Extracting Refined Rules from Knowledge-Based Neural Networks," *Machine Learning*, 13(1), 71–101 (1993).
6. L. Fu, *Neural Networks in Computer Intelligence*. McGraw-Hill, New York, 1994.
7. R. Setiono and H. Liu, "Understanding Neural Networks Via Rule Extraction," in *IJCAI–95, Proceedings International Joint Conference on Artificial Intelligence*, 1995.
8. C. Wallace and P. Freeman, "Estimation and Inference by Compact Function," *J. Roy. Statist. Soc. Series B*, 49B(3), 240–265 (1987).
9. S. M. Weiss and N. Indurkhya, "Optimized Rule Induction," *IEEE Expert*, 8(6), 61–69 (1991).
10. D. T. Pham and M. S. Aksoy, "An Algorithm for Automatic Rule Induction," *Artif. Intell. Eng.*, 8 (1994).
11. P. R. Cohen and E. A. Feigenbaum, *The Handbook of Artificial Intelligence III*. William Kaufmann Inc., 1982.
12. C. J. Thornton, *Techniques of Computational Learning*: *An Introduction*, Chapman & Hall, New York, 1992.
13. J. R. Quinlan, "Induction of Decision Trees," *Machine Learning*, 1(1), 81–106 (1986).
14. P. Clark and T. Niblett, "The CN2 Induction Algorithm," *Machine Learning*, 3, 261–283 (1989).
15. H. Liu and R. Setiono, "Chi2: Feature Selection and Discretization of Numeric Attributes," in *Proceedings of the 7th IEEE International Conference on Tools with Artificial Intelligence*, 1995.
16. H. Lu, R. Setiono, and H. Liu, "Neurorule: A Connectionist Approach to Data Mining," in *Proceedings of VLDB '95*, Elsevier Science Ltd, London, 1995, pp. 478–489.
17. H. Liu, "Efficient Rule Induction from Noisy Data," *Expert Syst. Appl.*, 10(2), 275–280 (1996).

18. D. Michie, D. J. Spiegelhalter, and C. C. Taylor, *Machine Learning, Neural and Statistical Classification*, Ellis Horwood, New York, 1994.
19. J. Han, Y. Cai, and H. Cercone, "Data-Driven Discovery of Quantitative Rules in Relational Databases," *IEEE Trans. Knowledge Data Eng.*, 5(1), 15–28 (1993).
20. R. A. Fisher, "The Use of Multiple Measurements in Taxonomic Problems," *Ann. Eugen.*, 7(2), 179–188 (1936).
21. P. M. Murphy and D. W. Aha, "UCI Repository of Machine Learning Databases," FTP from ics.uci.edu in the directory pub/machine-learning-databases, 1994.
22. P. W. Frey and D. J. Slate, "Letter Recognition Using Holland-Style Adaptive Classifiers," *Machine Learning*, 6(2), 161–182 (1991).

BIBLIOGRAPHY

Barr, A., P. R. Cohen, and E. A. Feigenbaum, *The Handbook of Artificial Intelligence, Vol. 4*, Addison-Wesley, Reading, MA, 1989.

Michie, D., D. Spiegelhalter, and C. Taylor. *Machine Learning, Neural and Statistical Classification*, Ellis Horwood, New York, 1994.

Quinlan, J., *C4.5: Programs for Machine Learning*, Morgan Kaufmann, San Mateo, CA, 1993.

Russell, S. and P. Norvig, *Artificial Intelligence: A Modern Approach*, Prentice-Hall, Englewood Cliffs, NJ, 1995.

Setiono, R. and H. Liu, "Symbolic Representation of Neural Networks," *IEEE Computer*, 71–77 (1996).

Shavlik, J. and T. Dietterich (eds.), *Readings in Machine Learning*, Morgan Kaufmann, San Mateo, CA, 1990.

Smith, M., *Neural Networks for Statistical Modeling*, Van Nostrand Reinhold, New York, 1993.

Weiss, S. M. and C. A. Kulikowski, *Computer Systems That Learn*, Morgan Kaufmann, San Mateo, CA, 1991.

HUAN LIU

GENETIC PROGRAMMING

INTRODUCTION

Genetic programming is a domain-independent problem-solving approach in which computer programs are evolved to solve, or approximately solve, problems. Genetic programming is based on the Darwinian principle of reproduction and survival of the fittest and analogs of naturally occurring genetic operations such as *crossover* (*sexual recombination*) and *mutation*.

John Holland's pioneering *Adaptation in Natural and Artificial Systems* (1) described how an analog of the evolutionary process can be applied to solving mathematical problems and engineering optimization problems using what is now called the *genetic algorithm* (GA). The genetic algorithm attempts to find a good (or best) solution to the problem by genetically breeding a population of individuals over a series of generations. In the genetic algorithm, each *individual* in the population represents a candidate solution to the given problem. The *genetic algorithm* (GA) transforms a *population* (set) of individuals, each with an associated *fitness* value, into a new *generation* of the population using reproduction, crossover, and mutation.

Books on genetic algorithms that include those that survey the entire field, such as those by Goldberg (2), Michalewicz (3), and Mitchell (4) as well as others that specialize in particular areas, such as the application of genetic algorithms to robotics (5), financial applications (6), image segmentation (7), pattern recognition (8), parallelization (9), and simulation on modeling (10), control and signal processing (11), and engineering design (12).

Edited collection of papers on genetic algorithms include Refs. 13–18. Recent work on genetic algorithms can often be found in conference proceedings, such as the International Conference on Genetic Algorithms (19), ICEC—International Conference on Evolutionary Computation (20), the annual Genetic Programming Conference (21), Parallel Problem Solving from Nature (22), Artificial Evolution (23), Genetic Algorithms in Engineering Systems: Innovations and Applications (24), Evolutionary Computing (25), Evolutionary Computation and its Applications (26), Frontiers of Evolutionary Algorithms (27), Simulated Evolution and Learning (28), International Conference on Evolvable Systems (29), International Conference on Artificial Neural Nets and Genetic Algorithms (30), and the Evolutionary Programming Conference (31).

Genetic programming addresses one of the central goals of computer science, namely automatic programming. The goal of automatic programming is to create, in an automated way, a computer program that enables a computer to solve a problem. Paraphrasing Arthur Samuel (32), the goal of automatic programming concerns

> How can computers be made to do what needs to be done, without being told exactly how to do it?

In genetic programming, the genetic algorithm operates on a population of computer programs of varying sizes and shapes (33). Genetic programming starts with a primordial ooze of thousands or millions of randomly generated computer programs composed of the available programmatic ingredients and then applies the principles of animal husbandry to breed a new (and often improved) population of programs. The breeding is done in a domain-independent way using the Darwinian principle of survival of the fittest, an analog of the naturally occurring genetic operation of crossover (sexual recombination) and occasional mutation. The crossover operation is designed to create syntactically valid offspring programs (given closure among the set of programmatic ingredients). Genetic programming combines the expressive high-level symbolic representation of computer programs with the near-optimal efficiency of learning of Holland's genetic algorithm. A computer program that solves (or approximately solves) a given problem often emerges from this process. See also Ref. 34.

Genetic programming breeds computer programs to solve problems by executing the following three steps:

1. Generate an initial population of random compositions of the functions and terminals of the problem (i.e., computer programs).
2. Iteratively perform the following substeps until the termination criterion has been satisfied:
    A. Execute each program in the population and assign it a fitness value using the fitness measure.
    B. Create a new population of computer programs by applying the following operations. The operations are applied to computer program(s) chosen from the population with a probability based on fitness.
        (i)   *Darwinian Reproduction*: Reproduce an existing program by copying it into the new population.
        (ii) *Crossover*: Create two new computer programs from two existing programs by genetically recombining randomly chosen parts of two existing programs using the crossover operation (described below) applied at a randomly chosen crossover point within each program.
        (iii) *Mutation*: Create one new computer program from one existing program by mutating a randomly chosen part of the program.
3. The program that is identified by the method of result designation is designated as the result for the run (e.g., the best-so-far individual). This result may be a solution (or an approximate solution) to the problem.

Multipart programs consisting of a main program and one or more reusable, parameterized, hierarchically called subprograms (called *automatically defined functions*) may also be evolved (35,36). An *automatically defined function* (ADF) is a function (i.e., subroutine, subprogram, DEFUN, procedure) that is dynamically evolved during a run of genetic programming and which may be called by a calling program (or subprogram) that is concurrently being evolved. When automatically defined functions are being used, a program in the population consists of a hierarchy of one (or more) reusable function-defining branches (i.e., automatically defined functions) along with a main result-producing branch. Typically, the automatically defined functions possess one or more dummy arguments (formal parameters) and are reused with different instantiations of these dummy arguments. During a run, genetic programming evolves different subprograms in the function-defining branches of the overall program, different main programs in the result-producing branch, different instantiations of the dummy arguments of the automatically defined functions in the function-defining branches, and different hierarchical references between the branches.

Architecture-altering operations enhance genetic programming with automatically defined functions by providing a way to automatically determine the number of such subprograms, the number of arguments that each subprogram possesses, and the nature of the hierarchical references, if any, among such subprograms (37). These operations include branch duplication, argument duplication, branch creation, argument creation, branch deletion, and argument deletion. The architecture-altering operations are motivated by the naturally occurring mechanism of gene duplication that creates new proteins (and hence new structures and new behaviors in living things) (38).

Recent research on genetic programming is described in Ref. 39, the proceedings of the annual Genetic Programming Conferences (40), and in most of the conferences cited earlier on evolutionary computation. Edited collection of papers on genetic programming include Refs. 41 and 42.

Before applying genetic programming to a problem, the user must perform five major preparatory steps. These five steps involve determining the following:

1. The set of terminals
2. The set of primitive functions
3. The fitness measure
4. The parameters for controlling the run
5. The method for designating a result and the criterion for terminating a run

The first major step in preparing to use genetic programming is to identify the set of terminals. The terminals can be viewed as the inputs to the as-yet-undiscovered computer program. The set of terminals (along with the set of functions) are the ingredients from which genetic programming attempts to construct a computer program to solve, or approximately solve, the problem.

The second major step in preparing to use genetic programming is to identify the set of functions that are to be used to generate the mathematical expression that attempts to fit the given finite sample of data. Each computer program (i.e., parse tree, mathematical expression, LISP S-expression) is a composition of functions from the function set $\mathcal{F}$ and terminals from the terminal set $\mathcal{T}$. Each of the functions in the function set should be able to accept, as its arguments, any value and data type that may possibly be returned by any function in the function set and any value and data type that may possibly be assumed by any terminal in the terminal set; that is, the function set and terminal set selected should have the closure property so that any possible composition of functions and terminals produces a valid executable computer program. For example, a run of genetic programming will typically employ a protected version of division (returning an arbitrary value such as zero when division by zero is attempted).

The evolutionary process is driven by the *fitness measure*. Each individual computer program in the population is executed and then evaluated, using the fitness measure, to determine how well it performs in the particular problem environment. The nature of the fitness measure varies with the problem. For many problems, fitness is naturally measured by the discrepancy between the result produced by an individual candidate program and the desired result. The closer this error is to zero, the better the program. In a problem of optimal control, the fitness of a computer program may be the amount of time (or fuel, or money, etc.) it takes to bring the system to a desired target state. The smaller the amount, the better. If one is trying to recognize patterns or classify objects into categories, the fitness of a particular program may be measured by accuracy or correlation. For electronic circuit design problems, the fitness measure may involve how closely the circuit's performance (say, in the frequency or time domain) satisfies user-specified design requirements. If one is trying to evolve a good randomizer, the fitness might be measured by means of entropy, satisfaction of the gap test, satisfaction of the run test, or some combination of these factors. For some problems, it may be appropriate to use a multiobjective fitness measure incorporating a combination of factors such as correctness, parsimony (smallness of the evolved program), efficiency (of execution), power consumption (for an electrical circuit), or manufacturing cost (for an electrical circuit).

The primary parameters for controlling a run of genetic programming are the population size, M, and the maximum number of generations to be run, G.

Each run of genetic programming requires specification of a *termination criterion* for deciding when to terminate a run and a method of *result designation*. One frequently used method of result designation for a run is to designate the best individual obtained in any generation of the population during the run (i.e., the *best-so-far-individual*) as the result of the run.

In genetic programming, populations of thousands or millions of computer programs are genetically bred for dozens, hundreds, or thousands of generations. This breeding is done using the Darwinian principle of survival and reproduction of the fittest along with a genetic crossover operation appropriate for mating computer programs. A computer program that solves (or approximately solves) a given problem often emerges from this combination of Darwinian natural selection and genetic operations.

Genetic programming starts with an initial population (generation 0) of randomly generated computer programs composed of the given primitive functions and terminals. Typically, the size of each program is limited, for practical reasons, to a certain maximum number of points (i.e., total number of functions and terminals) or a maximum depth (of the program tree). The creation of this initial random population is, in effect, a blind random parallel search of the search space of the problem represented as computer programs.

Typically, each computer program in the population is run over a number of different *fitness cases* so that its fitness is measured as a sum or an average over a variety of representative different situations. These fitness cases sometimes represent a sampling of different values of an independent variable or a sampling of different initial conditions of a system. For example, the fitness of an individual computer program in the population may be measured in terms of the sum of the absolute value of the differences between the output produced by the program and the correct answer to the problem (i.e., the Minkowski distance) or the square root of the sum of the squares (i.e., Euclidean distance). These sums are taken over a sampling of different inputs (fitness cases) to the program. The fitness cases may be chosen at random or may be chosen in some structured way (e.g., at regular intervals or over a regular grid). It is also common for fitness cases to represent initial conditions of a system (as in a control problem). In economic forecasting problems, the fitness cases may be the daily closing price of some financial instrument.

The computer programs in generation 0 of a run of genetic programming will almost always have exceedingly poor fitness. Nonetheless, some individuals in the population will turn out to be somewhat more fit than others. These differences in performance are then exploited.

The Darwinian principle of reproduction and survival of the fittest and the genetic operation of crossover are used to create a new offspring population of individual computer programs from the current population of programs.

The reproduction operation involves selecting a computer program from the current population of programs based on fitness (i.e., the better the fitness, the more likely the individual is to be selected) and allowing it to survive by copying it into the new population.

The crossover operation creates new offspring computer programs from two parental programs selected based on fitness. The parental programs in genetic programming are typically of different sizes and shapes. The offspring programs are composed of subexpressions (subtrees, subprograms, subroutines, building blocks) from their parents. These offspring programs are typically of different sizes and shapes than their parents.

For example, consider the following computer program (presented here as a LISP S-expression):

(+ (* 0.234 Z) (– X 0.789)),

which we would ordinarily write as

0.234 Z + X – 0.789.

This program takes two inputs (X and Z) and produces a floating-point output. Also, consider a second program:

(* (* Z Y) (+ Y (* 0.314 Z))).

One crossover point is randomly and independently chosen in each parent. Suppose that the crossover points are the * in the first parent and the + in the second parent. These two crossover fragments correspond to the underlined subprograms (sublists) in the two parental computer programs.

The two offspring resulting from crossover are as follows:

(+ (+ Y (* 0.314 Z)) (– X 0.789))
(* (* Z Y) (* 0.234 Z)).

Thus, crossover creates new computer programs using parts of existing parental programs. Because entire subtrees are swapped, the crossover operation always produces syntactically and semantically valid programs as offspring regardless of the choice of the two crossover points. Because programs are selected to participate in the crossover operation with a probability based on fitness, crossover allocates future trials to regions of the search space whose programs contains parts from promising programs.

The mutation operation creates an offspring computer program from one parental program selected based on fitness. One crossover point is randomly and independently chosen and the subtree occurring at that point is deleted. Then, a new subtree is grown at that point using the same growth procedure as was originally used to create the initial random population.

After the genetic operations are performed on the current population, the population of offspring (i.e., the new generation) replaces the old population (i.e., the old generation). Each individual in the new population of programs is then measured for fitness, and the process is repeated over many generations.

The hierarchical character of the computer programs that are produced is an important feature of genetic programming. The results of genetic programming are inherently hierarchical. In many cases, the results produced by genetic programming are default hierarchies, prioritized hierarchies of tasks, or hierarchies in which one behavior subsumes or suppresses another.

The dynamic variability of the computer programs that are developed along the way to a solution is also an important feature of genetic programming. It is often difficult and unnatural to try to specify or restrict the size and shape of the eventual solution in advance. Moreover, advance specification or restriction of the size and shape of the solution to a problem narrows the window by which the system views the world and might well preclude finding the solution to the problem at all.

Another important feature of genetic programming is the absence or relatively minor role of preprocessing of inputs and postprocessing of outputs. The inputs, intermediate results, and outputs are typically expressed directly in terms of the natural terminology of the problem domain. The programs produced by genetic programming consist of functions that are natural for the problem domain. The postprocessing of the output of a program, if any, is done by a *wrapper* (*output interface*).

Finally, another important feature of genetic programming is that the structures undergoing adaptation in genetic programming are active. They are not passive encodings (i.e., chromosomes) of the solution to the problem. Instead, given a computer on which to run, the structures in genetic programming are active structures that are capable of being executed in their current form.

Automated programming requires some hierarchical mechanism to exploit, *by reuse* and *parameterization*, the regularities, symmetries, homogeneities, similarities, patterns, and modularities inherent in problem environments. Subroutines do this in ordinary computer programs.

Automatically defined functions can be implemented within the context of genetic programming by establishing a constrained syntactic structure for the individual programs in the population. Each multipart program in the population contains one (or more) function-defining branches and one (or more) main result-producing branches. The result-producing branch usually has the ability to call one or more of the automatically defined functions. A function-defining branch may have the ability to refer hierarchically to other already-defined automatically defined functions.

Genetic programming evolves a population of programs, each consisting of an automatically defined function in the function-defining branch and a result-producing branch. The structures of both the function-defining branches and the result-producing branch are determined by the combined effect, over many generations, of the selective pressure exerted by the fitness measure and by the effects of the operations of Darwinian fitness-based reproduction and crossover. The function defined by the function-defining branch is available for use by the result-producing branch. Whether or not the defined function will be actually called is not predetermined, but instead, determined by the evolutionary process.

Because each individual program in the population of this example consists of function-defining branch(es) and result-producing branch(es), the initial random generation must be created so that every individual program in the population has this particular constrained syntactic structure. Because a constrained syntactic structure is involved, crossover must be performed so as to preserve this syntactic structure in all offspring.

Genetic programming with automatically defined functions has been shown to be capable of solving numerous problems (35). More importantly, the evidence so far indicates that, for many problems, genetic programming requires less computational effort (i.e., fewer fitness evaluations to yield a solution with, say, a 99% probability) with automatically defined functions than without them (provided the difficulty of the problem is above a certain relatively low break-even point).

Also, genetic programming usually yields solutions with smaller average overall size with automatically defined functions than without them (provided, again, that the problem is not too simple); that is, both learning efficiency and parsimony appear to be properties of genetic programming with automatically defined functions.

Moreover, there is evidence that genetic programming with automatically defined functions is scalable. For several problems for which a progression of scaled-up versions was studied, the computational effort increases as a function of problem size at a *slower rate* with automatically defined functions than without them. Also, the average size of solutions similarly increases as a function of problem size at a *slower rate* with automatically defined functions than without them. This observed scalability results from the profitable reuse of hierarchically callable, parameterized subprograms within the overall program.

When single-part programs are involved, genetic programming automatically determines the size and shape of the solution (i.e., the size and shape of the program tree) as well as the sequence of work-performing primitive functions that can solve the problem. However, when multipart programs and automatically defined functions are being used, the question arises as to how to determine the architecture of the programs that are being evolved. The *architecture* of a multipart program consists of the number of function-defining branches (automatically defined functions) and the number of arguments (if any) possessed by each function-defining branch. The architecture may be specified by the user, may be evolved using evolutionary selection of the architecture (35) or may be evolved using architecture-altering operations (37).

THE THRESHOLD OF PRACTICALITY

Genetic programming has been used to produce results that are competitive with human performance on certain nontrivial problems. In fields as diverse as cellular automata, space satellite control, molecular biology, and design of electrical circuits, genetic programming has evolved a computer program whose results were, under some reasonable interpretation, competitive with human performance on the specific problem. For example, genetic programming with automatically defined functions has evolved a rule for the majority classification task for one-dimensional two-state cellular automata with an accuracy that exceeds that of the original human-written Gacs–Kurdyumov–Levin (GKL) rule, all other known subsequent human-written rules, and all other known rules produced by automated approaches for this problem (43). Another example involves the near-minimum-time control of a spacecraft's attitude maneuvers using genetic programming (44). A third example involves the discovery by genetic programming of a computer program to classify a given protein segment as being a transmembrane domain without using biochemical knowledge concerning hydrophobicity (35,45). A fourth example illustrated how automated methods may prove to be useful in discovering biologically meaningful information hidden in the rapidly growing databases of DNA sequences and protein sequences. Genetic programming successfully evolved motifs for detecting the D-E-A-D box family of proteins and for detecting the manganese superoxide dismutase family that detected the two families either as well as, or slightly better than, the comparable human-written motifs found in the database created by an international committee of experts on molecular biology (46). A fifth example is recent work on facility layouts (47).

An additional group of examples is provided by work in which genetic programming has been used to evolve both the topology and numerical component values for electrical circuits, including low-pass filters, crossover (woofer and tweeter) filters, asymmetric bandpass filters, amplifiers, computational circuits, a time-optimal controller circuit, a temperature-sensing circuit, and a voltage reference circuit (21).

OPERATIONS ON COMPLEX DATA STRUCTURES

Ordinary computer programs use numerous well-known techniques for handling vectors of data, arrays, and more complex data structures. One important area for work on technique extensions for genetic programming involves developing workable and efficient ways to handle vectors, arrays, trees, graphs, and more complex data structures. Such new techniques would have immediate application to a number of problems in such fields as computer vision, biological sequence analysis, economic time series analysis, and pattern recognition where a solution to the problem involves analyzing the character of an entire data structure. Recent work in this area includes that of Langdon (48) in handling more complex data structures such as stacks, queues, rings, and lists, the work of Teller (49) in understanding images represented by large arrays of pixels, and the work of Handley (50) in applying statistical computing zones and iteration to biological sequence data and other problems.

EVOLUTION OF MENTAL MODELS

Complex adaptive systems usually possess a mechanism for modeling their environment. A mental model of the environment enables a system to contemplate the effects of future actions and to choose an action that best fulfills its goals. Brave (51) has developed a special form of memory that is capable of creating relations among objects and then using these relations to guide the decisions of a system.

Automatically Defined Functions, Automatically Defined Macros, and Modules

Computer programs gain leverage in solving complex problems by means of reusable and parameterizable subprograms. Automated machine learning can become scalable (and truly useful) only if there are techniques for creating large and complex problem-solving programs from smaller building blocks. Spector (52) has developed the notion of automatically defined macros (ADMs) for use in evolving control structures. Rosca (53) has analyzed the workings of hierarchical arrangements of subprograms in genetic programming. Angeline (54) has studied modules that are made available to all programs in the population through a genetic library.

Automatically defined functions and architecture-altering operations are used for creating useful electrical subcircuits (21).

CELLULAR ENCODING

Gruau (55) described an innovative technique, called *cellular encoding* or *developmental genetic programming* in which genetic programming is used to concurrently evolve the architecture of a neural network, along with the weights, thresholds, and biases of the individual neurons in the neural network. In this technique, each individual program tree in the population is a specification for developing a complete neural network from a starting point consisting of a very simple embryonic neural network containing a single neuron. Genetic programming is applied to populations of these network-constructing program trees in order to evolve a neural network to solve various problems.

Brave (56) has extended and applied this technique to the evolution of finite automata.

AUTOMATIC PROGRAMMING OF MULTIAGENT SYSTEMS

The cooperative behavior of multiple independent agents can potentially be harnessed to solve a wide variety of practical problems. However, programming of multiagent systems is particularly vexatious. Bennett's recent work (57) in evolving the number of independent agents while evolving the specific behaviors of each agent and the recent work by Luke and Spector (52) in evolving teamwork are opening this area to the application of genetic programming. See also Ref. 58.

AUTOPARALLELIZATION OF ALGORITHMS

The problem of mapping a given sequential algorithm into a parallel machine is usually more difficult than writing a parallel algorithm from scratch. The recent work of Walsh and Ryan (59) is advancing the autoparallelization of algorithms using genetic programming.

COEVOLUTION

In nature, individuals do not evolve in a vacuum. Instead, there is coevolution that involves interactions between agents and other agents as well as between agents and their physical environment (60,61).

COMPLEX ADAPTIVE SYSTEMS

Genetic programming has proven useful in evolving complex systems, such as Lindenmayer systems (62) and cellular automata (43) and can be expected to continue to be useful in this area.

EVOLUTION OF STRUCTURE

One of the most vexatious aspects of automated machine learning from the earliest times has been the requirement that the human user predetermine the size and shape of the ultimate solution to his problem (32). There can be expected to be continuing research on ways by which the size and shape of the solution can be made part of the *answer* provided by the automated machine learning technique, rather than part of the *question* supplied by the human user. For example, architecture-altering operations (37) enable genetic programming to introduce (or delete) function-defining branches, to adjust the number of arguments of each function-defining branch, and to alter the hierarchical references among function-defining branches. Brave (63) showed that recursion could be implemented within genetic programming. It is also possible to evolve iterations using genetic programming (46).

FOUNDATIONS OF GENETIC PROGRAMMING

Genetic programming inherits many of the mathematical and theoretical underpinnings from John Holland's pioneering work (1) in the field, including the near-optimality of Darwinian search. However, the genetic algorithm is a dynamical system of extremely high dimensionality. Many of the most basic questions about the operation of the algorithm and the domain of its applicability are only partially understood. The transition from the fixed-length character strings of the genetic algorithm to the variable-sized Turing-complete program trees (49) and even program graphs (64) of genetic programming further compounds the difficulty of the theoretical issues involved. There is increasing work on the grammatical structure of genetic programming (65) and the theoretical basis for genetic programming (66).

OPTIMIZATION

Recent examples of applications of genetic programming to problems of optimization include work (67) from the University of Idaho, the site of much early work on genetic programming techniques, and the work of Garces-Perez, Schoenefeld, and Wainwright (47).

EVOLUTION OF ASSEMBLY CODE

The innovative work by Nordin (68) in developing a version of genetic programming in which the programs are composed of sequence of low-level machine code offers numerous possibilities for extending the techniques of genetic programming (especially for programs with loops) as well as enormous savings in computer time. These savings can then be used to increase the scale of problems being considered. See also Ref. 39.

TECHNIQUES THAT EXPLOIT PARALLEL HARDWARE

Evolutionary algorithms offer the ability of solve problems in a domain-independent way that requires little domain-specific knowledge. However, the price of this domain independence and knowledge independence is paid in execution time. Application of genetic programming to realistic problems usually requires substantial computational resources. The long-term trend toward ever-faster microprocessors is likely to continue to make ever-increasing amounts of computational power available at ever-decreasing costs. However, for those using algorithms that can beneficially exploit parallelization (such as genetic programming), parallelization is even more important than microprocessor speed in terms of delivering large amounts of computational power. In genetic programming, the vast majority of computer resources are used on the fitness evaluations. The calculation of fitness for one individual in the population is usually independent and decoupled from the calculation of fitness of all other individuals. Thus, parallel computing techniques can be applied to genetic programming (and genetic algorithms in general) with almost 100% efficiency (69). In fact, the use of semi-isolated subpopulations often accelerates the finding of a solution to a problem using genetic programming and produces not just near-linear speedup, but superlinear speedup. Parallelization of genetic programming will be of central importance to the growth of the field.

EVOLVABLE HARDWARE

One of the newest areas of evolutionary computation involves the use of evolvable hardware (29,70). Evolvable hardware includes devices such as field programmable gate arrays (FPGA) and field programmable analog arrays (FPAA). The idea of evolvable hardware is to embody each individual of the evolving population *into hardware* and thereby exploit the massive parallelism of the hardware to perform evolution "in silicon." These devices are reconfigurable with very short configuration times and download times. Thompson (71) has pioneered the use of field-programmable gates arrays to evolve a frequency discriminator circuit and a robot controller using the recently developed Xilinix XC6216 chip. Considerable growth can be anticipated in the use of evolvable hardware to accelerate genetic programming runs and perform evolution.

FUTURE WORK

The presence of some or all of the following characteristics make an area especially suitable for the application of genetic programming:

- An area where conventional mathematical analysis does not, or cannot, provide analytic solutions
- An area where the interrelationships among the relevant variables are poorly understood (or where it is suspected that the current understanding may well be wrong)
- An area where finding the size and shape of the ultimate solution to the problem is a major part of the problem
- An area where an approximate solution is acceptable (or is the only result that is ever likely to be obtained)
- An area where there is a large amount of data, in computer-readable form, that requires examination, classification, and integration
- An area where small improvements in performance are routinely measured (or easily measurable) and highly prized

For example, problems in automated control are especially well suited for genetic programming because of the inability of conventional mathematical analysis to provide analytic solutions to many problems of practical interest, the willingness of control engineers to accept approximate solutions, and the high value placed on small incremental improvements in performance.

Problems in fields where large amounts of data are accumulating in machine-readable form (e.g., biological sequence data, astronomical observations, geological and petroleum data, financial time series data, satellite observation data, weather data, news stories, marketing databases) also constitute especially interesting areas for potential practical applications of genetic programming.

REFERENCES

1. J. H. Holland, *Adaptation in Natural and Artificial Systems*: *An Introductory Analysis with Applications to Biology, Control, and Artificial Intelligence*, University of Michigan Press, Ann Arbor, MI, 1975; second edition published by MIT Press, 1992.

2. D. E. Goldberg, *Genetic Algorithms in Search, Optimization, and Machine Learning*, Addison-Wesley, Reading, MA, 1989.

3. Z. Michalewicz, *Genetic Algorithms + Data Structures = Evolution Programs*, Springer-Verlag, Berlin, 1992.

4. M. Mitchell, *An Introduction to Genetic Algorithms*, MIT Press, Cambridge, MA, 1996.

5. Y. Davidor, *Genetic Algorithms and Robotics*, World Scientific, Singapore, 1991.

6. R. J. Bauer, Jr., *Genetic Algorithms and Investment Strategies*, John Wiley & Sons, New York, 1994.

7. B. Bhanu and S. Lee, *Genetic Learning for Adaptive Image Segmentation*, Kluwer Academic Publishers, Boston, 1994.

8. S. K. Pal and P. P. Wang, *Genetic Algorithms and Pattern Recognition*, CRC Press, Boca Raton, FL, 1996.

9. J. Stender (ed.), *Parallel Genetic Algorithms*, IOS Publishing, Amsterdam, 1993.

10. J. Stender, Hillebrand, and J. Kingdon (eds.), *Genetic Algorithms in Optimization, Simulation, and Modeling*, IOS Publishing, Amsterdam, 1994.

11. K. F. Man, K. S. Tang, S. Kwong, and W. A. Halang, *Genetic Algorithms for Control and Signal Processing*, Springer-Verlag, London, 1997.

12. M. Gen and R. Cheng, *Genetic Algorithms and Engineering Design*, John Wiley & Sons, New York, 1997.

13. L. Davis (ed.), *Genetic Algorithms and Simulated Annealing*, Pittman, London, 1987.

14. L. Davis, *Handbook of Genetic Algorithms*, Van Nostrand Reinhold, New York, 1991.

15. L. Chambers (ed.), *Practical Handbook of Genetic Algorithms: Applications: Volume I*, CRC Press, Boca Raton, FL, 1995.

16. J. Biethahn and V. Nissen (eds.), *Evolutionary Algorithms in Management Applications*, Springer-Verlag, Berlin, 1995.

17. D. Dasgupta and Z. Michalewicz (eds.), *Evolutionary Algorithms in Engineering Applications*, Springer-Verlag, Berlin, 1997.

18. T. Back, D. B. Fogel, and Z. Michalewicz (eds.), *Handbook of Evolutionary Computation*. Institute of Physics Publishing, Bristol, UK; Oxford University Press, New York, 1997.

19. T. Back (ed.), *Genetic Algorithms: Proceedings of the Fifth International Conference*. Morgan Kaufmann, San Francisco, CA, 1997.

20. IEEE, *Proceedings of the Fourth IEEE Conference on Evolutionary Computation*, IEEE Press, New York, 1997.

21. J. R. Koza, F. H. Bennett III, H. Forrest, D. Andre, M. A. Keane, and F. Dunlap, "Automated Synthesis of Analog Electrical Circuits by Means of Genetic Programming," *IEEE Trans. Evolutionary Computation, 1*(2) (1997).

22. H.-M. Voigt, W. Ebeling, I. Rechenberg, and H.-P. Schwefel (eds.), *Parallel Problem Solving from Nature—PPSN IV*, Springer-Verlag, Berlin, 1996.

23. J. M. Alliot, E. Lutton, E. Ronald, M. Schoenauer, and D. Snyers (eds.), *Artificial Evolution*: *European Conference, AE 95, Brest, France, September 1995, Selected Papers*. Lecture Notes in Computer Science Vol. 1063, Springer-Verlag, Berlin, 1995.

24. IEE, *Proceedings of the First International Conference on Genetic Algorithms in Engineering Systems*: *Innovations and Applications* (*GALESIA*), Institution of Electrical Engineers, London, 1995.

25. T. C. Fogarty (ed.), *Evolutionary Computing*: *AISB Workshop, Sheffield, U.K., April 1995, Selected Papers*. Lecture Notes in Computer Science Vol. 993, Springer-Verlag, Berlin, 1995.

26. E. D. Goodman (ed.), *Proceedings of the First International Conference on Evolutionary Computation and Its Applications*, Presidium of the Russian Academy of Sciences, Moscow, 1996.

27. P. P. Wang (ed.), *Proceedings of Joint Conference of Information Sciences*, 1997.

28. X. Yao, J.-H. Kim, and T. Furuhashi (eds.), *Simulated Evolution and Learning*, Lecture Notes in Artificial Intelligence Vol. 1285, Springer-Verlag, Heidelberg, 1997.

29. T. Higuchi, M. Iwata, and W. Lui (eds.), *Proceedings of International Conference on Evolvable Systems*: *From Biology to Hardware* (*ICES–96*), Lecture Notes in Computer Science Vol. 1259, Springer-Verlag, Berlin, 1997.

30. D. W. Pearson, N. C. Steele, and R. F. Albrecht, *Artificial Neural Nets and Genetic Algorithms*, Springer-Verlag, Vienna, 1995.

31. P. J. Angeline, R. G. Reynolds, J. R. McDonnell, and R. Eberhart (eds.), *Evolutionary Programming VI. 6th International Conference, EP97, Indianapolis, Indiana, USA, April 1997 Proceedings*. Lecture Notes in Computer Science Vol. 1213, Springer-Verlag, Berlin, 1997, pp. 125–136.

32. A. L. Samuel, "Some Studies in Machine Learning Using the Game of Checkers," *IBM J. Res. Devel.*, *3*(3), 210–229 (1959).

33. J. R. Koza, *Genetic Programming*: *On the Programming of Computers by Means of Natural Selection*, MIT Press, Cambridge, MA, 1992.

34. J. R. Koza and J. P. Rice, *Genetic Programming*: *The Movie*, MIT Press, Cambridge, MA, 1992.

35. J. R. Koza, *Genetic Programming II*: *Automatic Discovery of Reusable Programs*, MIT Press, Cambridge, MA, 1994.

36. J. R. Koza, *Genetic Programming II Videotape*: *The Next Generation*, MIT Press, Cambridge, MA, 1994.

37. J. R. Koza, "Gene Duplication to Enable Genetic Programming to Concurrently Evolve Both the Architecture and Work-Performing Steps of a Computer Program," in *Proceedings of 14th International Joint Conference on Artificial Intelligence*, Morgan Kaufmann, San Francisco, CA, 1995.

38. S. Ohno, *Evolution by Gene Duplication*, Springer-Verlag, New York, 1970.

39. W. Banzhaf, P. Nordin, R. E. Keller, and F. D. Francone, *Genetic Programming—An Introduction*. Morgan Kaufmann, San Francisco, CA, 1998.

40. J. R. Koza, K. Deb, M. Dorigo, D. B. Fogel, M. Garzon, H. Iba, and R. L. Riolo (eds.), *Genetic Programming 1997*: *Proceedings of the Second Annual Conference, July 13–16, 1997, Stanford University*, Morgan Kaufmann, San Francisco, CA, 1997.

41. K. E. Kinnear, Jr. (ed.), *Advances in Genetic Programming*, MIT Press, Cambridge, MA, 1994.

42. P. J. Angeline and K. E. Kinnear, Jr. (eds.), *Advances in Genetic Programming 2*, MIT Press, Cambridge, MA, 1996.

43. D. Andre, F. H. Bennett III, H. Forrest, and J. R. Koza, "Discovery by Genetic Programming of a Cellular Automata Rule That Is Better Than Any Known Rule of the Majority Classification Problem," in *Genetic Programming 1996*: *Proceedings of the First Annual Conference, July 28–31, 1996, Stanford University*, J. R. Koza, D. E. Goldberg, D. B. Fogel, and R. L. Riolo (eds.), MIT Press, Cambridge, MA, 1996.

44. B. Howley, "Genetic Programming of Near-Minimum-Time Spacecraft Attitude Maneuvers, in *Genetic Programming 1996: Proceedings of the First Annual Conference, July 28–31, 1996, Stanford University*, J. R. Koza, D. E. Goldberg, D. B. Fogel, and R. L. Riolo (eds.), MIT Press, Cambridge, MA, 1996.

45. J. R. Koza and D. Andre, "Evolution of Iteration in Genetic Programming," in *Evolutionary Programming V: Proceedings of the Fifth Annual Conference on Evolutionary Programming*, MIT Press, Cambridge, MA, 1996.

46. J. R. Koza and D. Andre, "Automatic Discovery of Protein Motifs Using Genetic Programming," in X. Yao (ed.), *Evolutionary Computation: Theory and Applications*, World Scientific, Singapore, 1996.

47. J. Garces-Perez, D. A. Schoenefeld, and R. L. Wainwright, "Solving Facility Layout Problems Using Genetic Programming," in *Genetic Programming 1996: Proceedings of the First Annual Conference, July 28–31, 1996, Stanford University*, J. R. Koza, D. E. Goldberg, D. B. Fogel, and R. L. Riolo (eds.), MIT Press, Cambridge, MA, 1996.

48. W. B. Langdon, "Using Data Structures Within Genetic Programming," in *Genetic Programming 1996: Proceedings of the First Annual Conference, July 28–31, 1996, Stanford University*, J. R. Koza, D. E. Goldberg, D. B. Fogel, and R. L. Riolo (eds.), MIT Press, Cambridge, MA, 1996.

49. A. Teller, "Turing Completeness in the Language of Genetic Programming with Indexed Memory," *Proceedings of The First IEEE Conference on Evolutionary Computation*, IEEE Press, New York, Vol. I, pp. 136–141.

50. S. Handley, "A New Class of Function Sets for Solving Sequence Problems," in *Genetic Programming 1996: Proceedings of the First Annual Conference, July 28–31, 1996, Stanford University*, J. R. Koza, D. E. Goldberg, D. B. Fogel, and R. L. Riolo (eds.), MIT Press, Cambridge, MA, 1996.

51. S. Brave, "The Evolution of Memory and Mental Models Using Genetic Programming," in J. R. Koza, D. E. Goldberg, D. B. Fogel, and R. L. Riolo (eds.), *Genetic Programming 1996: Proceedings of the First Annual Conference, July 28–31, 1996, Stanford University*, MIT Press, Cambridge, MA, 1996.

52. L. Spector, "Simultaneous Evolution of Programs and Their Control Structures," in *Advances in Genetic Programming 2*, P. J. Angeline and K. E. Kinnear, Jr. (eds.), MIT Press, Cambridge, MA, 1996.

53. J. P. Rosca, "Genetic Programming Exploratory Power and the Discovery of Functions," in *Evolutionary Programming IV: Proceedings of the Fourth Annual Conference on Evolutionary Programming*, J. R. McDonnell, R. G. Reynolds, and D. B. Fogel (eds.), MIT Press, Cambridge, MA, 1995.

54. P. J. Angeline, "Genetic Programming and the Emergence of Intelligence," in *Advances in Genetic Programming*, K. E. Kinnear, Jr. (ed.), MIT Press, Cambridge, MA, 1994.

55. F. Gruau, "Genetic Micro Programming of Neural Networks," *Advances in Genetic Programming*, K. E. Kinnear, Jr. (ed.), MIT Press, Cambridge, MA, 1994, pp. 495–518.

56. S. Brave, "Evolving Deterministic Finite Automata Using Cellular Encoding," in J. R. Koza, D. E. Goldberg, D. B. Fogel, and R. L. Riolo (eds.), *Genetic Programming 1996: Proceedings of the First Annual Conference, July 28–31, 1996, Stanford University*, MIT Press, Cambridge, MA, 1996.

57. F. H. Bennett III, "Automatic Creation of an Efficient Multi-agent Architecture Using Genetic Programming with Architecture-Altering Operations," in J. R. Koza, D. E. Goldberg, D. B. Fogel, and R. L. Riolo (eds.), *Genetic Programming 1996: Proceedings of the First Annual Conference, July 28–31, 1996, Stanford University*, MIT Press, Cambridge, MA, 1996.

58. H. Iba, "Multiple-Agent Learning for a Robot Navigation Task by Genetic Programming," in *Genetic Programming 1997: Proceedings of the Second Annual Conference, July 13–16, 1997, Stanford University*, J. R. Koza, K. Deb, M. Dorigo, D. B. Fogel, M. Garzon, H. Iba, and R. L. Riolo (eds.), Morgan Kaufmann, San Francisco, CA, 1997, pp. 195–200.

59. P. Walsh and C. Ryan, "Paragen: A Novel Technique for the Autoparallelisation of Sequential Programs Using Genetic Programming," in *Genetic Programming 1996: Proceedings of the First Annual Conference, July 28–31, 1996, Stanford University*, J. R. Koza, D. E. Goldberg, D. B. Fogel, and R. L. Riolo (eds.), MIT Press, Cambridge, MA, 1996.

60. P. J. Angeline and J. B. Pollack, "Coevolving High-Level Representation," in *Artificial Life III, SFI Studies in the Sciences of Complexity*, C. G. Langton (ed.), Addison-Wesley, Redwood City, CA, 1994, Vol. XVII, pp. 55–71.

61. J. B. Pollack and A. D. Blair, "Coevolution of a Backgammon Player," in *Artificial Life V: Proceedings of the Fifth International Workshop on the Synthesis and Simulation of Living Systems*, MIT Press, Cambridge, MA, 1996.

62. C. Jacob, "Evolving Evolution Programs: Genetic Programming and L-Systems," in *Genetic Programming 1996: Proceedings of the First Annual Conference, July 28–31, 1996, Stanford University*, J. R. Koza, D. E. Goldberg, D. B. Fogel, and R. L. Riolo (eds.), MIT Press, Cambridge, MA, 1996, pp. 107–115.

63. S. Brave, "Using Genetic Programming to Evolve Recursive Programs for Tree Search," *Proceedings of the Fourth Golden West Conference on Intelligent Systems*, International Society for Computers and Their Applications, Raleigh, NC, 1995, pp. 60–65.

64. A. Teller and M. Veloso, "PADO: A New Learning Architecture for Object Recognition," in *Symbolic Visual Learning*, K. Ikeuchi and M. Veloso (eds.), Oxford University Press, Oxford, 1996.

65. P. A. Whigham, "Search Bias, Language Bias, and Genetic Programming," in *Genetic Programming 1996: Proceedings of the First Annual Conference, July 28–31, 1996, Stanford University*, J. R. Koza, D. E. Goldberg, D. B. Fogel, and R. L. Riolo (eds.), MIT Press, Cambridge, MA, 1996.

66. R. Poli and W. B. Langdon, "A New Schema Theory for Genetic Programming with One-Point Crossover and Point Mutation," in *Genetic Programming 1996: Proceedings of the First Annual Conference, July 28–31, 1996, Stanford University*, J. R. Koza, D. E. Goldberg, D. B. Fogel, and R. L. Riolo (eds.), MIT Press, Cambridge, MA, 1997, pp. 278–285.

67. T. Soule, J. A. Foster, and J. Dickinson, "Code Growth in Genetic Programming," in *Genetic Programming 1996: Proceedings of the First Annual Conference, July 28–31, 1996, Stanford University*, J. R. Koza, D. E. Goldberg, D. B. Fogel, and R. L. Riolo (eds.), MIT Press, Cambridge, MA, 1996.

68. P. Nordin, "A Compiling Genetic Programming System That Directly Manipulates the Machine Code," in *Advances in Genetic Programming*, K. E. Kinnear, Jr. (ed.), MIT Press, Cambridge, MA, 1994.

69. D. Andre and J. R. Koza, "Parallel Genetic Programming: A Scalable Implementation Using the Transputer Network Architecture," in *Advances in Genetic Programming 2*. P. J. Angeline and K. E. Kinnear, Jr. (eds.), MIT Press, Cambridge, MA, 1996, Chap. 18.

70. E. Sanchez and M. Tomassini (eds.), *Towards Evolvable Hardware*, Lecture Notes in Computer Science Vol. 1062, Springer-Verlag, Berlin, 1996.

71. A. Thompson, "Silicon Evolution," in *Genetic Programming 1996: Proceedings of the First Annual Conference, July 28–31, 1996, Stanford University*, J. R. Koza, D. E. Goldberg, D. B. Fogel, and R. L. Riolo (eds.), MIT Press, Cambridge, MA, 1996.

JOHN R. KOZA

AN INCREMENTAL MEMORY ALLOCATION METHOD FOR MIXED WORKLOADS

INTRODUCTION

Database management systems (DBMS) are faced with increasingly demanding performance objectives. A large variety of applications require an acceptable performance for complex workloads consisting of a mix of decision-support activities and on-line transactions. There are several mechanisms in a DBMS engine which may be tuned in order to improve performance: multiprogramming level (MPL) control, disk and CPU scheduling, data placement, and memory management. We concentrate on memory management in this study, although a complete investigation of performance for a complex workload should probably include all of them.

Although the memory capacity of systems is constantly growing, memory management issues continue to be the focus of the database research community. Numerous studies have been devoted to static memory allocation and buffer management (1–5). A very few recent papers address techniques that adapt to a dynamic environment (6–10).

A hash-join algorithm requires a significant amount of memory to keep a hash table for efficient execution. This amount varies from the square root of the size of the inner relation to the full inner-relation size. The hash table must be held in memory for the entire period of join execution. A hash-join algorithm is divided into two phases: *building*, when a system reads the inner relation from a disk page by page and stores its tuples into a hash table, and *probing*, when pages of the outer relation are read and the system probes its tuples against the hash table. Both phases require a significant amount of time. During this period, there are many other components of a system workload that suffer as a result of insufficient memory. How can memory management help them to improve performance? One desirable answer would be to reduce the memory consumed by the hash-join. Several methods have been recently proposed to adapt the memory requirements for a join over the period of execution.

One method is to employ a virtual memory technique of paging a hash table. The DBMS maps the hash table into a smaller region of allocated memory, and the join operator does not need to worry about the actual size of memory. If the size of available memory is below a certain threshold, then the DBMS suspends the join. This simplifies the join operator but can cause serious performance drawbacks. Paging the hash table can lead to thrashing because of the random nature of hash table accesses, and suspending the join due to insufficient memory can result in underutilization of resources.

Another method is to adapt the memory allocated to the hash-join by requests from the DBMS. Several adaptive join algorithms have been published recently. They can

Reprinted from *Information Systems*, 1996, Vol. 21, No. 4, pp. 369–386, V. Soloviev, "An Incremental Memory Allocation Method for Mixed Workloads," with kind permission from Elsevier Science Ltd, The Boulevard, Langford Lane, Kidlington OX5 1GB, UK.

execute the join with a fluctuating amount of available memory. However, the performance of the join always suffers from reduced memory when available memory is decreased. The goal of adaptive join algorithms is to provide an efficient execution of a join when the join memory is changed due to management decisions external to the join. By contrast, we are looking for ways of saving the join memory for other jobs without penalizing the join.

A third method which takes into account the interests of other concurrently running jobs consists of monitoring performance for each class of workload components. If a performance requirement is not satisfied for a class, then the memory is adjusted between classes using a feedback mechanism. The *fragment fencing* method protects fragments of the shared buffer pool designated to each of the workload classes from an excessive page replacement. One drawback of this approach is that it is excessively general and does not use the specifics of query processing algorithms. In addition, fragment fencing is appropriate only for relatively stable workloads, because a feedback adjustment takes time.

In this study, we investigate a different approach, namely a monitoring of memory consumption by the hash-join operator. Under traditional memory management, the amount of memory allocated to the hash table is determined by an optimizer with or without consideration of the interests of other jobs in the workload. When the hash-join process starts, all reserved memory is allocated as a whole to the process.

However, the hash-join process does not need all the memory immediately. The hash-join process fills memory with tuples over the entire build phase of a hash-join execution. The total hash-table memory is insufficiently utilized over the build phase. Indeed, each of the hash-join algorithms has an average memory utilization of only about 50% during the build phase.

We propose to allocate memory for a hash table not as a whole at the beginning of the hash-join execution, but incrementally by smaller portions when the hash-join process is actually ready to utilize this memory. Memory that has been reserved for the hash table but not yet allocated to the join process can continue to be used as a part of the shared buffer pool by other concurrent processes. Primary beneficiaries of the temporarily increased buffer pool are short transactions that use the shared buffer as a cache for hot pages. This method is deadlock-free, because memory reserved for a join is never allocated to other processes.

Another advantage of incremental allocation is that optimizers are notoriously inaccurate in selectivity estimation and, hence, in estimating the memory to be consumed by a join. This method will reserve memory based on the optimizer estimate but may allocate much less.

The remainder of this article is organized as follows. We review existing work that is related to our study in the next section. The incremental memory allocation method is presented and discussed in the third section. We describe the simulation model used for evaluation of the method in the fourth section. The fifth section presents the results of that evaluation. Finally, our conclusions come in the last section.

RELATED WORK

As mentioned in the Introduction, the subject of memory allocation in database systems has been studied extensively. A significant number of studies involve the allocation of buffers to queries in order to reduce disk accesses. The most relevant articles are those that have addressed the problem of allocating buffers to queries in the context of multi-user relational DBMS. The hot-set model (2) and DBMIN (1) determine a query-specific memory allocation for each query. They allow a new query to start execution only when sufficient memory is available. The DBMIN algorithm was later upgraded to incorporate a predictive load control based on disk utilization (4).

Although each of these algorithms was designed to manage a multiclass workload, they suffer from focusing solely on *intraquery buffering* (i.e., these algorithms consider the buffer pool as being divided up among several concurrently executing queries). Other queries are required to wait until enough memory is available. None of these algorithms investigates the impact of *temporal interquery buffering*. Interquery buffering is sharing buffer frames between several transactions and queries that execute at different times. In addition, none of these methods handles memory allocation for hash-joins.

Interquery buffering is different from data sharing between concurrently executing queries. Data sharing refers to queries or transactions referencing the same data simultaneously. An example of data sharing is the sharing of low-level operators such as building and probing between multiple hash-join queries accessing common relations, which we studied for batch queries (11). Interquery buffering refers to sharing buffer frames that different jobs may use for storing their own data *at different times*. In interquery buffering, several jobs use a common buffer pool without demarcating bounds between separate jobs.

Interquery buffering was investigated in Refs. 8, 9, and 12 for a mixed workload of hash-join queries and short read transactions. Whereas Ref. 8 was a preliminary study comparing several policies of dividing memory between queries and transactions, two other articles (9,12) proposed the *fragment fencing* algorithm for managing a multiclass workload to meet response-time goals of each specific class and investigated its performance. The algorithm observes the per-class reference frequencies and helps the initial buffer allocation and page replacement mechanisms to avoid actions that may violate the individual class goals. A fragment is a statically determined set of database pages that have relatively uniform access probabilities. The fencing method provides individual fragments with something like temporary "soft working sets" of pages within a shared buffer pool.

For example, if transactions access one big indexed file and one small indexed file with equal frequencies, than a traditional three-level least recently used (LRU) page replacement mechanism with "love" and "hate" hints soon fills the shared buffer pool with index pages of both files. This page replacement algorithm always prefers index pages to data pages, but ignores differences between file sizes. However, the data pages of the small file may be referenced more often than the index pages of the large one, and it makes sense to give them a higher priority for buffering.

The fencing method restricts the number of buffer pages to remain within a certain range for each of the files. This range depends on a file temperature. Therefore, the fencing algorithm will provide the small file with a larger buffer set than under the three-level LRU replacement. Fragment fencing monitors the performance of individual classes and can adjust the ranges dynamically to meet performance goals.

Whereas fragment fencing dynamically moderates memory between job classes based on their performance goals, this method does not adjust memory during a lifetime of queries. However, the hash-join can take a long execution time and the DBMS may desire to appropriate a part of the join's memory to satisfy the memory requirements of higher-priority transactions. Several algorithms have been presented (6,7) for adjusting hash-joins to work with fluctuating memory. They differ one from another in the way they handle memory shortages and utilize excess memory. But each of them obviously causes the performance of the hash-join to deteriorate when memory is reduced by the external request. Also, none of these studies investigates the effect of dynamic memory withholding from the hash-join on the performance of the transaction class.

INCREMENTAL MEMORY ALLOCATION

First, we specify a memory management model that we assume as the environment for processing the database workload. At any point in time, some pages are being used for disk buffers (the *disk buffer region*) and some are being used for working storage (the *storage buffer region*) (9). A DBMS memory allocation policy is responsible for making the decision as to how many pages to devote to each region. A page replacement policy is responsible for pages residing in the disk buffer region. The disk buffer region is shared by all running jobs, that is, queries and transactions. When the memory manager starts a new job, it takes pages from the buffer region. Pages are returned to the buffer region after their release.

Although a number of different join algorithms have been proposed, we restrict our attention to the hybrid-hash join algorithm (13). This algorithm is executed in two phases, termed the *build* and *probe* phases. In the build phase, the inner relation is scanned and an in-memory hash table is constructed by hashing each tuple on the join attribute. In the probe phase, the outer relation is scanned and tuples are used to probe the hash table to test for matches. The matched tuples are then joined and produced as output.

As we mentioned in the Introduction, the two phases of the hash-join differ drastically in the way they utilize the allocated memory. In the build phase, memory is consumed gradually by newly arriving tuples of the inner relation read from disk. In the probe phase, all allocated memory has already been occupied for holding the tuples of the inner relation. The probing utilizes all available memory, but the build phase consumes memory one page at a time.

The build phase itself can be divided into two steps. The first step consists of the initial memory allocation for the entries of the hash table. Then, during the second step, the join process reads pages of the inner relation from disk and inserts their tuples into the hash table.

This second building step can take a prolonged period of time, even if disk cache memory is employed for prefetching pages. The join process clearly utilizes memory inefficiently. On the average, only about 50% of the allocated memory is used during the building phase.

We propose allocating memory for the hash-join incrementally (Fig. 1). The first portion must be sufficient for creation of hash-table entries. Each entry of that table takes enough space to store one pointer to a tuple.

Tuples are typically stored in the hash table using chaining as the method of collision resolution. Therefore, one more pointer per build tuple will be needed at the time when the tuple arrives. With chaining, the average number of probes in an unsuccessful search is about 1.18 when the hash table is half-full; even if the table is full, the average number of probes to insert the last element is about 2.10 (14). As the search length is

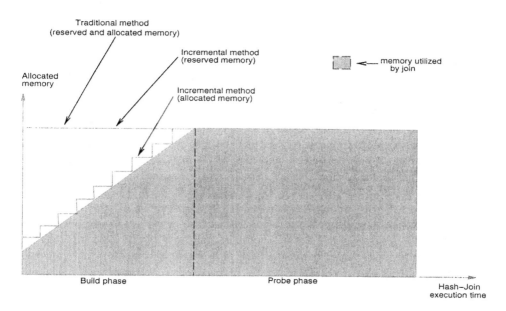

FIGURE 1   Incremental memory allocation for hash-join.

this small, it is sufficient to allocate one table entry per tuple, keeping the table full after hashing all tuples.

We estimate the memory needed for the hash table entries as $4N$ bytes, where N is the number of build tuples. This corresponds to 0.5 of the extra memory added by the "fudge factor" to the hash-table memory size. If F is a "fudge factor" used in the literature to account for extra memory for hashing tuples and L is the memory needed to store build tuples, then the first portion of the memory must be at least $L(F - 1)(0.5)$. We estimate the overhead as 8 bytes per tuple (i.e., one pointer for a hash-table entry and one for chaining). Then, for example, $F = 1.04$ for 200-byte tuples, and the first portion of memory may be as small as 2% of the join's memory.

Allocation of additional entries to the hash table leads to an insignificant increase of the first portion of memory. If we want to keep the average number of probes after the building phase equal to 1.50 instead of 2.10, the first portion of memory will still only increase to only to 3% of the join's memory.

All other portions may be of an arbitrary size. The simplest method to handle the allocation of portions would be to make them equal. The number of portions is a parameter of the method. When the join has filled the currently available memory with tuples, it requests another portion from the system.

Note that the memory manager reserves the total join's memory at the beginning of the join execution. This guarantees that all memory requests issued by the join process will be completed without a delay or deadlock, because the reserved memory cannot be allocated to any other jobs. Meanwhile, the memory that has been reserved but not yet allocated is still a part of the shared buffer pool. The larger shared buffer pool leads to a better performance of transactions.

The overhead of incremental memory allocation is negligible. Each of the memory allocation actions is implemented as a procedure call and does not require a system call. Let the cost to initialize the allocation of pages from the shared buffer pool be A instructions and the cost to get one page from the shared buffer pool to a requesting process be B instructions. Let m be the total number of pages allocated to the operator, with a cost of P instructions to allocate one page. Then, the traditional allocation of all pages in one action costs $A + Pm$. If we allocate memory incrementally by n portions, then the cost is $A + Pm/n + (n - 1)(A + Pm/n) = n(A + Pm/n) = nA + Pm$. Therefore, the overhead of the incremental allocation is $(n - 1)A$ instructions. We estimate A as 500 instructions.* n is a parameter of the method and we varied it from 2 to 100. When $n = 1$, incremental allocation is reduced to the traditional allocation of all the memory at the beginning of execution. We use p, the portion of reserved memory allocated per unit time, as a parameter of the algorithm in the performance section; that is, $p = 1/n$.

Consider the case of multibucket joins. If the memory buffer space is not large enough to hold the entire inner relation, the multibucket hybrid hash-join algorithm (13) divides the buffer space among the hash buckets such that all the blocks of the first bucket completely reside in memory. For each of the other hash buckets, only a single in-memory buffer is allocated. The remainder of the buckets are stored on disk. Whenever the in-memory buffer gets filled, its contents are written to a disk. At the end of the building phase, the first bucket resides wholly in memory, whereas each of the other buckets resides on disk except for at most one block of each bucket. For the probe phase, if a tuple of the outer relation hashes to the first bucket, it is joined with the matching record. If a tuple hashes to a bucket other than the first, it is written to disk into buckets for the outer relation. At the end of probing, all tuples that hash to the first bucket have been joined. To complete the join, we execute build and probe phases for each pair of the remaining buckets stored on disk.

We suggest applying incremental memory allocation only for processing the first bucket, for three reasons. First, the time of processing the first bucket is significantly larger than the time of processing the others. Therefore, the potential saving in processing the first bucket is much larger. Second, releasing memory after processing each bucket and allocating it again for another bucket causes high overhead, because each page of the hash table is added to and taken from the shared buffer pool more than once. Third, the period of time that released pages may spend in the buffer pool is too short and not sufficient for the pages to be "warmed up" for efficient utilization by transactions.

SIMULATION MODEL

The simulator used for this study was derived from a simulation model of the Gamma parallel database machine which has been validated against the actual Gamma implementation. This simulator has been used in a number of ongoing studies in scheduling and resource allocation for centralized and parallel database systems (8,9,10,11,15). The sim-

---

*We tried to get an evaluation of this number from commercial systems, but it turns out that very few of them use the shared-buffer model described above. Most of the systems allocate memory to queries from a separate buffer pool of free pages which is not used as the shared-buffer pool. One of the reasons for such a decision is that many DBMSs inherit the memory management schemas from operating systems under which they have been developed. We received an estimation only for Sybase, and this yielded about 250 instructions for A and a few dozen instructions for P. To be safe, we include a cost of 500 instructions for A in our experiments.

ulator is written in the CSIM/C++ process-oriented simulation language (16). For this study, we use a centralized configuration that consists of one processing node with a single CPU, memory, and two disks. The remainder of this section provides a more detailed description of the relevant portion of the simulation model and concludes with a table of the simulation parameters used for this investigation.

We followed Ref. 9 in our choice of system configuration, database, and workload model for a baseline experiment. However, we expanded them in some experiments by variations of multiprogramming level (MPL) and query file sizes. We also varied the system memory size and CPU speed to verify the scalability of experimental results.

Simulated System Configuration

The simulated terminals model the source of external workload for the system. Each terminal submits a stream of queries of a certain class, one after another. After a submission, the terminal waits for a response before sending the next query. Between submissions, the terminal "thinks," that is, waits for some amount of simulated time. The think time of a terminal can be chosen to be random (exponentially distributed) or constant. The number of terminals and the think times are important parameters to regulate average MPL and disk utilization.

The processing node of the system is modeled as a single CPU, two disk drives, and a buffer pool. The buffer pool models a set of main memory frames, each 8 kbytes in size. We use the three-level LRU page replacement policy with *love/hate* hints [like those used in the Starburst buffer manager (17)]. The hints are provided by the query operators when a page is unfixed. The hints determine three levels of the page value in the following way: Index pages are more valuable than data pages, and randomly accessed data pages are more valuable than sequentially accessed data pages. Pages are chosen for replacement in the following order: (i) unused frames, that is, frames not mapped to any database page; (ii) sequentially accessed pages using a most recently used (MRU) criterion; (iii) randomly accessed data pages using an LRU criterion; (iv) index pages using an LRU criterion. This policy, in particular, prevents the buffer pool from being flooded by pages from the sequential scan operator. A memory reservation system allows memory to be reserved by a particular operator in the working storage, preventing the reserved frames from being stolen. For example, this mechanism protects the hash-table frames of hash-join operators. The CPU is scheduled by a round-robin policy with a 5-ms time slice.

The simulated disks model a slightly simplified Fujitsu Model M2266 (1 GB, 5.25 in.) disk drive. This disk provides a 256-kbyte disk cache that is divided in the simulator into eight 32-kbyte cache contexts for prefetching pages of sequential scans. Each I/O request, along with the required page number, specifies whether or not prefetching is desired. If so, one context's worth of disk blocks (four pages) is read into a cache context, and the page originally requested is transferred from the disk to memory. Thus, five pages total are read from the disk media as a single non-preemptive disk read operation. Subsequent requests to one of the prefetched blocks can then be satisfied without incurring an I/O operation. A simple round-robin replacement policy is used to allocate a cache context if the number of concurrent prefetch request exceeds the number of available cache contexts. The disk queue is managed by an elevator algorithm.

The important parameters of the simulated DBMS are listed in Table 1. The CPU speed of 50 MIPS is typical of high-end workstations or mid-range computers. This

TABLE 1   Simulation Parameters

Configuration parameter	Value	CPU cost parameter	No. of instructions
Transaction terminals	100	Initiate join	40,000
Query terminals	1	Terminate join	10,000
CPU speed	50 MIPS	Initiate select	20,000
Number of disks	2	Terminate select	5,000
Page size	8 kbytes	Start an I/O	1,000
Memory size	512 pages	Copy 8K message	10,000
Disk cylinder size	83 pages	Test an index entry	50
Disk seek factor	0.617	Initiate memory allocation	500
Disk rotation time	16.667 m	Probe hash table	200
Disk settle time	2.0 m	Insert record in hash table	100
Disk transfer rate	3.09 m	Write record into buffer page	100
Disk cache context size	4 pages	Read record from buffer page	300

speed was chosen so that CPU utilizations could be kept close to 10% in order to be sure that two workload classes compete for memory, rather than CPU cycles. The workload keeps the system disk bound; the disk utilization of the transaction disk (see the next subsection) varies from 0.50 to 0.90. The system memory of 4 Mbytes is obviously small and was chosen solely to keep the simulation time low. The important factor for performance is not the actual size of the memory but its size relative to the database relations and working storage of workload units. Nevertheless, we also provide some simulation results for the case of large memory to demonstrate the scalability of experiments. The software parameters are based on actual instruction counts taken from Gamma (except the cost of memory allocation initialization as mentioned above). "Read Record from Buffer Page" is applied to all tuples of join file pages and transaction data pages read from disk to memory. "Write Record to Buffer Page" is applied to all tuples of pages stored on disk (e.g., to the bucket overflow tuples and to the tuples falling into buckets other than the first one). The disk characteristics approximate those of the Fujitsu Model M2266 disk drive described earlier. "Disk Seek Factor" is multiplied by the square root of the number of passed cylinders to obtain the seek time.

Database Model

The database consists of two sets of files. Files of the first set have associated B+ tree indices, one unclustered secondary index per file. This set of files is accessed through an index scan in a random (as opposed to a sequential) pattern. There are four data files together with their four index files in this set. Key sizes are 12 bytes. A pointer requires 4 bytes. The files, designated large, medium, small, and tiny, are used by the transaction class, which is described in the next subsection.

The second set represents the query files; these are 100 identical files for most of the experiments. These sets of files reside on separate disk to eliminate disk contention between transactions, which access the first set of files, and queries, which access the second set.

The parameters of the simulated database that we used in the baseline experiment are given in Table 2. All parameter deviations are described together with related experiments.

Workload Model

We are interested primarily in the effects of the replacement policy and buffer pool size variations on transaction performance. The key workload characteristics in our experiments are page reference patterns and working storage sizes. That is why the simulated workload classes are simple instances of variations in these two parameters. For this study, we choose a workload that is close to the workload used in Ref. 9. The workload consists of two classes: transactions and queries.

Transactions

The class of transactions models page reference behaviors typical of transactions in the TPC-A benchmark (18). Each transaction performs a nonclustered index select of a single record on one of four files: big, medium, small, and tiny. Terminals submit transaction by series in groups of four without a think time. Each series accesses each of four files once. A terminal think time appears between series. Because all the file indices are two levels deep, this adds up to a total of three random page references per transaction. Although all files have equal access frequencies, they will have different per-page access rates because of differences in file sizes. Transactions do not need a working storage, and their performance is determined by the buffer hit ratio and by the transaction MPL.

For every experiment in the performance analysis section, we fix the number of transaction terminals at 100. Their think times are varied in different experiments stipulating different levels of system load.

Queries

A query workload is modeled using binary relational joins of two randomly chosen query files. The primary factor of join performance is the amount of working storage allocated to them rather than their hit rates. The buffer hit rates of query relations are usually zero in our experiments. We use the hybrid hash-join algorithm (13) because it has an established reputation of good performance for different combinations of query and memory

TABLE 2   Database Characteristics

File name	No. of records	Record size	No. of pages
big file	100,000	100	1,234
big index	100,000	16	196
medium file	40,000	100	493
medium index	40,000	16	79
small file	10,000	100	123
small index	10,000	16	20
tiny file	1,000	100	12
tiny index	1,000	16	2
query files	20,100	200	502

sizes. Each hybrid hash-join operator creates two buckets. The first bucket is larger and can consumer all the system memory; the second bucket is smaller. (A special experiment is devoted to hash-joins with larger numbers of buckets.) The inner and outer join files have the same size in the baseline experiment, in order to avoid any possible effect of query optimization decisions. Because the relative proportion of the build and probe phases of the join is important in this study, we also consider the case of larger outer relations.

Because our objective is to evaluate the effect of query memory allocation on transaction performance, the possibility of more than one query executed simultaneously would interfere with the observation of buffer region size fluctuations. We therefore limited the number of terminals that submit queries to one in all our experiments. We varied the think time for this terminal from 0 to 15 s, because we are interested in the performance of a transaction class before a query execution starts and after a query is done.

PERFORMANCE RESULTS

This section describes the results of the performance evaluation of the incremental memory allocation method. A key parameter of the evaluation is the size of the allocated memory portion. We begin with a baseline model, and further experiments are carried out by varying a few parameters each time. The baseline experiment studies the effect of incremental memory allocation for initial system configuration and database. We evaluate an incremental memory allocation under different workload intensities; we achieve variations in intensity by changing the think time of transaction terminals.

In addition, we allow query terminal think time to vary independently. Besides varying workload, we also study the impact of total query memory on transaction performance. The second group of experiments is devoted to variations of join relation sizes; we investigate the case of a larger probe relation as well as the case of a multibucket join of two large relations. In the last series of experiments, we explore the scalability of results under some variations of system parameters. We also consider the case of a shared disk for storing both transaction and query files, to demonstrate the effect of disk contention.

The performance metric of interest here is the average transaction response time. For some experiments, we also demonstrate the behavior of such characteristics as the buffer hit ratio, the query response time, the 90th percentile transaction response time, and so forth. Each experiment described in the performance section has at least 60,000 transaction completions and 50 query completions. This provides a 99% confidence level that the results are within 1% accuracy for transactions and a 95% confidence level that the results are within 5% accuracy for queries.

Baseline Experiment

All the experiments in this section execute the workload for 30 min of simulated time. The results of experiments are presented in graphs. The numerical values of the baseline experiment are also submitted in tabular form in the Appendix. The incremental memory allocation has p, the portion of reserved memory allocated per time, as a parameter of the method. All experiments are performed for four values of p: 1.0, 0.5, 0.1, and 0.01. Note that $p = 1$ denotes traditional memory allocation.

Query Think Time Variations

The first experiment compares the transaction response time for a variety of query think time values. The four curves in Figure 2 show the performance of incremental memory allocation for different p values as a function of query think time. A query think time period takes the values 0, 1, 2, 3, 5, 7, and 10 s. This means that the system processes only transactions in these periods. In the first experiment, we fix the transaction think time of each of the 100 terminals as exponentially distributed with a mean of 2 s. We denote this as exp(2) later.

Of the 512 pages in the total memory of the system, the query memory size was chosen to be 410 pages (the storage buffer region for queries). This ensures that transactions never compete for memory during query executions. Indeed, a transaction can consume up to 3 pages, and depending on the response time experienced, there are an average of 2.8 to 3.7 transactions resident in the system at any moment with peaks of 20–25. The rest of memory is used as a cache and is occupied mostly by index pages of transaction files. The resulting transaction throughput is approximately 48 completions per second. We can see that the proposed method yields a significant reduction in the transaction response time even for $p = 0.5$ (i.e., when incremental allocation takes only a single additional allocation action compared to the traditional method). The allocation of memory for the join in 10 steps (i.e., $p = 0.1$) provides additionally about half the improvement reached by $p = 0.5$. Further increasing the number of allocations brings a very modest performance improvement, if any.

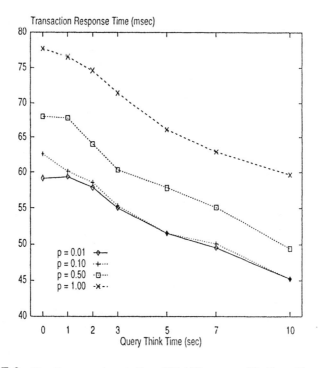

FIGURE 2   Baseline experiment: TransThinkTime = exp(2); QueryMemo = 410.

This behavior of incremental allocation remains correct for a variety of tested query think time values. A variation of the query think time adds the consideration of the buffer region behavior between query executions. The presence and length of gaps between query executions is essential, because it takes time for transactions to "warm up" the buffer region. Incremental allocation demonstrates the maximum improvement when the query think time is 3 s. A smaller time is not sufficient for transactions to fill the additional buffer pages with "hot" pages after the moment when the total query memory has been released at the end of the previous query execution. A larger query think time reduces the gain by lessening the number of query completions in the measured simulation time interval. Parameter behavior for a zero query think time is explained by the fact that extra buffer pages, provided by incremental allocation, have become available for buffer management very recently after the completion of the previous query. In such circumstances, even a small addition of extra pages over the later stage of building would not be useless for transactions, because the extra time spent by the pages in the buffer pool increases their chances of being hit. A decrease of the transaction response time for larger query think time values is obviously explained by the reduction of the query portion of the workload.

Figure 3 shows how the number of transaction buffer hits changes over different phases of query execution. Here, the query memory size is 410 pages, the query think time is 2 s, the transaction think time is exp(2). The period of time from the beginning of the query to the next query submission is about 20 s. The *y* axis shows the average

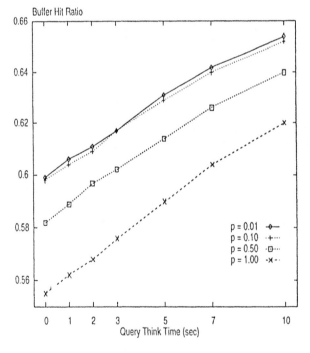

FIGURE 3   Average number of transaction buffer hits per 0.5-s interval during different phases of query execution.

number of transaction buffer hits during the previous 0.5 s interval (there are 40 intervals total). These average values are given for 350 query completions (simulated time is 2 h).

The cycle between queries may be divided into four phases. In the first phase, building, incremental allocation helps to increase sharply the buffer hits ($p = 0.1$ and $p = 0.01$) compared to the traditional method ($p = 1.0$). Note, that the case $p = 0.01$ has two advantages over $p = 0.1$. First, it preserves the peak in buffer hits a little longer. Second, it provides a larger number of buffer hits during the second part of building, due to allocating more memory when the buffer pages have already become "warm." The case $p = 0.5$ has a lower peak and falls earlier because half of the saved memory is allocated to the query in the middle of the build phase. The remaining three phases demonstrate about the same buffer bit performance as both the incremental and traditional methods. Although buffer hits remain volatile but flat during the probing phase, they increase when the processing of the first hash-join bucket is over and the system processes the second bucket. This is because the second bucket in our queries is much smaller and a significant portion of additional memory becomes available to transactions. In the last phase, the query think period, the query has been completed and the total memory of the system may be used by transactions. However, it takes time to warm up buffers and that is why the buffer hits increase steadily over the last two phases of the studied cycle.

Figure 4 displays the behavior of the transaction buffer hit ratio. Numerical values, including the transaction MPL, are given in Table A1 in the Appendix. We can see that the hit ratio increases steadily for smaller portions of allocated memory. As the query think time approaches 3 s, the lines for $p = 0.1$ and $p = 0.01$ draw nearer, and the gap increases between both of them and the line for $p = 1$. This fact reflects the fact that a

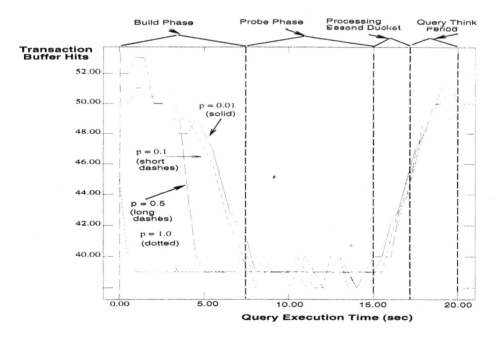

FIGURE 4   Baseline experiment: TransThinkTime = exp(2); QueryMemo = 410.

delay between queries is long enough to warm up the buffer region and the small addition provided by $p = 0.01$ compared with $p = .01$ is insignificant. Although the hit ratio is connected directly to the parameter values of the incremental allocation, this characteristic fails to reflect very precisely the behavior of the response time. The transaction MPL appears to be more appropriate for monitoring the response time than the hit ratio. The reason for this is that transaction MPL also includes a disk utilization factor that is not counted by the buffer hit ratio. Incremental allocation reduces the transaction MPL by improving the hit ratio, but disk contention remains sufficiently high for higher MPLs to influence the response time.

Transaction Think Time Variations

The second experiment demonstrates the impact of transaction intensity on incremental allocation performance. The query memory stays fixed at 410 pages, and the query think time is 3 s. Figure 5 presents the transaction response time for a variety of transaction think time values. Both absolute response time and relative gain from incremental allocation are reduced for lighter transaction loads. Although incremental allocation improves the response time by 23% for transaction think time equal to exp(2), the gain falls to 14% for exp(3) and to only 9% for exp(5). Note that the average transaction MPL of traditional allocation ($p = 1$) is 3.43 for exp(2), 1.24 for exp(3), and only 0.56 for exp(5). This demonstrates that incremental allocation provides more savings for heavier transaction loads.

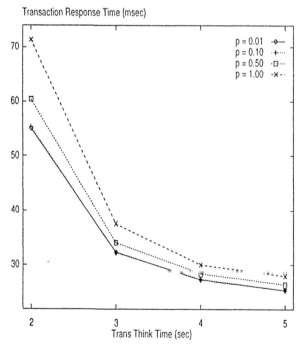

FIGURE 5   Baseline experiment: QueryThinkTime = 3; QueryMemo = 410.

Combining results from Figures 4 and 5, we conclude that an increasing query load is not a serious problem for the incremental allocation, whereas an increasing transaction load is an environment in which incremental allocation demonstrates its full potential. For that reason, we may suggest that incremental allocation is better suited for heavier-loaded systems, although it remains useful for less heavily loaded systems as well.

The query response time is stable in all experiments above, varying within 1% of the mean value of 17.5 s. The variation is independent of the p value. This shows that the overhead of incremental allocation is negligible even for $p = 0.01$ and can be ignored as a potential drawback of the method.

Figure 6 shows the performance for two transaction think time values exp(2) and exp(3), that correspond to heavier and lighter transaction loads, respectively. We show their performance as a function of p, the allocated memory portion. Although this picture is an orthogonal presentation of partial data in Figure 8 and can be derived from there, we have found it useful to include this as a separate figure for more convenient comparison with experimental results shown below. This comparison is intended to demonstrate the scalability of results for a variety of database and system configuration parameters.

Query Memory Variations

The last baseline experiment considers the performance for several sizes of query memory (Figs. 7 and 8). Numerical values are presented in Table A2 in the Appendix. We used query memory sizes of 52, 110, 210, 310, 410, and 500 pages, out of 512 total. A

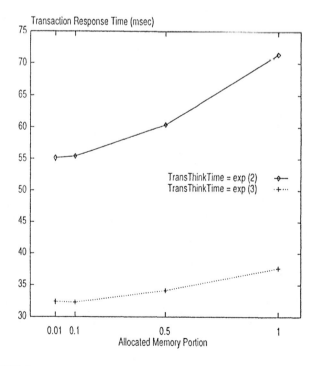

FIGURE 6   Baseline experiment: QueryThinkTime = 3; QueryMemo = 410.

dependency of the query response time on QueryMemo is almost linear, as shown in Figure 7. The query response time is independent of p values (see Appendix).

In Figure 8, the four graphs show the performance of incremental allocation for different p values. Due to a high variation of transaction response time in this experiment, the results are shown using a logarithmic scale. Transaction think time is exp(2) and query think time is 3 s in this experiment. Query memory sizes of 52 and 110 pages are too small to allow incremental allocation to have much effect on the transaction performance. When the query memory is 210 pages, the buffer pool consists of about 300 pages even at the time of query execution. This buffer pool size is almost sufficient for storing all 297 index pages. The extra memory provided by incremental allocation can still help transactions. It is useful to cache pages of the small and tiny files because these files have a higher temperature. Incremental allocation yields about a 13% improvement here. Note that the query response time is 24.0 s in this case.

The case of 310 query pages is intermediate for caching index pages; the gain for incremental allocation is up to 15%. The query response time equals 20.6 s in this case. The case of 410 query pages was described in detail above; as we said, the incremental allocation results in a 23% improvement, and the query response time is 17.7 s.

When queries are executed with 500 pages to maximize their performance, the buffer pool consists of a very few pages. Although queries achieve the best response time here, 13.5 s, the class of transactions is penalized heavily. Their mean response time rockets to 687 ms for $p = 1$ compared to 71.4 ms in the case of 410 pages, and the MPL soars to 5.31 compared to 3.43 for 410 pages. Incremental allocation can facilitate

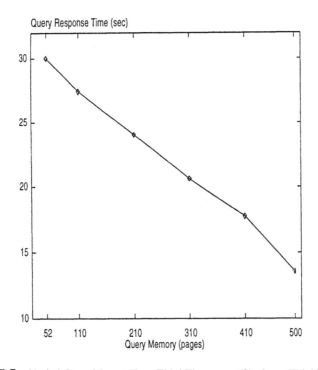

FIGURE 7   Varied QueryMemo: TransThinkTime = exp(2); QueryThinkTime = 3.

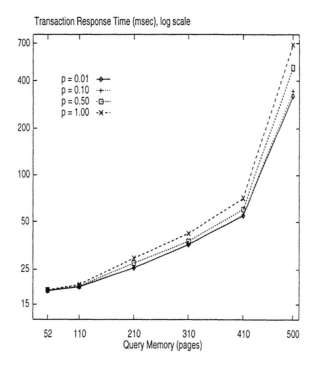

FIGURE 8   Varied QueryMemo: TransThinkTime = exp(2); QueryThinkTime = 3.

transaction performance in this case: Response time is 323 ms for $p = 0.01$ (i.e., less than half as large). Even a small addition of pages granted for a short time, which is provided by the case of smaller allocated portions ($p - 0.01$), has an impact on performance. The transaction MPL falls from 5.31 to 4.16 when $p = 0.01$.

The transaction throughput remains stable for all memory values except 500 pages, when it is significantly reduced. The choice of 410 pages given to the query (80% of total memory) is justified by the following two factors. First, increasing query memory from 52 pages to 410 pages reduces the transaction throughput by only 2%, whereas increasing it from 410 pages to 500 pages hurt the throughput significantly. Second, the amount of memory given to the query depends on a performance metric. One possible metric is to balance the transactions and the query by balancing the load of their disks. Utilizations of the query disk and transaction disk are balanced when QueryMemo = 410 pages, as is shown in the Appendix.

An overall conclusion of the baseline experiment is that $p = 0.01$ is best, although $p = 0.1$ is acceptable.

Each of the remaining experiments in the article has transaction think time exp(2) and query think time 3 s. Query memory is 410 pages in all the remaining experiments except the last one.

Query File Variations

In the baseline experiment, all query files have equal sizes. However, the outer files of joins are often larger than the inner files. This can result in a longer probe phase of the hash-join and, in turn, in erosion of the effect of incremental allocation.

In the next experiment, presented in Figure 9, we study the transaction performance for queries having larger outer files. We compare the cases when all probe relations are twice as large (Prob2 database) as build relations, when all probe relations are four times larger (Prob4 database), and the baseline case (Base) that we considered in the experiments above. File parameters are given in Table 3. Each line in Figure 9 presents the performance for a workload when query files are taken from a proper database. For each query, a build relation is chosen randomly from build files, and a probe relation is chosen from probe files. Although the number of probe files is less than that of build files in databases Prob2 and Prob4, the query buffer hit ratio always remains zero in this experiment. Simulated time in experiments with databases Prob2 and Prob4 was 1 h.

The response time for both Prob2 and Prob4 is obviously higher than for Base. Savings from incremental allocation is decreased for larger probe relations, but remains significant, with 22% for Prob2 and 13% for Prob4. For $p = 1$, the difference in performance between Base and Prob2 is much larger then between Prob2 and Prob4. This is caused by the following factors: On the one hand, each hash-join produces two buckets, and the second bucket is smaller. A join operator releases a part of memory when it completes probing the larger bucket and starts probing the smaller. This memory returns to the buffer pool, helping transactions. The time period to process the smaller bucket is longer for larger probing relations. Therefore, the extra memory from the join spends a longer time in the buffer, and transaction performance is improved. On the other hand, the number of queries during the simulated time period is larger for smaller probing

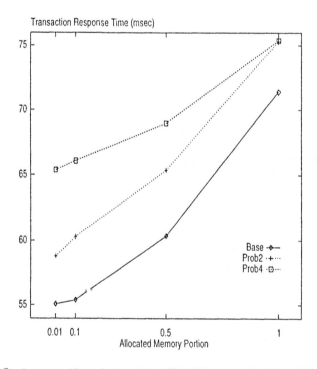

FIGURE 9   Large probing relations: TransThinkTime = exp(2); QueryThinkTime = 3.

TABLE 3   Query Databases

Database name	Database description	No. of files	No. of tuples per file	No. of pages per file	File size (Mbytes)
Base	Database for the baseline experiment	100	20,100	502	4.1
Prob2	Probe files are twice as large				
	Build files	100	20,100	502	4.1
	Probe files	50	40,200	1,004	8.2
Prob4	Probe files are four times as large				
	Build files	100	20,100	502	4.1
	Probe files	25	80,400	2,008	16.4
Multibucket2	All files are twice as large as in Base	100	40,200	1,004	8.2
Multibucket4	All files are four times as large as in Base	50	80,400	2,008	16.4

relations. The number of times when the query terminal thinks is larger as well. There-fore, the time during which transactions enjoy the possession of the whole buffer pool is larger for smaller probing relations. A combination of these two factors produces a non-linear dependence between the probe relation size and the transaction response time.

As we mentioned above, all hash-joins in previous experiments are executed with two buckets, one larger and one smaller. To ensure that our results are scalable to cases of several join buckets, we provide experiments with query relations twice as large (data-base Multibucket2, see Table 3), and four times as large (database Multibucket4, see Table 3). Simulated time in experiments with databases Multibucket2 and Multibucket4 was 2 h. Results of this experiment appear in Figure 10, where we also add numbers for queries taken from the baseline database (Base). Queries processing database Multi-bucket2 create three buckets per join, and those processing database Multibucket4 create six buckets per join. Figure 10 demonstrates that the performance of incremental alloca-tion is perfectly scalable to multibucket cases. The dependence of the gain on various ratios of build relation to memory size is given in Figure 11. This picture is an orthogonal presentation of data in Figure 8 and can be derived from there. Figure 11 shows that the gain depends almost linearly on the QueryMemo to BuildRelation ratio.

System Parameter Variations

The first experiment in this subsection considers a case of a single database disk. All transaction and query files from a baseline experiment share one disk. Parameters of this experiment are taken to be the same as for the experiment presented in Figure 7, except for the number of disks. Transaction response time appears in Figure 12, and query response time in Figure 13. Figures 12 and 13 show that incremental allocation improves the performance of both transactions and queries. This takes place because incremental allocation reduces the transaction MPL. As a result, disk contention is decreased for both queries and transactions. A comparison of Figures 12 and 7 demonstrates the scalability

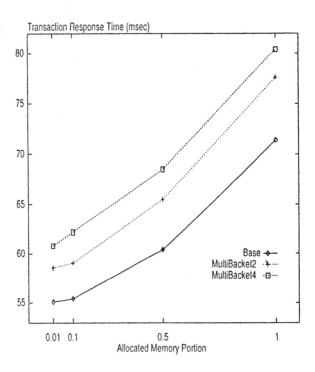

FIGURE 10   Multibucket queries: TransThinkTime = exp(2); QueryThinkTime = 3.

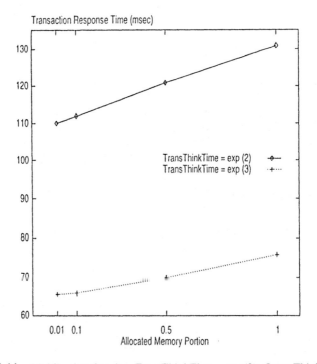

FIGURE 11   Multibucket Queries: TransThinkTime = exp(2); QueryThinkTime = 3.

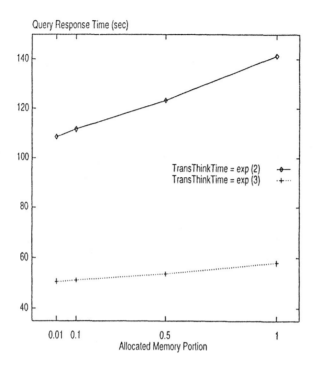

FIGURE 12   Shared Disk: QueryThinkTime = 3; QueryMemo = 410.

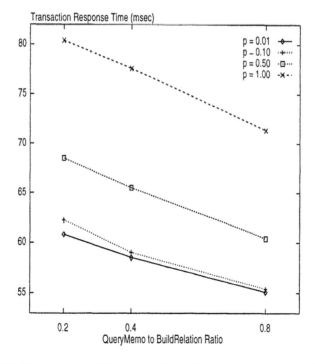

FIGURE 13   Shared Disk: QueryThinkTime = 3; QueryMemo = 410.

of incremental allocation performance for transactions in separated-disk and single-disk cases. Simulated time for experiments with a shared disk was increased to 2.5 h to ensure at least 50 query completions.

A combination of 50 MIPS and 4 Mbyte memory, which was chosen in order to keep the simulation time low, sounds unrealistic. In the last experiment, we increase memory to 24 Mbyte. Simulation results of the experiments for workload parameters taken from the experiment in Figure 7 appear for this configuration in Figures 14. All query and transaction files in the experiment with the large memory are increased by a factor of 6 compared with file sizes described in Table 2. Simulated time in experiments with the large memory is 2 h. The figure shows that the results of performance evaluation for 50 MIPS and 4 Mbyte memory are perfectly scalable to the case of larger memory.

CONCLUSIONS

In this article, we proposed the incremental memory allocation method for an execution of hash-joins. This method allows a later allocation of a significant amount of memory during the build phase of hash-join. We assumed a memory management mechanism in which free memory is allocated from a shared buffer pool. This pool is used as a cache by all database workload components. The effect of the later memory allocation to join queries appears in an increasing size of shared cache, which, in turn, improves the perfor-

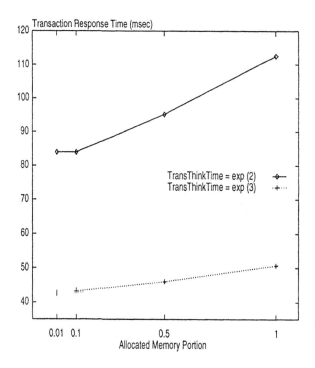

FIGURE 14   Memory 24 MB: QueryThinkTime = 3; QueryMemo = 2460.

mance of other jobs in the workload. The proposed method has a simple implementation and negligible performance overhead.

Using a detailed simulation model, we investigated the impact of incremental memory allocation on transaction performance for multiclass database workloads. Our results demonstrated that this method successfully reduces transaction response time for a variety of workload intensities, joining file sizes, and system configuration parameters. We conclude that incremental memory allocation appears promising as a means of better resource utilization for medium and heavy loaded database systems processing multiclass workloads.

The incremental memory allocation method complements rather than precludes the adaptive join algorithms proposed in Refs. 6 and 7. Both of these approaches may be used together, to provide even greater improvement in the performance of transactions. The incremental memory allocation method can be used at a lower level within an adjustable join algorithm. The incremental memory allocation method affects the *allocation* but not the *reservation* of memory in order to guarantee deadlock-free execution. Each time the adaptive join algorithm changes the number/sizes of buckets, the size of reserved memory might be affected. In turn, the incremental allocation algorithm works with memory already reserved by buckets and allocates this memory gradually to the buckets. Bucket memory saved temporarily by incremental allocation can be used only as a cache without redirecting to other buckets. Otherwise, a memory reservation must be changed, which can cause a deadlock.

Although this study explores incremental memory allocation only for hash-joins, we believe that this technique can be useful in processing some other memory-intensive database operators, such as sorting or a sort–merge join applied to files accessed through indexes. If an index scan is employed for reading file pages from disk, it may take a long time to fill the memory with data for further sorting. Memory can be allocated to the operator incrementally, helping other jobs to benefit from a larger cache size.

ACKNOWLEDGMENTS

The author would like to thank Kurt Brown for helpful discussions regarding the simulator details and the methodology of experiments, and other numerous writers of the original Gamma simulator without which the work would not have been possible.

APPENDIX

TABLE A1   Baseline Experiment: QueryMemory = 410 Pages

Query think time (s)	Trans think time (s)	p	Average TransResp time (ms)	90th % TransResp time (ms)	Hit Ratio	Query resp. time (s)	Trans. disk util.	Trans. per sec	Trans. MPL
0	exp(2)	0.01	59.2	138.2	0.599	17.7	0.81	48.3	2.86
		0.1	62.6	147.7	0.598	17.8	0.82	48.5	3.03
		0.5	68.0	157.7	0.582	17.7	0.84	48.3	3.28
		1.0	77.8	173.3	0.555	17.7	0.88	47.8	3.72
3	exp(2)	0.01	55.1	132.0	0.618	17.7	0.78	48.5	2.67
		0.1	55.4	133.4	0.617	17.7	0.78	48.3	2.68
		0.5	60.4	142.7	0.602	17.6	0.81	48.6	2.94
		1.0	71.4	166.2	0.576	17.7	0.85	48.0	3.43
10	exp(2)	0.01	45.2	110.5	0.654	17.6	0.72	48.9	2.21
		0.1	45.2	109.9	0.652	17.8	0.72	48.9	2.21
		0.5	49.6	122.8	0.640	17.7	0.74	48.5	2.41
		1.0	59.7	147.7	0.620	17.8	0.78	48.7	2.91
3	exp(3)	0.01	32.3	65.9	0.607	17.7	0.55	32.9	1.06
		0.1	32.2	65.6	0.606	17.8	0.56	33.0	1.06
		0.5	34.1	69.6	0.594	17.7	0.57	32.8	1.12
		1.0	37.6	76.1	0.568	17.7	0.61	32.9	1.24

TABLE A2   Baseline Experiment: TransThinkTime = exp(2); QueryThinkTime = 3 s.

QueryMemo pages (out of 512)	p	Average TransResp time (ms)	90th % TransResp time (ms)	Trans. hit ratio	Trans. per sec	QueryResp time (s)	Query disk util.	Trans. disk util.
52	0.01	18.2	36.1	0.758	49.4	30.0	0.88	0.52
	0.1	18.4	36.4	0.758	49.7	30.0	0.88	0.53
	0.5	18.4	36.1	0.758	49.4	30.0	0.88	0.52
	1.0	18.5	36.6	0.757	49.6	29.8	0.88	0.53
110	0.01	19.3	37.5	0.750	49.2	27.4	0.87	0.54
	0.1	19.5	38.0	0.749	49.8	27.5	0.87	0.54
	0.5	19.6	38.1	0.747	49.6	27.6	0.87	0.55
	1.0	20.0	38.7	0.745	49.7	27.6	0.87	0.55
210	0.01	25.6	48.3	0.707	49.3	24.0	0.85	0.62
	0.1	25.8	48.8	0.706	49.0	24.0	0.85	0.62
	0.5	27.3	51.4	0.698	49.5	23.8	0.85	0.64
	1.0	29.4	55.4	0.685	49.3	24.0	0.85	0.67
310	0.01	35.7	77.5	0.664	49.2	20.6	0.82	0.71
	0.1	35.9	78.0	0.662	49.0	20.6	0.82	0.71
	0.5	37.5	82.7	0.655	48.8	20.6	0.82	0.72
	1.0	42.0	91.8	0.636	49.0	20.6	0.82	0.76
410	0.01	55.1	132.0	0.618	48.5	17.7	0.79	0.78
	0.1	55.4	133.4	0.617	48.3	17.7	0.79	0.78
	0.5	60.4	142.7	0.602	48.6	17.6	0.79	0.81
	1.0	71.4	166.2	0.576	48.0	17.7	0.79	0.85
500	0.01	323.6	952.8	0.500	43.0	13.6	0.73	0.89
	0.1	345.4	969.7	0.489	42.4	13.5	0.73	0.89
	0.5	487.2	1124.3	0.444	40.3	13.6	0.73	0.92
	1.0	687.0	1201.8	0.358	37.2	13.5	0.73	0.97

REFERENCES

1. H. Chou and D. DeWitt, "An Evaluation of Buffer Management Strategies for Relational Database Systems," in *Proc. 11th Int'l VLDB Conf.*, Stockholm, Sweden (1985).
2. D. Sacca and M. Schkolnik, "Buffer Management in Relational Database Systems," in *ACM Trans. Database Sys.*, *11*(4), 473–498 (1986).
3. D. Cornell and P. Yu, "Integration of Buffer Management and Query Optimization in a Relational Database Environment," in *Proc. 15th Int'l VLDB Conf.*, Amsterdam (1989).
4. C. Faloutsos, R. Ng, and T. Sellis, "Predictive Load Control for Flexible Buffer Allocation," in *Proc. 17th Int'l VLDB Conf.*, Barcelona (1991).
5. E. O'Neil, P. O'Neil, and G. Weikum, "The LRU-K Page Replacement Algorithm for Database Disk Buffering," in *Proc. 1993 ACM–SIGMOD Conf. Management of Data*, Washington, DC (1993).
6. H. Zeller and J. Gray, "An Adaptive Hash Join Algorithm for Multiuser Environments," in *Proc. 16th Int'l VLDB Conf.*, Brisbane, Australia (1990).
7. H. Pang H, M. Carey, and M. Livny, " Partially Preemptible Hash Joins," in *Proc. 1993 ACM–SIGMOD Conf. Management of Data*, Washington, DC (1993).
8. K. Brown, M. Carey, D. DeWitt, M. Mehta, and J. Naughton, "Scheduling Issues for Complex Database Workloads," Computer Science Technical Report TR 1095, University of Wisconsin-Madison (1992).

9.   K. Brown, M. Carey, and M. Livny, "Managing Memory to Meet Multiclass Workload Response Time Goals," in *Proc. 19th Int'l VLDB Conf.*, Dublin (1993).

10. M. Mehta and D. DeWitt, "Dynamic Memory Allocation for Multiple-Query Workloads," in *Proc. 19th Int'l VLDB Conf.*, Dublin (1993).

11. M. Mehta, V. Soloviev, and D. DeWitt, "Batch Scheduling in Parallel Database Systems," in *Proc. 9th IEEE Int'l Data Engineering Conf.*, Vienna (1993).

12. K. Brown, M. Mehta, M. Carey, and M. Livny, "Towards Automated Performance Tuning for Complex Workloads," in *Proc. 20th Int'l VLDB Conf.*, Santiago, Chile (1994).

13. D. DeWitt, R. Katz, F. Olken, L. Shapiro, M. Stonebraker, and D. Wood, "Implementation Techniques for Main Memory Database Systems," in *Proc. 1984 ACM–SIGMOD Conf. Management of Data*, Boston (1984).

14. D. Knuth, *The Art of Computer Programming, Vol. 3*, Addison-Wesley, Reading, MA, 1973.

15. A. Shatdal and J. Naughton, "Using Shared Virtual Memory for Parallel Join Processing," in *Proc. 1993 ACM–SIGMOD Conf. Management of Data*, Washington, DC (1993).

16. H. Schwetman, "CSIM Users' Guide," MCC Technical Report No ACT-126-90, MCC, Austin, TX (1990).

17. L. Haas, L. Maas, W. Chang, G. Lohman, J. McPherson, P. Wilms, G. Liapis, B. Lindsay, H. Pizahesh, M. Carey, and E. Shekita, "Starburst Mid-Flight: As the Dust Clears," in *IEEE Trans. Knowledge Data Eng.*, KDE-2(1), 143–160 (1990).

18. J. Gray (ed.), *The Benchmark Handbook*. Morgan Kaufmann, San Mateo, CA, 1991.

VALERY SOLOVIEV

AN INTRODUCTION TO SOFTWARE REUSE

INTRODUCTION

In the past decade, software reuse has gradually started coming into the mainstream of research and practice as a viable subfield of software engineering. There have been many papers and articles in technical, professional, and trade publications dealing with the issues and prospects, the pros and cons, and the incentives and impediments of software reuse. The main themes addressed in these publications have been the investigation of reusability from the perspectives of management, cost, and human factors, as well as from technical perspectives. Because of the significant outstanding problems, it is expected that active interest in reuse will continue at a healthy pace from both the research and practice angles.

Reuse practice appears to exhibit considerable potential—far more than other ongoing activities—to enhance the software development process and to restructure not only the process of software construction but also the actual software development departments. Recent surveys and papers on the reusability of software indicate that software reuse is a major way to boost software engineering productivity (1). One survey indicated that 40–60% of all code is reusable from one application to another, 60% of the design and code on all business applications are reusable, and 75% of program functions are common to more than one program (1). The survey also indicated that only 15% of the code found in most programs is unique and novel to each specific application.

To accommodate and exploit software reuse, the management and organization of these departments have to be restructured, not just locally and in isolation but also in the context of the entire organization.

The potential payoff from replacing expensive development activities with relatively inexpensive reused parts is too attractive an opportunity to be ignored. Over the life cycle of a system, reuse can provide many advantages over traditional "designing from the ground up":

1. Shortens development cycles and lower production cost in future development efforts
2. Improves system reliability by reusing proven components and reducing the need for system testing
3. Reduce life-cycle maintenance cost by reducing the "ripple" effect of program changes through design abstraction
4. Enables the developing organization to recover its investment in existing software systems when producing new programs and conducting new design efforts.

The list of organizations that emphasized reuse was very short at the end of eighties. Today, most of the major software shops (public or private) consider development of reusable software or reusing existing software as a top priority. Special multinational projects in Europe have been organized to focus on the development of reusable software. Japanese software shops are considered one of the leaders in software factories which heavily emphasize reuse technology (2).

Software reuse could be implemented at several levels, including the specification level, design level, program/subprogram library level, code level, and object-code level. There is no single, widely accepted definition for reuse. Reuse has a distinct definition for each of the above-mentioned levels. Moreover, the techniques applied to organize and manage reuse are different from one level to another. The complexity of reuse methods and techniques increases from the specification level to the code and object-code levels. On the positive side, the time and space efficiency resulting from the application of reuse techniques improves in the same direction.

Reusability is not limited to code and design artifacts. All components and aspects of software (i.e., documents, planning, requirement analysis/specification, contracts, test plans/cases, etc.), should ideally be designed and prepared to be reused.

Regardless of the level of reuse, the design of a successful reuse environment should be able to address the following tasks:

1. Identification and access to a segment of reusable components based on user requirements (*locating*)
2. Facilitating program modification (*customization*)
3. Providing facilities to store, retrieve, and integrate the reusable components efficiently (*configuration/version management*) (2,3).

HISTORICAL BACKGROUND

The research and development activities on software reuse have been investigated from different prospectives. As far as this research is concerned, it could be broken down chronologically into three periods:

1. Pre-ITT workshop (1969–1983)
2. STARS workshops and reuse conferences/seminars (1983–1986)
3. Recent activities (1987–present)

The idea of the need for a library of scientific routines was originally proposed by Maurice Wilkes (1949) when the first set of programs was stored in the EDSAC computer at the University of Cambridge. McIlroy's visionary paper on software reuse in the NATO Software Engineering Conference of 1968 is considered by Neighbor as the seminal document on software reuse. In this paper, he presents the idea of a program component factory. The year 1969 regarded as year 0 in the first period (1969–1983) of software reuse (the pre-ITT workshops period).

Matsubara, the Japanese computer scientist, used the idea of "software factories" in 1977 in the Toshiba's computer division (4). The key factor for the successful undertaking by Japanese industry was that they were first in justifying the amortized cost of developing the crucial bulk of reusable software and the cost of the software engineering environment necessary to succeed. The effort of the Japanese computer industry started to pay off in the mid-eighties (4).

The significant work of Lanergan and Raytheon "Reusable Code: The Application Development Technique of the Future" was another milestone in software reuse. Another significant paper in this decade was by D. L. Parnas "On the Design and Development of Program Families." Other contributors to software reuse in this period include Blazer, Kernigham, Cheatham, Glass, Freeman, Denning, and Neighbor. Freeman and Neighbor made strong contributions in the last 3 years of this period. Neighbor wrote the first Ph.D. dissertation on reusable software (2).

In the early eighties some U.S. commercial organizations and government agencies (ITT and DoD) initiated the research and development of programs on software reuse. The first software reuse workshop was conducted in 1983 in Stamford, Connecticut. In the following sections, a survey of the related work is presented. This survey contains various approaches, issues, perspectives, and models that are of significance in software reuse.

ORGANIZATIONAL ISSUES OF SOFTWARE REUSE

Most of the up-to-date work by reuse researchers/practitioners is presented in technical workshops on software reuse. This potential isolation is one of the basic problems behind the lack of adequate progress in practical nontechnical issues. To remedy the situation, participation and collaboration of experts in fields such as organizational structure, management, human behavior, and economics are needed. These experts can assist in detailed impact studies on the economics of reuse and considerations of human behavior, and strategy setting and planning that would eventually lead to the reorganization of the software departments and the software development process. One can cite as precedent the Japanese success, the European promising start, and the reported progress in some U.S. government organizations which could not have been achieved without institution-wide planning (8).

The reuse community duly realizes the impact of organizational factors on the failure or success of developing reusable software. Nevertheless, due to the lack (or inadequacy) of organizationwide planning and commitment and the existence of organizational inhibitors, the development of systematic mechanisms to practice reuse effectively has not been entirely successful in most organizations. Planning for the development of reusable software is a long-term strategic decision. There is evidence to believe that the organizations that emphasize long-term planning have proven to be more successful in this venture. The lack of long-term planning could be voluntary, as in the case of some large organizations for which short-term budget reports constitute the main factor—if not the only factor—in planning; or it can be involuntary and simply based on the lack of required capabilities (such as typical small or medium-size software shops) (14).

Effective reuse of software requires a significant change in traditional software development practices. Standards must be set and enforced by a mature organizationwide software development process. Education and training within the organization are necessary to promote willing, enthusiastic participation in the software development process for which software reuse is an integral part. When projects and sites are thinking and speaking different languages, naming conventions, and documentation styles, reuse can become time-consuming and error-prone. This creates a significant up-front cost associated with reorganizing the company's policies and organizational structure and, therefore, requires a firm commitment by the organization to have reuse fully implemented and accepted by all sites and projects (5).

Benefits to the Organization

To achieve success from reuse, the benefits gained from reuse must outweigh the associated cost and risk incurred. Benefits received from software reuse within a project depend on the complexity and size of the software application and the usability of available reuse components. Because each organization is different culturally and will react differently to the same set of motivations, such as the history, composition, and mission of the organization (6), reuse will benefit each organization differently (7,8).

Software reuse, however, should be viewed as a capital investment for the organization. Not only can economic and quality assurance benefits be seen at the project level but also at the organization level through increased functional capability among different platform and software applications. Reusability among different projects and sites produces software that looks and performs the same across all the families of applications developed within the organization.

Software reuse also allows for more efficient use of existing organizational resources through information sharing of different projects and sites. Statistics show that only 15% of all program code is unique to a specific application and that 40–60% of all code is reusable from one application to another (9).

A good example of such a strategy is one of the DoD contractors. To ensure future competition with other DoD contractors, Bofors implemented a long-term reuse strategy to design a family of systems as opposed to numerous specific systems. Bofors made radical modifications to their development process to emphasize the development of common software applications. As a result, productivity doubled and $20 million in savings was achieved on the first contract won after implementing their new strategy; Bofors has not lost a major Ada proposal or follow-on contract since (10).

Economic Benefits

Software reuse decreases the life-cycle cost of development by an average of 8% (7) versus traditional development. This is attributed to the reduction in unique development for each project. In fact, when a software component is reused without modification, it costs 20% of what it would cost to develop the component from scratch (11). Reusing software also reduces the time spent at the requirements, design, specification, coding, testing, and maintenance stages of the software development process. This decrease in time will allow resources currently used in building software applications to shift to improving software development.

Currently, the cost of maintaining software is the most expensive aspect of software development. In fact, 50% of the maintenance cost for a system is spent by programmers trying to understand the system (12). However, future systems that share a common software architecture will lead to maintenance engineers who are familiar with a family of systems in the same domain and who do not require a learning curve to understand the individual systems. Also, redundant maintenance is reduced as problems found in one system are corrected via reusable software components and thus corrected in to all systems.

Measuring Software Reusability

Numerous research efforts have attempted to provide methodologies to quantify the success of reuse practice by organizations. These methodologies must be able to measure the progress and effectiveness of the reuse practice. Measuring the effect of reuse primarily focuses on the impact on software productivity, quality, and lead time. In order to be able to accomplish this task, the following data should be gathered:

1. Amount of work saved by reusing existing software components
2. Number of reduced errors
3. Reduced maintenance costs
4. Benefit of reusing components developed with the potential to be reused in future
5. Overhead costs of developing reusable software components

Productivity and quality can be evaluated on the level of product, project, and organization. Lead time is only measurable at the level of project and component (4).

Another important category of reuse measurement is process evaluation. This category of metrics uses past data to control and improve the currently running reuse process. Among the major metrics in this category are effort, size of project, number of pen questions, number of faults, and so forth.

Quality Assurance Benefits

Software reliability, maintainability, and interoperability can be improved by using reusable software components. Software components that are known to be reliable reduce the potential for unknown technical risks. Also, the ability to maintain software becomes easier by using well-designed, developed, and tested components that were designed specifically for reuse.

Software components designed for reuse have been certified to adhere to company standards and, therefore, contain fewer errors. The generic design of reusable components simplifies the interface and functionality and, therefore, allows designs to be tailored easier, which, in turn, increases the portability of the design. Components designed for reuse also have common attributes such as modularity and parameterization that serve to make them portable across multiple platforms. Therefore, systems produced with reusable components are better able to share information with other systems.

The results of improved, quality systems have been seen in many companies. GTE Data Services experienced a 20–30% increase in quality improvements and zero defects in software utilizing reusable components (9). Raytheon has also experienced great success in its industrial software lab. Reusable components improved the quality of code shipped to customers by a factor of 10 and resulted in better customer satisfaction (9).

Reason for Failures

Reuse, like any other technology, only provides benefits when used correctly. Organizations must determine if the potential benefits from reuse outweigh the associated costs and risks which must be incurred. The answer to this question is different for each organization and project. Organizations must determine whether there are sufficient resources such as technology, financial commitment, regulations, policies, and management commitment to pursue reuse. Projects must consider what components will be developed for reuse and which can be reused from existing components.

Another associated problem with reuse is that projects must invest about 20–50% more up front to develop reusable software (13) and then the software must be used at least three times within the organization for the effort to pay off (9). Reusable software development costs 1.25 to 2 times as much to develop than traditional software development methods (11) and 1.5 to 2.5 times if domain analysis is required (8). Specifically, development costs increase by 10% if a component is used in one project only, 30% if the component is used within a domain, and 50% if used within multiple domains (12).

Cultural factors within the organization also can become reuse inhibitors. The implementation of reuse will result in significant cultural changes in the way the organization currently does business. Cultural factors include the following: lack of vocal commitment or support for the concept of reuse at the highest management level; threaten to the concept due to its novelty; potential for disturbing the current status of software development; and the perceived "loss of control" by material developers. Because the magnitude of change is anticipated to be significant, nontechnical issues experienced by the organization may constitute the most critical factor in impeding the success of software reuse.

Considering the above-mentioned facts, the main inhibitors of software reuse could be classified into the following categories (30).

1. Inadequate representation technology
2. NIH (not invented here) factor
3. High initial capitalization

REUSE MODELS AND PROCESSES

In this section, we introduce the technical foundation and issues in software reuse. The first subsection describes the reuse process. Then, we will discusses the reuse types and models.

Reuse Process

In general, software can be developed *for* reuse, *with* reuse or in a hybrid process. The *for* reuse process is the development of reusable software components. The *with* reuse is the development of software from existing components. In reality, most of the reusable software practices use a hybrid approach. Practical software development should provide an environment that facilitates *systematic* development of software artifacts from either existing components or that develops new ones that can be reused in future software.

To be more specific, the reuse process infrastructure should be built based on four basic principles as defined in following (14):

Process-Driven Reuse: Ensures that reuse is an inseparable part of the software development process. This includes using off-the-shelf software for constructing prototypes to define requirements and standards for Critical Design Reviews.

Domain-Specific Reuse: Supports large-scale reuse by building applications through domain analysis which establishes a consensus for domain-specific architectures.

Architecture-Centric Reuse: Establishes reuse-oriented, flexible architectures for enterprise domains which are well supported by the community. Architectures are created from generic components that rely on principles and standards facilitating "black box" reuse.

Library-Based Reuse: Provides the ability to capture, locate, and share reusable components across domains and throughout the entire community through a network of interconnected reuse library systems.

Level of Reuse

The success of reuse depends on the usability of available software components. As only 15% of the code within an application is unique to that application and only a portion of that percentage can be reused within an application, reuse at the project level is very limited. However, at an organizational level, reuse can be achieved within the three different levels of application-specific, domain-independent, and domain-dependent reuse (7).

> **Application-Specific Reuse**: Refers to the customized code within an application. This type of reuse is limited to application-unique functions reused by the project team.
>
> **Domain-Independent Reuse**: Refers to general-purpose functions which can be shared by a wide range of applications or horizontal domains. Once common functions within the domains are discovered, developing standard architectures and templates facilitates reusing of these general-purpose functions. Some studies have reported a 50% productivity improvement in 6 years (10).
>
> **Domain-Dependent Reuse**: Refers to a family of related software applications within the same vertical domains built using the same set of standard components.

Reuse Models and Techniques

This section presents a summary of six major models of software reuse. In order to maintain consistency in the comparison of the different reuse models and techniques, the following criteria for model evaluation originally proposed by Krueger (15) is used:

1. Abstraction: The unit of reuse and the level of abstraction.
2. Selection: The method to select the reusable components.
3. Customization (also called specialization): How the components are customized for reuse.
4. Integration: How the components are integrated.

The reuse models considered in this study generally fall into three categories: accidental (ad hoc) reuse, design for reusing existing software, and design for reusability. The first two models *Design and Code Scavenging* and *Source Code* (components) are the main approaches in the accidental reuse or design *with* reusing existing software. The last three models are designs *for* reusability (15).

Design and Code Scavenging

Design and code scavenging (DCS) is an ad hoc "model" for using the design and fragments of an existing software system. The goal of this model is to reduce the amount of time and effort expended in the software development life cycle. The efficiency of DCS is based on the experience of and the information available to the designer/developer:

1. Abstraction: There is no formal abstraction; information on the components might be stored in a simple library.
2. Selection: Selection is either from the library or based on the programmer/designer's memory.
3. Customization: Manual editing of the code fragments. Understanding the dif-

ferences between the old and the new systems is a crucial factor in successful customization of this reuse model.

4. Integration: Integration and customization are actually merged into one phase in this model; the programmer/designer must have a good knowledge of the semantics of the language and understand the impact of the customization and integration on the modified components of the software system (15).

Source Code Components

Given the availability of a large number of software components, similar to the Japanese "software factory," one could ask, "Does a part exist that performs this function?" The goal of the off-the-shelf source code components (SCC) model is to provide an answer to the question. Compared to DCS, this model of reuse is more effective because the components are designed and developed for the purpose of reuse and are organized in a library. Examples of successful SCC are the SPSS statistical libraries and IMSL math library.

Modern languages such as Ada, Modula-2, C++, and Smalltalk-80 not only provide features for developing reusable components but also provide mechanisms to make a distinction between abstraction and implementation. Krueger believes that even though in a few narrow areas this model has been successful, the applicability of SCC in broader areas is not yet clear. Specific areas of engineering and mathematics are examples of the successful application of SCC. However, this model could become very effective where an environment that facilitates the SCC model of reusability exists (16).

1. Abstraction: In a limited domain with a set of short, well-defined specifications for the components, abstraction is a trivial task (e.g., with regression analysis and standard deviation as functions of a statistical library or abstract data types such as stack, queue, various types of trees, etc.). For other cases, a higher-level language is required to provide abstraction. For example, the Anna environment provides abstraction facilities for the formal specification and abstraction of the Ada programming environment.

2. Selection: Facilities such as Anna are difficult to understand and use, and are only partially helpful in selecting the components. One solution is the classification of the components and providing a manual or automatic search scheme to help the user/developer in finding the desired component(s). One example of this approach is the IMSL library. Employing a specification language to describe the components will also facilitate the selection; however, it is questionable whether this approach will be of any significant help in a large system without an appropriate abstraction and classification scheme or without the existence of an integrated software reuse environment.

3. Customization: Direct editing is the main method to customize the code for new applications. This method has the same basic problems that the DCS model has (i.e., the impact of modifications on other components). Krueger considers "work at a low level of abstraction" another drawback of this model. In fact, this is not a drawback for all cases. In some such environments as ROPCO (Reuse Of Persistent Code and Object code), the low level of work adds to the capabilities of the environment (16). Another approach for customization is using parameterized components such as the Ada generic package. The use of parameterized packages relieves the burden of validation of the

modified components (17). The generic parameter(s) of a parameterized package is declared in such a way that the type of element for which it is instantiated satisfies the parameter requirements.

4. Integration: Module Interconnection Languages (MIL) are used for the integration of the reusable components. The main problem with MILs is the issue of the name space. An efficient MIL must be able to help by resolving this problem (16,18).

Program Schemes

In this approach, the software components are designed to be reusable. The Program Scheme (PS) model emphasizes the reuse of algorithms and data abstractions rather than code. Each scheme consists of a variable part and a fixed part (analogous to an abstraction). The variable part describes the range of options for which a scheme can be instantiated, and the fixed part formally describes what computation or structure a scheme represents. The library of a PS system is a collection of program schemes. Aside from the specifications, each scheme needs to have other information, such as how to instantiate the scheme and assertions about the valid use of various scheme instantiations.

1. Abstraction: The main advantage of this model over DCS and SCC (which can be considered ad hoc models) is the use of abstraction. Formal semantic specification, such as plan calculus, combination of first-order logic and directed graph, temporal logic, and axioms and theories are employed to provide program specification and abstraction in PS.

2. Selection: A composition of a hierarchical classification scheme like the one presented by Prieto Diaz (19), a multiple abstraction specification exposition used in the TTL Data book of Texas Instrument, and an efficient search scheme form a good selection scheme. The size of the library is considered to be one of the major factors in the design of a software library. Large libraries need to use the (object-oriented) database technology with the capability of answering fuzzy questions about program schemes, as is the case in the PS model.

3. Customization: Customization is a continuation of selection and is considered as filling in the slots in a scheme structure. This phase could be an insertion, a choosing or both. In insertion, the variable parts of the scheme are filled by language constructs, code segments, nested schemes, or specifications. Choosing consists of selecting from the library a high level of abstraction to satisfy the variable part of the scheme.

4. Integration: The MIL of the implementation language could be used for the integration of the PSs. An MIL provides formal grammar constructs required to specify and eventually integrate the reusable components. The more sophisticated MILs, such as Gougen's LIL (17) and Perry's Inscape (20), provide semantic specifications and limit the components' interface to only correct syntactic and semantic compositions.

Very High-Level Languages

The goal of very high-level languages (VHLLs) is to construct an abstract model suitable for reasoning and to provide a concise and expressive formal notation for abstraction specification. Execution time optimization is not the primary objective of VHLL design, rather it is typically the ability to facilitate software development. The level of reuse in VHLLs is data and implementation specification. A VHLL employs its compiler to map abstraction specification directly into executable abstraction realization.

1. Abstraction: Mathematical methods are usually used for abstraction. VHLL modules consist of a fixed part (module functional semantics) and a variable part (objects specifications).
2. Selection: Selection and customization can take place at the two levels of the VHLL and the VHLL language constructs. The highest level consists of selecting the most closely appropriate VHLL for a specific problem, and the second level of choosing a suitable language construct for the problem specification. The selection of an appropriate VHLL applicable to the domain of a specific application obviously has a strong effect on the development process.
3. Customization: The major type of customization consists of recursively substituting the slots in the parameterized VHLL language constructs with the constructs of the appropriate type.
4. Integration: The integration of language constructs could take place through reasoning and verification. Data flow and control flow of components are unified and localized to function composition, function arguments, and return values to make the integration process simpler.

Transformation Systems

A transformation is a mapping from programs to programs. In this model (TS), two separate phases are employed for software development. The first phase involves providing the specification of software behavior in a high-level specification language like an executable VHLL. The second phase is transforming the specification produced in the first level into an enhanced executable system (21). The transformation process is mostly an interactive one and requires human-guided compilation. This is due to the lack of efficient automatic algorithm and data structure selection facilities.

1. Abstraction: VHLLs are used for the specification abstraction. According to Krueger, "transformation abstractions are typically expressed as match/substitution patterns" (15).
2. Selection: The appropriate transformations can be selected from a TS library using the expert system technology. A rule-based transformation–selection system should provide rules such as the transformation goal, stratgies, and selection rationale.
3. Customization: Transformation generally does not involve modification unless a complete match does not exist in the library. In the case of a no-match, the customization is the same as the VHLL model customization. Transformation mapping (from specification to code) is automatic and hidden from the user.
4. Integration: The integration of transformation is in the form of functional composition.

It should be noted that although the above-mentioned models present different categories of reuse models, in reality most of the existing reuse approaches utilize a combination of two or more of these models. Furthermore, currently there is no one model that can be shown to be the best one for software reuse. These models differ in their potential investment requirements and their potential degree of reusability. The following section present different types of reuse comprised of one or more models described.

Three types of reuse processes currently exist: Adaptive Reuse, Parameterized Reuse, and Engineered Reuse (22,23). Each of these three types can be applied to a different set of reuse requirements and provide a different set of risks and benefits for each project.

Adaptive Reuse

Most organizations already practice adaptive reuse. Adaptive reuse utilizes the results of previous development as the starting point to create new applications. This method is commonly referred to as code salvaging or scavenging, because the old software was not explicitly designed for reuse. Also, this method does not provide a means for selecting and retrieving potentially useful components for reuse like a software reuse library provides.

However, adaptive reuse requires little investment by the organization when porting systems from one environment to another. In fact, a cost-savings factor of 23 : 1 over new development can be achieved (12). Adaptive reuse can also support new development projects, provided only incremental changes from the previous application are required. In this case a cost-savings factor of 1.8 can be achieved by the project (12). Applications that require major modifications and upgrades will only achieve marginal benefits from adapting old software. To improve the cost-effectiveness of software reuse at an organizational level or across families of systems, parameterized reuse should be employed (22).

Parameterized Reuse

When the number of similar systems being produced by the organization grows beyond three, there is a cost benefit to collecting common components and standardizing them into domain-specific software reuse libraries. This approach has proven to be extremely successful in organizations that deliver large systems to a broad range of customers that meet similar sets of requirements. The Japanese Software Factories base reuse success on the establishment of a common architecture for a family of systems that can be applied through parameterization to a wide range of users (23).

Although this method requires a major investment for an organization because of the establishment of an infrastructure for all new implementations, there is a significant payoff, provided the domain is stable. However, in areas of new and evolving technology, a stable framework cannot be achieved. In the case in which requirements for new systems do not adhere to previously established standards, engineered reuse provides the most benefits.

Engineered Reuse

Whereas parameterized reuse is more appropriate in mature domains, reuse in domains that rely on emerging technology cannot standardize at the same level of parameterization. Applications within such a domain must relay on new techniques such as domain analysis to establish commonality and enable software reuse. By experts within the field examining related software systems and the underlying theory of the class of systems they represent, domain analysis can provide a generic description of the requirements of those systems. It can also propose a set of approaches for implementing new systems.

Engineered reuse also requires a major investment by the organization. However, software components must meet the requirements of a wide range of applications or this investment will not be cost-effective.

Domain analysis is a major factor in successful development of reusable software. The next section presents an introduction to domain analysis process.

DOMAIN ANALYSIS

Domain analysis is a process by which information used in developing software for a specific application problem area is identified, captured, and organized with the goal of making it reusable. Arrango sees reuse as a learning system (24). In his proposed model, software development is a self-improving process that draws from a knowledge source, which is named the reuse infrastructure and is integrated with the software development process. Reuse infrastructure consists of reusable resources and their descriptions.

Domain analysis is actually a family of disciplines. This family includes software specification, software implementation, conceptual modeling, knowledge engineering, knowledge representation, and traditional software engineering (24). The interdisciplinary nature of domain. In the reuse environment promoted by Arrango, the desired software is implemented (i.e., constructed) using the reuse infrastructure and the specification of the software to be built. The software produced is compared to the input to the system (i.e., the specification of the system).

Underlying domain analysis is an information infrastructure to support reuse. Prieto-Diaz (19) identifies the following components of the infrastructure: domain models, development standards, and libraries of reusable components. The libraries of reusable components contain more than just program code; they contain all aspects of the designs of software systems. This allows the reuser to decide whether or not a particular component can be used in a system that is currently under development.

Domain analysis is an ongoing process. The typical process of an integrated software development process and domain analysis is as follows. First. the reusable resources are identified and added to the system. Then, the reuse data are gathered and fed back to the domain analysis system for tuning the domain models and updating the resource library. Finally, the newly developed system, as a member of the existing system, is used to refine the reuse infrastructure. Domain engineering is the complete process of doing a domain analysis and building the infrastructure for reuse. Domain-specific kits are a set of reusable tools that are designed to facilitate development of applications in such a limited domain.

Arrango and Prieto-Diaz (1991) define a problem domain as a related class of problems with the following characteristics:

- There is comprehensive relationships among items of information.
- There is a community that has a stake in solving the problems.
- The community seeks software-intensive solutions to these problems.
- The community has access to knowledge that can be applied to solving the problems.

The lack of a formal and systematic methodology is the primary issue in domain analysis. Domain analysis is recommended for specific applications; therefore, domain analysis would be restricted to limited-domain software and not appropriate for general reusability environments. Representing knowledge explicitly is a problem that must be faced by domain analysts. Much of the knowledge that domain experts use is implicit and nonformal. To be reusable, the knowledge must be explicit and formal (24). According to Prieto-Diaz, for domain analysis to work, it needs to be formalized much like what happened in software development when the building of larger systems started (25).

Another problem that the domain analyst must tackle is how to make boundaries between different domains. The analyst must determine which objects to include in the domain and to what degree those objects need to be abstracted so that they can be reused later. The more an object is abstracted, the higher is its potential for being reused later.

Libraries, classification schema, and locating have been central issues in software reusability. The following section presents the foundation of these issues.

CLASSIFICATION AND IDENTIFICATION OF SOFTWARE

Locating reusable components is becoming an activity that is increasingly performed by automated systems, such as Gopher, the World Wide Web, and so forth, through bulletin boards, and news bulletins, or with information-brokerage applications. The most reusable software will not be reused if it cannot be found by potential users. The key to successful location of reusable software is the classification mechanism under which the software is organized and retrieved—tools that access the software under the classification scheme.

Software classification schemes have been considered a kernel for software reusability system. A collection of modules or program components is organized by attributes that define software structure, environment, function, implementation, and so on.

According to Prieto-Diaz, "classification is grouping like things together." All members of a group or class produced by classification share at least one characteristic that members of other classes do not possess. Classification displays the relationships that exist among things and among classes of things (19). A classification scheme is a tool to produce a systematic order based on a controlled and structured index vocabulary.

Prieto-Diaz (19) suggests that the characterization of a software component's functionality (what it does) and its environment (where it does it) suffice for classification. Burton and Argon (2) use an algorithm's description, documentation, testing history, and version management plus its functionality and environment as the classification attributes.

The Prieto-Diaz/Freeman classification method actually employs a controlled vocabulary technique for indexing software. They have used this technique to avoid duplicate and ambiguous descriptors of software components.

Another method of software classification and identification is abstraction. Abstraction has been used to help manage the intellectual complexity of software development. Abstraction contributes to simplification by secluding irrelevant attributes from the relevant one. In other words, to transform a problem to a simpler one, certain details within the original problem are overlooked. The most common types of abstraction of software are abstraction by parameterization and abstraction by specification.

Abstraction plays a central and oftentimes a limiting role in the ability to satisfactorily address the selection, customization, and integration of software components. Abstraction of software components is employed to help a user find, understand, and select the suitable components from a software collection system. Abstraction could help the selection process in all of the different reuse models. For reuse purposes, abstraction by specifications must express all information required for selection, customization, and integration. Abstraction can also play a significant role in the integration of software components in all levels of reuse. All parts involved in the integration (i.e., the interface specification, interconnection language, and version-control system) can use abstraction in order to provide various components' relevant specifications.

SOFTWARE ARCHITECTURE AND ITS IMPACT ON REUSABILITY

With the increasing complexity of software systems, the challenges of development have risen above the level of just algorithmic and design problems. Successes and failures are being tied more directly to the overall organization of a software system. This is referred to as the *software architecture* level of design (26). Although there is a considerable amount of ambiguity on the exact definition of software architecture, researchers and developers seem to have identified this concept as a crucial factor that drives a software of development project.

What Is a Software Architecture

A common theme in a variety of different research done on software architecture is its impact on software reuse. Although much of the work in the area of software reuse has been about constructing and managing software repositories, there still lies the problem of how to get developers to use these repositories in the most efficient and effective way. To solve this, efforts have been made in all possible directions, including monetary rewards and organizationwide recognition. Software architecture takes the view that in order to enhance reuse, there needs to be an architectural development methodology as found in other nonsoftware disciplines of engineering such as construction. This view relies on developers having an understanding of common component configurations (27). The architectural development methodology matches the problem domain to standard architectural models, and adapts the standard components associated with these models to meed domain requirements (27).

In terms of research topics in software reuse, there is a close relationship among architecture, domain analysis, frameworks, and reengineering. Whereas the common theme among these topics is to identify software systems in generic forms, called *architectures*, *domains*, *frameworks*, or *process flows*, these topics have their differences. These differences are not so much in terms of their functionality but more in their level of application and their scope. Software architecture actually embodies domain analysis, frameworks, reengineering, and reuse at different stages of its implementation.

An extensive part of software architecture is recognizing standard software development practices, categorizing them, and establishing new standards. Over the years, some software architectures have become common terms in development, such as "client–server architecture," "layered architecture," "object-oriented systems," "distributed architecture," and so on. According to Garlan and Shaw, architecture is a collection of computational components—or simply *components*—together with a description of the interactions between these components—the *connectors*. The significance of this definition is the fact that if an architecture is completely definable in terms of components and connectors, then, based on the commonality, many of these components and connectors can be reusable. Using this definition, each architecture style defines a family of such systems in terms of a pattern of structural organization. They also define a vocabulary of component and connector types. and a set of constraints on how they can be combined (26).

Market Demand of Software Components and Connectors

Like any other marketplace, commercial development has driven the software industry too. So far, software commodities have been in the form of end products; that is, software is bought and sold whole, not in parts. However, a closer inspection of the software development process reveals that there is no reason why the software industry could not evolve into something like the automobile industry, where along with the end products (the automobiles), a huge part of the business exists in the form of automobiles parts (your auto parts store, etc.). The difference here, again, is that automobile have specific standards of construction—a car has four wheels, a transmission, battery, and so forth, but what is there in terms of defining software? Although software products are not as distinct as automobiles, their parts can certainly be categorized. For example, if the spell checker part of a word processor is defined in terms of specific standards, users can buy spell checkers as independent products that will "plug" into a variety of word processing software.

Whitehead et al. (28) identify some existing components such as Unix filter and Visual Basic VBXs, and list some requirements on architectures for software component marketplaces:

1. Multiple component granularity
2. Substitutability of components
3. Parameterizable components
4. Customizable components
5. Component development in multiple programming languages
6. Component-specific help
7. Component-specific user-interface dialog and presentation properties
8. Easy distribution of components from seller to buyer
9. Support for multiple sales models

The trend in software development has been in the direction of higher levels of development languages and platforms, so it is certainly foreseeable to have an environment in which building software is more of a matter of putting components together, with the amount of actual coding becoming a very small part of it. However, we do need to be careful about this analogy of software components to hardware components because software is very people-specific and much more dynamic than hardware. Software components that are invisible to the users, such as search routines, numerical algorithms, and graphics routines, are more likely candidates for being standardized, but for the components for which creativity is important, such as user interfaces, standardization may not be so desirable.

Standardization And Its Challenges

Standardization is the key factor in enabling software architectures to enhance reuse. Unless there are clearly defined and commonly accepted software architectures, the reuse will be limited to the specific organization, or wherever the scope of the architecture ends. Standardization has always been a big challenge in the software industry, as seen in the case of operating systems, communication protocols, and so forth. If we take a closer look at some success stories in standardization, such as OSI reference layers, TCP/IP, ODBC, http, and the World Wide Web, the common theme is that they are not platform-specific and that they have extensions to be able to plug into a variety of other systems. For example, TCP/IP can be implemented on Unix machines, Windows NT, and Macintoshes without any significant changes to their original structure. It is the ease of implementation that has made all these standards possible.

Standardizing software architectures and thus enhancing reuse is going to speed up software development time, which is very desirable for the market. However, the market itself is very diverse, and not very flexible toward efforts for industrywide standardization. So if we are to be able to standardize allowing such diversity, the standards should focus more on the generic commonality of the existing systems. It will nevertheless require a lot of support from the market because the market has to be willing to play by the generic guidelines the standards will provide. Individual organizations will not be willing to throw away the methodologies they have developed on their own just to make sure their systems confirm to some standards, but if it is possible for them to adapt their methodologies to generic guidelines, they will be more likely to follow that route, given the promise of software reuse and relatively easy extensions of the system.

SUMMARY AND CONCLUSIONS

It can be argued that the concept of software reuse started when the first program was stored in a computer. The software crisis, coupled with impressive advances in computer hardware technology, have forced software developers to reconsider traditional ad hoc software development technologies and to initiate a systematic approach to software development. One important aspect of a comprehensive and systematic approach is exploiting the reuse potential of existing software. The significance of the role of reusable software in reducing the cost and effort of software development has been identified and widely recognized in the computing literature.

As mentioned earlier, a majority of the published work and experiences focus on the future of software by designing reuse models and techniques. The problem with that approach is not a technical one; no one can ignore the contributions made by reuse researchers to the field of software engineering. The main problem of that approach is that it can result in ignoring the millions of lines of existing code that may have potential for reuse. It is unrealistic to believe that the development of reusable software will just happen from a certain date in the relatively near future when practical and capable software environments are available that can produce reusable modules/programs. There are a large number of private and public organizations that cannot afford to switch from the old system to a new system not only because of budgetary constraints but also for the attendant operational problems. The proper solution of these organizations is a combination of both approaches: that is design for reuse hand in hand with reuse based on code scavenging.

> **Reuse Technology**: Reuse technology lacks a formal and complete picture of what to reuse and how to reuse it. Research in this area needs to focus on and to ascertain how to enhance the existing capabilities to capture, modify, and reuse a wide range of information in the development process. A rich machine-pro-

cessable representation and a clear strategy to lead to the optimum approach to reusability are specifically needed.

State of the Art: Techniques and methods to facilitate reusable software engineering (i.e., encapsulation, normalization, module interconnection language, organization and retrieval of software components in large repositories, and programming and detailed design techniques) are available or are emerging, but most of them need to be tailored to facilitate productive reuse.

State of the Practice: More and more organizations produce reusable software or systematically attempt to reuse existing software. The advantages of application of the reuse technology could be shown by long-term cost analysis.

Achieving high orders of software reuse requires changes in the way software is being developed, maintained, and reused. New policies and standards are needed to be used in the creation of infrastructure for software development projects (29).

REFERENCES

1. W. Tracz, "Software Reuse Myths," *Software Eng. Notes, ACM SIFSOFT*, 17–21 (January 1988).
2. M. Zand, "ROPCO—An Environment for Micro-Incremental Reuse," Ph.D. thesis, Department of Computer Science, Oklahoma State University, Stillwater, OK (1990).
3. M. Zand and M. Samadzadeh, "Software Reuse," *IEEE Potentials* (August/September 1994).
4. T. Matsubara et al., "SWB System: A Software Factory," *Software Engineering Environment*, North-Holland, Amsterdam, 1981, pp. 305–318.
5. K. D. Schwartz, "DoD Software Standard Sharpens Blurred Boundaries," *Gov. Computer News*, *12*(9), 58(1) (1993).
6. M. Wasmund, "Incentives Versus Targets—A Practical Experience," IBM Deutschland, Germany, 1988.
7. J. Poulin, "A Reuse Incentive Program for Domain-Independent Software," Federal Systems Company, IBM, Owego, NY (December 1993).
8. S. Isoda, "Experiences of a Software Reuse Project: Software Laboratories of Nippon Telegraph and Telephone Corporation (NTT), *J. Syst. Software* (September 1994).
9. C. McClure, *The Three Rs of Software Automation: Re-engineering, Repository, and Reusability*, Prentice-Hall, Englewood Cliffs, NJ, 1992.
10. Paramax, *Acquisition Handbook—Final, Central Archive for Reusable Defense Software* (*CARDS*), Department of Defense, 1993.
11. F. McGrath, "Cost Benefit from Investment in I-CASE," *Logicon* (July 1993).
12. Department of the Navy, *Software Reuse Implementation Plan*, Naval Information Systems Management Center, Washington, DC, 1993.
13. J. Endosos, "Audit Says DoD's Software Reuse Plan Faces Many Barriers," *Gov. Computer News*, *12*(6) 46(1) (1993).
14. Department of Defense, "Software Reuse Initiative: Vision and Strategy," DoD (July 15, 1992).
15. W. Krueger, "Models of Reuse in Software Engineering," Technical Report CMU-CS-89-188, Department of Computer Science, University of Carnegie Mellon, Pittsburgh, PA (December 1989).
16. M. Kazerooni-Zand, M. Samadzadeh, and K. M. George, "ROPCO—An Environment for Micro-Incremental Reuse," in *Proceedings of IEEE International Phoenix Conference on Computers and Communications*, IEEE, Pheonix, AZ, March 1990, pp. 347–355.
17. J. A. Gougen, "Reusing and Interconnecting Software Components," *IEEE Computer*, 16–28 (February 1986).

18. D. Perry, "Software Interconnection Models," in *Proceedings of the 9th International Conference on Software Engineering*, IEEE, Monterey CA, March 30–April 2, 1987, pp. 61–69.

19. R. Prieto-Diaz "Classification of Reusable Modules," in *Software Reusability*, T. Biggerstaff and A. Perlis (eds.), *ACM Press*, New York, NY, (1990).

20. D. Perry, "The Inscape Program Construction and Evolution Environment," Technical Report, Computer Technology Research Laboratory, AT&T Bell Lab, Murray Hill, NJ, (September 1986).

21. T. Cheatham et al., "Program Refinement by Transformation," in *Proceedings of the 5th International Conf. on Software Eng.*, IEEE Computer Society Press, Washington, DC, 1981, pp. 430–437.

22. A. S. Peterson, *Coming to Terms with Software Reuse Terminology: A Model-Based Approach*, Software Engineering Institute, Pittsburgh, PA, 1991.

23. S. Cohen, *Process and Products for Software Reuse and Domain Analysis*, Software Engineering Institute, Pittsburgh, PA, 1991.

24. G. Arango, "Domain Analysis Methods," in *Software Reusability*, W. Schaeffer, R. Prieto-Diaz, and M. Matsumoto (eds.), Ellis Horwood, New York, 1993, pp. 17–49.

25. R. Prieto-Diaz, "Domain Analysis for Reusability," in *Proceedings of COMPSAC '87*, IEEE, 1987, pp. 23–29.

26. D. Garlan and M. Shaw, "An Introduction to Software Architecture, *Adv. Software Eng. Knowledge Eng.*, *1*, Pittsburgh, PA, 1–39 (1993).

27. L. Best, Position Paper: Workshop on Architectures for Software Systems, ICSE-17, Seattle, WA (April 24–25, 1995), pp. 13–19.

28. E. J Whitehead, Jr, J. E. Robbins, N. Medvidovic, and R. N. Taylor, Software Architecture: Foundation of a Software Component Marketplace, *Proceedings of the First International Workshop on Architecture for Software Systems*, Seattle, WA, April 24–25, 1995, pp. 276–282.

29. M. Zand and M. Samadzadeh, "Software Reuse: Current Status and Trends," *J. Syst. Software*, 167–170 (September 1995).

30. W. Tracz, "Software Reuse: Motivators and Inhibitors," in *Proceedings of COMPCONS '87*, 1987, p. 358(5).

MANSOUR K. ZAND

KNOWLEDGE ACQUISITION PROBLEM IN MONOTONE BOOLEAN SYSTEMS

INTRODUCTION

Learning is the main property that characterizes an intelligent system. As similar situations will usually appear again and again in a given environment, the goal of learning is to gain experience that can be used to improve the performance of the system when similar situations occur in the future. Gaining experience often requires the system to build up an internal knowledge base that can efficiently fetch the information when needed.

The learning process can be divided into two phases: the knowledge acquisition phase and the rule generation phase. In the knowledge acquisition phase, it is relatively easy to gather a large amount of knowledge or facts. However, critical facts are usually difficult to collect or easy to neglect. Therefore, the time, manpower, and other resources spent on knowledge acquisition can be very large if this process is not managed properly.

This article examines the knowledge acquisition problem for learning in a monotone Boolean system. In such systems, it is assumed that all examples are represented by binary vectors in space E^n and each bit of a vector represents an attribute of the example. The attributes are assumed to be binary [i.e., to be either "True" or "False" ("0" or "1"), respectively]. All examples are divided into two classes and are thus regarded as positive and negative examples. The relation among the examples can be expressed in the form of a monotone Boolean function, in which an example is regarded as a positive example when the function value for the example is 1 and as a negative example when the function value is 0. The goal of the knowledge acquisition phase in a monotone Boolean system is to infer the function and thus be able to determine the class membership for all examples in the problem space.

MONOTONE BOOLEAN FUNCTIONS

To express the relationship among the examples in the form of a monotone Boolean function requires that the class membership of all examples be known. Determining the class membership of all examples is the same as to restoring the underlying monotone Boolean function; thus, this knowledge acquisition process is known as *monotone Boolean function inference*.

As discussed earlier, it could be very costly to determine the class membership of all examples in the problem space if the process is not arranged properly. For instance, to get the function value of all examples in space E^{10} could mean to test each one of the 1024 examples in that space. Even if each test requires only 30 min to get the result, this process could be too slow to be acceptable in many practical situations. Furthermore, the considerable costs related with each test could be another reason that prevents the use of this kind of testing.

When the details of different kinds of tests are omitted, each example submitted for testing can be regarded as posing a question and the results coming from the test can be regarded as getting an answer. Therefore, it is desirable to ask a sequence of appropriate questions (i.e., to test only a small number of examples from the problem space), so that the class membership of all examples in the space can be determined. The selection of the examples, or the question-asking strategy, is critical in reducing the number of questions.

When the relation among the examples is expressed as a general Boolean function, there is no way to determine the class membership of other examples based on the classified examples (training set). Therefore, every example should be examined if the relation among the examples (i.e., the inferred Boolean function) is required to be 100% correct. This means that the size of the examples in the training set will always be 2^n, the same as the number of all the examples in space E^n. However, the number of questions can be reduced when the relation can be expressed as a *monotone Boolean function* (to be discussed later). As the class membership of all examples in a monotone Boolean system satisfy the monotone property, it is possible that a small number of classified examples can be used to determine the class membership of new examples. This, in turn, can significantly expedite the learning process and thus reduce the costs. Under monotonicity, examples can be ordered as follows (1):

> *Let E^n denote the set of all binary vectors of length n; let x and y be two such vectors. Then, the vector $x = \langle x_1, x_2, \ldots, x_n \rangle$ **precedes** vector $y = \langle y_1, y_2, \ldots, y_n \rangle$ (denoted as $x \preccurlyeq y$) if and only if $x_i \leq y_i$ for $1 \leq i \leq n$. If, at the same time, $x \neq y$, then x **strictly precedes** y (denoted as $x < y$).*

According to this definition, the vectors in space E^2 can be ordered as follows:

$$\langle 11 \rangle > \langle 01 \rangle > \langle 00 \rangle$$

and

$$\langle 11 \rangle > \langle 10 \rangle > \langle 00 \rangle.$$

However, the vectors $\langle 01 \rangle$ and $\langle 10 \rangle$ cannot be compared according to the above definition.

Based on the order of the vectors, an *increasing monotone Boolean function* is defined as follows (1):

> *A Boolean function f defined in space E^n is said to be an increasing (isotone) monotone Boolean function if and only if for any vectors x, y $\in E^n$, such that $x \preccurlyeq y$, then $f(x) \leq f(y)$.*

Similarly, a *decreasing monotone Boolean function* is defined as follows (1):

> *A Boolean function f defined in space E^n is said to be a decreasing (antitone) monotone Boolean function if and only if for any vectors x, y $\in E^n$, such that $x \preccurlyeq y$, then $f(x) \geq f(y)$.*

In a monotone Boolean system, a function is either an increasing monotone Boolean function or a decreasing monotone Boolean function. However, as the method used to acquire the class memberships for the examples is the same for both cases, in this article it is assumed that a hidden function is always an increasing monotone Boolean function.

Monotonicity is a very strong constraint and, sometimes, cannot be easily satisfied. Fortunately, it can easily be proved that every general Boolean function $q(x_1, \ldots, x_n)$ can be described in terms of several increasing $g_i(x_1, \ldots, x_n)$ and decreasing $h_i(x_1, \ldots, x_n)$ monotone Boolean functions (2); that is,

$$q(x) = \bigvee_{i=1}^{m} \left(g_i(x) \wedge h_i(x) \right).$$

For the number $\psi(n)$ of monotone Boolean functions defined on the vectors in space E^n, it is known (3,4) that

$$\Psi(n) = 2^{\left\lfloor \frac{n}{n/2} \right\rfloor |1+\varepsilon(n)|},$$

where $0 < \varepsilon(n) < c(\log n)/n$, c is a constant, and $\lfloor n/2 \rfloor$ is the largest integer less than or equal to $n/2$.

A Boolean function can be of any form. All the forms are regarded as equivalent as long as they give the same correct true–false function values for all input Boolean vectors. However, it is convenient to represent a Boolean function in either the Conjunctive Normal Form (CNF) or the Disjunctive Normal Form (DNF) (see, for instance, Refs. 5–10). Peysakh (11) describes an algorithm for converting any Boolean expression into CNF. The CNF form can be described as follows:

$$\bigwedge_{j=1}^{k} \left(\bigvee_{i \in \rho_j} \alpha_i \right),$$

where a_i is either attribute A_i or its negation $\overline{A}_i$, j is the number of attribute combinations, and ρ_j is the jth index set for the jth attribute combination. Similarly, DNF can be described as follows:

$$\bigvee_{j=1}^{k} \left(\bigwedge_{i \in \rho_j} \alpha_i \right).$$

SHANNON FUNCTION AND THE HANSEL THEOREM

Suppose the relations among the binary examples in the problem space can be expressed with a monotone Boolean function f. This function f can be obtained by classifying all vectors with the help of the appropriate operator A_f (also called an *oracle*) which, when fed with a vector $x = (x_1, x_2, x_3, \ldots, x_n)$, returns the class membership [or function value $f(x)$] of vector x. Let $A = \{F\}$ be the set of all algorithms which can be used to determine the class membership of all vectors in the space, and $\varphi(F, f)$ be the number of accesses to the operator A_f required to obtain the monotone Boolean function $f \in M_n$ (where M_n is the set of all monotone Boolean functions defined on n variables). Based on the above notation, the *Shannon function* $\varphi(n)$ can be introduced as follows (12):

$$\varphi(n) = \min_{F \in A} \max_{f \in M_n} \varphi(F, f).$$

An upper bound on the number of questions needed to determine the class membership of all vectors and restore the underlying monotone Boolean function is given by the following equation (also known as *Hansel theorem*) (13):

$$\varphi(n) = \binom{n}{\lfloor n/2 \rfloor} + \binom{n}{\lfloor n/2 \rfloor + 1}.$$

The significance of the Hansel theorem is that the total number of questions needed to infer any monotone Boolean function defined by the relations among vectors in space E^n will not exceed $\varphi(n)$ if a proper question-asking strategy is applied.

Kovalerchuk et al. (14) proposed a method on how to classify the examples in a monotone Boolean system by issuing a sequence of membership inquires to an operator or "oracle." That method is based on the concept of *the Hansel chains* and is optimal in the sense of the *Hansel theorem* and the *Shannon function*.

HANSEL CHAINS

A *chain* in space E^n is a sequence of binary vectors. All binary vectors in space E^n can be organized into several chains, which are called *Hansel chains* (13). For any two adjacent vectors x and y in a Hansel chain (where y follows x), the vector x is required to be different than vector y by only 1 bit so that vector x strictly precedes vector y.

The Hansel chains in space E^n can be generated recursively based on the Hansel chains in space E^{n-1}. Algorithm 1, as shown in Figure 1, is a modified version of the method proposed by Hansel (13) to generate hansel chains in space E^n.

For space E^1, there is only a single Hansel chain that consists of two vectors, $\langle 0 \rangle$ and $\langle 1 \rangle$; that is

$$H^{1,1} = \{\langle 0 \rangle, \langle 1 \rangle\}.$$

To form the Hansel chains for space E^2, there are three steps to be followed:

Algorithm 1: Hansel Chains Generation in space E^n
Input: Dimension n, Hansel chains of dimension n-1;
Output: Hansel chains of dimension n;

Note that the Hansel chains of space E^{n-1} are assumed to be known and also $H^{1,1} = \{\langle 0 \rangle, \langle 1 \rangle\}$.

For each single chain C of the Hansel Chains in space E^{n-1} do the following:
Step 1: Form a new chain C^{min} in space E^n by attaching the element '0' to the front of each vector in chain C;
Step 2: Form a new chain C^{max} in space E^n by attaching the element '1' to the front of each vector in chain C;
Step 3: Move the last vector in chain C^{max} to C^{min};
Step 4: Add C^{min} to the Hansel Chains of dimension n;
Step 5: If after removing the last vector form C^{max} to C^{min}, C^{max} is not empty, then add chain C^{max} to the Hansel chains of dimension n;
The above 5 steps will be repeated until all chains in space E^{n-1} have been processed.

FIGURE 1   An algorithm for the generation of Hansel chains in space E^n.

Step 1: Attach the element "0" to the front of each vector in $H^{1,1}$ and get chain C^{2min}; that is,

$$C^{2min} = \{\langle 00 \rangle, \langle 01 \rangle\}$$

Step 2: Attach the element "1" to the front of each vector in $H^{1,1}$ and get chain C^{2max}; that is,

$$C^{2max} = \{\langle 10 \rangle, \langle 11 \rangle\}$$

Step 3: Move the last vector in chain C^{2max} (i.e., vector $\langle 11 \rangle$) to the end of C^{2min}. Now, the two Hansel chains in E^2 can be listed as follows:

$$H^{2,1} = \{\langle 00 \rangle, \langle 01 \rangle, \langle 11 \rangle\},$$
$$H^{2,2} = \{\langle 10 \rangle\}$$

To form the Hansel chains for space E^3, the previous three steps will be repeated:

Step 1: Attach the element "0" to the front of each vector in $H^{2,1}$ and $H^{2,2}$ and get chains $C^{3,1min}$ and $C^{3,2min}$, respectively, as follows:

$$C^{3,1min} = \{\langle 000 \rangle, \langle 001 \rangle, \langle 011 \rangle\},$$
$$C^{3,2min} = \{\langle 010 \rangle\}$$

Step 2: Attach the element "1" to the front of each vector in $H^{2,1}$ and $H^{2,2}$ and get chains $C^{3,1max}$ and $C^{3,2max}$, respectively, as follows:

$$C^{3,1max} = \{\langle 100 \rangle, \langle 101 \rangle, \langle 111 \rangle\},$$
$$C^{3,2max} = \{\langle 110 \rangle\}$$

Step 3: Move the last vector form $C^{3,1max}$ and $C^{3,2max}$ to the end of their counterparts $C^{3,1min}$ and $C^{3,2min}$, respectively, to form the Hansel chains in E^3 as follows:

$$H^{3,1} = \{\langle 000 \rangle, \langle 001 \rangle, \langle 011 \rangle, \langle 111 \rangle\},$$
$$H^{3,2} = \{\langle 100 \rangle, \langle 101 \rangle\},$$
$$H^{3,3} = \{\langle 010 \rangle, \langle 110 \rangle\}.$$

As there is only one vector in chain $C^{3,2max}$, this chain can be deleted after the vector $\langle 110 \rangle$ is moved to $C^{3,2min}$. So there are only three chains in the final set with Hansel chains, namely $H^{3,1}$, $H^{3,2}$, and $H^{3,3}$.

In general, the Hansel chains for space E^n can be generated recursively by repeating the three steps described above from the Hansel chains in space E^{n-1}. Table 1 lists the Hansel chains generated for space E^3.

THE SEQUENTIAL HANSEL CHAINS STRATEGY

An interactive learning approach based on Hansel chains was proposed by Kovalerchuk et al. (14) and can significantly reduce the number of inquiries needed to determine a hidden monotone Boolean function in space E^n. This interactive learning approach assumes that there is no example classified initially. By systematically choosing a set of vectors from the Hansel chains and by asking about their class memberships, all other vectors in the space can be classified. The algorithm proposed is optimal in the sense of the Shannon function and the Hansel theorem.

TABLE 1   Hansel Chains for E^3

Chain no.	Vector in-chain index	Vector
1	1	000
	2	001
	3	011
	4	111
2	1	100
	2	101
3	1	010
	2	110

The typical process of this interactive learning is as follows:

1. Generate the Hansel chains in space E^n.
2. Sort the Hansel chains in increasing order of the size (i.e., the number of vectors) of the Hansel chains.

Start from the first Hansel chain and do the following:

3. Start from the first unclassified vector in the chain and require the class membership of that vector.
4. Use the class membership of this classified vector to determine the class membership of as many undetermined vectors as possible.
5. If all the vectors in the chain are determined, then process the next Hansel chain.

Steps 3–5 will be repeated until all chains have been processed.

As in Step 3, the vectors are selected sequentially in each Hansel chain; the algorithm is therefore called a *Sequential Hansel Chains Approach*. The above steps are described in detail in Figure 2.

The following example is a step-by-step demonstration of how the sequential Hansel chains approach can be used to determine all positive and negative examples in space E^3 and eventually form the underlying hidden monotone Boolean function.

First, the Hansel chains for space E^3 are generated by using Algorithm 1, as are listed in Table 1. In Step 1, the previous Hansel chains are sorted in descending order of their size. Table 2 lists the sorted Hansel chains. The current chain pointer, *CurChain* = 1, indicates that the algorithm will begin to process from the first chain in that sequence.

After the Hansel chains are generated and sorted, Steps 2–5 will be repeated until all vectors in space E^3 are classified.

Iteration 1

Step 2: As *CurChain* = 1 and no vector has been classified, the vector $\langle 100 \rangle$ is selected for testing.

Step 3: Suppose the result of the test indicates that the class membership value of vector $\langle 100 \rangle$ is 0 (i.e., false).

Algorithm 2. Sequential Hansel Chains Question-Asking Approach

Input: Dimension n;
Output: Number of questions asked to determine the class membership of all the vectors for space E^n.

Step 0: {Hansel chain generation.}
Use algorithm 1 to generate all Hansel Chains for space E^n.
Step 1: {Initialization.}
SORT the Hansel chains in increasing order of the size of the chains.
Set the Current Chain Pointer *CurChain*=1;
Step 2: {Some vectors are unclassified.}
Select the first unclassified vector v in chain C_i, where i=*CurChain*;
Step 3: {Inquire the class membership of the vector};
Class(v) =ANSWER(v);
Step 4: {Mark the vectors whose value can be determined based on the monotonicity property and the value of v, and update the undetermined sequence of vectors in each Hansel chain.};
For(each chain C_j, for j=1, 2, 3, ..., K) Do
Begin {FOR}
MARK the class membership of vectors in C_j that can be determined;
End {FOR};
Step 5: {Check for completion condition}
IF(there are no unclassified vectors in the current chain) THEN
Begin{ IF}
IF (*CurChain*=2^n) THEN
Begin{ IF}
Output the class membership of all the vectors and the number of questions needed;
EXIT;
End {IF};
ELSE {There are other chains not processed}
CurChain=*CurChain*+1;
End {IF};
ELSE { There are unclassified vectors}
Goto Step 2;

FIGURE 2   A sequential Hansel chains question-asking approach.

Step 4: Based on the monotone property of the hidden Boolean function, the class membership of vector $\langle 100 \rangle$ indicates that vector $\langle 000 \rangle$ also has a class membership value of 0. Therefore, the vector $\langle 000 \rangle$ and vector $\langle 100 \rangle$ can be classified as negative.

Step 5: As there is an unclassified vector in chain 1, it is necessary to start another iteration and go back to Step 2.

The specifics of iteration 1 are given in Table 3, in which the symbol "<--" indicates the vector selected in this iteration.

TABLE 2   Sorted Hansel Chains

Chain no.	Vector in-chain index	Vector
1	1	100
	2	101
2	1	010
	2	110
3	1	000
	2	001
	3	011
	4	111

Iteration 2

Step 2: As $CurChain = 1$ and vector $\langle 101 \rangle$ has not been classified, it is selected for testing.

Step 3: Suppose the result of the test indicates that the membership value of vector $\langle 101 \rangle$ is 1.

Step 4: Based on the monotone property of the vectors, the class membership of vector $\langle 100 \rangle$ determines that vector $\langle 111 \rangle$ will also have a membership value of 1. Therefore, vectors $\langle 101 \rangle$ and $\langle 111 \rangle$ can be classified as positive.

Step 5: There is no unclassified vector in chain 1. However, as $CurChain = 1 < 3$, which indicates that not all the vectors have been classified, it is necessary to let $CurChain = 1 + 1 = 2$ so that the next iteration will begin with the vectors in Hansel chain 2. The result after iteration 2 is listed in Table 4.

Iteration 3

Step 2: As $CurChain = 2$ and the first vector $\langle 010 \rangle$ in chain 2 has not been classified, it is selected for testing.

Step 3: Suppose the result of the test determines that the membership value of vector $\langle 010 \rangle$ is 1.

TABLE 3   Vectors Classified in Iteration 1

Chain no.	Index of vectors in the chain	Vector	Vector membership	Selected vector in the iteration	Answer	Other vectors determined
1	1	100		<--	0	
	2	101				
2	1	010				
	2	110				
3	1	000				0
	2	001				
	3	011				
	4	111				

TABLE 4 Vectors Classified in Iteration 2

Chain no.	Index of vectors in the chain	Vector	Vector membership	Selected vector in the iteration	Answer	Other vectors determined
1	1	100	0			
	2	101		<--	1	
2	1	010				
	2	110				
3	1	000	0			
	2	001				
	3	011				
	4	111				1

Step 4: Based on the monotone property of the vectors, the class membership of vector $\langle 010 \rangle$ will determine that vectors

$\langle 110 \rangle$ and $\langle 011 \rangle$

will also have a membership value of 1 (another vector, vector $\langle 111 \rangle$, has already been classified by vector $\langle 101 \rangle$ in iteration 2). Therefore, the three vectors

$\langle 010 \rangle$, $\langle 110 \rangle$, and $\langle 011 \rangle$

can be classified as positive.

Step 5: There is no unclassified vector left in chain 2. However, as *CurChain* = 2 < 3, which indicates that not all vectors have been classified, it is necessary to increase *CurChain* to 3 so that the next iteration will start from Hansel chain 3.

The details of iteration 3 are listed in Table 5.

TABLE 5 Vectors Classified in Iteration 3

Chain no.	Index of vectors in the chain	Vector	Vector membership	Selected vector in the iteration	Answer	Other vectors determined
1	1	100	0			
	2	101	1			
2	1	010		<--	1	
	2	110				1
3	1	000	0			
	2	001				
	3	011				1
	4	111	1			

TABLE 6   Vectors Classified in Iteration 4

Chain no.	Index of vectors in the chain	Vector	Vector membership	Selected vector in the iteration	Answer	Other vectors determined
1	1	100	0			
	2	101	1			
2	1	010	1			
	2	110	1			
3	1	000	0			
	2	001		<--	1	
	3	001	1			
	4	111	1			

Iteration 4

Step 2: As *CurChain* = 3 and the first (and the only) vector has not been classified is $\langle 001 \rangle$, it is chosen for testing.

Step 3: Suppose the result of the test determines that the membership value of vector $\langle 001 \rangle$ is 1.

Step 4: As vector $\langle 010 \rangle$ is the only vector left unclassified, it is classified in this iteration.

Step 5: There is no unclassified vector in chain 3 and *CurChain* = 3. Therefore, all vectors in E^3 have been classified.

The number of questions needed to determine the class membership of all examples is 4, the same as the number of iterations. The details of the iteration are listed in Table 6. The class membership of all examples are listed in Table 7.

The hidden function is derived from Tables 3–6 as follows. We look at each one of the vectors which have been classified as positive by the oracle. Note that there are three such vectors, namely vectors $\langle 101 \rangle$, $\langle 010 \rangle$, and $\langle 001 \rangle$. Then, the attributes with

TABLE 7   The Class Membership of All Vectors in the Hansel Chains

Chain no.	Vector in-chain index	Vector	Function value
1	1	100	0
	2	101	1
2	1	010	1
	2	110	1
3	1	000	0
	2	001	1
	3	011	1
	4	111	1

value "1" in these vectors indicate the attributes present in the terms when the DNF format is used. Each such vector corresponds to one DNF term. Thus, from the above vectors, we get the following inferred monotone Boolean function:

$$f(x) = (x_1 \wedge x_3) \vee (x_2) \vee (x_3).$$

THE PROPOSED BINARY SEARCH/HANSEL CHAINS STRATEGY

The major advantage of the sequential Hansel chains approach is its conceptual simplicity. However, when the sequential Hansel chains approach is applied, the unclassified vectors in the Hansel chains are tested one by one. In this situation, the vectors are selected blindly and it is possible that some less effective vectors (as explained next) will be submitted for testing first.

One may note that before a vector is selected for membership inquiry, a "reward" value of the vector selection can be some how evaluated; that is, one can know *at least* how many other vectors can be classified as positive or negative if this vector is classified as positive or negative, respectively. By comparing these "reward" values of all unclassified vectors, one can select a vector which, when asked, can give the maximum "reward" value. However, the computation will be very heavy if the "reward" value for each vector has to be calculated. An alternative approach is to calculate and compare the "reward" values of only the middle vector of the unclassified vectors in each Hansel chain $H^{n,i}$ (for $i = 1, \ldots, k$, where k is the number of Hansel chains in space E^n) and select the middle vector that appears to be the most promising.

We call this new method the *Binary Search/Hansel Chains Strategy*. This method derives the main idea from the widely used binary search algorithm (see, for instance, Ref. 15). In summary, this binary search/Hansel chains strategy consists of the following steps:

Step 1: Select the middle vector of the unclassified vectors in each Hansel chain.

Step 2: Evaluate the "reward" value of each middle vector; that is, the number of vectors that can be classified as positive (denoted as P) if the middle vector is positive and the number of vectors that can be classified as negative (denoted as N) if the middle vector is negative.

Step 3: Compare the (P, N) pair of all middle vectors, and then select the most promising middle vector. Next ask the membership value of that vector.

Step 4: Based on the previous answer, classify other vectors that can be determined as result of the previous answer and the monotonicity property.

Step 5: Redefine the middle vectors of each Hansel chains as necessary.

Step 6: Go back to Step 2, unless all the vectors have been classified, in which case exit.

The detailed description of this algorithm is shown in Figure 3.

AN ILLUSTRATIVE EXAMPLE

To illustrate this binary search/Hansel chains question-asking strategy, an example is given for space E^3, in which there is a total of eight vectors. The Hansel chains are constructed as shown in Table 1. The underlying monotone Boolean function is the same

Algorithm 3: Binary Search/ Hansel Chains Question-Asking Approach

Input: Dimension n;

Output: Number of questions asked to determine the class of all the vectors in space E^n.

Step 0: {Initialization phase.}

  Use Algorithm 1 to form all Hansel Chains in space E^n.

  Let the j-th chain, denoted as C_j (for j=1, 2, 3, ..., K), be comprised by the sequence of vectors:

$$V_{j1}, ..., V_{j2}, ..., V_{jk}, \text{ for } j=1, 2, 3,..., K;$$

  Initialize the upper and lower borders, U_j and L_j, respectively, in each chain as follows:

$$U_j = V_{j1};$$
$$L_j = V_{jk};$$

  where K is the total number of vectors in Hansel chain C_j.

Step 1: {Some vectors are still unclassified.}

  For(each chain C_j, for j=1, 2, 3, ..., K) Do

  Begin {For}

    IF(Hansel chain C_j has some unclassified vectors) THEN

    Begin {IF}

      Get M_j $(j=\lfloor(U_j - L_j)/2\rfloor$, the "middle" vector of the sequence of unclassified vectors in chain C_j;

      PREDICT:

        POS(M_j)=Number of unclassified vectors which   would classified to TRUE if M_j were a positive example;

        NEG(M_j)=Number of unclassified vectors which would be classified to FALSE if M_j were a negative example;

    End{IF};

  End {For};

Step 2: {Inquire the value of the most "promising" unclassified example.}

  SELECT the most "promising" M_j according to a criteria;

  $M_y = M_j$;

  Inquire the value of M_y;

Step 3: {Mark the vectors whose value can be determined based on the monotonicity property and the value of M_y, and update the borders of undetermined sequence of vectors in each Hansel chain. }

  For(each chain C_j, for j=1, 2, 3, ..., K) Do

  Begin {FOR}

    MARK the value of vectors in C_j that can be determined;

    IF (M_y is TRUE) THEN

        UPDATE U_j

    ELSE {M_y is negative}

        UPDATE L_j;

  End {FOR};

Step 4: {Check for completion condition.}

  IF (no Hansel chain remains with unclassified vectors) THEN

  Begin{ IF}

    Output the class of all the vectors and the number of question needed;

    EXIT;

  End {IF};

  ELSE Goto Step 1;

FIGURE 3   A binary search/Hansel chains question-asking approach.

as the one is used in the previous section. At each iteration, a vector is selected as a question posed by the binary search/Hansel chains strategy.

At the beginning of iteration 1, the middle vector of each Hansel chain (as described in Step 1, above) is selected and marked with the "<--" symbol in the table. Then, according to Step 2, the "reward" value for each one of these middle vectors is calculated. For instance, if the second vector in chain 1 has a function value of 1, then there will be three other vectors (i.e., the vectors $\langle 000 \rangle$, $\langle 001 \rangle$, and $\langle 010 \rangle$) which can also be classified as positive because the inferred Boolean function is assumed to be *monotone*. Therefore, the total number of vectors that can be calculated to have a function value of 1 is $P = 4$, which is put under the entry " 'reward' value P if the middle vector is positive" of vector $\langle 001 \rangle$. Similarly, if it is calculated that the function value is 0, the "reward" value for the vector $\langle 001 \rangle$ will be $N = 2$; hence, this value is put in the entry " 'reward' value N if the middle vector is negative."

Once the "reward" values of all middle vectors have been evaluated, the most promising middle vector will be selected and its function value will be asked. Several selection criteria can be used to compare the (P, N) pairs of each middle vector and select the most promising vector. The one that is used here is to compare the smaller one of the (P, N) values [i.e., to determine $\min(P, N)$] of each vector and select the vector whose $\min(P, N)$ is the *largest* among all middle vectors. If the number of such vectors is more than one, then the tie will be broken randomly. Based on this criterion, vector 2 is chosen in chain 1 and marked with the "<--" symbol in its corresponding entry under the column "Selected middle vector with the largest $\min(P, N)$."

After getting the function value for vector $\langle 001 \rangle$, which is assumed to be 1 in this case, this value is put in the entry "answer." Then, this answer will be used to classify the vectors whose class membership can be determined by this answer and the monotonicity property. The middle vector of each Hansel chain will be updated as needed. The details of this iteration are shown in Table 8. As there are still undetermined vectors, at least one more iteration is required.

At iteration 2, the vector $\langle 100 \rangle$ is chosen in a similar manner, and based on the answer, the class membership of the vectors $\langle 100 \rangle$ and $\langle 000 \rangle$ is determined. This iteration is shown in detail in Table 9.

At iteration 3 (Table 10), as there is no unclassified vector left in Hansel chain 1 and Hansel chain 2, the middle vectors of these two chains do not need to be considered anymore. Therefore, an "X" is marked for each of the two chains in the column "middle vector in the chain." At iteration 3 the vector $\langle 010 \rangle$ is chosen and the remaining two vectors, $\langle 010 \rangle$ and $\langle 110 \rangle$, are determined. At this point, the class membership of all vectors has been determined and, thus, the question-asking process stops.

In a manner similar to the function inferred at the end of the previous section, the new function is generated from Tables 8–10:

$$f(x) = (x_2) \vee (x_3).$$

It is easy to confirm that these two functions are equivalent, although the second one is much simpler.

By using the binary search/Hansel chains question-asking strategy, the number of questions is able to be reduced to three from the previous four needed by the sequential Hansel chains approach. Although the difference between three and four queries is not significant, some test problems reported in Ref. 16 indicate that the new strategy requires on the average 50% queries less than the existing sequential Hansel chains approach.

TABLE 8   Details for Iteration 1

Chain no.	Index of vectors in the chain	Vector	Vector membership	Middle vector in the chain	Reward P if the vector is positive	Reward N if the vector is negative	Selected middle vector with the largest $\min(P, N)$	Answer	Other vectors determined
1	1	000							
	2	001		<--	4	2	<--	1	
	3	011							—
	4	111							—
2	1	100		<--	4	2			
	2	101							—
3	1	010		<--	4	2			
	2	110							

TABLE 9   Details for Iteration 2

Chain no.	Vector in-chain index	Vector	Vector membership	Middle vector in the chain	Reward P if the vector is positive	Reward N if the vector is negative	Selected middle vector with the largest min(P, N)	Answer	Other vectors determined
1	1	000		<--	4	1			0
	2	001	1						
	3	011	1						
	4	111	1						
2	1	100		<--	2	2	<--	0	
	2	101	1						
3	1	010		<--	2	2			
	2	110							

TABLE 10 Details for Iteration 3

Chain no.	Vector in-chain index	Vector	Vector membership	Middle vector in the chain	Reward P if the vector is positive	Reward N if the vector is negative	Selected middle vector with the largest min(P, N)	Answer	Other vectors determined
1	1	000	0						
	2	001	1	X					
	3	011	1						
	4	111	1						
2	1	100	0	X					
	2	101	1						
3	1	010		←-	2	1	←-	1	
	2	110							1

The illustrative examples in this article simply demonstrate the implementation of the proposed binary search/Hansel chains strategy.

The basic idea behind the binary search strategy is to select the most "promising" vector among all unclassified vectors in each iteration and submit it for testing. The selection of the most "promising" vector is based on the intuitive notion that once the selected vector is tested and classified, there will be more vectors that can be determined based on the testing results. In the above example, when the binary search/Hansel chains approach is used, the vectors submitted for testing are

$$\{\langle 001 \rangle, \langle 100 \rangle, \langle 010 \rangle\}.$$

In the example of the fourth section, when the sequential Hansel chains approach is used, the vectors submitted were

$$\{\langle 100 \rangle, \langle 101 \rangle, \langle 001 \rangle, \langle 010 \rangle\}.$$

in which vector $\langle 101 \rangle$ is not as effective as the other vectors.

CONCLUSION

This article discussed the knowledge acquisition problem in monotone Boolean systems. One of the main issues related to knowledge acquisition in such monotone Boolean systems is how to reduce the number of inquiries needed to classify all vectors in the problem space.

As it has been discussed above, by using Hansel chains in the sequential question-asking strategy (14), the number of possible questions will not exceed an upper bound as stated in the Hansel theorem. However, the performance of sequential question-asking strategy depends on the sequence of the Hansel chains and it may change dramatically when it is applied to different problems.

Therefore, a new guided vector selection approach; the binary search/Hansel chains approach is proposed to address this problem. When this new method is applied, the average number of inquiries can be further reduced and the performance of the method is relatively consistent compared to that of the sequential question-asking strategy (16).

ACKNOWLEDGMENT

The authors gratefully acknowledge the support from the Office of Naval Research (ONR) Grant N00014-95-1-0639.

REFERENCES

1. S. Rudeanu, *Boolean Functions and Equations*, North-Holland, Amsterdam, 1974.
2. B. Kovalerchuk, E. Triantaphyllou, and E. Vityaev, "Monotone Boolean Functions Learning Techniques Integrated with User Interaction," in *Proc. of Workshop "Learning from Examples vs. Programming by Demonstrations*," 1995, pp. 41–48.
3. D. V. B. Alekseev, "Monotone Boolean Functions," *Encyclopedia of Mathematics, Vol. 6*, Kluwer Academic Publishers, Norwell, MA, 1988, pp. 306–307.

4. D. Kleitman, "On Dedekind's Problem: The Number of Monotone Boolean Functions," *Proc. Am. Math. Soc.*, *21*, 677–682 (1969).
5. C. E. Blair, R. G. Jeroslow, and J. K. Lowe, "Some Results and Experiments in Programming Techniques for Propositional Logic," *Computers Oper. Res.*, *Vol. 3*, No. 13, 63–65 (1985).
6. T. M. Cavalier, P. M. Pardalos, and A. L. Soyster, "Modeling and Integer Programming Techniques Applied to Propositional Calculus," *Computers Oper. Res.*, *17*(6), 561–570 (1990).
7. J. N. Hooker, "Generalized Resolution and Cutting Planes," *Ann. Oper. Res.*, *12*(1–4), 217–239 (1988).
8. J. N. Hooker, "A Method of Producing a Boolean Function Having an Arbitrarily Prescribed Prime Implicant Table," *IEEE Trans. Computers*, *14*, 485–488 (1988).
9. R. G. Jeroslow, *Logic-Based Decision Support*, North-Holland, Amsterdam, 1988.
10. H. P. Williams, "Linear and Integer Programming Applied to Artificial Intelligence," Preprint series, University of Southampton, Faculty of Mathematical Studies, (1986), pp. 1–33.
11. J. Peysakh, "A Fast Algorithm to Convert Boolean Expressions into CNF," IBM Computer Science RC 12913 (#57971), 1987.
12. V. K. Korobkov, "On Monotone Boolean Functions of Algebra Logic," Problemy Cybernetiki, Nauka Publishers, Moscow, *Vol. 13*, 5–28 (1985) (In Russian).
13. G. Hansel, "Sur le Nombre des Fonctions Boolenes Monotones den Variables," *C. R. Acad. Sci. Paris*, *262*(20), 1088–1090 (1966).
14. B. Kovalerchuk, E. Triantaphyllou, A. S. Deshpande, and E. Vityaev, "Interactive Learning of Monotone Boolean Functions," *Inform. Sci.*, *94*(1–4), 87–118 (1996).
15. R. Neapolitan and K. Naimipour, *Foundations of Algorithms*, D. C. Heath and Company, New York, 1995.
16. J. Lu and E. Triantaphyllou, "The Binary Search/Hansel Chains Approach for Interactive Inference of Monotone Boolean Functions," Working Paper, Department of Industrial Engineering, Louisiana State University, Baton Rouge (1997).

EVANGELOS TRIANTAPHYLLOU

JIEPING LU

MAINTENANCE OF MATERIALIZED VIEWS: PROBLEMS, TECHNIQUES, AND APPLICATIONS

INTRODUCTION

What is a view? A view is a derived relation defined in terms of base (stored) relations. A view defines a function from a set of base tables to a derived table; this function is typically recomputed every time the view is referenced.

What is a materialized view? A view can be materialized by storing the tuples of the view in the database. Index structures can be built on the materialized view. Consequently, database accesses to the materialized view can be much faster than recomputing the view. A materialized view is like a cache—a copy of the data that can be accessed quickly.

Why use materialized views? Like a cache, a materialized view provides fast access to data; the speed difference may be critical in applications where the query rate is high and the views are complex so that it is not possible to recompute the view for every query. Materialized views are useful in new applications such as data warehousing, replication servers, chronicle or data recording systems (1), data visualization, and mobile systems. Integrity constraint checking and query optimization can also benefit from materialized views.

What is view maintenance? Just as a cache gets *dirty* when the data from which it is copied are updated, a materialized view gets dirty whenever the underlying base relations are modified. The process of updating a materialized view in response to changes to the underlying data is called view maintenance.

What is incremental view maintenance? In most cases, it is wasteful to maintain a view by recomputing it from scratch. Often, it is cheaper to use the heuristic of inertia (only a part of the view changes in response to changes in the base relations) and thus compute only the changes in the view to update its materialization. We stress that the above is only a heuristic. For example, if an entire base relation is deleted, it may be cheaper to recompute a view that depends on the deleted relation (if the new view will quickly evaluate to an empty relation) than to compute the changes to the view. Algorithms that compute changes to a view in response to changes to the base relations are called *incremental view maintenance* algorithms, and are the focus of this article.

Classification of the View Maintenance Problem

There are four dimensions along which the view maintenance problem can be studied:

- Information Dimension: The amount of information available for view maintenance. Do you have access to all/some the base relations while doing the maintenance? Do you have access to the materialized view? Do you know about integrity constraints and keys? We note that the amount of information used is orthogonal to the incrementality of view maintenance. Incrementality refers to a computation that only computes that part of the view that has changed; the information dimension looks at the data used to compute the change to the view.

- Modification Dimension: What modifications can the view maintenance algorithm handle? Insertion and deletion of tuples to base relations? Are updates to tuples handled directly or are they modeled as deletions followed by insertions? What about changes to the view definition? Or sets of modifications?
- Language Dimension: Is the view expressed as a select–project–join query (also known as a SPJ views or as a conjunctive query), or in some other subset of relational algebra—SQL or a subset of SQL? Can it have duplicates? Can it use aggregation? Recursion? General recursions, or only transitive closure?
- Instance Dimension: Does the view maintenance algorithm work for all instances of the database, or only for some instances of the database? Does it work for all instances of the modification, or only for some instances of the modification? Instance information is of two types—*database instance* and *modification instance*.

We provide a classification of the view maintenance problem along the above dimensions through examples. The first example illustrates the information and modification dimensions.

Example 1 (Information and Modification Dimensions)
Consider relation

part(part_no,part_cost,contract)

listing the cost negotiated under each contract for a part. Note that a part may have a different price under each contract. Consider also the view expensive_parts defined as

$$\text{expensive\_parts(part\_no)} = \Pi_{\text{part\_no}} \, \sigma_{\text{part\_cost}>1000}(\text{part})$$

The view contains the **distinct** part numbers for parts that cost more than $1000 under at least one contract (the projection discards duplicates). Consider maintaining the view when a tuple is inserted into relation part. If the inserted tuple has part_cost ≤ 1000, then the view is unchanged.

However, say part($p1$,5000,$c15$) is inserted that does have cost > 1000. Different view maintenance algorithms can be designed depending on the information available for determining if $p1$ should be inserted into the view.

- The materialized view alone is available: Use the old materialized view to determine if part_no already is presented in the view. If so, there is no change to the materialization; otherwise, insert part $p1$ into the materialization.
- The base relation part alone is available: Use relation part to check if an existing tuple in the relation has the same part_no but greater or equal cost. If such a tuple exists, then the inserted tuple does not contribute to the view.
- It is known that part_no is the key: Infer that part_no cannot already be in the view, so it must be inserted.

Another view maintenance problem is to respond to deletions using only the materialized view. Let tuple part($p1$,2000,$c12$) be deleted. Clearly, part $p1$ must be in the materialization, but we cannot delete $p1$ from the view because some other tuple, like part($p1$,3000,$c13$), may contribute $p1$ to the view. The existence of this tuple cannot be (dis)proved using only the view. Thus, there is no algorithm to solve the view maintenance problem for deletions using only the materialized view. Note, if the relation part was also available, or if the key constraint was known, or if the counts of number of view tuple derivations were available, then the view could be maintained.

With respect to the information dimension, note that the view definition and the actual modification always have to be available for maintenance. With respect to the modification dimension, updates typically are not treated as an independent type of modification. Instead, they are modeled as a deletion followed by an insertion. This model loses information, thereby requiring more work and more information for maintaining a view than if updates were treated independently within a view maintenance algorithm (2–4).

The following example illustrates the other two dimensions used to characterize view maintenance.

Example 2 (Language and Instance Dimensions)

Example 1 considered a view definition language consisting of selection and projection operations. Now let us extend the view definition language with the join operation, and define the view supp_parts as the equijoin between relations supp(supp_no, part_no,price) and part ($\bowtie$ part_no represents an equijoin on attribute part_no):

$$\text{supp\_parts(part\_no)} = \Pi_{\text{part\_no}}(\text{supp} \bowtie_{\text{part\_no}} \text{part})$$

The view contains the **distinct** part numbers that are supplied by at least one supplier (the projection discards duplicates). Consider using only the old contents of supp_parts for maintenance in response to insertion of part($p1$,5000,$c15$). If supp_parts already contains part_no $p1$, then the insertion does not affect the view. However, if supp_parts does not contain $p1$, then the effect of the insertion cannot be determined using only the view.

Recall that the view expensive_parts was maintainable in response to insertions to part using only the view. In contrast, the use of a join makes it impossible to maintain supp_parts in response to insertions to part when using only the view.

Note, view supp_parts is maintainable if the view contains part_no $p1$ but not otherwise. Thus, the maintainability of a view also depends on the particular instances of the database and the modification.

Figure 1 shows the problem space defined by three of the four dimensions, namely the information, modification, and language dimensions. The instance dimension is not shown here so as to keep the figure manageable. There is no relative ordering between the points on each dimension; they are listed in arbitrary order. Along the language dimension, *chronicle algebra* (1) refers to languages that operate over ordered sequences that may not be stored in the database (see the subsection Using Materialized Views and Some Base Relations: Partial Reference). Along the modification dimension, *group updates* (4) refers to insertion of several tuples using information derived from a single deleted tuple.

We study maintenance techniques for different points in the shown problem space. For each point in this three-dimensional (3-D) space, we may get algorithms that apply to all database and modification instances or that may work only for some instances of each (the fourth dimension).

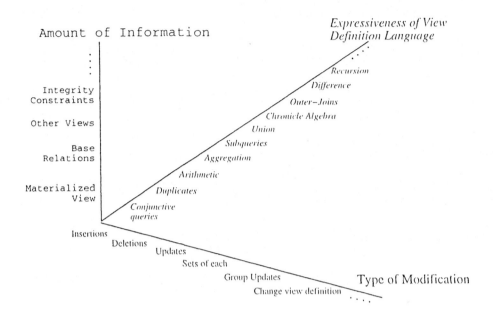

FIGURE 1   The problem space.

Paper Outline

We study the view maintenance problem with respect to the space of Figure 1 using the "amount of information" as the first discriminator. For each point considered on the information dimension, we consider the languages for which view maintenance algorithms have been developed and present selected algorithms in some detail. Where appropriate, we mention how different types of modifications are handled differently. The algorithms we describe in some detail address the following points in the problem space.

- Information dimension: Use *Full Information* (all the underlying base relations and the materialized view). Instance dimension: Apply to all instances of the database and all instances of modifications. Modification dimension: Apply to all types of modifications. Language dimension: Consider the following languages:

  SQL views with duplicates, UNION, negation, and aggregation (e.g., SUM, MIN)

  Outer-join views

  Recursive Datalog or SQL views with UNION, stratified aggregation and negation, but no duplicates

- Information dimension. Use *Partial Information* (materialized view and key constraints—views that can be maintained without accessing the base relations are said to be *self-maintainable*). Instance dimension: Apply to all instances of the database and all instances of modifications. Language dimension: Apply to SPJ views. Modification dimension: Consider the following types of modifications:

Insertions and deletions of tuples

Updates and group updates to tuples

We also discuss maintaining SPJ views using the view and some underlying base relations.

THE IDEA BEHIND VIEW MAINTENANCE

Incremental maintenance requires that the change to the base relations be used to compute the change to the view. Thus, most view maintenance techniques treat the view definition as a mathematical formula and apply a differentiation step to obtain an expression for the change in the view. We illustrate through an example.

Example 3 (Intuition)

Consider the base relation $link(S,D)$ such that $link(a,b)$ is true if there is a link from source node a to destination b. Define view hop such that $hop(c,d)$ is true if c is connected to d using two links, via an intermediate node:

$$\text{b}: \quad hop(X,Y) = \Pi_{X,Y}(link(X,V) \bowtie_{V=W} link(W,Y)).$$

Let a set of tuples $\Delta(link)$ be inserted into relation link. The corresponding insertions $\Delta(hop)$ that need to be made into view hop can be computed by mathematically differentiating definition b to obtain the following expression:

$$\Delta(hop) = \Pi_{X,Y}((\Delta(link)(X,V)) \bowtie_{V=W} link(W,Y))$$
$$\cup (link(X,V)) \bowtie_{V=W} \Delta(link)(W,Y))$$
$$\cup (\Delta(link)(X,V)) \bowtie_{V=W} \Delta(link)(W,Y))).$$

The second and third terms can be combined to yield the term $link^v(X,V) \bowtie_{V=W} \Delta(link)(W,Y)$ where $link^v$ represents the relation link with the insertions, for example, $link \cup \Delta(link)$.

In the above example, if tuples are deleted from link, then the same expression computes the deletions from view hop. If tuples are inserted into and deleted from relation link, then $\Delta(hop)$ is often computed by separately computing the set of deletions $\Delta^-(hop)$ and the set of insertions $\Delta^+(hop)$ (5,6). Alternatively, by differently tagging insertions and deletions, they can be handled in one pass as in Ref. 7.

USING FULL INFORMATION

Most work on view maintenance has assumed that all the base relations and the materialized view are available during the maintenance process, and the focus has been on efficient techniques to maintain views expressed in different languages—starting from select–project–join views and moving to relational algebra, SQL, and Datalog, considering features like aggregations, duplicates, recursion, and outer joins. The techniques typically differ in the expressiveness of the view definition language, in their use of key and integrity constraints, and whether they handle insertions and deletions separately or in one pass. (Updates are modeled as a deletion followed by an insertion.) All the techniques work on all database instances for both insertions and deletions. We will classify these techniques broadly along the language dimension into those applicable to nonrecursive views, those applicable to outer-join views, and those applicable to recursive views.

Nonrecursive Views

We describe the counting algorithm for view maintenance, and then discuss several other view maintenance techniques that have been proposed in the literature.

The counting Algorithm

This algorithm (7) applies to SQL vies that may or may not have duplicates and that may be defined using UNION, negation, and aggregation. The basic idea in the counting algorithm is to keep a count of the number of derivations for each view tuple as extra information in the view. We illustrate the counting algorithm using an example.

Example 4

Consider view hop from Example 3, now written in SQL.

> CREATE VIEW hop(S,D) as
> (**select distinct** $l1.S$, $l2.D$ **from** link $l1$, link $l2$ **where** $l1.D = l2.S$)

Given link = $\{(a,b),(b,c),(b,e),(a,d),(d,c)\}$, the view hop evaluates to $\{(a,c),(a,e)\}$. The tuple hop(a,e) has a unique derivation. hop(a,c), on the other hand, has two derivations. If the view had duplicate semantics (did not have the **distinct** operator), then hop(a,e) would have a count of 1 and hop(a,c) would have a count of 2. The counting algorithm pretends that the view has duplicate semantics and stores these counts.

Suppose the tuple link(a,b) is deleted. Then, we can see that hop can be recomputed as $\{(a,c)\}$. The counting algorithm infers that one derivation of each of the tuples hop(a,c) and hop(a,e) is deleted. The algorithm uses the stored counts to infer that hop(a,c) has one remaining derivation and therefore only deletes hop(a,e), which has no remaining derivation.

The counting algorithm thus works by storing the number of alternative derivations, count(t), of each tuple t in the materialized view. This number is derived from the multiplicity of tuple t under duplicate semantics (8,9). Given a program T defining a set of views $V_1, \ldots, V_k$, the counting algorithm uses the differentiation technique of the section The Idea Behind View Maintenance to derive a program T_Δ. The program T_Δ uses the changes made to base relations and the old values of the base and view relations to produce as output the set of changes, $\Delta(V_1), \ldots, \Delta(V_k)$, that need to be made to the view relations. In the set of changes, insertions are represented with positive counts, and deletions by negative counts. The count value for each tuple is stored in the materialized view, and the new materialized view is obtained by combining the changes $\Delta(V_1), \ldots,$ $\Delta(V_k)$ with the stored views $V_1, \ldots, V_k$. Positive counts are added in, and negative counts are subtracted. A tuple with a count of zero is deleted. The count algorithm is optimal in that it computes exactly those view tuples that are inserted or deleted. For SQL views counts can be computed at little or no cost above the cost of evaluating the view for both set and duplicate semantics. The counting algorithm works for both set and duplicate semantics and can be made to work for outer-join views (see the subsection Outer-Join Views).

Other Counting Algorithms

Reference 10 maintains select, project, and equijoin views using counts of the number of derivations of a tuple. They build data structures with pointers from a tuple τ to other tuples derived using the tuple τ. Reference 11 uses counts just like the **counting** algorithm, but only to maintain SPJ views. Also, they compute insertions and deletions separately, without combining them into a single set with positive and negative counts. Reference 12 describes "ViewCaches," materialized views defined using selections and one join, that store only the TIDs of the tuples that join to produce view tuples.

Algebraic Differencing: This was introduced in Ref. 13 and used subsequently in Ref. 5 for view maintenance. It differentiates algebraic expressions to derive the relational expression that computes the change to an SPJ view without doing redundant computation. Reference 14 provides a correction to the minimality result of Ref. 5, and Ref. 15 extends the algebraic differencing approach to multiset algebra with aggregations and multiset difference. They derive two expressions for each view; one to compute the insertions into the view, and another to compute the deletions into the view.

The Ceri–Widom Algorithm: This algorithm (16) derives production rules to maintain selected SQL views—those without duplicates, aggregation, and negation, and those where the view attributes functionally determine the key of the base relation that is updated. The algorithm determines the SQL query needed to maintain the view and invokes the query from within a production rule.

Recursive Algorithms: The algorithms described in the section Recursive Views also apply to nonrecursive views.

Outer-Join Views

Outer joins are important in domains like data integration and extended relational systems (17). View maintenance on outer-join views using the materialized view and all base relations has been discussed in Ref. 4.

In this section, we outline the algorithm of Ref. 4 to maintain incrementally full outer-join views. We use the following SQL syntax to define a view V as a full outer-join of relations R and S:

CREATE view V as select $X_1, \ldots, X_n$ **from** R **full outer join** S **on** $g(Y_1, \ldots, Y_m)$ is a conjunction of predicates that represent the outer-join condition. The set of modifications to relation R is denoted as $\Delta(R)$, which consists of insertions $\Delta^+(R)$ and deletions $\Delta^-(R)$. Similarly, the set of modifications to relation S is denoted as $\Delta(S)$. The view maintenance algorithm rewrites the view definition to obtain the following two queries to compute $\Delta(V)$.

(a): **select** $X_1, \ldots, X_n$ (b): **select** $X_1, \ldots, X_n$
    from $\Delta(R)$ **left outer join** S **from** R^v **right outer join** $\Delta(S)$
    on $g(Y_1, \ldots, Y_m)$ **on** $g(Y_1, \ldots, Y_m)$.

R^v represents relation R after modification. All other references in queries (a) and (b) refer either to the premodified extents or to the modifications themselves. Unlike with SPJ views, queries (a) and (b) do not compute the entire change to the view, as explained below.

Query (a) computes the effect on V of changes to relation R. Consider a tuple r^+ inserted into R and its effect on the view. If r^+ does not join with any tuple in s, then

r^+.NULL (r^+ padded with nulls) has to be inserted into view V. If, instead, r^+ does join with some tuple s in S, then $r^+.s$ (r^+ joined with tuple s) is inserted into the view. Both these consequences are captured in query (a) by using the left outer-join. However, query (a) does not compute a possible side effect if r^+ does join with some tuple s. The tuple NULL.s (s padded with nulls) may have to be deleted from the view V if NULL.s is in the view. This will be the case if, previously, tuple s did not join with any tuple in R.

Similarly, a deletion r^- from R not only removes a tuple from the view, as captured by query (a), but may also precipitate the insertion of a tuple NULL.s if, before deletion, r^- is the only tuple that joined with s. Query (b) handles the modifications to table S similar to the manner in which query (a) handles the modifications to table R, with similar possible side effects. The algorithm of Ref. 4 handles these side effects.

Recursive Views

Recursive queries or views often are expressed using rules in Datalog (18), and all the work on maintaining recursive views has been done in the context of Datalog. We describe the **DRed** (**Deletion and Rederivation**) algorithm for view maintenance, and then discuss several other recursive view maintenance techniques that have been proposed in the literature.

The *DRed* algorithm

This algorithm (7) applies to Datalog or SQL views, including views defined using recursion, UNION, and stratified negation and aggregation. However, SQL views with duplicate semantics cannot be maintained by this algorithm. The **DRed** algorithm computes changes to the view relations in three steps. First, the algorithm computes an overestimate of the deleted derived tuples: A tuple t is in this overestimate if the changes made to the base relations invalidate *any* derivation of t. Second, this overestimate is pruned by removing (from the overestimate) those tuples that have alternative derivations in the new database. A version of the original view restricted to compute only the tuples in the overestimated set is used to do the pruning. Finally, the new tuples that need to be inserted are computed using the partially updated materialized view and the insertions made to the base relations. The algorithm can also maintain materialized views incrementally when rules of defining derived relations are inserted or deleted. We illustrate the **DRed** algorithm using an example.

Example 5

Consider the view hop defined in Example 4. The **DRed** algorithm first deletes tuples hop(a,c) and hop(a,e) because they both depend on the deleted tuple. The **DRed** algorithm then looks for alternative derivations for each of the deleted tuples. hop(a,c) is rederived and reinserted into the materialized view in the second step. The third step of the **DRed** algorithm is empty because no tuples are inserted into the link table.

None of the other algorithms discussed in this section handle the same class of views as the **DRed** algorithm; the most notable differentiating feature being aggregations. However, some algorithms derive more efficient solutions for special subclasses.

The PF (*Propagation/Filtration*) Algorithm

This algorithm (6) is very similar to the **DRed** algorithm, except that it propagates the changes made to the base relations on a relation by relation basis. It computes changes in *one* derived relation due to changes in *one* base relation, looping over all derived and base relations to complete the view maintenance. In each loop, an algorithm similar to the delete/prune/insert steps in DRed is executed. However, rather than running the deletion step to completion before starting the pruning step, the deletion and the pruning steps are alternated after each iteration of the seminaive evaluation. Thus, in each seminaive iteration, an overestimate for deletions is computed and then pruned. This allows the PF algorithm to avoid propagating some tuples that occur in the overestimate after the first iteration but do not actually change. However, the alternation of the steps after each seminaive iteration also causes some tuples to be rederived several times. In addition, the PF algorithm ends up fragmenting computation and rederiving changed and deleted tuples again and again. Reference 19 presents improvements to the PF algorithm that reduce rederivation of facts by using memoing and by exploiting the stratification in the program. Each of DRed and the PF algorithms can do better than the other by a factor of *n*, depending on the view definition (where *n* is the number of base tuples in the database). For nonrecursive views, the DRed algorithm always works better than the PF algorithm.

The Kuchenhoff Algorithm

This algorithm (20) derives rules to compute the difference between consecutive database states for a stratified recursive program. The rules generated are similar in spirit to those of Ref. 7. However, some of the generated rules (for the *depends* predicates) are not safe, and the delete/prune/insert three-step technique of Refs. 6 and 7 is not used. Further, when dealing with positive rules, the Kuchenhoff algorithm does not discard duplicate derivations that are guaranteed not to generate any change in the view as early as the DRed algorithm discards the duplicate derivations.

The Urpi–Olive Algorithm

This algorithm (3) for stratified Datalog views derives transition rules showing how each modification to a relation translates into a modification to each derived relation, using existentially quantified subexpressions in Datalog rules. The quantified subexpressions may go through negation and can be eliminated under certain conditions. Updates are modeled, directly; however, because keys need to be derived for such a modeling, the update model is useful mainly for nonrecursive views.

Counting-Based Algorithms

These algorithms can sometimes be used for recursive views. The counting algorithm of Ref. 21 can be used effectively only if every tuple is guaranteed to have a finite number of derivations,* and even then, the computation of counts can significantly increase the cost of computation. The BDGEN system (23) uses counts to reflect not all derivations, but only certain types of derivations. Its algorithm gives finite even counts to all tuples, even those in a recursive view, and can be used even if tuples have infinitely many derivations.

---

*An algorithm to check-finiteness appears in Refs. 9 and 22.

Transitive Closures

This algorithm (24) derives nonrecursive programs to update right-linear recursive views in response to insertions into the base relation. Reference 25 gives nonrecursive programs to update the transitive closure of specific kinds of graphs in response to insertions and deletions. The algorithm does not apply to all graphs or to general recursive programs. In fact, there does not exist a nonrecursive program to maintain the transitive closure of an arbitrary graph in response to deletions from the graph (26).

Nontraditional Views

This algorithm (27) extends the DRed algorithm to views that can have nonground tuples. Reference 28 gives a maintenance algorithm for a rule language with negation in the head and body of rules, using auxiliary information about the number of certain derivations of each tuple. They do not consider aggregation and do not discuss how to handle recursively defined relations that may have an infinite number of derivations.

USING PARTIAL INFORMATION

As illustrated in the Introduction, views may be maintainable using only a subset of the underlying relations involved in the view. We refer to this information as *partial information*. Unlike view maintenance using full information, a view is not always maintainable for a modification using only partial information. Whether the view can be maintained may also depend on whether the modification is an insertion, deletion, or update. So the algorithms focus on checking whether the view can be maintained, and then on how to maintain the view.

We will show that treating updates as a distinct type of modification lets us derive view maintenance algorithms for updates where no algorithms exist for deletions + insertions.

Using No Information: Query Independent of Update

There is a lot of work on optimizing view maintenance by determining when a modification leaves a view unchanged (2,11,29,30). This is known as the "query independent of update," or the "irrelevant update" problem. All these algorithms provide checks to determine whether a particular modification will be irrelevant. If the test succeeds, then the view stays unaffected by the modification. However, if the test fails, then some other algorithm has to be used for maintenance.

References 2 and 11 determine irrelevant updates for SPJ views, whereas Ref. 29 considers irrelevant updates for Datalog. Further, Ref. 30 can determine irrelevant updates for Datalog with negated base relations and arithmetic inequalities.

Using the Materialized View: Self-Maintenance

Views that can be maintained using only the materialized view and key constraints are called *self-maintainable* views in Ref. 4. Several results on self-maintainability of SPJ and outer-join views in response to insertions, deletions, and updates are also presented in Ref. 4. Following Ref. 4 we provide the following definitions.

Definition 1 (Self-Maintainability with Respect to a Modification Type): A view *V* is said to be self-maintainable with respect to a modification type (insertion, deletion, or update) to a base relation R if for all database states, the view can be self-maintained in response to all instances of a modification of the indicated type to the base relation R.

Example 6

Consider view supp—parts from Example 2 that contains all **distinct** part—no supplied by at least one supplier. Also, let part—no be the key for relation part (so there can be at most one contract and one part—cost for a given part).

If a tuple is deleted from relation part, then it is straightforward to update the view using only the materialized view (simply delete the corresponding part—no if it is present). Thus, the view is self-maintainable with respect to deletions from the part relation.

By contrast, let tuple supp($s1,p1,100$) be deleted when the view contains tuple $p1$. The tuple $p1$ cannot be deleted from the view because supp may also contain a tuple supp($s2,p1,200$) that contributes $p1$ to the view. Thus, the view is not self-maintainable with respect to deletions from supp. In fact, the view is not self-maintainable for insertions into either supp or part.

Some results from Ref. 4 are stated after the following definitions.

Definition 2 (Distinguished Attribute):   An attribute A of a relation R is said to be distinguished in a view V if attribute A appears in the **select** clause defining view V.

Definition 3 (Exposed Attribute):   An attribute A of a relation R is said to be exposed in a view V if A is used in a predicate. An attribute that is not exposed is referred to as being non-exposed.

Self-Maintainability with Respect to Insertions and Deletions

Reference 4 shows that most SPJ views are not self-maintainable with respect to insertions, but they are often self maintainable with respect to deletions and updates. For example:

- An SPJ view that takes the join of two or more distinct relations is not self-maintainable with respect to insertions.
- An SPJ view is self-maintainable with respect to deletions to R_1 if the key attributes from each occurrence of R_1 in the join are either included in the view or are equated to a constant in the view definition.
- A left or full outer-join view V defined using two relations R and S, such that

   The keys of R and S are distinguished
   All exposed attributes of R are distinguished

   is self-maintainable with respect to all types of modifications to relation S.

Self-Maintainability with Respect to Updates

By modeling an update independently and not as a deletion + insertion, we retain information about the deleted tuple that allows the insertion to be handled more easily.

Example 7

Consider, again, relation part(part—no,part—cost,contract), where part—no is the key. Consider an extension of view supp—parts:

supp_parts(supp_no,part_no,part_cost) =
Π_{part_no}(supp $\bowtie_{part\_no}$ part)

The view contains the part_no and part_cost for the parts supplied by each supplier. If the part_cost of a part $p1$ is updated, then the view is updated by identifying the tuples in the view that have part_no $= p1$ and updating their part_cost attribute.

The ability to self-maintain a view depends on the attributes being updated. In particular, updates to nonexposed attributes are self-maintainable when the key attributes are distinguished. The complete algorithm for self-maintenance of a view in response to updates to nonexposed attributes is described in Ref. 4 and relies on (a) identifying the tuples in the current view that are potentially affected by the update and (b) computing the effect of the update on these tuples.

The idea of self-maintenance is not new—autonomously computable views were defined in Ref. 2 as the views that can be maintained using only the materialized view for all database instances, but for a given modification instance. They characterize a subset of SPJ views that are autonomously computable for insertions, deletions, and updates, where the deletions and updates are specified using conditions. They do not consider views with self-joins or outer-joins, do not use key information, and do not consider self-maintenance with respect to all instances of modifications. The characterization of autonomously computable views in Ref. 4 for updates is inaccurate—for instance, Ref. 4 determines, incorrectly, that the view "**select** X **from** r(X)" is not autonomously computable for the modification "Update(R(3) to R(4))".

Instance Specific Self-Maintenance

For insertions and deletions only, a database instance-specific self-maintenance algorithm for SPJ views was discussed first in Ref. 31. Subsequently, this algorithm has been corrected and extended in Ref. 32.

Using Materialized View and Some Base Relations: Partial Reference

The partial-reference maintenance problem is to maintain a view given only a subset of the base relations and the materialized view. Two interesting subproblems here are when the view and all the relations except the modified relation are available, and when the view and modified relation are available.

Modified Relation Is not Available (Chronicle Views)

A chronicle is an ordered sequence of tuples with insertion being the only permissible modification (1). A view over a chronicle, treating the chronicle as a relation, is called a chronicle view. The chronicle may not be stored in its entirety in a database because it can get very large, so the chronicle view maintenance problem is to maintain the chronicle view in response to insertions into the chronicle, but without accessing the chronicle. Techniques to specify and maintain such views efficiently are presented in Ref. 1.

Only Modified Relation Is Available (Change-Reference Maintainable)

Sometimes a view may be maintainable using only the modified base relation and the view, but without accessing other base relations. Different modifications need to be treated differently.

Example 8

Consider maintaining view supp_parts using relation supp and the old view in response to deletion of a tuple t from relation supp. If t.part_no is the same as the part_no of some other tuple in supp, then the view is unchanged. If no remaining tuple has the same part_no as tuple t, then we can deduce that no supplier supplies t.part_no and, thus, the part number has to be deleted from the view. Thus, the view is change-reference maintainable.

A similar claim holds for deletions from part but not for insertions into either relation.

Instance Specific Partial-Reference Maintenance

References 32 and 33 give algorithms that successfully maintain a view for some instances of the databases and modification, but not for others. Their algorithms derive conditions to be tested against the view and/or the given relations to check if the information is adequate to maintain the view.

APPLICATIONS

New and novel applications for materialized views and view maintenance techniques are emerging. We describe a few of the novel applications here, along with a couple of traditional ones.

Fast Access, Lower CPU and Disk Load

Materialized views are likely to find applications in any problem domain that needs quick access to derived data, or where recomputing the view from base data may be expensive or infeasible. For example, consider a retailing database that stores several terabytes of point of sale transactions representing several months of sales, and supports queries giving the total number of items sold in each store for each item the company carries. These queries are made several times a day, by vendors, store managers, and marketing people. By defining and materializing the result, each query can be reduced to a simple lookup on the materialized view; consequently, it can be answered faster, and the CPU and disk loads on the system are reduced. View maintenance algorithms keep the materialized result current as new sale transactions are posted.

Data Warehousing

A database that collects and stores data from several databases is often described as a data warehouse. Materialized views provide a framework within which to collect information into the warehouse from several databases without copying each database in the warehouse. Queries on the warehouse can then be answered using the materialized views without accessing the remote databases. Provisioning, or changes, still occurs on the remote databases and are transmitted to the warehouse as a set of modifications. Incremental view maintenance techniques can be used to maintain the materialized views in response to these modifications. Although the materialized views are available for view maintenance, access to the remote databases may be restricted or expensive. Self-maintainable views are thus useful for maintaining a data warehouse (4). For cases where the view is not self-maintainable and one has to go to the remote databases, besides the cost of remote accesses, transaction management is also needed (34).

Materialized views are used for data integration in Refs. 4 and 35. Objects that reside in multiple databases are integrated to give a larger object if the child objects "match." Matching for relational tuples using outer joins and a *match* operator is done in Ref. 4, whereas more general matching conditions are discussed in Ref. 35. The matching conditions of Ref. 35 may be expensive to compute. By materializing the composed objects, in part or fully, the objects can be used inexpensively.

Reference 36 presents another model of data integration. The authors consider views defined using some remote and some local relations. They materialize the view partially, without accessing the remote relation, by retaining a reference to the remote relation as a constraint in the view tuples. The model needs access to the remote databases during queries and, thus, differs from a typical warehousing model.

Chronicle Systems

Banking, retailing, and billing systems deal with a continuous stream of transactional data. This ordered sequence of transactional tuples has been called a chronicle (1). One characteristic of a chronicle is that it can get very large, and it can be beyond the capacity of any database system to even store, far less access, for answering queries. Materialized views provide a way to answer queries over the chronicle without accessing the chronicle.

Materialized views can be defined to compute and store summaries of interest over the chronicles (the balance for each customer in a banking system, or the profits of each store in the retailing system). View maintenance techniques are needed to maintain these summaries as new transactions are added to the chronicle, but without accessing the old entries in the chronicle (1).

Data Visualization

Visualization applications display views over the data in a database. As the user changes the view definition, the display has to be updated accordingly. An interface for such queries in a real estate system is reported in Ref. 37, where they are called *dynamic queries*. Data archaeology (38) is a similar application where an archaeologist discovers rules about data by formulating queries, examining the results, and then changing the query iteratively as his/her understanding improves. By materializing a view and incrementally recomputing it as its definition changes, the system keeps such applications interactive. Reference 39 studies the "view adaptation problem," for example, how to incrementally recompute a materialized view in response to changes to the view definition.

Mobile Systems

A common query in a personal digital assistant (PDA) is of the form, Which freeway exits are within a 5 mile radius? One model of computation sends the query to a remote server that uses the position of the PDA to answer the query and sends the result back to the PDA. When the PDA moves and asks the same query, data transmission can be reduced by computing only the change to the answer and designing the PDA to handle answer differentials.

Integrity Constraint Checking

Most static integrity constraints can be represented as a set of views such that if any of the views is nonempty, then the corresponding constraint is violated. Then, checking constraints translates to a view maintenance problem. Thus, view maintenance techniques can be used to incrementally check integrity constraints when a database is modified. The expression to check integrity constraints typically can be simplified when the constraint holds before the modification; for example, the corresponding views initially are empty (40–45).

Query Optimization

If a database system maintains several materialized views, the query optimizer can use these materialized views when optimizing arbitrary queries, even when the queries do not mention the views. For instance, consider a query in a retailing system that wants to compute the number of items sold for each item. A query optimizer can optimize this query to access a materialized view that stores the number of items sold for each item and store, and avoid access to a much larger sales-transactions table.

References 36 and 46 discuss the problem of answering a conjunctive query (SPJ query) given a set of conjunctive view definitions. Optimization of aggregation queries using materialized views is discussed in Refs. 47–49. The view adaptation results of Ref. 39 can be used to optimize a query using only one materialized view.

OPEN PROBLEMS

This section describes some open problems in view maintenance, in the context of Figure 1. Many points on each of the three dimensions remain unconsidered, or even unrepresented. It is useful to extend each dimension to unconsidered points and to develop algorithms that cover entirely the resulting space because each point in the space corresponds to a scenario of potential interest.

View maintenance techniques that use all the underlying relations, for example, full information, have been studied in great detail for large classes of query languages. We emphasize the importance of developing comprehensive view maintenance techniques that use different types of partial information. For instance:

- Use information on functional dependencies, multiple materialized views, general integrity constraints, and horizontal/vertical fragments of base relations (for example, simple views).
- Extend the view definition language to include aggregation, negation, and outer join for all instances of the other dimensions. The extensions are especially important for using partial information.
- Identify *subclasses* of SQL views that are maintainable in an instance-independent fashion.

The converse of the view maintenance problem under partial information, as presented in the section Using Partial Information is to identify the information required for efficient view maintenance of a given view (or a set of views). We refer to this problem as the "information identification (II)" problem. Solutions for view maintenance with partial information indirectly apply to the II problem by checking if the given view falls into one of the classes for which partial-information-based techniques exist. However, direct and more complete techniques for solving the II problem are needed.

An important problem is to implement and incorporate views in a database system. Many questions arise in this context. When are materialized views maintained—before the transaction that updates the base relation commits, or after the transaction commits? Is view maintenance a part of the transaction or not? Should the view be maintained before the update is applied to the base relations, or afterward? Should the view be maintained after each update within the transaction, or after all the updates? Should active rules (or some other mechanism) be used to initiate view maintenance automatically or should a user start the process? Should alternative algorithms be tried, based on a cost-based model, to choose between the options? Some existing work in this context is in Refs. 16, 23, 50, and 51. Reference 16 considers using production rules for doing view maintenance and Ref. 23 presents algorithms in the context of a deductive DB system. Reference 50 does not discuss view maintenance but discusses efficient implementation of deltas in a system that can be used to implement materialized views. Reference 51 describes the ADMS system that implements and maintains simple materialized views, "ViewCaches," in a multidatabase environment. The ADMS system uses materialized views in query optimization and addresses questions of caching, buffering, access paths, and so forth.

The complexity of view maintenance also needs to be explored. The dynamic complexity classes of Ref. 52 and the incremental maintenance complexity of Ref. 1 characterize the computational complexity of maintaining a materialized copy of the view. Reference 52 shows that several recursive views have a first-order dynamic complexity, whereas Ref. 1 defines languages with constant, logarithmic, and polynomial incremental maintenance complexity.

ACKNOWLEDGMENTS

We thank H. V. Jagadish, Leonid Libkin, Dallan Quass, and Jennifer Widom for their insightful comments on the technical and presentation aspects of this article.

REFERENCES

1. H. V. Jagadish, I. S. Mumick, and A. Silberschatz, "View Maintenance Issues in the Chronicle Data Model," in *14th PODS*, 1995, pp. 113–124.
2. J. A. Blakeley, N. Coburn, and P. Larson, "Updating Derived Relations: Detecting Irrelevant and Autonomously Computable Updates," *ACM Trans. Database Syst.*, *14*(3), 369–400 (1989).
3. T. Urpi and A. Olive, "A Method for Change Computation in Deductive Databases," in *VLDB 1992*.
4. A. Gupta, H. V. Jagadish, and I. S. Mumick, "Data Integration Using Self-Maintainable Views," Technical Memorandum 113880-941101-32, AT&T Bell Laboratories (November 1994).
5. X. Qian and G. Wiederhold, "Incremental Recomputation of Active Relational Expressions," *IEEE TKDE*, 3, 337–341 (1991).

6. J. V. Harrison and S. Dietrich, "Maintenance of Materialized Views in a Deductive Database: An Update Propagation Approach," in *Workshop on Deductive Databases, JICSLP*, 1992.

7. A. Gupta, I. S. Mumick, and V. S. Subrahmanian, "Maintaining Views Incrementally," in *SIGMOD 1993*, pp. 157–167. (Full version in AT&T Technical Report 9921214-19-TM.)

8. I. S. Mumick, "Query Optimization in Deductive and Relational Databases," Ph.D. thesis, Stanford University (1991).

9. I. S. Mumick and O. Shmueli, "Finiteness Properties of Database Queries," in *Advances in Database Research: Proc. of the 4th Australian Database Conference*, 1993, pp. 274–288.

10. O. Shmueli and A. Itai, "Maintenance of Views," in *SIGMOD 1984*, pp. 240–255.

11. J. A. Blakeley, P. Larson, and F. Tompa, "Efficiently Updating Materialized Views," in *SIGMOD 1986*.

12. N. Roussopoulos, "The Incremental Access Method of View Cache: Concept, Algorithms, and Cost Analysis," in *ACM–TODS*, *16*(3), 535–563 (1991).

13. R. Paige, "Applications of Finite Differencing to Database Integrity Control and Query/Transaction Optimization," in *Advances in Database Theory*, Plenum Press, New York, 1984, pp. 170–209.

14. T. Griffin, L. Libkin, and H. Trickey, "A Correction to 'Incremental Recomputation of Active Relational Expressions' by Qian and Wiederhold," *IEEE TKDE*, to appear.

15. T. Griffin and L. Libkin, "Incremental Maintenance of Views with Duplicates," in *SIGMOD 1995*.

16. S. Ceri and J. Widom, "Deriving Production Rules for Incremental View Maintenance," in *VLDB*, 1991.

17. B. Mitschang, H. Pirahesh, P. Pistor, B. Lindsay, and N. Sudkamp, "SQL/XNF—Processing Composite Objects as Abstractions over Relational Data," in *Proc. of 9th IEEE ICDE*, 1993.

18. J. D. Ullman, *Principles of Database and Knowledge-Base Systems, Vol. 2*. Computer Science Press.

19. A. Gupta and I. S. Mumick, "Improvements to the PF Algorithm," Report TR STAN-CS-93-1473, Stanford University.

20. V. Kuchenhoff, "On the Efficient Computation of the Difference Between Consecutive Database States," in *DOOD*, Springer-Verlag, Berlin, 1991.

21. A. Gupta, D. Katiyar, and I. S. Mumick, "Counting Solutions to the View Maintenance Problem," in *Workshop on Deductive Databases, JICSLP*, 1992.

22. I. S. Mumick and O. Shmueli, "Universal Finiteness and Satisfiability," in *PODS 1994*, pp. 190–200.

23. J. M. Nicolas and Yazdanian, "An Outline of BDGEN: A Deductive DBMS," in *Inform. Process.*, 705–717 (1983).

24. G. Dong and R. Topor, "Incremental Evaluation of Datalog Queries," in *ICDT*, 1992.

25. G. Dong and J. Su, "Incremental and Decremental Evaluation of Transitive Closure by First-Order Queries," in *Proceedings of the 16th Australian Computer Science Conference*, 1993.

26. G. Dong, L. Libkin, and L. Wong, "On Impossibility of Decremental Recomputation of Recursive Queries in Relational Calculus and SQL," in *Proc. of the Intl. Wksp. on DB Prog. Lang.*, 1995.

27. A. Y. Levy, A. O. Mendelzon, Y. Sagiv, and D. Srivastava, "Answering Queries Using Views," in *PODS 1995*, pp. 95–104.

28. O. Wolfson, H. M. Dewan, S. J. Stolfo, and Y. Yemini, "Incremental Evaluation of Rules and Its Relationship to Parallelism, in *SIGMOD 1991*, pp. 78–87.

29. C. Elkan, "Independence of Logic Database Queries and Updates," in *9th PODS*, 1990, pp. 154–160.

30. A. Y. Levy and Y. Sagiv, "Queries Independent of Updates," in *19th VLDB*, 1993, pp. 171–181.

31. J. A. Blakeley and F. W. Tompa, "Maintaining Materialized Views without Accessing Base Data," *Inform. Syst.*, *13*(4), 393–406 (1988).

32. A. Gupta and J. A. Blakeley, "Maintaining Views Using Materialized Views," Unpublished.

33. A. Gupta, "Partial Information Based Integrity Constraint Checking," Ph.D. Thesis, Stanford University (1995).

34. Y. Zhuge, H. Garcia-Molina, J. Hammer, and J. Widom, "View Maintenance in a Warehousing Environment," in *SIGMOD 1995*, pp. 316–327.

35. G. Zhou, R. Hull, R. King, and J-C. Franchitti, "Using Object Matching and Materialization to Integrate Heterogeneous Databases," in *Proc. of 3rd Intl. Conf. on Cooperative Inform. Syst.*, 1995, pp. 4–18.

36. J. Lu, G. Moerkotte, J. Schu, and V. S. Subrahmanian, "Efficient Maintenance of Materialized Mediated Views," in *SIGMOD 1995*, pp. 340–351.

37. C. Williamson and B. Shneiderman, "The Dynamic HomeFinder: Evaluating Dynamic Queries in a Real-Estate Information Exploration System," in *Sparks of Innovation in Human–Computer Interaction* B. Shneiderman (ed.), Ablex Publishing, Norwood, NJ, 1993.

38. R. J. Brachman et al., "Integrated Support for Data Archaeology," *Int. J. Intell. Coop. Inform. Syst.*, 2, 159–185 (1993).

39. A. Gupta, I. Singh Mumick, and K. A. Ross, "Adapting Materialized Views After Redefinitions," in TR CUCS-010-95, Columbia University, (March 1995); also in *SIGMOD 1995*, pp. 211–222.

40. P. O. Buneman and E. K. Clemons, "Efficiently Monitoring Relational Databases," *ACM Trans. Database Syst.*, 4(3), 368–382, 1979.

41. J. M. Nicolas, "Logic for Improving Integrity Checking in Relational Data Bases," *Acta Inform.*, 18(3), 227–253 (1982).

42. P. A. Bernstein and B. T. Blaustein, "Fast Methods for Testing Quantified Relational Calculus Assertions," in *SIGMOD 1982*, pp. 39–50.

43. F. Bry, R. Manthey, and B. Martens, "Integrity Verification in Knowledge Bases," in *Logic Programming*, Springer-Verlag, Berlin, 1992, pp. 114–139.

44. J. W. Lloyd, E. A. Sonenberg, and R. W. Topor, "Integrity Constraint Checking in Stratified Databases," *J. Logic Program.*, 4(4), 331–343 (1987).

45. S. Ceri and J. Widom, "Deriving Production Rules for Constraint Maintenance," in *VLDB*, 1990.

46. A. Rajaraman, Y. Sagiv, and J. D. Ullman, "Answering Queries Using Templates with Binding Patterns," in *PODS 1995*, pp. 105–112.

47. S. Chaudhuri, R. Krishnamurthy, S. Potamianos, and K. Shim, "Query Optimization in the Presence of Materialized Views," in *11th IEEE Intl. Conference on Data Engineering*, 1995.

48. S. Dar, H. V. Jagadish, A. Y. Levy, and D. Srivastava, "Answering SQL Queries with Aggregation Using Views," Technical report, AT&T (1995).

49. A. Gupta, V. Harinarayan, and D. Quass, "Generalized Projections: A Powerful Approach to Aggregation," in *VLDB*, 1995.

50. S. Ghandeharizadeh, R. Hull, and D. Jacobs, "Heraclitus[Alg,C]: Elevating Deltas to be First-Class Citizens in a Database Programming Language," Technical Report USC-CS-94-581, University of Southern California (1994).

51. N. Roussopoulos, C. Chun, S. Kelley, A. Delis, and Y. Papakonstantinou, "The ADMS Project: Views 'R' Us," in *IEEE Data Eng. Bull.*, 18(2) (1995). Special Issue on Materialized Views and Data Warehousing.

52. S. Patnaik and N. Immerman, "Dyn-fo: A Parallel, Dynamic Complexity Class," in *PODS 1994*.

ASHISH GUPTA

INDERPAL SINGH MUMICK

MASSIVELY PARALLEL PROCESSING USING OPTICAL INTERCONNECTIONS

INTRODUCTION

Small-scale parallel systems of two or more processors have been used commercially since the 1970s. Some of these systems were used to maintain large databases while the user waited for the next advance in technology to provide more power in a single processor. Other users were working at the forefront of engineering and scientific disciplines, where difficult problems could be solved only with large amounts of computational power. At the other end of the computer power spectrum, microcomputers, developed in the early 1980s, found a large market and were put to use in a wide variety of applications. This fueled the development of successively more powerful, yet low-cost microprocessors. The computational power available on a desktop today often exceeds the power once available only on "mainframe" computers.

As challenging engineering and scientific problems have grown larger and the cost of high-end processors has increased, researchers have investigated ways to provide powerful, low-cost processing systems by coupling a large number of microprocessors and putting them to work in parallel. To do this effectively requires significant changes from the familiar serial approach to computing. These changes affect virtually all areas of computing, including computer architecture, network architecture, operating systems, language compilers, and computational algorithms.

To understand the changes that are required, a large number of parallel systems have been designed and built by both research and commercial organizations over the last two decades. These systems have used different models of parallel operation, often described as single-instruction, multiple-data (SIMD) and multiple-instruction, multiple-data (MIMD). A review of parallel systems issues and a description of many of the machines that were built is provided in Ref. 1. Some of the systems described in this review were intended to interconnect over 100 processors. Examples include the NYU Ultracomputer, the Intel Paragon, and the IBM GF11. The Thinking Machines CM-2 system was built from very simple microprocessors and designed to interconnect over 64,000 of them. Other massively parallel systems that have been marketed commercially include the KSR-1 from Kendall Square Research and the TC2000 from BBN Systems. Systems currently being marketed include the Fujitsu VPP700 (2), the Hitachi SR2201 (3), the NEC SX-4 (4), the IBM SP-2 (5), and the Cray T3E (6). The latter two are built from microprocessors, and up to 2048 microprocessors can be combined in a single system.

The focus of this article is on the use of optical technology to interconnect a very large number of processors. Although networks such as the Internet can connect an extremely large number of processors and may use optical links, this type of processor interconnection represents distributed processing rather than parallel processing. Parallel processing requires extremely short communication delays so that a processor can use the network with minimal impact on its computation speed. In many parallel architectures, processors use the network to access parts of memory. As a result, specialized networking hardware and techniques are required rather than a general-purpose network such as the Internet. Despite the use of specialized networks, communication speed in parallel systems is still much slower than computation speed. Parallel algorithms are, therefore, designed to minimize the amount of communication required.

In the remainder of this article, we will discuss optical devices, architectures, and control techniques that can be used to build high-speed interconnection networks to improve overall system performance. In the next section, we will describe the potential advantages of optical interconnections over electrical interconnections. A number of relevant optical technologies and devices are discussed briefly in the third section. In the fourth section, we review some proposed optical architectures and discuss the techniques used to control them. Some final observations are given in the last section.

WHY OPTICS?

The characteristics of electronic signals and optical signals have been compared for purposes ranging from connecting continents via telecommunication links to connecting gates on a Very Large Scale Integration (VLSI) circuit (7). Some studies are theoretical in nature in order to understand the fundamental physical limitations (8). Although optics have been used for telecommunication systems for many years, studies such as Refs. 9–11 have concluded that optical interconnections can be cost-effective over distances as short as those between circuit boards. The advantage of optical connections increases as distance and data rate increase. Thus, optical interconnection networks can often provide better performance than electronic networks. Two key measures used to describe network performance are latency and bandwidth.

- *High bandwidth*. The bandwidth of a communication link is the rate at which data can be sent through the link. For optical networks, the rate is independent of the distance the signal is to be transmitted. For electronic networks however, the attenuation of a signal is related to its frequency. With a fixed amount of power, increasing the data rate of a signal reduces the distance over which it can be transmitted. Thus, optical links have an advantage when higher data rates (for example, above 200 Mb/s) or longer distances (for example, above 1 m) are required (10).

  To understand how large the potential optical bandwidth is, consider a hypothetical processor that operates at 500 MHz and produces a 64-bit result every cycle. To transmit these results over a network requires a bandwidth of 32 Gb/s. Current electronic busses may transmit a maximum of 1–10 Gb/s using parallel transmission lines each operating at a rate of hundreds of Mb/s. Optical systems in research labs have been shown to operate at burst speeds of up to 250 Gb/s over a single optical link (12). Although practical systems operating at such speeds are years away, optics have the potential to increase communication bandwidth by orders of magnitude.

- *Low latency*. Latency refers to the end-to-end delay in communication. Because optical signals can readily be converted to and from electronic form, low-latency designs for electronic networks can be adapted for optics. Latency may be reduced further if the network can provide all-optical connections.

Optical interconnections also have advantages for system construction and packaging:

- *Reduced electrical power and cooling requirements.* In high-density VLSI chips, electrical power consumption and the resultant need for cooling are important issues. It has been estimated that in a massively parallel system such as the CM-5, 60–80% of the power is consumed by the interconnection network (7). Optical connections require less power than electrical connections as the data rate and distance of the connection increases.
- *Increased fan-out.* Fan-out refers to sending a signal from a single transmitter to multiple receivers, such as when a signal is placed on a bus. The fan-out of an electronic signal is limited by the need for termination devices at each receiver to prevent unwanted signal reflections. Optical signals do not have this problem and can support a much larger degree of fan-out.
- *Immunity to electromagnetic interference.* The conductors in electronic circuits act as antennas for electromagnetic radiation. This is a source of noise on an electrical connection. Photons do not interact with each other or with other radiation, thus extending the range of operating environments for optical systems.
- *Increased connection density.* Electronic signals interfere with each other when placed close together, thus limiting the density of interconnections. The amount of interference is related to the frequency of the signal, so that circuit density decreases as bandwidth increases. Light beams do not interact in this way. This increases both the flexibility of circuit design and the possible interconnection density.

Although there are advantages to optical interconnections, it is not clear when they will become common in parallel processing systems. The introduction of optical technology requires the mass production of optical devices with suitable function, cost, reliability, performance, and packaging characteristics, and on the general acceptance of massively parallel systems.

OPTICAL TECHNOLOGIES IN COMPUTER INTERCONNECTION NETWORKS

Overview

In this section, we review basic optical technologies and their application to computer interconnection networks. The intent is to provide a high-level overview of the operation of optical devices and to describe the types of technological advances that are necessary to make optical interconnection networks a reality.

Optical devices have a wide range of applications including telecommunications, image processing, pattern recognition, neural networks, printers, CD players, data storage, remote sensing, and defense applications such as radar, sonar, and electronic warfare. This wide range of applications has fostered research into devices with a correspondingly wide range of functions. In some cases, devices that perform similar functions have characteristics that make them most suitable for different applications. The result is an enormous variety of devices and technologies from which to choose the components of an optical network.

Initial developments in optical technologies were used by the telecommunications industry. Telecommunications networks require the propagation of a large number of low-bandwidth signals over long distances with bit error rates of about 10^{-9}. High-speed trunk connections are essentially point-to-point and equipment must often function reliably in extreme physical environments. Optical-fiber characteristics are a significant concern in network design. For practical implementations, research has been directed toward miniaturizing devices, increasing their reliability, and developing a means to manufacture large quantities at low cost. The resulting technology is, however, not sufficient to meet the needs of shorter distance communications. Applications such as cable TV, local-area networking, and multimedia require increased signal processing capabilities from optoelectronic devices. Parallel processor interconnection networks are extremely sensitive to network latency and require high performance, as well. For example, an interconnection network requires the transmission of accurately synchronized, high-bandwidth signals over short distances. It may require frequent switching or large fan-out and requires error rates of 10^{-12} or less. The integration of more complex optical circuitry into semiconductor devices has fostered the development of new semiconductor materials and manufacturing techniques.

In the remainder of this section, we list several types of optical devices and the underlying physical principles that are used to generate, convey, manipulate, and detect optical signals. A more complete overview is available from many sources such as Refs. 13–15; detailed discussions on devices are available from Refs. 16–20. The physical principles are covered in, for example (27,57).

Physical Basis of Optical Technologies

An optical signal is generated in a semiconductor when electrons and holes recombine across the junction between differently doped materials and emit photons. The same principal is behind both lasers and light-emitting diodes. However, lasers use higher electrical currents so that stimulated emissions dominate spontaneous emissions, resulting in a coherent beam of light with a very narrow spectrum. The wavelengths emitted are a complex function of the physical characteristics of the device. Photodetectors receive optical signals by essentially the reverse process. Light energy is converted to electrical energy by the absorption of photons and the creation of electron-hole pairs in the semiconductor. These pairs move through the semiconductor material to create an electrical current.

Optical waveguides such as optical fibers are able to conduct light using the principle of *total internal reflection*. This occurs when a thin, transparent material is surrounded by materials with a lower index of refraction. Light traveling along the waveguide which strikes the interface with the surrounding material is reflected back into the waveguide. The physical characteristics of the waveguide affect the distance the signal can be carried.

The need to increase device capabilities for routing and filtering optical signals has fostered the development of new semiconductor materials and the advancement of new technologies that provide electronic control over optical signals. In some crystals, the speed at which light travels depends on the polarization of the light and on the direction it is traveling relative to the crystal structure. These crystals are called *birefringent*, and light passing through them will emerge as two images, each with a different polarization. This birefringence property may be altered by the presence of an externally applied electric field. This change is known as the *electrooptic effect*. Electrooptic crystals include quartz (SiO_2), lithium niobate ($LiNbO_3$), and gallium arsenide (GaAs).

The *acoustooptic effect* is similar to the electrooptic effect in that it changes the refractive index of a crystal. In this case, the changes are due to the mechanical strain produced by an acoustic wave. An acoustic transducer is used to inject an acoustic wave into the crystal, creating a periodic variation in the crystal's refractive index. This variation can be used to diffract an input optical signal or to change its polarization, based on its wavelength. Materials widely used in acoustooptic devices include lithium niobate ($LiNbO_3$), tellurium dioxide (TeO_2), and fused quartz (SiO_2).

These physical effects have been exploited to produce a wide variety of devices. These devices can be placed into two categories based on their means of conveying optical signals. One category of devices is most suited for use with optical fibers, whereas the other is appropriate for handling optical signals conveyed directly through free space.

Fiber-Based Systems

Fiber-optic interconnection networks use optical fibers as "wires" between light sources, switching and routing devices, and detectors. The operation of a device may either determine or depend on the wavelength of the optical signal, making wavelength sensitivity an important device characteristic.

- **Sources**

  Light-emitting diodes emit light with a broad range of wavelengths. An electronic signal can be used to modulate the intensity of the emitted light. As with electronic data transmission, digital data is transmitted in an optical signal through the use of an encoding technique (for example, NRZ, pulse bipolar, etc.).

  Lasers emit a narrow spectrum of coherent light. For low-loss transmission over glass optical fibers, the wavelengths most often used are in the infrared regions around 850, 1300, or 1550 nm. For the short distances involved in interconnections networks, the choice of wavelength is probably not critical. A common semiconductor laser design is the Fabry–Perot laser. Mirrored surfaces placed at both ends of an active region of the semiconductor are used to obtain the lasing effect. The width of the emitted spectrum can be reduced by distributed feedback (DFB) and distributed Bragg reflector (DBR) designs. Rather than using mirrors, these designs use a grating inside the laser cavity in order to select the wavelength of the light that propagates within the active region.

  Tunable lasers based on the DBR and DFB designs can be made by electronically altering the index of refraction of the material within a section of the laser cavity. The current injected into this section determines the density of carriers, which, in turn, affects the material's index of refraction and the output wavelength. Multiple quantum well (MQW) designs have even narrower linewidths and a broader tuning range.

  Alternatively, wavelength control may be obtained by selecting a desired laser from an array of lasers that emit at different, fixed wavelengths. It may also be possible to select the desired wavelength from a source with a wide spectral bandwidth by using a narrow-bandwidth tunable filter.

- **Propagation**

    Optical fibers have characteristics such as dispersion and attenuation that affect the intensity and shape of the propagating signal. For long-distance transmissions, *single-mode* glass fibers with a core diameter of 2–10 μm and an overall diameter of 125 μm may be used. Amplification and reshaping of the optical pulses are required periodically. If amplification alone is needed, erbium-doped fiber amplifiers may be used to amplify a wide range of wavelengths simultaneously (19). These are not primary concerns in an interconnection network, however, where the distances are short enough that it may be possible to transmit satisfactory signals over low cost optical fibers made from polymers (21).

- **Routing**

    Optical signals can be routed under electrical control using the electrooptic and acoustooptic effects described earlier. Devices that use these effects can often be designed as either switches or filters. Two key characteristics of a device include the range of wavelengths over which the device operates and the speed of operation.

    To understand how the electrooptic effect can be used, consider the optical directional coupler in Figure 1. In this device, electrodes are deposited over two waveguides which have been routed closely together in a semiconductor. An optical signal is input at one end of one waveguide. A voltage is applied across the electrodes, creating an electric field that affects the index of refraction in the two waveguides in opposite ways. In effect, this field changes the amount of internal reflection experienced by the input signal, allowing light to leak out of one waveguide and become trapped in the other. By carefully choosing the device geometry and the applied voltage, the portion of the signal appearing at each of the output ports can be controlled. Thus, this device can be operated as either a modulator or a switch.

    Optical filters can be used to separate signals based on wavelength or polarization (22). A Fabry–Perot filter consists of two highly reflective mirrors in parallel, forming a resonant cavity. At certain wavelengths determined by geometry, light passes through the cavity. The other wavelengths are trapped inside the cavity by the reflective surfaces.

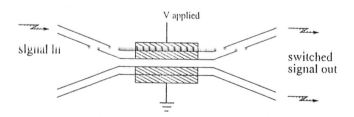

FIGURE 1   An optical directional coupler.

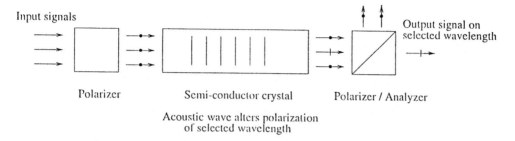

Input signals

Output signal on selected wavelength

Polarizer

Semi-conductor crystal

Polarizer / Analyzer

Acoustic wave alters polarization
of selected wavelength

FIGURE 2   An acoustooptic filter.

An electronically tunable optical filter can be built using the acoustooptic effect. The basic geometry of the filter is shown in Figure 2 (23). Polarized incoming light passes through a crystal of, for example, lithium niobate. A transducer places an acoustic signal into the crystal. The interaction between the acoustic and optic signals in the crystal results in a change in the polarization of light at a selected wavelength. A polarization filter is then used to remove the unwanted signals from the output light beam. By driving the transducer with several acoustic signals, this device can be used to select several corresponding optical signals. Its tuning time is in the microsecond range. Electrooptical filters can be built with tuning times in the nanosecond range, but over a much narrower range of wavelengths.

A *passive star coupler* is essentially a glass hub with optical fibers from transmitters entering at one end and optical fibers to receivers leaving at the other end. The light signal from any transmitter is diffused by the coupler so that it is distributed equally to all of the fibers leading to the receivers. The coupler is called *passive* because it uses no electrical power and performs no logical or routing functions. It simply diffuses and transmits light. Signal routing is accomplished by using wavelength-sensitive devices and/or suitable network control techniques. When the same set of nodes is connected to the input and output fibers as shown in Figure 3, the passive star has the logical appearance of a bus.

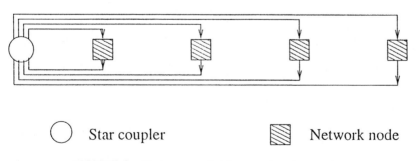

◯ Star coupler   ▨ Network node

FIGURE 3   Nodes connected to a passive star coupler.

- **Detection**

    Photodiodes and *phototransistors* may be used to detect an optical signal. Direct detection is used when the signal modulates the intensity of the light. Coherent detection is used when the signal has been modulated onto a continuous wave. The detected signal must be amplified, reshaped, and decoded by receiver circuitry to convert it to the form used by the electronics.

    Tunable detectors. An alternative to using a tunable transmitter is to use a tunable receiver. This effect can be obtained by placing a tunable filter in front of the detector.

Free-Space Systems

One of the advantages of optical interconnections is that optical signals can propagate close to each other, and even pass through each other without interacting. To exploit the high connection density possible with optical signals, two-dimensional arrays of light sources and detectors are used. This, in effect, creates a single, two-dimensional optical beam. The information content of the beam can be independently controlled at each location within its cross section by using *spatial light modulators*. To direct the light in free space, lenses, mirrors, and beam splitters are used. A simple free space system is depicted in Figure 4.

- **Sources**

    Two-dimensional arrays of lasers can be built using *vertical-cavity surface-emitting laser* (VCSEL) technology and gallium arsenide (GaAs) substrates (24). Previous semiconductor lasers emitted light from the edge of the substrate rather than the surface, and hence could not be built in two-dimensional arrays.

    It is also possible to produce a two-dimensional array of signals using optical *modulators*. In such systems, the signal from a single laser source is imaged into an array of spots which illuminate the modulators in the array. The modulators may be self-electrooptic effect devices (SEEDs), which use an electronic signal to control the reflectivity of the surface of the

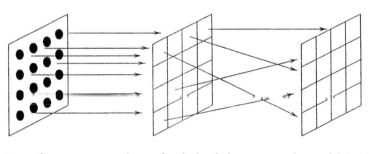

Array of sources   Array of optical switches   Array of detectors

FIGURE 4   Simple free-space interconnections.

device. Reflection of the "read-out" beam by the SEED array produces a modulated two-dimensional optical beam of signals.

- **Propagation**

  Lenses are used to focus and collimate beams of light between sources and detectors. There are two approaches. *Microoptics* refers to components that range in size from microns to millimeters and which can be manufactured in arrays and mounted on a substrate (7). For example, a lenslet array is an array of small lenses each of which focuses the signal from a single light source. *Bulk optics* refers to objects that operate on the entire cross section of the beam. These objects require more space than integrated optics.

  A critical issue in using free-space optical transmission in parallel processing is establishing and maintaining the proper alignment of the optical components (7,25). High-quality lenses are needed to focus light precisely, and each component must be carefully aligned in three spatial and three angular coordinates to within very narrow tolerances. This alignment is sensitive to thermal and vibrational influences in the environment. This requirement has fostered the development of misalignment tolerant designs (25) and the integration of optical components onto substrates (26).

- **Routing**

  A *spatial light modulator* (SLM) is a two-dimensional array of cells which operates on the cross section of an optical beam. The operation of each cell can be controlled individually by electronic or optical means. Each cell may be transparent or may modify a characteristic of the incident light, such as the intensity, polarization, direction, or phase. The key characteristics of an SLM are the cell density and the speed of cell operation. Many implementations of SLMs have been proposed using magnetic garnets, liquid crystals, multiple quantum well (MQW) structures, deformable mirrors, and devices using the electrooptic and acoustooptic effects (7).

  A *hologram*, like a lens, can be used to create an optical image of an object (13,27). Unlike a lens, the hologram contains an optical interference pattern with all the information necessary to recreate the image. The image is reproduced by illuminating the hologram with a laser. An image consisting of a pattern of spots can be used to route the input signal to one or more different locations.

  The interference pattern in the hologram of a single spot at a given location can be computed and reproduced on a black-and-white printer. This can be used to generate the pattern that would be present if the hologram was produced photographically and is known as a *computer-generated hologram* (CGH). Similarly, subject to the limits of computational complexity, a CGH can be created for any pattern of spots that represents a desired signal routing. An SLM may be designed with each cell as a CGH that routes the corresponding signal in the cross section of the optical beam.

  A *beam splitter* is a semitransparent mirror often placed at a 45° angle to the incident signal. A portion of the signal is reflected in a new direction and the remaining signal passes through unaffected. The portion of the beam that is reflected is determined by the amount of reflective coating at each location of the mirror. A beam splitter that reflects/transmits light based on its polarization is called a *polarizer* or *analyzer*.

- **Detection**

    An array of photodetectors is used to receive the signal beam from an array of transmitters. In many designs, electronic processing logic is combined with photodetectors, VCSELs, or modulators into cells of an array built into a single chip. This arrangement is called a *smart pixel array*. It functions much like an SLM with increased processing flexibility, in that each signal within the beam can be independently received, processed, and, if desired, retransmitted.

OPTICAL INTERCONNECTION NETWORKS

With an understanding of the general capabilities of optical devices, we now turn our attention to how the devices can be used in optical interconnection networks for massively parallel processing. Systems can be built from several different models or parallel computation, so that a network may interconnect processors, memories, microcomputers, or clusters of components. We will refer to these devices attached to the network as *nodes*.

To fully understand an interconnection network, we need to know not only the internal components and how they are connected but also the techniques that are used to control the message traffic in the network. We begin this discussion by describing the requirements of a network used for typical parallel applications.

Network Requirements

A network must not only support the communication needs of the application but must do so in a cost-effective manner. Some considerations for each of these follow.

Communication in Parallel Applications

Algorithms used in parallel applications often decompose the problems to be solved into regular structures. Each processor is assigned a piece of a problem and must communicate with processors working on related pieces. In the most general case, any node of a parallel system may communicate with any other node, and the interconnection network must be able to provide for this. However, a more typical case is that a node will communicate with only a small number of other nodes, and in a regular pattern (28). Typical communication patterns found in parallel applications include the following.

- *Broadcast and multicast.* In a multicast, one processor communicates the same information to a set of processors. If the set includes all processors, then it is referred to as a broadcast.

- *Reduction.* This is the inverse of a multicast. A set of processors communicates some information to a single processor. This processor then combines the information in some way. Often, a reduction is followed by a broadcast.
- *Nearest neighbor.* This pattern is often found in algorithms in which the processors are logically arranged as an *n*-dimensional array called a *mesh*. Information held by one processor affects only the processors adjacent to it along a dimension of the array. This pattern is found in some matrix multiplication algorithms, in algorithms for solving linear systems of equations, and in algorithms that use a systolic or pipelined data flow.
- *Hypercube.* In this pattern, every bit in a *b*-bit processor address represents a dimension of a binary hypercube with 2^b processors (i.e., a *b*-dimensional binary array). Processors communicate only with the *b* processors whose address is exactly 1 bit different from their own. There are two variations on the use of this pattern. In *divide-and-conquer*, all processors communicate across a given dimension at one time. This pattern is found in a wide variety of applications such as sorting. Another variation is the *recursive doubling* pattern. In this pattern, 2^{i-1} processors send messages over dimension *i*, in sequence from $i = 1$ to $i = b$. This can be used to propagate information from one processor to all other processors. The hypercube pattern is efficient because only *b* steps are required to exchange information between 2^b processors.

Many parallel applications are built from loops consisting of synchronized phases of computation and communication. One consequence of this is that message traffic may arrive in bursts. Another is that the communication pattern may be repetitive. Thus, nodes tend to communicate often with a small subset of other nodes. The localized, repeating aspects of a communication pattern are often described as the *communication locality of reference*. Processor caches and virtual memory systems are used to exploit locality of memory references to improve computer performance. Similarly, it is desirable to build a network that exploits locality of communication references to improve performance.

The size of a message in a parallel application can range from a few bytes to a few thousand bytes, depending on the application and on the design of the parallel system. Fast programming techniques can reduce software communication overhead to a few microseconds (29). To avoid becoming a performance bottleneck, switching and control operations for network hardware must be performed in the nanosecond range.

Network Structure and Scalability

A straightforward way of providing fast communication between any pair of network nodes is with a direct connection through a crossbar switch. A crossbar switch allows any of its *N* inputs to be independently connected directly to any of its outputs. Many different approaches have been used for designing small optical crossbars ($N \leq 32$) using fibers or other waveguides.

- One approach fans out each input signal to a column in an $N \times N$ array of optical switches and couples the signals from each row of switches into a single output fiber (7).
- A passive star coupler with *N* wavelengths may be used as a crossbar. Each node receives messages on a unique wavelength. Network control must handle or avoid collisions.

- A highly integrated crossbar has been proposed in Ref. 30, where light and sound interact in a thin crystal film deposited on the surface of a semiconductor. A lens is created at each end of the film, bracketing the area where the acoustooptic interaction occurs. The acoustic signal that determines the switch settings is a combination of acoustic signals that control the diffraction of each optical input. With this approach, an integrated crossbar of approximately 12×12 may be possible.
- An electronic crossbar switch with optical inputs and outputs is described in Ref. 31. Bytes of data are transmitted using a separate wavelength for each bit. These wavelengths are then multiplexed into an optical fiber. At the switch, the bits are demultiplexed, spatially separated, and switched through a set of parallel 1-bit wide electronic crossbars. The output optical signal is regenerated and combined in the same way as the input signal. This design is expected to connect up to 64 nodes.

Although the performance of a crossbar switch interconnecting N nodes increases linearly with the number of nodes, the increase in internal complexity is $O(N^2)$. Complexity is an estimate of the number of switches, wires, transmitters, receivers, or other network components that are required by a design. Designs like a crossbar perform well because they can provide a direct connection between any pair of nodes simultaneously. However, they present an enormously complex wiring problem and have a significant hardware cost. A crossbar network for 1000 processors would require millions of components. Thus, this approach is impractical for massively parallel processing.

It is desirable to have an architecture where both performance and cost increase linearly with the number of nodes. Such an architecture is said to be *scalable*. Although a perfectly scalable architecture does not exist, there are a wide variety of designs reflecting different trade-offs between cost and performance. Optical interconnection networks often use designs similar to those used for electronic networks. These designs include buses, meshes, multistage interconnection networks, and trees.

The simplest hardware arrangement is a bus, which connects all nodes to a single shared communication link. A set of access control procedures must be defined to handle communication. As we will see, many optical architectures use a bus-based approach.

A *mesh* is an *n*-dimensional array of nodes with a fixed number of nodes in each dimension. A common electronic design called a *hypercube* has exactly two nodes in each dimension. When nodes at the edge of the array are connected to the nodes at the opposite, parallel edge of the array, the network is called a *torus*. In many electronic designs, each node is connected only to its nearest neighbors along each dimensional axis of the array. Fiber-optic designs for an *n*-dimensional array of nodes have been proposed using several different physical interconnection patterns.

In a *multistage interconnection network* (MIN), sets of routers or switches are interconnected in stages. A message is sent through a path consisting of one router at each stage. Well-known MINs include the omega, butterfly, shuffle, and Clos networks. Both electronic and optical MINs can be constructed by interconnecting a large number of small (for example, 2×2) crossbar switches. Compared to a crossbar, a MIN offers less performance [$O(\log N)$ for latency], but has less complexity [$O(N \log N)$].

A tree or hierarchical arrangement has also been used in both fiber-optic and electronic designs. The processing nodes are placed at the leaves of the tree, and the branches of the tree are formed by links between switches or routers.

Controlling an Optical Network

The object of network control is to provide communication paths for the exchange of data between nodes when the number of connections the network can provide simultaneously is limited. These paths are provided by controlling when, where, and how the optical signal is transmitted. After some general discussion, we will look more closely at techniques that can be used to control one simple network, the optical bus.

Managing Connections

Two approaches are commonly used to pass data through a network. In *packet switching*, messages are routed between senders and receivers through intermediate nodes. This is done using routing information added to each message. While research is being done to decode addresses and route messages optically at rates up to 250 Gb/s (32), in the near term, packet switching will require electronic processing. This means that an optical signal must be converted to electronic form, stored in a buffer for processing, and retransmitted optically over the next link toward the destination. A message may be delayed when the link is in use for another message or a buffer is not available at the next node in the path. Packet-switched networks require mechanisms to ensure that messages make continued progress toward their destinations and that traffic congestion does not degrade performance. Adaptive routing may be provided so that component failures can be tolerated. Because routing latency can be much larger than transmission time in an optical network, the best performance is normally obtained when the number of routing steps is minimized.

Another approach is to use *circuit switching*, in which the network provides a direct physical connection between the source and destination of a message. With an all-optical connection, circuit switching can exploit the full performance capability of optics. However, circuit-switched networks require complex controls to coordinate the entire network to provide the nodes with the connections needed by the parallel application. For example, when the connection passes through optical switches, filters, or other electronically controlled devices, message transmission must be coordinated with device control. This coordination can be predetermined and implemented from the duration of the parallel application. This is called *static* control. Alternatively, *dynamic* control can be used to establish circuits that meet the immediate needs of the parallel application. Dynamic control can be implemented in a *centralized* manner in which a single network controller determines how circuits should be provided in response to application needs. However, in a large system, the controller can become a performance bottleneck, and if it breaks, the entire system will halt. To avoid this, a *distributed* approach can be used in which the nodes themselves control the network using a protocol for establishing circuits.

Optical Circuits

Optical circuits can be provided using the following two techniques.

- We can exploit the wavelength sensitivity of optical devices and reduce the number of network components (hence, cost) by managing the use of wavelengths for circuit establishment. Because signals on different wavelengths do not interfere with each other, they can be sent simultaneously through optical fibers and couplers and separated only when they need to be routed or received. This is known as *wavelength division multiplexing* (WDM) (33) and is shown in Figure 5 for three wavelengths, λ_1, λ_2, and λ_3. WDM is often used with tunable transmitters and/or receivers. It allows a structure such as a passive star to provide many connections simultaneously, as well as offering broadcast and multicast capability. WDM is not a complete solution for massively parallel processing, however, because the number of different wavelengths available in a network in the near term is likely to be on the order of tens rather than thousands.

- Another technique often used to coordinate circuit establishment is time division multiplexing (TDM) (34). In TDM, the operation of the network is divided into small time intervals. Through the use of a global clock, these intervals, or *time slots*, are synchronized across all network components and attached nodes. During each time slot, the network provides a specified set of connections. A sequence of these sets is created, and the network automatically cycles through this sequence so that all required connections are established in turn.

  The length of a time slot is chosen to allow the devices and nodes to establish a new set of connections and transmit a message. Because the connection requirements are predetermined, device control signals are prespecified and new connections can be established very quickly. A 10-Gb/s network could transmit four words of 64 bits in a time slot of 30 ns.

  Although TDM can be used in either optical or electronic networks, the large optical bandwidth exceeds the requirements of a single processor and makes multiplexing especially attractive in optical networks (35).

Both WDM and TDM are most often used in fiber-based architectures. Free-space architectures normally exploit the high connection density provided by the cross section of a two-dimensional optical beam, often referred to as *spatial parallelism*. The use of TDM and WDM together is referred to as *time–wavelength division multiplexing* (TWDM).

As an all-optical connection is required to fully exploit the potential performance of an optical network, we will look more closely at the performance of a circuit-switched network. Static control of a circuit-switched optical network can be implemented using a TWDM schedule built from prior knowledge of the application's overall communication pattern. However, in some cases, a static schedule will provide a large number of unused or seldom used connections. For example, when the communication pattern of an application cannot be precisely determined in advance, a static schedule may need to provide all

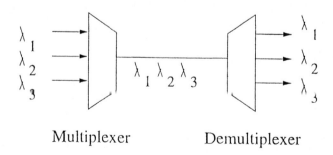

Multiplexer   Demultiplexer

FIGURE 5   Multiplexing three wavelengths together.

possible connections. The number of time slots required can be very large, and a message may have a long *access delay* until the network provides the connection it needs.

To handle situations where the communication pattern cannot be determined in advance, a dynamic protocol may be used to establish connections. As with packet switching, this network control is performed in the electronic domain. This *establishment delay* can be long relative to the time needed to transmit a message in a high-bandwidth optical network.

A more flexible implementation of TDM can be used to balance these two types of delay. In some cases, a compiler can use sophisticated algorithms to identify communication patterns similar to the ones described earlier (36) and multiplex these patterns together (37). This use of *compiled communication* reduces establishment delays by providing the network with TDM to change connections rapidly. It also reduces access delay by establishing a sequence of connections tailored to the application's immediate needs. TDM can also be combined with dynamic protocols such as those described in the next section. It may also be possible to manage connections with TDM using dynamic techniques analogous to those used to manage pages in virtual memory (35).

Optical Busses

A bus architecture is a simple, well-studied design that is easily implemented in optics. Like a 2×2 switch, a bus can be used as the building block of more complex networks. A optical bus can be logically implemented with a variety of physical designs, or through a passive star as shown in Figure 3 (38). These designs exploit the fan-out capability of optics and do not require complex optical switches. A wide variety of approaches for controlling these networks have been studied. In general, a wavelength and a time interval is reserved for communication between a particular set of nodes (34). Some designs restrict the set to a single source and a single destination; others employ a multicast capability or a protocol to handle conflicts in data transmission. The choice of protocol depends on the number and type of transmitters and receivers at each node (for example, fixed, tunable).

One simple technique is known as *broadcast-and-select*. All nodes transmit and receive using the same wavelength. A message and the address of its destination are broadcast to all nodes, which then process the information. The destination node selects (for example, receives) the message, and all other nodes discard it. All nodes must examine all message traffic, placing a large processing load on the network interface electronics. *Collisions* occur when two nodes transmit messages at the same time on the same wavelength. Because all nodes receive the same wavelength, these collisions can be detected and messages resent using a randomized algorithm such as those used in electronic networks.

Performance may be improved by the use of multiple wavelengths for message transmission. For example, each node may have a tunable transmitter and a receiver tuned to a unique, fixed wavelength. This arrangement provides *self-routing* of messages. Each node receives only traffic destined for itself. Self-routing allows full use of optical bandwidth without overwhelming the electronics with message processing. Collisions occur only for transmission to the same destination node. However, the sending nodes cannot detect these collisions because they do not receive on the wavelength used by the destination node. Thus, some kind of reservation or acknowledgment scheme must be used.

A static TWDM reservation scheme can be developed using $N - 1$ time slots. In time slot i, the node at address A can transmit messages to the node at address $(A + i)$ mod N. When the number of wavelengths is limited, a static reservation scheme can still be developed by extending the length of the fixed schedule.

An acknowledgment scheme can be implemented dividing time slots into two sub-slots: one for message transmission and a second for acknowledgment. Messages that are successfully transmitted are acknowledged in the subsequent subslot. Unacknowledged messages are assumed to have been in a collision, and a random retransmission scheme is used.

The considerations are slightly different when each node is provided with a tunable receiver and a fixed, unique transmission wavelength. In this design, a media access protocol must be used to inform the destination node that a message is coming. Again, a fixed TWDM allocation scheme can be used for this purpose. An alternative is to use a separate control channel and reservation protocol, requiring an additional fixed receiver at each node.

We can further increase the performance (and cost) of the network if each node is provided with multiple transmitters or receivers. For example, consider a network where each node has a tunable transmitter and a receiver on every wavelength. In such networks, control protocols must resolve *destination conflicts*. These occur when several nodes transmit messages to the same destination at the same time, but on different wavelengths. The control scheme must allocate both a wavelength and a time slot to each connection.

The additional receivers allow each node to detect collisions for all destinations. This provides an alternative to increasing the length of a static TWDM schedule when the number of wavelengths in the network is limited. At low loads, the number of time slots required may be reduced by allowing multiple senders to transmit in any time slot, detecting and recovering from collisions as necessary.

Many protocols have been developed to dynamically allocate connections rather than use a static TWDM schedule. These protocols often use a control channel to allow a sender to reserve an optical wavelength for communication to a receiver. *Slotted* protocols use synchronized time slots in a communication channel. *Contention* protocols rely on collision detection and recovery. Both kinds of protocol have been proposed for use in the control channel and in the data channel. Various assumptions have been made about the speed with which network devices can be tuned. These designs can be characterized by the number of transmitters and receivers required at each node, as well as by the use of fixed or tunable devices. A survey of these protocols is provided in Refs. 39 and 40.

In addition to performance consideration, networks built from a single passive star are limited in size by the *optical power budget*. This refers to the amount of the emitted signal that arrives at the detector. Emitted signal strength and detector sensitivity are characteristics of the device and can be related to electrical power consumption. Signal losses during transmission are affected by the number and type of network components and the amount of fan-out required. The physical restriction on the size of a passive star means that networks to interconnect thousands of processors will require more complex architectures.

Fiber-Based Architectures

One approach to building an optical network is to simply replace electronic links with optical links. This approach does not account for the advantages or the limitations of optics (41). One way to exploit the optical advantages of high fan-out and multiple signal wavelengths is to use passive stars as the building blocks of larger networks. Each star can be controlled using techniques described in the previous section. Because optical components are complex and costly, the number of these components is an important consideration in network design.

Packet-Switched Architectures

Packet switching is commonly used in mesh and MIN electronic architectures. Both architectures can be built with routers that process message headers to determine the next link in the path to the destination. Many optical networks have been designed to interconnect an *n*-dimensional array of nodes using passive stars to form connections along the dimensions. Exploiting the fan-out of the passive star greatly reduces the number of routing steps required compared to electronic mesh networks. The optical designs differ in the arrangement of the connections, the routing algorithms, and the number and type of network components required. Three examples are described:

- A *wavelength division multiple access channel hypercube* (WMCH) is proposed in Ref. 38. Nodes are arranged in a mesh, and all processors that share a dimensional axis are connected via a single passive star. Figure 6 shows an example of a small two-dimensional mesh. Tunable transmitters or receivers can be used with WDM so that messages are sent directly to the desired node along any one dimension using the techniques described earlier. Messages pass through

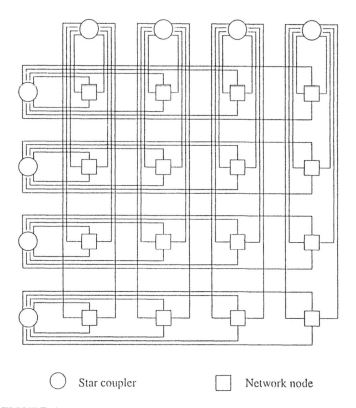

◯   Star coupler   ▢   Network node

FIGURE 6   A small WMCH mesh connected with optical passive stars.

the array one dimension at a time until they reach their destination. Using passive star couplers with a fan-out of 256, a network of 64K nodes could be constructed with a maximum of one intermediate routing step. Compared to networks with point-to-point connections, the WMCH uses fewer transmitters and receivers and requires far fewer message routing steps.

- A *bus–mesh* architecture is described in Ref. 42 for a two-dimensional array of nodes. Each bus connects the transmitters from a row of nodes to the receivers of a column of nodes. There are no nodes at the diagonal locations of the mesh. Each row of nodes transmits at a unique wavelength and each column receives at a unique wavelength. This allows all busses to be implemented with a single passive star coupler. TDM is used to give each node an equal opportunity to transmit. Multiple nodes can occupy a mesh location as shown in Figure 7 by adding additional TDM slots. Routing requires a maximum of two steps.

- The *dBus* architecture for interconnecting processors in a mesh based on de Bruijn digraphs is described in Ref. 43. An optical bus is used to connect the transmitters of nodes along one dimension to the receivers of nodes along another dimension. For example, in a three-dimensional array, the nodes at array locations (x, a, b) transmit to nodes at locations (a, b, x), where a and b are any fixed values and x represents all locations connected by the bus along a dimension of the array. A two-dimensional dBus array is shown in Figure 8. Each node has only one transmitter and one receiver. The busses may be implemented by a star coupler and WDM can be used to allow multiple messages to be sent on the bus at one time. Compared to the WMCH architecture, the dBus requires significantly fewer star couplers, transmitters, and receivers, at the cost

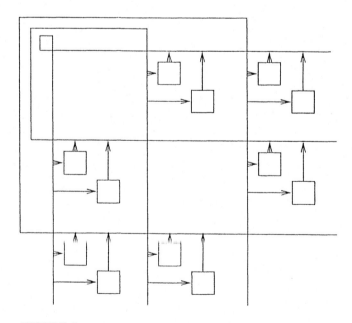

FIGURE 7   A bus–mesh with two nodes at each mesh location.

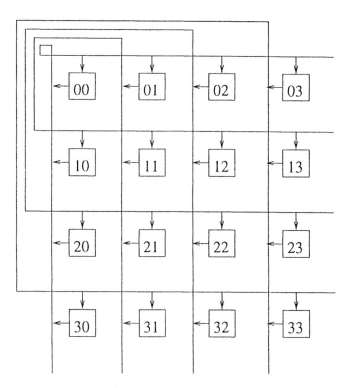

FIGURE 8   A dBus array.

of a slightly larger average number of routing steps between nodes. A dBus array can also be implemented using TWDM and a MIN architecture known as a dilated slipped banyan network (44).

Circuit-Switched Architectures

Whereas the packet-switched architectures use large fan-out to reduce the number of routing steps, circuit-switched architectures avoid routing entirely by providing direct connections. Circuit-switched architectures that have been proposed include the following:

- An optical bus may be used to interconnect a small number of nodes. Optical busses may be bidirectional or unidirectional. Different designs and control techniques have been analyzed in studies such as Refs. 38 and 45.
- A MIN can be constructed from electronically controlled optical switches. When the switches can be set to provide an all-optical path for any connection, the MIN implements circuit switching. A circuit-switched MIN that provides all-to-all connectivity is described in Ref. 44. A distributed protocol that can be used to establish all-optical paths in MINs is given in Ref. 46.
- Figure 9 depicts a circuit-switched *optical mesh* constructed by attaching electronically controlled optical switches to the processing nodes and interconnecting the switches in a mesh arrangement using optical fibers. Signals can be sent

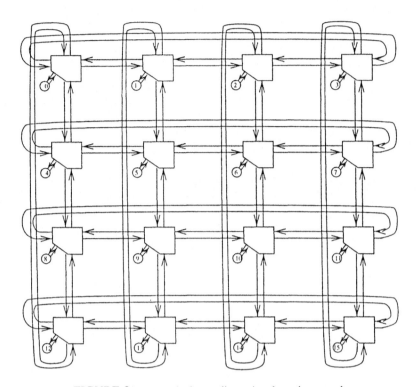

FIGURE 9   An optical two-dimensional mesh network.

between switch controllers using a mesh network that parallels the optical network and consists of low-bandwidth electronic links. The optical switches can be set to provide all-optical, TDM connections using a reservation protocol between the controllers, as described in Ref. 47.

- A hierarchical optical architecture based on the Fat-Tree network is proposed in Ref. 48. The *space–wavelength hierarchical architecture* (SWHA) places processing nodes at the leaves of a hierarchy and uses switches called *FatNodes* inside the hierarchy. A FatNode is a space–wavelength switch constructed from passive couplers and an acoustooptic tunable filter (AOTF). Signals from the processing nodes are sent up the hierarchy using WDM. At each level, the incoming signals are coupled. The AOTF then separates the wavelengths, switching them either up or down the hierarchy. A coupler at each level merges the signals switched back down the hierarchy with signals heading down from higher levels.

The number of wavelengths heading up/down the hierarchy can be reconfigured to meet the traffic requirements of the application and can provide increased bandwidth at the top of the hierarchy. Spatial reuse of wavelengths is achieved by partitioning wavelengths consistently at each level of the hierarchy. For example, a set of wavelengths can be reserved for communication between processing nodes joined by a level 1 FatNode. Because these wavelengths will never be switched to a level 2 FatNode, each group of processing nodes that communicates through a level 1 FatNode can use the same wavelengths without conflict.

Once the wavelengths have been partitioned at different levels of the hierarchy, each processor can be assigned a frequency on which to receive messages from processors communicating through each different level. Thus, each processor must have a receiver capable of receiving one wavelength per level of hierarchy. A fixed TWDM schedule can be constructed to provide each processor with a direct optical connection to every other processor connected through a given hierarchical level using a broadcast-and-select approach.

- Another way to interconnect a large number of nodes using passive star couplers is with the *partitioned optical passive star* (POPS) topology described in Ref. 49. As shown in Figure 10, the nodes are divided into g equal-sized groups. Transmitters from a group of nodes are connected to receivers in another group via a single passive star. Thus, communication between groups requires one dedicated transmitter and receiver at each node. Overall, each node requires g transmitters and receivers for communicating with each group, including its own. Complete interconnection of these g groups requires g^2 couplers. Communication takes place in time slots used alternately for control and data.

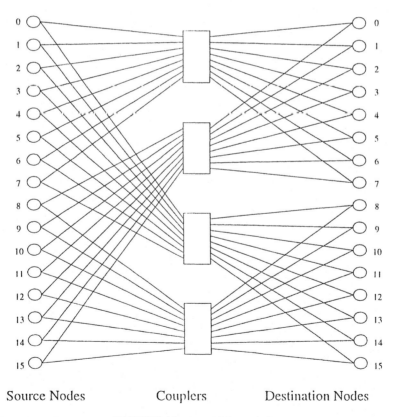

Source Nodes   Couplers   Destination Nodes

FIGURE 10   A POPS network.

A two-step procedure is used to establish connections dynamically. In the first step, each node submits a connection request to a controller node within the group. The group controller resolves contention for the use of the couplers through which the group transmits. The resolution of these conflicts can be arranged in a TDM cycle to reduce the frequency of request submissions to the group controller. The second step consists of an exchange of control information. The controllers simultaneously broadcast the intended use of the couplers to all nodes in each group. Each node examines the broadcasts to determine if it is the destination of multiple messages. The nodes resolve these destination conflicts and respond with status information indicating which node should be allowed to transmit.

The control protocol makes use of the broadcast capability of passive stars and exploits locality of references to reduce the frequency of control operations and to share the high bandwidth of the optical network.

- A power-optimal network built from interconnected passive stars is described in Ref. 50. Groups of log N transmitting nodes are connected to all N receiving nodes in a manner, based on addresses so that no two receivers hear identical sets of transmitters. To allow for a small number of transmitters and receivers at each node, extra stages of couplers are placed in the optical path to fan-out and fan-in the optical signals. Interconnections for all N nodes can be established in a power-optimal manner with three stages of couplers. A static TDM schedule is used to provide all-to-all communications.

Free-Space Optical Architectures

Within the confines of a parallel processor, optical signals need to travel only short distances in a carefully controlled environment free of dust and other particles. Thus, processors can exchange optical signals directly through free space. The emergence of smart pixel technology has given free-space architectures a boost by providing a signal processing capability not easily achieved through prior SLMs. Proposed architectures for free-space optical networks include the following:

- Small crossbar switches are the building blocks of multistage interconnection networks. A Banyan MIN built from 2×2 free-space optical switches is described in Ref. 51. Larger free-space crossbar switches that can be used to build MINs are described in Ref. 52. Both designs use birefringent computer-generated holograms which are sensitive to the polarization of light. The polarization of the input signals is adjusted by electronically controlled polarization modulators, thus affecting the path of the signal through the hologram and thereby switching the signal.
- The interconnection-cached network (ICN) described in Refs. 53 and 54 is one design for a large free-space interconnection network. This design is based on circuit boards which contain a cluster of processors. Within the cluster, an electronic crossbar network is used. Between clusters, an optical backbone network is used. The backbone provides a high data rate but is slow to reconfigure. Thus, the distribution of work to processors must take into account communication patterns between clusters of processors to avoid the need to reconfigure the backbone network.

As shown in Figure 11, circuit boards containing processors are stacked in

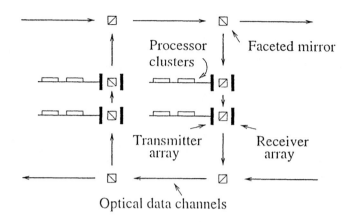

Optical data channels

FIGURE 11   The ICN architecture.

one or more columns. Each board is connected to an array of transmitters and an array of receivers. Optical signals traveling is a beam along a column are reflected to receivers by a faceted mirror. Similarly, transmitted signals can be inserted into the beam. At one end of the column, the beam is merged into a unidirectional ring that encompasses all columns, again using faceted mirror splitter/combiner cubes. At the other end of the column, a splitter cube is used to direct a portion of the beam into the column. A direct connection from any cluster to any other cluster is formed by a careful arrangement of the mirror facets and subarrays of transmitters and receivers used for each connection. Because the path from any VCSEL transmitter ends at a unique photodiode detector, an all-optical connection is provided between every pair of clusters.

• Smart pixels are used in the hyperplane and intelligent backplane designs described in Refs. 55 and 56. Each node in the network is electronically attached to a smart pixel array which serves as its interface to the optical backplane. The design looks much like Figure 4 without the need for an array of switches. The pixel arrays are arranged in a column, and signals are sent from one array to another in a daisy-chained fashion to form a unidirectional ring. A subarray of pixels is allocated to a communication channel, allowing parallel data transmission. Electronic logic in the pixel array determines the use of each channel. Signals may be injected from the node into the channel, extracted from the channel to the node, or retransmitted along the channel.

CONCLUSIONS

In the past decade, advances have been made in a wide range of areas related to the use of optics in interconnection networks. Developments have included new materials, fabrication techniques, devices, and the network architectures and control techniques that tie them all together. Electronic interconnection networks have been built with a wide range of architectures, and optical device capabilities can only increase the number of design options. It remains to be seen which device technologies can be developed to meet the cost, function, and performance requirements of practical parallel systems. In the meantime, electronic technologies will also improve, raising the bar for the introduction of optical interconnection networks.

For massively parallel processing to become commonplace, significant issues of cost, performance, and programmability must be addressed. Optical interconnection networks are likely to be successful to the extent that computing techniques in general are successful in exploiting the power of massive parallelism. Optical technology is capable of extending the size of usable parallel systems beyond that possible with electrical interconnections. Continued advances in this field will be necessary, however, before this potential can be realized.

REFERENCES

1. K. Hwang, *Advanced Computer Architecture*, McGraw-Hill, New York, 1993.
2. Fujitsu, marketing brochure, 1996.
3. Hitachi, marketing brochure, 1996.
4. NEC Corporation, marketing brochure, 1996.
5. IBM Corporation, http://ibm.tc.cornell.edu/ibm/pps.
6. Cray Research Inc., marketing brochure, 1996.
7. H. Arsenault and Y. Sheng, *An Introduction to Optics in Computers*, Tutorial Texts in Optical Engineering Vol. TT8, *Tutorial Texts in Optical Engineering*, SPIE Optical Engineering Press, Bellingham, WA, 1992.
8. H. Ozaktas, "Comparison of Fully Three-Dimensional Optical, Normally Conducting and Superconducting Interconnections," in *11th International Parallel Processing Symposium, Workshop on Optics and Computer Science*, IEEE Comp. Soc. Press, Los Alamitos, CA, April 1997 (only available on CD-ROM version).
9. D. A. B. Miller, "Optics of Low-Energy Communication Inside Digital Processors: Quantum Detectors, Sources and Modulators as Efficient Impedance Converters," *Opt. Lett.*, *14*(2), 146–148 (1989).
10. R. A. Nordin, A. F. J. Levi, R. N. Nottenburg, J. O'Gorman, T. Tanbun-Ek, and R. A. Logan, "A Systems Perspective on Digital Interconnection Technology," *J. Lightwave Technol.*, *10*(6), 811–827 (1992).
11. C. W. Stirk and J. Neff, "The Cost of Optical Interconnects vs. MCMs," in *Optics in Computing*, OSA Technical Digest Series, Vol. 8, Optical Society of America, Washington, DC, 1997, pp. 21–23.
12. P. Prucnal, I. Glesk, and J. Sokoloff, "Demonstration of All-Optical Self-Clocked Demultiplexing of TDM Data at 250 Gb/s," in *Proceedings of the First International Workshop on Massively Parallel Processing Using Optical Interconnections*, IEEE Comp. Soc. Press, Los Alamitos, CA, April 1994, pp. 106–117.
13. D. Feitelson, *Optical Computing: A Survey for Computer Scientists*, The MIT Press, Cambridge, MA, 1988.
14. *IEEE Commun. Mag.*, *27*(10) (1989), special issue on lightwave systems and components.
15. J. Powers, *An Introduction to Fiber Optic Systems*, 2nd ed., Irwin, Homewood, IL, 1997.
16. N. Berg and J. Pellegrino (eds.), *Acousto-optic Signal Processing*, 2nd ed., Marcel Dekker, Inc., New York, 1996.
17. H. Ghafouri-Shiraz and B. S. K. Lo, *Distributed Feedback Laser Diodes*, John Wiley & Sons, New York, 1996.
18. P. E. Green, Jr., *Fiber Optic Networks*. Prentice-Hall, Englewood Cliffs, NJ, 1993.

19. D. Spirit and M. O'Mahony (eds.), *High Capacity Optical Transmission Explained*. John Wiley and Sons, 1995.

20. T. Tamir, G. Griffel, and H. Bertoni (eds.), *Guided-Wave Optoelectronics*, Plenum Press, New York, 1995.

21. Y. Li and T. Wang, "Side-Coupling Polymer Fiber Optics for Optical Interconnections," in *Optics in Computing*, OSA Technical Digest Series, Vol. 8, Optical Society of America, Washington, DC, 1997, pp. 255–257.

22. H. Kobrinski and K.-W. Cheung, "Wavelength-Tunable Optical Filters: Applications and Technologies," *IEEE Commun. Mag.*, 27(10), 53–63 (1989).

23. I. Chang, "Acousto-Optic Tunable Filters," in *Acousto-optic Signal Processing*, 2nd ed., N. Berg and J. Pellegrino, Marcel Dekker, Inc., New York, 1996, pp. 139–167.

24. J. Zhou, J. He, and M. Cada, "Optimal Design of Combined Distributed-Feedback/Fabry–Perot Structures for Vertical Cavity Surface Emitting Semiconductor Lasers," in *Guided-Wave Optoelectronics*, edited by T. Tamir, G. Griffel, and H. Bertoni (eds.), Plenum Press, New York, 1995, pp. 75–81.

25. F. A. P. Tooley, "Challenges in Optically Interconnecting Electronics," *IEEE J. Selected Topics Quantum Electron.*, 2(1), 3–13 (1996).

26. L. Y. Lin, J. L. Shen, S. S. Lee, and M. C. Wu, "Surface-Micromachined Micro-XYZ Stages for Free-Space Micro-Optical Bench," *IEEE Photon. Technol. Lett.*, 9(3), 345–347 (1997).

27. A. Ghatak and K. Thyagarajan, *Optical Electronics*, Cambridge University Press, Cambridge, 1989.

28. D. Lahaut and C. Germain, "Static Communications in Parallel Scientific Programs," in *PARLE '94 Parallel Architecture and Languages*, Springer-Verlag, Berlin, July 1994.

29. M. Welsh, A. Basu, and T. von Eicken, "ATM and Fast Ethernet Network Interfaces for User-Level Communication," in *Proceedings of the 3rd International Symposium on High Performance Computer Architecture, HPCA '97*, IEEE Comp. Soc. Press, Los Alamitos, CA, February 1997, pp. 332–342.

30. R. Weverka, K. Wagner, R. McLeod, K. Wu, and C. Garvin, "Low-Loss Acousto-Optic Photonic Switch," in *Acousto-optic Signal Processing*, 2nd ed., N. Berg and J. Pellegrino (eds.), Marcel Dekker, Inc., New York, 1996, pp. 479–573.

31. A. V. Krishnamoorthy, J. E. Ford, R. W. Goosen, J. A. Walker, B. Tseng, S. P. Hui, J. E. Cunningham, W. Y. Jan, T. K. Woodward, M. C. Nuss, R. G. Rozier, F. E. Kiamilev, and D. A. B. Miller, "The Amoeba Chip: An Optoelectronic Switch for Multiprocessor Networking Using Dense-wdm," in *Proceedings of the Third International Conference on Massively Parallel Processing Using Optical Interconnections*, IEEE Comp. Soc. Press, Los Alamitos, CA, October 1996, pp. 94–100.

32. I. Glesk and P. Prucnal, "Demonstration of 250 gb/s All-Optical Routing Control of a Phonotic Crossbar Switch," in *Guided-Wave Optoelectronics*, edited by T. Tamir, G. Griffel, and H. Bertoni (eds.), Plenum Press, New York, 1995, pp. 25–33.

33. C. A. Brackett, "Dense Wavelength Division Multiplexing Networks: Principles and Applications," *IEEE J. Selected Areas Commun.*, 8(6), 948–964 (1990).

34. I. Chlamtac and A. Ganz, "Channel Allocation Protocols in Frequency-Time Controlled High Speed Networks," *IEEE Trans. Commun.*, 36(4), 430–440 (1988).

35. D. M. Chiarulli, S. P. Levitan, R. G. Melhem, and C. Qiao, "Locality Based Control Algorithms for Reconfigurable Optical Interconnection Networks," *Appl. Opt.*, 33, 1528–1537 (1994).

36. J. Li and M. Chen, "Compiling Communication-Efficient Programs for Massively Parallel Machines," *IEEE Trans. Parallel Distrib. Syst.*, 2(3), 361–375 (1991).

37. C. Qiao and R. Melhem, "Reconfiguration with Time Division Multiplexing MINs for Multiprocessor Communications," *IEEE Trans. Parallel Distrib. Syst.*, 5(4), 337–352 (1994).

38. P. Dowd, "Wavelength Division Multiple Access Channel Hypercube Processor Interconnection," *IEEE Trans. Computers*, 42(10), 1223–1241 (1992).

39. B. Mukherjee, "WDM-Based Local Lightwave Networks Part i: Single-Hop Systems," *IEEE Network*, 6(3), 12–27 (1992).

40. B. Mukherjee, "WDM-Based Local Lightwave Networks Part ii: Multihop Systems," *IEEE Network*, 6(4), 20–31 (1992).

41. R. Chamberlain and R. Krchnavek, "Architectures for Optically Interconnected Multicomputers," in *GLOBECOM '93: Proceedings of the IEEE Global Telecommunication Conference*, IEEE, November 1993, pp. 1181–1186.

42. K. A. Williams, T. Q. Dam, and D. H.-C. Du, "A Media-Access Protocol for Time- and Wavelength-Division Multiplexed Passive Star Networks," *IEEE J. Selected Areas Commun.*, 11(4), 560–567 (1993).

43. G. Liu, K. Lee, and H. Jordan, "*n*-Dimensional Processor Arrays with Optical dBuses," in *Proceedings of the Second International Workshop on Massively Parallel Processing Using Optical Interconnections*, IEEE Comp. Soc. Press, Los Alamitos, CA, October 1995, pp. 116–123.

44. R. Thompson, "The Dilated Slipped Banyan Switching Network Architecture for Use in an All Optical Local Area Network," *IEEE J. Lightwave Technol.*, 9(12), 1780–1787 (1991).

45. Z. Guo, R. Melhem, R. Hall, D. Chiarulli, and S. Levitan, "Pipelined Communication in Optically Interconnected Arrays," *J. Parallel Distrib. Comput.*, 12, 269–281 (1991).

46. C. Salisbury, R. Melhem, and C. Qiao, "Distributed Path Management in Switched Optical Banyan Networks," in *Optics in Computing*, OSA Technical Digest Series, Vol. 8, Optical Society of America, Washington, DC, 1997, pp. 195–197.

47. X. Yuan, R. Melhem, and R. Gupta, "Compiled Communication for All-Optical TDM Networks," in *Supercomputing '96*, IEEE Comp. Soc. Press, Los Alamitos, CA, November 1996.

48. P. Dowd, K. Bogineni, K. Aly, and J. Perreault, "Hierarchical Scalable Photonic Architectures for High-Performance Processor Interconnection," *IEEE Trans. Computers*, 42(9), 1105–1120 (1993).

49. D. M. Chiarulli, S. P. Levitan, R. G. Melhem, J. P. Teza, and G. Gravenstreter, "Partitioned Optical Passive Star (POPS) Multiprocessor Interconnection Networks with Distributed Control," *J. Lightwave Technol.*, 14(7), 1601–1612 (1996).

50. Y. Birk, "Power-Optimal Layout of Passive, Single-Hop, Fiber-Optic Interconnections Whose Capacity Increases with the Number of Stations," in *INFOCOM '93: 12th Joint Conference of the Computer and Communication Societies*, IEEE Comp. Soc. Press, Los Alamitos, CA, March 1993, pp. 565–572.

51. D. M. Marom, P. Shames, F. Xu, R. R. Rao, and Y. Fainman, "Compact Free-Space Multistage Interconnection Network Demonstration," in *Optics in Computing*, OSA Technical Digest Series, Vol. 8, Optical Society of America, Washington, DC, 1997, pp. 192–194.

52. N. Cohen, D. Mendlovic, B. Leibner, and E. Marom, "Folded Architecture for Modular All-Optical Switch," in *11th International Parallel Processing Symposium, Workshop on Optics and Computer Science*, IEEE Comp. Soc. Press, Los Alamitos, CA, April 1997 (only available on CD-ROM version).

53. S. Araki, M. Katija, K. Kasahara, K. Kubota, K. Kurihara, I. Redmond, E. Schenfeld, and T. Suzaki, "Experimental Free-Space Optical Network for Massively Parallel Computers," *Appl. Opt.*, 35(8), 1269–81 (1996) .

54. Y. Lyuu and E. Schenfeld, "MICA, a Mapped Interconnection-Cached Architecture," *Proc. of Frontiers of Massively Parallel Computation*, IEEE Comp. Soc. Press, Los Alamitos, CA, 1995, pp. 80–89.

55. H. Hinton and T. Szymanski, "Intelligent Optical Backplanes," in *Proceedings of the Second International Workshop on Massively Parallel Processing Using Optical Interconnections*, IEEE Comp. Soc. Press, Los Alamitos, CA, October 1995, pp. 133–143.

56. T. Szymanski and H. Hinton, "Design of a Terabit Free-Space Photonic Backplane for Paral-

lel Computing," in *Proceedings of the Second International Workshop on Massively Parallel Processing Using Optical Interconnections*, IEEE Comp. Soc. Press, Los Alamitos, CA, October 1995, pp. 16–27.

57. W. B. Leigh (ed.), *Devices for Optoelectronics*, Marcel Dekker, Inc., New York, 1996.

CHARLES SALISBURY

RAMI MELHEM

.

MEASURING THE STRENGTH OF CRYPTOSYSTEMS

INTRODUCTION

Modern communication networks such as the Internet are vulnerable to attack. In many cases, it is a relatively easy task for a hacker to eavesdrop on communications. To prevent such attacks, it may be necessary to provide confidentiality of information. It may also be required to provide mechanisms to ensure the integrity of information and a method for users to sign electronic documents. Finally, there may be a need for users to prove their identity before they gain access to computer networks. Cryptography is the method used to secure networks by providing such mechanisms using encryption algorithms (ciphers). These algorithms are combined together in a security architecture. The complete system, including the algorithm, architectures, and key management procedure, is called a cryptosystem. The aim of this article is to describe methods for measuring the security of cryptosystems.

The basic tool of cryptography is a cipher. A cipher consists of encrypting and decrypting operations used to transform plaintext into ciphertext and back again, respectively. Also, a cipher has secret information (key) shared by two users. The encryption operation, E, of a cipher transforms a message, M, into a cryptogram, C, under the influence of an encryption key, K. This can be represented as $E(P, K) = C$. The decryption operation, D, of a cipher transforms C back to M under the influence of a decryption key K'. This can be represented as $D(C, K') = P$.

Although the aim of a cryptographer is to design strong ciphers, the objective of the cryptanalyst is to find techniques to overcome this security. The aim of the cryptanalyst may be to find meaning in an intercepted cryptogram obtained from wiretapping. Other objectives of an attacker may be concerned with inserting modifications into a message or masquerading as a legitimate user.

Over the past 200 years, efficient techniques for attacking ciphers have evolved. This is especially the case in the last 50 years with the development of high-speed computers which may allow for fast, exhaustive key attacks, sophisticated mathematical attacks, or fully automated attacks on cryptograms using statistical analysis.

In measuring the security of a cipher, the following are usually assumed:

1. The cryptanalyst has a complete knowledge of the cipher system, so the security depends entirely on the strength of the algorithm and the secrecy of the key.
2. The cryptanalyst has obtained the cryptogram.
3. The cryptanalyst knows the plaintext equivalent of some ciphertext (i.e., known plaintext attack).

In addition, it may be assumed that the cryptanalyst has obtained ciphertext from plaintext selected by the attacker. This is referred to as the case of a chosen plaintext attack. In this case, the cryptanalyst may have the assistance of an insider.

Ciphers are classified as either symmetric or asymmetric. In symmetric ciphers, the encryption and decryption keys are equal, or one can be easily deduced from the other. In this case, the legitimate sender and receiver of the cryptogram hold the same secret information. There are two types of symmetric ciphers, namely block and stream ciphers.

In a symmetric block cipher, the plaintext is divided into blocks of equal length. Each block, P, is then encrypted using the same key, K, to form a ciphertext block, $C = E(P, K)$, for transmission. In this transformation, each ciphertext bit should be a Boolean function of all the bits of the corresponding plaintext block as well as all the bits of the key. At the receiving end, the ciphertext block is decrypted using the same key, $P = E^{-1}(C, K)$ (or a key which can easily be deduced from the encryption key). This process is outlined in Figure 1. It should be noted that, in practice, blocks are "chained" together by adding modulo 2 the previous ciphertext block to the plaintext before encryption. This prevents attacks based on a building up a dictionary of commonly used blocks. The most commonly used symmetric cipher is the Data Encryption Standard (DES) algorithm (1). The DES has a block length of 64 bits and a key length of 56 bits.

Stream ciphers encrypt each symbol (bit, byte, etc.) in the plaintext, in turn. The state of the cipher changes after each symbol transformation, so that the same symbol recurring in the plaintext may produce different ciphertext characters. In the most commonly used stream cipher, the plaintext is divided into bits. Let $p(t)$ denote the tth term of the binary plaintext stream. A binary keystream is produced by a pseudorandom or random number generator, denoted by $z(t)$. The ciphertext bit, $c(t)$, is produced by the exclusive- or combination of $p(t)$ and $z(t)$. The receiver decrypts by producing the same keystream $z(t)$ and exclusive-oring with $c(t)$ to recover $p(t)$. This process is outlined in Figure 2.

In the case where $z(t)$ is produced by a purely random process, a stream cipher is called a *Vernam one-time pad*. Otherwise, the keystream is pseudorandom, produced by a deterministic process. The pseudorandom generator is usually run with some initial seed. This seed can be regarded as the key for the stream cipher.

Asymmetric, or public key, ciphers have different keys for encryption and decryption, and it is computationally infeasible to derive at least one of the keys from knowledge of the other. In this case, "computationally" infeasible indicates that the operation is theoretically possible but would require an enormous amount of time and space using massive computer power. In public key ciphers, the sender and receiver need not share

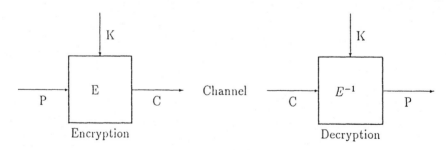

FIGURE 1   Block cipher.

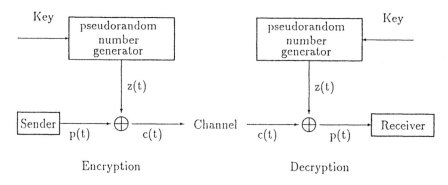

FIGURE 2   Stream cipher.

the same secret knowledge in order to communicate securely. This provides a method to exchange keys for symmetric ciphers as well as a method to form verifiable digital signatures and one-time passwords to access networks.

In a public key cipher, let $PK(A)$ and $SK(A)$ denote a person A's public and secret key pair, respectively. A standard application of such a system in a communications network is to store a copy of $PK(A)$, together with a *certificate*, in a public directory. The certificate is a copy of $PK(A)$ plus A's identity, which has been digitally signed by some widely trusted entity, and it prevents an attacker from replacing $PK(A)$ with a different public key. One use of the public key cipher is then to exchange keys as follows:

1. B selects key K.
2. B looks up A's public key, $PK(A)$, in the directory.
3. B encrypts K using $PK(A)$ [i.e., $E(K, PK(A)) = C$].
4. B transmits C to A over an insecure channel.
5. A decrypts C using $SK(A)$ [i.e., $D(C, SK(A)) = K$].

It should be noted that in practice, a key-exchange protocol will require additional mechanisms to prevent replay of old keys and to allow authentication of the key's origin.

Another use of public key ciphers is to form digital signatures as follows:

- Signature by Person A
  1. A forms the hash value of m, $f(m)$.
  2. A encrypts $f(m)$ using secret key $SK(A)$ to form signature, s [i.e., $s = E(f(m), SK(A))$].
  3. A transmits m and s to B.
- Verification by Person B
  1. B forms hash value $f(m)$.
  2. B looks up A's public key, $PK(A)$, in the directory.
  3. B forms $D(s, PK(A))$ and checks if this value is $f(m)$. If true, then B accepts A's signature.

It should be noted that in addition a one-way hash function is usually required. A hash function is a function that inputs an arbitrary-length string and outputs a fixed-length string, the hash value. A one-way hash function is a hash function in which it is easy to compute the hash value but is hard to generate a message that hashes to a particular value. Commonly used one-way hash functions are MD5 (2) and SHA (3), which have a hash length of 128 and 160 bits, respectively.

In measuring the security of a cryptosystem, one needs to examine both the ciphers and the protocols which are used in the design. A *communications protocol* is a set of rules which determines the possible messages which each entity involved is able to send, as well as the format of those messages. A *cryptographic protocol* is a communications protocol in which cryptography is used to allow entities to deduce security properties about other entities or certain messages that are sent or received. A familiar example of a communications protocol might be one used to send electronic mail. The protocol will include specifications of the fields that should be in the message header and their formats. A cryptographic mail protocol might add encryption to hide the contents and subject line of messages, or allow authentication of the sender's identity.

MODELS FOR MEASURING THE SECURITY OF CIPHERS

There are two models which are used to measure the security of ciphers. The first is an information-theoretic model from Shannon (4), namely the concept of *perfect security*. A cipher is said to offer perfect security (or be unconditionally secure) if observation of the ciphertext provides no information about the plaintext or key to an attacker. Shannon showed, for perfect secrecy, that a cipher requires the key size to be at least as large as the message. An example of such a scheme is the Vernam one-time pad.

In analyzing the problems concerned with the theoretical secrecy of a cipher system, Shannon (4) shows that information may be conveniently measured by means of entropy. Entropy may be defined as the amount of information required to reproduce the message, or as a measure of uncertainty.

Given a set of possibilities with probabilities $p_1, p_2, \ldots, p_n$, the entropy H is given by

$$H = -\Sigma \, p_i \log_2 p_i. \tag{1}$$

The average amount of information obtained when a message M is chosen, $H(M)$, is given as $H(M) = -\Sigma \, P(M) \log_2 P(M)$, the summation being over all possible messages with positive probability. Similarly, there is an entropy (uncertainty) associated with the choice of the key, $H(K)$, given by $H(K) = -\Sigma \, P(K) \log_2 P(K)$. In a perfect system in which the number of messages, keys, and cryptograms are all equal to the same value n, then the amount of information in the message is at most $\log_2 n$ and occurs when all messages are equiprobable. In the case of a binary message of length L, $n = 2^L$ and the amount of information is $\log_2 2^L = L$. The amount of information in the message can be concealed completely only if the key uncertainty is at least $\log_2 n$, as the amount of uncertainty we can introduce into the solution cannot be greater than the key uncertainty (4). For a cipher system with a finite key, it is desirable to maximize the length of the intercepted cryptogram that is required before the uncertainty about the message is reduced close to zero. In practice, this cannot be achieved to any great extent due to the inherent redundancy in languages, even when compression algorithms are applied.

The second model for measuring the security of a cipher is that of computational security. Computational security is measured in relation to the number of operations needed to break the cipher. We measure these operations in relation to both the time and space complexity required. We may also consider the amount of money required to build the hardware necessary to conduct such an attack on the cipher. For example, we might consider the cost for building special-purpose hardware and time required to conduct an exhaustive key search attack on a symmetric block cipher.

Another approach to computational security is to measure the security in relation to the solution of a difficult mathematical problem. For example, many of the public key ciphers are measured in relation to the difficulty of factoring integers which are the product of two large primes. It should be noted that many of the ciphers in this class are sometimes called provably secure. In most cases, this is incorrect, as a cipher is said to be provably secure only if the difficulty of attacking the system is equivalent to solving some well-known problem. Most public keys ciphers are not provably secure because there may be another more efficient method (yet unknown) for breaking the algorithm which does not require the solution of this hard problem.

In general, when describing the security of a cipher, we can only give some practical ad hoc measures based on perceived resources of an adversary and available techniques for attacking the algorithm. These clearly change over time, owing to the design of cheaper and more efficient computer resources as well as the creation of new techniques for attacking particular algorithms.

MEASURING THE STRENGTH OF STREAM CIPHERS

The security of a stream cipher depends on the keystream. If the keystream is a one-time pad, then the cipher is unconditionally secure. However, in this case, the size of the key shared by the receiver and sender needs to be as long as the actual message. In most commercial communications systems, this is not practical. Instead, the keystream is produced by a pseudorandom number generator. The goal in designing a secure pseudorandom number generator is to produce a sequence which has the appearance of a random sequence. There are five measures which are commonly used to analyze the level of security of such a keystream generator:

- Key length
- Period
- Linear complexity
- Vulnerability to statistical attack
- Vulnerability to correlation attack

The key for a pseudorandom number generator is usually defined to be the initial seed. If the length of this seed is n, then the total number of keys is 2^n. In certain cases, the actual Boolean function used to form the keystream may be kept secret also. If this is the case, it may be possible to greatly strengthen the cipher from an exhaustive key attack.

In general, a pseudorandom number generator is deterministic and ultimately periodic. The period, p, of the keystream is the smallest number such that $z(t) = z(t + p)$ for all t greater than or equal to some fixed constant integer T (many pseudorandom streams may have some initial nonperiodic terms at the start). The value of p should be large (i.e., much greater than the length of any cryptogram). Otherwise, if the keystream repeats itself, it may be possible to perform automated ciphertext attacks on the cryptogram by combining two sections of the same cryptogram, or different cryptograms which have been encrypted using the same part of the keystream (5). Such an attack was proposed in Ref. 6, using the redundancy of the plaintext, and a fully automated attack, based on the knowledge of the plaintext statistics only (7), has been shown to be successful. In fact, to avoid such attacks, any large subsection of the keystream should not be repeated.

Two methods for analyzing keystreams for repetitions of large substrings are the autocorrelation test and the Ziv–Lempel complexity measure. The autocorrelation test compares a binary string with a shifted version of itself. This can be used to define a statistic (8) to measure any periodic behavior within a string. The Ziv–Lempel complexity measure, which is used in data compression (9), examines the number of new patterns in a string. If the number of new patterns is too small, then this could indicate the existence of repetitions.

Any periodic sequence satisfies a unique linear recurrence relation of shortest length. The length of this linear recurrence relation is the linear complexity of the sequence. If the linear complexity is L, then given $2L$ consecutive terms of the sequence, it is possible to reconstruct the entire sequence by finding the recurrence relation. There is a fast algorithm to do this reconstruction, namely the Berlekamp–Massey algorithm (10). Upon gaining any portion of the keystream, a cryptanalyst would naturally seek to determine the linear complexity, L, and the corresponding recurrence relation of the stream. Knowledge of the recurrence relation will then enable the cryptanalyst to produce the complete keystream and hence decrypt the entire intercepted cryptogram. Because it would require knowledge of $2L$ terms of the sequence to gain this information, the linear complexity of the keystream should be large in order to avoid this attack.

If the distribution of zeros and ones in the keystream is not random, it contains a redundancy which causes leakage of information in the ciphertext. An attacker may be able to use this information to attack an intercepted cryptogram. In order to be assured that such attacks are not feasible, we need to study sample keystreams for vulnerability to a statistical attack. Empirical tests may be applied to sample keystreams to test for local randomness. If a keystream of length n is analyzed, the measures that are applied test the hypothesis that this string was based on n Bernoulli trials (11) with the probability of obtaining a one on each trial being $\frac{1}{2}$. Several statistical test have been designed for testing this hypothesis. These include tests on the following: uniformity of bits (frequency test) and uniformity of subblocks (poker test); uniformity of overlapping subblocks (binary derivative or serial test); distribution of runs; subblock repetitions (repetition test); and subblock memory (universal test). A description of these tests can be found in Refs. 8 and 12. It should be noted that these tests are black-box procedures, in that to apply them, only the output of the keystream generator is required. It is not necessary to know the format of the actual generator.

The design of many keystream generators involves the combination of simpler systems (see Refs. 13 and 14), where a different component of the key is used to seed each subsystem. In such designs, it may be possible to conduct the so-called divide-and-conquer correlation attacks (15). The correlation coefficient between two binary variables A and B is defined by $c = 2p - 1$, where p is the probability that A and B are distinct, and $1 - p$ is called the correlation probability. If the correlation probability between two binary variables A and B is $\frac{1}{2}$, then their correlation coefficient is zero. This means that knowing one of the variables gives no information about the other one. But if p is not $\frac{1}{2}$, then there is information leakage between two binary variables. The essence of divide-and-conquer correlation attacks is to use this information leakage to conduct attacks on each of the input systems. These attacks may determine the seed of each component independently of the other components. In certain cases, it may be possible to conduct such attacks using knowledge of ciphertext alone (15). In other cases, it may be possible to replace the actual generator with another one which is a close approximation and which may provide simple methods to attack (13). Both basic (15) and fast (16) correlation attacks have been designed. The attacks are successful only if the correlation coefficient is large enough in magnitude. This value provides another measure of the security of a keystream generator.

MEASURING THE STRENGTH OF SYMMETRIC BLOCK CIPHERS

After the design and widespread usage of the DES algorithm, many new techniques for attacking block ciphers have been developed, and new block ciphers have been designed to overcome these attacks. There are three different methods for measuring the security of a symmetric block cipher, namely:

- Size of key
- Black-box analysis
- Analysis of algorithm

In 1977, Diffie and Hellman (17) argued that it may be possible to build a machine at a cost of $20,000,000 (U.S. dollars) that could exhaustively search for all DES keys and find the correct key in 1 day given a small number of known plaintext–ciphertext pairs of blocks. They also argued that the cost of this machine would decrease rapidly with time. In 1993, Wiener (18) demonstrated that the building of such a machine was now feasible. The rapid development in electronic devices over the previous 16 years meant that such a machine could now be built relatively inexpensively. Wiener's estimate for the costs in U.S. dollars and the time to complete the attack are given in Table 1.

Several of the new ciphers which have been proposed recently, such as the IDEA cipher (19), have a larger key size which should prevent such exhaustive key search attacks. Also, it is possible to enhance the security of an existing symmetric block cipher such as the DES algorithm by using multiple encryption. Under the principle of multiple encryption, there are several keys. A plaintext block is encrypted using the first key, the resulting block is then encrypted using the second key, and so forth. If two keys are used in double encryption, there is a time—memory trade-off which, effectively, reduces the number of keys the cryptanalyst needs to try, to the same number of keys as in a single key attack (20), provided the attacker has a suitability large storage space available. In

TABLE 1   Cost and Key Search Time for Wiener's Machine

Key search machine cost	Expected search time
$100,000	35 h
$1,000,000	3.5 h
$10,000,000	21 min

order to prevent such an attack, one can use triple encryption with either two or three keys (21).

There is an increasing trend to use block ciphers known only to the designers. Also, the cost of conducting an in-depth analysis of a new design can be very expensive. The designers and users of both publicly available block ciphers and proprietary algorithms need a systematic method to examine these systems prior to using them to raise their confidence that they are secure from cryptanalytic attack, within at least commercial bounds.

Black-box techniques, such as those described in Ref. 8, provide a method to conduct a preliminary analysis of block ciphers. These tests are black box in that to apply them, knowledge of the actual encryption algorithm is not required. All that is needed is an implementation of the cipher, either executable code or a hardware version, which allows one to input keys, and plaintext blocks and obtain output ciphertext blocks. There are several important properties of a block cipher that can be analyzed in this fashion. These include the following:

Completeness: A block cipher is said to be complete if, in an output ciphertext block, each ciphertext bit depends on all of the plaintext bits of an input block. Each ciphertext bit should depend on all the bits of the key.

Independence of plaintext and ciphertext blocks: The ciphertext blocks should appear to be independent of the plaintext blocks. For example, highly patterned plaintext blocks should output random ciphertext blocks.

Randomness of block differences: There are several relationships which can be measured in terms of differences of ciphertext blocks brought about by changes in plaintext blocks. First, there are the plaintext and key avalanche effects. A block cipher satisfies the plaintext (key) avalanche effect if a one-bit change in the plaintext (key) results in an average of one-half of the ciphertext bits changing (22). These are properties which a block cipher should have. Another property based on block differences which we do *not* want a block cipher to satisfy is the complementation property. This property states that for all plaintext blocks P and all keys K, given $C = E(P, K)$, then $C' = E(P', K')$, where C', P', and K' are the complements of C, P, and K, respectively. If a cipher satisfies the complementation property, then it may be possible to conduct an exhaustive key attack by searching one-half of the key space. It is known that DES satisfies this property. However, this is not regarded as a serious weakness.

Linear relationships: In general, a block cipher should not determine linear relationships which can be exploited by an attacker. There are several linear relationships that we can analyze using black-box techniques. First, we can determine if the block cipher is affine. A block cipher with block length n is said to be affine if for each key there exists an $n \times n$ matrix A and a binary column vector B of length n such that

$$C = AP + B$$

for all plaintext–ciphertext pairs of blocks (P, C). It is possible to attack an affine cipher given $n + 1$ known plaintext–ciphertext pairs. Also, we can determine if there are any linear relationships defined in subblocks of input and output bits. Such relationships would assist an attacker.

It should be noted that the black-box techniques provide a first-step sieve. These provide an inexpensive method for analyzing a block cipher. A cipher which fails any one of these tests should, in most cases, be regarded as insecure. However, in order to obtain a better understanding of the security of a block cipher, it is necessary to undertake an in-depth analysis of the actual algorithm.

Two important methods of analyzing block ciphers which depend on knowing complete details of the algorithm are differential (23) and linear (24) cryptanalysis. Differential cryptanalysis is a chosen plaintext attack which examines pairs of plaintext blocks whose "difference" is fixed. The resulting "differences" in ciphertext blocks is called a characteristic. From the examination of the algorithm, plaintext differences are selected which give characteristics that have a higher probability of occurring. Differential cryptanalysis uses these characteristics to assign probabilities to probable keys, and, eventually, the correct key is found, provided sufficient pairs are examined. In the case of the DES algorithm, the best characteristic requires 2^{47} chosen plaintext pairs in order to find the correct key.

Linear cryptanalysis examines the probability that the exclusive-or sum of certain plaintext and ciphertext bits is equal to the exclusive-or sum of certain key bits. The attack relies on finding bit positions which give a probability, p, such that $|p - \frac{1}{2}|$ is far from $\frac{1}{2}$. The attack is a known plaintext attack. The bit positions giving the best probabilities are found by examination of the algorithm. In the case of the DES algorithm, Matsui conducted such an attack to recover the correct key using 2^{43} plaintext–ciphertext pairs of blocks. This attack required the use of 12 HP9735/PA—RISC 99Mhz computers taking 50 days (25).

MEASURING THE STRENGTH OF KEY GENERATORS

Besides the strength of the encryption algorithms, the security of cryptographic devices used in large communication networks such as the Internet depends on the secrecy of the keys used. Cryptographic keys may be generated by using hardware devices or by using software that includes pseudorandom algorithms (26,27). It is important that the hardware or software devices that are employed to generate these keys be tested periodically to ensure the randomness of the output blocks. An attacker may find it easier to determine the key used in encryption by searching a small set of possible keys than to investigate any possible weakness in the cipher. For example, a potentially serious flaw was discovered in the key generation process for the Netscape Navigator (28) that reduced the key space to far below the 128 bits allowed. Hence, it is of fundamental importance that the method of generating the keys is itself secure. In general, there are two steps involved in key generation for symmetric ciphers:

1. An initial seed is selected from some random process.
2. The initial seed is input into a one-way function whose output is the key.

It should be noted that the entropy of the key generation procedure is derived from Step 1. A one-way function, such as a hash function, does not increase the actual entropy.

To generate initial seeds, either especially built hardware devices such as a random-bit generator (29) or software are used. A hardware device, in general, offers a secure method for seed generation. However, this is more expensive than a software-based solution. A popular approach to seeding using software has been to gather information from a system clock, other system identification numbers, or the timing between external events (e.g., keystrokes or mouse movements). Unfortunately, such procedures have been found to obtain a limited number of variable values for the seed and may provide insufficient unpredictability (26).

There are two methods for measuring the security of a key generation procedure. If the actual technique used is known, it may be possible to conduct an in-depth analysis of the procedure and to identify any weakness. This was the case in the analysis of the key generation process for the Netscape Navigator (28). On the other hand, the designers may wish to keep the key generation process secret from the actual users. In this case, it is necessary to apply black-box techniques to measure the entropy of the key generation process. Such methods are described in Ref. 30. These testing procedures only require the output keys from the key generator.

The most powerful of the methods in Ref. 30 is the repetition test. The repetition test provides a method to approximate the actual entropy in the key generator. This test relies on an application of the birthday paradox (31); that is, if we generate a sample of K random keys from a total possible N keys and if K is approximately $\sqrt{N}$, then the probability of at least one repetition is 0.5. As K increases, then there should be more than one repetition. If K is approximately $8\sqrt{N}$, then the number of repetitions should follow a Normal distribution with mean 32 and variance 32 (8). An example of the application of this procedure would be when we find 100 repetitions in a sample of 1,000,000 keys. In this case, we can say with a probability exceeding 0.995 that the true entropy of the key is less than 34 bits, irrespective of the actual key length.

Although the repetition test is useful in measuring the entropy of a key generator, there are computational limitations to its use, depending on the storage capacity and speed of the computer used in applying the procedure. For example, to show that the entropy is 40 bits, a sample of approximately 8,000,000 keys would be required for storage and sorting.

MEASURING THE STRENGTH OF PUBLIC KEY CIPHERS

The security of public key ciphers is determined in relation to the difficulty of solving for the secret key from knowledge of the public key. In general, this is measured in relation to the difficulty of solving a particular mathematical problem. The most commonly used public key ciphers are the RSA algorithm, which is based on the integer factorization problem, and a set of related ciphers based on the discrete logarithm problem.

The RSA algorithm was designed by Rivest, Shamir, and Adleman (32). The procedure used in the RSA algorithm for key generation, encryption, and decryption is given below.

RSA Algorithm

Key Generation
- Select two large primes p and q.
- Select e relatively prime to $(p - 1)(q - 1)$.
- Compute d, where $ed = 1 \bmod (p - 1)(q - 1)$.
- Public key e, n.
- Secret key d.

TABLE 2 Factoring Records

Year	No. of decimal digits
1983	71
1985	80
1988	90
1989	100
1993	120
1994	129
1996	130

Encryption
- Plaintext message block $m < n$
- Ciphertext message block $c = m^e \bmod n$

Decryption
- $m = c^d \bmod n$

The security of the RSA algorithm depends on the difficulty of factoring a large integer which is the product of two large primes. Over the past few years, there has been a dramatic improvement in factoring. This is shown in Table 2, which lists the largest "difficult" number factored in a given year as reported in the open literature. This improvement in factoring techniques has been brought about by the design of more powerful computers and more efficient factoring algorithms. For many years, the most powerful factoring algorithms was the quadratic sieve (33), which was responsible for most of the factorizations referred to in Table 2. Recently, a new algorithm called the number field sieve (34) has proven to be even better. Both of these algorithms can be implemented in parallel by the use of massively parallel computers or the use of large computer networks, such as the Internet using the idle time of computers.

Many applications of public key cryptography may require a very long period of security. For example, digital signatures may be needed to be kept secure for a period of 50 years. In order to provide this level of security, one should select numbers for RSA with a very large modulus. For example, Table 3 gives recommended modulus sizes in bits for the RSA algorithm.

The discrete log ciphers are based on the difficulty of solving the discrete log

TABLE 3 Recommended Public Key Lengths (in Bits)

Year	vs. Individual	vs. Corporation	vs. Government
1995	768	1280	1536
2000	1024	1280	1536
2005	1280	1536	2048
2010	1280	1536	2048
2015	1536	2048	2048

Source: Ref. 35.

problem over some finite set. Let G denote a finite set and $*$ a binary operation defined on G which is closed (i.e., for x and y in G, then $x * y$ belongs to G). We use the standard exponential notation where for integer n, x^n means $x * x * \cdots * x$ (where there are n, x's). Over G, then, the discrete log problem is: Given x and y, find integer n such that $y = x^n$. Several different encryption algorithms have been designed based on the difficulty of solving the discrete log problem, including the Diffie–Hellman algorithm (17) and ElGamal cryptosystem (36). It should be noted that the ElGamal cryptosystem is the analog of the RSA algorithm in that both algorithms can be used for encryption as well as providing digital signatures.

For the discrete log ciphers, various choices of the finite set G have been proposed, including the integers modulo a large prime, Galois fields $GF(2^n)$, and the points on an elliptic curve (see Ref. 37). Over a large prime, solving the discrete log problem has a similar level of difficulty of factoring an integer of the same size. Hence, the ElGamal cipher defined over a large prime offers the same level of security as the RSA algorithm over a modulus of equivalent size. On the other hand, the discrete log ciphers over an elliptic curve, depending on the choice of the curve (38), offer a higher level of security.

MEASURING THE STRENGTH OF ONE-WAY HASH FUNCTIONS

As was mentioned in the Introduction, the security of digital signatures depends on both the security of the public key cipher and the one-way hash function used. The security of a one-way hash function is measured primarily in relation to the degree by which the algorithm is collision-free. A hash function is said to be strongly collision-free if it is computationally difficult to find two messages which result in the same hash value. The difficulty of finding such collisions is measured, first, in relation to the number of bits produced in the hash value. By the birthday paradox, if the number of bits is n, then an attacker would need to hash on the average about $2^{n/2}$ messages before discovering two messages which have the same hash value. As pointed out in Ref. 39, these changes to a message could be very slight and not easily detectable. In order to avoid such an attack, most hash functions are usually designed with a hash value of at least 128 bits. To conduct such an attack, in this case, would require that one evaluates, stores, and then sorts 2^{64} hash values. This is regarded as an intractable problem using current technology.

A second measure of the difficulty of finding collisions depends on the strength of the one-way hash algorithm. There may be a weakness in the design which an attacker can exploit to find collisions which require testing far less than $2^{n/2}$ messages for collisions. For example, Dobbertin (40) recently demonstrated how to attack the MD4 hash function (41) due to a weakness in the internal design of the algorithm. This attack required, on the average, testing 2^{20} messages for a collision instead of 2^{64} indicated in the brute force attack, from a hash function of 128 bits.

OTHER SECURITY MEASURES FOR CRYPTOSYSTEMS

The methods that we have described for analyzing the security of a cryptosystem relate to examining the actual algorithms used. Two other important areas in measuring the security of a cryptosystem relate to the method of implementation of the algorithms used and the security of the protocol in the system.

There have been a number of new attacks on the implementation of certain algorithms which have broken otherwise secure ciphers. The first type of implementation attacks are the *timing attacks* on public key ciphers as reported by Kocher (42). For their success, these attacks depend on taking advantage of the method used to implement a particular algorithm. For example, Kocher described attacks on the RSA algorithm implemented with the RSAREF tool-kit (43). The attack on the RSA algorithm derives the secret exponent. The timing attacks have now been extended to breaking certain symmetric block ciphers. For example, in Ref. 44, a method for attacking certain implementations of the IDEA cipher was described. This attack may allow an attacker to obtain 80 bits of the 128-bit key. There are techniques to avoid these timing attacks provided one changes the method used to implement a particular algorithm. For example, in the case of the RSA algorithm, multiplying each block to be encrypted by a different random number prior to encryption and removing this encrypted random number prior to transmission prevents the timing attacks (42). In the case of the IDEA cipher, one can prevent the attacks by using lookup tables for the multiplication modulo $2^{16} + 1$ used in the algorithm (44). In order to measure whether an implementation of a cipher is secure from timing attacks, one needs to be provided with the source code used.

Another class of implementation-based attacks depends on the platform on which a cryptosystem is implemented. Typically, cryptosystems are implemented either in software or hardware (or a combination of both). Software-based cryptosystems are, in general, more inexpensive and flexible than hardware-based solutions. However, there are serious security problems in most cases if a purely software-based cryptosystem is used. In general, software is susceptible to attacks from outside influences, such as hackers and viruses. In particular, most cryptosystems require that keys be stored in some method for future use. If these are stored, unencrypted, in software files, they are clearly open to attack. Tamperproof hardware devices such as security modules or smart cards are more secure. In particular, such devices have been used both as a secure method for storage of cryptographic keys and for implementation of the ciphers. However, recent attacks have shown that it may be possible to break schemes implemented in tamperproof modules. These attacks fall into three broad categories:

Random hardware faults: These are transient faults which only affect the current data. For example, a bit stored may spontaneously change. In Ref. 45, it has been shown that it may be possible to use such a fault to form an attack on the RSA algorithm.

Induced faults: These attacks require physical access to the hardware device and the ability to alter the data inside the device during computation. It has been shown that it may be possible to use such methods to attack hardware devices which implement public key ciphers (46) and symmetric block ciphers (47,48).

Physical attacks: These attacks take advantage of specific hardware and system design restrictions. Numerous attacks are summarized in Ref. 49, including attacks on early pay television schemes, low-voltage attacks, and ultraviolet attacks. Some of these attacks are relatively inexpensive and simple to implement, whereas others are more sophisticated.

A measure of the security of a cryptosystem, which uses tamperproof hardware, may require extensive examination of the device and its use within the system.

Another important measure of the security of a cryptosystem is the degree to which the cryptographic protocols in the design can be attacked. In recent years, formal, and semiformal, techniques have been successfully applied to communications protocols to analyze them and prove that they possess certain desirable properties such as an absence of "deadlock." Attempts to analyze and prove security properties of cryptographic protocols have been less successful; although significant progress has been made, there is intense research continuing in this area. The reason that the problem for cryptographic protocols is much harder than for general communications protocols is that a malicious entity must now be added to the protocol whose actions are completely unconstrained. It must be assumed that the attacker is able not only to read all messages but also to manipulate them in any way, including the following:

- Capturing and deleting any message
- Altering the contents of a message in any way
- Delaying messages until a later time, including reordering messages
- Inserting totally fabricated messages purporting to come from any other entity

There are many instances of protocols that have been broken, in many cases many years after publication. A catalog of protocol attacks, together with common-sense measures to avoid the commonly encountered ones, is given by Abadi and Needham (50). Experience has shown that there are often very subtle bugs in protocols that are very difficult to detect and which may involve the attacker taking on multiple roles and interleaving several protocol runs.

During a communications exchange, basic security services such as confidentiality and integrity can be provided by a fairly straightforward application of the chosen cryptographic algorithms. However, the use of such algorithms requires the communicating entities to share one or more secret keys (for performance reasons, symmetric algorithms are nearly always used for bulk encryption). In a distributed communications environment, it is not reasonable to expect each pair of entities to share such a secret key initially. Furthermore, it is standard practice to ensure that each communication session has a new key (a *session key*) so that compromise of one session will not affect previous or subsequent sessions. The majority of effort in the development of cryptographic protocols has been devoted to *key establishment* protocols, which are used at the start of a communications session to provide each entity involved with a new session key. Key establishment protocols can be divided into two broad groups:

Key distribution protocols: In these protocols, one entity selects the new session key and transmits it securely to the other entities that require it. Two common models are used, depending on whether symmetric or asymmetric cryptography is employed. With symmetric cryptography, a trusted server is required, who shares long-term secret keys with each user. The server usually selects the new session key and distributes it to each entity that requires it, protected with the long-term key that is shared with that entity. If asymmetric cryptography is used, session keys may be generated and distributed directly between entities that require them protected by the relevant public keys (for confidentiality) or private keys (for integrity). The general paradigm for key distribution was established in the seminal paper of Needham and Schroeder (51). This paper includes specific proposed protocols which have, subsequently, been found to be flawed.

Key agreement protocols: By contrast, these protocols require that each entity contribute to the generation of the session key. Usually, these protocols are used in combination with public key cryptography, but this is not really necessary.

The archetypal key agreement protocol is based on the Diffie–Hellman key exchange mentioned earlier. In order to ensure that a new session key is established each time, the two entities involved cannot use the same public key as a basis of the exchange. They must, therefore, choose random "public" values which are exchanged. However, in order to allow authentication of the origin of messages, additional security measures must be employed. A well-known protocol that incorporates Diffie–Hellman key exchange with digital signatures to provide key agreement is the station-to-station protocol (52).

Attempts to determine the strength of key establishment protocols has largely concentrated on analysis techniques which model the protocol in a chosen formalism. There are two main categories of analysis techniques. *Logical methods* model the "beliefs" of entities and how they are modified on receipt of protocol messages (53). *Algebraic methods* model the actions of each entity (including the attacker) and attempt to find attacks which break the protocol because the attacker achieves undesired goals (54).

Protocol analysis techniques give a yes/no answer on the security of a protocol: The protocol is either good or bad. From this viewpoint, there is no quantitative measure of the strength of a protocol. However, such a measure is clearly available by reference to the cryptographic algorithms used in a protocol's implementation. It is not unreasonable to ask that a protocol be as hard to break as it is to break the weakest of the cryptographic algorithms it employs. Furthermore, the protocol designer can make careful use of the cryptographic algorithms to maximize the difficulty in attacking a protocol. For example, a number of protocols have been designed to protect against the poor choice of passwords of typical system users. The EKE protocol (55) assumes the existence only of a shared password but, as far as is known, the only way to break it is as hard as breaking with Diffie–Hellman key exchange when a cryptographically strong key is used. It has also been shown that very specific protocols can be designed within a very formal framework through which it can be proven that the resulting protocol is impossible to break (in a specific sense) as long as a certain cryptographically strong function exists.

Largely as a result of the experience gained from finding new attacks, basic designs of good key establishment protocols are now widely accepted. However, the instances of bad protocols do not appear to be diminishing. One problem is that many protocols try to achieve aims additional to, or just plain different from, those of key establishment. In many cases, it is not clear exactly what properties are required, and there is no established formalism in which to capture the requirements. This problem is particularly acute in relation to the many emerging protocols for electronic commerce. These are typically an order of magnitude more complex than key establishment protocols, and their goals are much more varied, including issues of nonrepudiation with respect to three or more mutually suspicious parties. It is doubtful whether existing analysis techniques are capable of handling these protocols effectively and it is a challenging research problem to find new ways to design and analyze these protocols which will quickly become a part of all our lives.

CONCLUSION

The computer revolution of the past 30 years has completely changed the international economy. Most corporations rely on using computers to store and transmit information. The security of such systems depends on using cryptosystems which cannot be easily broken. One needs a toolbox of techniques in order to measure this security. As we have described, this toolbox should contain techniques for analyzing ciphers, both in their design and method of implementation as well as the procedure used in key generation and protocols involved in the cryptosystem.

New and more sophisticated techniques for attacking cryptosystems are being developed. Hence, there is a need to develop new methods for analyzing cryptosystems. As well, there is a need to design new ciphers and protocols to prevent these attacks.

During the 20th century, there have been several revolutionary developments, both in the design and methods for attacking ciphers, which were beyond the imagination of any science fiction writer in the year 1900. The developments in the science of cryptology over the next 100 years may be just as revolutionary. For example, if startling developments are made in either the application of Quantum (56) or DNA Computing (57), which are infeasible to implement under current technology, then public key cryptography could have real problems.

REFERENCES

1. NBS (National Bureau of Standards), "Data Encryption Standard," *Federal Information Processing Standards*, Publication 46, U.S. Department of Commerce, Washington, DC, 1977.
2. R. L. Rivest, The MD5 Message Digest Algorithm, RFC 1321, April 1992.
3. "Proposed Federal Information Processing Standard for Secure Hash Standard," *Fed. Reg.*, *57*(21), 3747–3749 (1992).
4. N. J. A. Sloane and A. D. Wyner (eds.), *Claude Elwood Shannon Collected Papers*, IEEE Press, New York, 1993.
5. R. R. Junemann, "Analysis of Certain Aspects of Output-feedback Mode," *Advances in Cryptology: Proceedings of Crypto '82*, Plenum, New York, 1983, pp. 99–127.
6. F. Rubin, "Computer Methods for Decrypting Random Stream Ciphers," *Cryptologia, 2*(3), 215–231 (1978).
7. E. Dawson and L. Nielsen, "Automated Cryptanalysis of *XOR* Plaintext Strings," *Cryptologia, 20*(2), 165–181 (1996).
8. H. M. Gustafson, "Statistical Analysis of Symmetric Ciphers," Ph.D. thesis, Queensland University of Technology, Australia (1996).
9. A. Lempel and J. Ziv, "On the Complexity of Finite Sequences," *IEEE Trans. Inform. Theory, IT-22*, 75–81 (1976).
10. J. L. Massey, "Shift Register Sequences and BCH Decoding," *IEEE Trans. Inform. Theory, IT-15*, 122–127 (1969).
11. G. Bhattacharyya and R. Johnson, *Statistical Concepts and Methods*, John Wiley & Sons, New York, 1977.
12. H. Beker and F. Piper, *Cipher Systems: The Protection of Communications*, John Wiley & Sons, New York, 1982.
13. J. Dj. Golić, "Linear Cryptanalysis of Stream Ciphers," in *Fast Software Encryption—Leuven '94*, Springer-Verlag, New York, 1995, pp. 154–169.
14. R. Rueppel, *Analysis and Design of Stream Ciphers*, Springer-Verlag, Berlin, 1986.
15. T. Siegenthaler, "Decrypting a Class of Stream Ciphers Using Ciphertext Only," *IEEE Trans. Computers, C-34*, 81–85 (1985).
16. W. Meier and O. Staffelbach, "Fast Correlation Attacks on Certain Stream Ciphers," *J. Cryptol., 1*(3), 159–167 (1989).
17. W. Diffie and M. E. Hellman, "Exhaustive Cryptanalysis of the NBS Data Encryption Standard," *Computer, 10*(6), 74–84 (1980).

18. M. J. Wiener, "Efficient DES Key Search," Technical Report TR-244, School of Computing Science, Carelton University (May 1994).

19. X. Lai, *On the Design and Security of Block Ciphers*, ETH Series in Information Processing, Vol. 1, Hartung-Gorre Verlag, Konstanz, 1992.

20. R. C. Merkle and M. Hellman, "On the Security of Multiple Encryption," *Commun. ACM*, *24*(7), 465–467 (1981).

21. W. Tuchman, "Hellman Presents No Shortcut Solutions to DES," *IEEE Spectrum*, *16*(7), 40–41 (1979).

22. A. E. Webster and S. E. Tavares, "On the Design of S-boxes," in *Advances in Cryptology—CRYPTO '85*, Springer-Verlag, Berlin, 1986, pp. 523–530.

23. E. Biham and A. Shamir, "Differential Cryptanalysis of DES-like Cryptosystems," *J. Cryptol.*, *4*(1), 3–72 (1991).

24. M. Matsui, "Linear Cryptanalysis Method for DES Cipher," in *Advances in Cryptology—EUROCRYPT '93*, Springer-Verlag, Berlin, 1993, pp. 386–397.

25. M. Matsui, "The First Experimental Cryptanalysis of the Data Encryption Standard," in *Advances in Cryptology—CRYPTO '94*, Springer-Verlag, Berlin, 1994, pp. 1–11.

26. D. Eastlake, S. Crocker, and J. Schiller, *RFC1750: Randomness Recommendations for Security*, Internet Activities Board, December 1994.

27. A. J. Menezes, P. C. van Oorschot, and S. A. Vanstone, *CRC Handbook of Applied Cryptography*, CRC Press, Boca Raton, FL, 1996.

28. I. Goldburg and D. Wagner, "Randomness and the Netscape Browser," *Dr Dobbs J.*, *21*(1), 66–70 (1996).

29. Calmos RBG1210 Random Bit Generator, *Newbridge Microsystems Databook*, Newbridge Microsystems, Ontario, Canada, 1990, pp. 3-28–3-21.

30. E. P. Dawson and H. M. Gustafson, "Statistical Methods for Testing the Strength of Key Generators," in *Proceedings of the 1st International Conference on the Theory and Applications of Cryptology, PRAGOCRYPT '96*, October 1996, pp. 452–466.

31. C. H. Meyer and S. M. Matyas, *Cryptography—A New Dimension in Data Security*, John Wiley & Sons, New York, 1982.

32. R. L. Rivest, A. Shamir, and L. M. Adleman, "A Method for Obtaining Digital Signatures and Public Key Cryptosystems," *Commun. ACM*, *21*(2), 120–126 (1978).

33. C. Pomerance, "The Quadratic Sieve Factoring Algorithm," in *Advances in Cryptology: Proceedings of EUROCRYPT '84*, Springer-Verlag, Berlin, 1985, pp. 169–182.

34. A. K. Lenstra and H. W. Lenstra, Jr. (eds.), *The Development of the Number Field Sieve*, Springer-Verlag, Berlin, 1993.

35. B. Schneier, *Applied Cryptography: Protocols, Algorithms, and Source Code in C*, 2nd ed., John Wiley & Sons, New York, 1996.

36. T. ElGamal, "A Public-Key Cryptosystem and a Signature Scheme Based on Discrete Logarithms," in *Advances in Cryptology: Proceedings of CRYPTO '84*, Springer-Verlag, New York, 1985, pp. 10–18.

37. I. F. Blake, X. Gao, R. C. Mullin, S. A. Vanstone, and T. Yaghoobian, *Applications of Finite Fields*, A. J. Menezes (ed.), Kluwer Academic Publishers, Boston, 1993.

38. G. Harper, A. Menezes, and S. Vanstone, "Public-key Encryptions with Very Small Key Length," in *Advances in Cryptology EUROCRYPT '92*, Springer-Verlag, Berlin, 1993, pp. 163–173.

39. G. Yuval, "How to Swindle Rabin," *Cryptologia*, *3*(3), 187–190 (1979).

40. H. Dobbertin, "Cryptanalysis of MD4," in *Fast Software Encryption*, Springer-Verlag, Berlin, 1996, pp. 53–69.

41. R. L. Rivest, "The MD4 Message Digest Algorithm," in *Advances in Cryptology—CRYPTO '90 Proceedings*, Springer-Verlag, Berlin, 1991, pp. 303–311.

42. P. C. Kocher, "Timing Attacks on Implementations of Diffie-Hellman, RSA, DSS, and Other

Systems," in *Advances in Cryptology—CRYPTO '96*, Springer-Verlag, Berlin, 1997, pp. 104–113.

43. RSA Laboratories, *RSAREF: A Cryptographic Toolkit, Version 2.0*, RSA Laboratories, 1994; available via FTP from rsa.com.

44. J. Kelsey, "Idea and Timing Attacks," presented at Rump Session at *Crypto '95*.

45. D. Boneh, R. A. DeMillo, and R. J. Lipton, *On the Importance of Checking Computations*, Math and Cryptography Research Group, Bellcore, http://www.bellcore.com/PRESS/ADVSRY96/medadv.html.

46. F. Bao, R. Deng, Y. Han, A. Jeng, D. Narasimhalu, and T. H. Nagir, *New Attacks to Public Key Cryptosystems on Tamperproof Devices*, Information Security Group, Institute of Systems Science, National University of Singapore, 29 October 1996, http://www.itd.nrl.navy.mil/ITD/5540/ieee/cipher/newsitems/961029.sgtamper.html.

47. E. Biham and A. Shamir, *A New Cryptanalytic Attack on DES*, Israel, 18 October 1996; http://jya.com/dfa.htm.

48. S. Moriai, "More Practical Differential Fault Analysis of Block Ciphers, Telecommunications Advancement Organization of Japan," in *Fast Software Encryption*, Springer-Verlag, New York, 1997.

49. R. Anderson and M. Kuhn, "Tamper Resistance—A Cautionary Note," *Usenix Electron. Commerce, 96* (19 November 1996).

50. M. Abadi and R. Needham, "Prudent Engineering Practice for Cryptographic Protocols," *IEEE Trans. Software Eng.*, 22(1), 6–15 (1996).

51. R. Needham and M. Schroeder, "Using Encryption for Authentication in Large Networks of Computers," *Commun. ACM, 21*, 993–999 (1978).

52. W. Diffie, P. van Oorschot, and M. Wiener, "Authentication and Authenticated Key Exchange," *Designs Codes Cryptogr.*, 2, 107–125 (1992).

53. M. Burrows, M. Abadi, and R. Needham, "A Logic for Authentication," *Proc. Roy. Soc.*, 426, 223–271 (1989).

54. R. Kemmerer, C. Meadows, and J. Millen, "Three Systems for Cryptographic Protocol Analysis," *J. Cryptol.*, 79–130 (1994).

55. S. Bellovin and M. Merritt, "Encrypted Key Exchange: Password Based Protocols Secure against Dictionary Attacks," in *1992 IEEE Symposium on Research in Security and Privacy*, IEEE Computer Society Press, Washington, DC, 1992, pp. 72–84.

56. P. W. Shor, "Algorithms for Quantum Computation: Discrete Log and Factoring," in *Proceedings of the 35th Symposium on Foundations of Computer Science*, 1994, pp. 124–134.

57. L. M. Adleman, "Molecular Computation of Solutions to Combinatorial Problems," *Science*, 226(11), 1021 (1994).

ED P. DAWSON

HELEN M. GUSTAFSON

COLIN BOYD

NEURAL NETWORKS FOR IDENTIFICATION, CONTROL, ROBOTICS, AND SIGNAL AND IMAGE PROCESSING

INTRODUCTION

Researchers have always been fascinated by the massively computational processing skills of the human brain, in particular by its ability in performing parallel tasks, partitioning complex problems into smaller ones, reconstructing concepts from partial information, and deducing and inferring new features and behaviors from the available knowledge by exploiting similarity and generalization; all of the above is obtained only on the basis of learning from examples, by means of analytical inspection, understanding, interpolation, and feature extraction. Artificial neural networks were initially studied to model and better understand the structure and the behavior of the natural counterpart; nowadays, they are considered as independent computational paradigms suited to afford the solution of several industrial applications, whenever an algorithmic approach is not known, feasible, or performs badly.

In the early stages, neural computational paradigms have proven to be effective only in solving very simple problems. Later, advances in theoretical research and the availability of suitable Very Large Scale Integration (VLSI) technologies sustained and pushed major research efforts to overcome the limits of current processing systems and challenge complex real-world cases. To this end, in the last several years, neural technologies clearly revealed their abilities in a variety of applications, hence proposing themselves as one of the most widely accepted and common model-free design tools.

This article is a critical review of the state of the art and the use of neural technologies in relevant industrial aspects, such as system identification, control, robotics, and signal and image processing. In particular, the use and the relevance of neural paradigms will be considered in the identification of nonlinear static and dynamic functions, prediction of nonlinear dynamic systems and time series, control of nonlinear dynamic systems, signal and image processing, filtering, feature and texture extraction, sensor fusion, high-level measurement, classification, and recognition. These applications are fundamental in the applied research and in the industry allowing for designing advanced monitoring and control systems for plants, robots, engines, complex devices and systems, in which adaptability, flexibility, and generalization ability are relevant features for the system effectiveness.

First, the article introduces the basic concepts related to neural computation, namely the definition of neural topology, the configuration procedures, the evaluation of the model performances, the neural model optimization, and the sensitivity of the model performance to the parameters. Implementation aspects will also be treated.

Then, the use of the neural techniques in industrial applications, their potential benefits, and limits will be discussed. Finally, attention will be focused on the methodological aspects related to the design and use of neural techniques in industrial applications. Limits and capabilities as well as design guidelines will be given.

THEORETICAL FOUNDATIONS OF THE NEURAL COMPUTATION FOR INDUSTRIAL APPLICATIONS

An artificial neural network is a parallel and distributed computational paradigm whose structure, processing sequence, and dependencies among data are defined by a directed graph. The nodes (or *neurons*) are the processing units, whereas the arcs (or *synapses*) represent the interconnections along which data flows among neurons. The external world communicates with the neural networks via the *network inputs*, a set of virtual neurons (or *input neurons*) which redistribute (usually without any manipulation) the information to subsequent neurons. The results of the computation performed by the whole neural network constitute the *network outputs*, delivered to the external world by neurons (or *output neurons*). Neurons without any direct (either input or output) connection to the external world are called *hidden neurons*. Hidden and output neurons compute their own outputs by applying suitable nonlinear operations to the incoming inputs (provided by input or proper neurons). To modulate the influence of a neuron output onto the subsequent neural computation, an interconnection weight (or *synaptic weight*) is associated to each arc. In other words, the weight represent the strength of the connection between the two neurons; its final effect is to amplify or reduce the signal flowing along that connection.

With reference to Figure 1, any ith neuron (except for the input ones) receives n inputs $x_j, j = 1, \ldots, n$ from previous neurons and computes an *excitation value* e_i, (which depends on the inputs $x_j, j = 1, \ldots, n$ and the weights $w_j, j = 1, \ldots, n$). A common excitation function is given by the weighted summation of the neuron's inputs; one of the most common is $e_i = \sum_{j=1}^{n} w_{ij}x_j + \theta_i$ where θ_i is a *threshold* term. More complex excitation functions can be used: excitatory and inhibitory input signals can be considered to give more flexibility to the interneural relationships, whereas cumulated pulsed inputs can be adopted to simulate the asynchronous operation of a natural neuron instead of synchronously evaluating the excitation directly onto the current inputs. A nonlinear transfer function (or *activation function*) $f_i(e_i)$ is then applied to the excitation value to produce the neuron's output x_i. Among the most common activation functions experimented with in the literature, we find continuous functions (e.g., linear, piecewise linear, sigmoid, and tangentoid) and discontinuous ones (e.g., step and multisteps). The excitation and activation functions characterize the processing ability of the individual neuron as well as of the neurons' ensemble. It should be noted that it is not required that the network to be a

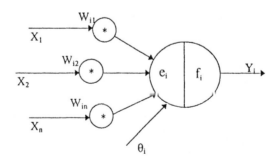

FIGURE 1   The schematic diagram of a neuron.

priori, composed of identically behaving neurons, even if this is the most common case.

In the literature, several topologies have been suggested to deal with different classes of applications and provide neural models able to approximate static input/output mappings, cluster or classify data, gather information about unknown input distributions, and modeling or representing dynamic systems. Basically, two principal types of neural topologies can be identified: the static and the dynamic.

Static networks are directed to solve problems in which no explicit dynamics is considered; that is, they are effective in any kind of problem that can be logically reduced to a mapping (e.g., pattern classification, filtering, signal/image restoration, and identification of static functions).

The simplest topology (called Madaline) consists of two layers of neurons (the input and the output layers); its ability is in classifying linearly separable classes. Output neurons are connected to all input neurons but not to each other. The computation leads to an acyclic graph and a feed-forward data flow.

To solve nonlinearly separable classification problems, we must provide more power to the network, as can be obtained by inserting a hidden layer. This happens with *multilayered* feed-forward networks (Fig. 2a) which contain a cascade of more than one Madaline. It has been proven that such networks are universal function approximators (i.e., that they are able to approximate any static function with an arbitrary precision). Several different models can be found in the literature based on the multilayered feed-forward networks. Some of them consider lateral interconnections between neurons belonging to the same layer to influence the current excitation of neighboring neurons.

Another interesting neural model is the self-organizing map (Fig. 2b). The network is composed of a single-layered network in which each neuron is connected to all network inputs and the outputs of the other neurons. Such networks are useful to cluster and classify input data by estimating the input distribution.

Other models incorporate backward connections and can be used as associative memories. Bidirectional associative memories are multilayered networks with connections linking neurons in adjacent layers both in the forward and the backward directions. A particularly relevant case is Hopfield's network (see Fig. 2c), a single-layer network in which each neuron receives a single network's input and the output coming from all the other neurons. The neuron output is obtained at the steady state by fixing the input pattern and letting the network to evolve accordingly.

Dynamic networks have been designed to deal with applications characterized by the presence of dynamics. This is the typical case of applications addressing dynamic systems, as happens, for example, in system identification, prediction, control, Infinite Impulse Response (IIR) filtering, and related problems such as monitoring, what–if simulations, control, motion, and high-level vision. The simplest structure of a dynamic network reproduces the computational scheme of a classic sequential machine, composed by a set of memory elements holding the system state and a combinatorial circuit evaluating the output and the next-state functions. For each new input, the combinatorial circuit provides the machine output according to the current input and the internal state as well as generating the control signals to store the next state into the memory elements.

One of the most common neural network topologies resembling such a structure consists of a multilayered feed-forward network having external memory elements connected to it by *external feedback loops* (Fig. 2d). The network outputs holding information about the state of the modeled dynamic system are fed back to the network's inputs through memory elements. In general, the network's inputs are the current and the past

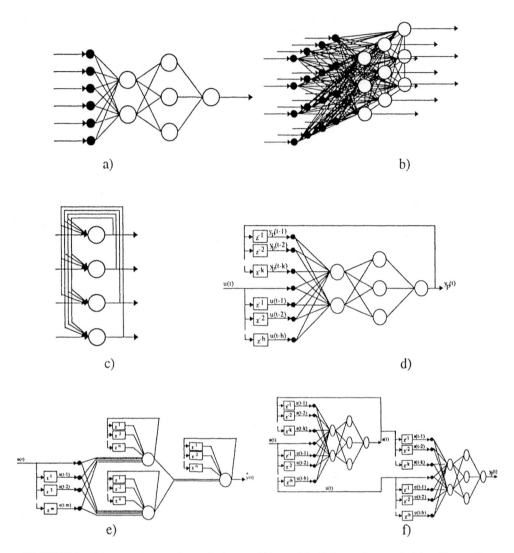

FIGURE 2 The neural network topologies: multilayered feed-forward network (a), self-organizing map (b), Hopfield's network (c), external feedback loops (d), local feedback loops (e), state-output network (f).

primary inputs of the dynamic system as well as the current and the past predicted outputs or the actual past outputs; to increase the accuracy, it is sometimes necessary to take into account the past prediction errors also. The number of past inputs and outputs that need to be taken into account is related to the internal dynamics of the system and can often be deduced—at least in a first approximation—by studying a rough physical model of the real system and the related differential equations. This structure has been widely shown to be effective in many practical cases of prediction, identification, control, and filtering. This approach has been shown to be feasible also when the state variables of the modeled system cannot be measured or explicitly defined.

Memory elements can be also introduced within the network at the level of each layer by creating feedback loops similar to the global ones; these complex structures have not shown any practical enhancement with respect to the previous case. Feedback loops can be introduced *locally* at the level of the individual neuron (Fig. 2e); this leads to a high number of degrees of freedom and states (due to the high number of interconnections and neurons, respectively) and, as a consequence, to a higher complexity in the configuration procedure.

The *state-space* model of the classic system theory ruled by

$$s(t) = f_x(s(t-1), \ldots, s(t-k), u(t), \ldots, u(t-h)),$$
$$y_p = f_y(s(t-1), \ldots, s(t-k), u(t), \ldots, u(t-h))$$

suggests a network structure as in Figure 2f: the relationships addressing the state variables are modeled by a recurrent network and the ones related to the output by a static network depending on the state values and the inputs. Extension to multiple outputs system is straightforward. Such a topology, even if particularly suitable to represent dynamic system, may be difficult to be configured if the state (or the states) are not (or not easily) measurable. In such a case, the network may be constructed to present some virtual states, without physical meaning but necessary to give the model enough dynamic degrees of freedom.

All the above neural model families contain parameters (namely the interconnection weights, the thresholds, and possible parameters in the activation functions) that need to be tailored onto the specific application case to obtain the specific model able to solve the given problem. The procedure used to configure the parameters of a neural network is called *learning*. Basically, it consists of determining suitable values for the synaptic weights: it rarely involves tuning of the thresholds and the parameters associated with the activation functions. In most neural networks, learning is an iterative procedure which progressively adjusts the network's parameters so as to minimize a given figure of merit. Network configuration is achieved by learning the desired behavior of the model from examples, by resembling the acquisition of knowledge in the biological neural systems.

Two main classes of training procedures can be identified: the supervised and the unsupervised learning. In *supervised learning*, for each network input, the actual outputs are compared to the expected ones provided by an external independent entity (the supervisor): The difference measured between a pair of actual and expected outputs for a given network input is the network output error associated to such actual network output. The *learning error* is some function of the network output error evaluated by applying the input data set used for training. Basically, the learning procedure updates the current weights with quantities that are a function of the current learning error.

Several rules have been proposed in the literature to realize the weight adjustment; the most common ones rely on indirect minimization methods based on the training error function (e.g., Hebbian, Widrow–Hoff, delta, and gradient-descent rules). In multilayered networks, weight updating through the whole structure is achieved by evaluating the learning error at the network outputs and, then, by propagating it backward up to the input layer, so that a specific neuron error is derived for the application of the update rule. The main drawback of this approach is the mandatory need of a priori knowledge about the expected network output so that the supervisor can provide the pairs of network input and the corresponding expected output.

The supervised learning is the typical technique adopted in the literature to configure many static and dynamic kind of networks (e.g., multilayered networks and dynamic networks with external feedback loops).

In *unsupervised learning*, weights are adjusted according to the minimization of a specific function of the current outputs and weights only: it is suitable whenever the expected network output for a given input is not a priori known. This approach is typical of self-organizing maps, recirculating networks, and Boltzmann's machines. According to the specific network structure, some rules have been proposed in the literature to achieve network configuration autonomously. For example, at each iteration in the self-organizing maps, weights are adjusted to strengthen the input–output correlation of the neurons having the highest output values for the current network input; this leads autonomously to create cumulating points (or regions) in the network, each of them being particularly active for a specific class of input examples. In the recirculating networks, the network output is fed back to the input so as to reconstruct the current input itself: weights are adjusted in order to minimize the difference between actual and reconstructed inputs.

To perform learning, suitable examples must be presented to the network: The set of data used for the learning phase is called the *training data* set. Examples must cover the input space as much as possible in order to excite the network at the farthest limits and allow it to experience a high number of different behaviors spread out over the whole input space. The number of examples used for training must be large enough to allow the network to obtain a clear and comprehensive (even if not necessarily complete) understanding of the expected behavior. When data are lacking, suitable techniques can be adopted to avoid the network to focus on a limited subset of the input space and, thus, to learn only a part of the whole expected behavior. Training data must be presented several times to the network in order to force a deep capturing of the essence of each of them, a good understanding, and memorization of the expected behavior.

The learning error in supervised learning (or similar figures in the unsupervised approaches) decreases during training as long as the network is able to use its degrees of freedom; decreasing may not be monotonous and may even temporarily increase according to the local weight optimization choices. Therefore, learning could be terminated when the learning error becomes practically steady or falls below a given application-dependent threshold. A deep training on the training set biases the neural model to such data. This ability is interesting but limits the usefulness of the neural approach because the network is constrained to reproduce only the behavior of the system over the observed training points, and performances on different data may be poor. On the other hand, when solving a problem, we are mostly interested in developing a model able to provide good performance over the whole input dominion (or a subpart of it): this property is called generalization and the test of the model performance is the validation procedure. To monitor the evolution of the performance of the neural model over training time, we consider a *testing set* (i.e., a separate set of data similar to the training one). Estimation of the performance is obtained by suspending temporarily the normal training evolution and presenting the testing set to the network. The test error, namely the error on such set, is computed, and if learning needs to be continued (i.e., the performance on the test set is not sufficient for the application), the training procedure—including the weights configuration—is resumed.

The error computed on the testing set gives a biased estimate of the generalization ability possessed by the network in the presence of unknown inputs. Once the training phase has been completed, one has to measure the *generalization ability* of the neural network by computing the performances of the model on the *validation set*, an additional data set similar to the testing one but never used to guide the learning procedure. The validation set is applied only once at the end of the whole training: the validation error corresponding to such network inputs is an unbiased measure of the generalization ability. This error tends to be higher if we prolong the learning too much because the network is more and more focused to match the training set (*overfitting*). The learning procedure therefore needs to be terminated *as soon as* a reasonable learning error has been achieved, before the network loses the generalization ability.

When the network configuration is completed, the neural model parameters (e.g., the interconnection weights) are frozen. The nominal operation of the network can thus be started and the learned behavior reproduced: This phase is called *recall*. The learned behavior is reproduced for the known inputs, and a suitable behavior is extrapolated from the available information acquired during learning so as to produce outputs hopefully close to the expected ones. Generalization is accurate when the input space has been sufficiently explored to cover the system operating range and detailed to provide a fine-granularity interpolation.

A suitable learning phase leads to a model which reproduces the real system accurately. Variations of the model parameters (even if small in percentage) may modify the behavior with respect the desired one in a relevant way: *Sensitivity* of the neural behavior to the model parameters must, therefore, be considered and evaluated, in particular for critical applications. Variations can be due, for example, to the intrinsic tolerance in the fabrication process, the finite-digit representations, the approximated function evaluations, the errors induced by faults, and the natural drift related to thermal or electric effects and aging.

Learning can be applied only once before starting the recall phase (*static* learning) or periodically (*periodic* learning) to readapt the model to slowly evolving environments. In this second case, recall is suspended to update the model parameters. If the modeled system changes its behavior frequently or rapidly, *on-line* learning could be envisioned in parallel to recall, even if a too frequent parameter adaptation may lead to a massive computational overhead without any accuracy increment.

Learning can be performed *off-board* by a system completely independent from the neural network used in recall (e.g., by software simulation on a traditional computing system or hardware emulation on a development system). The selected model parameters are then transferred into the neural model realization for recall. Alternatively, learning can be executed *on-board* by including the suitable supports directly into the adopted neural model realization.

As its biological counterpart, the neural model may be redundant for the envisioned application, as an a priori minimum dimensioning is often difficult or even impossible to be identified. Overdimensioning leads to a higher computational complexity of the neural model and, as a consequence, to a more complex implementation (namely a larger circuit complexity for hardware realizations or a slower computer program for software solutions). Besides, the generalization ability is usually reduced because additional difficulties occur in configuring the higher number of degrees of freedom in the model, whereas, on the other hand, learning prolongation may induce overfitting effects. In the literature, some techniques have been presented to optimize the network structure during or after the learning phase (e.g., by weight decay, optimal brain damage, covariance matrix, spectral decomposition, or Final Prediction Error Biased (FPEB)).

Similarly, network underdimensioning may not allow for the capture of the complete system behavior due to lack of enough degrees of freedom in the model, and, as a consequence, the generalization ability is usually poor.

HARDWARE ARCHITECTURES AND SOFTWARE IMPLEMENTATIONS

In the literature, a number of approaches have been explored to implement the neural paradigms by exploiting existing computing structures as well as by developing new hardware solutions. This research was, and still is, constrained by the balance of realization costs versus the system performance and features with respect to the specific application characteristics and requirements. Difficulties in designing and implementing hardware solutions for complex applications make the availability and reusability of traditional computing structures attractive.

The high complexity of the neural computational paradigms and the large number of their possible alternatives and variations usually require an extensive numerical experimentation in order to deduce some characteristics behaviors and derive a theoretic framework for a specific class of neural models. On the other hand, design of a neural solution for an application problem needs the complete identification of the neural model capable of solving the problem (i.e., the neural topology, the neuron functions, the interconnection weights). To achieve this goal, it is necessary to be able to create and evaluate alternative design approaches—before implementing them—so as to satisfy the application requirements and constraints concerning both functional aspects and performance.

In addition, actual usability of neural networks in real industrial applications need to take into account system performance, in particular, for real-time applications to execute the massive computations associated to such models. All the above leads to the basic need of high-performance computing systems in order to support research, design, and use of the neural paradigms.

Unfortunately, before the eighties, technologies used in building computing systems were not able to produce VLSI devices suitable for the massive demand of the neural paradigms in a real (or even reasonable) time. The computational capability of mainframes and minicomputers available up to that time was not sufficient to provide a realistic support to research and experimentation; as a consequence, only some theoretical analysis was performed on the neural networks as a modeling of the natural brain.

In the eighties, the market was dominated by mainframes, minicomputers, and some vector computers for batch processing massively computing applications: Personal computers were just coming out as an attractive solution to low-cost, low-performance office automation. Advances in integration technologies soon started to allow the realization of more powerful general-purpose computing systems and, in turn, provided a reasonably efficient support for research in artificial intelligence and, specifically, on neural networks. For this reason, research and application experiments flourished again, producing results that were barely competitive with existing approaches.

The initial research phase was mainly performed on *general-purpose computing architectures* in order to minimize the costs and the time of setting up the experimental environment, because these computers were already available. On these systems, the neural paradigms are implemented by using suitable *software simulators*, which reproduce the nominal operations of the massively parallel neural networks by scheduling them on the traditional computer architecture according to the precedence ordering defined in the neural processing itself. This solution is still the most flexible for the high flexibility and the openness of the environment which allows for easy design and implementation. Different classes of general-purpose computing architectures have been considered and experimented for this purpose: monoprocessor machines, multiprocessor machines, and multicomputer systems.

The *monoprocessor* machines have a traditional "Von Neumann" structure; they typically range from the minicomputer (or even mainframe) systems down to the workstations and personal computers. The use of vector processors (or coprocessors) has been experimented with to speed up the execution of the neural operations.

Multiprocessor systems encompass several kinds of structure. The simplest case is a computer composed by traditional "Von Neumann" processors tightly coupled by a system bus, with or without shared memory. Simulation is partitioned in subtasks related to the operations of groups of neurons; each subtask is executed by a processor, eventually in parallel with the others to exploit the computational parallelism available in the multiprocessor system. More complex interconnection structures among processors can be used to reduce the conflicting use of the shared bus and, as a consequence, to speed up the simulation: Solutions based on dedicated hypercube and omega networks have been reported in the literature. Local interconnections have been studied leading to *array processors*.

The multicomputer systems consists of networked computers which cooperate in the simulation by distributing the computation over the computer network. This allows the creation of very high-performance systems by using widely commercially available computers and interconnection technologies (e.g., personal computers and workstations connected through a computer local area network).

Software simulation of neural paradigms on these computing systems may include both learning and recall phases. In the first case, the designer defines the uncommitted network topology and applies the learning algorithm until the desired configuration is found; then, the network user starts the recall on the tailored network with the obtained weight distribution.

The use of software simulators permits the more accurate study of the behavior of the neural network by observing, monitoring, and controlling data and operations. The software simulator can, in fact, also manage these aspects by storing and retrieving information which are interesting for the system designer or the application user. This is appreciated by researcher and developers who are studying in detail new neural paradigms, new training algorithms, and new applications. Another great advantage is the intrinsic programmability and modifiability of the software solution with respect to a hardware implementation, as cost and development time are of concerned. This is highly appreciated in the design of a new system or a new neural paradigm, in particular when the application specification is not completely known or it is evolving. This allows the upgrade of the neural model according to the new requirements of the theoretical aspects or the applications.

Several approaches have been presented in the literature for software simulation. We may identify two classes: the general-purpose and the dedicated software simulators. The *general-purpose software simulators* are software tools and environments realized to study and develop any neural network (or at least a large class). The user can specify the network topology, operation, and learning by selecting among a predefined set of solutions directly supported by the simulator: The network designer or user needs to choose a limited number of parameters characterizing the network structure and behavior, by interacting with a simple user-friendly (often graphical) simulator interface. This is suitable for many researchers and application developers who are not concerned with the internal characteristics and theoretical aspects of the neural paradigms: They are, in fact, looking for a tool capable of solving their application problem and they are often considering such a tool as a black box with given specifications and instructions of use. In the case where a more detailed access to the internal features and operations of the neural networks is required (e.g., by researcher studying new paradigms and training procedures, or by developers working on system optimization), the simulation can be configured and performed by activating suited observation and monitoring tools. In some cases, the detailed structure and operations of the whole neural network, or the learning procedure, or the distribution of the tasks composing the neural computation in a multiprocessor or multicomputer architecture need to be specified, created, run, and monitored by the simulator user in order to have a better and very detailed view of the neural computation as well as of the simulator activities. The network definition can be created by specifying each individual operation in a suitable (either textual or visual) language; the simulator interprets such a user-defined specification and executes the neural paradigm simulation according to it. The network configured by the simulator can be stored and retrieved later for recall. Example of these simulation environments are NeuralWorks by NeuralWare, Explorenet 3000 by HNC, and Matlab with Neural Networks Toolbox by Mathworks.

Dedicated software simulators are tools which are usually developed to solve specific problems, whenever general-purpose environments are not considered suitable enough. This is the case, for example, when they do not allow a way to easily define some characteristics of new neural paradigms, or they do not allow the observation and the easily or effectively control the network under study, or they are too slow for the actual use of the neural network in the real environment (possibly in the presence of real-time constraints). The dedicated simulators are used to afford either the learning phase or the recall or both, according to the specific needs of the application, the system developer, or the application user. They consist of computer programs specifically written in a programming language for the envisioned hardware architecture. All information can be available to the system designer and, possibly, even to the application user; however, a lot of effort is required to set up the system and to verify the correctness not only of the neural paradigm but also of the dedicated software simulator itself. Even if higher performance can be achieved, time to market as well as system modifiability, adaptability, reusability, expandability and generalizability will be reduced.

Simulation can be performed by using two of the above approaches separately for learning and recall, according to the specific interests, application requirements, and constraints. If the research focus is on the training problems or on new network structures, the designer will benefit from the use of a dedicated simulator or general-purpose one having suitable configurable features for user-defined neural paradigms and learning; the result of the research will be the description of the neural paradigm, including the specific interconnection weights. This result will be used in a simplified dedicated simulator for recall only in the case of application constraints on the performance, or in a general-purpose simulator capable of supporting recall for the envisioned paradigm. If the application requires strict real-time operation, a dedicated simulator can be implemented to achieve a high efficiency, whereas the network topology definition and the weight evaluation through learning can be performed on a general-purpose simulator suitable for that topology to save programming efforts. Moving from one simulator to another introduces some problems related to the compatibility of the data representation and, in particular, accuracy. Different approaches may lead to approximation in the neural model parameters and, in turn, in the actual behavior with respect to the theoretically expected one. Model stability and sensitivity therefore needs to be addressed in the design of the neural solution.

In many strict real-time applications, the use of software simulators may lead to adopt high-performance computers to deal with the time constraints (i.e., to high costs). These costs may become so high that the neural paradigms are of no practical use, even if theoretically attractive and accurate. In some complex applications, the computations required by the computing system may be so massive that no general-purpose architecture is available. On the other hand, even if available, these computing systems may be so huge that it cannot be used for the envisioned application when it also imposes dimensional constraints. In all the above cases, a definite speedup and size limitation for the neural computation is necessary: The use of a hardware realisation therefore becomes mandatory.

In the literature, several researches presented effective and efficient implementations based on *hardware realization* of the neural paradigms. A large spectrum of solutions were explored, ranging from dedicated neural architectures to general-purpose neurocomputers. Realization of such structures for networks having practical use is feasible since the middle of the eighties due to the advances in the VLSI integration technologies as well as in wafer-scale and multichip module technologies which allow for implementing complex systems. When the neural paradigm becomes very complex, physical realization may require several separate integrated circuits or systems that need to be connected into a single computing system, possibly having a multiboard structure. Theoretical research on neural paradigm optimization was performed to minimize the complexity of the neural model so as to allow or enhance the physical realizability; model compactness also obviously influences the efficiency of software simulation.

Initially, analog approaches were experimented with for individual components, as direct realization of each neural operator by means of a dedicated device was more promising in terms of the density of neural operators. The drawback was the limited control on the fabrication parameters and, as a consequence, the relevant impact on the accuracy and reproducibility of the neural computation; this is the same limit shown by traditional analog computers.

Digital approaches have been shown to be more robust and flexible from this point of view, because the digital system operation relies only on the binary discretized value of the analog quantities representing the electrical signals. In some cases, these solutions may be less compact than the analog counterpart; however, often the digital technologies may be downsized much easier than the analog ones and, as a consequence, may lead to smaller circuits.

Dedicated hardware architectures implement the neural operations of a specific type of paradigm into a dedicated device. In the literature, three basic classes of architectures can be found: direct mapped, time multiplexed, and pipelined structures. A *direct-mapped architecture* is a structure realized by considering a one-to-one mapping of each neural operation (i.e., weight multiplication, addition, application of the nonlinear activation function, output distribution) onto a dedicated component. To increase system throughput, *pipelined architectures* can be created by pipelining the cascade of neural operations in the direct-mapped architecture at the level of the whole neuron or even within the individual neuron. When pipelining is applied at the neuron level, the time between two network outputs will be limited to the neuron latency, and it will be further reduced to the stage latency in the case of pipelining operations within the individual neuron. To decrease the overall circuit and interconnection complexity, *time-multiplexed architectures* can be designed by multiplexing some components implementing the neural operations (e.g., multipliers, adders, interconnections), and weights might need to be stored in circular shift registers. Suitable timing is considered to present the operands at the proper time. System performance is obviously reduced with respect to the other approaches. The hardware overhead for multiplexing must be accurately taken into account as it may greatly limit the circuit complexity reduction.

The powerfulness of the dedicated architectures is their very impressive computational capability. Conversely, being dedicated may be a severe limit because it reduces the reusability of the structure and often needs a longer design and fabrication time. To speed up the realization of a hardware solution, programmable dedicated devices are now available, such as the FPGAs: The circuit to be implemented is described in a high-level specification language and then translated into the device configuration signals by a compiler. This implies, however, the execution of all design steps as for a dedicated architecture.

To simplify neural design, some computing structures oriented to the neural paradigm realization, even if not dedicated to a specific neural paradigm, have been proposed in the literature. These structure are called *neurocomputers*. They are able to execute a large number of neural models, when the proper configuration of the computer is loaded, specifying the neuron number and operations, the interconnection topology and weights, and possibly the learning algorithm. Loading such a configuration is equivalent to loading a program in a traditional "Von Neumann" computer. Programmability of the neural operation is the key factor that makes attractive the use of neurocomputer in experimenting, developing, and prototyping neural solutions for high-performance applications having very strict real-time constraints.

The detailed structure of the hardware implementations and the configuration of the neural model parameters (namely the interconnection weights) need to be defined by taking into account accuracy and precision aspects in the neural computation and their influence on behavior, stability, and convergence of the neural paradigms. The arithmetic units are, in fact, built for finite-representation operands (integer, full-fractional, or floating-point numbers) and for the related finite-ring operations, both in the computing architectures supporting the software simulators and the hardware neural architectures, whereas the theoretical analysis and design is often performed on a data representation having a higher precision.

The accuracy issues can be observed a posteriori in the realized system to certify the correctness of its behavior. Alternatively, they can be included as additional guidelines in the learning procedure so as to reduce the network sensitivity to data discretization moving from the theoretical data representation used for the neural paradigm definition to the actual representation for recall; by construction, this usually allows the guarantee of the correctness of the network behavior operating of discrete-valued data.

In hardware realization, learning and recall can be tackled either separately or jointly in the same architecture. Usually, the highly demanding constraints and requirements which are imposed on the hardware solution are strictly mandatory for recall, being the relevance of timing relevant only during the actual use of the neural system. Because learning is performed only once (or a most rarely), it is acceptable not to consider the real-time system operation but only a virtual time completely unrelated with the actual one: the goals are, in fact, correctness and accuracy of the network behavior, not timing. As a consequence, generally, learning is performed *off-board*, out of the hardware neural architecture, in software simulators on a separated general-purpose computing architecture. The resulting neural paradigm configuration is then downloaded in the hardware structure for subsequent recall.

Conversely, if a self-contained neural system is envisioned or high performance is required also for learning (e.g., because data are directly extracted from the real application environment, or very time-consuming learning procedures need to be sped up), an *on-board* approach must be considered. The hardware neural architecture must be extended to deal also with the operations required by learning so that it is able to compute the network parameters and, then, to reproduce the learned behavior in recall, even if the hardware realization exploited for learning may be different from the one used in recall. When different implementations (either software or hardware) are used for learning and recall, accuracy and precision problems discussed above becomes crucial for guaranteeing the correct behavior of the neural model.

APPLICATIONS OF NEURAL PARADIGMS

Traditional information processing technologies execute a deterministic algorithm to identify the desired solution for the specific application case. In several applications related to approximated reasoning and associative problems, the complexity of the traditional algorithms is too high, or it is too difficult to develop the algorithm itself, or the algorithm is unknown or cannot be completely specified. This occurs in many cases for system identification, control, prediction, robotics, signal processing, filtering, image processing, vision, and pattern classification (i.e., whenever reasonable solutions can be found by exploiting strategies typical of the human reasoning, such as similarity, analogy, generalization, interpolation, extrapolation, and multiple-goal optimization). In this section, the most widely known and explored application areas are summarized to show the versatility and adaptability of the neural paradigms; many problems can be tackled by means of these technologies. The ones recalled here are directed to prove the effectiveness and the efficiency of the neural networks as modeling and problem-solving tools.

System identification takes a relevant role in large industrial application areas because it allows capturing the system behavior (i.e., its characteristics parameters) from the analysis of real measurements, even in the presence of noise. This is important whenever it is necessary to model a system in order to study and reproduce its behavior as well as to experiment with its operation possibly in abnormal or rare working conditions. Neural techniques have been shown to be effective and useful in situations where a model-based or parametric approach is difficult to formulate.

In particular, it was shown in the literature that neural networks are universal approximators of any nonlinear static functions (i.e., can very accurately model any linear on nonlinear system in which the outputs depend only on the current inputs). This property does not hold for any dynamic system [i.e., when the outputs depend also on the current state of the system (in other words, it is the whole history of the system which influences the generation of the current output)]. In most cases, the neural paradigms provide good models, even if the approximation may be partially reduced (it is worth to note that also traditional modeling techniques suffer for the inaccuracy due to the difficulties in capturing and describing the system dynamics).

Industrial applications have been realized for neural-based advanced sensors to detect and measure physical quantities; for example, artificial retinas, chocleas, and muscular tension have been realized by using integrated circuits, as well as infrared and high-energy detectors based on CCD technologies. Nonintrusive and noninteracting instruments can be implemented by observing physical quantities related to the desired one; magnetic resonance, echography, or reflected light can be used to measure the state of an object (e.g., the roughness of a surface or the position in the space). Nonlinear characteristics of traditional sensors can be smoothed and linearized to ease subsequent use more efficiently and accurately than with a lookup table or a specific algorithm which can be too large or time-consuming.

Availability of a system model is also useful for measuring characteristics whenever this operation is difficult to perform in the real system due to the operating environment (e.g., radiation, pollution, physical unreachability, unsafety) or to the system itself (e.g., unavailability of sensors during operation). Many examples of neural models for complex dynamic systems have been reported in the literature, often proving the attractiveness and the efficiency of these techniques with respect to more traditional approaches, in particular as adaptability and configuration through learning by examples are concerned. Systems envisioned include simple machinery, electrical systems, thermal machines, bridges, civil structures, up to complete plants (e.g., chemical and thermoelectric).

Neural modeling of dynamic systems or time series generated by dynamic process is the theoretical base for *prediction* of the expected output that will be produced after a given time interval from the current time. The expected output is evaluated starting from current and past inputs and past outputs (either real or extracted from the model). This is often useful in several applications to foresee the system or process behavior enough in advance to take correct decisions. A number of examples are available in complex systems, industrial plants, medicine, biology, chemistry, environmental sciences, and several other fields—just to mention some cases: temperature and pressure prediction, induction current in electric motors and generators, position and speed prediction of moving objects, fluid-flow estimation, load estimation for electric power distribution, fault prediction in machinery and plants, production estimation for plant management, stock exchange trends of shares and currencies, load forecast in computer networking and telephone switching systems, food industry, product quality assessment, seismic events, weather forecasting, effectiveness of medical treatments, sensitivity of drugs, and diseases forecast.

A particular use of prediction is the "what–if" simulation: quite accurate simulations are performed in a very limited time to foresee the machine/plant reactions to different possible actions without actually applying them, so that the supervisor is able to select the most suitable one.

Neural networks have been shown to be effective also in the *control* of nonlinear systems, involving both static and dynamic cases. With respect to traditional techniques, neural paradigms are attractive when the nonlinearities are very strong, the dynamics are complex, and the system behavior is not completely known. The main goal is to maintain the desired working point of the system despite possible variations of the operating conditions and environment; alternatively, in evolving systems, control is directed to guarantee that the system moves along the desired trajectory in the state space with a predefined accuracy.

Several neural models have been experimented with that deal with a large variety of application systems, environments, and conditions. High accuracy can be achieved for single-input single-output systems, by taking into account different classes of data observability (e.g., explicit or hidden states and physical quantities) and error models (namely output error, noise). Systems having multiple inputs and/or outputs may be modeled with increased difficulties due to higher complexity. Often, accuracy is anyway competitive with the one reported by using traditional approaches suitable for dynamic linear, linearized, or nonlinear systems.

A large number of industrial applications have been reported in the literature, among which are machinery operation, rotation and forces in motors, fuel distribution in combustion engines, electric power stabilizers, inverter control, motion of robotic arms, industrial manipulators, navigation in moving platforms and robots, flight control, orientation and navigation of space satellites, electronic control system for automotive, vibration, fluid flow in pipelines, pressure and temperature control in machinery, systems, and production processes, fluid level in machinery and plants, chemical processes, distillation, food state and manipulation, calibration of advanced instruments, environment control, pollution, signal equalization in electronic amplifiers, image quality in camera and reproduction devices, and prosthesis control.

Another large area of successful application of the neural techniques is *signal processing*. Different goals and perspectives can be considered in manipulating continuous sequences of data generated by a physical processes. Signal transformation through *signal filtering* is one of the classical techniques for modifying the characteristics of the signal itself or extract relevant information. As in traditional approaches (e.g., Finite Impulse Response (FIR) and IIR filtering as well as Fourier or cosine transformations), the signal is observed through a sampling window sliding in time over the signal itself. Whenever the observation window photographs a set of signal samples, the filtering or transformation is applied, generating the output view of the incoming signal. A number of cases have been reported in the literature for signals produced in different application areas (e.g., in electronics, electrical engineering, mechanical systems, chemical plants, biomedical systems, radio transmissions). Noise cancellation in any kind of continuous signal is one of the most effective cases. The prediction and cross-correlation ability of neural network can be exploited for signal reconstruction whenever the noise makes the signal poorly understandable or even when the sensor observing the signal is occasionally or temporarily unable to operate (e.g., for transient or intermittent faults).

Neural implementation of some classical transformations (e.g., Walsh, Hough) is also been experimented with to benefit from the adaptive abilities of the neural paradigms in configuring the filter coefficients; harmonic analysis of the signal by using neural networks constitutes a high-level transformation able to extract the relevant characteristics of the signal itself.

Filtering can be used also for feature extraction from the input signal; for example, to detect the occurrence of characteristics waveforms, pulses, spikes, and regularities. Several applications are in speech and sound processing (e.g., for automatic typewriters, phoneme and word recognition, speech understanding, automatic translators, voice and sound compression, equalization and manipulation, voice and sound synthesis). Other industrial applications are in the identification of the operating conditions of machinery, plants, and production processes by observing sensor data, as well as preliminary analysis and data cleaning for system diagnosis.

Availability of data coming from a number of sensors in parallel often requires some preprocessing to merge and compare information coming from the different sources into a single highly compact data flow, avoiding redundancies and removing possible local errors. This allows also for the extraction of relevant information for the application from a massive amount of data.

Sensor signal fusion is the basis of high-level data processing in the presence of many signal sources. Examples can be found in electromagnetic field modeling, multisource remote sensing for geophysics, radar signal analysis, complex structures (e.g., bridges) analysis and monitoring, location determination for mobile robots, weather forecast, life signals analysis, and monitoring for medicine.

Signal processing can be used with sensor fusion to create *high-level signal sensors*. As for any traditional physical quantity, we can, in fact, define a feature in the system under observation and a measurement procedure to evaluate quantitatively such a feature. The neural network can extract information from inputs coming from real sensors, and manipulate and merge them in order to create an instrument capable of performing a high-level measurement (possibly indirect) of the desired feature. The simplest example of these high-level approaches consists of measuring a quantity defined as a function of physical quantities observed by sensors; other, more abstract examples are the membership of the inputs to predefined classes and the identification of features (e.g., pulses, spikes, specific waveforms, regularities).

Several practical cases have been reported in the literature and used in the industry: tactile exploration for robots, speed and incline estimation for moving objects, classification of dielectric anomalies, classification of materials, classification of surface characteristics, product quality inspection for computer-aided manufacturing, electric load monitoring, classification of electrical partial discharges, radar and sonar signal categorization, phoneme recognition, classification of vibration and seismic signals, security assessment in plants, biological tissue classification, and waveform classification in electrocardiograms and electroencephalograms.

A high-level measurement may also be used for the diagnosis of complex systems and the identification of the fault and/or the faulty component. Examples are available in the literature for sensors, motors, complex systems, and plants, in particular in electrical, electronic, mechanical, aerospace, civil, and chemical engineering fields.

Similar to signal processing is the use of neural networks for *image processing*. The basic difference is in the intrinsic structure of the treated data being bidimensional, instead of monodimensional as it happens in simple signal processing. Also, image processing has a wide application area and provides attractive results, which are often competitive with the traditional algorithmic techniques.

Image filtering is directed to the same goal as signal filtering. Noise removal and image transformation are applied to clean the images and to extract relevant features from them, as well as to enhance their quality. Typical applications explored by research and often exploited in the industry are image cleaning and restoration, edge detection, contour identification, segment and texture extraction, and quality control.

Sensor image fusion has been experimented with for example, in human or robot motion analysis from image observation and in artificial stereo vision for robots. High-abstraction measurements can be performed on images, similar to simple signals. *High-level image sensors* can be defined to process the rough images in order to extract characteristic features. Several examples are available in the literature, mainly related to classification and recognition problems: object recognition from visual observation, classification of target radar images, cloud classification, motion understanding from visual analysis, vision understanding, character recognition, complex image (e.g., human face) recognition, classification of images of biological tissues, analysis and classification of nuclear magnetic resonance images, fingerprint recognition, pattern recognition and classification, quality assessment by visual inspection, and system diagnosis from visual inspection.

DESIGN METHODOLOGIES

Design and implementation of neural paradigms to solve real-world application problems is often a complex and not well-defined task. In the literature, there are many theoretical papers addressing the fundamental and methodological aspects as well as application examples showing the effectiveness of neural technologies in wide areas. However, a well-structured general methodology or, at least, a set of them suited for specialized application areas are not yet available, or well assessed, or widely accepted, or practically effective. Partial strategies and many suggestions are presented in the literature by abstracting from the application examples, but they usually are suitable only in a very narrow area, or they address a specific topic, or they are too abstract to be of some practical use for the given problem. This lack of methodology and the difficulties in using them are often due to the relative novelty and intrinsic complexity of these computational paradigms, the number of theoretical and practical application problems involved, the possible uncertainty and incomplete definition in the applications, and the superficiality and the lack of technical knowledge about the application and the related background that are shown by some practitioners in affording the applications. Unfortunately, the designer needs to rely mainly on previous experiences and intuitively generalize the information and results currently available.

In this section, some basic design phases and hints are summarized to provide a general framework for an effective and successful approach to the use of neural technologies in industrial applications; however, the designer needs to refer to more specialized examples in the literature to find previous experiences similar to his application case, so as to exploit possible results already available.

The first design phase is *partitioning* of the complex application problem into well-separated subproblems interconnected by a limited number of system variables. This allows limiting the complexity of each problem to be treated and make it more manageable, in particular because it becomes relatively easier to choose the neural paradigms suitable for the specific problem, possibly by looking in the literature for similar cases. Moreover, training a large neural network capable of capturing the behavior of the whole system requires a longer and more accurate procedure to avoid possible biasing of the network behavior on some of the system relationships.

Typical partitioning guidelines are subsystem simplicity, functional decoupling, physical or topological separation, interconnection clusters, observability and measurability of variables, and controllability of subsystems inputs. Best results are often achieved by decomposing the system in Single Input Single Output (SISO) or Multiple Input Single Output (MISO) subsystems with possible reconvergent paths. They are described by observing and measuring input or internal system variables while either one system output or one internal system measurable variable is generated.

It is necessary that each subproblem be solved by using neural techniques: in many cases, neural techniques are highly desirable because an algorithmic approach is not known or efficient. However, whenever such an approach exists and can be implemented satisfying the application constraints (e.g., real-time operation), it should be adopted unless a neural approach is proved to have higher performance or accuracy (when they are desired in the application). This allows the selection of the best problem-solving strategy for each individual subproblem by exploiting the characteristics of each technology (namely algorithms, neural networks, or even, in general, fuzzy logic, genetic algorithms, expert systems, etc.), which is a single approach usually not suitable, effective, or accurate for the whole problem as for the specialized ones.

Configuration of a neural model for one of the above subproblems means defining its parameters so that to reproduce the behavior of the system or the physical process. In many cases, the whole input domain is not completely used by the application because the application is defined in a subdomain. An accurate neural solution needs to be found only in these subspaces: despite of the generalization ability, we cannot grant good performances from them (even if it is reasonable to wait for a degrading loss in performance). The second phase in neural design is *selection of working ranges*, by analyzing the characteristic behavior of the application and its constraints.

Sample generation for learning, testing, and validation must be performed according to the specific characteristics of the application. If the problem is reducible to that of pattern classification, samples need to be extracted so as to cover the input/output space as possible.

If the application is related to analysis and modeling of a static physical process (i.e., with outputs related only to the current inputs), the process must be observed and sampled; sampling should be performed at each variation of the process input variables which control the process behavior. If the process inputs can be controlled, they should be excited, with values covering the whole input space so as to fully explore the system behavior in it.

If the system to be modeled is a dynamic process or a system, training data generation does not simply consist in observing and collecting input–output pairs, but must take into account the whole dynamic response of the process (i.e., a sequence of input–output pairs). If the system to be modeled is an autonomous dynamic process without any external control parameter, the training data must be extracted from the observation of the process itself.

Conversely, if the system has inputs that can be controlled and stimulated by the designer, adequate excitation signals for each of them must be identified to fully excite all system dynamics so as to achieve an accurate model from an extensive observation of the system behavior under the widest operating conditions. A good approximation of the ideal white-noise signal is a random signal composed of steps and ramps with random amplitudes, periods, and steepnesses, covering the input working space. If system inputs are naturally not independent due to the physical characteristics of the system or to the presence of control loops, independent excitations may be not feasible and, as a consequence, part of the dynamics may be not captured completely, leading to possible inaccuracy. Some uncorrelation signals can be artificially introduced to enhance the quality of the neural model by adding small perturbations to subsystem feedback signals. The training data are extracted by *sampling* inputs and (if a supervised learning is envisioned) outputs of the dynamic system. Sampling is performed with a period T suitable to capture all typical system dynamics. The ideal sampling period should be at least half of the shortest time constant of the system in order to observe all dynamics correctly. In the practice, it can be derived either by studying a rough mathematical model of the system or by spectral analysis of input and output signals being the sampling frequency at least double of the maximal cut frequency for which the signal is bandwidth; estimation uncertainty suggests reducing such approximated sampling period by a correction factor while limiting massive oversampling to preserve training speed and avoid overfitting.

As already stated, three different sets of samples should be generated independently in this way for training the neural model: *learning*, *testing*, and *validation sets*. They are respectively used to evaluate the functional optimization and weights corrections in learning, to verify the learning termination by considering the approximation error and the generalization ability, and to evaluate the quality of the model at the end of learning.

If the neural model must perform a static mapping of inputs to outputs, each element in any of these sets is either an input–output pair or an input value only for supervised or unsupervised learning, respectively. If the neural network is used to model a dynamic process or system, the element is a sequence of input–output pairs—supervised learning usually being adopted—covering the system response to the input event triggering it. Theoretically, this response lasts an infinite time, but it can be practically considered exhausted in a suitable finite time. However, because the input excitation is composed of a random signal (or its approximation), the resulting total response is actually the composition of the responses to the individual exciting events: As a consequence, the total response should still be in infinite sequence. A good approximation can be built by cascading random finite-time subsequences, each of which is obtained by exciting the system, as discussed above, and guaranteeing the signal continuity between adjacent subsequences; a finite (but large enough) number of different subsequence is created to guarantee the virtual randomness. Typically, a subsequence is about few tens times the largest system line constant and few tens of different subsequence are required. Due to the possible relevant length of the system response, an observation window is used to extract a subset of contiguous samples from the sequence at each iteration; the window slides along the sequence at each iteration of the learning algorithm so as to present the whole dynamics.

Usually, inputs and outputs do not have the same order of magnitude: This may lead to learning to focus on capturing the behavior related more to large inputs or outputs than to the others. Data *normalization* is thus necessary to guarantee correctness and effectiveness of the training algorithm and to limit the possible dominance of some inputs or outputs with respect to the others. Data normalization scales data amplitude into the same range of values (typically, $[-1, 1]$).

Similarly, if the observation window used for dynamic systems has a variable size for capturing the signal characteristics, it needs to be normalized to a given size in order to match the number of network inputs. Samples in the normalized window are generated by interpolating the actual samples in the variable-sized window and by extracting the desired samples from the interpolating function in the actual window scaled to the normalized size.

The subsequent design phase is concerned with the *selection of the neural paradigm*. The family of neural models (namely the network topology and the neuron operation) is chosen for the application envisioned, according to experience. Then, the specific structure of the neural model must be defined (i.e., the number of layers, the numbers of neurons in each layer); also, this step is accomplished by exploiting the personal experience. If no satisfactory guideline is found, an "intelligent" exploration of the possible structures is needed.

For the adopted neural paradigm, *selection of the learning algorithm* must be performed among the techniques summarized in the section Theoretical Foundations of the Neural Computation for Industrial Applications. Because training is strictly related to the paradigm structure, this step basically consists of adopting the training approach proposed in the literature for the envisioned neural model, even if a limited selection among some variations or alternative techniques as well as some optimization may be available. Also, in this case, the literature and the personal experience are usually of great help in identifying a good or, at least, reasonable approach.

It is worth noting that, because selection of both the neural model and the learning algorithm rely mainly on designer knowledge and expertise, the quality and the effectiveness of the neural solution for a given application is often difficult to be a priori foreseen.

To apply the learning algorithm, it is necessary to define the *training scheme* (i.e., the arrangement of inputs, outputs, and learning algorithm) according to the specific application and the adopted training procedure. The training scheme for classification applications or modeling static processes and systems is shown in Figures 3a and 3b for supervised and unsupervised learning, respectively. Current inputs are presented to the network, which, in turn, generate the current outputs. In supervised learning, current and expected system outputs are delivered to the training procedure to evaluate the weight adjustment from the actual error. In unsupervised learning, only the current output is used by the training algorithm to determine the weight adjustment. The new weights are then applied to the model.

The training scheme for prediction in dynamic processes and systems has the typical structure shown in Figure 3c (where Z is the delay operator). Current and past inputs are presented to the network with the past actual system outputs; the network generates the current expected outputs which are compared to the expected ones for weight adjustment. The real past data are, in fact, available to foresee the future outputs.

The training scheme for neural identification is given in Figure 3d: The past actual outputs are replaced by the corresponding outputs generated by the network in the past. Alternatively, if the absolute error is quite small with respect to the signals, the neural paradigm can be configured faster by using the training scheme for prediction, and the past expected output are replaced by the actual ones during recall.

For dynamic system control, neural identification of the system to be controlled may be performed first: this provides a model from which it is often easier to extract the training data for the controller. In the *indirect control* approach, the controller is synthesized as a neural identifier whose inputs are the outputs of the controlled systems and the reference input, whereas the outputs are the inputs of the controlled system. White noise is added to achieve a more robust identification. If the static behavior is not completely captured by the model, a feed-forward neural controller is introduced to generate an additive correction.

If the dynamics are not limited or the expected controlled behavior cannot be derived from the system description, the *direct control* approach must be adopted. The neural controller is trained by using the system outputs and the reference input as inputs, whereas its outputs are delivered to the actual system and to the system neural model; the error between the model and system outputs is back-propagated through the neural model in order to evaluate the error induced at the controller outputs, and such last error Is, In turn, used to adjust the weights of the neural controller.

The subsequent phase is the *application of the learning procedure*. During such a task, the learning data set is presented to the network several times in order to guarantee enough understanding of the desired behavior. Learning data are extracted randomly from the data set and presented to the network: uniform extraction provides a balanced and unbiased learned behavior. The number of repetitions is related to the complexity of

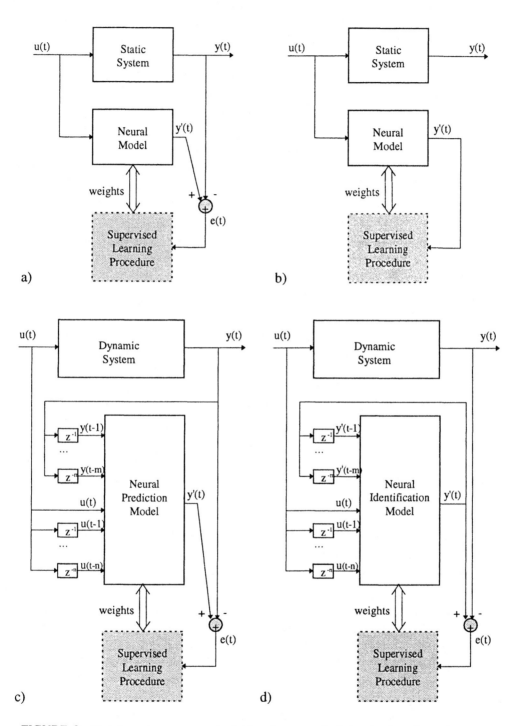

FIGURE 3   Training schemes: supervised (a) and unsupervised (b) algorithm in static neural networks, prediction (c), and identification (d) in dynamic networks.

the problem: it should be determined from the experience and from the accurate analysis of the literature. The termination test is applied to decide about the continuation of learning.

If the obtained network is overdimensioned with respect to the problem, *network optimization* techniques can be envisaged, as already discussed earlier. They reduce the topological complexity by removing unnecessary neurons or interconnections either by pruning at the end of the training phase or by modifying the figure of merit used during learning which penalizes unnecessary degrees of freedom.

Finally, to evaluate the model quality (e.g., the learning error and the generalization ability), *validation* is performed by applying the validation data set at the end of learning.

CONCLUSIONS

Basic theoretical aspects of artificial neural networks have been reviewed in this article. The main application areas related to prediction, identification, control, robotics, and signal and image processing have been explored to show the effectiveness and the efficiency of these adaptive computational paradigms. The relative novelty of these techniques and their intrinsic complexity have not yet allowed the definition of a standard design methodology for any application. However, the main common steps have been discussed in this article to provide practical guidelines. Because complete design still depends on the experience and the ability of the designer rather than on a well-assessed methodology, the successful use of these techniques is often not guaranteed.

Positive results achieved in many cases, and the apparent simplicity of these techniques induced many users to consider them as the ideal approach whenever a complex problem is concerned or an algorithmic solution is not known. Also, these paradigms have their own limits and drawbacks. The designer should try to adopt the most suited approach to tackle each subproblem, leading to create heterogeneous systems in which classic algorithmic solutions and neural components are mixed to exploit the specific capabilities of each technology. Similarly, other soft-computing approaches (such as fuzzy logic, genetic algorithm, expert systems, chaos) should be integrated as well.

BIBLIOGRAPHY

Anderson, J. A. and E. Rosenfeld (eds.), *Neurocomputing*: *Foundations of Research*, MIT Press, Cambridge, MA, 1988.

Anderson, J. A., Pellionisz, A., and E. Rosenfeld (eds.), *Neurocomputing 2*: *Directions for Research*, MIT Press, Cambridge, MA, 1990.

Baughmann, D. R. and Y. A. Liu, *Neural Networks in Bioprocessing and Chemical Engineering*, Academic Press, San Diego, CA, 1995.

Cichocki, A. and R. Unbehauen, *Neural Networks for Optimization and Signal Processing*, John Wiley & Sons, New York, 1993.

Dowla, F. U. and L. L. Rogers, *Solving Problems in Environmental Engineering and Geosciences with Artificial Neural Networks*, MIT Press, Cambridge, MA, 1995.

Gelenbe, E. (ed.), *Neural Networks Advances and Applications*, 2, Elsevier Science Publishers, Amsterdam, 1992.

Hassoun, M. H., *Fundamentals of Artificial Neural Networks*, MIT Press, Cambridge, MA, 1995.

Haykin, S., *Neural Networks*: *A Comprehensive Foundation*, McMillan and IEEE Computer Society, New York, 1994.

Hertz, J., A. Krogh, and R. G. Palmer, *Introduction to the Theory of Neural Computation*, Addison-Wesley, Redwood City, CA, 1991.

Hecht-Nielsen, R., *Neurocomputing*, Addison-Wesley, Reading, MA, 1990.

Khanna, T., *Foundations of Neural Networks*, Addison-Wesley, Reading, MA, 1990.

Kosko, B., *Neural Networks and Fuzzy Systems*, Prentice-Hall, Englewood Cliffs, NJ, 1992.

Linggard, R., D. J. Myers, and C. Nightngale (eds.), *Neural Networks for Vision, Speech and Natural Language*, Chapman & Hall, London, 1992.

Maren, A., C. Harston, and R. Pap, *Handbook of Neural Computing Applications*, Academic Press, San Diego, CA, 1990.

Miller, W. T., III, R. S. Sutton, and P. J. Werbos (eds.), *Neural Networks for Control*, MIT Press, Cambridge, MA, 1990.

Narendra, K. S., R. Ortega, and P. Dorato, *Advances in Adaptive Control*, IEEE Press, New York, 1991.

Pham, D. T. and X. Liu, *Neural Networks for Identification, Prediction and Control*, Springer-Verlag, London, 1995.

Sanchez-Sinencio, E. and C. Lau, *Artificial Neural Networks*, IEEE Press, New York, 1992.

Sheu, B. J. and J. Choi, *Neural Information Processing and VLSI*, Kluwer Academic Publishers, Boston, 1995.

Siu, K.-Y., V. Roychowdhury, and T. Kailath, *Discrete Neural Computation: A Theoretical Foundation*, Prentice-Hall, Englewood Cliffs, NJ, 1995.

Takefuji, Y. (ed.), *Analog VLSI Neural Networks*, Kluwer Academic Publishers, Boston, 1993.

Touretsky, D. S. (ed.), *Advances in Neural Information Processing Systems, 1*, Morgan Kaufmann, San Mateo, CA, 1989.

Touretsky, D. S. (ed.), *Advances in Neural Information Processing Systems, 2*, Morgan Kaufmann, San Mateo, CA, 1990.

Weigend, A. S. and N. A. Gershenfeld (eds.), *Time Series Prediction: Forecasting the Future and Understanding the Past*, Addison-Wesley, Reading, MA, 1994.

White, D. A. and D. A. Sofge (eds.), *Handbook of Intelligen Control: Neural Fuzzy and Adaptive Approaches*, Van Nonstrand Reinhold, New York, 1992.

Zurada, J. M., *Introduction to Artificial Neural Systems*, West Publishing Company, St. Paul, MN, 1992.

IEEE Transactions on Neural Networks, yearly edition, since 1989.

INNS Journal on Neural Networks, yearly edition, since 1989.

Proceedings in Advances in Neural Information Processing Systems NIPS, yearly edition, since 1989.

IEEE Proceedings of the International Conference on Neural Networks ICNN, published in 1987, 1988, 1993, 1994, 1995, 1996.

IEEE–INNS Proceedings of the International Joint Conference on Neural Networks IJCNN, published in 1989, 1990 (two issues), 1991, 1992 (two issues), 1997.

INNS Proceedings of the World Congress on Neural Networks WCNN, published in 1993, 1994, 1995, 1996.

CESARE ALIPPI

VINCENZO PIURI

REAL-TIME SITUATION MANAGEMENT:
A JAVA APPLICATION

INTRODUCTION

Communication: A process by which information is exchanged among individuals through a common system.

Coordination: An activity in which various parts or units act together in a smooth, synchronized manner for the most effective results.

In many organizations, plans are constructed for activities, and all the activities that a particular individual, unit, or resource is responsible for are grouped together as an activity list. This list serves to remind the individual what activities are his/her responsibility and acts as evidence of the completion of activities.

Plans are constructed for a wide range of activities:

- ISO 9000 compliance
- Safety checks for mines or ships
- Evidence gathering at large disasters
- Power plant (nuclear and electrical) situation response
- Launching of trains, airplanes, ships (cruise and freight), military operations, space operations, and other major events such as marketing, sports events, and so on
- Emergency situations with police, medical, disaster, fire, government, rail, airline (crashes), and ships (oil spills)
- Legal or regulatory compliance
- Just-in-Time (JIT) manufacturing

In these situations, the coordination and communication between individuals and an understanding of the status of the current state of the plan's implementation are of prime importance. The organization(s) is responsible for managing the situation to an optimal conclusion.

In many organizations, situations occur either spontaneously, as in the case of a natural disaster, or are planned, as in the case of launching a spacecraft. The organization is responsible for managing the situation to its optimal conclusion. This typically involves having previously considered the situation's occurrence and developed a plan for it.

Typically, the organization involved is not so concerned with budgets and schedules, as in the case of long-term projects. Although the schedule is still of interest, its focus is shifted to ensure that all required tasks are completed. In such situations, the

---

Java is a trademark of Sun Microsystems Inc. Other trademarks appearing in this article, such as Macintosh and SUN SPARC, are trademarks of their respective companies.

individuals involved are concerned with the completion of the tasks in the shortest time possible.

Typically, many situations are of short duration, ranging from hours to a few days. In such situations, the individuals involved are concerned with synchronization, coordination, and communication with minimal time delays.

Let us now explore a few examples. One such example could be for emergency response organizations, such as fire, police, medical, and power-generating stations (nuclear and hydro). In such organizations, plans are usually derived for different situations. However, the exact time of occurrence of the situation is unknown. Once the situation occurs, a tool could be used to ensure that the many different organizations that could be involved are kept coordinated and everyone is kept current of the status of the situation.

Another example is similar to the first, but the timing of the occurrence of the situation is known in advance, for example, in a space launch, cruise ship departure, or military operation, and so on. The difference in the two types of examples is that in this example, a set of activities preceding the start of the situation usually occurs. For example, in a space launch, many tasks must be complete before launch clearance can be given. In this situation, there is a point at which the person with overall responsibility must decide to begin the execution of the project. Understanding the status of the organization prior to making that go/no-go decision is crucial.

For a third example, consider that before a ship can leave port, a number of tasks, such as loading a wide variety of materials and supplies, must be complete.

In many such situations, the coordination and communication between individuals is critical. For example, in a civil emergency, the activities of the fire, police, and medical resources must be coordinated to maximize effectiveness.

In many situations, tasks that are performed are also guided by regulations or laws. For example, in nuclear power plants or in oil spills, ensuring that the appropriate response is completed is very important.

JAVA

The APEXM development project began by first developing the required functionality and then considering the hardware/software platform. Once the required functionality was decided upon, a number of design constraints were issued.

It was determined that the target hardware platforms could be a mix of Macintoshes, PCs and SUNs. However, there was no certainty of that mix or which platform could be the server; the server being the computer which contains the database. Thus, the possibly that the hardware platform might be, for example, Macintoshes and PCs with either a Macintosh or PC as the server had to be considered. In addition, many other factors were considered; for example, APEXM had to

- Interact without a UNIX operating system
- Interact without expensive X-Window-type software
- Have communication between remote units over the Internet to lower long-distance phone costs
- Have no additional costs for database software
- Have little memory or disk space requirements
- Cut development costs by not having separate versions of the software for each type of operating system

At first, the team considered using a computer language called C++, which would have required UNIX (which allows multiple users) and special user terminal software to allow each user to operate on the server. Although this violated the design constraints, the technology was mature and well known.

The computer language called Java was then considered. It was newly available and reportedly would fit all the design constraints and functionality requirements.

Java* is a language that is constructed using the common capabilities across computers and their operating systems. It allows the developer to write a software program and use a compiler to translate that program into code applicable for an operating system. A compiler is an automatic code translation program, and depending on machine speed, it takes a few minutes to complete the translation.

Upon deciding to examine the capabilities of Java, experimental code was developed to further understand the language's level of maturity and capability. It became obvious that Java would satisfy the design constraints and functionality requirements.

APEXM OVERVIEW

APEXM, a plan which is a set of activities, can be represented, and the software allows each team member to indicate the status of each activity item. The activity list serves to remind the user which items have been completed and which have not. Activity items of interest to other individuals can be connected. This could be the case when one individual wants to know the status of another individual's activity item, perhaps for information purposes or in order to begin a follow-on activity.

This connection function allows both horizontal and vertical connections. Thus, activity items can be connected to other individuals and used to indicate that a successive activity can now begin; or the activity items can be connected to managers for information purposes in order for them to know the status of the organization before making decisions. Another function, designed to enhance the understanding of the status of the organization, allows activity lists to be grouped by relevance. Each user can then view the completion status of all relevant activity lists.

In many organizations, either for analysis or legislative purposes, a great concern is knowing exactly when activity items were completed; thus APEXM will record the time the user indicated that each activity item was completed.

The APEXM system consists of two main packages: a plan editor and a situation monitor.

For each plan, the plan editor provides the facilities to define the various activities to be performed by each team member and to interlink those activities that influence or affect other personnel. Thus, for example, if there is a chemical spill, the cleanup crews may need to know when it is safe to begin work based on the activity of another team member.

The situation monitor provides the various team personnel with a reminder of the activities to perform for a given situation. The situation monitor also provides a mechanism to pass information to people who require it before being able to complete their own activities.

---

*For more information on Java see httpd//www.javasoft.com on the Internet.

As shown in Figure 1, users can be connected through the intranet and Internet while using the situation monitor.

In most situations the current response systems being used often rely on using paper checklists or long telephone/radio communications (widely used in the military and emergency response organizations).

The Java system thus offers many advantages, including the following:

1. Global and timely view of the action of all the participants.
2. Coordination across the participants.
3. The system captures the various activities and processes that must be implemented, thus reducing training time and loss of detail.
4. The completed activity lists form archival data that offer evidence of the execution of the procedures in the correct time sequence.
5. The responses can be reviewed for appropriateness, and gaps or inappropriate interconnections can be corrected easily and preserved for the future.
6. The worldwide interconnectivity of the Internet offers a low-cost medium ac-

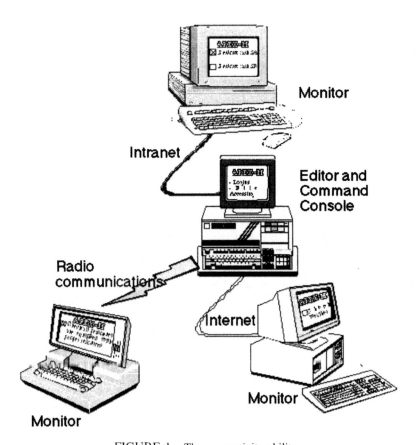

FIGURE 1   The connectivity ability.

cessible to everyone. Access to the system is therefore possible to anyone who has telephone access.

7. The product is machine independent and will run on the existing computing platforms.
8. Using a laptop and a modem, the system is totally portable, allowing any official to move around and keep up to date at the same time.
9. Plan coordinators can change the plans and all people involved can be updated with new activity lists.

Figures 2–4 show the editor and the monitor.

DEVELOPMENT AND TESTING RESULTS

The development of the project took place on a Macintosh, and when testing took place several Java deficiencies came to light. Laboratory testing consisted of several machines connected together to simulate a 20-user setup. The machines included a SUN SPARC

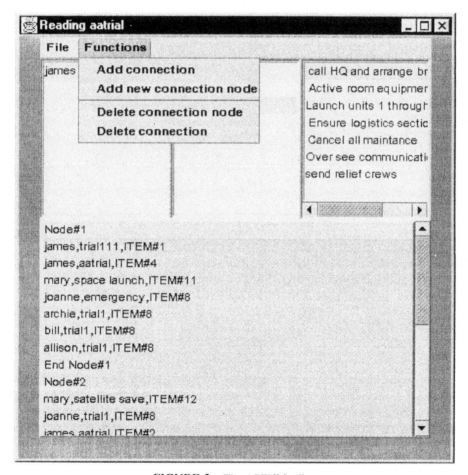

FIGURE 2   The APEXM editor.

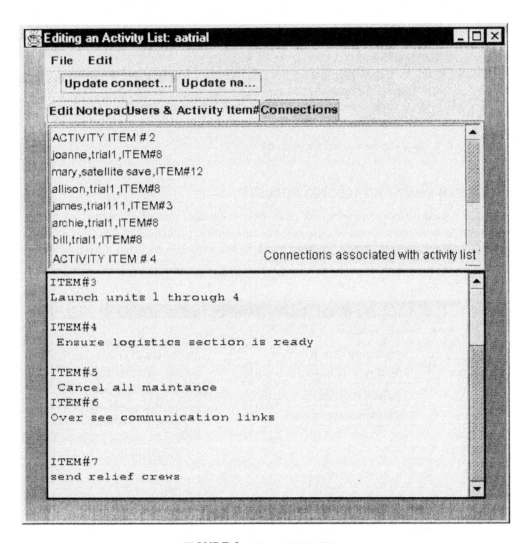

FIGURE 3   The APEXM Editor.

5, Macintoshes, Power Macintoshes, a Power Book Macintosh, and a 486 PC running Windows 95. The setup involved both remote log-in over the Internet and local-area-network (LAN)-based computers. The 486 and the SUN took turns in separate tests as the central computer. A series of tests was conducted, and all machines had been preset to have synchronized internal clocks.

Testing was successful. In addition to the 20-user simulations, some testing involved initialing two users on the SUN SPARC and having the operator check activity

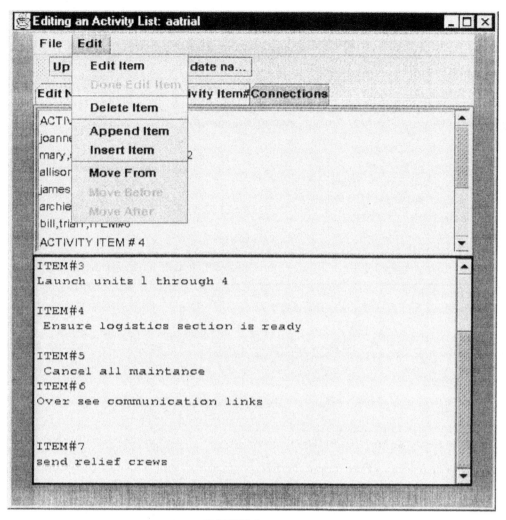

FIGURE 3   Continued.

items in such a fast sequence that items were checked off as true and then false within 1 s and an activity item of a second activity list was modified within the same second.

However, whereas the entire system worked on the SUN SPARC station, problems occurred on the PC and Macintosh. On the PC using Java version 1.1, the text does not appear properly on the screen and some screens crash the system.

The Macintosh version 1.0.2 contained many more glitches: The echo-back character on the text fields did not work, the cursor could not be seen on Power Macintoshes, the list component did not screen refresh properly, and, finally, most serious of all for this, application, the Macintosh would not listen to more than two ports at a time.

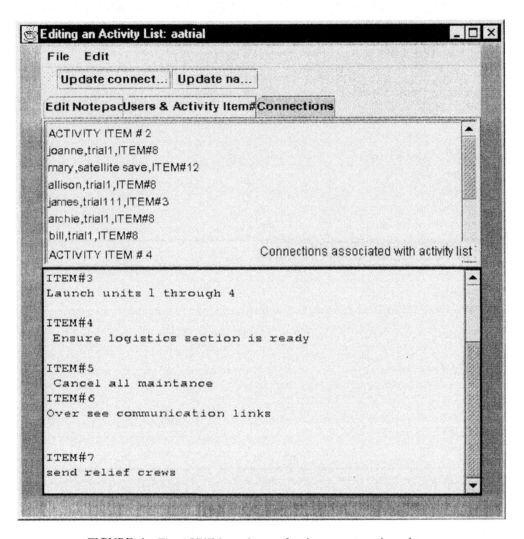

FIGURE 4   The APEXM monitor performing an automatic update.

CONCLUSION

The original recommendation to develop the application using Java is still considered valid and the author believes glitches will be removed as the language matures.

GLOSSARY

Activity list: A set of tasks or activities for which one individual is responsible.

Activity item: One activity or task on an activity list.

Central computer: The computer in which the APEXM editor software resides and the APEXM database. This computer is also accessed by the computers containing the APEXM monitor software to access the database.

Plan: A set of tasks or activities that must be completed.

Project management: Most individuals are familiar with the concept of project management and related software tools. With project management software, the user is able to represent a plan for a project in terms of activities or tasks. Each task has resources, typically people and equipment, associated with it. In addition, each task has a cost and time duration associated with it. Tasks can have sequential relationships to other tasks. Once the tasks are linked, budgets and schedules can be derived.

During the execution of the project, actual time and money expenditures can be entered and the impact on the schedule and budget determined. Typically, such software produces various reports and has many analysis capabilities.

Real time: Information or data presented in real time is current and up to date. In the case of APEXM, the status of the activity lists is always current to approximately one minute.

Situation: A complex, trying, or critical problem or circumstance.

Situation management: The ability to make the appropriate guiding decisions during a situation so that the situation comes to an optimal solution.

BIBLIOGRAPHY

Cornell, G. and C. S. Horstman, "*Core Java*", SunSoft Press, Mountain View, CA.
Daconta, M. C., *Java for C/C++ Programmers*, John Wiley & Sons, New York.
Flanagan, D., *Java in a Nutshell*, O'Reilly & Associates, Sebastopol, CA.
Newman, A., *Special Edition Using Java*, Que Corporation, Indianapolis, IN.

JAMES E. BOWEN

RISK MANAGEMENT

TERMS AND DEFINITIONS

Risk

There are a number of definitions and uses for the term risk, but no universally accepted definition.

What all definitions have in common is agreement that risk has two characteristics (1, p. 7):

- *Uncertainty*: An event may or may not happen.
- *Loss*: An event has unwanted consequences or losses.

Example Risk Definitions

Three example definitions of risk are shown below:

Risk is the potential for realization of unwanted negative consequences of an event (2, p. 24).

Risk is the measure of the probability and severity of adverse effects (3, p. 94).

Risk is the possibility of suffering loss, injury, disadvantage, or destruction (4, p. 1961).

SEI Definition of Risk

The SEI uses the Webster's Dictionary definition of risk: *Risk* is the possibility of suffering loss.

In a development project, the loss describes the impact to the project which could be in the form of diminished quality of the end product, increased costs, delayed completion, or failure.

Risk vs. Opportunity

Risk and opportunity go hand in hand. Many development projects strive to advance current capabilities and achieve something that hasn't been done before. The opportunity for advancement cannot be achieved without taking risk. "Risk in itself is not bad; risk is essential to progress, and failure is often a key part of learning. But we must learn to balance the possible negative consequences of risk against the potential benefits of its associated opportunity" (5, p. 3).

Special permission to reprint portions of the *Continuous Risk Management Guidebook.* © 1996 by Carnegie-Mellon University is granted by the Software Engineering Institute.

SEI Risk Statement

For a risk to be understandable, it must be expressed clearly. Such a statement must include

- A description of the current conditions that may lead to the loss
- A description of the loss or consequence

Risk Example

A company has introduced object-oriented (OO) technology into its organization by selecting a well-defined project "X" with hard schedule constraints to pilot the use of the technology. Although many "X" project personnel were familiar with the OO concept, it had not been part of their development process, and they have had very little experience and training in the technology's application. It is taking project personnel longer than expected to climb the learning curve. Some personnel are concerned, for example, that the modules implemented to date might be too inefficient to satisfy project "X" performance requirements.

The risk is: Given the lack of OO technology experience and training, there is a possibility that the product will not meet performance or functionality requirements within the defined schedule.

Non-Risk Example

Another company is developing a flight control system. During system integration-testing, the flight control system becomes unstable because processing of the control function is not quick enough during a specific maneuver sequence.

The instability of the system is not a risk since the event is a certainty—it is a problem.

CONTINUOUS RISK MANAGEMENT DEFINITION

Background

The term *risk management* is applied in a number of diverse disciplines. People in the fields of statistics, economics, psychology, social sciences, biology, engineering, toxicology, systems analysis, operations research, and decision theory, to name a few, have been addressing the field of risk management (1, p. 8).

Kloman summarized the meaning of risk management in the context of a number of different disciplines in an article for *Risk Analysis*:

> What is risk management? To many social analysts, politicians, and academics it is the management of environmental and nuclear risk, those technology-generated macro-risks that appear to threaten our existence. To bankers and financial officers it is the sophisticated use of such techniques as currency hedging and interest rate swaps. To insurance buyers and sellers it is coordination of insurable risks and the reduction of insurance costs. To hospital administrators it may mean "quality assurance." To safety professionals it is reducing accidents and injuries. (6, p. 20).

Kloman Paraphrase of Rowe

Risk management is a discipline for living with the possibility that future events may cause adverse effects (6, p. 203).

SEI Definition

Continuous Risk Management is a software engineering practice with processes, methods, and tools for managing risks in a project. It provides a disciplined environment for proactive decision-making to

- Assess continuously what could go wrong (risks)
- Determine which risks are important to deal with
- Implement strategies to deal with those risks

Note: The SEI definition emphasizes the continuous aspect of risk management—hence the name Continuous Risk Management (CRM).

Continuous Risk Management Example

When using Continuous Risk Management, risks are assessed continuously and used for decision-making in all phases of a project. Risks are carried forward and dealt with until they are resolved or they turn into problems and are handled as such.

Non-Continuous Risk Management Example

In some projects, risks are assessed only once during initial project planning. Major risks are identified and mitigated, but risks are never explicitly looked at again.

This is not an example of Continuous Risk Management because risks are not continuously assessed and new risks are not continuously identified.

SEI RISK MANAGEMENT PARADIGM

Risk Management Paradigm

The SEI risk management paradigm is depicted in Figure 1 (5, p. 9). The paradigm illustrates a set of functions that are identified as continuous activities throughout the life cycle of a project.

Functions of Continuous Risk Management

The functions of Continuous Risk Management are introduced below (7,8). Each risk nominally goes through these functions sequentially but the activity occurs continuously, concurrently (e.g., risks are tracked in parallel while new risks are identified and ana-

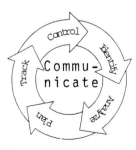

FIGURE 1   The SEI risk management paradigm.

lyzed), and iteratively (e.g., the mitigation plan for one risk may yield another risk) throughout the project life cycle.

Function	Description
Identify	Search for and locate risks before they become problems.
Analyze	Transform risk data into decision-making information. Evaluate impact, probability, and timeframe, classify risks, and prioritize risks.
Plan	Translate risk information into decisions and mitigating actions (both present and future) and implement those actions.
Track	Monitor risk indicators and mitigation actions.
Control	Correct for deviations from the risk mitigation plans.
Communicate	Provide information and feedback internal and external to the project on the risk activities, current risks, and emerging risks.
	Note: Communication happens throughout all the functions of risk management.

Principles and the Paradigm

The SEI risk management paradigm sets forth a practice for managing risks within a project. The following paragraphs summarize what principles apply to each paradigm function. These need to be kept in mind as methods and tools are selected and implementation details are determined for a specific project. While it is difficult to measure the effectiveness of the principles, it is easy to detect their absence in any implemented risk management practice.

Identify

The principles applicable during the **Identify** function are

- Effective risk management requires that risks be identified as part of a continuous process, not a one-time-only activity at the start of the project.
- Risk identification must employ both open communication and a forward-looking view to encourage all personnel to bring forward new risks and to look beyond their immediate problems.
- Although individual contributions play a role in risk management, teamwork improves the chances of identifying new risks by allowing personnel to combine their knowledge and understanding of the project.

Analyze

The principles applicable during the **Analyze** function are

- Conditions and priorities often change on a project and can affect the important risks to a project—risk analysis must be a continuous process.
- Analysis requires open communication so that prioritization and evaluation is accomplished using all known information.

- A forward-looking view enables personnel to consider long-range impacts of risks.
- A global perspective and a shared product vision allow project personnel to consider their risks in the larger scheme of the end product, the customer's needs, and organizational goals.

Plan

The principles applicable during the **Plan** function are

- Planning risks is a continuous process of determining what to do with new risks as they are identified, to enable efficient use of resources.
- Integrated management is needed to ensure mitigation actions do not conflict with project or team plans and goals.
- A shared product vision and global perspective are needed to create mitigation actions that ultimately benefit the project, customer, and organization.
- The focus of risk planning is to be forward-looking, to prevent risks from becoming problems.
- Teamwork and open communication enhance the planning process by increasing the amount of knowledge and expertise that can be applied to the development of mitigation actions.

Track

The principles applicable during the **Track** function are

- Open communication about a risk's status stimulates the project and risk management processes.
- Tracking is a continuous process—current information about a risk's status is conveyed periodically to the rest of the project.
- When project personnel review tracking data with a forward-looking view and a global perspective, they can interpret the data to reveal adverse trends and potential risks.
- Integrated management combines risk tracking with routine project monitoring processes, creating a synergy that better predicts and identifies new issues.

Control

The principles applicable during the **Control** function are

- Open communication is important for effective feedback and decision-making, a critical aspect of Control.
- Risk control is also enhanced through integrated management—combining it with routine project management activities enables comprehensive project decision-making.
- Shared product vision and a global perspective support control decisions that are effective for the long-term success of the project and organization.

Communicate

The principles applicable during the **Communicate** function are

- Risk communication is often difficult because it deals with probability and negative consequences—it relies upon open communication to be effective and must encourage a free flow of information within and between all project levels.
- Communication must value the individual voice as well as promote teamwork to support the effectiveness of the other functions.

REFERENCES

1. R. J. Kirkpatrick, J. Walker, and R. Firth, "Software Development Risk Management: An SEI Appraisal," *Software Engineering Institute Technical Review '92* (CMU/SEI-92-REV), Software Engineering Institute, Carnegie Mellon University, Pittsburgh, 1992.
2. W. D. Rowe, *An Anatomy of Risk*, Robert E. Krieger, Malabar, FL, 1988.
3. W. W. Lowrance, *Of Acceptable Risk*. William Kaufmann, Los Altos, CA, 1976.
4. *Webster's Third New International Dictionary*, Merriam-Webster, Springfield, MA. 1981.
5. R. L. Van Scoy, *Software Development Risk: Opportunity, Not Problem* (CMU/SEI-92-TR-30, ADA 258743), Software Engineering Institute, Carnegie Mellon University, Pittsburgh, 1992.
6. H. F. Kloman, "Risk Management Agonists," *Risk Anal.*, *10*(2), 201–205 (1990).
7. Software Engineering Institute, "The SEI Approach to Managing Software Technical Risks," *Bridge* 19–21 (October 1992).
8. R. P. Higuera, and D. P. Gluch, "Risk Management and Quality in Software Development," *Proceedings of the Eleventh Annual Pacific Northwest Software Quality Conference*, October 18–20, 1993. Portland.

RONALD P. HIGUERA

SCALABLE COMPUTERS

INTRODUCTION AND GENESIS OF PARALLEL COMPUTING

It is widely recognized that computer technology has become a critical component of everyday life of a modern society. The computer has become ubiquitous in manufacturing, services, products, and entertainment. Computers have been changing ways in which we conduct business, produce goods, and do science.

Parallel processing is currently a small fraction of overall computer technology and the Computer Revolution. Yet, there are two compelling reasons for parallel processing to have increasing importance in the future. The first one is that parallel processing supports the largest computations which became an integral part of sciences, medicine, and manufacturing. Large-scale computer modeling enabled by parallel processing impacts decision making in banking, finance, military, and government. Parallel computers empower decision-makers, such as high-level managers, military leaders, and chief scientists with the ability to gather, access, and synthesize information, as well as to simulate real-life processes to measure the impact of social, economical, and industrial decisions. The quality of the simulations and synthesized information strongly depends on the amount of applied computational power. Today, even the largest uniprocessor computers are too slow for the more challenging problems of this kind.

The second reason for the growing importance of parallel processing is that improvements in the speed of sequential computing are approaching technological limits. The semiconductor industry has been doubling processor speed every 18 months for the last few decades, but this rate of improvement cannot last as processor design technology is maturing. In addition to economical forces (the cost of hardware needed to fabricate chips with smaller dimensions is an exponential function of the size improvement), the basic laws of physics limit the speed of a uniprocessor. The speed of signal transmission in a computer cannot exceed the speed of electrons in the transmission media, which is ~25,000 km/s for silicon. Consequently, it takes one-billionth of a second for a signal to propagate in a silicon chip of an inch in diameter. However, one signal propagation can support at most one floating-point operation. Hence, a sequential computer built with a chip of such size can provide at most one gigaflops of performance, merely one-thousandth the speed delivered by the fastest parallel computer available today.

The quest for higher-speed machines has been fueled by computationally intensive problems with profound economical and social impacts, referred to as Grand Challenges (1). Typically, such problems include the following:

- High-resolution weather forecasting crucial for agriculture, disaster prevention, and so forth
- Pollution studies that include cross-pollutant interactions, important in environmental protection

- Global modeling of atmosphere–ocean–biosphere interactions to measure the long-term impact of human activities on the stability of the global ecosystem
- Human genome sequencing that will assist in recognizing, preventing, and fighting genetic diseases
- The design of new and more efficient drugs to cure cancer, AIDS, and other diseases
- High-temperature superconductor design that can revolutionize computer design, electrical devices, and so on
- The aerodynamic design of aerospace vehicles (airflow modeling) and improvements in automotive engine design (ignition and combustion modeling) that can lead to more efficient use of depletable fossil fuels in transportation
- The design of quantum switching devices important for building more powerful computers

It is estimated that achieving interactive response time for Grand Challenge problems, in the order of minutes for smaller instances and hours for larger ones, with require a machine with performance measured in teraflops (i.e., in thousands of billion floating-point operations per second). Today's largest machines can achieve this kind of performance on a limited range of algorithms for very large, highly localized, finely tuned, and often simplified applications. The real drawback is in the software and programmer's ability to find enough useful parallelism in an application to utilize all of the processors of a parallel computer most of the time. Yet, parallel processing is the only feasible option for sustained growth in computer performance in view of the invitable slowdown in the rate of improvements in the semiconductor industry mentioned earlier.

SPEEDUP, EFFICIENCY, AND SCALABILITY OF PARALLEL COMPUTATION

Let $s(p)$ denote the *speedup* of a program when executed on p processors and $t(i)$ be the execution time of this program on an i processor machine. Then,

$$s(p) = \frac{t(1)}{t(p)} \,.$$
[1]

The *parallel efficiency* is defined as

$$e(p) = \frac{s(p)}{p} \,.$$
[2]

The speedup is linear when $s(p) = p$ (hence, the efficiency is 1), superlinear when $s(p) > p$, and sublinear (the most common case) when $s(p) < p$. Superlinear speedup is rarely encountered and can usually be attributed to the larger total cache and main memory of a parallel machine than the cache and memory of the sequential machine used to measure $t(1)$. An interesting case of superlinearity arises in some combinatorial searches when knowledge of a bound for the sought value speeds up processing branches of the search tree. The parallel algorithm explores several branches concurrently and the bounds found in them speed up the search for all processors, whereas a sequential search may find these bounds later in the execution, so branches processed earlier cannot benefit from them. Of course, parallel execution can be emulated on a sequential machine, but then the required memory will have to contain all the investigated branches at once, likely exceeding the memory size of the sequential computer. In the following discussion, we will focus on the typical case of the sublinear speedup.

In Eqs. (1) and (2), we assumed a constant problem size. As in the theory of algorithms, we are also interested in speedup and efficiency as a function of the problem size N. The corresponding definitions then become

$$S(N, p) = \frac{T(N, 1)}{T(N, p)} \quad \text{and} \quad E(N, p) = \frac{S(N, p)}{p}, \qquad [3]$$

where $S(N, p)$, $T(N, p)$, and $E(N, p)$ are speedup, execution time, and parallel efficiency, respectively, of a program with the problem size N and executed on a p processor machine.

Similarly, as in theory of algorithms, we are often interested not only in the exact functions expressing S and E in terms of N or p but also in their $O(\ )$ order. $O(\ )$ notation can be formally defined as

$$f(x) \in O(g(x)) \quad \text{iff} \quad (\exists c, X : (\forall x > X : f(x) < c * g(x))).$$

In other words, there is such a constant c that for all sufficiently large values of arguments (bigger than X), the value of $f(x)$ is smaller than $c * g(x)$. Instead of saying that $f(x) \in O(g(x))$, we often write $f(x) = O(g(x))$. For example, $f(x) = 0.0000001 * x^2 + x$ belongs to $O(x^2)$ [and also $f(x) = O(x^3)$, etc.] but not to $O(x)$, even though for small x, $f(x) \approx x$.

By definition, efficiency measures how well an investment in additional hardware (cost of p processors) pays off. For linear speedup, efficiency is 1, meaning that 100% of the power of newly added processors contributes directly to the solution, an ideal case. In practice, adding processors introduces overheads such as load balance (the problem has to be divided between a larger number of participating processors, so the partitioning may become uneven), synchronization (more processors must be synchronized), and communication (the partitions are smaller, so more data must be exchanged between larger number of processors). Hence, the typical case is the sublinear speedup with efficiency $E(N, p) < 1$.

Because efficiency is a function of two arguments, we may consider how it behaves when one of them is fixed. If we set a problem size to a constant, say N_c, then clearly when the number of processors becomes large enough, some of them would be idle and efficiency would suffer. In particular, $E(N_c, p) < T(N_c, 1)/p$ and $T(N_c, 1)$ is a constant; therefore, efficiency asymptotically decreases to 0 when the number of processors increases to infinity. This very simple analysis indicates that for a fixed-size problem, there is a limit to how much parallelism can be profitably applied. Kuck (2) defines several efficiency limits that can be used to quantify what "profitably" in this context means. The most modest limit is that at which $S(N_c, p) > S(N_c, p + 1)$ [or equivalently $E(N_c, p) > pE(N_c, p + 1)/(p + 1)$]. More restrictive is the requirement that $E(N_c, p) > 1/(2 \log_2 p)$, and the highest limit corresponds to the demand that $E(N_c, p) > 1/2$. We will refer to these limits as *threshold*, *intermediate*, and *high-performance* limits, respectively. There is also the corresponding bound on the number of processors that can be used at each level of efficiency. These bounds are denoted as p_t, p_i, and p_h, respectively. For scalable computers and algorithms, typically $p_t > p_i > p_h \geq 1$ (see Fig. 1). Sometimes, however, the value of p_t could be smaller than p_i, or even p_h. For example, an inherently sequential algorithm has $p_t = 1$ and therefore p_t is no bigger than p_h or p_i.

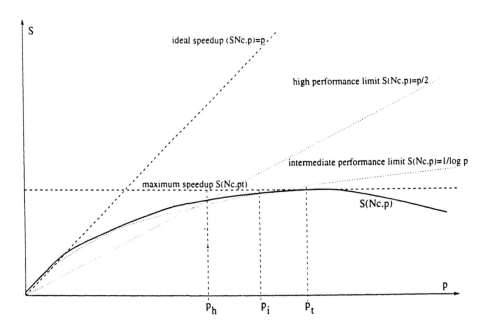

FIGURE 1   Constant problem size speedup.

Very similarly, we can consider the efficiency function for a fixed number of processors, p_c (see Fig. 2). For small problem sizes, the speedup rises quickly when the problem size grows. However, even for well-parallelizable problems, the speedup $S_{max} = p_c$ is an asymptotic value; so for large problem sizes, there is very little improvement in the speedup when the problem size grows. Similarly, as in the previous plot, we can define two boundary values of the problem sizes: N_i which is the minimum size for which the speedup is at least $p_c/(2 \log_2 p_c)$, and N_h, for which the speedup is $p_c/2$. It should be noted that for many algorithms, the speedup may never reach the high-performance limit, regardless of the problem size considered. Moreover, the available memory limits the maximum size of the problem that can be run on a machine with a fixed number of processors. If this limit is exceeded, the performance of the system will degrade significantly. However, the same degradation will be observed on a sequential machine, which usually has less memory than the parallel machines, so, at least formally, the speedup may not suffer. Nevertheless, the execution time will increase in such a case, and therefore running programs with sizes beyond the memory limit is not practical (see Ref. 2 for more detailed discussion of this limit).

Combining the two presented plots, we obtain the three-dimensional plot of the speedup as a function of the problem size and the number of processors used. However, to normalize this new plot for different algorithms, we will use the execution time on a single processor $T(N, 1)$ as an argument in place of the problem size N. The value $T(N, 1)/p$ defines the computational load on each processor, independently of the algorithm used. In Figure 3, we show the constant speedup curves on the $p \times T(N, p)$ plane. On this plane, the constant computational workload curves are represented as straight lines originating at the origin of the axes (one such line is drawn in Fig. 3). For some

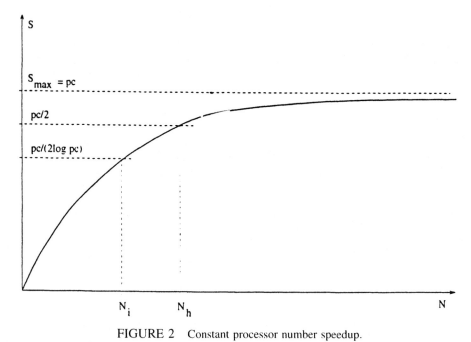

FIGURE 2   Constant processor number speedup.

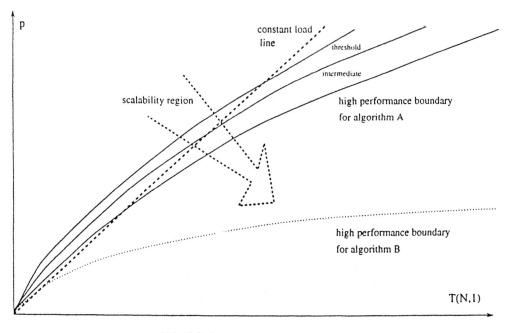

FIGURE 3   Constant speedup curves.

unspecified algorithm A, three curves are shown. For each computational load $T(N, 1)$, the threshold performance curve identifies the number of processors that deliver the highest speedup. The intermediate performance curve defines the minimum number of processors, p_i, for which the speedup $S(N_i, p_i) \geq p_i/(2 \log_2 p_i)$ for the given load $T(N_i, 1)$. The high-performance curve represents the speedup equal to half of the number of processors used. As shown, the high-performance region is the smallest, contained within the intermediate performance region, which, in turn, is within the threshold performance region. For the linear speedup, the constant performance curve is a straight line. Most often, however, such curves are convex, showing that the performance benefit of adding an additional processor to the system is decreasing with the size of the system.

How large the high-performance region is depends both on the architecture and the algorithm. In Figure 3, algorithm B is less amenable to parallelization than algorithm A because its high-performance curve is within the high-performance curve of algorithm A. Howver, these curves can also represent performance of the same algorithm on two different architectures, in which case the curve B corresponds to less scalable architecture. Hence, intuitively, scalability of a computer describes its ability to use additional computing power (more processors) to solve larger problems fast. In other words, scalability measures how the number of processors used must increase to keep the solution time constant or small when the problem size increases.

Definition 1:   A computer is scalable for the range of processors $[p_{smin}, p_{smax}]$ and the range of problem sizes $[N_{smin}, N_{smax}]$ if and only if $\forall p \in [p_{smin}, p_{smax}]$, $N \in [N_{smin}, N_{smax}]$: $S_{lim}(p) \leq S(N, p) \leq S(N, p + 1)$, where $S_{lim}(p)$ is either $p/2$ or $p/(2 \log_2 p)$.

The size of the scalability region is a measure of the scalability of an architecture and/or algorithm.

To illustrate these notions on a concrete algorithm, let us consider a simple *addition problem* which requires summing N numbers using a p processor machine. The algorithm is very simple: Each processor first adds N/p numbers in as many steps, and then all processors sum their subresults to find the answer. The first architecture that we consider has a ring interconnection which requires $p - 1$ steps to add the subresults (each step involves one addition and a communication of one value). The second one uses a tree interconnection, so the addition of subresults takes about $2 \log_2 p$ steps (on each level of tree, except the bottom, there are two communication steps, each sending a value and two addition steps; see Fig. 4). Hence, the execution time, speedup, and efficiency in these two cases can be expressed as

$$T_t(N, p) = O\left(\frac{N}{p} + \log_2 p\right) \quad \text{and} \quad T_r(N, p) = O\left(\frac{N}{p} + p\right),$$

$$S_t(N, p) = O\left(\frac{p}{1 + (p \log_2 p)/N}\right) \quad \text{and} \quad S_r(N, p) = O\left(\frac{p}{1 + p^2/N}\right),$$

$$E_t(N, p) = O\left(\frac{1}{1 + (p \log_2 p)/N}\right) \quad \text{and} \quad E_r(N, p) = O\left(\frac{1}{1 + p^2/N}\right),$$

Setting the constant problem size to N_c yields a plot of the speedup as a function of the number of processors:

$$S_t(N_c, p) = \frac{p}{1 + (p \log_2 p)/N_c} \quad \text{and} \quad S_r(N_c, p) = \frac{p}{1 + p^2/N_c}.$$

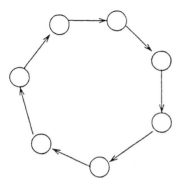

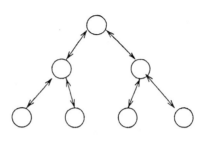

Ring Interconnection   Tree Interconnection

FIGURE 4   Tree and ring interconnections.

As seen from Figure 5, the speedups have unique maxima, which are achieved at

$$p_{t,\max} = N_c \ln 2 \quad \text{with the corresponding speedup } S_{t,\max}(N_c) \approx \frac{N_c}{\log_2 N_c},$$

$$p_{r,\max} = \sqrt{N_c} \quad \text{with the corresponding speedup } S_{r,\max}(N_c) = \frac{\sqrt{N_c}}{2} = \frac{p_{r,\max}}{2}.$$

For the ring architecture, the high-performance level is obtained only at the optimum number of processors. The tree architecture reaches the high-performance level for

$$p_{t,h} = \frac{N_c}{\log_2 N_c}.$$

The numbers of processors for which intermediate performance is achieved for these architectures are defined as

$$p_{t,i} \approx 2N_c \quad \text{and} \quad p_{r,i} \approx \sqrt{N_c \log_2 N_c}.$$

It should be noted that tree architecture delivers much better performance for the given problem size than ring architecture. The fastest computation for the given problem size N_c is $\log_2 N_c$ for tree architecture and $2\sqrt{N_c}$ for ring architecture.

Plots of the constant speedup curves for this algorithm are shown in Figure 6. These plots were obtained from the general formula that defines the problem size N needed to achieve performance S using p processors:

$$N_t = \frac{S * p \log_2 p}{p - S} \quad \text{and} \quad N_r = \frac{S * p^2}{p - S}. \qquad [4]$$

It is easy to find the equations defining the high- and intermediate-performance limits from Eq. (4):

$$N_{t,h} = p \log_2 p; \quad N_{t,i} = \frac{p \log_2 p}{2 \log_2 p - 1} \approx \frac{p}{2}$$

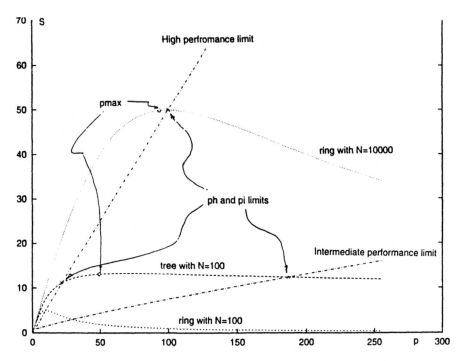

FIGURE 5   Constant problem size speedup for addition algorithm.

and

$$N_{r,h} = p^2; \quad N_{r,i} = \frac{p^2}{2 \log_2 p - 1} \approx \frac{p^2}{2 \log_2 p}.$$

Hence, the region of scalability for the tree architecture is much larger than such region for the ring architecture, demonstrating that the former is more scalable than the latter.

SCALABILITY OBSTACLES

The speedup that can be achieved by an application is limited by the following two parallel program needs:

1. To synchronize processors during parallel execution
2. To distribute data and programs to processors before and during execution

Synchronization introduces two kinds of overheads:

- *Load imbalance overhead* that keeps some processors idle waiting for others to reach a synchronization point
- *Communication overhead* associated with sending and receiving synchronization signals

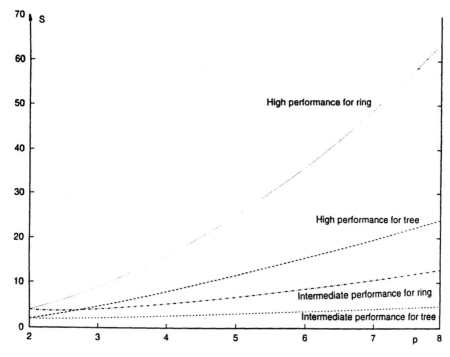

FIGURE 6   Constant speedup curves for addition algorithm.

Load imbalance appeares in several forms. First, for any given problem size N_c, there is a limit into how many pieces a program of this size can be divided. This divisibility limit is rarely encountered in practice because the required number of processors is extremely large for large problems and it is clear that running small problems on a machine with a large number of processors cannot be effective. For example, in the addition problem presented in the previous section, the divisibility limit is N_c. For $p = N_c$, all addition operations involve sending arguments between processors. Using more processors than N_c leaves some of them without unique data and, therefore, idle.

The second form of load imbalance arises when the load does not divide evenly among processors. The best balance that the load distribution can achieve for a computational step of $T(N_c, 1)$ complexity is to execute it in $\lceil T(N_c, 1)/p \rceil$ time, which is, of course, longer than $T(N_c, 1)/p$, but often the difference is negligible. For example, using $N_c - 1$ processors in the addition problem will force all processors (except one) to idle for one step during which the only processor with two numbers assigned to it sums them.

The third form of load imbalance arises when at several points of program execution, the number of parallel pieces that can be created is smaller than the number of available processors. The most common case of this situation happens when there are fragments of code that must be executed sequentially. This case is governed by Amdahl's Law (3) which describes how the nonparallelizable part of the code limits the speedup. More precisely, if f is the fraction of the sequential execution time spent on code which is inherently sequential (so-called Amdahl's fraction), then

$$s(p) = \frac{p}{(p-1)*f+1} \, .$$ [5]

Hence, independently of the number of processors used, $s(p) \leq 1/f$ [simply because $f *$ $t(1) \leq t(p)$].

Amdahl's Law can be generalized by introducing a sequence of fractions $f_1, f_2, \ldots,$ f_{p-1}, where f_i denotes a fraction of the execution time devoted to a fragment of code which can be split into i parallel tasks. Then, the speedup is

$$s(p) = \frac{p}{\sum_{i=1}^{p-1} f_i * (p/i - 1) + 1} \, .$$ [6]

Amdahl's Law seems very pessimistic; after all, every program has sequential parts and even if these parts are small and limited to few percent of the code, the speedup is still limited to less than a hundred times (see Fig. 7).

Fortunately, often the execution time of sequential parts of the algorithm do not change, or change slowly with the growth of the problem size, whereas the execution time of parallelizable parts changes rapidly when the problem size is increased. Hence, Amdahl's fraction is dependent on the problem size and, as such, it could be written as $f(N)$. For a wide class of problems, $f(N)$ can be made arbitrarily small by selecting a

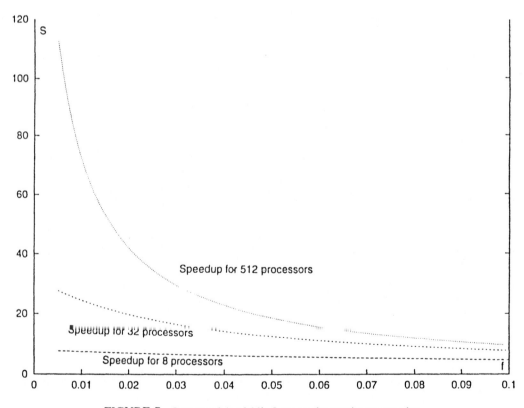

FIGURE 7   Impact of Amdahl's Law on the maximum speedup.

sufficiently large problem size. Consequently, for such problems, the speedup can be made arbitrarily large, showing that the algorithm is scalable. More formally, this requirement can be stated as follows.

Definition 2: An algorithm is computationally scalable if

$$\forall p > 1: \lim_{N \to \infty} f_p(N) = 0. \tag{7}$$

Definition 2 uses the generalized Amdahl's Law [compare Eq. (6)] and it simplifies to the requirement

$$\lim_{N \to \infty} f(N) = 0$$

for the original Amdahl's fraction $f(N)$.

Often the problems computed on parallel machines are too large to fit on a uniprocessor, so measuring Amdahl's fraction for them is either impossible or difficult. Gustafson (4) proposed a different measure, A, that represents a fraction of parallel execution time during which the parallel machine executed the sequential part of the code. Therefore, the speedup is

$$s(p) = p - (p - 1) * A. \tag{8}$$

The nice feature of this formula is that it clearly shows how to improve the speedup. If we start adding processors (i.e., increasing p) but keep the work of all processors the same, then, most likely, A will stay the same and the speedup will grow. Likewise, with the constant number of processors, we decrease A by increasing the problem size. The final conclusion is similar to what Amdahl's Law implies: By selecting a problem large enough to keep all processors occupied for a long time, the impact of the sequential parts of the program could be made negligible.

It should be noted, that Amdahl's and Berstis' fractions are different even for the same program. Consider a program that requires initial setup and postprocessing cleanup steps that must be done sequentially (see Fig. 8) and each requires one time unit. The parallelizable part of the program requires six time units. On a sequential machine, Amdahl's fraction, f, is equal to $2/8 = 0.25$, so the speedup on a six-processor machine is then [see Eq. (5)] $s(p) = 8/3$. However, during parallel execution, two time units are

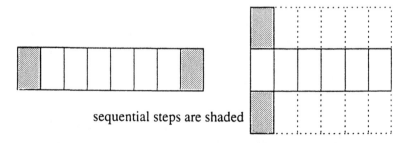

sequential steps are shaded

Amdahl's fraction f=1/4   Berstis's fraction A=2/3

FIGURE 8   Amdahl's and Berstis' fractions for the same program.

spent on sequential execution, so Berstis' fraction is $A = 2/3 \neq f$, but the speedup is the same, 8/3 according to Eq. (8).

There is yet another form of load imbalance that is very difficult to handle. This is a load imbalance that arises at run time in response to evolving computations. To eliminate it, the program must change data and task allocations to processors during execution, which increases execution time. The program must also devote part of its execution time to monitoring load balance and to finding new data and task distributions. Monitoring, finding a new distribution, and moving data and tasks all contribute to the overhead which decreases speedup and efficiency of parallel computation. These issues are still unresolved and they are the subject of ongoing research (e.g., see Ref. 5).

Communication overhead associated with sending and receiving synchronization signals is of the same nature as communication overhead arising during distribution of data and tasks to parallel processors. The initial distribution cost is usually a small percentage of the overall computation costs because it is proportional to the data size N, whereas the computation is a much faster growing function of N, often in $O(N^2)$ or higher. Hence, we will concentrate on assessing communication overhead incurred during parallel execution. This overhead is dependent on the volume of data communicated, its granularity, and the properties of interconnecting network of a parallel machine.

Similar to the case of Amdahl's fraction, there is a large body of algorithms that have an amount of computation growning faster than the volume of data that need to be communicated. A very important subset of such algorithms includes scientific computation that evaluate a function at many points of a physical domain. In such computations, the volume of data to be communicated is proportional to the surface of a subdomain assigned to a single processor. The computation is proportional to the volume of each subdomain. Hence, for two-dimensional and three-dimensional domains, the communication to computation ratios $r(N)$ are

$$r_{2D}(N) = O\left(\frac{1}{\sqrt{T(N, p_c)}} \right) \quad \text{and} \quad r_{3D}(N) = O(T(N, p_c)^{-1/3}).$$

Although $r_{3D}(N)$ decreases slower than $r_{2D}(N)$, the decrease is still significant and converges to 0 when problem size grows to infinity.

Definition 3: An algorithm is *efficiently parallelizable* if its communication to the computation ratio $r(N)$ satisfies the condition

$$\lim_{N \to \infty} r(N) = 0.$$

Conclusion

A computation is *scalable* if an efficiently parallelizable and computationally scalable algorithm is run on an architecture with a scalable interconnection network.

The scalability of parallel architectures is discussed in the following section; here, we discuss scalability of interconnection networks. The basic problem with the networks is that they have either scalable cost or scalable performance, but not both. At one extreme are scalable performance networks, such as the fully interconnected network or a crossbar switch. In such networks, the distance between any two components is independent of the number of interconnected components. However, the cost for such networks grows proportionally to the square of the number of interconnected components. Hence, the machine with p processors will cost $p + c * p^2$, where c is the ratio of the cost of a processor to the cost of wire or a switch. As a result, as the size of the machine increases, the proportion of the money spent on the computing power p decreases as $1/(1 + cp)$, making the computation more and more expensive. On the other hand, the cost-scalable solution (e.g., a ring or a tree) provides the diminishing network performance with the growth of the number of components because the total bandwidth for the data communication is constant and shared among all processors.

The solutions used most commonly today are located between these two extremes, using interconnections such as a hypercube, a switching network with $\log_2 p$ stages, or a fat tree (6). In a hypercube, processors are arranged into a $\log_2 p$-dimensional cube, each having $\log_2 p$ direct neighbors (see Fig. 9). Switching networks have p switches at each stage and shuffle messages at each switch, effectively emulating the fully interconnected network. Finally, fat trees provide higher-level nodes with multiple links to accommodate higher communication traffic flowing through them (see Fig. 9). All these interconnection networks incur the cost of $O(p \log_2 p)$ for connecting p components. The distance between any two components is $O(\log_2 p)$. As a result, both the communication overhead and the ratio of interconnection to the total cost of the machine grow slowly with the size of the parallel machine.

CLASSIFICATION OF PARALLEL MACHINES AND LIMITATIONS OF THEIR SCALABILITY

The basic classification of parallel machines was proposed by Flynn (7), who characterized classes of architectures according to their instruction and data streams. Sequential machines are Single Instruction Single Data class, or SISD for short. Very Large Instruc-

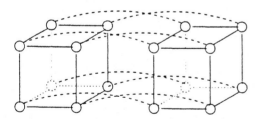

4-cube created by connecting two 3-cubes

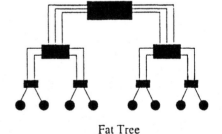

Fat Tree

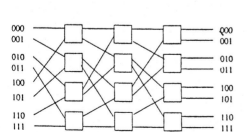

Switching network (Omega) with 8 nodes

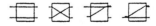

The four switch functions for an omega switch

FIGURE 9   Scalable interconnection networks.

tion Word (VLIW) machines (8) are Multiple Instruction Single Data (MISD) because their instruction word contains several ordinary instructions and their processors include several copies of functional units that execute these instructions concurrently. VLIW machines rely on a compiler to pack several instructions into one word. However, the code produced by the compilers of high-level languages contains only short sequences of instructions uninterrupted by conditional jumps. Therefore, a complex program analysis, called *trace scheduling* (9) is needed to support even modest parallelism of the order of several to a few dozen. Hence, MISD architectures are inherently nonscalable.

The next class of parallel machines is characterized by a Single Instruction and Multiple Data streams (SIMD). The same instruction is executed by all processors, each working on different data. For limited class of algorithms, including scientific computations with a compile-time defined data structures, these machines are scalable. Their limitations are discussed below (see also Ref. 10).

The final class of machines uses Multiple Instruction and Multiple Data (MIMD) streams. Such machines come in two flavors: either with memory shared among all processors or memory distributed to exclusive use of individual processors. Shared-memory machines are easy to program because they directly support global address space for parallel programs. However, modern processors are equipped with caches, and maintaining cache coherence is expensive and limits scalability of these architectures.

In distirbuted-memory machines, the programmer is explicitly responsible for distributing data and tasks to each processor and for moving data around the processors during execution. The data movements are encoded as the communication primitives that either are a part of a communication library [such as Message Passing Interface (MPI) Library (11)], or are embedded directly into the programming language (6). As discussed in the previous section, providing a scalable interconnection network is a challenge for all architectures, but, in general, MIMD distributed-memory machines are considered the most scalable.

To reap the benefits of both the shared-memory simple programming model owing to global address space and scalability supported by distributed memory, several modern architectures support the shared-memory model via distributed-memory hardware (12). Such an approach was encouraged by increasing similarities between shared-memory architectures with large local caches and the distributed-memory machines. The scalability and performance of these machines are still not fully understood, but more evaluations and research on these topics are under way.

The issue of scalability cannot be considered without looking at parallel programming paradigms. The increasing importance of parallel processing prompted growth in the body of standardization in parallel programming languages and tools. Yet, there is no evidence of convergence of the supported programming paradigms to a single model. Currently, there are two most popular models for parallel program design: data parallelism and message passing.

Data parallelism is popular because of its simplicity. In this model, a single program (and, therefore, a single thread of execution) is replicated on many processors, and each copy operates on a separate part of data. Depending on the tightness with which the execution of programs is synchronized, there are two modes of using data parallelism. When each instruction of the program is synchronically executed on all processors, then the Single Instruction Multiple Data (SIMD) mode is used. Such tight synchronization requires hardware support.

From the software engineering point of view, SIMD machines are easy to program because there is a single flow of control on all processors. The main focus of parallelization is to find large data structures that can be distributed to all processors to keep them all occupied. Another concern is to minimize the data movements necessary to provide data to processors that are to execute them. Due to the small granule of parallelism (single instruction), SIMD machines consist of a very large number of simple processors (tens or hundred thousands of processors in a single machine is not unusual). Each of these processors must either execute the same statement as all the others or idle, so SIMD machines achieve poor efficiency on programs that do not contain sufficiently large data structures. They also do not perform well on programs which require irregular data references (list structures, dynamic memory, etc.). The consensus is that SIMD architecture has a very specialized niche of applications (e.g., visual information and scene processing), but it is not the best choice for general parallel processing.

Data parallelism can also be used in a loosely synchronized mode, when the program execution consists of two stages:

1. Computational stage, when copies of the same program are executed in parallel on each processor locally. The execution can differ in the conditional branches taken, number of loop iteration executed, and so forth.
2. Data exchange stage, when all processors concurrently engage in exchanging nonlocal data.

It should be noted that the data exchange stage is very simple in case of shared-memory machines (when it can be enforced by use of locks or barriers). The frequency of synchronization in the SPMD model can be adjusted to correspond to the latency of the interconnection network. The SPMD model is very adequate for scientific computing, which often requires applying basically the same algorithm at many points of computational domain. SPMD parallel programs are conceptually simple because the same program executes on all processors, but they are more complex than SIMD programs.

For more complex applications, running a single program across the parallel machine may be unnecessarily restrictive. In particular, dynamically changing programs with unpredictable execution times result in poorly balanced parallel computations when implementend in SPMD mode. This is because in the SPMD model, processors synchronize at the data exchange stage, and none of the processors can proceed to the next computational stage until all others reach the data exchange stage.

The SPMD model was abstracted into a Bulk-Synchronous Parallelism (BSP) model (13). This model provides an abstraction of parallel algorithm description that lends itself to performance and scalability analysis. The model also became a basis for a library that facilitates the creation of portable parallel software (14).

The BSP model consists of three components:

1. Processors that execute sequential code
2. A router which provides point-to-point communication between pairs of processors
3. A synchronization mechanism that synchronizes all or a subset of the processors at selected points of execution

In the BSP model, computation consists of a sequence of supersteps. In each superstep, a processor performs some local computation and transmits messages to other processors. After each superstep, all processors synchronize, and the next superstep starts. In the BSP model, the data transmitted are not guaranteed to be available at the destination until after the end of the superstep at which they were sent.

A BSP computer is characterized by the four parameters: number of processors p, processor speed s, synchronization periodicity L, and ratio of the global computation to communication speed g. The synchronization periodicity L is the smallest number of processor operations that can be executed between sucessive synchronization operations. The ratio g is equal to the total number of local operations performed by all processors in a time unit divided by the total number of words delivered by the communication network in the same unit. Processor speed s is measured in flops (floating-point operations per second). The synchronization parameter, L, is measured in floating-point operations and the ratio g is measured in floating-point operations per word. The values of parameters L and g depend on the number of processors p, so we will often write them as functions $L(p)$ and $g(p)$, respectively.

The BSP parameters allow for algorithm performance and scalability analysis. For example, consider a superstep that needs to communicate h words of data. Because it takes $g * h$ time units for the communication network to deliver the data to its destination and L units to synchronize all the processors performing the superstep, at least $L + g * h$ units of computation are needed to keep the processors busy; an amount of computation less than this threshold would result in idling of some processor and, therefore, would be a source of inefficiency.

In terms of the BSP parameters, parallel machines are often characterized by large values of s, owing to their fast processors, and low values of L and g thanks to communication links with low latency and large bandwidth. A general-purpose network of workstations, on the other hand, is characterized by values of s that are somewhat lower than for the parallel machines and values of L and g that are much larger than the corresponding values for the parallel machines because of high latency and low bandwidth of its communication interconnections. The importance of interconnection networks for architecture scalability can be seen from the difference in the dependence of L and g on the number of interconnected components. The asymptotic values of BSP parameters for various architectures are shown in Figure 10. The ideal values, $L = g = O(1)$, can be achieved only on an idealized PRAM (Parallel Random Access Machine) which has an unattainable scalable shared memory. Thanks to this memory, PRAM can execute communication and synchronization in one instruction cycle. However, modern networks using optical links and hypercube or staged switches are relatively close to this ideal.

To illustrate scalability analysis using BSP, consider once again the adition problem introduced in the second section. There is one superstep with N/p computational steps followed by $\log_2 p$ supersteps, each requiring a one-word communication and one addition. Hence, the BSP cost of the algorithm is

$$O\left(\frac{N}{p} + (g + L + 1)\log_2 p\right).$$

To keep the other steps of the same order as the first one, the number of processors used must satisfy the following inequalities:

$$\log_2 p \leq \frac{N}{p} \quad \text{so } p \in O\left(\frac{N}{\log_2 N}\right),$$

$$(L + g)\log_2 p \leq \frac{N}{p} \quad \text{so } pg(p)\log_2 p, pL(p)\log_2 p \in O(N).$$

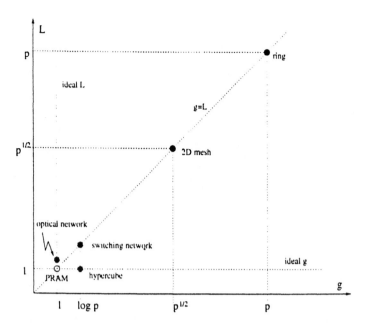

FIGURE 10   BSP parameters for selected architectures.

For the tree architecture, $L(p) = g(p) = O(\log_2 p)$; therefore, $p \in O(N/\log_2^2 N)$. However, for ring architecture, $L(p) = g(p) = O(p)$ and, consequently, $p \in O(\sqrt{N}/\log_2 N)$. Hence, as we found in the second section, the tree architecture is more scalable than the ring one, and more processors can be used efficiently for the given problem size by the former than the latter.

Similar analysis can be used to analyze the different algorithms to find out under what conditions one is better than the other. A somewhat simplified example of this kind of analysis would be to consider another algorithm for the addition problem in which all processors send their subresults to one processor which then does the final additions. Hence, there are just two supersteps and the cost is $O(N/p + p + L + gp)$, because the processor receiving the partial sums must read them sequentially. Hence, the restrictions for the number of processors yield $p \in O(\sqrt{N})$ and $pL(p), p^2 g(p) \in O(N)$. For ring architectures, the corresponding limit is $p \in N^{1/3}$. Comparing it with the limit for the first algorithm, we find that when $\log_2^3 N > N$ (which is true for $N < 16$), the second algorithm is better than the first.

The BPS analysis indicates that the most scalable parallel architecture would have the functions $g(p)$ and $L(p)$ as close as possible to $O(1)$. As seen in Figure 10, the modern architectures move toward this goal.

CONCLUSION AND FUTURE TRENDS

There is a clear trend toward widening the base of parallel processing both in hardware and software. On the hardware side, that means using off-the-shelf, commercially available components (processor, interconnection switches) which benefit from the rapid pace of technological advancement fueled by the large customer base. The other effect is the convergence of different architectures, thanks to spreading the successful solutions among all of them. Workstations, interconnected by a fast network approach the performance of parallel machines. Shared-memory machines with multilevel caches and sophisticated prefetching strategies execute programs with efficiency similar to distributed-memory machines.

On the software side, widening the base of users currently relies on standardization of parallel programming tools. By protecting the programmer's investment in software, standardization promotes development of libraries, tools, and application kits that, in turn, will attract more end users to parallel processing. Standardization supports scalable solutions that can be applied across different architectures and configurations of parallel machines, depending on the data size of the problem instant at hand. These trends increase importance of predictable performance and scalability analysis of both algorithms and architectures.

REFERENCES

1. National Research Council, *Evolving High Performance Computing and Communications Initiative to Support the Nations's Information Infrastructure*, National Academy Press, Washington, DC, 1995.
2. D. J. Kuck, *High Performance Computing*, Oxford University Press, New York, 1996.
3. G. M. Amdahl, "The Validity of the Single Processor Approach to Achieving Large Scale Computing Capabilities," *AFIPS Proc. Summer Joint Computer Conference*, Vol. 30, 1967.
4. J. L. Gustafson, "Reevaluating Amdahl's Law," *Commun. ACM*, *31*(5), 532–533 (1988).
5. C. Bottasso et al., "The Quality of Partitions by an Iterative Load Balancer," in *Languages, Compilers and Run-Time Systems for Scalable Computers*, B. K. Szymanski (ed.), Kluwer Academic Publishers, Boston, 1996, pp. 265–278.
6. M. Quinn, *Parallel Computing, Theory and Practice*, McGraw-Hill, New York, 1994.
7. M. J. Flynn, "Some Computer Organizations and Their Effectiveness," *IEEE Trans. Computers*, *C-21*, 948–960 (1972).
8. J. A. Fisher and J. J. O'Donnel, "VLIW Machines: Multiprocessors We Can Actually Program," *COMPCON Proc.*, 1984, pp. 299–305.
9. J. Ellis, *Bulldog: A Compiler for VLIW Architecture*, MIT Press, Cambridge, MA, 1985.
10. J. Hennessy and D. A. Patterson, *Computer Architectures: A Quantitative Approach*, Morgan Kaufman Publishers, San Mateo, CA, 1990.
11. P. S. Paccecho, *Parallel Programming with MPI*, Morgan Kaufman, San Mateo, CA, 1997.
12. K. Hwang, *Advanced Computer Architectures: Parallelism, Scalability, Programmability*, McGraw-Hill, New York, 1993.
13. L. Valiant, "A Bridging Model for Parallel Computation," *Commun.* ACM, *33*(8), 103–111 (1990).
14. R. Miller and J. L. Reed, "The Oxford BSP Library: Users' Guide," Version 1.0, Oxford Parallel Technical Report, Oxford University, 1994.

BOLESLAW K. SZYMANSKI

A SEMANTIC JUSTIFICATION OF THE FUZZY CONTROL METHOD

1. INTRODUCTION

The so-called fuzzy control method (in the sense of Mamdani) has become a popular tool for controlling engineering systems. In particular, its application to such systems is popular, which can also be controlled manually by experienced experts; in these cases, it mostly requires considerably less (technical and intellectual) effort than the classical procedures of control engineering. The method is often criticized because its semantic basis is not clear. Indeed, its protagonists refer only to a vaguely described semantic by asserting that "fuzzy control" simulates the way in which experts control systems by hand. However, this is just not conclusively justified anywhere. On the other hand, it makes sense to start from the assumption that experts orient themselves (at least unconsciously) by any elementary principle when controlling a system by hand, and before the asserted simulation-idea has a chance of being plausible at all, this principle has to be clearly formulated as a hypothesis at least. This requirement is not fulfilled in the case of the fuzzy control method [unless one is willing to accept that experts, when controlling a system by hand, make (consciously or unconsciously) use of so-called fuzzy logic which is at best doubtful]. Thus, it only remains to hope that afterwards one has the good fortune that the fuzzy control method proves to be compatible with such a principle. It is the aim of the present article to demonstrate that this is really the case. Within the next section, the standard of the fuzzy control method will be described briefly and commented on critically. The third and fourth sections then deal with the announced justification of the fuzzy control method within the framework of an elementary principle of human behavior. Finally, in the fifth section, it will be explained why, by the latter principle, the use of a special type of acceptability functions (synonyms: "fuzzy sets," "membership functions") is suggested.

2. THE STANDARD OF THE FUZZY CONTROL METHOD

The starting point of each application of the fuzzy control method is, as already mentioned, the problem of controlling a certain engineering system (e.g., a steam engine). That is, one has to supervise the operation of the system, and to take care by adequate measures that it will remain as constant as possible in a certain state. The supervision may be restricted to the observation of certain (real-valued) measured quantities $\xi_1, \ldots,$ ξ_n (e.g., let $n = 2$ and ξ_1, ξ_2 be the pressure, resp. the change of pressure) which are relevant to the operation of the system (the notations will be chosen following Ref. 2).

Let us suppose that ξ_i $(1 \leq i \leq n)$ can take values in an interval $X_i \subset \mathbb{R}$, and that the desired state of the system is represented by a convex subset of the set of possible values for the vector $(\xi_1, \ldots, \xi_n)$. Furthermore, the catalog of measures may amount to nothing more than the possibility of adjusting arbitrarily a (real-valued) regulated quantity η (e.g., the heat) which has some influence on the operation of the system, and which can take values in an interval $Y \subset \mathbb{R}$. The basic idea of the fuzzy control method consists of disregarding the development of a mathematical model for the engineering system, and making use of the experience of an expert, instead, who is able to control the system by hand. In this connection, one imagines that the expert's experience is represented by a list of k vaguely formulated rules of conduct $R_1, \ldots, R_k$, such as

> R_1: If ξ_1 is great and ξ_2 is moderate and ... and ξ_n is approximately zero, then adjust η approximately to "1.8."
>
> R_2: If ξ_1 is small and ξ_2 is approximately 4.3 and ... and ξ_n is great, then adjust η to a small value.
>
> $\vdots$
>
> R_k: If ξ_1 is approximately zero and ξ_2 is small and ... and ξ_n is small, then adjust η to a moderate value.

As soon as the rules are known, one first carries out a certain degree of formalization within the fuzzy control method:

For $i \in \{1, \ldots, n\}$, one defines p_i functions $\alpha_1^i, \ldots, \alpha_{p_i}^i$ on X_i (which are called "acceptability functions" in the following) taking values in $[0, 1]$. These functions are interpreted as formal representatives of the vague circumscriptions occurring in the rules of conduct $R_1, \ldots, R_k$. Thus, for $j_i \in \{1, \ldots, p_i\}$ and $x_i \in X_i$, $\alpha_{j_i}^i(x_i)$ expresses how acceptable it is to use the by $\alpha_{j_i}^i$ represented linguistic circumscription with respect to the realization x_i of ξ_i. That is, if, for instance, $\alpha_{j_i}^i$ represents the circumscription "ξ_i is great," then $\alpha_{j_i}^i(x_i)$ indicates how acceptable it is to denote the value x_i as "a great realization of ξ_i" (the extreme functional values "1" and "0" stand for "absolute acceptable," resp. "completely unacceptable"). Quite analogously, one models the uncertain circumscriptions, concerning the regulated quantity η, by p functions $\alpha_1, \ldots, \alpha_p$. Finally, let $\alpha_{(r)}^i$ denote the function representing that circumscription which has concretely been used in rule R_r $(1 \leq r \leq k)$ for circumscribing the degree to which ξ_i is realized, and $\alpha_{(r)}$ the function representing the circumscription which has been used in rule R_r for circumscribing the degree to which η is realized.

Remark 2.1. In almost every case, the functions $\alpha_{(r)}^i$, resp. $\alpha_{(r)}$, $1 \leq i \leq n$, $1 \leq r \leq k$, are silently (i.e., without an explicit explanation) chosen in such a way that each of their graphs together with a line along the ordinate forms a trapezoid or a triangle or is at least similar to such a figure (compare Section 5). Trapezoid-like, resp. triangle-like functions [in the sense of Definition 2.2(i)] in particular are unimodal [in the sense of Definition 2.2(ii)].

Definition 2.2.

(i) A continuous function $\gamma: X(\subset \mathbb{R}) \to [0, 1]$ shall be called "trapezoid-like" ("triangle-like") if there exist real numbers $e_1 < e_2 < e_3 < e_4$ $(g_1 < g_2 < g_3)$ in X such that:

(a) $\gamma(x) = 0 \ \forall \, x \in X: x \leq e_1 \lor x \geq e_4$ $[\gamma(x) = 0 \ \forall \, x \in X: x \leq g_1 \lor x \geq g_3]$

(b) $\gamma(x) = 1 \; \forall \, x \in [e_2, e_3]$ ($\gamma(x) = 1$ for $x = g_2$)

(c) The restriction of γ to the interval $[e_1, e_2]$ ($[g_1, g_2]$), resp. $[e_3, e_4]$ ($[g_2, g_3]$), takes all values in $[0, 1]$ and is monotonously increasing, resp. monotonously decreasing.

(ii) A function $\gamma: X(\subset \mathbb{R}) \to [0, 1]$ shall be called unimodal if for all $\lambda \in [0, 1]$ and for all $x, x' \in X: \gamma(\lambda x + (1 - \lambda)x') \geq \min\{\gamma(x), \gamma(x')\}$ (roughly, this means that the graph of γ has only one peak).

If, now, at a certain time the values $x_1, \ldots, x_n$ are measured as realizations of the quantities $\xi_1, \ldots, \xi_n$, then, within the frame of the fuzzy control method, the quantity η will be adjusted to a value y^0, which is mostly computed according to one of the following three variants (see Ref. 2):

Variant I (Max-Criterion Procedure). Choose y^0 as an arbitrary element of the set

$$\text{MAX}[\hat{\alpha}_{x_1, \ldots, x_n}] := \{y \in Y \mid \hat{\alpha}_{x_1, \ldots, x_n}(y') \leq \hat{\alpha}_{x_1, \ldots, x_n}(y) \quad \forall \, y' \in Y\},$$

where

$$\hat{\alpha}_{x_1, \ldots, x_n} : Y \to [0, 1]$$

with

$$\hat{\alpha}_{x_1, \ldots, x_n}(y) = \max_{r \in \{1, \ldots, k\}} \{\min\{\alpha^1_{(r)}(x_1), \ldots, \alpha^n_{(r)}(x_n), \alpha_{(r)}(y)\}\}.$$

Variant II (Mean-of-Maximum Procedure). If $\left|\text{MAX}[\hat{\alpha}_{x_1, \ldots, x_n}]\right| < \infty$, choose y^0 according to

$$y^0 = \frac{1}{\left|\text{MAX}[\hat{\alpha}_{x_1, \ldots, x_n}]\right|} \sum_{\text{MAX}|\hat{\alpha}_{x_1, \ldots, x_n}|} y.$$

Otherwise, choose y^0 according to

$$y^0 = \frac{1}{\int_{\text{MAX}|\hat{\alpha}_{x_1, \ldots, x_n}|} dy} \int_{\text{MAX}|\hat{\alpha}_{x_1, \ldots, x_n}|} y \, dy.$$

Variant III (Center-of-Area Procedure). Choose y^0 according to

$$y^0 = \frac{1}{\int_{y \in Y} \hat{\alpha}_{x_1, \ldots, x_n}(y) \, dy} \int_{y \in Y} y \hat{\alpha}_{x_1, \ldots, x_n}(y) \, dy.$$

As already mentioned in Section 1, the heart of the criticism of the fuzzy control method is directed against the fact that it is applied without referring to a transparent semantic basis; thus, Variant I is usually motivated within the framework of the so-called fuzzy logic. As for its effectiveness, it is popular to make use of the following argument (here a bit schematized):

The expert who provides his experience in the form of the rules of conduct $R_1, \ldots, R_k$ is able to control the engineering system by hand. While controlling, he essentially does nothing else but apply fuzzy logic on the background of these rules. Because, on the other hand, Variant I is motivated just by fuzzy logic, it is suitable for simulating the expert, and thus, as he, for controlling the technical system.

(For instance, Mamdani seems to argue in this way when he writes in Ref. 3: "The essence of this work is simply that if an experienced operator can provide the protocol for achieving such a control in qualitative linguistic terms, then fuzzy logic can be used to successfully implement this strategy.")

In this connection, the adequacy of fuzzy logic as a model of what happens in the expert's head remains unclear. Its underlying formalism (the minimum rule, resp. maximum rule, the defuzzification, etc.) is handled as axiomatic, although its usefulness is by no means obvious, which, however, should be the case with the axiomatic of a practical theory. An axiomatic which is not obvious, just like all that follows from it, is no longer checkable with respect to its practical adequacy. Thus, with regard to the fuzzy control method, one can at best refer to a certain intuition and to the fact that it works satisfactorily in special applications; however, even in such cases, one is not able to give conclusive reasons for this. In fact, semantic questions are almost never treated in the literature about the fuzzy control method, and if (e.g., in Ref. 2) they are, the proposed semantic is so complicated that one greatly feels how it has afterwards been brought into line with the already existing formalism whose motivating basis it really should form instead. But for the most part, semantic questions are dismissed out of hand by pointing out in a wholesale way that the fuzzy control method simulates the behavior of human experts, and that, in connection with controlling an engineering system, such a simulation may sometimes make more sense than the development of a mathematical model of the underlying physical process. One refers to situations where there is an extreme discrepancy between the effort needed for the development of a model and the ease with which an expert can control the system by hand. So, an appropriately trained person can balance (cycle, surf, etc.) with ease, although the development of a corresponding mathematical model surely would not be easy. Indeed, a mathematical formalism for simulating human experts in comparable situations would be a very useful instrument (to find such formalisms is a typical aim in many projects of artificial intelligence)—but, of course, only if one is able to conclusively explain why the actually given formalism really ensures the simulation. The absence of this explanation, however, is the real weak point of the fuzzy control method. Within the next section, such an explanation will be provided by demonstrating that the fuzzy control method models the behavior of an expert who is guided by his memories of successful reactions to system states in the past.

3. FUZZY CONTROL EMBEDDED IN AN ELEMENTARY SEMANTIC BASE MODEL

What does an expert do when controlling an engineering system of the above considered type, that is, when cycling, getting a car into a parking space, balancing a stick, and so on? Of course, it is in the nature of things that one can only conjecture as to this question. However, it is hard to suppose that he makes theoretical considerations, that he determines mathematical solutions, or makes use of such solutions at all (as is the case in conventional control procedures). It seems to be much more plausible that he simply makes use of memories of successful behavior in the past. In other words, he tries to react to each situation (given by the realizations $x_1, \ldots, x_n$ of the quantities $\xi_1, \ldots, \xi_n$) in such a way, which is as similar as possible to his reaction to a similar situation in the past when he achieved a satisfying result. Now, the "memory of similar behavior in similar situations" is a very subjective process, and the question arises as to how to formalize it adequately. It is remarkable that this can be managed by making use of the same formal pieces of equipment which already served in Section 2 for describing the fuzzy control method; one only has to adequately change the interpretation of the involved notion of "acceptability." Thus, it will prove useful to interpret degrees of acceptability as measures for the subjectively estimated closeness of certain objects. The transition to this meaning may be seen as the main idea of the article. In the following, it will be demonstrated that, in particular, Variants I–III in Section 2 can sufficiently be justified on this background.

Definition 3.1 A reaction of the expert who controls the system is an $(n + 1)$-tuple

$$(\underline{x}, y) := (x_1, \ldots, x_n, y) \in \mathfrak{R} := \left(\overset{n}{\underset{i=1}{X}} X_i \right) \times Y.$$

The vector $(x_1, \ldots, x_n)$ of realizations of the measured quantities $\xi_1, \ldots, \xi_n$ represents a possible situation (a certain state) that the system may arrive at while operating, and the value y (concerning the regulated quantity η) stands for the measure taken by the expert then.

Now, it will be assumed that the expert has k vague memories of behavior patterns at his disposal. "Vague memory of behavior patterns" means that the expert in general is not able to definitely tie himself down to k concrete reactions $(\underline{x}, y)_1, \ldots, (\underline{x}, y)_k$. Instead, he is only able to specify k sets of reactions $\mathfrak{B}_1, \ldots, \mathfrak{B}_k$. All reactions within one and the same set $\mathfrak{B}_r$ $(1 \leq r \leq k)$ he considers to be fully acceptable prototypes of his rth behavior pattern (in other words, the elements within one and the same set $\mathfrak{B}_r$ "harmonize" maximally with the expert's memory, seem to be ideal representatives of this memory to him, etc.). Suppose that the expert specifies the sets $\mathfrak{B}_r$ $(1 \leq r \leq k)$ by making use of the acceptability functions according to

$$\mathfrak{B}_r := \{(\underline{x}, y) \in \mathfrak{R} \mid \alpha_{(r)}^1(x_1) = 1, \ldots, \alpha_{(r)}^n(x_n) = 1, \alpha_{(r)}(y) = 1\}.$$

(From now on, it will be assumed that $\mathfrak{B}_r \neq \emptyset$ for $1 \leq r \leq k$.)

Then, obviously,

$$\mathfrak{B}_r = \{(\underline{x}, y) \in \mathfrak{R} \mid x_1 \in \text{MAX}[\alpha_{(r)}^1], \ldots, x_n \in \text{MAX}[\alpha_{(r)}^n], y \in \text{MAX}[\alpha_{(r)}]\},$$

where

$$\text{MAX}[\alpha_{(r)}^i] := \{x_i \in X_i \mid \alpha_{(r)}^i(x_i') \leq \alpha_{(r)}^i(x_i) \quad \forall x_i' \in X\} \quad \text{for } 1 \leq i \leq n$$

and

$$\text{MAX}[\alpha_{(r)}] := \{y \in Y \mid \alpha_{(r)}(y') \leq \alpha_{(r)}(y) \quad \forall y' \in Y\}.$$

Definition 3.2

(i) The set $\mathfrak{B}_r$ $(1 \leq r \leq k)$ shall be denoted as the "rth behavior pattern" of the expert.

(ii) A reaction $(x_1, \ldots, x_n, y) \in \mathfrak{B}_r$ shall be denoted as a "prototype of the rth behavior pattern."

(iii) A situation $(x_1, \ldots, x_n) \in (X_{i=1}^n X_i)$ with

$$\alpha_{(r)}^1(x_1) = 1, \ldots, \alpha_{(r)}^n(x_n) = 1$$

(i.e., with $x_1 \in \mathrm{MAX}[\alpha_{(r)}^1], \ldots, x_n \in \mathrm{MAX}[\alpha_{(r)}^n]$) shall be denoted as the "basis of the rth behavior pattern."

The above specification of the sets $\mathfrak{B}_1, \ldots, \mathfrak{B}_k$ gives expression to be a change in meaning of the functions $\alpha_{(r)}^1, \ldots, \alpha_{(r)}^n, \alpha_{(r)}$. While, within the framework of the conventional meaning, "$\alpha_{(r)}^i(x_i)$" ($1 \leq i \leq n$, $1 \leq r \leq k$, $x_i \in X_i$) expresses how compatible the value x_i is with the linguistic circumscription of the realization of ξ_i, represented by $\alpha_{(r)}^i$ (see Section 2), from now on, "$\alpha_{(r)}^i(x_i)$" shall be interpreted as the subjectively estimated degree of correspondence between x_i and the expert's vague memory of the ith component of a situation in which he successfully had proceeded according to the rth behavior pattern while controlling the system by hand. Analogously, for $y \in Y$, "$\alpha_{(r)}(y)$" shall be interpreted as the subjectively, by the expert, estimated degree of correspondence between y and the expert's memory of the measure which has to be taken within the framework of the rth's behavior pattern. The above interpretation quite naturally results in the following interpretation of the numbers "$1 - \alpha_{(r)}^i(x_i)$," resp. "$1 - \alpha_{(r)}(y)$" which will serve as a semantic basis from now on.

Interpretation.   For $i \in \{1, \ldots, n\}$, $r \in \{1, \ldots, k\}$, $x_i \in X_i$, $y \in Y$, the number "$1 - \alpha_{(r)}^i(x_i)$," resp. "$1 - \alpha_{(r)}(y)$" represents a kind of subjectively estimated distance, expressing how far x_i, resp. y differs from the picture the expert forms (via memory) of the ith, resp. $(n + 1)$th component of a prototype of the rth behavior pattern.

With this background, it is easy to imagine the behavior of a controlling expert who is guided by his memory of successful behavior in the past, as follows:

Suppose, while operating, the system gets into the situation $(x_1, \ldots, x_n)$ [from now on, it will be supposed that the variable $(x_1, \ldots, x_n)$ takes an arbitrary but fixed chosen value; this will simplify the notations in connection with notions that depend on the system's actual situation because one thus spares the tiresome reference to $(x_1, \ldots, x_n)$]. Then, the expert, controlling by hand, reacts according to one of the k remembered (learned) behavior patterns $\mathfrak{B}_1, \ldots, \mathfrak{B}_k$—of course, according to one which fits the situation $(x_1, \ldots, x_n)$ as well as possible. Ideally, $(x_1, \ldots, x_n)$ is a basis of one of the behavior patterns $\mathfrak{B}_1, \ldots, \mathfrak{B}_k$, for instance, of the rth behavior pattern ($r \in \{1, \ldots, k\}$). In this case, the expert behaves in full agreement with his memory if, by choosing an adequate $y \in Y$, he supplements the situation $(x_1, \ldots, x_n)$ to a prototype $(x_1, \ldots, x_n, y)$ of the rth behavior pattern, and then behaves according to this prototype (i.e., if he adjusts the quantity η to the value y). If $(x_1, \ldots, x_n)$ is not a basis of one of the behavior patterns $\mathfrak{B}_1, \ldots, \mathfrak{B}_k$, and therefore cannot be supplemented to a prototype of a behavior pattern, he will try to determine a behavior pattern $\mathfrak{B}_r \in \{\mathfrak{B}_1, \ldots, \mathfrak{B}_k\}$ and a value $y \in Y$ in such a way that "the distances" $1 - \alpha_{(r)}^1(x_1), \ldots, 1 - \alpha_{(r)}^n(x_n), 1 - \alpha_{(r)}(y)$ become at least as small as possible against all other possible choices of $\mathfrak{B}_r$ and y, and then behave according to the behavior pattern $(x_1, \ldots, x_n, y)$ (i.e., to adjust η to the value y). First, of course, one has to clarify the importance of the "smallness of each single distance" for the "smallness of these distances on the whole." The simplest and most natural way to do this is to specify a metric d on $\mathbb{R}^{n+1}$, and to modify the vague task of minimizing the single distances $1 - \alpha_{(r)}^1(x_1), \ldots, 1 - \alpha_{(r)}^n(x_n), 1 - \alpha_{(r)}(y)$ to the more concrete task of minimizing the distance between the vector $(1, \ldots, 1) \in \mathbb{R}^{n+1}$ and the vector

$$(\alpha_{(r)}^1(x_1), \ldots, \alpha_{(r)}^n(x_n), \alpha_{(r)}(y)) \in \mathbb{R}^{n+1}$$

with regard to $\mathfrak{B}_r$ and y.

Altogether, the following base model for the behavior of an expert controlling by hand seems to be sufficiently motivated (not meaning that it would be inevitable):

Base Model. Given the situation $(x_1, \ldots, x_n)$, an expert, controlling by hand, endeavors to choose $\mathfrak{B}_r$ and y [for short: (r, y)] in such a way that, with an adequately chosen metric d on $\mathbb{R}^{n+1}$, the distance

$$d[(\alpha_{(r)}^1(x_1), \ldots, \alpha_{(r)}^n(x_n), \alpha_{(r)}(y)), (1, \ldots, 1)] \tag{1}$$

is minimized [where $(1, \ldots, 1) \in \mathbb{R}^{n+1}$]. Afterwards, he supplements the situation $(x_1, \ldots, x_n)$ to the reaction $(x_1, \ldots, x_n, y)$ and behaves accordingly; that is, he adjusts the quantity η to the value y.

This base model embodies a plausible variant of the natural behavior of an expert. Possible candidates for d are all metrics which are compatible with the intuitive idea of spatial proximity. This especially applies to all those metrics d which can be represented according to

$$d[\underline{z}, \underline{z}'] = m(|z_1 - z_1'|, \ldots, |z_{n+1} - z_{n+1}'|) \tag{2}$$

for all $\underline{z} := (z_1, \ldots, z_{n+1})$, $\underline{z}' := (z_1', \ldots, z_{n+1}') \in \mathbb{R}^{n+1}$, with a function $m: X_{i=1}^{n+1}\mathbb{R}^+ \to \mathbb{R}$, that increases monotonously with regard to all its arguments. Examples are the Euclidean Metric, the Maximum Metric ($d[\underline{x}, \underline{x}'] := \max_i |x_i - x_i'|$), and the Taxi Metric ($d[\underline{x}, \underline{x}'] := \Sigma_i |x_i - x_i'|$).

Definition 3.3. Let $\delta: Y \to [0, 1]$, with

$$\delta(y) = \frac{\min_{1 \le r \le k} d[(\alpha_{(r)}^1(x_1), \ldots, \alpha_{(r)}^n(x_n), \alpha_{(r)}(y)), (1, \ldots, 1)]}{d[(0, \ldots, 0), (1, \ldots, 1)]}$$

and $\alpha: Y \to [0, 1]$, with

$$\alpha(y) = 1 - \delta(y).$$

Then, for $y \in Y$, $\alpha(y)$ shall be denoted as the "suitability of y."

Motivation of Definition 3.3. The above considerations suggest the following interpretation. The larger (smaller) $\delta(y)$, the less (more) the reaction $(x_1, \ldots, x_n, y)$ corresponds to the expert's idea of that behavior pattern to which $(x_1, \ldots, x_n, y)$ fits best. The factor $\{d[(0, \ldots, 0), (1, \ldots, 1)]\}^{-1}$ in the definition of $\delta(y)$ does not affect this interpretation. It is merely a standardizing constant, ensuring that $0 \le \delta(y), \alpha(y) \le 1$ for all $y \in Y$. Thus, the interpretation of $\alpha(y)$ as a measure for the subjectively estimated suitability of the potential adjustment value y is obvious.

Definition 3.4.

(i) Given a situation $(x_1, \ldots, x_n)$ and a metric d, let $\mathfrak{M}$ denote the set of all pairs (r, y) that minimize Eq. (1).

(ii) $\mathfrak{M}_Y := \{y \in Y \mid \exists r \in \{1, \ldots, k\} : (r, y) \in \mathfrak{M}\}$ shall be denoted as the "set of adjustment values which are optimal in the situation $(x_1, \ldots, x_n)$."

Remark 3.5.

(i) From the above explanations, it obviously follows for each $\hat{y} \in \mathfrak{M}_Y$ and for each $y \in Y$: $\delta(y) \ge \delta(\hat{y})$, resp. $\alpha(y) \le \alpha(\hat{y})$. That is, the expert believes the reaction $(x_1, \ldots, x_n, \hat{y})$ to be at least as suitable in the situation $(x_1, \ldots, x_n)$

as any other. Conversely, every value $y \in Y$ which maximizes α is by definition also an element of $\mathfrak{M}_Y$. Thus, within the framework of the base model, it is easy to interpret $\mathfrak{M}_Y$ as the set of adjustment values which in the expert's opinion are optimal, given the situation $(x_1, \ldots, x_n)$.

(ii)   From $\alpha(y) \leq \alpha(\hat{y})$ for all $y \in Y$, it immediately follows that α is constant on $\mathfrak{M}_Y$.

(iii) If $\alpha^i_{(r)}$, $\alpha_{(r)}$ $(1 \leq i \leq n, 1 \leq r \leq k)$ are good-natured enough (e.g., trapezoid-like, resp. triangle-like), then, with the background of the limitation to metrics which allow a representation according to Eq. (2), it is not difficult to see that $\mathfrak{M}$, $\mathfrak{M}_Y \neq \emptyset$.

Making use of the set $\mathfrak{M}_Y$, the behavior of an expert who orients himself by the above base model may also be described in a much shorter way:

Shortened Form of the Base Model.   Given the situation $(x_1, \ldots, x_n)$, an expert, controlling by hand, endeavors to behave in the situation $(x_1, \ldots, x_n)$ according to a reaction $(x_1, \ldots, x_n, \hat{y})$, where $\hat{y} \in \mathfrak{M}_Y$.

Theorem 3.6. *If d is the Maximum Metric, then*:

(i) $\alpha = \hat{\alpha}_{x_1, \ldots, x_n}$

(ii) $\mathfrak{M}_Y = \mathrm{MAX}[\hat{\alpha}_{x_1, \ldots, x_n}]$.

($\hat{\alpha}_{x_1, \ldots, x_n}$ *and* $\mathrm{MAX}[\hat{\alpha}_{x_1, \ldots, x_n}]$ *are defined as in connection with Variant 1 in Section 2.*)

Proof. If d is the Maximum Metric, then obviously, $d[(0, \ldots, 0), (1, \ldots, 1)] = 1$, and thus, for all $y \in Y$:

$$\alpha(y) = 1 - \min_{1 \leq r \leq k} d[(\alpha^1_{(r)}(x_1), \ldots, \alpha^n_{(r)}(x_n), \alpha_{(r)}(y)), (1, \ldots, 1)]$$

$$= 1 - \min_{1 \leq r \leq k} \{\max\{|\alpha^1_{(r)}(x_1) - 1|, \ldots, |\alpha^n_{(r)}(x_n) - 1|, |\alpha_{(r)}(y) - 1|\}\}$$

$$= 1 - \min_{1 \leq r \leq k} \{1 - \min\{\alpha^1_{(r)}(x_1), \ldots, \alpha^n_{(r)}(x_n), \alpha_{(r)}(y)\}\}$$

$$= 1 - \{1 - \max_{1 \leq r \leq k} \{\min\{\alpha^1_{(r)}(x_1), \ldots, \alpha^n_{(r)}(x_n), \alpha_{(r)}(y)\}\}\}$$

$$= \max_{1 \leq r \leq k} \{\min\{\alpha^1_{(r)}(x_1), \ldots, \alpha^n_{(r)}(x_n), \alpha_{(r)}(y)\}\}$$

$$= \hat{\alpha}_{x_1, \ldots, x_n}(y)$$

and thus part (i).

(ii)   According to part (i) of Remark 3.5, we have $\mathfrak{M}_Y = \{y \in Y \mid \alpha(y') \leq \alpha(y) \, \forall y' \in Y\}$. Together with part (i) of the theorem, it follows that

$$\mathfrak{M}_Y = \{y \in Y \mid \hat{\alpha}_{x_1, \ldots, x_n}(y') \leq \hat{\alpha}_{x_1, \ldots, x_n}(y) \quad \forall y' \in Y\}$$

and by the definition of $\mathrm{MAX}[\hat{\alpha}_{x_1, \ldots, x_n}]$

$$\mathfrak{M}_Y = \mathrm{MAX}[\hat{\alpha}_{x_1, \ldots, x_n}]. \qquad \square$$

Remark 3.7.   Theorem 3.6 implies that, if d is specially chosen as the Maximum Metric, and if, given the situation $(x_1, \ldots, x_n)$, the adjustment value is chosen as an element $y^0 \in \mathfrak{M}_Y$—that is, if, while controlling the engineering system, one orients oneself by the above base model—this will lead to the same result as if, according to Variant I in Section 2 (Max-Criterion Procedure), one would determine the adjustment value as an element $y \in Y$ that maximizes $\hat{\alpha}_{x_1, \ldots, x_n}$. That is, Variant I is nothing other than a special case of the base model!

4. TWO NATURAL MODIFICATIONS OF THE BASE MODEL

Modification 1.

The set $\mathfrak{M}_Y$, consisting of all adjustment values which are optimal in the sense of the base model, does not, in general, contain only one element. Within the framework of the base model, the expert does justice to this circumstance by arbitrarily choosing any element in $\mathfrak{M}_Y$. This arbitrariness corresponds to the fact that the expert is not able to differentiate between the single qualities of elements within $\mathfrak{M}_Y$—not meaning that differences in quality really do not exist. If they exist, however, extreme mistakes are possible in connection with an arbitrary choice (this is valid all the more, the more the adjustment values scatter in $\mathfrak{M}_Y$). The question arises as to how to prevent such mistakes by a modification of the base model. One possibility is to use an average value as y^0, computed in such a way that each element of $\mathfrak{M}_Y$ has the same influence on it. It is plausible to compute this average value according to

$$
y^0 = \begin{cases} \dfrac{1}{|\mathfrak{M}_Y|} \displaystyle\sum_{y \in \mathfrak{M}_Y} y, & \text{if } |\mathfrak{M}_Y| < \infty \\[2ex] \dfrac{1}{\int_{\mathfrak{M}_Y} dy} \int_{\mathfrak{M}_Y} y \, dy, & \text{otherwise.} \end{cases}
\tag{3}
$$

For the most common—in the sense of Remark 2.1—acceptability functions $\alpha^i_{(r)}$, $\alpha_{(r)}$ ($1 \leq i \leq n$, $1 \leq r \leq k$), the integral on the right side of Eq. (3) is always defined if $\mathfrak{M}_Y$ contains more than a finite number of elements. This immediately follows from Theorem 4.1.

Theorem 4.1. *If the acceptability functions* $\alpha^i_{(r)}$, $\alpha_{(r)}$ ($1 \leq i \leq n$, $1 \leq r \leq k$) *are unimodal [see part (ii) of Definition 2.2], then* $\mathfrak{M}_Y$ *can be represented as a union set of a finite number of (eventually degenerated) intervals.*

Proof. Obviously, for $r \in \{1, \ldots, k\}$, we have $\mathfrak{M}_Y = \bigcup_{r \in \{1, \ldots, k\}} \mathfrak{M}_Y(r)$, with $\mathfrak{M}_Y(r)$:= $\{y \in Y \mid (r, y) \in \mathfrak{M}\}$. It remains to show that the sets $\mathfrak{M}_Y(r)$ are intervals for all r-values. Now, suppose that $y_1, y_2 \in \mathfrak{M}_Y(r)$, for an arbitrary but fixed chosen $r \in \{1, \ldots, k\}$. Without loss of generality, suppose that $\alpha_{(r)}(y_1) \leq \alpha_{(r)}(y_2)$.

Let y be an arbitrary element of Y with $y_1 \leq y \leq y_2$. By definition of $\mathfrak{M}_Y(r)$ it follows that the pairs (r, y_1), (r, y_2) minimize Eq. (1). Because of the assumed unimodality of the function $\alpha_{(r)}$ [see part (ii) of Definition 2.2], it follows that $\alpha_{(r)}(y) \geq \alpha_{(r)}(y_1)$, and thus, because of the limitation to such metrics which allow a representation according to Eq. (2), it follows that Eq. (1) does not take a greater value at "(r, y)" than at "(r, y_1)." That is, (r, y) also provides a minimum of Eq. (1), and thus $y \in \mathfrak{M}_Y$. $\square$

Remark 4.2. The adjustment value y^0 itself, computed according to Eq. (3), does not have to be in $\mathfrak{M}_Y$. But if it is in $\mathfrak{M}_Y$, then its choice is as well in accord with the base model as with Modification 1.

Remark 4.3. If one specially chooses the Maximum Metric for d, then by part (ii) of Theorem 3.6, $\mathfrak{M}_Y = \text{MAX}[\hat{\alpha}_{x_1,\ldots,x_n}]$. Thus, in order to compute y^0 within the framework of the above modification of the base model, one only has to replace the set $\mathfrak{M}_Y$ in Eq. (3) by the set $\text{MAX}[\hat{\alpha}_{x_1,\ldots,x_n}]$. Then, one obtains the same adjustment value as if applying Variant II (Mean-of-Maximum Procedure), described in Section 2. That is, Variant II is nothing other than a special case of Modification 1 of the base model!

Modification 2.

The idea of computing an average value in order to prevent extreme adjustment values may also be taken into account in a more consequent way than has occurred until now. Until now, the average value was computed only on the basis of adjustment values which are elements of $\mathfrak{M}_Y$, that is, only on the basis of values which maximize α or, equivalently, on the basis of such values which are equally optimal in the expert's opinion. Because it is not possible to determine differences in their quality [see part (ii) of Remark 3.5], they all are weighted equally, and thus have the same influence on Eq. (3). On the other hand, values outside $\mathfrak{M}_Y$ (i.e., values not maximizing α) are not taken into consideration at all, although they need not be worse adjustment values de facto: If, for two values y^*, $y^\# \in Y$, it is valid that $\alpha(y^*) \leq \alpha(y^\#)$, then this only means that in the situation $(x_1, \ldots, x_n)$, the suitability of $y^\#$ as an adjustment value is subjectively assessed higher by the expert than that of y^*, and not that $y^\#$ is definitely better. Thus, because, while choosing an adequate adjustment value y^0 one has no choice but to rely on the expert's subjective estimation, represented by the function α, it is adequate to take this estimation at least completely into consideration. That is, it presents itself to extend the computation of the average value over all $y \in Y$ and to take into account each y according to its presumed suitability $\alpha(y)$, that is, to choose y^0 according to

$$y^0 = \frac{1}{\int_Y \alpha(y)\, dy} \int_Y y\alpha(y)\, dy. \tag{4}$$

Remark 4.4. If α is interpreted physically as mass distribution along an axis of possible adjustment values, then an adjustment value y^0, computed according to Eq. (4), also may be interpreted as the center of gravity of this mass distribution. This obviously is also the case if the adjustment value has been computed according to Eq. (3); however, with the difference that, there, instead of α, its restriction to the set $\mathfrak{M}_Y$ is used; that is, one only takes into account that part of the whole mass which is regularly distributed over $\mathfrak{M}_Y$ [compare with part (ii) of Remark 3.5], meaning that one is not willing to attach any importance to a value y outside $\mathfrak{M}_Y$ as an alternative adjustment value. On the other hand, in the case $0 < \alpha(y) < 1$, in advance one already has explicitly attached importance to such a value y via α, which is not consistent, as discussed above.

Remark 4.5. If d is specially chosen as the Maximum Metric, then by part (i) of Theorem 3.6, we have $\alpha = \hat{\alpha}_{x_1,\ldots,x_n}$. Thus, in order to compute y^0 within the framework of Modification 2 of the base model, one only has to replace in Eq. (4) the function α by the function $\hat{\alpha}_{x_1,\ldots,x_n}$. The resulting adjustment value is obviously the same as the one provided by applying Variant III (Center-of-Area Procedure), described in Section 2. That is, Variant III is nothing other than a special case of the second modification of the base model!

5. THE CONSISTENT CHOICE OF THE ACCEPTABILITY FUNCTIONS

In Section 3, for $x_i \in X_i$, resp. $y \in Y$ the number "$1 - \alpha^i_{(r)}(x_i)$," resp. "$1 - \alpha_{(r)}(y)$" has been interpreted as a kind of subjective measure, expressing how much x_i differs from the idea, which the expert forms, of a certain measured value, resp. of a certain adjustment value (see Section 3). The base model (together with its two modifications) was based on rationally handling this meaning. In addition, a kind of "natural profile" of the acceptability functions $\alpha^i_{(r)}, \alpha_{(r)}$, $1 \le i \le n$, $1 \le r \le k$, which the expert has to specify, may also be derived from this meaning: So, it is easy to start from the assumption that these acceptability functions, as far as they are compatible with the "distance-semantic," fulfill the following requirements:

I: Let $i \in \{1, \ldots, n\}$ and $r \in \{1, \ldots, k\}$. Then, both in X_i and Y there is at least one element to which $\alpha^i_{(r)}$, resp. $\alpha_{(r)}$ attaches the value "1."

Requirement I already played a role in deriving the base model (see the comment in parentheses on page 233). Thus, it requires no further explanation.

II: Let $i \in \{1, \ldots, n\}$ and $r \in \{1, \ldots, k\}$. The set $\mathrm{MAX}[\alpha^i_{(r)}]$, resp. $\mathrm{MAX}[\alpha_{(r)}]$ of all those elements of X_i, resp. of Y to which $\alpha^i_{(r)}$, resp. $\alpha_{(r)}$ attaches the value "1" is an interval.

That is, those elements which harmonize maximally with the experts memory lie de facto close together too.

III: The acceptability functions $\alpha^i_{(r)}$, $\alpha_{(r)}$ are continuous for $i \in \{1, \ldots, n\}$, $r \in \{1, \ldots, k\}$.

The true distance between $x_i \in X_i$ and the set $\mathrm{MAX}[\alpha^i_{(r)}]$ is a continuous function of x_i. Thus, the term "$1 - \alpha^i_{(r)}(x_i)$" [and consequently the term "$\alpha^i_{(r)}(x_i)$"] as a measure of the subjectively estimated difference between x_i and the expert's idea of a remembered prototype-value should also be a continuous function, unless arguments are against this which result from the semantic of "$1 - \alpha^i_{(r)}(x_i)$ the term." This, however, is just not the case within the framework of the distance-semantic propagated here (compare the interpretation in Section 3). Quite analogously, one may argue with regard to $\alpha_{(r)}$.

IV: For all $i \in \{1, \ldots, n\}$ and $r \in \{1, \ldots, k\}$, there exist elements $x^-_{i,r}, x^+_{i,r} \in X_i$, $y^-_r, y^+_r \in Y$ with

$$\alpha^i_{(r)}(x_i) = 0 \quad \text{for } x_i \in (-\infty, x^-_{i,r}] \cup [x^+_{i,r}, \infty),$$
$$\alpha_{(r)}(y) = 0 \quad \text{for } y \in (-\infty, y^-_r] \cup [y^+_r, \infty).$$

That is, one starts from the assumption that all values, which lie sufficiently far on the right or on the left of $\mathrm{MAX}[\alpha^i_{(r)}]$, resp. $\mathrm{MAX}[\alpha_{(r)}]$, run absolutely counter to the expert's idea.

V: For all $i \in \{1, \ldots, n\}$, $r \in \{1, \ldots, k\}$ and for all $x'_i, x''_i \in X_i$, $y', y'' \in Y$, it is valid that

$$x'_i \le x''_i \le \inf \mathrm{MAX}[\alpha^i_{(r)}] \Rightarrow \alpha^i_{(r)}(x'_i) \le \alpha^i_{(r)}(x''_i),$$
$$x'_i \ge x''_i \ge \sup \mathrm{MAX}[\alpha^i_{(r)}] \Rightarrow \alpha^i_{(r)}(x'_i) \le \alpha^i_{(r)}(x''_i),$$
$$y' \le y'' \le \inf \mathrm{MAX}[\alpha_{(r)}] \Rightarrow \alpha_{(r)}(y') \le \alpha_{(r)}(y''),$$
$$y' \ge y'' \ge \sup \mathrm{MAX}[\alpha_{(r)}] \Rightarrow \alpha_{(r)}(y') \le \alpha_{(r)}(y'').$$

In other words, the one of two x_i-values (y-values) lying on the same side of $MAX[\alpha^i_{(r)}]$ ($MAX[\alpha_{(r)}]$) which is closer to $MAX[\alpha^i_{(r)}]$ ($MAX[\alpha_{(r)}]$) than the other should harmonize with the expert's idea at least to such an extent as the one lying further away.

One easily realizes that acceptability functions which fulfill the requirements I–V have to be—up to a certain extent, specified by Definition 2.2—similar to trapezoids or triangles; that is, they have to be just of that type which is so often used in applications of the fuzzy control method (see Remark 2.1).

6. FINAL REMARKS

It has been demonstrated by simple means how an expert may be simulated, who controls an engineering system by hand, and who, while doing this, is guided by his memory of successful behavior in the past. There was no need to use fuzzy logic in this connection. While within fuzzy logic one makes calculations with numbers in [0, 1], which shall express the subjectively estimated acceptability of certain statements and which are interpreted as "generalized truth-values" (degrees of possibility, degrees of membership), the considerations, made in the present article, are only based on the rational usage of numbers in [0, 1], which have been specified in order to subjectively circumscribe certain distances. In connection with a fuzzy-logically motivated control method, one has to state certain rules (so-called t-norms and t-conorms) in advance as to how to handle the "pseudo-truth-values." The justification of such rules is problematic, and often it is simply omitted; in connection with the approach propagated here, one only has to specify a metric in order to describe the actually intended interpretation of "distance." The distance-semantic is more convenient as a basis for deriving a control method because it is more elementary: so, the consequences of fixing a certain metric are surely more transparent than those which result from fixing fuzzy logical rules about how to judge the "truth" of statement-compositions. While, within the framework of the distance-semantic, the choice of the metric represents a natural degree of freedom, the weighing up between adequate fuzzy logical rules is—because of the unclear consequences—mostly seen as an unpleasant problem, and is often made taboo by simply fixing this rule axiomatically without referring to a semantic base. Beyond that, the distance- semantic is subsumptive; thus, the control method, derived from it, surprisingly coincides with the conventional control method especially if the Maximum Metric is chosen (see Remarks 3.7, 4.3, and 4.5). In this sense, the distance-semantic in retrospect provides an elementary justification of the fuzzy control method, and may help to clear up an essential part of the objections to it. Thus, the fact that the fuzzy control method is often successfully used for controlling engineering systems without previously having to analyze the actual underlying physical process may, with the background of its semantically unclear derivation by means of fuzzy logic, easily give the impression of being a kind of miracle cure. That is, at first sight it seems as if it were possible to extract more from the method than one has invested, which, of course, is suspicious with justification. If, however, one starts from the assumption that an expert is able to control the considered engineering system by hand, and if it is sufficiently reasonable to assume that the expert, while controlling the system by hand, does nothing else but retrieve memories of successful behavior in past situations in the form of subjective circumscriptions of certain distances (what seems to be plausible), then one also has sufficient grounds for believing that the fuzzy control method is suitable for controlling the system.

REFERENCES

1. H. Becker, "A Semantic Base for the Fuzzy Extension Principle, *Computers Artif. Intell.*, *16*(4), 337–353, 1997.
2. R. Kruse, J. Gebhardt, and F. Klawonn, *Fuzzy Systeme: Leitfäden und Monographien der Informatik*, Teubner Verlag, 1993.
3. E. H. Mamdani, "Application of Fuzzy Logic to Approximate Reasoning Using Linguistic Synthesis," *IEEE Trans. Computers*, *26*, 1182–1191 (1977).

Received 29 March 1995; revised 27 May 1995, 1 October 1995

HELMUT BECKER

SENSITIVITY ASPECTS OF INEQUALITY MEASURES

INTRODUCTION

It is intuitively easy to understand what is meant by inequality measures, because applications occur in very sensitive situations: rich versus poor persons or countries, high productivity versus low productivity (in various aspects: economic, scientific, biological, etc.). Inequality applies to virtually every aspect of human and nonhuman life. It is, therefore, not surprising that one wishes to measure "degrees" of inequality. Such inequality measures (also called concentration measures) have the property that the larger the value, the more unequal (uneven, concentrated) the situation is. Usually these measures are "normalized" so that they range between 0 and 1, but this is not necessary.

Sometimes one is not interested in the degree of inequality but in the opposite aspect: how even is a situation (e.g., in biology where one is interested in the diversity of species that are available). Large concentrations of some species imply the rare (or non) occurrence of other spaces and this is considered as an impoverishment of the situation. However, a special theory on evenness measures or diversity measures is only needed if one wants to study specific problems in specific domains of the sciences (e.g., in biodiversity studies). General aspects of these evenness measures indeed follow immediately from the analog ones of concentration measures. Indeed, let f be a concentration measure bounded by, for example, 0 and 1. Then it is intuitively clear that

$$g = 1 - f \tag{1}$$

is an evenness measure (e.g., the most concentrated situation gives $f = 1$ and hence $g = 0$, and the most even situation gives $f = 0$ and hence $g = 1$).

Therefore, we will limit ourselves mainly to the study of concentration measures, also because in computer science and technology and in information theory, it is far more important to study inequality than to study equality. The intuitive reason for this is clear: The more unequal a situation is, the better we can exploit this in order to optimize certain situations. Let us give an example: The more unequal symbols or words occur in a "text", the better this text can be compressed by giving the shorter codes (e.g., binary codes) to these symbols or words that occur most. An example of application is the Huffman compression technique, which we will discuss briefly in the context of entropy.

Unequal situations are often encountered in the information sciences: Only a few scientists are prolific (publish a lot), but many publish little; a scientific discipline has only a few "top journals", whereas many journals occasionally publish in this area. In linguistics, computer sciences, and information sciences, one has the law of Zipf stating that the occurrence of words in a text (the tokens as one says in linguistics) is inversely proportional to the rank of this word ("type" in linguistics) (rank according to the occurrence of this word in the text).

Unequal situations can be explained by studying probabilistic properties such as the so-called "Success Breeds Success" principle that states (simplifying) that prolific sources have a higher probability to produce a new item than less prolific ones. In this article, we do not go into these probabilistic aspecs: We limit our attention to the problem of "how to measure inequality."

For more on these probabilistic aspects of inequality, we refer the reader to Refs. 1 and 2, and references therein.

PRINCIPLES OF INEQUALITY

Basic Principles

In the sequel, we will use the terminology of sources that produce items (e.g., words and their uses in texts, authors producing publications, etc.). We want to measure the degree of inequality (i.e., the degree of the differences in production quantities of these sources). Related to this, one could mention the so-called 80/20 rule which states that 20% of the most prolific sources produce 80% of all items. Of course, in general other numbers might occur. It is clear that a 90/10 result gives a more concentrated situation than a 80/20 result, whereas a 70/25 result is more even. Not directly comparable with 80/20 is, for example, a 90/30 result. We will go into this later.

These "generalized" 80/20 rules will be encountered in the sequel as an application of our more general framework in which we want to produce a single number that measures concentration (rather than two as above).

Let us define some notation. Let N be the total number of sources. For source $i \in \{1, \ldots, N\}$, denote by x_i its production ($x_i \in \mathbb{R}^+$). It is clear that a concentration measure must be a function of the N-tuple $(x_1, \ldots, x_N)$, preferably with positive values:

$$f: (x_1, \ldots, x_N) \rightarrow f(x_1, \ldots, x_N) \in \mathbb{R}^+.$$

We will assume (although it is not strictly necessary) that the values of f are bounded (i.e., min f and max f exist in $\mathbb{R}$). Most commonly these are 0 and 1 and it will be clear from the sequel that any good bounded concentration measure can be transformed into one where min $f = 0$ and max $f = 1$. These situations must occur in the following cases. Let $X = (x, 0, \ldots, 0)$ [i.e., one source (here the first one) produces everything ($x \in \mathbb{R}^+$)], then $f(X) = 1$. In the other extreme, if $Y = (y, y, \ldots, y)$ ($y \in \mathbb{R}^+$) [i.e., all sources produce the same quantity y], then $f(Y) = 0$. We will call this principle (Z):

$$f(x, 0, \ldots, 0) = 1 \tag{2}$$

[or, more generally, max $f(X)$, where the maximum is taken over all $X = (x_1, \ldots, x_N)$ such that $\sum_{i=1}^{N} x_i = x$]
and

$$f(y, y, \ldots, y) = 0 \tag{3}$$

[or, more generally, min $f(X)$, where the minimum is taken over all $X = (x_1, \ldots, x_N)$ for which $\sum_{i=1}^{N} x_i = Ny$, hence $\bar{X} = y$, where $\bar{X}$ denotes the average of the values $x_1, \ldots, x_N$].

The next principle is called the "Permutation Invariance" and is denoted by (P). It states that concentration is not a labeled property; that is, the concentration value is not changed if, for example, names of persons are interchanged. Formulated exactly, we state that for every $(x_1, \ldots, x_N)$ and every permutation π

$$\pi: \{1, 2, \ldots, N\} \rightarrow \{1, 2, \ldots, N\}$$

of the numbers $1, \ldots, N$, we have that

$$f(x_1, \ldots, x_N) = f(x_{\pi(1)}, \ldots, x_{\pi(N)}).$$ [4]

Concentration measures should be "normalized" w.r.t. the total production $\sum_{i=1}^{N} x_i$. Indeed, we need, for example, to compare the concentration of words in texts and this comparison may not be dependent on the size of the text: Independent of the size of the database, one should, indeed, be able to determine the optimal compression technique. It is even so that the size of a database is not always known or at least cannot be predicted (e.g., when considering the growth of such databases). An example from econometrics also illustrates this principle very clearly: Concentration must be independent of the units; for example, when measuring wealth, the value of f must be independent of the currency used (U.S. dollars, yen, pound, Euro, etc.). This principle is called "Scale Invariance," (S): For every $(x_1, \ldots, x_N)$ and every $c > 0$,

$$f(cx_1, \ldots, cx_N) = f(x_1, \ldots, x_N).$$ [5]

Last but not least, at the real heart of concentration theory, it should be obvious that "if one takes away from the poor and gives it to the rich, inequality concentration must increase". Obviously, this principle is called the "Transfer Principle", (T): For every $(x_1, \ldots, x_N)$ and if $i, j \in \{1, \ldots, N\}$ are such that $x_i \leq x_j$, and if $0 < h \leq x_i$, then

$$f(x_1, \ldots, x_i - h, \ldots, x_j + h, \ldots, x_N) > f(x_1, \ldots, x_i, \ldots, x_j, \ldots, x_N)$$ [6]

(h is the amount that is taken away from the "poorer" source i and given to the "richer" source j). This is a very natural principle. It also includes several other principles:

Principle (R): If the richest gets richer, inequality increases. For every $(x_1, \ldots, x_N)$, if $x_i = \max\{x_1, \ldots, x_N\}$ and if there exists a $k \neq i$ such that $x_k \neq 0$, then, for every $h > 0$,

$$f(x_1, \ldots, x_i + h, \ldots, x_N) > f(x_1, \ldots, x_i, \ldots, x_N).$$ [7]

Principle (N): The principle of the nominal increase: For every $(x_1, \ldots, x_N)$ where not all x_i are equal, and every $h > 0$,

$$f(x_1 + h, \ldots, x_N + h) < f(x_1, \ldots, x_N).$$ [8]

All these principles are in accordance with our intuitive feeling about inequality. Of course, independent of all these principles, one is not yet sure that such functions f exist. That they exist (abundantly) will be clear in the sequel. As stated, (T) $\Rightarrow$ (R) and (T) $\Rightarrow$ (N). Therefore, we only consider the set of principles

$$(B) = \{(Z), (P), (S), (T)\}$$ [9]

and consider (B) as a minimum requirement for a good concentration measure. Further refinements of Principle (T) will lead to finer requirements for concentration measures and hence to a reduction of their quantity. This will be the main purpose of this survey article: feeling the sensitivity of concentration measures with respect to diverse transfer principles such as (T).

The Lorenz Curve and Lorenz Order

The Lorenz curve and order are two of the most important findings in contemporary mathematics with basic applications in concentration theory. The concept is simple and beautiful. Let us consider one situation $X = (x_1, \ldots, x_N)$: N sources where source i has a production of x_i items. Consider the "normalized" vector

$$A_x = (a_1, \ldots, a_N),$$

where, for every $i = 1, \ldots, N$,

$$a_i = \frac{x_i}{\displaystyle\sum_{k=1}^{N} x_k} \, . \tag{10}$$

Then consider the set of points

$$\left(\frac{i}{N}, \sum_{j=1}^{i} a_j \right) \tag{11}$$

(i.e., the cumulative fraction of the items in the first i sources). Let us suppose that X is decreasing (if it is not, a rearrangement of the coordinates in X will yield a decreasing vector, still called X). In this case, by interconnecting the points in the term [11], and linking the first point with (0, 0) yields a concavely increasing polygonal curve. For example, Figure 1 shows the Lorenz curve for the vector $X = (1, 4, 3, 10)$, rearranged to yield a decreasing vector (10, 4, 3, 1). We could, of course, also consider increasing vectors. In this case, our Lorenz curve is convexely increasing, being the mirror image of the first one over the diagonal [connecting (0, 0) and (1, 1)] of the unit square.

That the Lorenz curve has something to offer to concentration theory is already clear from its very definition. It contains all applicable forms of the so-called 80/20 rule. Indeed, every vertical line indicates an abscissa x which corresponds with an ordinate y given by the Lorenz curve. Hence, a $100y/100x$ rule is obtained and this for every value of $x \in [0, 1]$.

In informetrics, one has the so-called Bradford curves (cf. Ref. 1). They are nothing else than the Lorenz curves, but where the fractions are replaced by their counts (i.e., i versus $\sum_{j=1}^{i} x_j$) and where the ordinates are given in a logarithmic scale. The use of these so-called semilogarithmic scales yielded additional information on the type of bibliography (here sources are journals and items are the articles in these journals) under study. For more on this, we refer the reader to Ref. 1.

We are now in a position to introduce the Lorenz order between two vectors $X = (x_1, \ldots, x_N)$ and $X' = (x'_1, \ldots, x'_N)$. We suppose that both X and X' are decreasing and that

$$\sum_{i=1}^{N} x_i = \sum_{i=1}^{N} x'_i.$$

Then we say that X' dominates X (in notation $X \prec X'$ or $X' \succ X$) if

$$\sum_{i=1}^{j} x_i \leq \sum_{i=1}^{j} x'_i \tag{12}$$

for every $j = 1, \ldots, N - 1$. Because

$$\sum_{i=1}^{N} x_i = \sum_{i=1}^{N} x'_i,$$

inequality (12) is also valid for $j = N$. Because of this equality and by Eq. (10), we have now that $X \prec X'$ if and only if the Lorenz curve of X is always below the one of X' (i.e., the Lorenz curve of X never intersects the one of X'). The order expressed by $\prec$ (a partial order) is called the Lorenz order.

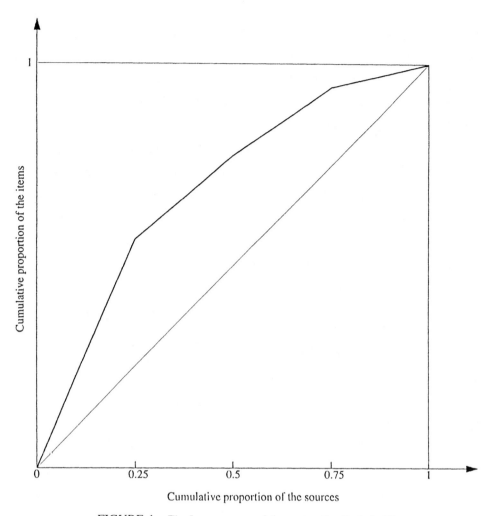

Cumulative proportion of the sources

FIGURE 1   The Lorenz curve of the vector $X = (1, 4, 3, 10)$.

The Lorenz order is very important in mathematics (e.g., in the study of convex function inequalities, geometric inequalities, combinatorial analysis, and matrix theory). For more on this, see Ref 3. The importance for the topic discussed in this article will become apparent from the next definition and theorem.

Let f be a function as above. We say that f satisfies Principle (L) if it satisfies Principles (Z), (P), and (S) and whenever $X = (x_1, \ldots, x_N) \prec X' = (x'_1, \ldots, x'_N)$ and $X \neq X'$, we have

$$f(X) < f(X'). \qquad\qquad [13]$$

Functions for which $X \prec X'$ implies $f(X) \leq f(X')$ are sometimes called Schur convex functions.

Theorem: *(L) is equivalent to (B).*

In other words, the preservation by f of the Lorenz dominance order is equivalent to the transfer principle. The transfer principle was hinted at by Pigou (4) in 1912 but was first exactly described by Dalton in 1920 (5). The Lorenz curve was introduced in Ref. 6 in 1905. The Lorenz order was introduced (as notation and terminology) by Hardy et al. (7). It is therefore, a bit surprising to state that the above theorem was essentially known (of course, in other terminology) by Muirhead in 1903; see Ref. 8 and also Ref. 9.

The above theorem offers a geometric "visualization" of what is required of a good concentration measure. It summarizes in one graph and one notation ($\prec$) of what, more or less, concentration is all about.

Of course, all the definitions and results mentioned so far are empty if we cannot give concrete examples of good inequality measures.

CONCENTRATION MEASURES

Let $X = (x_1, \ldots, x_N)$ be an arbitrary vector.

The Coefficient of Variation *V*

This is the most well-known concentration measure. This measure V is defined as the quotient of the standard deviation σ of X and of the average (mean) μ of X:

$$V = \frac{\sigma}{\mu}.$$ [14]

Recall that

$$\mu = \frac{1}{N} \sum_{i=1}^{N} x_i$$

and that

$$\sigma^2 = \frac{1}{N} \sum_{i=1}^{N} (x_i - \mu)^2 = \frac{1}{N} \sum_{i=1}^{N} x_i^2 - \mu^2.$$

The Yule Characteristic *K*

This measure is derived from V:

$$K = \frac{V^2}{N}.$$ [15]

The measure is used in linguistics.

Pratt's Measure and the Gini Index

We suppose here that X is decreasing.

Denote

$$q = \sum_{i=1}^{N} i a_i$$

with a_i as in Eq. (10). Then Pratt's measure C is defined as

$$C = \frac{2[((N+1)/2 - q)]}{N - 1} \qquad [16]$$

and Gini's index by

$$G = \frac{N-1}{N} C. \qquad [17]$$

It must, however, be remarked that Gini's index was introduced in 1909 in econometrics (cf. Ref. 10), long before Pratt's measure was, namely in 1977 (cf. Ref. 11), the latter one in informetrics. Originally, the Gini index G was defined as twice the area between the Lorenz curve and the straight line joining (0, 0) and (1, 1) (i.e., the Lorenz curve of a uniform distribution). That they are essentially the same [cf. Eq. (17) with N usually very high] was only seen in 1979—see Ref. 12. This is a typical example of "reinventing the wheel," not so surprising with this highly interdisciplinary subject!

The measures V, C, and G are generalized as follows. Define, for $r \geq 1$,

$$P(r) = \frac{\left\{ [1/2N(N-1)] \sum_{i,j=1}^{N} |x_i - x_j|^r \right\}^{1/r}}{\mu}, \qquad [18]$$

the so-called generalized Pratt measure, essentially introduced in Ref 13. It can be shown (cf. Ref. 14) that

$$P(1) = C \quad \text{and} \quad P(2) = \sqrt{\frac{N}{N-1}} V.$$

Theil's Measures Th and *L*

These measures were introduced in 1967 in Ref. 15 as follows:

$$\text{Th} = \frac{1}{N} \sum_{i=1}^{N} \left(\frac{x_i}{\mu} \right) \ell n \left(\frac{x_i}{\mu} \right) \qquad [19]$$

and

$$L = -\left(\ell n(N) + \frac{1}{N} \sum_{i=1}^{N} \ell n(a_i) \right), \qquad [19']$$

again with a_i as in Eq. (10).

We close this nonexhaustive list with the Atkinson indices.

The Atkinson Indices *A(e)*

For $0 < e < 1$, define

$$A(e) = 1 - \left[\frac{1}{N} \sum_{i=1}^{N} \left(\frac{x_i}{\mu} \right)^{1-e} \right]^{1/(1-e)} \qquad [20]$$

and for $e = 1$

$$A(1) = 1 - \frac{(x_1 \cdots x_N)^{1/N}}{\mu} ; \qquad\qquad\qquad [21]$$

cf. Ref. 16. As is clear from the above, most of these measures originate from econometrics or sociometrics.

We refer to Ref. 14 for the proofs that all these measures satisfy Principle (L) and, hence, are to be considered good concentration measures.

Note 1: The Theil measures are also called Theil's entropy measures. Indeed, they resemble the well-known average entropy formula—known in information theory—

$$\bar{H} = -\sum_{i=1}^{N} a_i \log_2 a_i. \qquad\qquad\qquad [22]$$

Stated in this form, $\bar{H}$ is a valuable measure but is not a concentration measure, but a measure of evenness. Of course, upon normalization and the application of the tranformation (1), we obtain a concentration measure. Do not be mistaken: The measures Th and *L are* concentration measures.

Note 2: So far we have always supposed that N is fixed. This, of course, excludes dynamic studies of concentration (or evenness or diversity) because if time is variable, N is variable too, in most cases. Especially in biology, the variability of N has an implication on possibilities of studying diversity of species. We assume that the N-variability is less important in computer science and technology as well as in informetrics: There, one can still compare concentration values of, for example, databases of different sizes and draw professional conclusions based on these comparisons. An example of this is given in the next section.

N-dependent theories can be developed as follows. It is clear that it is possible to draw a Lorenz curve for any vector $X = (x_1, \ldots, x_N)$ and any N. Now, we generalize the Lorenz order, introduced earlier (cf. Ref. 12) by stating that the N vector X dominates the N' vector X' if the Lorenz curve of X' never lies above the Lorenz curve of X. This will be denoted as $X' \prec\prec X$. This requirement generalizes the partial order introduced for fixed N.

A good concentration measure should respect this generalized Lorenz order. This means that such a concentration measure f should satisfy the following relation:

$$X' \neq X \quad \text{and} \quad X' \prec\prec X \Rightarrow f(X') < f(X). \qquad\qquad [23]$$

Related to this, we introduce the cell-replication axiom [introduced by Dalton (5)]. First, we define the mathematical operator REPEAT_c, with c a nonzero natural number, as

$$\text{REPEAT}_c(x_1, \ldots, x_N) = (x_1, \ldots, x_1, x_2, \ldots, x_2, \ldots, x_N, \ldots, x_N), \qquad [24]$$

where every x_i is repeated c times. Then, a function f satisfies the cell-replication axiom if

$$f(\text{REPEAT}_c(X)) = f(X). \qquad\qquad\qquad [25]$$

Note that the Lorenz curve of X and of $\text{REPEAT}_c(X)$ coincide, so that this is a very natural requirement.

It can be shown Ref. 17 that if a function is a good concentration measure for fixed N and, moreover, satisfies the cell-replication axiom, then it satisfies relation (23).

Now, the coefficient of variation, V, the Gini index, G, Theil's measures Th and

L, and all Atkinson indices $A(e)$ satisfy this additional requirement. Hence, they can be used to compare situations in which the number of sources is different. The Yule characteristic, K, and Pratt's measure, C, on the other hand, do not satisfy this additional axiom.

Finally, we note that it is possible to introduce other requirements to compare situations with a different number of sources. These requirements take the number of sources explicitly into account (17).

SOME APPLICATIONS IN COMPUTER SCIENCE, INFORMATION SCIENCE, AND LINGUISTICS

Huffman Compression of Codes

It is obvious that the occurrence of words in texts is very dependent on the words: some words occur very often (e.g., the, a, of, for, etc.) for grammatical reasons and some only occur a few times. It is then logical (and it is so in most cases) that the words that occur more often should be the shortest ones. This is often the case in natural language, although not in an optimal way. It is for this reason that one often uses abbreviations, acronyms, and so forth.

In the same way, codes for symbols should be shorter if the symbols occur more often than others. Let us give an example with an alphabet of only eight symbols A, B, C, D, E, F, G, H. As is always the case in practice, we will suppose that these symbols do not occur the same number of times. Suppose we have already ordered the symbols in decreasing order of occurrence. Suppose their fraction (probability) of occurrence is as follows: A, 0.338; B, 0.203; C, 0.135; D, 0.088; E, 0.081; F, 0.061; G, 0.054; H, 0.040.

For the sake of simplicity we only look at binary coding of these eight symbols, but any n-ary coding can be studied in the same way. It is clear that binary codes of length 3 suffice, as $2^3 = 8$. We could then code these eight symbols as follows: A = $\phi\phi\phi$, B = $\phi\phi1$, C = $\phi1\phi$, D = $\phi11$, E = $1\phi\phi$, F = $1\phi1$, G = 11ϕ, and H = 111. Hence, the average length per symbol is 3. There is, however, the following theorem, which can be used to decrease the average length required to code this alphabet.

Theorem [Huffman (18)]. *There exists a non-fixed-length decodable coding which is optimal in the sense that no shorter average length per symbol is possible. The average length per symbol of this coding is $\overline{H}$ as given by formula (22).*

This coding is called the Huffman coding. In the above example, one can calculate (using $a_1 = 0.338$, $a_2 = 0.203$, and so on, and $N = 8$, of course) that $\overline{H} = 2.65 < 3$. One cannot give the "shortest" binary coding A = ϕ, B = 1, C = $\phi\phi$, D = $\phi1$, E = 1ϕ, F = 11, G = $1\phi\phi$, and H = $1\phi1$ because this coding is not decodable. The (up to a permutation of ϕ and 1) unique solution is A = $\phi\phi$, B = 1ϕ, C = $\phi11$, D = 111, E = $\phi1\phi\phi$, F = $\phi1\phi1$, G = $11\phi\phi$, and H = $11\phi1$, with average length per symbol equal to 2.7, very close to 2.65 and a serious improvement (i.e., compression) w.r.t. the fixed-length coding with length 3. There is a simple algorithm to find this solution. The reader is referred to Ref. 19 for this as well as for much more on compression of texts. Note that the Huffman coding is decodable, as no code is the beginning of a larger code. So is it clear that the text $\phi11111111\phi11\phi\phi\phi\phi11\phi111\phi\phi$ is uniquely decodable as CDDCAAHG.

Zipf's Law and Mandelbrot's Law

One can ask the question: How do we obtain the probabilities (fractions) for the occurrence of the symbols as in the above example? More generally, how can we know the fraction of occurrence of the different words or letters in a text? The general answer is that this can be done statistically by sampling and then calculate confidence intervals for these sampled fractions. We must warn the reader that calculating confidence intervals for a large number of fractions is requiring very high sample sizes (cf. Ref. 20). If this cannot be executed, we can put all our hopes to known distributions of these multinomial fractions. They will give a good approximation of the concrete situation of the text and hence [also because the Huffman technique is very stable wrt the initial input parameters (i.e., the fractions of occurrence)] will yield an optimal or at least a quasi-optimal compression of the text. We will discuss two "classical" distributions.

The Law of Zipf

The law of Zipf (21,22) is a distribution that is encountered in linguistics. It states that if one orders the words in a text in decreasing order of their occurrence in this text, then the number of occurrences is inversely proportional to its rank. In mathematical notation, if r denotes the rank of the word and $y(r)$ the fraction of the number of times this word occurs in the text, then

$$y(r) = \frac{C}{r}, \qquad\qquad [26]$$

where C is a constant for the text. It is clear that formula (26) expresses the unequal occurrence of words in the text. In Ref. 23, I calculated the measure of Pratt, expressing the degree of concentration and found, for example, for a text of 10,000 words, a value of $C = 0.80$.

The Law of Mandelbrot

Even in linguistics, it is clear that the law of Zipf is not always valid. Often, one finds better approximations (of the data derived from the text) by using an extra parameter [e.g., r^α instead of r in formula (26)]. Of a different nature is the law of Mandelbrot (24,25). Stated more generally in terms of sources and items, it can be formulated as follows: if we rank the sources in decreasing order of the number of items they produce and if r denotes the rank of the source and $y(r)$ its fraction of the total production, then

$$y(r) = \frac{A}{1 + Br}, \qquad\qquad [27]$$

where A and B are constants. This law is encountered very often in informetrics (e.g., when describing inequality in publication patterns by authors or journals in a certain field). For this law, one finds the value $C = 0.61$ for Pratt's measure of inequality (again for 10,000 sources).

We see that this value is much lower than the one found for Zipf's law. Hence, Zipf's law expresses a more concentrated situation than Mandelbrot's. This result is somewhat surprising but can be explained—philosophically—as follows. In all situations where Zipf's or Mandelbrot's law applies, we clearly deal with an unequal situation:

Few sources produce a lot of items and many sources produce not many items. But in cases where Mandelbrot's law applies, the most prolific sources refrain their high production a bit: This is so in the case of author–publication patterns—here the most prolific authors will only publish their best work; this is also the case in the journal–article pattern—the more important a journal develops in a certain discipline the more strict (by applying heavy refereeing procedures) it will be in accepting papers for publication. This is not so in, for example, texts (where Zipf's law usually applies): The most heavily used words are continued to be used in that pace, no matter how long the text is, due to grammatical reasons. This creates the more concentrated situation, which is not a bad result from the point of view of compression of the text: the use of many small words and possibly of abbreviations (e.g., Prof., Dr., etc.) of heavily used words that are somewhat longer.

In the same way, one also finds the following result on the generalized 80/20 rule: The higher the average number of items per source, the smaller the fraction of the most prolific sources one needs in order to have a fixed cumulative fraction of the items. This has applications in libraries: The higher the average number of circulations per book (say per year) in a library, the smaller is the fraction of the most heavily used books needed to cover say 95% of all circulations. In other words (as is the case in public libraries as compared to scientific libraries), the weeding problem is easier in such libraries, as there a larger fraction (now of the least used books) can be taken that accounts for a very low fixed percentage of the circulations. In general, one could also say that the higher the average number of items per source, the higher the Lorenz curve is situated in the unit square.

In the next section, we will study some refinements of the transfer principle (T), as it is the basis in concentration theory. Most of these refinements go in the direction of the study of sensitivity properties of concentration measures with respect to transfers.

OTHER TRANSFER PRINCIPLES AND SENSITIVITY WITH RESPECT TO TRANSFERS

The classical transfer principle (T) deals with "taking away from one poor and giving it to one rich." Of course, as is also reflected in the theorem in the subsection The Lorenz Curve and Lorenz Order, consecutive compositions of bilateral transfers are possible, yielding the same inequality for our concentration measure f. But real life is more complicated! It can be that—to stay within the appealing econometric terminology—so many transfers happen, giving an overall bonus to the richer sources but in which there are also bonuses for some poor sources. The next transfer principle, stronger than (T) goes in this direction.

The Transfer Principles *E(p)*

It is immediately verified that the change of $X = (x_1, \ldots, x_i, \ldots, x_j, \ldots, x_N)$ into $X' = (x_1, \ldots, x_i - h, \ldots, x_j + h, \ldots, x_N)$, where $x_i \leq x_j$ and where $0 < h \leq x_i$ [as in the definition of the transfer principle (T)], implies that the variance of the vector X' is strictly larger than the variance of the vector X. Hence, a good generalization of Principle (T), hereby possibly affecting all sources, is as follows (cf. Ref. 9):

Let f be as always. We say that it satisfies the principle $E(p)$ $(p \geq 1)$ if for every $X = (x_1, \ldots, x_N)$ and $X' = (x_1', \ldots, x_N')$ such that

$$\sum_{i=1}^{N} x_j = \sum_{i=1}^{N} x'_j$$

and such that

$$\sum_{i,j=1}^{N} |x_i - x_j|^p < \sum_{i,j=1}^{N} |x'_i - x'_j|^p, \qquad [28]$$

we have that

$$f(x_1, \ldots, x_N) < f(x'_1, \ldots, x'_N). \qquad [29]$$

Note that

$$\frac{1}{2N^2} \sum_{i,j=1}^{N} |x_i - x_j|^p \qquad [30]$$

is the p variance of the vector X and also that it is equal to σ^2 if $p = 2$. The above definition can even be extended by replacing the function $x \rightarrow |x|^p$ by any convex function. In Ref. 9, it is shown that $E(p) \Rightarrow (T)$ for every $p \geq 1$; hence, we have at our disposition a stronger transfer principle. Hence, the concentration measures encountered so far, which also satisfy a principle $E(p)$ ($p \geq 1$), are stronger (better) measures than those which satisfy (T) but not $E(p)$.

Obviously, V and K satisfy $E(2)$, and in Ref. 14, it was shown that C and G satisfy $E(1)$ [in essence because $P(1) = C$, with $P(1)$ as in Eq. (18) with $r = 1$]. Obviously, $P(r)$ satisfies $E(r)$ for every $r \geq 1$. That any $E(p)$ is strictly stronger than (T) follows from the fact that neither Th nor $A(e)$ ($0 < e < 1$) satisfy any $E(p)$, whereas they all satisfy (T). It is shown in Ref. 26 that the validity of one $E(p)$ ($p \geq 1$) excludes the validity of any $E(q)$ ($q \geq 1$, $q \neq p$) at least if $N \geq 3$, which is always the case in practice. It is also so for $N = 3$ except for $p = 2$, $q = 4$, as here $E(2) = E(4)$. Because $E(2)$ relates to the classical variance, we could consider it to be the most important $E(p)$-principle and, hence, we can consider V, K, or other from V derived measures to be the most important concentration measures. Also, its formulation $V = \sigma/\mu$ is very simple. The principle $E(2)$ is equivalent with the following desirable transfer principle. Let $X = (x_1, \ldots, x_N)$ and $X' = (x'_1, \ldots, x'_N)$ be such that $x'_i = x_i + h_i$ ($i = 1, \ldots, N$) with

$$\sum_{i=1}^{N} h_i = 0$$

and such that

$$\sum_{i=1}^{N} h_i (x_i + x'_i) \geq 0. \qquad [31]$$

If $X \neq X'$ then

$$f(x_1, \ldots, x_N) < f(x'_1, \ldots, x'_N).$$

The proof can be found in Ref. 9.

Sensitivity Aspects of Inequality Measures with Respect to Transfers

It is very difficult to express what is meant by "sensitivity" of inequality measures. It is a "second-order" aspect, describing how dependent a measure is w.r.t. a transfer (apart from the fact that we have a strict inequality).* Let us go back to the original definition of the transfer principle (T). It states that when $x_i \leq x_j$ and when $0 < h \leq x_i$,

---

*We do not deal with statistical sensitivity (e.g., the dependence of the sensitivity of statistical methods w.r.t. the sample size).

$$f(x_1, \ldots, x_i, \ldots, x_j, \ldots, x_N) < f(x_1, \ldots, x_i - h, \ldots, x_j + h, \ldots, x_N). \qquad [32]$$

In this formulation, it is in no way stated how the difference

$$\Delta f = f(x_1, \ldots, x_i - h, \ldots, x_j + h, \ldots, x_N) - f(x_1, \ldots, x_N)$$

is dependent of x_i or i or x_j or j or even $x_j - x_i$ or $j - i$, and so forth (dependence on the indices presupposes, of course, a certain ordering of the x_i's). Discussions around this theme in econometrics can be found in Ref. 16 and for sociometrics in Ref. 13. In Ref. 27, Allison pleads for measures that are sensitive for differences (such as $x_j - x_i$). This plea is given in the context of publications and citations and, indeed, it is our feeling that sensitivity must be studied within the context of the application.

In Ref. 14, one has found that ΔV^2 is linearly dependent on $x_j - x_i$ but independent of i or j. Dependence of the latter is found for ΔG and ΔC, whereas, not surprisingly, ΔTh is dependent on $\ln(x_j) - \ln(x_i)$.

We will now look at (T) in another way. It is an easy consequence of (T) that [by applying Inequality (32) $N - 1$ times] (supposing $x_1 = \max\{x_i; i = 1, \ldots, N\}$ x_i and using property (P), this can always be realized)

$$f(x_1, \ldots, x_N) < f\left(x_1 + h, x_2 - \frac{h}{N-1}, \ldots, x_N - \frac{h}{N-1}\right) \qquad [33]$$

if $0 < h < \min\{(N-1) x_i; i = 1, \ldots, N\}$ $(N-1)x_i$.

This principle is related to moonlighting: One source (here the first one) gets richer (e.g., by not paying taxes), which is detrimental to all other citizens. In scientometrics, we have an example whereby the most important research group in a certain domain is recognized by a subsidizing authority (such as a government), thereby donating an important amount of money to this group, which is then not available any more for all the other groups.

Now, it is clear that Inequality (33) is rather artificial: What happens if the second largest source grows at the cost of all the others, and so on? It is intuitive that if x_1 is "above average production," then Inequality (33) should be valid. What average can we use? This will become clear in the sequel. Let us fix some notation. Let $X = (x_1, x_2, \ldots, x_N)$ be rearranged in such a way that the transfer h occurs at the first source (not necessarily anymore the source with maximum production). Denote

$$Y = \left(1, -\frac{1}{N-1}, -\frac{1}{N-1}, \ldots, -\frac{1}{N-1}\right), \qquad [34]$$

where there are $N - 1$ coordinates with value $-1/(N-1)$. Then, Inequality (33) is equivalent to

$$f(X + hY) - f(X) > 0. \qquad [35]$$

This only compares two situations: X (before the transfer) and $X' = X + hY$ (after the transfer). In these cases, a total transfer of $h > 0$ is involved and the inequalities should change if $h < 0$ and, furthermore, any small $|h|$ can be used. This boils down to calculate (for every "small" h)

$$\frac{f(X + hY) - f(X)}{h} \qquad [36]$$

and examining the sign of this number, now irrespective of the sign of h. This leads to the use of the directional derivative

$$f'(X; Y) = \lim_{h \to 0} \frac{f(X + hY) - f(X)}{h}$$

$$= \sum_{i=1}^{N} \frac{\partial f}{\partial x_i}(X) y_i,$$

where $Y = (y_1, \ldots, y_N)$ as in Eq. (34). Hence,

$$f'(X; Y) = \frac{\partial f}{\partial X_1}(X) - \frac{1}{N-1} \sum_{i=2}^{N} \frac{\partial f}{\partial x_i}(X). \tag{37}$$

This leads us to several new transfer principles (which will lead us to the notion of sensitivity): Let $M(X)$ denote any average (e.g., arithmetic, geometric, harmonic, median, etc.). We say that f satisfies transfer principle (T_M) if $x_1 > M(X)$ implies

$$f'(X; Y) > 0. \tag{38}$$

This transfer principle has been introduced in Ref. 28. Also in Ref. 28, it is noted that the value of $f'(X; Y)$ is a measure for the sensitivity of f w.r.t. transfers. Note that the sign of $f'(X; Y)$ changes for evenness measures and hence the value of $f'(X; Y)$ [or rather $|f'(X; Y)|$] can also be used for evenness measures. Here, however, we restrict ourselves to concentration measures.

Let us fix some notations for the different averages of a vector $X = (x_1, \ldots, x_N)$.

$$\mu = \frac{1}{N} \sum_{i=1}^{N} x_i \tag{39}$$

the arithmetic mean,

$$g = (x_1 \cdots x_N)^{1/N} \tag{40}$$

the geometric mean,

$$h = \frac{N}{\sum_{i=1}^{N} \left(\frac{1}{x_i}\right)} \tag{41}$$

the harmonic mean, and by m the median, that is, x_m for which

$$m = \frac{N+1}{2} \tag{42}$$

(and in case N is even, take the average of the two middle x_i-values).

In these cases, we can talk of the transfer principles (T_μ), (T_g), (T_h), and (T_m).

In Ref. 28, the following theorem has been proved, based on Eq. (34) and Inequality (35).

Theorem
(1) $V'(X; Y) = \dfrac{1/(\mu\sqrt{N})}{\sqrt{\sum_{i=1}^{N} (x_i - \mu)^2}} \left((x_1 - \mu) - \sum_{i=2}^{N} \dfrac{(x_i - \mu)}{N - 1} \right).$ [43]

Hence, V satisfies (T_μ). Hence, also, K satisfies (T_μ).

(2) $\mathrm{Th}'(X;\, Y) = \dfrac{1}{N\mu}\left[\left(\ell n\!\left(\dfrac{x_1}{\mu}\right) + \mu\right) - \dfrac{1}{N-1}\sum_{i=2}^{N}\left(\ell n\!\left(\dfrac{x_i}{\mu}\right) + \mu\right)\right].$ [44]

Hence, Th satisfies (T_g).

(3) $L'(X;\, Y) = -\dfrac{1}{N}\left(\dfrac{1}{x_1} - \dfrac{1}{N-1}\sum_{i=2}^{N}\dfrac{1}{x_i}\right).$ [45]

Hence, L satisfies (T_h). Also, $A(1)$ satisfies (T_h).

(4) $G'(X;\, Y) = -\dfrac{2(N+1-i)}{\mu N^2} + \dfrac{2}{\mu N^2(N-1)}\sum_{j\neq i}(N+1-j).$ [46]

Hence, G satisfies (T_m). Hence, also, C satisfies (T_m).

The respective values of $f'(X;\, Y)$ for $f = V$, Th, L, or G give the sensitivity of these measures w.r.t. trasnfers. To the best of our knowledge, in Ref. 28, it is the first time that a connection has been found between these classical measures of concentration and these different averages of a vector $X = (x_1, \ldots, x_N)$. In Ref. 28, some other concentration measures have been linked with some other (T_M) transfer properties (for generalized averages M).

This theory of sensitivity w.r.t. transfers is exact in the sense that it uses a clear definition [$f'(X;\, Y) > 0$] involving a derivative, which is expected for the study of sensitivity. Yet, it allows for differences in nature of the diverse concentration measures (w.r.t. the used average). The appearance of the four basic averages (arithmetic, geometric, harmonic, and the median) is remarkable. Overall, this sensitivity theory can be considered as a mathematical solution to some problems raised (with partial solutions) in Refs. 13, 16, and 27.

SUMMARY AND CONCLUSION

This review paper dealt with various ways of describing inequality (or concentration) as is occurring in virtually every aspect of life. The emphasis here is on computer science, linguistics, and information science. We underline the importance of unequal situations (as opposed to evenness studies as, for example, in biology) in these domains (e.g., in applications such as compression of databases and texts).

The Lorenz curve gives a visual method of studying concentration. The relation with the so-called 80/20 rule is given. We also give basic principles ("axioms") that good concentration measures should satisfy, among which is the appealing transfer principle. The article then continues by giving examples of good concentration measures such as V (the coefficient of variation), Pratt's measure C, and the Gini index G and their generalizations, Theil's measures Th and L, and, finally, the Atkinson indices $A(e)$ ($0 < e < 1$). In this connection, the entropy formula from information theory is described and applied to aspects of compression (cf. the Huffman compression of codes). Also, the concentration aspects of the laws of Zipf and Mandelbrot are discussed. Some remarks are made about the N dependence of these theories (i.e., the dependence on the number of sources).

The rest of the article dealt with the sensitivity of concentration measures w.r.t. transfers. New transfer principles, stronger than the classical one, are introduced and we indicate which concentration measures satisfy which generalized transfer principles. A nice class of transfer principles can be defined as follows. Let f be a concentration measure and denote by $f'(X; Y)$ the directional derivative in X (in the direction Y). Let

$$Y = \left(1, -\frac{1}{N-1}, \ldots, -\frac{1}{N-1} \right) \in \mathbb{R}^N.$$

Then x_1 greater than a certain average of X should lead to $f'(X; Y) > 0$. This is the case for V with the arithmetic average, for Th with the geometric average, for L with the harmonic average, and for G and C for the median of X. The values of $f'(X; Y)$ can be used as a measure of sensitivity of the measure f w.r.t. transfers.

The merit of this sensitivity theory for concentration measures is that it presents a clear and exact definition of what sensitivity means, yet it allows for differences in nature of the diverse concentration measures (as revealed by the use of four different averages of X).

ACKNOWLEDGMENT

The author is indebted to Prof. Dr. R. Rousseau for valuable comments on both the content as well as the style of this article.

REFERENCES

1. L. Egghe and R. Rousseau, *Introduction to Informetrics. Quantitative Methods in Library, Documentation and Information Science*, Elsevier, Amsterdam, 1990.
2. L. Egghe and R. Rousseau, *Math. Comput. Model.*, *23*, 93–104 (1996).
3. A. W. Marshall and I. Olkin, *Inequalities: Theory of Majorization and its Applications*, Academic Press, New York, 1979.
4. L. Pigou, *Wealth and Welfare*, Macmillan, New York, 1912.
5. H. Dalton, *Econom. J.*, *30*, 348–361 (1920).
6. M. O. Lorenz, *J. Am. Statist. Assoc.*, *9*, 209–219 (1905).
7. G. H. Hardy, J. E. Littlewood, and G. Polya, *Inequalities*, 1st ed., Cambridge University Press, Cambridge, 1934; 2nd ed., 1952.
8. R. F. Muirhead, *Proc. Edinburgh Math. Soc.*, *21*, 144–157 (1903).
9. L. Egghe and R. Rousseau, *J. Am. Soc. Inform. Sci.*, *42*, 479–489 (1991).
10. C. Gini, *Giornale Econom.*, *11*, 37 (1909).
11. A. D. Pratt, *J. Am. Soc. Inform. Sci.*, *28*, 285–292 (1977).
12. M. P. Carpenter, *J. Am. Soc. Inform. Sci.*, *30*, 108–110 (1979).
13. P. D. Allison, *Am. Sociol. Rev.*, *43*, 865–880 (1978).
14. L. Egghe and R. Rousseau, "Elements of Concentration Theory," in *Informetrics 89/90*, edited by L. Egghe and R. Rousseau, Elsevier, Amsterdam, 1990, pp. 97–137.
15. H. Theil, *Economics and Information Theory*, North Holland, Amsterdam, 1967.
16. A. B. Atkinson, *J. Econ. Theory*, *30*, 244–263 (1970).
17. R. Rousseau, *Belgian J. Oper. Res., Statist. Computer Sci.*, *32*, 99–126 (1992).
18. D. A. Huffman, *Proc. IRE*, *40*, 1098–1101 (1952).
19. J. A. Storer, *Data Compression. Methods and Theory*, Computer Science Press, Rockville, MD, 1988.
20. L. Egghe and N. Veraverbeke, *Int. J. Scientometr. Informetr.*, *1*, 183–193 (1995).

21. G. K. Zipf, *Selected Studies of the Principle of Relative Frequency in Language*, Harvard University Press, Cambridge, MA, 1932.
22. G. K. Zipf, *The Psycho-Biology of Language: An Introduction to Dynamic Philology*, Houghton Mifflin, New York, 1935; reprinted by MIT Press, Cambridge, MA, 1965.
23. L. Egghe, *J. Am. Soc. Inform. Sci.*, *38*, 288–297 (1987).
24. B. Mandelbrot, *Word*, *10*, 1–27 (1954).
25. B. Mandelbrot, *The Fractal Geometry of Nature*, Freeman, New York, 1977.
26. L. Egghe, *Scientometrics*, *25*, 167–191 (1992).
27. P. D. Allison, *Soc. Stud. Sci.*, *10*, 163–179 (1980).
28. L. Egghe and R. Rousseau, *Inform. Proc. Manag.*, *31*, 511–523, 1995.

BIBLIOGRAPHY

Allison, P. D., "Measures of Inequality," *Am. Sociol. Rev.*, *43*, 865–880 (1978).
Arnold, B. C., *Majorization and the Lorenz Order: A Brief Introduction*, Springer-Verlag, Berlin, 1987.
Egghe, L., and R. Rousseau, *Introduction to Informetrics. Quantitative Methods in Library, Documentation and Information Science*, Elsevier, Amsterdam, 1990.
Gini, C., *Memorie di Metodologia Statistica, Vol. 1: Variabilità e Concentrazione*, Libreria Eredi Virgilio Veschi, Rome, 1955.
Hardy, G. H., J. E. Littlewood, and G. Polya, *Inequalities*, 1st ed., Cambridge University Press, Cambridge, 1934; 2nd ed., 1952.
Lambert, P. J., *The Distribution and Redistribution of Income: A Mathematical Analysis*, 2nd ed., Manchester University Press, Manchester, UK, 1993.
Magurran, A., *Ecological Diversity and its Measurement*, Chapman & Hall, London, 1991.
Marshall, A. W., and I. Olkin, *Inequalities: Theory of Majorization and its Applications*, Academic Press, New York, 1979.
Sen, A. K., *On Economic Inequality*, Clarendon Press, Oxford, 1973.
Storer, J. A., *Data Compression. Methods and Theory*, Computer Science Press, Rockville, MD, 1988.
Theil, H., *Economics and Information Theory*, North-Holland, Amsterdam, 1967.
Zipf, G. K., *Human Behavior and the Principle of Least Effort*, Addison-Wesley, Cambridge, MA, 1949; reprinted by Hafner, New York, 1965.

LEO EGGHE

SYMBOLIC–NUMERIC ALGEBRA FOR POLYNOMIALS

INTRODUCTION

Polynomials arise in a variety of scientific and engineering applications and can be manipulated either algebraically or numerically. Symbolic and exact methods, despite their power, often lack the speed required by real-time industrial applications. On the other hand, numeric and approximation techniques often fail to guarantee the accuracy or the completeness of their output. This survey aspires to overview a relatively new area of research that lies at the intersection of the two traditional approaches to polynomial computation. Symbolic–numeric methods combine the mathematical veracity of algebraic reasoning with the efficiency of numeric computation in order to devise more powerful algorithms. A practical motivation is to treat polynomials with inexactly known coefficients, typically encountered when we rely on physical measurements or calculations of limited accuracy.

The prime feature of symbolic computation is *exactness*: in the produced output, the given input, as well as the arithmetic used. This is also known as exact algebraic computation. On the other hand, numeric computation can handle *approximate* inputs, uses floating-point arithmetic of fixed precision, and produces approximate output. Different problems call for different types of computation, but this survey shall concentrate on examples that require both symbolic and numeric computation. For instance, in solving polynomial systems by resultant matrices, the matrix construction must be exact and involves the manipulation of symbolic quantities. In operating on this matrix, we are mostly interested in speed; hence, numeric computation is preferred.

The connection between fixed precision and approximate computation is explained by a discussion on precision and accuracy. *Precision* denotes the number of digits used to represent a value. So, we speak of fixed precision in computer operations that use operands of size independent of the values they represent, and of arbitrary precision when the length of the operands changes in order to express exactly the values. Using more digits obviously yields better approximations or, even, the exact result in the case of arbitrary precision. This is the case with symbolic algorithms, albeit at the expense of higher computational cost. Exact arithmetic is mainly implemented by integers of arbitrary length, modular or p-adic methods. *Accuracy* measures the error in the computed value with respect to the exact value that would have been computed under arbitrary precision. Numeric algorithms are compared on the accuracy of their result, given a certain precision.

Approximate computation does not imply lack of rigor when an appropriate analysis of the problem's conditioning and the algorithm's stability is undertaken. *Conditioning* examines whether the given instance is far from being singular, in a sense that depends on the particular context; for a square matrix, singularity means a zero determinant. *Stability* captures the sensitivity of the algorithm to round-off error. A numerically stable algorithm applied to a well-conditioned problem delivers an output with small and bounded error. Numeric algorithms, especially the nonstable ones, are not suitable for ill-conditioned instances—for example, in inverting an almost singular matrix. In symbolic algebra, the respective issues concern the bit size of the output and the precision required in intermediate computations. These shall assess the amount of computational resources required, namely the time and space *complexity* in terms of *bit* (or Boolean) *operations*. Time complexity bounds are simpler for numeric algorithms over fixed precision, because they are given by the number of arithmetic operations.

Numeric computation has been studied for a long time, because it was historically the first motivation for building computing machines. A large body of literature and software exists, mainly for univariate or linear algebra problems. Independent packages for symbolic manipulation have been proposed since the 1950s. Nonetheless, *symbolic–numeric* computation has been present, in some form, in computer science and its applications since the dawn of computers. This interaction is most exciting when it calls for the design of new algorithms. It becomes manifest in two basic ways:

- Symbolic preprocessing is used to improve on the conditioning of inputs, or to handle ill-conditioned subproblems. Then a numeric algorithm can complete the overall task. An example is the construction of resultant matrices that reduce nonlinear system solving to a problem in numeric linear algebra; see the subsection System Solving by Resultant Matrices. Another example is the symbolic treatment of singularities during numeric curve tracing in modeling and graphics; see the subsection Modeling and Graphics.
- Numeric tools are used in accelerating certain parts of an otherwise symbolic algorithm, or in computing approximate answers from which the exact results can be recovered. For instance, once we have achieved a sufficiently large separation between the roots of a polynomial, a numeric approximation may be applied; see the algorithm of the subsection The Weyl–Pan Exclusion Algorithm. In computing approximate greatest common divisors, there exist gap theorems in terms of the polynomial coefficients that guarantee the divisor degree. Then, a numeric procedure can be applied for computing the divisor itself, as explained in subsection Approximate Greatest Common Divisor.

The most basic computations are arithmetic operations over the integers, the floating-point numbers, and the polynomials, in addition to polynomial evaluation and interpolation. Knuth (1), in his seminal work *The Art of Computer Programming*, introduces the volume covering these operations as follows: "The algorithms discussed in this book deal directly with *numbers*; yet I believe they are properly called *seminumeric*, because they lie on the borderline between numeric and symbolic calculation."

A choice of certain aspects of symbolic–numeric polynomial algebra was imposed by the richness of the field. For coherence, we have concentrated on methods for solving polynomials and have tried to focus on approaches that show currently vivid activity. Some elementary knowledge of arithmetic and polynomial operations is assumed. The most advanced material of the survey also requires certain concepts from linear algebra. For background information on these two areas, refer to Refs. 1–5. However, each section progresses gradually from basic to deeper notions and includes defintions of key ideas and tools that should give a feeling of the area even to the uninitiated reader. By following the references given for each topic, one may acquire a better background and explore further the subtleties of the field.

Besides fundamental polynomial arithmetic, the next most straightforward problem concerns the computation of all roots of a univariate polynomial. The next section examines the approximation with sufficient accuracy of all complex solutions. The subsection Overview of Polynomial Solving Methods overviews different approaches and the subsection The Weyl–Pan Exclusion Algorithm presents a classic approach that has rekindled recent interest. This problem naturally leads to the question of computing the greatest divisor of two or more polynomials. When the input is given with limited accuracy, the output is necessarily an approximation: this is the problem explored in the subsection Approximate Greatest Common Divisor.

The third section extends the discussion to systems of polynomials in several variables. The subsection Overview of System Solving Methods overviews two traditional approaches, one symbolic, namely Gröbner bases, and one numeric, namely homotopy continuation. Resultant-based methods are exposed in more detail in order to show the interplay of their symbolic and numeric subtasks in the subsection System Solving by Resultant Matrices.

The fourth section discusses applications of theoretical as well as practical nature. In particular, we discuss briefly certain aspects of polynomial computation that are not developed in this survey, and we mention several areas enhanced by the links of symbolic and numeric algebra. More emphasis, in purpose of illustration, is put on modeling and graphics applications in the subsection Modeling and Graphics.

Open problems are presented in each corresponding section. The fifth section presents a list of major references for further study and adds relevant references that were not cited elsewhere. An extensive bibliography follows.

UNIVARIATE POLYNOMIALS

Polynomials in a single variable are the most basic objects in our study. Consider such a polynomial.

$$f(x) = a_d x^d + a_{d-1} x^{d-1} + \cdots + a_1 x + a_0,$$

where x is the unknown variable, or indeterminate, and $d = \deg f(x)$ is the polynomial degree in this variable. The coefficients $a_d, \ldots, a_0$ are assigned specific values from a field. In this article, the coefficients are most often rational but could also be complex. The fundamental computational problem of algebra is to compute all values of x for which the polynomial evaluates to zero. These values are called *zeros*, *roots*, or *solutions* of the polynomial. Their study has motivated several scientific breakthroughs in mathematics through the centuries and has led to important new algorithms in computer science. We next present a brief overview of the extensive literature on root-finding and discuss in some detail one particular method, originally due to Weyl, in subsection The Weyl–Pan Exclusion Algorithm. When there are two or more polynomials, we are interested in their common roots. These are the values of x that make all polynomials evaluate to zero. The common roots are the roots of the greatest common divisor (GCD), and the subsection Approximate Greatest Common Divisor considers the problem of computing the GCD numerically.

Overview of Polynomial Solving Methods

By the fundamental theorem of algebra, the solutions of a polynomial with real coefficients are, in general, complex. Computing only the real roots is a separate problem, briefly examined in the fourth section. The general question has motivated much of the work by the brilliant mathematician E. Galois. His most well-known result states that, for arbitrary degree, there is no closed-form formula using radicals which may express the solution. Therefore, our efforts must be directed toward numeric algorithms that yield an approximation of each root. Yet, most modern-day methods employ some kind of exact computation.

There exists a wide variety of different techniques that solve this problem successfully for most small- and medium-degree polynomials, say of degree up to 20. However, fast and numerically stable implementations, needed to cope with large-degree polynomials such as those encountered in system solving, constitute an area of active research. For an extensive bibliography, see Ref. 6, and for an historical and comparative presentation, see Ref. 7. More detailed accounts are given in two of the milestones in the field (8,9).

Analytic Methods

Maybe the oldest general approach still in use today is Newton's method; see, for instance, its implementation in Ref. 10. Newton's method offers a general tool for improving an existing approximation and exhibits very fast convergence, provided it is given a good initial approximation. It is an *iterative* analytic approach; that is, it computes successively closer approximations to a target root. It terminates when the distance between the computed approximation and the exact root is sufficiently small. A limitation of the original method concerns roots of high multiplicity—in other words, repeated roots. A multiple root requires special attention because rounding off makes it appear as a *cluster* of roots, and clusters are hard to deal with by approximation methods. Standard techniques in Refs. 11 and 12 suffer from similar shortcomings. Nonetheless, the implementations based on the latter three approaches have proved very valuable in solving most polynomials encountered in practice, with degree up to 20.

Other Newton-based methods use a *homotopy*, or path-lifting technique (13) and can generalize to systems of polynomial equations (14). Root refinement methods that integrate symbolic and numeric computing include Ref. 15. Simultaneous approximation methods (16,17) are also analytic methods, but recent work (18) combines them with symbolic subroutines in order to achieve adaptive precision. *Adaptive precision* decreases computational cost because it identifies the areas where we can compute with fewer digits and still have a satisfactory result. This is usually due to the well-conditioning of some particular computation. The opposite would be *blind precision*, which is the naive approach and uses the same number of digits for all operations without discrimination.

Geometric Methods

More significant interaction of symbolic and numeric approaches is seen in recursive splitting, or divide-and-conquer, methods. In general, *divide-and-conquer* is useful when the original problem has higher complexity than the aggregate cost of the two subproblems and of the partitioning. The partitioning here consists in defining a circle in the complex space that splits the set of roots in two subsets. Geometric techniques regard complex space as a two-dimensional real plane. Several variants of this approach have been proposed and some have been implemented (19–23). We should underline here the heavy use of structured matrices (e.g., in Ref. 21), as well as algebraic factorization and cluster-based reasoning, both stressed in Ref. 22. The algorithms of Refs. 20 and 23 have led to the current record asymptotic upper bound on time complexity for the problem. Their principal breakthrough has been the design of a method for solving the geometric subproblem of identifying a splitting circle, so that the two subsets of roots are always well balanced. This method uses symbolic algrebra such as polynomial remainder and Sturm sequences. The asymptotic complexity is satisfactory, but the hidden overhead is so high that it excludes its application to polynomials of small degree.

Exclusion algorithms use geometric reasoning as well. The first algorithm of the kind was proposed by Weyl (24) and later impoved in Refs. 25 and 26. It is studied in detail below. Another representative algorithm is in Ref. 27.

The Weyl–Pan Exclusion Algorithm

This section examines in some detail the geometric exclusion algorithm proposed by Weyl (24), under the improvements suggested in Refs. 25 and 26; see also Ref. 7 for an overview. The main construction behind Weyl's algorithm is a quadtree partition of the complex plane, represented by a tree with four children per node. Purely numeric sub-tasks are defined in this process for reducing the overall complexity.

Basic Strategy

To search a certain region of the complex plane, we partition it into four squares and exclude those that are guaranteed not to contain any roots, as in Figure 1. This is a two-dimensional analog of a binary search on a line interval. The *quadtree* paradigm has been also successfully applied to other areas of computer science like image processing and *n*-body particle simulation. The algorithm starts with an initial suspect square that contains all the roots of the given polynomial. Finding this square is straightforward by application of known bounds on the size of roots (1,3,4,28). Alternatively, we may be interested only in solutions lying in a given region of the complex plane. The algorithm is especially suitable for this situation. The initial square is partitioned into four disjoint subsquares whose union is the original square. For each one, we check whether it contains any roots or not. This is carried out by a *proximity test* that estimates the distance to the closest root of the polynomial. If the test guarantees that no root lies in it, the

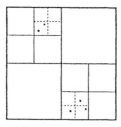

FIGURE 1   Quadtree partition of the complex plane. Black dots represent the roots of the poly-nomial and the thickness of the lines shows the order in which squares were defined, starting with the thickest and ending with the dashed edges.

square is discarded. The remaining squares are called suspect and each one undergoes the same process of partition. The recursion stops when, for every root, we have found a unique square that contains it.

The proximity test is based on Turan's technique (29). The details of this test are technical, but we should note the use of the so-called *Graeffe's iteration* to improve accuracy. This iteration has been independently discovered by Dandelin, Lobachevsky, and Graeffe, but it is customarily named after the latter (8). Interestingly, it was the most prestigious algorithm for root calculation in the 19th century, used by people paid specifically to perform such calculations. These people were known as "computers" (30). The merit of Weyl's technique is robustness, and this depends on the accuracy of the proximity test. For this, it is advisable to apply Turan's test to the kth Graeffe iterate, because then the error factors are powers of $1/k$. To define the iteration, suppose $f_0(x)$ is a polynomial of degree d, where the most significant coefficient $a_d = 1$. Then, its kth iterate is

$$f_k(x) = (-1)^d f_{k-1}(\sqrt{x}) f_{k-1}(-\sqrt{x}), \quad k \geq 1.$$

The zeros of $f_k(x)$ are the squares of the zeros of $f_{k-1}(x)$. Hence, they are better separated assuming that there is enough precision to express the new coefficients and that the roots of $f_{k-1}(x)$ lie outside the unit disk. The multiplication is performed by means of the fast Fourier transform, Karatsuba's algorithm, or a combination of both (1,4,28,31,110). The two methods represent a trade-off among asymptotic time complexity, numeric stability, and memory storage requirements.

Improvements

Pan's main contribution is the acceleration of Weyl's algorithm by means of an iterative process to refine the root approximations, once a sufficiently good isolation has been obtained. This relies on the observation that after some recursive steps, all roots are included into a few strongly isolated squares. It is possible to distinguish the squares containing isolated roots from those containing part of a cluster. The latter kind of squares are combined into a larger one in order to encompass an entire cluster. The iterative process applied to the larger square will shrink it until the side length becomes comparable to the cluster diameter. For individual roots, the iterative process will stop when it approximates them closely enough. Weyl's exclusion procedure restarts on the squares corresponding to clusters, until some separation is achieved that makes it possible to apply the iterative refinement again.

In summary, we are able to approximate all d zeros in an initial square of diameter D after h partitioning steps with accuracy $D/2^{h+1}$, by using order of $n^2 \log n \log(h \log n)$ arithmetic operations. In the worst case, the operations involve operands of bit size hn. It is easy to see that this is the necessary precision if we consider the following classic polynomial:

$$f(x) = x^d - 2^{bd}, \quad \text{has roots } 2^b e^{2k\pi i/d}, \quad \text{for } k = 0, \ldots, d-1.$$

Here, $e \simeq 2.71828$, $\pi \simeq 3.14158$, and $i = \sqrt{-1}$. Perturbing the constant coefficient by one bit at position bd produces polynomial x^d, with all roots equal to zero. This means that a much more significant bit changes in the roots, namely the bth bit. This shows that, in a sense, root-finding is ill-conditioned and that the above precision is needed in the worst case. Current work focuses on redesigning some parts of the algorithm in order to use adaptive precision. There is an extension of the algorithm to computing only the real roots of the given polynomial (32).

Approximate Greatest Common Divisor

We study the approximate greatest common divisor (GCD) of two univariate polynomials given with limited accuracy. This is a polynomial whose roots are the common roots of the two given polynomials. Equivalently, an approximate GCD is the exact GCD of the perturbations of the input polynomials, within some prescribed tolerance. The question becomes relevant whenever laboratory measurements are involved, as in graphics, modeling, robotics, and control theory, where noise corrupts the input (33–37). It can also be seen as a stepping stone toward problems on polynomial systems, where the given data is characterized by limited accuracy.

Consider the following pair of polynomials from Ref. 37. Their exact GCD is 1 but, under some tolerance $\varepsilon > 0$, there is a quadratic ε-GCD:

$$f_1(x) = x^5 + 5.503x^4 + 9.765x^3 + 7.647x^2 + 2.762x + 0.37725,$$
$$f_2(x) = x^4 - 2.993x^3 - 0.7745x^2 + 2.007x + 0.7605,$$
$$\varepsilon\text{-gcd}(f_1, f_2)(x) = x^2 + 1.007x + 0.2534, \qquad \varepsilon = 1.6 \ 10^{-4}.$$

Here, we have fixed a measure of distance between polynomials. The polynomial ε-gcd$(f_1, f_2)(x)$ is the exact GCD of a pair of polynomials whose distances from $f_1(x)$ and $f_2(x)$ are both bounded by ε. By definition, the ε-GCD is the polynomial that satisfies these conditions and has a maximum possible degree. This illustrates a typical situation in numeric computation, where the approximate solution of the input problem is obtained as the exact solution of a perturbed instance. The intuition behind this principle is a continuity property that ensures that a small change in the polynomial coefficients causes a small change of the root values. For a formal treatment of this concept see, for example, Ref. 38. Maximizing the degree in the presence of noise is a natural approach, corresponding to perturbing the polynomials in order to achieve the maximum number of common roots. The dual problem of minimizing the perturbation for a fixed degree has also been examined (39).

The univariate GCD identifies the common roots of the given polynomials. The inverse viewpoint reduces approximate GCD to univariate polynomial solving and combinatorial matching of the roots (40). A widely used approach is based on variants of the Euclidean algorithm for the exact GCD (22,41). This algorithm, described in the *Elements* of Euclid about 2300 years ago, is the oldest algorithm in the history of mankind still in use. In the approximate context, however, the extensions of Euclid's algorithm cannot maximize the degree and yield only a lower bound on it. A different approach consists in regarding the problem as an optimization question (39). An approximate GCD under a different computational model is studied in Ref. 42.

Using the Singular Values

In the rest of this section, we concentrate on methods that use matrices defined by the polynomial coefficients and the numeric rank of each matrix. Algebraically, these matrices give precise information on the degree of the GCD and allow its computation. The first of these matrices, denoted $S(f_1, f_2)$, has the following property, assuming that the polynomial degrees are deg $f_1(x) = d_1$ and deg $f_2(x) = d_2$.

$S(f_1, f_2)$ is of rank $d_1 + d_2 - r \Leftrightarrow \deg(\gcd(f_1, f_2)) = r$.

The matrix $S(f_1, f_2)$ is Sylvester's resultant matrix; the subsection Systems Solved by Resultant Matrices expands on this matrix. The matrices of the sequence are called subresultant matrices and provide analogous and more accurate information on the GCD degree (3,28,43). Numerically, the Singular Value Decomposition (SVD) is a stable procedure for computing the rank and the singular values of a rectangular matrix (2,5).

The Sylvester matrix was used in Ref. 37 to compute an approximate GCD, but there was no guarantee that the ε-GCD degree was maximized. This motivates the use of all matrices in the subresultant sequence (44,45). This approach yields a gap theorem on the singular values of two successive subresultant matrices which certifies the degree of the ε-GCD. The proof is constructive and leads to a numeric algorithm:

- Compute the necessary singular values of all subresultant matrices starting with Sylvester's matrix and until the hypotheses of the gap theorem are satisfied. If this does not happen for any pair of subresultants, then the algorithm fails.
- Use SVD on the last subresultant matrix to define an *approximate syzygy*, or Bézout's relationship. This amounts to specifying polynomials $g_1(x)$ and $g_2(x)$ which are relatively prime within ε, such that $g_1(x)f_1(x) - g_2(x)f_2(x)$ is almost zero.
- It remains to compute the perturbed polynomials within ε such that they possess an exact GCD of the calculated degree. This reduces to polynomial division and the solution of a linear system defined by a Sylvester matrix.

Extensions

The Bézout matrix can be used instead of Sylvester's matrix in the above algorithm. Its numerical stability may be better, due to its smaller size, albeit with a higher complexity for its construction. The comparative merits of each matrix constitute an active area of research; see the subsection Systems Solved by Resultant Matrices for more information. An algorithm similar to the one above has recently been proposed in connection to an asymptotically optimal gap theorem (46).

The latter method has been extended to the case of an arbitrary number n of univariate polynomials $f_1(x), \ldots, f_n(x)$. The main step is a generalization of the subresultant matrices (46). In particular, the Sylvester matrix is generalized to

$$
S(f_1, \ldots, f_n) =
\begin{bmatrix}
-f_2 & f_1 & 0 & \cdots & 0 \\
-f_3 & 0 & f_1 & \cdots & 0 \\
\vdots & \vdots & & \ddots & \vdots \\
-f_n & 0 & \cdots & 0 & f_1
\end{bmatrix},
$$

where each f_i represents a submatrix containing the coefficients of polynomial $f_i(x)$, in the same fashion as in the Sylvester matrix. The resulting algorithm is significantly more efficient and numerically stable than if one applied the algorithm designed for two polynomials $n - 1$ times.

Open questions naturally include the extension to higher dimensions. Further work on matrix methods is highly probable to converge with ongoing research in multivariate polynomial systems based on resultant theory. An example is presented in Refs. 37 and

47. The main premise of this prospect is that multivariate resultant matrices are generalizations of the Sylvester matrix studied above or of the Bézout matrix.

MULTIVARIATE POLYNOMIALS

In this section, we focus on the solution of systems of polynomials in several variables. After a sample of symbolic–numeric approaches in the next section, we discuss matrix-based methods in the subsection System Solving by Resultant Matrices. They use purely symbolic computation for the matrix construction, which essentially reduces the nonlinear problem to a problem in linear algebra. Then, they rely on numeric techniques for approximating all common roots.

We are concerned with polynomials with rational coefficients. As in the univariate case, their solutions do not necessarily lie in real space, so we consider the problem of computing their complex roots. Approaches exist to compute directly the real roots, surveyed in the fourth section.

Overview of System Solving Methods

Gröbner bases offer a powrful algebraic tool for analyzing polynomial systems (3,43,48). So far, the inputs, all intermediate computation, and the outputs have all been considered to be exact. Recently, numeric computation on inexact data is being examined. This yields efficient solutions of practical problems (49) and leads to a notion of approximate basis (50). Gröbner bases can be used to reduce the nonlinear problem to a problem in linear algebra by constructing matrices with analogous properties like the resultant matrices. Then, numeric linear algebra is heavily used, such as Jordan decomposition for dealing with multiple roots (51).

Another approach that combines purely combinatorial constructions with numeric computation is sparse, or polyhedral, *homotopy continuation*. Traditional continuation (14,52) has put the emphasis on numeric methods for path following and avoiding degenerate situations. Exploiting algebraic properties has led to significant improvements (53, 54). More general and stronger structure properties are being investigated in light of the advances in sparse elimination theory. This theory, presented in the next section, has introduced sparse homotopies. The goal of sparse homotopies is to exploit the monomial structure of a given polynomial system in order to follow a smaller number of paths than those in classical continuation (55–58). The symbolic part consists in computing a polyhedral subdivision, which yields a rather tight bound on the number of paths and defines a starting system for the homotopy. In the numeric part, all paths are followed until they arrive at approximations of the root values. The polyhedral subdivision can be modified in order to define paths that are relatively smooth near their beginning, thus addressing a major issue in numeric tracing.

Further efficient approaches exist for system solving, covering the entire range from purely symbolic to purely numeric ones; see for example, Refs. 9, 28, 43, 59, and 60.

System Solving by Resultant Matrices

Strong interest in *multivariate resultants* has been recently revived since resultant-based methods have been found to be very efficient for solving certain classes of small and medium-size problems, say of dimension up to 10. Moreover, they can strongly exploit the structure of the input system and yield structured matrices. The various matrix formulations of the resultant reduce the computation of the common roots of a nonlinear system to an eigenproblem, which is a well-studied problem in linear algebra.

Classical elimination theory and the classical multivariate resultant have a long and rich history that includes such luminaries as Euler, Bézout, Cayley and Macaulay; see Refs. 61 and 62. Having been at the crossroads between pure and computational mathematics, it became the victim, in the second quarter of this century, of the polemic led by the promoters of abstract approaches. Characteristically, the third edition of van der Waerden's *Modern Algebra* has a chapter on elimination theory and resultants that has disappeared from later editions. Moreover, when the number of variables exceeds three or four, elimination methods lead to matrices which are too large for hand calculations. However, the advent of modern computers has revived this area. The last decade has seen efficient resultant-based solutions of certain algorithmic as well as applied problems. Some of these problems were impossible to tackle with other methods in real time. These areas include robotics (63,64), the theory of the reals (65), and modeling (66).

The *resultant* is typically defined when all polynomial coefficients are symbolic. For a system of $n + 1$ arbitrary polynomial equations in n variables, it is a polynomial in the coefficients; hence, it eliminates n variables. The easiest example is the Sylvester resultant, when $n = 1$. Then, the resultant equals the determinant of Sylvester's matrix. For generic polynomials $f_1(x)$ and $f_2(x)$ of degrees 1 and 2, respectively, Sylvester's matrix S is as follows:

$$\begin{cases} f_1(x) & = a_1 x + a_0 \\ f_2(x) & = b_2 x^2 + b_1 x + b_0 \end{cases} \quad \text{and} \quad S = \begin{bmatrix} a_1 & a_0 & 0 \\ 0 & a_1 & a_0 \\ b_2 & b_1 & b_0 \end{bmatrix}. \tag{1}$$

The resultant is det $S = a_1^2 b_0 + a_0^2 b_2 - a_0 a_1 b_1$. Another example is the determinant of the coefficient matrix of $n + 1$ linear polynomials. Under certain technical conditions, the resultant vanishes for a particular specialization of all polynomial coefficients if and only if the given polynomial system has a nontrivial solution.

Resultant Matrices

A variety of methods exist for constructing *resultant matrices*; that is, matrices whose determinant is ideally the resultant or, otherwise, a nontrivial multiple of it. All methods are symbolic. They can be classified in two categories, following the two original formulations, named after Sylvester and Bézout. The former has been illustrated above, and the entries are constrained to be either zero or some polynomial coefficient. For more than two polynomials, a generalization of the method has been obtained by Macaulay (61,62,67).

Resultants in classical elimination theory, as well as Macaulay matrices, are completely defined by the total degrees of the input polynomials. More recently, *sparse elimination* theory has modeled polynomials by their nonzero monomials, or supports, in order to obtain tighter bounds and exploit sparseness. This theory has close links with combinatorial geometry. Polynomials are specified by their support and its convex hull. Sparse elimination defines the sparse resultant, whose degree depends on these convex polytopes instead of the total degrees (67–70). Constructing matrices whose determinant is a nontrivial multiple of the sparse resultant involves algebraic and geometric computation and yields matrices that generalize those of Sylvester and Macaulay (67,69–72).

The second branch of resultant matrix constructions stems from Bézout's method for the resultant of two univariate polynomials. For the example system in the matrices (1), the resultant matrix is

$$\begin{bmatrix} a_0b_1 - a_1b_0 & a_0b_2 \\ a_0 & a_1 \end{bmatrix}.$$

[2]

Notice that both matrices (1) and (2) have the same determinant which is equal to the resultant within a sign. Bézout's matrix has been generalized to arbitrary systems. It is sometimes named after Dixon, who introduced the first generalizations. In general, the Bézout/Dixon matrix has a smaller size than Sylvester's, Macaulay's, and the sparse resultant matrix, respectively. On the other hand, its entries are polynomials in the input coefficients. Another difference is that the matrices of Sylvester type are constructed combinatorially, whereas the Bézout/Dixon matrix construction is based on discrete differentials and requires some polynomial computation. This is costly but may be performed numerically. There is a rich algebraic theory behind Bézout/Dixon's matrix and a number of applications that exploit its compact size (4,28,62,73,74). An open problem is to classify the problems for which each resultant formulation is preferable by taking into account the complexity of matrix construction and the numerical stability of matrix-based system solving.

All resultant matrices are characterized by strong *structure* properties. More formally, they can be partitioned in blocks, each of which has a structure that generalizes the Toeplitz or Hankel structure. Generally, structured matrices allow us to store and compute with matrices in complexities that are typically an order of magnitude smaller than for dense unstructured matrices (4). The reason is that structured matrices can be defined by a significantly smaller number of elements than the full number of matrix entries. This is also the case here. For instance, the Sylvester matrix (1) can be vertically partitioned into two blocks with two and one rows, respectively. Each block has Toeplitz structure —in other words, constant diagonals. An essential aspect of the quasi-Toeplitz or quasi-Hankel structure of resultant matrices is that their multiplication with a vector can be performed in almost linear time rather than quadratic time. Hence, we can take advantage of Lanczos' numeric algorithm to decrease complexity by nearly one order of magnitude in constructing the matrix, computing the resultant polynomial, and solving certain polynomial systems (75–77). What is under investigation is how to exploit structure in the matrix manipulations described below for system solving.

System Solving

The principal merit of resultant matrices is that they reduce the solution of a nonlinear system to a matrix problem, where we can use an arsenal of numeric linear algebra techniques and software. In what follows, we concentrate on systems whose solution set contains a finite number of points. Several extensions have been explored (78) or are currently under investigation. By construction, the existence of common solutions implies a decrease of matrix rank. In most applications, we deal with systems of $n + 1$ polynomials in $n + 1$ unknowns. To obtain an overconstrained system, for which the resultant is defined, we should either add an extra polynomial or "hide" a variable in the coefficient field (61,65,67,70). We illustrate the latter method in the case of a system of two polynomials:

$$f_1(x, y) = 2x + y - 2, \qquad f_2(x, y) = 2x^2 + 4x - y + 2.$$

[3]

Hiding y yields a system of univariate polynomials as in matrix (1). The resultant is now a polynomial in y, namely $2(y - 2)(y - 8)$. Solving the resultant yields the values of y at the roots or, in general, the projections of the roots on the axis of the hidden variable.

However, evaluation of a matrix determinant is numerically unstable. Therefore, it is preferable to reduce the problem to computing the eigenvalues and eigenvectors of a square matrix (67,70,79,80). This is expressed by an equation of the form $(A - \lambda I)v = 0$, where A denotes a square matrix, I is the identity matrix of the same dimension, λ is an unknown value, and v an unknown vector. The premise of this transformation is that multiplication of the resultant matrix by an appropriate column vector yields multiples of the input polynomials. For the Sylvester matrix of system (3), this gives

$$\begin{bmatrix} 2 & y-2 & 0 \\ 0 & 2 & y-2 \\ 2 & 4 & -y+2 \end{bmatrix} \begin{bmatrix} x^2 \\ x \\ 1 \end{bmatrix} = \begin{bmatrix} xf_1(x, y) \\ f_1(x, y) \\ f_2(x, y) \end{bmatrix}.$$

If we specialize x and y at the roots, the product vector will be zero. Inversely, to solve the system, it suffices to find the values of y for which the matrix is singular and to compute the nonzero vectors in its kernel. Among these vectors, we restrict attention to those that correspond to a specialization of x. This is equivalent to solving the following problem:

$$\left(\begin{bmatrix} 2 & -2 & 0 \\ 0 & 2 & -2 \\ 2 & 4 & 2 \end{bmatrix} + y \begin{bmatrix} 0 & 1 & 0 \\ 0 & 0 & 1 \\ 0 & 0 & -1 \end{bmatrix} \right) v = 0.$$

This can be transformed to an eigenproblem by setting $y = -1/\lambda$ and by performing certain matrix operations. Depending on the condition number of the matrix, we may instead choose to solve a generalized eigenproblem (2,5). The *condition number* of a matrix expresses the distance of this matrix from the closest singular matrix, in some appropriate matrix space (2,5,81). Therefore, a well-conditioned matrix is one on which we may safely operate numerically. The above matrix operations generalize to the case when the degree of the hidden variable is higher than 1. This approach applies to Macaulay, sparse resultant and Bézout/Dixon matrices of arbitrary size. Powerful numeric methods exist for computing all eigenvalues λ and eigenvectors v (2,5), as well as public-domain implementations such as LAPACK (82). In addition, such software packages provide estimators of the matrix conditioning and a choice between fast but less stable routines against slower but more accurate ones.

Special attention is required when there are roots of high multiplicity which give rise to eigenspaces of high dimension. Current work is concentrating on numeric methods for transforming the matrix problem in a numerically stable way so that multiple roots are identified. Schur factorization has been proposed in this respect (47,66). Another problem arising in practice is when the matrix determinant vanishes for all values of the hidden variable and is, therefore, a trivial multiple of the resultant polynomial. This can be handled by a perturbation method (83,84). More practically, a numeric approach, reminiscent of deflation, yields a generically nonsingular submatrix which is singular at the system's roots (73,85,86). A more general question is how to change the symbolic construction of the resultant matrix in order to palliate such numeric issues.

A standard question in elimination theory is to what extent we should proceed with eliminating variables at the expense of increasing the degree. This trade-off is evident even in linear systems, where eliminating variables symbolically creates equations of higher degree. Algebraically, the problem does not change, but its numeric solution may become substantially more intricate. The two classes of resultant matrix formulations offer different approaches to this trade-off. The Sylvester-type matrices are larger but have linear entries in the input coefficients, whereas the Bézout/Dixon matrix is more compact with higher-degree entries.

APPLICATIONS

This section surveys diverse areas that benefit from interleaving symbolic and numeric polynomial algebra. Before we discuss modeling and graphics to some detail, we mention other relevant areas to show the diversity of the field.

Determining the sign of a rational expression can be performed fast and robustly by a combination of fixed-precision floating-point arithmetic and exact algebraic techniques such as *p*-adic lifting and modular arithmetic (59,87–90). Sign determination is a basic operation in computational geometry and solid modeling, where tests are typically formulated as determinant signs. More generally, it is a critical operation whenever one computes with real numbers, say by means of Sturm sequences. We omit a detailed presentation of real algebra and real quantifier elimination, because the methods involved are mostly symbolic (43,91,92).

Further examples of symbolic–numeric interaction can be found in rational and polynomial arithmetic—for instance binary segmentation methods, numeric algorithms achieving arbitrary precision, and structured matrix operations; see, for example, Ref. 4. Ideas from symbolic–numeric algebra have been exploited in integration and the solution of differential equations (3,93,94), optimization (65,95), as well as Riemannian geometry by means of discrete groups (96). Turning to more applied fields, computational economics and game theory (97,98), the forward and inverse kinematics of robots and mechanisms, as well as the computation of their motion plans (35,63,64,99), structure and motion in machine vision (100), the geometric structure of molecules (101,102), problems in physics (103), and signal processing (37,49), have all benefited from the use of symbolic–numeric algebra.

Modeling and Graphics

A major application area that thrives on the integration of numeric and symbolic techniques is the general domain of geometric and solid modeling, graphics, and computer-aided design. Surface intersection is discussed in some detail below, as a fundamental problem in these areas. In addition, the computation of offset curves and surfaces, of distances between points and surfaces, of birational maps, spline and finite-element approximations of real surfaces, mesh generation, constraint-based sketching, and data fitting have all benefited from this cross-fertilization (33,36,104–106). The monograph (34) provides a very appropriate introduction.

Representation

For different problems, different representations of curves and surfaces may be suitable. The need arises to be able to convert between rational parametric and implicit representations. The former gives every point coordinate as a rational expression in one or two parameters and is preferred for tracing, rendering, and fitting. Implicit, or algebraic, representations express a curve or a surface as the set of points which satisfy a single polynomial and are, thus, better suitable for testing membership. The following example is of a parabola parametrized by polynomials in a parameter t, then expressed implicitly by a single equation:

$$x = t + 1, \quad y = t^2 + 1 \Leftrightarrow x^2 - 2x - y + 2 = 0.$$

Computing surface intersections can be reduced to expressing the given surfaces in the two distinct representations. Symbolic–numeric techniques are used to convert from one representation to the other (33,34,36,48,66,107), where the main algebraic tools include Gröbner bases and resultant matrices. Observe that the implicit representation above is given precisely by the resultant of the parametric system if we consider it as a univariate system in t, with x and y belonging to the coefficient field. The resultant can be computed as the determinant of Sylvester's matrix (1) or Bézout's matrix (2), where we specialize $a_1 = 1$, $a_0 = 1 - x$ and $b_2 = 1$, $b_1 = 0$, $b_0 = 1 - y$.

Surface Intersection

The bulk of computation in modeling and graphics is typically performed over fixed-precision floating-point arithmetic for reasons of speed. The drawbacks of purely numeric computation concern accuracy and robustness. Today, it is becoming clear that robustness issues impose the use of some exact manipulation of geometric objects at degenerate configurations. For instance, the intersection of two surfaces is usually a one-dimensional curve, whereas three surfaces meet at a point. A modeler that has to deal with two tangent surfaces intersecting at a single point, or three surfaces whose intersection is a curve may be in trouble if it relies exclusively on numeric calculations. Even in the generic case of two surfaces intersecting at a curve, approximate results may not be sufficiently accurate when the curve contains singular points. The incorporation of symbolic methods to cope with singularities seems to offer the accuracy required to guarantee robustness, and the performance penalty remains reasonable. Of course, a judicious choice must be made in order to balance the use the symbolic and numeric computation, and this question is far from being considered as closed.

Suppose that two surfaces are given in some convenient representations. One approach is to map the space curve of their intersection into the plane, *trace* the plane curve, then map it back to the space curve. There are algebraic methods for performing these transformations. Tracing is done for the most part numerically, thus achieving good performance. It uses some linear local approximation to advance on the curve by moving along the tangent direction; then, it uses some correction mechanism to stay on the curve. The numeric approximation fails at singular points, though, because the behavior of the curve is highly nonlinear. Symbolic computation is used to transform the traced curve to an equivalent one that has no singularity at the corresponding point. Once we have safely passed the singularity, we have to go back to the original plane curve because completing the tracing on the new curve is not possible. This situation is depicted in Figure 2. A major issue is locating the singularity, and this can be done to any desired precision by Gröbner bases, multivariate resultants, and real root isolation. This and other methods to surface intersection are an active area of research. For further discussion, consult Refs. 34, 78, 107, and 108.

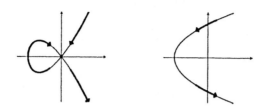

FIGURE 2   Tracing at a singularity. The thick arrows represent the actual tracing by the overall algorithm. The original curve, shown at left, has a singularity at the origin, whereas the new curve, shown at right, is regular at that point.

FURTHER INFORMATION

The following references contain general information on the topics discussed here, with emphasis on the following:

- Symbolic computation (3,28,43,48,67,94,109).
- Numeric computation (2,5,9,59,60,81,110). In particular, Ref. 5 contains an extensive bibliography on numeric linear algebra.
- References 1, 4, and 31 discuss the juxtaposition of numeric and symbolic computation. Some recent nonregular conferences and workshops have the same focus (111–113). The forthcoming Ref. 114 should cover further relevant topics on univariate polynomial solving.

The standard research journals in this area include *Journal of Applied Algebra to Engineering and Code-Correcting, Journal of Symbolic Computation, Linear Algebra and Its Applications, Mathematics of Computation, Numerische Mathematik, Numerical Algorithms*, and *SIAM Journal of Scientific Computing*. We should mention the special issue of *Journal of Symbolic Computation* devoted precisely on symbolic–numeric algebra for polynomials and expected to appear in 1998. New implementations are reported in the *ACM Transactions on Mathematical Software*.

There are well-known libraries and packages of subroutines for the most popular numeric linear algebra operations—in particular EISPACK (115), LAPACK (82), and LINPACK (116). Symbolic computation is implemented in modern computer algebra packages, such as *Axiom* (117), *Mathematica* (118), *Maple* (119), and *Reduce* (120), which have also several numeric routines. A stronger emphasis on numeric computation has been placed in *Matlab* (121). A current effort to implement a public-domain library for nonlinear algebra is undertaken by the European ESPIRIT project FRISCO (Framework for the Integration of Symbolic-Numeric Computing) (122).

ACKNOWLEDGMENTS

I wish to thank Dario Bini, Victor Pan, Frank Sottile, and Hans Stetter for their comments on an early draft, and Gabriel Dos Reis for his help with the figures.

REFERENCES

1. D. E. Knuth, *The Art of Computer Programming*: *Seminumerical Algorithms*, Addison-Wesley, Reading, MA, 1981, Vol. 2.
2. J. Wilkinson, *The Algebraic Eigenvalue Problem*, Oxford University Press, London, 1965.
3. B. Buchberger, G. E. Collins, R. Loos (eds.), *Computer Algebra: Symbolic and Algebraic Computation*, 2nd. ed., volume 4 of *Computing Supplementum*. Springer-Verlag, Wien, 1982.
4. D. Bini and V. Y. Pan, *Polynomial and Matrix Computations, volume 1: Fundamental Algorithms*, Birkhäuser, Boston, 1994.
5. G. H. Golub and C. F. Van Loan, *Matrix Computations*, 3rd. ed., The Johns Hopkins University Press, Baltimore, MD, 1996.
6. J. M. McNamee, "A Bibliography on Roots of Polynomials," *J. Comput. Appl. Math.*, *47*, 391–394 (1993).
7. V. Y. Pan, "Solving a Polynomial Equation: Some History and Recent Progress," *SIAM Rev.*, *39*(2), 187–220 (1997).
8. A. S. Householder, *The Numerical Treatment of a Single Nonlinear Equation*, McGraw-Hill, Boston, 1970.
9. P. Henrici, *Applied and Computational Complex Analysis, Volume 1*, John Wiley & Sons, New York, 1974.
10. K. Madsen and J. Reid, "Fortran Subroutines for Finding Polynomial Zeros," Technical Report HL75/1172 (C.13), Computer Science and Systems Division, Oxford University (1975).
11. E. Hansen, M. Patrick, and J. Rusnak, "Some Modifications of Laguerre's Method," *BIT*, *17*, 409–417 (1977).
12. M. A. Jenkins and J. F. Traub, "A Three Stage Variable Shift Iteration for Polynomial Zeros and Its Relation to Generalized Rayleigh Iteration," *Numer. Math.*, *14*, 252–263 (1970).
13. S. Smale, "The Fundamental Theorem of Algebra and Complexity Theory," *Bull. Am. Math. Soc.*, *4*(1), 1–36 (1981).
14. M. Shub and S. Smale, "On the Complexity of Bezout's Theorem V: Polynomial Time," *Theoret. Computer Sci.*, *133*(1), 141–164 (1994).
15. G. E. Collins and W. Krandick, "A Tangent-Secant Method for Polynomial Complex Root Calculation," in *Proc. ACM Int. Symp. on Symbolic and Algebraic Computation*, 1996, pp. 137–141.
16. E. Durand, *Solutions Numériques des Equations Algébriques. Equations du Type* $F(X) = 0$; *Racines d'un Polynôme, volume 1*, Masson, Paris, 1960.
17. O. Aberth, "Iteration Methods for Finding All Zeros of a Polynomial Simultaneously," *Math. Comput.*, *27*, (122), 339–344 (1973).
18. D. Bini, "Numerical Computation of Polynomial Zeros by Means of Aberth's Method," *Numer. Algorithms* (1997).
19. A. Schönhage, "The Fundamental Theorem of Algebra in Terms of Computational Complexity," Unpublished manuscript (1982).
20. C. A. Neff and J. H. Reif, "An $o(n^{1+\varepsilon} \log b)$ Algorithm for the Complex Root Problem," in *Proc. IEEE Symp. Foundations of Computer Science*, 1994, pp. 540–547.
21. J. P. Cardinal, "On Two Iterative Methods for Approximating the Roots of a Polynomial," in *The Mathematics of Numerical Analysis* J. Renegar, M. Shub, and S. Smale (eds.), *Lectures in Applied Mathematics* Vol. 32, American Mathematical Society, Providence, RI, 1996.
22. H. J. Stetter, "Analysis of Zero Clusters in Multivariate Polynomial Systems," in *Proc. ACM Intern. Symp. on Symbolic and Algebraic Computation*, 1996, pp. 127–135.
23. V. Y. Pan, "Optimal and Nearly Optimal Algorithms for Approximating Polynomial Zeros," *Comp. Math. (with Appl.)*, *31*, 97–138 (1996).
24. H. Weyl, "Randbemerkungen zu Hauptproblemen der Mathematik, II, Fundamentalsatz der Algebra and Grundlagen der Mathematik," *Math. Z.*, *20*, 131–151 (1924).

25. P. Henrici and I. Gargantini, "Uniformly Convergent Algorithms for the Simultaneous Approximation of All Zeros of a Polynomial," in *Constructive Aspects of the Fundamental Theorem of Algebra*, B. Dejon and P. Henrici (eds.), John Wiley & Sons, London, 1969.

26. V. Y. Pan, "On Approximating Complex Polynomial Zeros: Modified Quadtree (Weyl's) Construction and Improved Newton's Iteration," Technical Report 2894, INRIA, Sophia-Antipolis, France (May 1996).

27. J.-P. Dedieu and J.-C. Yakoubsohn, "Computing the Real Roots of a Polynomial by the Exclusion Algorithm," *Numer. Algorithms*, 4, 1–24 (1993).

28. R. Zippel, *Effective Polynomial Computation*. Kluwer Academic Publishers, Boston, 1993.

29. P. Turan, *On a New Method of Analysis and its Applications*, John Wiley & Sons, New York, 1984.

30. A. Hyman, *Charles Babbage, Pioneer of the Computer*, Princeton University Press, Princeton, NJ, 1982.

31. A. Borodin and I. Munro, *The Computational Complexity of Algebraic and Numeric Problems*, American Elsevier, New York, 1975.

32. V. Y. Pan, M.-H. Kim, A. Sadikou, X. Huang, and A. Zheng, "On Isolation of Real and Nearly Real Zeros of a Univariate Polynomial and Its Splitting into Factors," *J. Complexity*, 12(4), 572–594 (1996).

33. T. W. Sederberg and J. Snively, "Parametrization of Cubic Algebraic Surfaces," in *The Mathematics of Surfaces II*, R. Martin (ed.), Oxford University Press, Oxford, 1987.

34. C. M. Hoffmann, *Geometric and Solid Modeling*, Morgan Kaufmann, San Mateo, CA, 1989.

35. J.-P. Merlet, *Les Robots Parallèles*, Traités de Nouvelles Technologiques, Hermès, Paris, 1990.

36. D. Manocha, "Solving Systems of Polynomial Equations," *IEEE Comp. Graphics Appl.*, 46–55, 1994; special issue on solid modeling.

37. R. M. Corless, P. M. Gianni, B. M. Trager, and S. M. Watt, "The Singular Value Decomposition for Polynomial System," in *Proc. ACM Int. Symp. on Symbolic and Algebraic Computation*, 1995, pp. 195–207.

38. A. M. Ostrowski, *Solution of Equations and Systems of Equations*, 2nd ed., Pure and Applied Mathematics, Academic Press, New York, 1966.

39. N. Karmarkar and Y. N. Lakshman, "Approximate Polynomial Greatest Common Divisors and Nearest Singular Polynomials," in *Proc. ACM Int. Symp. on Symbolic and Algebraic Computation*, 1996, pp. 35–43.

40. V. Y. Pan, "Numerical Computation of a Polynomial GCD and Extensions," Technical Report 2969, INRIA, Sophia-Antipolis, France (August 1996).

41. M.-T. Noda and T. Sasaki, "Approximate GCD and Its Application to Ill-Conditioned Algebraic Equations," *J. Computat. Appl. Math.*, 38, 335–351 (1991).

42. A. Schöhage, "Quasi-GCD Computations," *J. Complexity*, 1, 118–137 (1985).

43. B. Mishra, *Algorithmic Algebra*, Springer-Verlag, New York, 1993.

44. I. Z. Emiris, A. Galligo, and H. Lombardi, "Numerical Univariate Polynomial GCD," in *The Mathematics of Numerical Analysis*, J. Renegar, M. Shub, and S. Smale (eds.), *Lectures in Applied Mathematics* Vol. 32, American Mathematic Society, Providence, RI, 1996, pp. 323–343.

45. I. Z. Emiris, A. Galligo, and H. Lombardi, "Certified Approximate Univariate GCDs," *J. Pure Appl. Algebra 117* and *118*, 229–251 (1997); special issue on effective methods in algebraic geometry.

46. D. Rupprecht, "Approximate GCD of *n* Univariate Polynomials, Unpublished manuscript (1997).

47. R. M. Corless, P. M. Gianni, and B. M. Trager, "A Reordered Schur Factorization Method for Zero-Dimensional Polynomial Systems with Multiple Roots," in *Proc. ACM Int. Symp. on Symbolic and Algebraic Computation*, 1997, pp. 133–140.

48. D. Cox, J. Little, and D. O'Shea, *Ideals, Varieties, and Algorithms*, Undergraduate Texts in Mathematics, Springer-Verlag, New York, 1992.

49. J. C. Faugère, F. Moreau de Saint-Martin, and F. Rouillier, "Synthèse de bancs de filtres et ondelettes bidimensionnels par le calcul formel," Rapport interne CCETT, CNET (1996).

50. H. J. Stetter, "Stabilization of Polynomial Systems Solving with Groebner Bases," in *Proc. ACM Int. Symp. on Symbolic and Algebraic Computation*, 1997, pp. 117–124.

51. H. M. Möller and H. J. Stetter, "Multivariate Polynomial Equations with Multiple Zeros Solved by Matrix Eigenproblems," *Numer. Math.*, *70*, 311–329 (1995).

52. E. Allgower and K. Georg, *Numerical Continuation Methods*, Springer-Verlag, Berlin, 1990.

53. A. P. Morgan, A. J. Sommese, and C. W. Wampler, "A Product Decomposition Bound for Bézout Numbers," *SIAM J. Numer. Anal. 32*(4) (1994).

54. C. Wampler, "Forward Displacement Analysis of General Six-in-Parallel SPS (Stewart) Platform Manipulators Using Soma Coordinates," Technical Report 8179, General Motors R & D (1994).

55. J. Verschelde, P. Verlinden, and R. Cools, "Homotopies Exploiting Newton Polytopes for Solving Sparse Polynomial Systems," *SIAM J. Numer. Anal.*, *31*(3), 915–930 (1994).

56. B. Huber and B. Sturmfels, "A Polyhedral Method for Solving Sparse Polynomial Systems," *Math. Computat.*, *64*(212), 1542–1555 (1995).

57. T. Y. Li, T. Wang, and X. Wang, "Random Product Homotopy with Minimal BKK Bound," in *The Mathematics of Numerical Analysis*, J. Renegar, M. Shub, and S. Smale (eds.), Lectures in Applied Mathematics Vol. 32, American Mathematical Society, Providence, RI, 1996.

58. J. Verschelde, K. Gatermann, and R. Cools, "Mixed Volume Computation by Dynamic Lifting Applied to Polynomial System Solving," *Discrete and Computat. Geom.*, *16*(1), 69–112 (1996).

59. G. Alefeld and R. D. Grigorieff (eds.), *Fundamentals of Numerical Computation*, volume 2 of *Computing Supplementum*. Springer-Verlag, Wein, 1980.

60. N. J. Higham, *Accuracy and Stability of Numerical Algorithms*, SIAM, Philadelphia, 1996.

61. B. L. van der Waerden, *Modern Algebra*, 3rd ed., F. Ungar Publishing Co., New York, 1950.

62. D. Kapur and Y. N. Lakshman, "Elimination Methods: An Introduction," in *Symbolic and Numerical Computation for Artificial Intelligence*, B. Donald, D. Kapur, and J. Mundy (eds.), Academic Press, New York, 1992, pp. 45–89.

63. J. F. Canny, *The Complexity of Robot Motion Planning*, MIT Press, Cambridge, MA, 1988.

64. D. Manocha and J. F. Canny, "Efficient Inverse Kinematics for General 6R Manipulators," *IEEE Trans. Robotics Automation*, *10*(5), 648–657 (1994).

65. J. Renegar, "On the Computational Complexity of the First-Order Theory of the Reals," *J. Symbol. Computat.*, *13*(3), 255–352 (1992).

66. D. Manocha and J. Demmel, "Algorithms for Intersecting Parametric and Algebraic Curves II: Multiple Intersections," *Graphical Models Image Process.*, *57*(2), 81–100 (1995).

67. D. Cox, J. Little, and D. O'Shea, *Using Algebraic Geometry*, Springer-Verlag, New York, 1998.

68. I. M. Gelfand, M. M. Kapranov, and A. V. Zelevinsky, "Hyperdeterminants," *Adv. Math.*, *96*(2) (1992).

69. B. Sturmfels, "On the Newton Polytope of the Resultant," *J. Algebr. Combinat.*, *3*, 207–236 (1994).

70. I. Z. Emiris, "On the Complexity of Sparse Elimination," *J. Complexity*, *12*, 134–166 (1996).

71. J. Canny and I. Emiris, "An Efficient Algorithm for the Sparse Mixed Resultant," in *Proc. Intern. Symp. on Applied Algebraic Algor. and Error-Corr. Codes*, G. Cohen, T. Mora, and O. Moreno (eds.), Lecture Notes in Comp. Science 263, Springer-Verlag, New York, 1993, pp. 89–104.

72. I. Z. Emiris and J. F. Canny, "Efficient Incremental Algorithms for the Sparse Resultant and the Mixed Volume," *J. Symbol. Computat.*, *20*(2), 117–149 (1995).

73. J.-P. Cardinal and B. Mourrain, "Algebraic Approach of Residues and Applications," in *The Mathematics of Numerical Analysis*, J. Renegar, M. Shub, and S. Smale (eds.), Lectures in Applied Mathematics Vol. 32, American Mathematical Society, Providence, RI, 1996, pp. 189–210.

74. D. Kapur and T. Saxena, "Comparison of Various Multivariate Resultant Formulations," in *Proc. ACM Int. Symp. on Symbolic and Algebraic Computation*, 1995, pp. 187–194.

75. J. F. Canny, E. Kaltofen, and Y. Lakshman, "Solving Systems of Non-linear Polynomial Equations Faster," in *Proc. ACM Int. Symp. on Symbolic and Algebraic Computation*, 1989, pp. 121–128.

76. B. Mourrain and V. Y. Pan, "Solving Special Polynomial Systems by Using Structured Matrices and Algebraic Residues," in *Proc. Workshop on Foundations of Computational Mathematics*, F. Cucker and M. Shub (eds.), Springer-Verlag, Berlin, 1997, pp. 287–304.

77. I. Z. Emiris and V. Y. Pan, "The Structure of Sparse Resultant Matrices," in *Proc. ACM Int. Symp. on Symbolic and Algebraic Computation*, 1997, pp. 189–196.

78. S. Krishnan and D. Manocha, "Numeric–Symbolic Algorithms for Evaluating One-Dimensional Algebraic Sets," in *Proc. ACM Int. Symp. on Symbolic and Algebraic Computation*, 1995, pp. 59–67.

79. W. Auzinger and H. J. Stetter, "An Elimination Algorithm for the Computation of All Zeros of a System of Multivariate Polynomial Equations, in *Proc. Int. Conf. on Numerical Math.*, International Series of Numerical Mathematics Vol. 86, Birkhäuser, Basel, 1988, pp. 12–30.

80. D. Manocha and J. Canny, "Multipolynomial Resultant Algorithms," *J. Symbol. Computat.*, *15*(2), 99–122 (1993).

81. E. Tyrtyshnikov, *Brief Introduction to Numerical Analysis*, Birkhäuser, Boston, 1997.

82. E. Anderson, Z. Bai, C. Bischof, J. Demmel, J. Dongarra, J. Du Croz, A. Greenbaum, S. Hammarling, A. McKenney, S. Ostrouchov, and D. Sorensen, *LAPACK Users' Guide*, 2nd ed., SIAM, Philadelphia, 1995.

83. J. Canny, "Generalised Characteristic Polynomials," *J. Symbol. Computat.*, *9*, 241–250 (1990).

84. J. M. Rojas, "Toric Laminations, Sparse Generalized Characteristic Polynomials, and a Refinement of Hilbert's Tenth Problem," in *Proc. Workshop on Foundations of Computational Mathematics*, F. Cucker and M. Shub (eds.), Springer-Verlag, Berlin, 1997, pp. 369–381.

85. D. Manocha, Y. Zhu, and W. Wright, "Conformational Analysis of Molecular Chains Using Nano-kinematics," *Computer Applic. Biol. Sci.*, *11*(1), 71–86 (1995).

86. B. Mourrain, "Solving Polynomial Systems by Matrix Computations," unpublished manuscript (1997).

87. K. L. Clarkson, "Safe and Effective Determinant Evaluation," in *Proc. IEEE Symp. Foundations of Computer Science*, 1992, pp. 387–395.

88. S. Fortune and C. J. Van Wyk, "Efficient Exact Arithmetic for Computational Geometry," in *Proc. ACM Symp. on Computational Geometry*, 1993, pp. 163–172.

89. J. R. Shewchuk, "Robust Adaptive Floating-Point Geometric Predicates," in *Proc. ACM Symp. on Computational Geometry*, 1996, pp. 141–150.

90. H. Brönnimann, I. Z. Emiris, V. Pan, and S. Pion, "Computing Exact Geometric Predicates Using Modular Arithmetic with Single Precision," in *Proc. ACM Symp. on Computational Geometry*, 1997, pp. 174–182.

91. G. E. Collins and R. Loos, "Real Zeros of Polynomials," in *Computer Algebra: Symbolic and Algebraic Computation*, B. Buchberger, G. E. Collins, and R. Loos (eds.), 2nd ed., Springer-Verlag, Wien, 1982.

92. S. Basu, R. Pollack, and M.-F. Roy, "Computing Roadmaps of Semialgebraic Sets on a Variety," in *Proc. Workshop on Foundations of Computational Mathematics*, F. Cucker and M. Shub (eds.), Springer-Verlag, Berlin, 1997, pp. 1–15.

93. E. Tournier (ed.), *Computer Algebra and Differential Equations*, Academic Press, New York, 1988.

94. J. H. Davenport, Y. Siret, and E. Tournier, *Computer Algebra*, Academic Press, London, 1988.

95. G. L. Nemhauser, A. H. G. Rinnooy Kan, and M. J. Todd (eds.), *Optimization*, Handbooks in Operations Research and Management Science, North-Holland, Amsterdam, 1989.

96. M. Seppälä and T. Sorvali, *Geometry of Riemann Surfaces and Teichmüller Spaces*, Mathematics Studies, Vol. 169, North-Holland, Amsterdam, 1992.

97. R. D. McKelvey and A. McLennan, "The Maximal Number of Regular Totally Mixed Nash Equilibria," Technical Report 865, Division of the Humanities and Social Sciences, California Institute of Technology, Pasadena (July 1994).

98. J. M. Rojas, "A New Approach to Counting Nash Equilibria," in *Proc. IEEE/IAFE Conf. Computational Intelligence for Financial Engineering*, 1997, pp. 130–136.

99. M. Raghavan and B. Roth, "Solving Polynomial Systems for the Kinematics Analysis and Synthesis of Mechanisms and Robot Manipulators," *Trans. ASME 117*, 71–79 (1995); special 50th anniversary design issue.

100. S. J. Maybank, "Applications of Algebraic Geometry to Computer Vision," in *Computational Algebraic Geometry*, F. Eyssette and A. Galligo (eds.), Birkhäuser, Boston, 1993, pp. 185–194.

101. A. W. M. Dress and T. F. Havel, "Distance Geometry and Geometric Algebra," *Found. Phys.*, *23*(10), 1357–1374 (1991).

102. L. M. Balbes, S. W. Mascarella, and D. B. Boyd, "A Perspective of Modern Methods in Computer-Aided Drug Design," in *Reviews in Computational Chemistry, Volume 5*, K. B. Lipkowitz and D. B. Boyd (eds.), VCH, New York, 1994, pp. 337–379.

103. V. A. Sarychev and S. A. Gutnik, "Equilibria of Satellite Under the Influence of Gravitational and Static Torques," *Cosmic Res.* (*Kosmicheskie Isslidovaniya*), *32*(4–5), 386–391 (1995).

104. G. Farin, *Curves and Surfaces for Computer Aided Geometric Design*, Academic Press, Boston, 1988.

105. C. L. Bajaj and S. Evans, "Splines and Geometric Modeling," in *Handbook of Discrete and Computational Geometry*, J. Goodman and J. O'Rourke (eds.), CRC Press, Boca Raton, FL, 1997.

106. R. T. Farouki, "Conic Approximations of Conic Offsets," *J. Symbol. Computat.*, *23*, 301–313 (1997); special issue on parametric algebraic curves and applications.

107. T. W. Sederberg, R. Goldman, and H. Du, "Implicitizing Rational Curves by the Method of Moving Algebraic Curves," *J. Symbol. Computat.*, *23*, 153–175 (1997); special issue on parametric algebraic curves and applications.

108. N. M. Patrikalakis, "Surface-to-Surface Intersections," *IEEE Computer Graphics Applic.*, *13*(1), 89–95 (1993).

109. K. O. Geddes, S. R. Czapor, and G. Labahn, *Algorithms for Computer Algebra*, Kluwer Academic Publishers, Norwell, MA, 1992.

110. R. E. Crandall, *Projects in Scientific Computation*, Springer-Verlag, New York, 1994.

111. J. Renegar, M. Shub, and S. Smale (eds.), *The Mathematics of Numerical Analysis*, Lectures in Applied Mathematics Vol. 32, American Mathematical Society, Providence, RI, 1996.

112. R. Corless, I. Z. Emiris, A. Galligo, B. Mourrain, and S. M. Watt (eds.), *Proc. Workshop on Symbolic–Numeric Algebra for Polynomials* (*SNAP-96*), 1996; http://www.inria.fr/safir/MEETING/snap.html.

113. F. Cucker and M. Shub (eds.), *Proc. Workshop on Foundations of Computational Mathematics*, Springer-Verlag, Berlin, 1997.

114. D. Bini and V. Y. Pan, *Polynomial and Matrix Computations, Volume 2: Selected Topics*, Birkhäuser, Boston, 1998.

115. B. T. Smith, J. M. Boyle, J. J. Dongarra, B. S. Garbow, Y. Ikebe, V. C. Klema, and C. B. Moler, *Matrix Eigensystem Routines—EISPACK Guide*, Lecture Notes in Computer Science Vol. 6, Springer-Verlag, Berlin, 1976.

116. J. Bunch, J. Dongarra, C. Moler, and G. W. Stewart, *LINPACK User's Guide*, SIAM, Philadelphia, 1979.

117. R. D. Jenks and R. S. Sutor, *AXIOM: The Scientific Computation System*. Springer-Verlag, New York, 1992; supported by The Numerical Algorithms Group; http://www.nag. co.uk/symbolic/AX.html.

118. S. Wolfram, *The Mathematica Book*, 3rd ed., Cambridge University Press, Cambridge, 1996.

119. B. W. Char, K. O. Geddes, G. H. Gonnet, B. L. Leong, M. B. Monagan, and S. M. Watt, *First Leaves: A Tutorial Introduction to Maple V*, Springer-Verlag, New York, 1992; http://www.maplesoft.com.

120. A. C. Hearn (ed.), *REDUCE User's Manual Version 3.6*. Rand Corporation, Santa Monica, CA, 1995; http://ftp.rand.org/software_and_data/reduce.

121. The MathWorks, Inc., *The Student Edition of MATLAB Version 4 User's Guide*. Prentice-Hall, Englewood Cliffs, NJ, 1995.

122. FRISCO (Framework for the Integration of Symbolic–Numeric Computing). ESPIRIT Long Term Research Project 21.024, 1996–1999; http://extweb.nag.co.uk/projects/FRISCO.html.

IOANNIS Z. EMIRIS

THE TRANSPUTER FAMILY OF PRODUCTS AND THEIR APPLICATIONS IN BUILDING A HIGH-PERFORMANCE COMPUTER

INTRODUCTION

The transputer is a specially constructed microprocessor manufactured by the British company Inmos (now a division of SGS-Thomson) with the intention of satisfying the need for the next generation of computers to handle parallel processing. The major difference between the transputer and an ordinary microprocessor is that the transputer can readily be built into high-performance computing networks/arrays to exploit programs with a high degree of concurrency.

A transputer is a programmable Very Large Scale Integrated (VLSI) device which provides all the resources of a computer including processing, memory, and concurrent communications on a single chip. It is a small, but a complete von Neumann computer. The reason that the terms concurrency and parallelism are associated with the transputer is that transputers can readily be built into networks and arrays, each working on its own job using its own local memory. A single transputer executes programs sequentially. It can execute parallel processes only insofar as it shares processing time between currently active processes, changing from one process to another when the current process has to wait for communication.

There are 16-bit and 32-bit transputers available. The IMS T800 and IMS T9000 series transputers have on-chip floating-point hardware support. Each transputer has four bidirectional links (except the IMS T400 which has only two links). Each link is serial and supports memory-to-memory block transfer. The transfers occur concurrently with processor execution, and all links can operate simultaneously. Each link consists of two channels, one for input and one for output. The output channel of a link on one transputer is connected to the input channel of a link on another transputer, and vice versa. The two-wire, point-to-point connections between two transputers are described as "links." Communication via a channel takes place when both the inputting and the outputting processes are ready. Consequently, the process which first becomes ready must wait until the second one is also ready.

Transputers can be programmed in most high-level languages and are designed to ensure that compiled programs will be efficient. However, to gain most benefit from the transputer architecture, the whole system should be programmed in Occam. Hardware and software have largely been developed in isolation in the past. In developing the transputer and the Occam language, Inmos developed them in harmony. The synergy between hardware and software is most clearly apparent when studying Occam, and the user should be aware that many of the features traditionally implemented in hardware are best realized in transputer systems in software, and vice versa.

The links of transputers are serial. One important benefit of using serial links is that it is easy to implement a full crossbar in VLSI, even with a large number of links.

The VLSI implementation of crossbar switches allows messages to be passing through all links at the same time, making the best possible use of the available bandwidth. The transfer of a message between one pair of links does not affect the data rate for another message passing between a second pair of links. Inmos division of SGS-Thomson Micro-electronics has developed three crossbar switches: IMS C004, IMS C104, and IMS C103 chips. The IMS C004 and IMS C104 are 32 × 32-way crossbars; the IMS C004 is designed for IMS T200, IMS T400, and IMS T800 family of transputers and the IMS C104 is designed for the IMS T9000 transputers. These switches can be connected to transputers of the same type for, or they can be used to construct networks having different types of transputers, via protocol converter chips (such as the IMS C100). The IMS C103 is a smaller version of the IMS C104 switch; it is an 8 × 8-way crossbar switch.

A brief description of the IMS C104 switch is given here. The IMS C104 is a nonblocking packet routing switch. An IMS C104 can be used to interconnect 32 IMS T9000 transputers that are not directly connected. The links of the IMS C104 can also be connected to other IMS C104's. This feature of the switch allows the construction of multicomputers having more than 32 nodes. A message on an IMS C104 chip is transmitted as a sequence of packets. The packets from different messages may be interleaved over each physical link. Interleaving packets from different messages allows any number of processes to communicate simultaneously via each physical link. To ensure that packets which are parts of different messages can be routed, each packet contains a header data. The chip uses the header of each packet arriving to determine the link to be used to output the packet. The data after the header is treated as the packet body until the packet terminator is received. This approach allows the transmission of packets of varying lengths. The IMS C104 uses the wormhole routing technique, in which the routing decision is taken as soon as the packet header is received. A packet may be passing through several switches at any one time. Thus, latency is minimized and transmission can be continuous.

THE TRANSPUTER FAMILY

The transputer family is a range of system components including processors, memory, network switches, and links. Currently, most transputer products are no longer in production. Some members of the transputer family are listed below:

IMS T200   This is a series of transputer families. Each IMS T2xx has a 16-bit integer processor, 2 kbytes of on-chip RAM, and 4 bidirectional links to other transputer products.

IMS T400   A 32-bit integer processor, 2 kbytes of on-chip RAM, and 2 bidirectional links to other transputer products.

IMS T414   A 32-bit integer processor, 2 kbytes of on-chip RAM, and 4 bidirectional links to other transputer products.

IMS T425   A 32-bit integer processor, 4 kbytes of on-chip RAM, and 4 bidirectional links to other transputer products.

IMS T800   A 32-bit processor, 4 kbytes of on-chip RAM, on-chip floating-point unit, 4 bidirectional links to other transputer products.

TIMS 805   A 32-bit processor, 4 kbytes of on-chip RAM, on-chip floating-point unit, 4 bidirectional links to other transputer products. This transputer is more powerful than the T800 in terms of processor and link speeds.

IMS T9000   A 32-bit integer processor, a 64-bit floating-point processor, 16 kbytes of on-chip RAM, 4 bidirectional links to other transputer products. This transputer is the highest-performance member of the transputer family. It is capable of a peak performance of about 250 MIPS and 30 MFLOPS. The four communication links provide a total of 80 Mbytes/s bidirectional bandwidth.

IMS C004   This is a communication support device for IMS T200, IMS T400, and IMS T800 series of transputers. It is a 32×32-way crossbar switch.

IMS C100   This is a communication support device. It is a protocol converter. It allows transputer networks built by IMS C103 switches to communicate with transputer networks built by IMS C103 and/or IMS C104 switches.

IMS C103   This is a communication support device for IMS T9000 transputers. It is a complete routing switch on a single chip. It connects eight links to each other via a 8×8 way, nonblocking crossbar switch with submicrosecond latency. Multiple C103s can be connected together to make larger and more advanced networks.

IMS C104   This is a communication support device for transputers. It is a complete routing switch on a single chip. The C104 connects 32 links to each other via a 32×32-way, nonblocking crossbar switch with submicrosecond latency. Multiple C104s can be connected together to make larger and more advanced networks.

A TRANSPUTER-BASED RECONFIGURATION PARALLEL SYSTEM—AN EXAMPLE

This section illustrates how a high-performance computer can be built using the transputer products. The motivation behind developing such a system is also presented.

Introduction

Recent studies have shown that a particular network of processors, which has been named the MultiRing network, can support a wide variety of algorithms and applications. The effectiveness of the MultiRing system is founded in its *reconfigurability*; the interconnections between processors can be adjusted to meet phase-specific requirements. The Multi-Ring network consists of 2^n processors connected in a ring, with the capability to be reconfigured, into R rings of D processors each, with corresponding elements of each ring linked, for any R and D whose product is 2^n. The total number of processors could be any composite number, but the use of a power of 2 maximizes the number of factorizations. For illustrative purposes, a network of $R = 4$ rings, each of size $D = 8$ processors, with corresponding elements linked, is shown in Figure 1.

The following subsection a background summary of the motivation behind this work is presented. The remaining subsections a brief description of the MultiRing is given, the problem of simulating the hypercube network on the MultiRing is addressed, various broadcasting mechanisms are discussed, a simpler computer vision problem utilizing the MultiRing network is described, and finally, the problem of building the Multi-Ring using the Inmos transputer products is discussed.

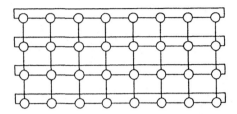

FIGURE 1   One possible configuration of a 32-node MultiRing network.

Background

It has been shown by Anderson (1) that as a general-purpose interconnection network, the simple ring (i.e., a single ring) is more *cost-effective* than many other well-known interconnection networks, such as systolic array, tree, and shuffle exchange. Karia et al. (2) describe algorithms that find ring networks of varying sizes within other networks; such algorithms are used in Gaussian elimination. Beck et al. (3) built a parallel system with essentially a simple ring interconnection network, called RAP (Ring Array Processor). RAP has been used quite successfully in speech research and neural network applications. There are also many other published research articles that describe algorithms targeted at ring-based topologies.

The ring interconnection network has many attractive properties. One important property is that each processor in a ring requires a fixed number of links (only two) irrespective of the size of the network; this makes a system with the ring interconnection network truly scalable. Such systems have simpler wiring and are therefore relatively inexpensive to build. The ring interconnection network does have one serious drawback—inefficient interprocessor communication between processors that are not neighbors. Consequently, *broadcasting* at the interconnection level is a problem. These difficulties have limited the usefulness of the simple ring for a large number of interesting problems and applications, but the reconfigurable MultiRing does address them.

The problem of parallelizing a number of algorithms that have different intrinsic parallelization characteristics have been addressed in Refs. 4–14. From these studies, it emerged that a network consisting of a number of processor rings in various configurations supports all the major parallelization strategies; this network is referred to as the *MultiRing*. The MultiRing network provides an efficient and general interprocessor communication and broadcasting mechanism at the interconnection level (unlike the simple ring network). The MultiRing network can be embedded in the hypercube interconnection network; elsewhere, it has been shown that all possible configurations of the MultiRing topology are subsets of the hypercube (15). Further investigations showed that at *any* interprocessor communication phase, the vast majority of algorithms *designed* for and successfully implemented on hypercube-based architectures *do not* use all the links provided by the hypercube. Examples of such algorithms include problems in artificial intelligence (16–19), fluid dynamics (20–23), image processing (24–31), partial differential equation solvers and matrix manipulation problems (32–36), simulation (37), sorting (38), and structural analysis (39,40). It has been observed that at any given time during the execution of these algorithms and many others not cited here, the interconnection subset actually being utilized (within the cube) was a configuration of the MultiRing topology. This observation strongly implies that the MultiRing topology provides the same generality *in practice* as the hypercube.

The MultiRing Network of Processors and Parallelization Issues

Data-Decomposition and Process-Decomposition are the two basic parallelization strategies that are widely used in parallel algorithm design. The MultiRing system encourages more general parallelization strategies to be used than those currently used—these can incorporate a combination of the two basic strategies. Some examples that use a combination of the two basic parallelization strategies can be found in Refs. 6, 7, and 14.

The example network shown in Figure 1 (processors are represented by circles and the links are denoted by lines) supports all major parallelization approaches. The network is made up of a number of rings of processors (four rings in this example); each processor in a ring is connected to the corresponding processors in the neighboring rings. For each processor, the maximum number of links for any number and size of rings required for this setup is *four* links. A problem whose process is decomposed into R subprocesses and whose data is decomposed into D smaller portions can exploit a network made up of R rings where each ring has D processors. In the network shown in Figure 1, $D = 8$ and $R = 4$.

MultiRing processor networks support the major parallelization strategies. An algorithm parallelized using the Data-Decomposition approach can run on one ring of processors (i.e., $R = 1$ and $D = v$, where v is the number of data portions). Similarly, an algorithm parallelized using Process-Decomposition can run on a linear processor network (i.e., $R = h$ and $D = 1$, where h is the number of subprocesses); here, each processor is executing a subprocess and it may cooperate with other processors to complete its operation. The combination of the two parallelization approaches is also supported by networks based on ring topology; such networks must have more than one ring of processors (as shown in Fig. 1). In addition, the MultiRing network supports many application-oriented parallelization schemes. As an example, it has been shown (41) that for imaging problems, the MultiRing network provides Image-Parallelism, Data-Parallelism, Process-Parallelism, and IDP-Parallelism (this is the combination of any of the first three parallelization schemes).

The MultiRing interconnection network contains within it the mesh *nearest-neighbor* interconnection network where each processor is directly connected to its four nearest neighbors; as an example, the network shown in Fig. 1 contains within it the 4×8 (or 8×4) mesh. This is significant because there is a rich set of algorithms already developed that exploit mesh interconnection networks.

One problem with the MultiRing network is that different algorithms require different configurations: One may require a single ring, whereas another may require more rings linked together in the manner shown in Figure 1. This problem will be addressed in this article and it will be shown how the topology of the processor rings can be reconfigured to cover all the numerically balanced configurations within a system having *any* composite number of processors.

Ring Reconfigurability

In this subsection, the scheme developed to reconfigure the MultiRing is described. The process of reconfiguration presented here is not physical; that is, it is not necessarily suitable for direct implementation in hardware. Therefore, the term "node" rather than "processor" is used to emphasis this.

A network having R rings each containing D nodes, where R and D are constants, is too restrictive for many applications. For example, a problem may have two or more phases: in one phase, it may require more (or fewer) rings than another phase. The network configuration used in one phase needs to be reconfigured to yield the network required in the other phase. In general, a MultiRing having 2^n nodes can be reconfigured into $n+1$ different configurations. Each of these configurations is referred to as the "numerically balanced ring" or "balanced ring." The balanced rings of a 2^n node system are 2^{n-s} rings, each having 2^s nodes, where s is an integer and $0 \le s \le n$. For example, the balanced rings of a 16-node system are 16 rings of 1 node each, 8 rings of 2 nodes each, 4 rings of 4 nodes each, 2 rings of 8 nodes, and 1 ring of 16 nodes.

The hypercube interconnection network supports the MultiRing topology; all possible numerically balanced rings of nodes can be mapped to subsets of the hypercube interconnection network. One can use the hypercube network for problems that utilize MultiRing topology. But the hypercube provides more connections than necessary. Recall that in the MultiRing network, there are at most four links required for each node; an n-dimensional hypercube provides more then four links for each node when $n > 4$. Therefore, the problem is to find a network of nodes that supports the MultiRing topology where each node has only a fixed number of links. Such a system has been designed and is described here.

Consider a ring of $t(t = 2^n)$ nodes where $P_0 \leftrightarrow P_1$, $P_1 \leftrightarrow P_2, \ldots, P_{t-1} \leftrightarrow P_0$ ($\leftrightarrow$ denotes a bidirectional link). This network contains within it (as its subsets), one ring of t nodes and t rings of one node each. In order to construct R rings of D nodes each ($R \times D = t$), two extra links for each node, P_i, need to be added to the network; they can be found with the aid of Eq. (1):

$$P_i \leftrightarrow P_{(i+R)\bmod t},$$
$$P_i \leftrightarrow P_{(i+t-R)\bmod t}. \tag{1}$$

As an example, consider the 16-node node ring shown in Figure 2a (note that the technique is applicable to any composite number of nodes, not just 16).

In order to construct two rings of eight nodes each (i.e., $R = 2$, $t = 16$, and $D = 8$), the following links need to be added to the network [found using the two equations, Eq. (1), for each node]: $P_0 \leftrightarrow P_2$, $P_1 \leftrightarrow P_3$, $P_2 \leftrightarrow P_4$, $P_3 \leftrightarrow P_5$, $P_4 \leftrightarrow P_6$, $P_5 \leftrightarrow P_7$, $P_6 \leftrightarrow P_8$, $P_7 \leftrightarrow P_9$, $P_8 \leftrightarrow P_{10}$, $P_9 \leftrightarrow P_{11}$, $P_{10} \leftrightarrow P_{12}$, $P_{11} \leftrightarrow P_{13}$, $P_{12} \leftrightarrow P_{14}$, $P_{13} \leftrightarrow P_{15}$, $P_{14} \leftrightarrow P_0$, and $P_{15} \leftrightarrow P_1$. This will result the network shown in Figure 2b which consists of two rings of eight nodes each. The two rings within Figure 2b are formed by (P_0, P_2, P_4, P_6, P_8, P_{10}, P_{12}, P_{14}) and (P_1, P_3, P_5, P_7, P_9, P_{11}, P_{13}, P_{15}). In addition, each node is connected to the corresponding node in the other ring (i.e., $P_0 \leftrightarrow P_1$, $P_2 \leftrightarrow P_3$, and so on).

As another example, in order to construct four rings of four nodes each (i.e., $R = 4$, $t = 16$, and $D = 4$), the following links need to be added to the original network shown in Figure 2a [found using Eq. (1) for each node]: $P_0 \leftrightarrow P_4$,
$P_1 \leftrightarrow P_5$, $P_2 \leftrightarrow P_6$, $P_3 \leftrightarrow P_7$, $P_4 \leftrightarrow P_8$, $P_5 \leftrightarrow P_9$, $P_6 \leftrightarrow P_{10}$, $P_7 \leftrightarrow P_{11}$, $P_8 \leftrightarrow P_{12}$, $P_9 \leftrightarrow P_{13}$, $P_{10} \leftrightarrow P_{14}$, $P_{11} \leftrightarrow P_{15}$, $P_{12} \leftrightarrow P_0$, $P_{13} \leftrightarrow P_1$, $P_{14} \leftrightarrow P_2$, and $P_{15} \leftrightarrow P_3$. This will result the network shown in Figure 2c which consists of four rings of four nodes each. The four rings within Figure 2c are formed by (P_0, P_4, P_8, P_{12}), (P_1, P_5, P_9, P_{13}), (P_2, P_6, P_{10}, P_{14}), and (P_3, P_7, P_{11}, P_{15}). In addition, each node is connected to the corresponding nodes in the other rings (i.e., $P_0 \leftrightarrow P_1$, $P_1 \leftrightarrow P_2$, $P_2 \leftrightarrow P_3$, $P_4 \leftrightarrow P_5$, $P_5 \leftrightarrow P_6$, $P_6 \leftrightarrow P_7$, $P_8 \leftrightarrow P_9$, and so on). All other ring configurations can be constructed in a similar way.

It is important to note that the $R \times D$ (or $D \times R$) mesh nearest-neighbor interconnec-

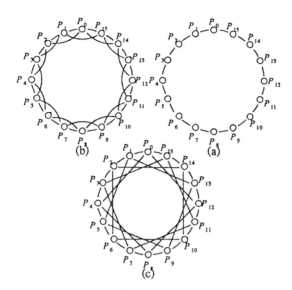

FIGURE 2   Construction of 16-node MultiRing.

tion network is contained within each configuration. For example, the network shown in Figure 2b contains within it the 2×8 (or 8×2) mesh network; similarly, the network shown in Figure 2c contains within it the 4×4 mesh network.

The Hypercube Network Within the MultiRing Network

Recent studies show that any parallel algorithm designed for a hypercube-based system can readily utilize the MultiRing interconnection network. The only overhead on the MultiRing would be the reconfiguration, which can be very efficient. This makes a Multi-Ring-based system very cost-effective compared to a hypercube-based system. Here, it is shown how a hypercube of a given size can be found within the MultiRing network of the same size.

A MultiRing with 2^n nodes can be reconfigured into $n + 1$ configurations. For example, a 16-node MultiRing (i.e., $n = 4$) can be reconfigured into five configurations: 1 ring of 16 nodes (Fig. 2a), 2 rings of 8 nodes each (Fig. 2b), 4 rings of 4 nodes each (Fig. 2c), 8 rings of 2 nodes each (not shown in the figure), and 16 rings of 1 node each. The last configuration of a MultiRing (16 rings of 1 node in our example) of any size is always a subset of the first configuration (1 ring of 16 in the example). Therefore, the last configuration of a MultiRing is not explicitly considered, because it is contained within the first configuration.

Consider the 16-node network shown in Figure 3 (although the method described here is illustrated with 16-node systems, it is applicable to any positive power-of-2 node system). A node in Figure 3 is represented by a bullet (•) and the numbers next to each node are the node identification numbers. Figure 3a shows 1 ring of 16 nodes; it has the same topology as the network shown in Figure 2a. Figure 3a combined with (using the union operation) Fig. 3b will result two rings of eight nodes each; the two rings are interconnected. The combined result has the same topology as the network shown in

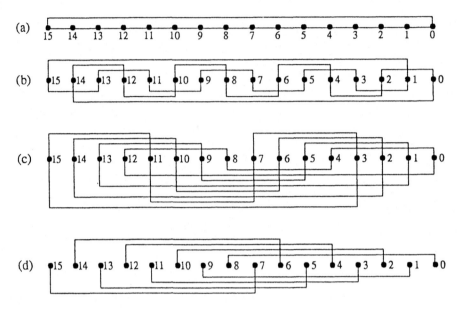

FIGURE 3   The 4 single-stage topologies of a 16-node MultiRing.

Figure 2b. Figure 3a combined with Figure 3c will result in four rings of four nodes each; the four rings are interconnected. The combined result has the same topology as the network shown in Figure 2c. Finally, Figure 3a combined with Figure 3d will result in eight rings of two nodes each; the eight rings are interconnected. Therefore, as illustrated, Figure 3 shows a 16-node MultiRing.

A hypercube of dimension n can be represented as n single-stage topologies (42). Figure 4 shows the four single-stage topologies of hypercube of dimension 4 (i.e., a 16-

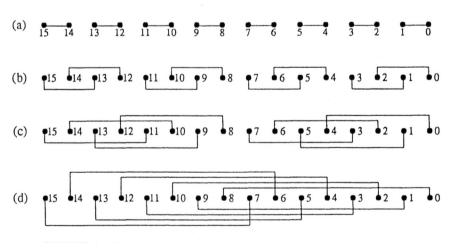

FIGURE 4   The four single-stage topologies of hypercube of dimension 4.

node system). Combining (union of) Figures 4a–d will result a hypercube of dimension 4.

As can be seen, the network shown in Figure 4a is a subset of the network shown in Figure 3a. Similarly, Figure 4b is a subset of Figure 3b; Figure 4c is a subset of Figure 3c; and Figure 4d is a subset of Figure 3d. As illustrated by Figures 3 and 4, each of the single-stage topologies of the hypercube is contained within the corresponding configuration of the MultiRing. Therefore, in this way, the hypercube network can very naturally be simulated by the MultiRing network.

Utilizing the MultiRing Network—Broadcasting Mechanism

In almost all parallel problems, some form of data broadcasting is required. The Multi-Ring network supports broadcasting at the interconnection level. Each of the broadcasting operations performs on the order Mn on the MultiRing network where the length of the message is M and there are 2^n nodes. This is very efficient. This broadcast time can be shown optimal among networks which are 4-regular, to within a multiplicative constant that is independent of the size of the network. Below, three broadcasting mechanisms are briefly described. In the following descriptions, the node adjacent to the current node in the counterclockwise direction within a ring is referred to as the next node.

Simple Broadcasting

In simple broadcasting, a block of data in one node is to be broadcast to all the other nodes. The operation is performed as follows (assume that A is the data to be broadcast and initially there is one ring of nodes; refer to Figure 2a): One node sends a copy of A counterclockwise to the next node; reconfigure the system to yield two rings (refer to Fig. 2b); within each of the two rings, two nodes each send a copy of A counterclockwise to the next node; reconfigure the system to yield four rings (refer to Fig. 2c); within each of the four rings, four nodes each send a copy of A to the next node; continue this process n times. After n steps, each of the 2^n nodes will have a copy of A.

Image Tile Broadcasting

This broadcasting operation has many appliations; it is a particularly useful operation for parallel image processing and recognition (this broadcasting method together with the one described below have many applications in imaging operations: both in low-level and high-level imaging problems). In imaging problems, it is often necessary to subdivide the image into tiles by horizontal and/or vertical cuts and assign each tile to a separate processor for parallel execution. If one node has a copy of all the image tiles in its local memory, the problem is to assign particular image tiles to particular nodes. After performing this assignment, node P_0 will contain $tile_0$, P_1 will contain $tile_1$, and so on. This operation is performed as follows (assuming that initially the image tiles are in one node in the order: $tile_0$, $tile_1$, $tile_2$, and so on): Send all those image tiles that are numbered with an odd number (subscript) to the next node in the ring (only the node with all the data will perform this first task); reconfigure the system to yield two rings, within each of the two rings send all those image tiles whose number (subscript) $div2$ (div denotes the integer division operator) is an odd number to the next node in the ring; reconfigure the system to yield four rings, within each of the four rings send all those image tiles whose number (subscript) $div4$ is an odd number to the next node in the ring; continue this process *n* times. After *n* steps, node P_0 will contain $tile_0$, P_1 will contain $tile_1$, and so on.

Each Node Broadcasting Its Data to the Entire System—Gossiping

In this type of broadcasting, each node has a block of data that needs to be broadcast to all other nodes in the system. Therefore, at the end of this operation, the data in each node will be the same as the data in the other nodes; that is, every node will have a copy of all the blocks of data. This operation is very similar to the simple broadcasting operation and is performed as follows (assuming that initially there is one ring of nodes): Each node sends a copy of its data to the next node; reconfigure the system to yield two rings; within each of the two rings each node sends a copy of its data to the next node; reconfigure the system to yield four rings, within each of the four rings each node sends a copy of its data to the next node; continue this process *n* times.

A Simple Vision Application on the MultiRing

The detection or recognition of useful features from a sequence of digitized images, captured from the same scene at different times, is an important problem with many possible applications, including military problems [tracking of multiple targets from image data; target detection and recognition in Forward Looking Infrared (FLIR) image sequences], industrial problems (dynamic monitoring of industrial processes by robot vision), medical imaging (study of cell motion by microcinematography; study of heart motion from x-ray movies), meteorology (cloud tracking), and transportation (highway traffic monitoring). Here, the problem of processing a sequence of digitized images captured from the same scene at different times into one single image suitable for standard detection (feature extraction) operation is addressed. The entire operation is referred to as the detection procedure/operation. The detection procedure described in this section has two phases. In the first phase, a sequence of images is preprocessed into one image. This single image will be suitable for feature extraction and recognition. To illustrate the approach, a standard four-stage vision preprocessing operation is used: noise reduction, boundary highlighting, conversion of the result to black-and-white (i.e., to binary), and combination of the images in a particular way (refer to Ref. 43 for the details of each). More sophisticated approaches can build on this same framework. In the second phase, the resultant image is searched for a number of features/objects. These two phases can be implemented efficiently by exploiting the reconfigurable MultiRing network for real-time applications.

Although simple, the first phase of the operation is computationally intensive. Each of the preprocessing operations requires many thousands (millions for high-resolution images) of arithmetic operations for each picture frame. The parallelism used in preprocessing a single image frame is different from the parallelism used in preprocessing a sequence of images. Preprocessing a single frame involves manipulating a large amount of data. Therefore, a common parallelization approach used to preprocess a single digitized image is the Data-Decomposition approach, in which the data representing the image is divided, and each partial image is allocated to its own processor. As an example, the image shown in Figure 5 has been divided into four subimage tiles. Each of the tiles shown in Figure 5 (the part of the image that overlaps a tile area) is allocated to a processor for execution. Now, each processor can preprocess its own tile independently. It will be shown how this can be done on the MultiRing reconfigurable network.

FIGURE 5   An image space divided into four tiles.

The operations involved in preprocessing a sequence of images can be pipelined as shown in Figure 6. The example shows a four-level pipeline setup; while the image taken at time t, i.e., $image_t$, is being processed in P_2, the images taken at times $t + 1$ and $t + 2$, i.e., $image_{t+1}$ and $image_{t+2}$, are being processed in P_1 and P_0, respectively. Most of the algorithms for preprocessing a sequence of digitized images include a final procedure which combines processed images in a particular way. In this example, processor P_3 is allocated to perform this combine operation. This operation is application dependent, but typically involves subtracting/adding one image from/to another. Processor P_3 is initialized with a null resident image. When P_3 receives an image from P_2, it will combine the new image with the resident image and the combination will become the new resident image. At the end of a sequence of preprocessed images, the result will be a single combined image residing in P_3. If the processing is correct and if the combining procedure is properly chosen, the combined image will contain the most important features of the sequence of images that P_3 has received.

A distinct algorithm is performed by each of the processors in the pipeline. For example, in a four-stage preprocessing operation (refer to Fig. 6), P_0 is assigned to remove noise, P_1 is assigned to highlight the boundaries, P_2 is assigned to convert gray values of each pixel to binary values, and P_3 is assigned to perform the combination operation.

The processed images exiting P_2 are smoothed, have important features highlighted, and have been converted to black and white (i.e., to binary). As each becomes available, the binary images are passed to P_3 to perform the combine operation. While the entire sequence of images has gone through the pipeline, P_3 will have one summary image in a suitable form for higher-level operations such as recognition tasks. Hence, preprocessing a sequence of digitized images consists of a number of processes (four in our example), each allocated to a processor for execution. This approach is known as Process-Decomposition; this is the decomposition of a process into a number of subprocesses and allocating each subprocess to a processor (or a group of processors) for execution.

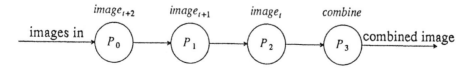

FIGURE 6   A four-level pipeline.

Here, it is beneficial to use an approach which utilizes both Process-Decomposition and Data-Decomposition.

Utilizing the Reconfigurable MultiRing Network

The reconfigurable MultiRing processor network can be used effectively to support the vision application described above. The MultiRing algorithm presented here has been devised with scalability in mind. It is assumed that there are 16 processors in the network and the image space is divided into four equal tiles as shown in Figure 5. The first phase of the algorithm, the pipeline, can efficiently utilize the MultiRing configuration shown in Figure 7. Each of the four image tiles is assigned to a processor in R_0. This assignment is done using a modified image tile broadcasting operation described earlier in the sub-section Image Tile Broadcasting (data broadcasting is achieved by exploiting the reconfiguration mechanism of the MultiRing network).

The MultiRing configuration shown in Figure 7 is suitable for a problem which is decomposed into four subproblems (because there are four rings) and in which its data are decomposed into four smaller portions (because there are four nodes in each ring).

Preprocessing operations (low-level image processing operations) are performed in basically two ways: on a point-to-point basis (pixel by pixel) or mask-oriented operations. For example, the addition of two images is accomplished on a pixel-by-pixel basis. The idea behind mask operations is to let the processed value of pixel be a function of its input value and the input values of its neighboring pixels. For instance, consider the subimage area shown in Figure 8a and suppose we wish to apply the mask shown in Figure 8b.

After performing the mask operation, the new intensity value of the centered pixel in Figure 8a will be:

$$\text{New value} = aw_1 + bw_2 + cw_3 + dw_4 + ew_5 + fw_6 + gw_7 + hw_8 + iw_9.$$

Mask operations are used widely in image processing applications. By properly selecting the coefficients and applying the mask at each pixel position in an image, it is possible to perform a variety of useful operations, such as noise reduction (smoothing), region thinning, edge highlighting. However, applying a mask at each pixel location is a computationally intensive task. For example, applying a 5×5 mask to a 512×512 image

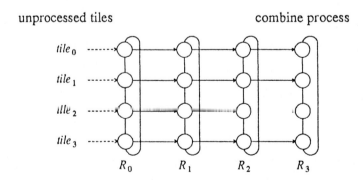

FIGURE 7   Four rings of four processors each.

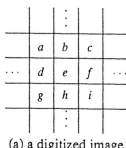

(a) a digitized image   (b) a 3 × 3 mask

FIGURE 8   The mask operation.

requires 25 multiplications and 24 additions at each pixel position; therefore, to process one digital image, 6.5 million multiplications and 6.2 million additions need to be performed. It should be noted that a mask cannot be applied to the boundaries of an image; consequently, the size of a processed image will be slightly smaller than the original one. For example, an $N \times N$ pixel image passed through a 3×3 mask will become an $(N - 2) \times (N - 2)$ pixel image. If the resultant image is passed, once more, through another 3×3 mask, then the result would be an $(N - 4) \times (N - 4)$ pixel image.

Consider the four-stage preprocessing operation (as discussed earlier): noise reduction (a mask operation), boundary highlighting (a mask operation), gray to binary conversion (a pixel-by-pixel operation), and combination of images (a pixel-by-pixel operation). The first ring, R_0, can be assigned to perform the noise reduction operation; the second R_1, can be assigned to perform the boundary highlighting operation; the third, R_2, can be assigned to perform gray to binary conversion, and the fourth, R_3, can be assigned to perform the combination operation. When the sequence of processed image tiles is provided to R_3, the combine operation will be performed, and R_3 will contain the tiles of a single image which will be in a suitable form for higher-level operations, the second phase (this phase will briefly be addressed later).

Unfortunately, the setup outlined above will not work if the image space is divided into tiles like those shown in Figure 5. The reason for this is that when an image is processed using a mask operator (in our case, the noise reduction and the boundary highlighting masks), the resultant image or tiles become smaller. Consequently, when the tiles in R_3 are *stitched* together to form a complete image (a necessary operation in the second phase), the pixels overlapping the tiles boundaries will have incorrect values.

The pixel values around each tile will be correct if the processors in each ring are allowed to communicate with each other (to get the required neighboring pixel values before applying each mask operation) during the execution of the algorithm; or, the image space can be divided into tiles that overlap each other by L pixels, where the value of L depends on the size of the masks used. For example, if the size of each of the two masks (noise reduction and boundary highlighting masks) is 3×3 (Figure 8b), then each tile in the original digital image must overlap with its neighbors by four pixels in each direction, as shown in Figure 9. Now the processors in each ring can perform their tasks independently without any communications within each ring.

In the second phase of the algorithm, the system searches for some particular fea-

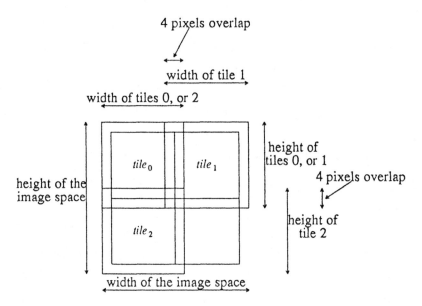

FIGURE 9   An image space divided into four overlapping tiles (only three are shown).

tures in the combined image; because this task is very application dependent, the details will not be addressed in this article (refer to Ref. 44 for one example). Here, it is shown, in a generic way, that particular features of the combined image can be detected efficiently on the MultiRing.

Each processed image tile of the combined image (residing in R_3) is made available to all the processors of the MultiRing. Therefore, after performing this operation, each processor will have a copy of the entire combined image (i.e., after a tile *stitching* operation) in its memory. This can be done efficiently using the reconfiguration capability of the MultiRing. This is a particular broadcasting operation (named gossiping) which has been described in the subsection Each Node Broadcasting Its Data to the Entire System—Gossiping. With its own copy of the combined image, each processor in the MultiRing can independently search for a particular feature in the image. In our example, a Multi-Ring with 16 processors, 16 different objects/features can be searched for simultaneously (refer to Ref. 45 for a number of standard searching techniques used in recognizing features in a sequence of digitized images).

Note that in the first phase of the algorithm, the processes assigned to rings R_0 and R_1 are more computationally expensive than the ones assigned to R_2 and R_3. Consequently, for each image, R_2 and R_3 will be idle for a period of time. Analysis of the algorithm indicates that the processors in R_0 and R_1 will be idle for approximately 5% of their times, whereas the processors in R_2 and R_3 will be idle for approximately 36% of their times.

Constructing the MultiRing Network

This subsection addresses the problem of constructing the MultiRing network using off-the-shelf components developed by the Inmos transputer products. The components that will be required include the Inmos transputer (46) and crossbar switch chips (46). Here,

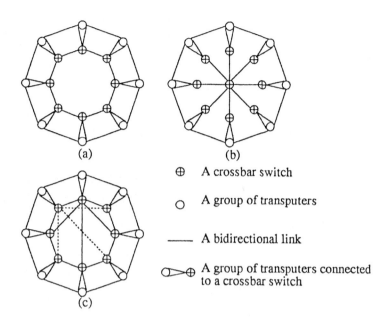

FIGURE 10   The construction of a MultiRing using crossbar switches.

it is shown that the MultiRing network can be built by using transputers as nodes and crossbar switches as the network configurer.

Constructing a Large-Scale MultiRing Using Transputer Products

Here, the problem of constructing the MultiRing network using the existing crossbar switching technology is addressed. Constructing a 32-node MultiRing (or smaller) is straightforward. An IMS C104 switch and 32 Inmos transputers linked to it will form a completely connected network. This network can be used as a 32-node MultiRing.

A more interesting problem to address is the case where the number of nodes in the network is greater than the number of connections allowed in a single crossbar switch (e.g., greater than 32 in the case of IMS C104). There are three solutions to this problem, as shown in Figure 10.

A link over which an excessive amount of communication is required to take place at any instant is referred to as a *hot-spot* link. In all three arrangements shown in Figure 10, the links that interconnect the crossbar switches are potential "hot spots." Preliminary studies have shown that the setup in Figure 10a is suitable for applications that mostly demand a few large rings of processors. This is due to the fact that as the number of rings increase, there would potentially be more traffic over the links that interconnect the switches. However, the setup is very simple and is very naturally scalable. The setup shown in Figure 10b, is found to be suitable for applications that mostly demand a few large rings of processors. But, compared to the arrangement shown in Figure 10a, there would potentially be less traffic over the links that interconnect the switches. This network is also quite scalable but requires special care when the number of links to the center switch becomes greater than the number of connections allowed to that switch.

The switch links in the setup shown in Figure 10c generates less traffic than the other two arrangements (Figure 10c shows only a subset of the switch links). But it is not as scalable as the other two.

REFERENCES

1. A. J. Anderson, *Multiple Processing—A Systems Overview*, Prentice-Hall, Englewood Cliff, NJ, 1989, pp. 232–233.
2. R. Karia and A. Teruel, "Mapping Rings onto Arbitrary Transputer Networks," in *Proc. 4th Conf. of North American Transputer Users Group (NATUG 4)*, New York, 1990, pp. 30–35.
3. J. Beck and N. Morgan, "Ring Array Processor Project Update," *Int. Computer Sci. Instit. Newslett.*, 4(1), 8–11 (1991).
4. H. R. Arabnia, "A Computer Input Device for Severely Disabled People," in *Proc. 2nd Conf. of North American Transputer Users Group (NATUG 2)*, Durham, NC, 1989, pp. 53–61.
5. H. R. Arabnia, "A Multi-Ring Transputer Network for the Arbitrary Rotation of Raster Images," in *Proc. 1990 Int. Conf. on Parallel Processing*, Vol. I of III (Architecture), Chicago, IL, 1990, pp. 591–593.
6. H. R. Arabnia, "A Parallel Algorithm for the Arbitrary Rotation of Digitized Images using Process-and-Data-Decomposition Approach," *J. Parallel Distrib. Computing*, 10(2), 188–193, 1990.
7. H. R. Arabnia, "Real-Time Preprocessing of Multiple Images Using an Unconventional Pipeline Approach," in *Proc. 4th Conf. of North American Transputers Users Group (NATUG 4)*, New York, 1990, pp. 57–66.
8. H. R. Arabnia, "Towards a General-Purpose Parallel System for Imaging Operations," in *Proc. 1991 Inter. Conf. on Parallel Processing I, Architecture*, CRC Press, Boca Raton, FL, 1991, pp. 644–646.
9. H. R. Arabnia, "Two Parallel Sort Algorithms: Pipelined-Sort and MultiRing-Sort," in *Proc. 5th Conf. of North American Transputer Users Group (NATUG 5)*, 1992, pp. 1–11.
10. H. R. Arabnia and M. A. Oliver, "Fast Operations on Raster Images with SIMD Machine Architectures," *Int. J. Eurograph. Assoc. (Computer Graphics Forum)*, 5(3), 179–189 (1986).
11. H. R. Arabnia and M. A. Oliver, "A Transputer Network for the Arbitrary Rotation of Digitised Images," *Computer J.*, 30(5), 425–433 (1987).
12. H. R. Arabnia and M. A. Oliver, "Arbitrary Rotation of Raster Images with SIMD Machine Architectures," *Int. J. of Eurograph. Assoc. (Computer Graphics Forum)*, 6(1), 3–12 (1987).
13. H. R. Arabnia and M. A. Oliver, "A Transputer Network for Fast Operations on Digitised Images," *Int. J. Eurograph. Assoc. (Computer Graphics Forum)*, 8(1), 3–12 (1989).
14. H. R. Arabnia and M. R. Robinson, "Parallelizing Using Process-and-Data-Decomposition (PADD) Approach on a Multi-Ring Transputer Network—An Example," in *Proc. 3rd Conf. of North American Transputer Users Group (NATUG 3)*, Sunnyvale, CA, 1990, pp. 107–118.
15. H. R. Arabnia and M. A. Oliver, "A Reconfigurable Network of Processors," in *The International Conference on Parallel and Distributed Processing Techniques and Applications (PDPTA '95)*, Nov. 3–4, Athens, GA, 1995, pp. 134–148.
16. W. Allen and A. Saha, "Parallel Neural-Network Simulation Using Back-Propagation for the ES-Kit Environment," in *Proc. 4th Conf. on Hypercubes, Concurrent Computers, and Applications*, March 1989, pp. 1097–1102.
17. M. Celenk and C. K. Lim, "Hypercube Mapped Ring and Mesh Implementations of Low-Level Vision Algorithms," in *Proc. 4th Conf. on Hypercubes, Concurrent Computers, and Applications*, March 1989, pp. 1103–1110.
18. D. J. Kleikamp and R. W. Wilkerson, "Associative–Commutative Unification in a Multicom-

puter Environment," in *Proc. 4th Conf. on Hypercubes, Concurrent Computers, and Applications*, March 1989, pp. 901–908.

19. P. C. Nelson, "Parallel Heuristic Search Using Islands," in *Proc. 4th Conf. on Hypercubes, Concurrent Computers, and Applications*, March 1989, pp. 909–915.

20. R. K. Agarwal, "Development of a Navier–Stokes Code on a Connection Machine," in *Proc. 4th Conf. on Hypercubes, Concurrent Computers, and Applications*, March 1989, pp. 917–924.

21. I. G. Angus and W. T. Thompkins, "Data Storage, Concurrency, and Portability: An Object Oriented Approach to Fluid Mechanics," in *Proc. 4th Conf. on Hypercubes, Concurrent Computers, and Applications*, March 1989, pp. 925–932.

22. E. Barszcz, "Performance of an Euler Code on Hypercubes," in *Proc. 4th Conf. on Hypercubes, Concurrent Computers, and Applications*, March 1989, pp. 933–940.

23. M. E. Braaten, "Computational Fluid Dynamics on Hypercube Parallel Computers," in *Proc. 4th Conf. on Hypercubes, Concurrent Computers, and Applications*, March 1989, pp. 949–952.

24. J. H. Baek and K. A. Teague, "Parallel Edge Detection on the Hypercube," in *Proc. 4th Conf. on Hypercubes, Concurrent Computers, and Applications*, March 1989, pp. 983–986.

25. J. H. Baek and K. A. Teague, "Parallel Object Representation Using Straight Lines on the Hypercube Multiprocessor Computer," in *Proc. 4th Conf. on Hypercubes, Concurrent Computers, and Applications*, March 1989, pp. 987–990.

26. A. N. Choudhary, S. Das, N. Ahuja, and J. H. Patel, "Surface Reconstruction from Stereo Images: An Implementation on a Hypercube Multiprocessor," in *Proc. 4th Conf. on Hypercubes, Concurrent Computers, and Applications*, March 1989, pp. 1045–1048.

27. H. I. Christensen and J. P. Jones, "Concurrent Multi-Resolution Image Analysis," in *Proc. 4th Conf. on Hypercubes, Concurrent Computers, and Applications*, March 1989, pp. 1031–1038.

28. H. Embrechts and R. Dirk, "Efficiency and Load Balancing Issues for a Parallel Component Labeling Algorithm," in *Proc. 4th Conf. on Hypercubes, Concurrent Computers, and Applications*, March 1989, pp. 1005–1008.

29. B. A. Huntsberger and T. L. Huntsberger, "Hypercube Algorithms for Multi-spectral Texture Analysis," in *Proc. 4th Conf. on Hypercubes, Concurrent Computers, and Applications*, March 1989, pp. 1009–1012.

30. S. Ranka and S. Sahni, "Image Transformations on Hypercube and Mesh Multicomputers," in *Parallel Architectures and Algorithms for Image Understanding*, V. K. Prasanna Kumar (ed.), Academic Press, San Diego, CA, 1991, pp. 227–271.

31. D. A. Simoni, B. A. Zimmerman, J. E. Patterson, C. Wu, and J. C. Peterson, "Synthetic Aperture Radar Processing Using the Hypercube Concurrent Architecture," in *Proc. 4th Conf. on Hypercubes, Concurrent Computers, and Applications*, March 1989, pp. 1023–1030.

32. C. C. Christara and E. N. Houstis, "A Domain Decomposition Spline Collocation Method for Elliptic Partial Differential Equations," in *Proc. 4th Conf. on Hypercubes, Concurrent Computers, and Applications*, March 1989, pp. 1267–1273.

33. G. L. Hennigan, S. P. Castillo, and E. Hensel, "The Feasibility of the FFT Applied to the Transient Solution of Field Problems Using Finite Elements," in *Proc. 4th Conf. on Hypercubes, Concurrent Computers, and Applications*, March 1989, pp. 1279–1286.

34. K. Hwang and F. A. Briggs, *Computer Architecture and Parallel Processing (SIMD Matrix Multiplication)*, McGraw-Hill, New York, 1985, pp. 355–361.

35. E. F. Van de Velde, "Multicomputer Matrix Computations: Theory and Practice," in *Proc. 4th Conf. on Hypercubes, Concurrent Computers, and Applications*, March 1989, pp. 1303–1308.

36. D. E. Womble, "Two Time Stepping Algorithms for Parallel Computers," in *Proc. 4th Conf. on Hypercubes, Concurrent Computers, and Applications*, March 1989, pp. 1291–1295.

37. S. Mattisson, L. Peterson, A. Skjellum, and C. L. Seitz, "Circuit Simulation on a Hypercube,"

in *Proc. 4th Conf. on Hypercubes, Concurrent Computers, and Applications*, March 1989, pp. 1297–1301.

38. K. Hwang and F. A. Briggs, *Computer Architecture and Parallel Processing (Parallel Sorting on Array Processors)*, McGraw-Hill, New York, 1985, pp. 361–367.

39. S. Hutchingson, S. Castillo, and E. Hensel, "A Basic Finite Element Code on the Connection Machine," in *Proc. 4th Conf. on Hypercubes, Concurrent Computers, and Applications*, March 1989, pp. 1339–1342.

40. J. G. Malone, "Automated Mesh Decomposition and Concurrent Finite Element Analysis for Hypercube Multiprocessor Computers," *Computer Methods Appl. Mech. Eng., 70*, 27–58 (1988).

41. H. R. Arabnia and J. W. Smith, "A Reconfigurable Interconnection Network for Imaging Operations and Its Implementation Using A Multi-Stage Switching Box," *1993 High Performance Computing: New Horizons*, Alberta, Canada, June 1993.

42. K. Hwang and F. A. Briggs, "*Computer Architecture and Parallel Processing (Cube Interconnection Networks)*," McGraw-Hill, New York, 1985, pp. 342–345.

43. R. C. G. Gonzalez and P. Wintz, *Digital Image Processing*, 2nd ed., Addison-Wesley, Reading, MA, 1987.

44. S. M. Bhandarkar and H. R. Arabnia, "Parallel 3-D Object Recognition," in *Proc. 1993 Int. Conf. on Signal Processing (ICSP '93)*, 1993.

45. T. S. Huang (ed.), *Image Sequence Analysis*, Springer-Verlag, New York, 1981.

46. Inmos, *The T9000 Transputer, Product Overview*, SGS-Thomson Microelectronics, Bristol, United Kingdom, 1991; DS-Links. Tech. Inform. X3T9.2/92-80R0, April 1992, pp. 10–17.

HAMID R. ARABNIA

TREES, CYCLES, AND COCYCLES OF FUZZY GRAPHS

FUZZY SUBSETS

History

Imprecise and vague concepts abound in natural language. For example, consider the following statement from the financial section of a city newspaper. "A strong rally in technology shares pulled the stock market higher by midday Wednesday, erasing losses that were tied to a sharp and surprising rise in the nation's durable-goods orders." Even simple statements such as "Paul is tall" or "It is very windy today" are difficult to reword into more precise statements without losing some of their semantic value. However, these types of statements give richness to a language. In fact, these kind of statements are frequently important in expert systems.

In 1965, Zadeh published his seminal article "Fuzzy Sets" (1) which described fuzzy set theory and, consequently, fuzzy logic. The purpose of Zadeh's article was to develop a theory which could deal with ambiguity and imprecision of certain classes or sets in human thinking, particularly in the domains of pattern recognition, communication of information, and abstraction. This theory proposed making the grade of membership of an element in a subset of a universal set a value in the closed interval [0, 1] of real numbers. With this idea in mind, if Paul were 6 ft tall, he might be assigned the grade of membership 3/4, say, in the "set" of tall people.

Zadeh's ideas have found applications in computer science, artificial intelligence, decision analysis, information science, system science, control engineering, expert systems, pattern recognition, management science, operations research, and robotics. Theoretical mathematics has also been touched by fuzzy set theory. The ideas of fuzzy set theory have been introduced into topology, abstract algebra, geometry, graph theory, and analysis. In this article, we discuss some of the ideas of fuzzy graph theory. In particular, we focus on the notions of trees, cycles, and cocycles of fuzzy graphs. We also discuss some applications of fuzzy graphs. Our approach follows that of Rosenfeld, the father of fuzzy abstract algebra, in his article (2) on fuzzy graphs.

Fuzzy Subsets and Fuzzy Relations

Let S be a set. A *fuzzy subset* σ of S is a mapping $\sigma: S \to [0, 1]$ which assigns to each element $x \in S$ a degree of membership, $0 \leq \sigma(x) \leq 1$. Similarly, a *fuzzy relation* on S is a fuzzy subset of the Cartesian product, $S \times S$, of S with itself; that is, a mapping $\mu: S \times S \to [0, 1]$ which assigns to each ordered pair of elements (x, y) a degree of membership, $0 \leq \mu(x, y) \leq 1$. In the special cases where σ and μ can only take on the values 0 and 1, they become the characteristic functions of an ordinary subset of S and an ordinary relation on S, respectively; that is, if X is a subset of S and $\sigma: S \to \{0, 1\}$ is defined by $\sigma(x) = 1$ if $x \in X$ and $\sigma(x) = 0$ if $x \notin X$, then σ is the characteristic function of X in S.

If T is a subset of S and $R \subseteq S \times S$ a relation on S, then R is a relation on T provided that $(x, y) \in R$ implies $x \in T$ and $y \in T$ for all $x, y \in S$. Let τ and ρ be the characteristic functions of T and R, respectively. Then, this condition can be restated as

$$\rho(x, y) = 1 \text{ implies } \tau(x) = \tau(y) = 1$$

for all x, y in S. This is implied by

$$\rho(x, y) \leq \tau(x) \wedge \tau(y)$$

for all x and y in S, where $\wedge$ means "minimum." We also use the notation $\wedge$ to denote the infimum of a subset of $[0, 1]$.

Returning to the general case where σ is a fuzzy subset of S and μ a *fuzzy relation* on S, we shall say that μ is a *fuzzy relation* on σ if and only if

$$\mu(x, y) \leq \sigma(x) \wedge \sigma(y)$$

for all x and y in S. In other words, for μ to be a fuzzy relation on σ, we require that the degree of membership of a pair of elements never exceed the degree of membership of either of the elements themselves. (If we think of the elements as nodes in a graph and the ordered pairs as arcs, this amounts to requiring that the "strength" of an arc can never exceed the strengths of its end nodes.)

Let μ be a fuzzy relation on σ. Then, μ is called the strongest fuzzy relation on σ if for all fuzzy relations ν on σ, $\nu \leq \mu$; that is,

$$\nu(x, y) \leq \mu(x, y)$$

for all $x, y \in S$.

Given a fuzzy subset σ of S, we define $\mu_\sigma : S \times S \to [0, 1]$ by $\mu_\sigma(x, y) = \sigma(x) \wedge \sigma(y)$ for all $x, y \in S$. Clearly, μ_σ is a fuzzy relation on σ. Let ν be any fuzzy relation on σ. Then, for all $x, y \in S$, $\nu(x, y) \leq \sigma(x) \wedge \sigma(y) = \mu_\sigma(x, y)$. Thus, μ_σ is the *strongest fuzzy relation* on σ that is a fuzzy relation on S.

Let μ be a fuzzy relation on S and let σ be a fuzzy subset of S. Then, σ is called the *weakest fuzzy subset* of S on which μ is a fuzzy relation if $\forall$ fuzzy subsets τ of S on which μ is a fuzzy relation, $\sigma(x) \leq \tau(x) \ \forall x \in S$.

Given a fuzzy relation μ on S, define the fuzzy subset σ_μ of S by

$$\sigma_\mu(x) = \sup\{\mu(x, y) \vee \mu(y, x) \mid y \in S\}$$

for all $x \in S$, where $\vee$ means "maximum." (The notation $\vee$ is also used to denote the supremum of a subset of $[0, 1]$.) Then $\sigma_\mu(x) \wedge \sigma_\mu(y) = \sup\{\mu(x, z) \vee \mu(z, x) \mid z \in S\} \wedge \sup\{\mu(y, w) \vee \mu(w, y) \mid w \in S\} \geq \mu(x, y) \wedge \mu(x, y) = \mu(x, y) \ \forall x, y \in S$ and so μ is a fuzzy relation on σ_μ. Let τ be any fuzzy subset of S on which μ is a fuzzy relation. Then, $\sigma_\mu(x) = \sup\{\mu(x, y) \vee \mu(y, x) \mid y \in S\} \leq \sup\{(\tau(x) \vee (\tau(y)) \vee \tau(y) \vee \tau(x)) \mid y \in S\} \leq \tau(x)$. Hence, σ_μ is the weakest fuzzy subset of S on which μ is a fuzzy relation.

For any t, $0 \leq t \leq 1$, the set $\sigma_t = \{x \in S \mid \sigma(x) \geq t\}$ is often called a *t-cut* or a *level* subset of S with respect to σ. The t-cut

$$\mu_t = \{(x, y) \in S \times S \mid \mu(x, y) \geq t\}$$

is a relation on S. Now, suppose that μ is a fuzzy relation on σ. Then, $\mu(x, y) \leq \sigma(x) \wedge \sigma(y)$. Let $(x, y) \in \mu_t$, where $0 \leq t \leq 1$. Then, $t \leq \mu(x, y)$. Hence, $t \leq \sigma(x)$ and $t \leq \sigma(y)$. Thus, $x, y \in \sigma_t$. Therefore, we can conclude that μ_t is a relation on σ_t. If $\mu_t = \emptyset$, then μ_t is vacuously a relation σ_t.

Composition of Fuzzy Relations

Throughout this section, μ and ν are fuzzy relations on σ, where σ is a fuzzy subset of a set S. The *composite* of μ and ν is the fuzzy subset $\mu \circ \nu$ of $S \times S$ defined by

$$(\mu \circ \nu)\,(x,\,z) = \sup\{\mu(x,\,y) \wedge \nu(y,\,z) \mid y \in S\}$$

for all x and z in S. This definition is often called a *sup-min composition*. It is motivated, in part, by the notion of a chain being as strong as its weakest link.

For all $x,\,y,\,z \in S$, we have $\mu(x,\,y) \le \sigma(x) \wedge \sigma(y)$ and $\nu(y,\,z) \le \sigma(y) \wedge \sigma(z)$. Thus, $\mu(x,\,y) \wedge \nu(y,\,z) \le \sigma(x) \wedge \sigma(y) \wedge \sigma(z) \le \sigma(x) \wedge \sigma(z)$ for every $y \in S$, so that $(\mu \circ \nu)(x,\,z) = \sup\{\mu(x,\,y) \wedge \nu(y,\,z) \mid y \in S\} \le \sigma(x) \wedge \sigma(z)$ for all $x,\,z \in S$. This shows that $\mu \circ \nu$ is a fuzzy relation on σ.

It is well known that composition of fuzzy relations is associative; that is, for all μ, ν, and ρ, we have $\mu \circ (\nu \circ \rho) = (\mu \circ \nu) \circ \rho$. We can, thus, uniquely define the powers of a fuzzy relation as $\mu^1 = \mu$, $\mu^2 = \mu \circ \mu$, $\mu^3 = \mu \circ \mu^2 = \mu \circ \mu \circ \mu$, and so on. We shall also define μ^∞ as follows:

$$\mu^\infty(x,\,y) = \sup\{\mu^k(x,\,y) \mid k = 1,\,2,\,\dots\}$$

for all $x,\,y \in S$. Finally, it is convenient to define

$$\mu^0(x,\,y) = \begin{cases} 0 & \text{if } x \ne y \\ \sigma(x) & \text{if } x = y \end{cases}$$

for all x and y in S.

It is not difficult to show for all t, $0 \le t \le 1$, that $(\mu \circ \nu)_t \supseteq \mu_t \circ \nu_t$ and that $(\mu \circ \nu)_t = \mu_t \circ \nu_t$ if S is finite.

Let μ, ν, and ρ be fuzzy relations on S such that $\mu \le \nu$ and $\lambda \le \rho$. Let $x,\,z \in S$. Then, $(\mu \circ \lambda)\,(x,\,z) = \sup\{\mu(x,\,y) \wedge \lambda(y,\,z) \mid y \in S\} \le \sup\{\nu(x,\,y) \wedge \rho(y,\,z) \mid y \in S\} = (\nu \circ \rho)\,(x,\,z)$. Thus, $\mu \circ \lambda \le \nu \circ \rho$; that is, $\mu \le \nu$ and $\lambda \le \rho$ implies $\mu \circ \lambda \le \nu \circ \rho$.

Reflexivity, Symmetry, and Transitivity

In this section, we define the notions of reflexivity, symmetry, and transitivity for fuzzy relations. We state, without proof, some of their basic properties. The proofs can be found in Ref. 2

Throughout this section, μ is a fuzzy relation on σ, where σ is a fuzzy subset of a set S.

We call μ *reflexive* if $\mu(x,\,x) = \sigma(x)$ for all $x \in S$. [This generalizes the usual definition, which requires $\mu(x,\,x) = 1$ for all $x \in S$.]

Proposition 1. *If μ is reflexive, then $\mu(x,\,y) \le \mu(x,\,x)$ and $\mu(y,\,x) \le \mu(x,\,x)$ for all $x,\,y \in S$.*

Proposition 2. *If μ is a reflexive fuzzy relation on σ, then for any $0 \le t \le 1$, μ_t is a reflexive relation on σ_t.*

Proposition 3. *Suppose that μ is reflexive. Then, the following conditions hold:*

1. *If ν is a fuzzy relation on S, $\mu \circ \nu \ge \nu$ and $\nu \circ \mu \ge \nu$.*
2. *If ν is a reflexive fuzzy relation on S, then $\mu \circ \nu$ is reflexive.*
3. *$\mu \le \mu \circ \mu$.*

4. $\mu^0 \le \mu^1 \le \mu^2 \le \cdots \le \mu^\infty$.
5. $\mu^0(x, x) = \mu^1(x, x) = \mu^2(x, x) = \cdots \mu^\infty(x, x) = \sigma(x)$ *for all* $x \in S$.

We call μ symmetric if $\mu(x, y) = \mu(y, x)$ for all x and y in S. It is clear that if μ is symmetric, so is μ_t for any threshold t. Note that the symmetric property does not depend on the choice of fuzzy subset σ, unlike reflexivity.

Proposition 4.   *If μ and v are symmetric, then $\mu \bigcirc v$ is symmetric if and only if* $\mu \bigcirc v = v \bigcirc \mu$.

Corollary 5.   *If μ is symmetric, so is every power of μ.*

We call μ *transitive* if $\mu \bigcirc \mu \le \mu$. Note that, like symmetry, this property does not depend on σ. Clearly, transitivity implies $\mu^k \le \mu$ for all k, so that $\mu^\infty \le \mu$. It is also easily seen that for any μ, μ^∞ is transitive.

Proposition 6.   *If μ is symmetric and transitive, then $\mu(x, y) \le \mu(x, x)$ for all x and y in S.*

Proposition 7.   *If μ is a transitive relation on σ, then for any $0 \le t \le 1$, μ_t is a transitive relation on σ_t.*

Proposition 8.   *Let μ, v, and ρ be fuzzy relations on S.*

1. *If μ is transitive and v and ρ are each $\le \mu$, then $v \bigcirc \rho \le \mu$.*
2. *If μ is transitive, v is reflexive, and $v \le \mu$, then $v \bigcirc \mu = v \bigcirc \mu = \mu$.*
3. *If μ is reflexive and transitive, then $\mu \bigcirc \mu = \mu$.*
4. *If μ is reflexive and transitive, then $\mu^0 \le \mu^1 = \mu^2 = \cdots = \mu^\infty$.*
5. *If μ and v are transitive and $\mu \bigcirc v = v \bigcirc \mu$, then $\mu \bigcirc v$ is transitive.*

FUZZY GRAPHS

Fuzzy Graphs

Any relation $R \subseteq S \times S$ on a set S can be regarded as defining a *graph* with node set S and arc set R. Similarly, any fuzzy relation $\mu : S \times S \to [0, 1]$ can be regarded as defining a *weighted graph*, or *fuzzy graph*, where the arc $(x, y) \in S \times S$ has weight $\mu(x, y) \in [0, 1]$. In this and the following sections, we shall use graph terminology and introduce fuzzy analogs of several basic graph-theoretical concepts. For simplicity, we will consider only undirected graphs (i.e., we assume that our fuzzy relation is symmetric) so that all arcs can be regarded as unordered pairs of nodes. {We will never need to consider loops [i.e., arcs of the form (x, x)]; we can assume, if we wish, that our fuzzy relation is reflexive.}

Formally, a fuzzy graph $G = (\sigma, \mu)$ is a pair of functions $\sigma : S \to [0, 1]$ and $\mu : S \times S \to [0, 1]$ where for all x and y in S, we have $\mu(x, y) \le \sigma(x) \land \sigma(y)$. The fuzzy graph $H = (\tau, v)$ is called a *fuzzy subgraph* of G if

$\tau \le \sigma$ [i.e., $\tau(x) \le \sigma(x)$ for all $x \in S$]

and

$v \le \mu$,   [i.e., $v(x, y) \le \mu(x, y)$ for all $x, y \in S$].

It may be noted that the definition of a fuzzy subgraph used here is the one used in Ref. 2. It differs from the one in Ref. 3. According to Ref. 3, H is a partial fuzzy subgraph of G.

For any threshold t, $0 \leq t \leq 1$, we recall that $\sigma_t = \{x \in S \mid \sigma(x) \geq t\}$ and $\mu_t = \{(x, y) \in S \times S \mid \mu(x, y) \geq t\}$. Then, as seen earlier, we have $\mu_t \subseteq \sigma_t \times \sigma_t$ so that $\sigma_t, \mu_t)$ is a graph with the node set σ_t and arc set μ_t.

Proposition 9. *If $0 \leq u \leq v \leq 1$, then (σ_v, μ_v) is a subgraph of (σ_u, μ_u).*

Proposition 10. *If (τ, ν) is a fuzzy subgraph of (σ, μ), then for any threshold t, $0 \leq t \leq 1$, (τ_t, ν_t) is a subgraph of (σ_t, μ_t).*

We say that the fuzzy subgraph (τ, ν) spans the fuzzy graph (σ, μ) if $\tau(x) = \sigma(x)$ for all x. In this case, the two graphs have the same fuzzy node set; they differ only in the arc weights.

For any fuzzy subset τ of σ [i.e., such that $\tau(x) \leq \sigma(x)$ for all x], the fuzzy subgraph of (σ, μ) induced by τ is the maximal fuzzy subgraph of (σ, μ) that has fuzzy node set τ. Evidently, this is just the fuzzy graph (τ, ν), where

$$\nu(x, y) = \tau(x) \wedge \tau(y) \wedge \mu(x, y)$$

for all $x, y \in S$. We will assume from now on that the underlying set S of a fuzzy graph is always finite.

Paths and Connectedness

A *path* ρ in a fuzzy graph is a sequence of distinct nodes $x_0, x_1, \ldots, x_n$ such that $\mu(x_{i-1}, x_i) > 0, 1 \leq i \leq n$; here, $n \geq 0$ is called the *length* of ρ. The consecutive pairs (x_{i-1}, x_i) are called the arcs of the path. The *strength* of ρ is defined as $\bigwedge_{i=1}^{n} \mu(x_{i-1}, x_i)$. In other words, the strength of a path is defined to be the weight of the weakest arc of the path. If the path has length 0, it is convenient to define its strength to be $\sigma(x_0)$. We call ρ a *cycle* if $x_0 = x_n$ and $n \geq 3$.

Two nodes that are joined by a path are said to be *connected*. It is evident that "connected" is a reflexive, symmetric relation, and it is readily seen to be transitive also. In fact, x and y are connected if and only if $\mu^\infty(x, y) > 0$. The equivalence classes of nodes under this relation are called connected components of the given fuzzy graph; they are just its maximal connected fuzzy subgraphs. A *strongest path* joining any two nodes x and y has strength $\mu^\infty(x, y)$; we shall sometimes refer to this as the strength of connectedness between the nodes.

Proposition 11. *If (τ, ν) is a fuzzy subgraph of (σ, μ), then $\nu^\infty(x, y) \leq \mu^\infty(x, y)$ for all x and y in S.*

Bridges and Cutnodes

Let $G = (\sigma, \mu)$ be a fuzzy graph, let x and y be any two distinct nodes, and let G' be the fuzzy subgraph of G obtained by deleting the arc (x, y) [i.e., $G' = (\sigma, \mu')$, where $\mu'(x, y) = 0$ and $\mu' = \mu$ for all other pairs]. We say that $x, y)$ is a *bridge* in G if $\mu'^\infty(u, v) < \mu^\infty(u, v)$ for some u, v; in other words, if deleting the arc (x, y) reduces the strength of connectedness between some pair of nodes. Evidently, (x, y) is a bridge if and only if there exist u and v such that (x, y) is an arc of every strongest path from u to v.

Theorem 12. *The following statements are equivalent:*

1. (x, y) *is a bridge.*
2. $\mu'^{\infty}(x, y) < \mu(x, y).$
3. (x, y) *is not the weakest arc of any cycle.*

Let w be any node in S and let G' be the fuzzy subgraph of G obtained by deleting the node w; that is, G' is the fuzzy subgraph induced by σ', where $\sigma'(w) = 0$ and $\sigma'(x) = \sigma(x)$ for all $x \in S \backslash \{w\}$. Note that in $G' = (\sigma', \mu')$, we must have $\mu'(w, z) = 0$ for all z. We say that w is a *cutnode* in G if $\mu^{*\infty}(u, v) < \mu^{\infty}(u, v)$ for some u, v (other than w); in other words, if deleting the node w reduces the strength of connectedness between some other pair of nodes. Evidently, w is a cutnode if and only if there exist u, v, distinct from w, such that w is on every strongest path from u to v.

G is called *nonseparable* (or, sometimes, a *block*) if it has no cutnodes. It should be pointed out that a block may have bridges. (This cannot happen for nonfuzzy graphs.) For example, in Figure 1, arc (x, y) is a bridge because its deletion reduces the strength of connectedness between x and y from 1 to $\frac{1}{2}$. However, it is easily verified that no node of this fuzzy graph is a cutnode.

If between every two nodes x and y of G there exist two strongest paths that are disjoint (except for x and y themselves), G is evidently a block. This is analogous to the "if" of the nonfuzzy graph theorem that G is a block (with at least three nodes) if and only if every two nodes of G lie on a common cycle. The "only if," on the other hand, does not hold in the fuzzy case, as the example just given shows.

Forests and Trees

We recall that a (nonfuzzy) graph that has no cycles is called *acyclic*, or a *forest*, and a connected forest is called a *tree*. For a fuzzy graph, we define a forest and a fuzzy forest. Similarly, we introduce the concepts of a tree and a fuzzy tree for a fuzzy graph. We shall call a fuzzy graph a *forest* if the graph consisting of its nonzero arcs is a forest, and a *tree* if this graph is also connected.

We call the fuzzy graph $G = (\sigma, \mu)$ a *fuzzy forest* if it has a fuzzy spanning subgraph $F = (\sigma, \nu)$ which is a forest, where for all arcs (x, y) not in F [i.e., such that $\nu(x, y) = 0$], we have $\mu(x, y) < \nu^{\infty}(x, y)$. Thus, if $(x, y) \in G$, but $(x, y) \notin F$, there is a path in F between x and y whose strength is greater than $\mu(x, y)$. It is clear that a forest is a fuzzy forest.

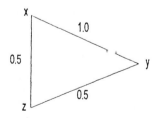

FIGURE 1   Fuzzy graph with a bridge; but no cutnodes.

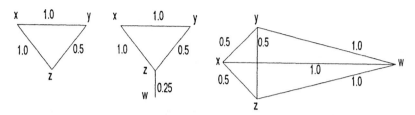

FIGURE 2   Fuzzy forests.

The fuzzy graphs in Figure 2 are fuzzy forests; the fuzzy graphs in Figure 3 are not fuzzy forests.

If G is connected, clearly so is F (any arc of a path in G is either in F, or can be diverted through F). In this case, we call G a *fuzzy tree*. The examples of fuzzy forests given in Figure 2 are all fuzzy trees.

Note that if we replaced $\mu(x, y) < v^{\infty}(x, y)$ by $\mu(x, y) \leq v^{\infty}(x, y)$ in the above definition, then even the graph in Figure 4 would be a fuzzy forest, as it has subgraphs such as the one given in Figure 5.

Let G be a fuzzy graph and let (x, y) be an arc, belonging to a cycle of G such that $\mu(x, y) < \mu'^{\infty}(x, y)$, where the prime denotes deletion of the arc (x, y) from G and $\mu(x, y)$ is the smallest. If we delete (x, y), the resulting fuzzy subgraph satisfies the path property of a fuzzy forest. If there are still cycles in this graph, we can repeat the process. Note that at each stage, no previously deleted arc is stronger than the arc being currently deleted; hence, the path guaranteed by the property of the theorem involves only arcs that have not yet been deleted. When no cycles remain, the resulting fuzzy subgraph is a forest F. Let (x, y) not be an arc of F; thus, (x, y) is one of the arcs that we deleted in the process of constructing F, and there is a path from x to y that is stronger than $\mu(x, y)$ and that does not involve (x, y) nor any of the arcs deleted prior to it. If this path involves arcs that were deleted later, it can be diverted around them using a path of still stronger arcs; if any of these were deleted later, the path can be further diverted, and so on. This process eventually stabilizes with a path consisting entirely of arcs of F. Thus, G is a fuzzy forest.

Conversely, if G is a fuzzy forest, let ρ be any cycle; then, some arc (x, y) of ρ is not in F. Thus, by the definition of a fuzzy forest, we have $\mu(x, y) < v^{\infty}(x, y) \leq \mu'^{\infty}(x, y)$. Thus, we have the following result.

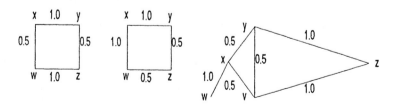

FIGURE 3   Fuzzy graphs, but not fuzzy forests.

FIGURE 4   Fuzzy forest if $\mu(x, y) \leq 2^\infty (x, y)$ replaces $\mu(x, y) < 2^\infty (x, y)$.

Theorem 13.   *G is a fuzzy forest if and only if in any cycle of G, there is an arc (x, y) such that $\mu(x, y) < \mu'^\infty(x, y)$, where the prime denotes deletion of the arc (x, y) from G.*

Note that if G is connected, so is the constructed F in our discussion above because no step of the construction disconnects. Theorem 13 leads to the next result.

Proposition 14.   *If there is at most strongest path between any two nodes of G, then G must be a fuzzy forest.*

The converse of Proposition 14 is false; G can be a fuzzy forest and still have multiple strongest paths between nodes. This is because the strength of a path is that of its weakest arc, and as long as this arc lies in F, there is little constraint on the other arcs. For example, the fuzzy graph in Figure 6 is a fuzzy forest; here, F consists of all arcs except (a, y). The strongest paths between x and y have strength $\frac{1}{4}$, due to the arc (x, a); both $x, a, b, y,$ and x, a, y are such paths, where the former lies in F but the latter does not.

This leads to the next proposition.

Proposition 15.   *If G is a fuzzy forest, the arcs of F are just the bridges of G.*

By this last proposition, if G is a fuzzy forest, its spanning forest F is unique.

Trees, Cycles, and Cutsets

Let $\sigma^* = \{x \in S \mid \sigma(x) > 0\}$, the *support* of σ, and $\mu^* = \{(x, y) \in S \times S \mid \mu(x, y) > 0\}$. Because $\mu(x, y) \leq \sigma(x) \wedge \sigma(y)$, $(x, y) \in \mu^*$ implies $x, y \in \sigma^*$. Thus, (σ^*, μ^*) is a graph.

We now recall some definitions and give some new ones.

FIGURE 5   Subgraph of theograph in Figure 4.

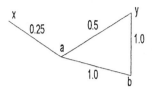

FIGURE 6   Fuzzy forest.

Definition 16.   Let (σ', μ') be a fuzzy subgraph of (σ, μ). Then, (σ', μ') is a *fuzzy spanning subgraph* of (σ, μ) if and only if $\sigma' = \sigma$.

Definition 17.

1. (σ, μ) is a *tree* if and only if (σ^*, μ^*) is a tree.
2. (σ, μ) is a *fuzzy tree* if and only if (σ, μ) has a fuzzy spanning subgraph (σ, ν) which is a tree such that $\forall (u, v) \in \mu^* \backslash \nu^*$, $\mu(u, v) < \nu^\infty(u, v)$ [i.e., there exists a path in (σ, ν) between u and v whose strength is greater than $\mu(u, v)$.]

Definition 18.

1. (σ, μ) is a *simple cycle* if and only if (σ^*, μ^*) is a simple cycle.
2. (σ, μ) is a *simple fuzzy cycle* if and only if (σ^*, μ^*) is a simple cycle and $\nexists$ unique $(x, y) \in \mu^*$ such that $\mu(x, y) = \min\{\mu(u, v) \mid (u, v) \in \mu^*\}$.
3. (σ, μ) is a *fuzzy cycle* if and only if (σ, μ) is a cycle and every fuzzy subgraph (σ', μ') of (σ, μ) which is a simple cycle is a simple fuzzy cycle.

Example 19.   Let $S = \{u, v, w, s, t\}$ and $X = \{(u, v), (u, w), (v, w), (w, s), (w, t), (s, t)\}$. Let $\sigma(x) = 1$ for all $x \in S$ and let μ be the fuzzy subset of X defined by $\mu(u, v) = \frac{1}{2}$, $\mu(u, w) = \mu(v, w) = \mu(w, s) = \mu(w, t) = \mu(s, t) = 1$. Then, (σ, μ) is neither a fuzzy cycle nor a fuzzy tree.

Example 20.   Let $S = \{w, u, v\}$ and $X = \{(w, u), (w, v), (u, v)\}$. Let $\sigma(x) = 1$ for all $x \in S$ and μ and μ' be fuzzy subsets of X defined by $\mu(w, u) = \mu(w, v) = 1$, $\mu(u, v) = \frac{1}{2}$ and $\mu'(w, v) = 1$, $\mu'(w, u) = \mu'(u, v) = \frac{1}{2}$. Then, (σ, μ) is a fuzzy tree, but not a tree and not a simple fuzzy cycle, whereas (σ, μ') is a simple fuzzy cycle, but not a fuzzy tree.

Example 20 illustrates the next result.

Theorem 21.   *Let (σ, μ) be a simple cycle. Then, (σ, μ) is a simple fuzzy cycle if and only if (σ, μ) is not a fuzzy tree.*

Theorem 22.   *If $\exists q \in (0, 1]$ such that (σ^*, μ_q) is a tree, μ_q a q-cut, then, (σ, μ) is a fuzzy tree. Conversely, if (σ, μ) is a simple cycle and (σ, μ) is a fuzzy tree, then $\exists q \in (0, 1]$ such that (σ^*, μ_q) is a tree.*

We now illustrate Theorem 22.

Example 23. Let $S = \{s, t, u, v \, w\}$ and $X = \{(s, t), (s, u), (t, u), (u, v), (u, w), (w, v)\}$. Let $\sigma(x) = 1$ for all $x \in S$ and let μ be the fuzzy subset of X defined by $\mu(s, t) = \frac{1}{4}$, $\mu(s, u) = \mu(t, u) = \frac{3}{8}$, $\mu(u, v) = \frac{1}{2}$, and $\mu(u, w) = 1$. Then, $\nexists \, q \in (0, 1]$ such that (σ^*, μ_q) is a tree. However (σ, μ) is a fuzzy tree.

(Fuzzy) Cutsets

Before proceeding further, we explain some concepts from graph theory. We associate with a graph G, two vector spaces over the field of scalars $\hat{z}_2 = \{0, 1\}$, where addition and multiplication is modulo 2. Then, for $1 \in \hat{z}_2$, $1 + 1 = 0$. Let $S = \{v_1, \ldots, v_n\}$ denote the set of vertices of G, and $X = \{e_1, \ldots, e_m\}$ the set of edges. A 0-*chain* of G is a formal linear combination $\Sigma \, \varepsilon_i v_i$ of vertices and a 1-*chain* a formal linear combination of edges $\Sigma \, \varepsilon_i e_i$, where the $\varepsilon_i \in \hat{z}_2$. The *boundary operator* ∂ is a linear function which maps 1-chains to 0-chains such that if $e = (x, y)$, then $\partial(e) = x + y$. The *coboundary operator* δ is a linear function which maps 0-chains to 1-chains such that $\delta(v) = \Sigma \, \varepsilon_i e_i$, where $\varepsilon_i = 1$ whenever e_i is incident with v.

Example 24. Let $G = (S, X)$, where $S = \{v_1, \ldots, v_6\}$ and $X = \{e_1, \ldots, e_9\}$ and where $e_1 = (v_1, v_2)$, $e_2 = (v_1, v_3)$, $e_3 = (v_2, v_3)$, $e_4 = (v_2, v_4)$, $e_5 = (v_2, v_5)$, $e_6 = (v_3, v_5)$, $e_7 = (v_3, v_6)$, $e_8 = (v_4, v_5)$, and $e_9 = (v_5, v_6)$ (see Fig. 7). The 1-chain $\gamma_1 = e_1 + e_2 + e_4 + e_9$ has boundary $\partial(\gamma_1) = (v_1 + v_2) + (v_1 + v_3) + (v_2 + v_4) + (v_5 + v_6) = v_3 + v_4 + v_5 + v_6$. The 0-chain $\gamma_0 = v_3 + v_4 + v_5 + v_6$ has coboundary $\delta(\gamma_0) = (e_2 + e_3 + e_6 + e_7) + (e_4 + e_8) + (e_5 + e_6 + e_8 + e_9) + (e_7 + e_9) = e_2 + e_3 + e_4 + e_5$.

A 1-chain with boundary 0 is called a *cycle vector* of G which we can think of as a set of line disjoint cycles. The collection of all cycle vectors, called the *cycle space*, form a vector space over $\hat{z}_2$. A *cutset* of a connected graph is a collection of edges whose removal results in a disconnected graph. A *cocycle* is a minimal cutset. A *coboundary* of G is the coboundary of some 0-chain in G. The coboundary of a subset of S is the set of all edges joining a point in this subset to a point not in the subset. Hence, every coboundary is a cutset. Because any minimal cutset is a coboundary, a cocycle is just a minimal nonzero coboundary. The collection of all coboundaries of G is a vector space over $\hat{z}_2$ and is called the *cocycle space* of G. A basis of this space which consists entirely of cocycles is called a *cocycle basis* for G.

Let G be a connected graph. Then, a *chord* of a spanning tree T is an edge of G which is not in T. The subgraph of G consisting of T and any chord of T has only one cycle. The set $C(T)$ of cycles obtained in this way is independent. Every cycle C depends

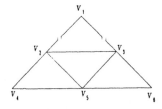

FIGURE 7   Graph illustrating the boundary and coboundary operators.

on the set $C(T)$ because C is the symmetric difference of the cycles determined by the chords of T which lie in C. We define $m(G)$, the *cycle rank*, to be the number of cycles in a basis for the cycle space of G. This discussion yields the following result.

Theorem 25(4). *The cycle rank of a connected graph G is equal to the number of chords of any spanning tree in G.*

Similar results can be derived for the cocycle space. Again, assume that G is a connected graph. The *cotree* T' of a spanning tree T of G is the spanning subgraph of G containing exactly those edges which are not in T. A cotree of G is the cotree of some spanning tree T. The edges of G which are not in T' are called its *twigs*. The subgraph of G consisting of T' and any one of its twigs contains exactly one cocycle. The collection of cocycles obtained by adding twigs to T', one at a time, is a basis for the cocycle space of G. The cocycle rank $m'(G)$ is the number of cocycles in a basis for the cocycle space of G. A more detailed account can be found in Ref. 4.

Theorem 26(4). *The cocycle rank of a connected graph G is the number of twigs in any spanning tree of T.*

Let $x \in S$ and let $t \in [0, 1]$. Define the fuzzy subset x_t of S by $\forall y \in S$, $x_t(y) = 0$ if $y \neq x$ and $x_t(y) = t$ if $y = x$. Then, x_t is called a *fuzzy singleton* in S. If $(x, y) \in S \times S$, then $(x, y)_{\mu(x, y)}$ denotes a fuzzy singleton in $S \times S$.

Definition 27. Let E be a subset of μ^*.

1. $\{(x, y)_{\mu(x, y)} \mid (x, y) \in E\}$ is a *cutset* of (σ, μ) if and only if E is a cutset of (σ^*, μ^*).
2. $\{(x, y)_{\mu(x, y)} \mid (x, y) \in E\}$ is a *fuzzy cutset* of (σ, μ) if and only if $\exists\ u, v \in \sigma^*$ such that $\mu'^{\infty}(u, v) < \mu^{\infty}(u, v)$ where μ' is the fuzzy subset of $S \times S$ defined by $\mu' = \mu$ on $\mu^* \backslash E$ and $\mu'(x, y) = 0\ \forall\ (x, y) \in E$; that is, the removal of E from μ^* reduces the strength of connectedness between some pair of vertices of (σ, μ).

When E is a singleton set, a cutset is called a *bridge* and a fuzzy cutset is called a *fuzzy bridge*.

The following is an example of a fuzzy graph (σ, μ) which has no fuzzy bridges and where μ is not a constant function.

Example 28. Let $S = \{t, u, v, w\}$ and $X = \{(t, u), (u, v), (v, w), (w, t), (t, v)\}$. Let $\sigma(x) = 1$ for all $x \in S$ and $\mu(t, u) = \mu(u, v) = \mu(v, w) = \mu(w, t) = 1$ and $\mu(t, v) = \frac{1}{2}$. Then, μ is not constant, but (σ, μ) does not have a fuzzy bridge because the strength of connectedness between any pair of vertices of (σ, μ) remains 1 even after the removal of an edge.

Theorem 29. *Let $S = \{v_1, \ldots, v_n\}$ and $C = \{(v_1, v_2), (v_2, v_3), \ldots, (v_{n-1}, v_n), (v_n, v_1)\}$, $n \geq 3$.*

1. *Suppose that $\mu^* \supseteq C$ and that $\forall\ (v_j, v_k) \in \mu^* \backslash C$, $\mu(v_j, v_k) < \max\{\mu(v_i, v_{i+1}) \mid i = 1, \ldots, n\}$ where $v_{n+1} = v_1$. Then, either μ is a constant on C or (σ, μ) has a fuzzy bridge.*
2. *Suppose that $\emptyset \neq \mu^* \subset C$. Then, (σ, μ) has a bridge.*

Theorem 30. *Suppose that the dimension of the cycle space of* (σ^*, μ^*) *is* 1. *Then,* (σ, μ) *does not have a fuzzy bridge if and only if* (σ, μ) *is a cycle and* μ *is a constant function.*

(Fuzzy) Chords, (Fuzzy) Cotrees, and (Fuzzy) Twigs

We assume throughout this section that (σ^*, μ^*) is connected.

Definition 31. Let (σ, ν) be a spanning fuzzy subgraph of (σ, μ) which is a tree. If (σ, ν_f) is a fuzzy tree such that $\nu \subseteq \nu_f \subseteq \mu$, $\nu_f = \mu$ on ν_f^*, and $\nexists$ a fuzzy tree (σ, ν') such that $\nu_f \subset \nu' \subseteq \mu$ and $\nu' = \mu$ on ν'^*, then (σ, ν_f) is called a *fuzzy spanning tree* of (σ, μ) with respect to ν.

Clearly, given (σ, ν) and (σ, μ) of Definition 3, (σ, ν_f) exists. We note that (σ, ν) is a spanning fuzzy subgraph of (σ, ν_f).

In Example 28, let ν, ν_f, and ν_f' be the fuzzy subsets of X defined as follows: $\nu = \mu$ on $\{(t, u), (t, v), (t, w)\}$ and $\nu(w, v) = \nu(u, v) = 0$, $\nu_f = \mu$ on $\{(t, u), (t, v), (t, w), (u, v)\}$, and $\nu_f(w, v) = 0$ and $\nu_f' = \mu$ on $\{(t, u), (t, v), (t, w), (w, v)\}$ and $\nu_f'(u, v) = 0$. Then, both (σ, ν_f) and (σ, ν_f') are fuzzy spanning trees of (σ, μ) with respect to ν; that is, given ν and ν_f in Definition 31 is not necessarily unique.

Consider the fuzzy graph (σ, μ) of Example 20. Define the fuzzy subset ν of X by $\nu(w, u) = \nu(u, v) = 1$. Because (σ, μ) is not a fuzzy cycle, the addition of $(u, v)_{1/2}$ to (σ, ν) does not create a fuzzy cycle. This fact motivates the definition of a fuzzy chord below.

Definition 32. Let (σ, ν) be a fuzzy spanning subgraph of (σ, μ) which is a tree. Let $(x, y) \in \mu^*$.

1. $(x, y)_{\mu(x, y)}$ is a *chord* of (σ, ν) if and only if $(x, y) \notin \nu^*$ [i.e., (x, y) is a chord of (σ^*, μ^*)].
2. $(x, y)_{\mu(x, y)}$ is a *fuzzy chord* of (σ, ν_f) if and only if $(x, y) \notin \nu_f^*$.

Example 33. Let $S = \{s, t, u, v, w\}$ and $X = \{(w, s), (w, t), (w, u), (w, v), (s, t), (u, v)\}$. Define the fuzzy subsets σ of S and μ and ν of X by $\sigma(x) = 1$ for all $x \in S$ and $\mu(x, y) = 1$ for all (x, y) in $X \setminus \{(w, u)\}$ and $\mu(w, u) = \frac{1}{2}$, $\nu(x, y) = 1$ for all (x, y) in Y, where $Y = X \setminus \{(w, s), (w, u)\}$. Then, $\nu_f = \mu$ on $X \setminus \{(w, s)\}$ and $\nu_f(w, s) = 0$. Also, $(w, s)_1$ and $(w, u)_{1/2}$ are chords of (σ, ν) and $(w, s)_1$ is a fuzzy chord of (σ, ν_f). If we define the fuzzy subset ν' of X by $\nu' = \nu_f$ on ν_f^* and $\nu'(w, s) = t$ where $0 < t < 1$, then (σ, ν') is a fuzzy tree such that $\nu_f \subset \nu'$. However, $\nu' \neq \mu$ on ν'^*.

Definition 34. Let (σ, ν) be a spanning fuzzy subgraph of (σ, μ) which is a tree.

1. Let ν' be a fuzzy subset of $S \times S$. Then, (σ, ν') is the *cotree* of (σ, ν) if and only if $\forall (x, y) \in \mu^*$, $\nu'(x, y) = 0$ if $\nu(x, y) > 0$ and $\nu'(x, y) = \mu(x, y)$ if $\nu(x, y) = 0$.
2. Let ν_f' be a fuzzy subset of $S \times S$. Then, (σ, ν_f') is the fuzzy *cotree* of (σ, ν_f) if and only if $\forall (x, y) \in \mu^*$, $\nu_f'(x, y) = 0$ if $\nu_f(x, y) > 0$ and $\nu_f'(x, y) = \mu(x, y)$ if $\nu_f(x, y) = 0$.

Let (σ, ν') be a cotree of (σ, ν), where (σ, ν) is a spanning fuzzy subgraph of (σ, μ) which is a tree. Then, (σ^*, ν'^*) is a cotree of (σ^*, ν^*) because $\nu'^* \cap \nu^* = \emptyset$, $\nu'^* \cup \nu^* = \mu^*$, and (σ^*, ν^*) is a tree.

Definition 35. Let (σ, ν) be a fuzzy spanning subgraph of (σ, μ) which is a tree and let $(x, y) \in \mu^*$.

1. Let (σ, ν') be a cotree of (σ, ν). Then, $(x, y)_{\mu(x, y)}$ is a *twig* of (σ, ν') if and only if $\nu'(x, y) = 0$.
2. Let (σ, ν'_f) be a fuzzy cotree of (σ, ν_f). Then, $(x, y)_{\mu(x, y)}$ is a *fuzzy twig* of (σ, ν'_f) if and only if $\nu'_f(x, y) = 0$.

Example 36. Let (σ, μ), (σ, ν), and (σ, ν_f) be the fuzzy subgraphs of Example 33. Let (σ, ν') be the cotree of (σ, ν) and (σ, ν'_f) be the fuzzy cotree of (σ, ν_f). Then, the twigs of (σ, ν') are $(s, t)_1$, $(w, t)_1$, $(w, v)_1$, and $(u, v)_1$. The fuzzy twigs of (σ, ν'_f) are $(s, t)_1$, $(w, t)_1$, $(w, v)_1$, $(u, v)_1$, and $(w, u)_{1/2}$.

(Fuzzy) 1-Chain with Boundary 0, (Fuzzy) Coboundary, and (Fuzzy) Cocycles

We recall that a pair $(M, *)$ is a semigroup if M is a nonempty set and $*$ is an associative binary operation on M. We let $G = (\sigma, \mu)$.

Definition 37. Let $(x, y) \in S \times S$. Then, (x, y) is called *exceptional* in G if and only if $\exists$ a cycle $C \subseteq S \times S$ such that $(x, y) \in C$ and (x, y) is unique with respect to $\mu(x, y) = \min\{\mu(u, v) \mid (u, v) \in C\}$. Let $E = \{(x, y) \in S \times S \mid (x, y) \text{ is exceptional}\}$. Let μ_E be the fuzzy subset of $S \times S$ defined by $\mu_E = \mu$ on $S \times S \backslash E$ and $\mu_E(x, y) = 0$ $\forall (x, y) \in E$.

Let $S_\mu = \{(x, y)_t \mid (x, y) \in \mu^*, t \in (0, 1]\} \cup \{0_t \mid t \subset (0, 1]\}$. Let the addition of elements of μ^* be a formal addition modulo 2 [i.e., $\forall (x, y), (u, v) \in \mu^*$, we write $(x, y) + (u, v)$ if $(x, y) \neq (u, v)$ and $(x, y) + (u, v) = 0$ if $(x, y) = (u, v)$]. Then, $\forall (x, y)_t, (u, v)_s \in S_\mu$, $(x, y)_t + (u, v)_s = ((x, y) + (u, v))_r$ where $r = \min\{t, s\}$. Also, $\forall (x, y)_t \in S_\mu$, $(x, y)_t + 0_s = (x, y)_r$ and $0_t + 0_s = 0_r$, where $r = \min\{t, s\}$. Clearly, $(S_\mu, +)$ is a commutative semigroup with identity 0_1. If $\backslash$ is a set of fuzzy singletons of a set W, we let $\text{foot}(\backslash) = \{w \in W \mid w_t \in \backslash\}$.

Let $\mathcal{Z}_2 = \{0, 1\}$ denote the field of integers modulo 2. Then, $1 + 1 = 0$. We have that $\Sigma \, \varepsilon_i(x_i, y_i)_{\mu(x_i, y_i)} + \Sigma \, \varepsilon'_i(x_i, y_i)_{\mu(x_i, y_i)} = \Sigma \, (\varepsilon_i + \varepsilon'_i)(x_i, y_i)_{\mu(x_i, y_i)}$, $\varepsilon_i(x_i, y_i)_{\mu(x_i, y_i)} = (x_i, y_i)_{\mu(x_i, y_i)}$ if $\varepsilon_i = 1$ and $\varepsilon_i(x_i, y_i)_{\mu(x_i, y_i)} = 0_{\mu(x_i, y_i)}$ if $\varepsilon_i = 0$, $\varepsilon_i, \varepsilon'_i \in \mathcal{Z}_2$. We have that $\Sigma \, \varepsilon_i(x_i, y_i)_{\mu(x_i, y_i)} = [\Sigma \, \varepsilon_i(x_i, y_i)]_m$, where $m = \min_i\{\mu(x_i, y_i)\}$.

Definition 38.

1. $\Sigma \, \varepsilon_i(x_i, y_i)_{\mu(x_i, y_i)}$ is a *1-chain with boundary* 0 in (σ, μ) where $(x_i, y_i) \in \mu^*$ if and only if $\Sigma \, \varepsilon_i(x_i, y_i)$ is a 1-chain with boundary 0 in (σ^*, μ^*).
2. $\Sigma \, \varepsilon_i(x_i, y_i)_{\mu(x_i, y_i)}$ is a *fuzzy 1-chain with boundary* 0 in (σ, μ) where $(x_i, y_i) \in \mu_E^*$ if and only if $\Sigma \, \varepsilon_i(x_i, y_i)$ is a 1-chain with boundary 0 in (σ^*, μ_E^*).

A (fuzzy) 1-chain with boundary 0 in (σ, μ) is called a (*fuzzy*) *cycle vector*.

Definition 39.

1. $\Sigma\ \varepsilon_i(x_i,\ y_i)_{\mu(x_i,\ y_i)}$ is a *coboundary* of $(\sigma,\ \mu)$ where $(x_i,\ y_i) \in \mu^*$ if and only if Σ $\varepsilon_i(x_i,\ y_i)$ is a coboundary of $(\sigma^*,\ \mu^*)$.

2. $\Sigma\ \varepsilon_i(x_i,\ y_i)_{\mu(x_i,\ y_i)}$ is a *fuzzy coboundary* of $(\sigma,\ \mu)$ where $(x_i,\ y_i) \in \mu^*_E$ if and only if $\Sigma\ \varepsilon_i(x_i,\ y_i)$ is a coboundary of $(\sigma^*,\ \mu^*_E)$.

$S' \subseteq \setminus_\mu$ is called a *(fuzzy) cocycle* of $(\sigma,\ \mu)$ if and only if foot($\setminus'$) is a cocycle of $((\sigma^*,\ \mu^*_E))$ $(\sigma^*,\ \mu^*)$.

(Fuzzy) Cycle Set and (Fuzzy) Cocycle Set
Definition 40.

1. The set of all (fuzzy) cycle vectors of $(\sigma,\ \mu)$ is called the *(fuzzy) cycle set* of $(\sigma,\ \mu)$.
2. The set of all (fuzzy) coboundaries of $(\sigma,\ \mu)$ is called the *(fuzzy) cocycle set* of $(\sigma,\ \mu)$.

The following examples show that the fuzzy cycle, cycle, fuzzy cocycle, and cocycle sets are not and do not necessarily generate vector spaces over $\dot{z}_2$.

Example 41. Let $S = \{t,\ u,\ v,\ w\}$ and $X = \{(t,\ u),\ (u,\ v),\ (v,\ w),\ (w,\ t),\ (t,\ v)\}$. Define the fuzzy subsets σ of S and μ of X as follows: $\sigma(x) = 1$ for all $x \in S$, $\mu(t,\ u) = \mu(u,\ v) = 1$, $\mu(v,\ w) = \mu(w,\ t) = \frac{1}{2}$, and $\mu(t,\ v) = \frac{1}{4}$. Then, the cycle set is $\{(t,\ u)_1 + (u,\ v)_1 + (t,\ v)_{1/4},\ (v,\ w)_{1/2} + (w,\ t)_{1/2} + (t,\ v)_{1/4},\ (t,\ u)_1 + (u,\ v)_1 + (v,\ w)_{1/2} + (w,\ t)_{1/2},\ 0_{1/4},\ 0_{1/2}\}$. The fuzzy cycle set is $\{(t,\ u)_1 + (u,\ v)_1 + (v,\ w)_{1/2} + (w,\ t)_{1/2},\ 0_{1/2}\}$. The cocycle set is $\{(t,\ u)_1 + (t,\ v)_{1/4} + (w,\ t)_{1/2},\ (u,\ v)_1 + (t,\ v)_{1/4} + (v,\ w)_{1/2},\ (t,\ u)_1 + (u,\ v)_1,\ (v,\ w)_{1/2} + (w,\ t)_{1/2},\ (w,\ t)_{1/2} + (t,\ v)_{1/4} + (u,\ v)_1,\ (t,\ u)_1 + (t,\ v)_{1/4} + (v,\ w)_{1/2},\ (w,\ t)_{1/2} + (t,\ u)_1 + (u,\ v)_1 + (v,\ w)_{1/2},\ 0_{1/4},\ 0_{1/2}\}$. The fuzzy cocycle set is $\{(t,\ u)_1 + (w,\ t)_{1/2},\ (u,\ v)_1 + (v,\ w)_{1/2},\ (t,\ u)_1 + (u,\ v)_1,\ (v,\ w)_{1/2} + (w,\ t)_{1/2},\ (w,\ t)_{1/2} + (u,\ v)_1,\ (t,\ u)_1 + (v,\ w)_{1/2},\ (w,\ t)_{1/2} + (t,\ u)_1 + (u,\ v)_1 + (v,\ w)_{1/2},\ 0_{1/2}\}$. The cycle set and cocycle set are not and do not generate vector spaces over $\dot{z}_2$ because of the presence of $0_{1/2}$ and $0_{1/4}$. Note also that in the cycle set, $((t,\ u)_1 + (u,\ v)_1 + (t,\ v)_{1/4}) + ((v,\ w)_{1/2} + (w,\ t)_{1/2} + (t,\ v)_{1/4}) = (t,\ u)_1 + (u,\ v)_1 + (v,\ w)_{1/2} + (w,\ t)_{1/2} + 0_{1/4} \neq (t,\ u)_1 + (u,\ v)_1 + (v,\ w)_{1/2} + (w,\ t)_{1/2}$. The fuzzy cycle set is a vector space over $\dot{z}_2$ in this example. The fuzzy cocycle set is not a vector space over $\dot{z}_2$ because $((v,\ w)_{1/2} + (w,\ t)_{1/2}) + ((w,\ t)_{1/2} + (t,\ u)_1 + (u,\ v)_1 + (v,\ w)_{1/2}) = (t,\ u)_1 + (u,\ v)_1 + 0_{1/2} \neq (t,\ u)_1 + (u,\ v)_1$.

Example 42. Let S, σ, and X be as in Example 41. Let $X' = X \cup \{(u,\ w)\}$. Define the fuzzy subset μ' of X' by $\mu' = \mu$ on X and $\mu'(u,\ w) = \frac{1}{8}$. Then the fuzzy cycle set and the fuzzy cocycle set of $(\sigma,\ \mu')$ coincides with the cycle set and the cocycle set of $(\sigma,\ \mu)$ of Example 41, respectively.

Examples 41 and 42 illustrate the results which follow.

Let $\mathcal{C}\setminus(\sigma,\ \mu)$, $\mathcal{FC}\setminus(\sigma,\ \mu)$, $\mathcal{C}\setminus(\sigma,\ \mu)$, and $\mathcal{FC}\setminus(\sigma,\ \mu)$ denote the cycle set, the fuzzy cycle set, the cocycle set, and the fuzzy cocycle set of $(\sigma,\ \mu)$, respectively. When the fuzzy graph $(\sigma,\ \mu)$ is understood, we sometimes write $\mathcal{C}\setminus$, $\mathcal{FC}\setminus$, $\mathcal{C}\setminus$, and $\mathcal{FC}\setminus$ for these sets, respectively.

We now show that even though $\mathcal{C}\setminus$, $\mathcal{FC}\setminus$, $\mathcal{C}\setminus$, and $\mathcal{FC}\setminus$ are not necessarily vector spaces over $\mathbb{Z}_2$, they are nearly so. In fact, it will be clear by the following results that the concepts of (fuzzy) twigs and (fuzzy) chords introduced here will have consequences similar to what their counterparts have in the crisp case.

For ease of notation, we sometimes use the notation e, f, or g for members of μ^*.

Clearly, CS, $\mathcal{T}CS$, C_cS, and $\mathcal{T}C_cS$ are subsets of $S_\mu = \{e_t \mid e \in \mu^*, t \in (0, 1]\} \cup \{0_t \mid t \in (0, 1]\}$. Let s be a subset of S_μ. We let $\langle s \rangle$ denote the intersection of all subsemigroups of S_μ which contain s. Then, $\langle s \rangle$ is the smallest subsemigroup of S_μ which contains s. Let $s^+ = \{(e_1)_{t_1} + \cdots + (e_n)_{t_n} \mid (e_i)_{t_i} \in s, i = 1, \ldots, n, n \in \mathbb{N}\}$, where $\mathbb{N}$ denotes the set of positive integers. Then, s^+ is a subsemigroup of S_μ.

Theorem 43. $\langle CS \rangle = (CS)^+ = CS \cup \{e_a + 0_b \mid e_a \in CS, 0_b \in (CS)^+\}$. $\langle CS \rangle$ has 0_m as its identity, where $m = \max\{b \mid 0_b \in (CS)^+\}$.

Corollary 44. $\langle \mathcal{T}CS \rangle = (\mathcal{T}CS)^+ = \mathcal{T}CS \cup (e_a + 0_b \mid e_a \in \mathcal{T}CS, 0_b \in (\mathcal{T}CS)^+\}$. $\langle \mathcal{T}CS \rangle$ has 0_m as its identity, where $m = \max\{b \mid 0_b \in (\mathcal{T}CS)^+\}$.

In a similar manner, we obtain the next two results.

Theorem 45. $\langle C_cS \rangle = (C_cS)^+ = C_cS \cup \{e_a + 0_b \mid e_a \in C_cS, 0_b \in (C_cS)^+\}$. $\langle C_cS \rangle$ has 0_m as its identity, where $m = \max\{b \mid 0_b \in (C_cS)^+\}$.

Corollary 46. $\langle \mathcal{T}C_cS \rangle = (\mathcal{T}C_cS)^+ = \mathcal{T}C_cS \cup \{e_a + 0_b \mid e_a \in \mathcal{T}C_cS, 0_b \in (\mathcal{T}C_cS)^+\}$. $\langle \mathcal{T}C_cS \rangle$ has 0_m as its identity, where $m = \max\{b \mid 0_b \in (\mathcal{T}C_cS)^+\}$.

Because CS, $\mathcal{T}CS$, C_cS, and $\mathcal{T}C_cS$ are nearly vector spaces over $\mathbb{Z}_2$, we can define the (fuzzy) cycle rank and (fuzzy) cocycle rank of a fuzzy graph in a meaningful way.

Definition 47. The *cycle rank* of (σ, μ), written $m(\sigma, \mu)$, is defined to be

$$m(\sigma, \mu) = \max\left\{\sum_{i=1}^{n} t_i \mid (e_i)_{t_i} \in CS, i = 1, \ldots, n, \{e_1, \ldots, e_n\} \text{ is a basis for foot}(CS)\right\}.$$

The *fuzzy cycle rank* of (σ, μ), written $fm(\sigma, \mu)$, is defined to be the cycle rank of (σ, μ_E). If $\{e_1, \ldots, e_n\}$ is a basis for foot (CS) such that $m(\sigma, \mu) = \Sigma_{i=1}^n t_i$, where $(e_i)_{t_i} \in CS$, $i = 1, \ldots, n$, then $\{e_1, \ldots, e_n\}$ is called a *cycle basis* of $\langle CS \rangle$. If $\{e_1, \ldots, e_n\}$ is a basis for foot($\mathcal{T}CS(\sigma, \mu)$) such that $fm(\sigma, \mu) = \Sigma_{i=1}^n t_i$, where $(e_i)_{t_i} \in \mathcal{T}CS(\sigma, \mu)$, $i = 1, \ldots, n$, then $\{e_1, \ldots, e_n\}$ is called a *fuzzy cycle basis* of $\langle CS(\sigma, \mu) \rangle$.

Theorem 48. Let $\{e_1, \ldots, e_n\}$ be a cycle basis of $\langle CS \rangle$. Then, $\forall e_t \in CS$, there is a reordering of $e_1, \ldots, e_n$ such that $e_t = (e_1)_{t_1} + \cdots + (e_m)_{t_m}$, $m \leq n$, where $t_i = \mu(e_i)$, $i = 1, \ldots, m$.

Corollary 49. Let $\{e_1, \ldots, e_n\}$ be a fuzzy cycle basis of $\langle CS(\sigma, \mu) \rangle$. Then, $\forall e_t \in \mathcal{T}CS(\sigma, \mu)$, there is a reordering of $e_1, \ldots, e_n$ such that $e_t = (e_1)_{t_1} + \cdots + (e_m)_{t_m}$, $m \leq n$, where $t_i = \mu(e_i)$, $i = 1, \ldots, m$.

The graphs in Figure 8 have the same cycle rank, but they are, of course, not isomorphic as one has four nodes and the other has five nodes.

Definition 50. The *cocycle rank* of (σ, μ), written $m_c(\sigma, \mu)$, is defined to be

$$m_c(\sigma, \mu) = \max\left\{\sum_{i=1}^{n} t_i \mid (e_i)_{t_i} \in C_cS, i = 1, \ldots, n, \{e_1, \ldots, e_n\} \text{ is a basis for foot}(C_cS)\right\}.$$

FIGURE 8   Nonisomorphic graphs with the same cycle rank.

The *fuzzy cocycle rank* of (σ, μ), *written* $fm_c(\sigma, \mu)$, is defined to be the cocycle rank of (σ, μ_E). If $\{e_1, \ldots, e_n\}$ is a basis for foot $(c \cdot)$ such that $m_c(\sigma, \mu) = \Sigma_{i=1}^{n} t_i$, where $(e_i)_{t_i} \in c \cdot$, $i = 1, \ldots, n$, then $\{e_1, \ldots, e_n\}$ is called a *cocycle basis* of $\langle c \cdot \rangle$. If $\{e_1, \ldots, e_n\}$ is a basis for foot$(\mathcal{7}c \cdot(\sigma, \mu))$ such that $fm_c(\sigma, \mu) = \Sigma_{i=1}^{n} t_i$, where $(e_i)_{t_i} \in \mathcal{7}c \cdot(\sigma, \mu)$, $i = 1, \ldots, n$, then $\{e_1, \ldots, e_n\}$ is called a *fuzzy cocycle basis* of $\langle c \cdot(\sigma, \mu) \rangle$.

In a similar manner, we obtain the next two results.

Theorem 51.   *Let* $\{e_1, \ldots, e_n\}$ *be a cocycle basis of* $\langle c \cdot \rangle$. *Then,* $\forall\, e_t \in c \cdot$, *there is a reordering of* $e_1, \ldots, e_n$ *such that* $e_t = (e_1)_{t_1} + \cdots + (e_m)_{t_m}$, $m \leq n$, *where* $t_i = (\mu(e_i)$, $i = 1, \ldots, m$.

Corollary 52.   *Let* $\{e_1, \ldots, e_n\}$ *be a fuzzy cocycle basis of* $\langle c \cdot(\sigma, \mu) \rangle$. *Then* $\forall\, e_t \in \mathcal{7}c \cdot(\sigma, \mu)$, *there is a reordering of* $e_1, \ldots, e_n$ *such that* $e_t = (e_1)_{t_1} + \cdots + (e_m)_{t_m}$, $m \leq n$, *where* $t_i = \mu(e_i)$, $i = 1, \ldots, m$.

APPLICATIONS

Pattern Classification Based on Fuzzy Relations

Let S be a set of patterns. A classification fuzzy relation μ on S is a fuzzy relation satisfying the following two conditions:

C1 $\mu(x, x) = 1$
C2 $\mu(x, y) = \mu(y, x)$

Note that condition C1 states that a pattern x is identical with itself. Thus, the relation is reflexive. Condition C2 means that any relation used to classify patterns has to be symmetric. Because μ is reflexive, $\mu \subseteq \mu^2 \subseteq \mu^3 \subseteq \cdots \subseteq \mu^\infty$. Note that μ^∞ is a fuzzy equivalence relation. So, for any $0 \leq t \leq 1$, $(\mu^\infty)_t$ is an equivalence relation on S. Let P^t denote the partition of S induced by the equivalence relation $(\mu^\infty)_t$.

Lemma 53.   *For all* $x, y, z \in S$,

$$\mu^\infty(x, z) \geq \min\{\mu^\infty(x, y), \mu^\infty(y, z)\}.$$

Theorem 54.   *Suppose that for all* $x, y \in X$, $\mu(x, y) \neq 1$ *if and only if* $x \neq y$. *Then,* $\rho(x, y) = 1 - \mu(x, y)$ *satisfies the properties of a metric; that is,*

1. $\rho(x, y) = 0$ if and only if $x = y$
2. $\rho(x, y) = \rho(y, x)$
3. $\rho(x, z) \le \rho(x, y) + \rho(y, z)$

Example 55. Let $S = \{x_1, x_2, x_3, x_4, x_5\}$ and $\mu(x_i, x_j)$ be as follows:

	x_1	x_2	x_3	x_4	x_5
x_1	1.0				
x_2	0.82	0			
x_3	0.0	0.43	1.0		
x_4	0.14	0.0	0.0	1.0	
x_5	0.22	0.91	0.0	0.54	1.0

Now $\mu^\infty = \mu^3$ is given by

	x_1	x_2	x_3	x_4	x_5
x_1	1.0				
x_2	0.82	1.0			
x_3	0.43	0.43	1.0		
x_4	0.54	0.54	0.43	1.0	
x_5	0.82	0.91	0.43	0.54	1.0

and we have the partitions

$$P^0 = P^{0.3} = \{\{x_1, x_2, x_3, x_4, x_5\}\},$$
$$P^{0.45} = \{\{x_1, x_2, x_4, x_5\}, \{x_3\}\},$$
$$P^{0.55} = \{\{x_1, x_2, x_5\}, \{x_4\}, \{x_3\}\},$$
$$P^{0.85} = \{\{x_1\}, \{x_2, x_5\}, \{x_4\}, \{x_3\}\},$$
$$P^{1.0} = \{\{x_1\}, \{x_2\}, \{x_5\}, \{x_4\}, \{x_3\}\}.$$

Thus, there are many partitions possible, and depending on the level of detail, one could classify the patterns based on equivalence relations. Note that if $s \ge t$, then P^s is a refinement of P^t.

Experimental Result

We now present an experiment done by Tamura et al. (5). Portraits obtained from 60 families were used in their experiment, each of which is composed of between 4 and 7 members. The reason why they chose the portraits is that even if parents do not have a facial resemblance, they may be connected through their children, and, consequently, they could classify the portraits into families. First, they divided the 60 families into 20 groups, each of which was composed of 3 families. Each group was, on the average, composed of 15 members. The portraits of each group were presented to a different student to give the values of the subjective similarity $\mu(x, y)$ between all pairs on a scale of 1 to 5. The reason why they used the 5-rank representation instead of continuous-value representation is that it had been proved that the human being cannot distinguish into more than five ranks. Twenty students joined in this experiment. Because the levels of the subjective values are different according to individuals, the threshold was determined in each group as follows. As the threshold was lowered, the number of classes decreased. Hence, under the assumption that the number of classes c to be classified was known to be three, lowering the threshold they stopped at the value which divided the patterns into three classes (collection of the patterns composed of more than two patterns that have a stronger relation than λ with each other) and some nonconnected patterns. However, as in the present case, when some $\mu(x, y)$ take the same value, sometimes there is no threshold by which the patterns are divided into just c given classes. In such a case, they made it possible to divide them into just c classes by stopping the threshold at the value where the patterns are divided into less than c classes and separating some connections randomly that have a minimum $\mu(x, y)$ of connections that have the stronger relation than the threshold. The correctly classified rates, the misclassified rates, and the rejected rates of 20 groups were within the range of 50–94%, 0–33%, and 0–33%, respectively, and they obtained the correctly classified rate 75% of the time, the misclassified rate 13%, and the rejected rate 12% as the averages of the 20 groups. Here, because the classes made in this experiment have no label, they calculated these rates by making a one-to-one correspondence between three families and three classes, so as to have the largest number of correctly classified patterns.

The method of classification proposed here is based on the procedure of finding a path connecting two patterns. Therefore, this method may be combined with nonsupervised learning and may also be applicable to information retrieval and path detection.

Clustering Analysis

The usual graph-theoretical approaches to clustering analysis involve first obtaining a threshold graph from a fuzzy graph, and then applying various techniques to obtain clusters as maximal components under different connectivity considerations. These methods have a common weakness, namely the weight of edges are not treated fairly in that any weight greater (less) than the threshold is treated as 1(0). In this section, we will extend these techniques to fuzzy graphs. It will be noted that the fuzzy graph approach is more powerful.

Various graph-theoretical techniques for clustering analysis can be found in Ref. 3. In the following definition, clusters will be defined based on various connectivities of a fuzzy graph.

Definition 56. Let $G = [V, R]$ be a symmetric graph. A cluster of type i is defined by condition i, $i = 1, 2, 3, 4$, in the following: (1) maximal ε-*connected subgraphs, for some* $0 < \varepsilon \leq 1$; (2) maximal τ-degree connected subgraphs; (3) maximal τ-edge connected subgraphs; (4) maximal τ-vertex connected subgraphs.

It follows from the previous definition that clusters of type 1, 2, and 3 are hierachical with different ε and τ, whereas clusters of type 4 are not due to the fact that τ-vertex components need not be disjoint.

It is also easily seen that all clusters of type 1 can be obtained by the single-linkage procedure. The difference between the two procedures lies in the fact that ε-connected subgraphs can be obtained directly from a certain matrix representation of μ^∞ by at most $n - 1$ matrix multiplication (where n is the rank of the matrix representation of μ), whereas in the single-linkage procedure, it is necessary to obtain as many threshold graphs as the number of distinct fuzzy values in the graph.

Theorem 57. *The τ-degree connectivity procedure for the construction of clusters is more powerful than the k-linkage procedure.*

Let G be a symmetric fuzzy graph. For $0 < \varepsilon \leq 1$, let G' be a graph obtained from G by replacing these weights less than ε in G by 0. For any k used in the *k-linkage* procedure, set $\tau = k\varepsilon$. It is seen that a set is a cluster obtained by applying *k-linkage* procedure to G if and only if it is a cluster obtained by applying the τ-*degree* connectivity procedure to G'.

Theorem 58. *The τ-edge connectivity procedure for the construction of clusters is more powerful than the k-edge connectivity procedure.*

Theorem 59. *The τ-vertex connectivity procedure for the construction of clusters is more powerful than the k-vertex connectivity procedure.*

For more details and examples, the reader is referred to Reference 3.

BASIC READINGS FOR FURTHER STUDY

For a study of the basic concepts of graph theory, we recommend the text by Harary (4). The topics appear in a logical order. Many figures are presented to illustrate concepts and results of graphs. The text contains three appendices with diagrams of graphs, directed graphs, and trees. The text emphasizes theory rather than algorithms or applications. For algorithms and applications of graph theory, we recommend References 6–8.

For a study of the fundamental concepts of fuzzy graphs, we recommend the articles of Rosenfeld (2) and Yeh and Bang (3). These two articles are the cornerstones, to date, of fuzzy graph theory. Both papers contain applications to cluster analysis. Most of the proofs of the results in latter part of the second section can be found in Ref. 9. Extensive work has been done in this area and the reader is referred to the bibliography.

REFERENCES

1. L. A. Zadeh, "Fuzzy Sets," *Inform. Control, 8,* 338–353 (1965).
2. A. Rosenfeld, "Fuzzy Graphs," in *Fuzzy Sets and Their Applications,* L. A. Zadeh, K. S. Fu and M. Shimura (eds.), Academic Press, New York, 1975, pp. 77–95.
3. R. T. Yeh and S. Y. Bang, "Fuzzy Graphs, Fuzzy Relations, and Their Applications to Cluster Analysis," in *Fuzzy Sets and Their Applications,* L. A. Zadeh, K. S. Fu and M. Shimura (eds.), Academic Press, New York, 1975, pp. 125–149.
4. F. Harary, *Graph Theory,* Addison-Wesley, Reading, MA, 1973.
5. S. Tamura, S. Higuchi, and K. Tanaka, "Pattern Classification Based on Fuzzy Relations," *IEEE Trans., SMC-1,* 61–66 (1971).
6. G. Chartrand and O. R. Oellermann, *Applied and Algorithmic Graph Theory,* McGraw-Hill, New York, 1993.
7. N. Deo, *Graph Theory with Applications to Engineering and Computer Science,* Prentice-Hall, Englewood Cliffs, NJ, 1974.
8. F. R. Foulds, *Graph Theory Applications,* Springer-Verlag, New York, 1991.
9. J. N. Mordeson and P. S. Nair, "Cycles and Cocycles of Fuzzy Graphs," *Inform. Sci., 90,* 39–49 (1996).

BIBLIOGRAPHY

Adamo, J. N., "Fuzzy Decision Trees," *Fuzzy Sets Syst.*, *4*, 207–219 (1980).

Arya, S. P., and D. Hazarika, "Functions with Closed Fuzzy Graph," *J. Fuzzy Math.*, *2*, 593–600 (1994).

Augustson, J. G., and J. Miner, "An Analysis of Some Graph Theoretical Cluster Techniques," *JACM*, *17*, 571–588 (1970).

Bellman, R., R. Kalaba, and L. Zadeh, "Abstraction and Pattern Classification," *J. Math. Anal. Applic.*, *13*, 1–7 (1966).

Bezdek, J. C., and J. D. Harris, "Fuzzy Partitions and Relations: An Axiomatic Basis for Clustering," *Fuzzy Sets Syst.*, *1*, 111–127 (1978).

Bhattacharya, P., "Some Remarks on Fuzzy Graphs," *Pattern Recogn. Lett.*, *6*, 297–302 (1987).

Bhutani, K. R., "On Automorphisms of Fuzzy Graphs," *Pattern Recogn. Lett.*, *9*, 159–162 (1989).

Bonner, R. E., "On Some Clustering Techniques," *IBM J. Res. Dev.*, *8*(1), (1964).

Cerruti, U., "Graphs and Fuzzy Graphs," in *Fuzzy Information and Decision Processes*, North-Holland, Amsterdam, 1982, pp. 121–131.

Chen, Q. J., "Matrix Representation of Fuzzy Graphs," *Math. Practice Theory*, *1*, 41–46 (1990) (in Chinese).

Chu, S. Y., "Fuzzy Tree Grammar and Fuzzy Forest Grammar," in *Advances in Fuzzy Sets, Possibility Theory, and Applications*, Plenum Press, New York, 1983, pp. 149–179.

Delgado, M., J. L. Verdegay, and M. A. Vila, "On Fuzzy Tree Definition," *Eur. J. Oper. Res.*, *22*, 243–249 (1985).

Delgado, M., J. L. Verdegay, and M. A. Vila, "On Valuation and Optimization Problems in Fuzzy Graphs: A General Approach and Some Particular Cases," *ORSA J. Comput.*, *2*, 74–83 (1990).

Ding, B., "A Clustering Dynamic State Method for Maximal Trees in Fuzzy Graph Theory," *J. Numer. Methods Comput. Applic.*, *13*, 157–160 (1992) (in Chinese).

El-Ghoul, M., "Folding of Fuzzy Graphs and Fuzzy Spheres," *Fuzzy Sets Syst.*, *58*, 355–363 (1993).

EL-Ghoul, M., "Folding of Fuzzy Torus and Fuzzy Graphs," *Fuzzy Sets Syst.*, *80*, 389–396 (1996).

Gitman, I., and M. D. Levine, "An Algorithm for Detecting Unimodal Sets and Its Application as a Clustering Technique," *IEEE Trans. Computers*, *C-19*, 583–593 (1970).

Goetschel, R. H., "Introduction to Fuzzy Hypergraphs and Hebbian Structures," *Fuzzy Sets Syst.*, *76*, 113–130 (1995).

Goetschel, R. H., W. L. Craine, and W. Voxman, "Fuzzy Transversals of Fuzzy Hypergraphs," *Fuzzy Sets Syst.*, *84*, 235–254 (1996).

Gould, R., *Graph Theory*, Benjamin/Cummings Publishing, Menlo Park, CA, 1988.

Halpern, J., "Set Adjacency Measures in Fuzzy Graphs," *J. Cybern.*, *5*, 77–87(1976).

Jardine, N., and R. Sibson, "A Model for Taxonomy," *Math. Biosci.*, *2*, 465–482 (1968).

Jardine, N., and R. Sibson, "The Construction of Hierarchic and Non-hierarchic Classifications," *Computer J.*, *11*, 177–184 (1968).

Kaufmann, A., *Introduction a la Theorie des Sous-Ensembles Flous, Vol. 1*, Masson, Paris, 1973, pp. 41–189.

Kiss, A., "An Application of Fuzzy Graphs in Database Theory, Automata, Languages and Programming Systems," *Pure Math. Appl. Ser. A*, *1*, 337–342 (1991).

Klein, C. M., "Fuzzy Shortest Path," *Fuzzy Sets Syst.*, *39*, 27–41 (1991).

Koczy, L. T., "Fuzzy Graphs in the Evaluation and Optimization of Networks," *Fuzzy Sets Syst.*, *46*, 307–319 (1992).

Lance, G. N., and W. T. Williams, "A General Theory of Classificatory Sorting Strategies, 1. Hierarchial Systems," *Computer J.*, *9*, 373–380 (1967).

Leenders, J. H., "Some Remarks on an Article by Raymond T. Yeh and S. Y. Bang Dealing with Fuzzy Relations; Fuzzy relations, Fuzzy Graphs, and Their Applications to Clustering

Analysis; Fuzzy Sets and Their Applications to Cognitive and Decision Processes," *Simon Stevin*, *51*, 93–100 (1977/78).

Ling, R. F., "On the Theory and Construction of *k*-Cluster," *Computer J.*, *15*, 326–332 (1972)

Luo, C.-S., "The Theorems of Decomposition and Representation for Fuzzy Graphs," *Fuzzy Sets Syst.*, *42*, 237–243 (1991).

Matula, D. W., "Cluster Analysis via Graph Theoretic Techniques," in *Proc. of Louisiana Conf. on Combinatrics, Graph Theory, and Computing*, March 1970, pp. 199–212.

Matula, D. W., "*k*-Components, Clusters, and Slicings in Graphs," *SIAM J. Appl. Math.*, *22*, 459–480 (1972).

McAllister, M. L. N., "Fuzzy Intersection Graphs," *Comput. Math. Applic.*, *15*, 871–886 (1988).

Mo, Z. W., and L. Su, "An Effective Method for Describing High-Dimensional Distorted Patterns—Fuzzy Tree Grammars," *Sichuan Shifan Daxue Xuebao Ziran Kexue Ban*, *16*, 9–13 (1993) (in Chinese).

Mori, M., and Y. Kawaahara, "Fuzzy Graph Rewritings. Theory of Rewriting Systems and Its Applications," *Surikaisekikenkyusho Kokyuroku*, *918*, 65–71 (1995) (in Japanese).

Mordeson, J. N., "Fuzzy Line Graphs," *Pattern Recogn. Lett.*, *14*, 381–384 (1993).

Mordeson, J. N., and P. S. Nair, "Successor and Source of (Fuzzy) Finite State Machines and (Fuzzy) Directed Graphs," *Inform. Sci.*, *95*, 113–124 (1996).

Mordeson, J. N., and C.-S. Peng, "Operations on Fuzzy Graphs," *Inform. Sci.*, *79*, 159–170 (1994).

Morioka, M., H. Yamasita, and T. Takizawa, "Extraction Method of the Difference Between Fuzzy Graphs," in *Fuzzy Information, Knowledge Representation and Decision Analysis*, IFAC Proc. Ser. 6, IFAC, Laxenburg, 1984, pp. 439–444.

Nair, P. S., "Triangle and Parallelogram laws on Fuzzy Graphs," *Pattern Recogn. Lett.*, *15*, 803–805 (1994).

Nance, R. E., R. R. Korfhage, and U. N. Bhat, "Information Networks: Definitions and Message Transfer Models," Technical Report CP-710011, Computer Science/Operation Research Center, SMU, Dallas, TX (July 1971).

Ramamoorthy, C. V., "Analysis of Graphs by Connectivity Considerations," *JACM*, *13*, 211–222 (1966).

Roubens, M., and P. Vincke, "Linear Fuzzy Graphs," *Fuzzy Sets Syst.*, *10*, 79–86 (1983).

Ruspini, E. H., "A New Approach to Clustering," *Inform. Control*, *15*, 22–32 (1969).

Ruspini, E. H., "A Theory of Fuzzy Clustering," in *Proceedings of the IEEE Conference on Decision Control*, 1977, pp. 1378–1383.

Sarma, R., and N. Ajmal, "Category and Functions with Closed Fuzzy Graph," *Fuzzy Sets Syst.*, *63*, 219–226 (1994).

Sibson, R., "Some Observations on a Paper by Lance and Williams," *Computer J.*, *14*, 156–157 (1971).

Singer, D., "Fuzzy Mason Graphs," *Fuzzy Sets Syst.*, *50*, 35–46 (1992).

Shannon, A., and K. Atanassov, "Intuitionistic Fuzzy Graphs from α, β and $\alpha\beta$-Levels," *Notes IFS*, *1*, 32–35 (1995).

Sunouchi, H., and M. Morioka, "Some Properties on the Connectivity of a Fuzzy Graph," *Bull. Sci. Eng. Res. Lab. Waseda Univ.*, *132*, 70–78 (1991) (in Japanese).

Takeda, E., "Connectivity in Fuzzy Graphs," *Tech. Rep. Osaka Univ.*, *23*, 343–352 (1973).

Takeda, E., and T. Nishida, "An Application of Fuzzy Graphs to the Problem Concerning Group Structure," *J. Oper. Res. Soc. Japan*, *19*, 217–227 (1976).

Tong, Z., and D. Zheng, "Connectedness in a Fuzzy Graph," in *Proceedings of the Twenty-sixth Southeastern Conference on Combinatorics, Graph Theory and Computing*, (1995); *Congr. Numer. 112*, 65–67 (1995).

Wu, L. G., and T. P. Chen, "Some Problems Concerning Fuzzy Graphs," *J. Huazhong Inst. Tech.* (special issue on fuzzy math.), *iv*, 28–60 (1980) (in Chinese).

Yamashita, H., and M. Morioka, "On the Global Structure of a Fuzzy Graph," *Anal. Fuzzy Inform.*, *1*, 167–176 (1987).

Yamashita, H., "Approximation Algorithm of a Fuzzy Graph," *Bull. Centre Inform.*, 2, 59–60 (1985) (in Japanese).

Yamashita, H., "Structure Analysis of Fuzzy Graph and Its Application," *Bull. Sci. Eng. Res. Lab. Waseda Univ.*, *132*, 61–69 (1991) (in Japanese).

Yeh, R. T., "Toward an Algebraic Theory of Fuzzy Relational System," Technical Report 25, Department of Computer Science, The University of Texas (July 1973).

Zadeh, L. A., "Similarity Relations and Fuzzy Orderings," *Inform. Sci.*, *3*, 177–200 (1971).

Zhu, R. Y., "The Critical Number of the Connectivity Degree of a Fuzzy Graph," *Fuzzy Math.*, 2, 113–116 (1982) (in Chinese).

Zhu, S. Y., "Fuzzy Tree Grammars and Fuzzy Forest Grammars," *Fuzzy Math.*, *16*, 45–64 (1981) (in Chinese).

Zhu, S. Y., "Error-Correcting Fuzzy Tree Grammars I," *Fuzzy Math.*, *3*, 15–26 (1983) (in Chinese).

Zhu, S. Y., "Error-Correcting Fuzzy Tree Grammars II," *Fuzzy Math.*, *3*, 9–22 (1983) (in Chinese).

JOHN N. MORDESON

PREMCHAND S. NAIR

UNIFORM RANDOM NUMBER GENERATION

INTRODUCTION

Random numbers generators (RNGs) can be found in most software libraries or systems. They are a key ingredient for several types of computations, such as for Monte Carlo simulation, statistical methods, probabilistic algorithms in different areas, computer games, cryptography, casino machines, and so on. From the user's point of view, the output of a RNG is usually considered as a sequence of independent and identically distributed (i.i.d.) random variables, often with the uniform distribution over the interval [0, 1]. The RNGs should at least *appear* to behave as such. In reality, however, they are simple computer programs whose behavior is completely deterministic after their initial state is chosen. Hence, the name *pseudorandom* is often employed. Attempts have been made to construct *truly random* generators based on physical devices such as noise diodes, gamma-ray counters, and so on, but these remain largely impractical and unreliable. See Ref. 1 for a discussion.

We define a *random number generator* (see Refs. 2 and 3) as a structure $\mathcal{G} = (S, \mu, T, U, G)$, where S is a finite set of *states*, μ is a probability distribution on S used to select the *initial state* (or *seed*) s_0, the mapping $T: S \rightarrow S$ is the *transition function*, U is a finite set of *output* symbols, and $G: S \rightarrow U$ is the *output function*.

The state of the generator starts at s_0 and evolves according to the recurrence $s_n = T(s_{n-1})$, for $n \geq 1$. The output at step n is $u_n = G(s_n)$. These u_n are the so-called *random numbers*. Note that the number of states in S can be much larger than the number of distinct output values, so different states can be mapped to the same output, in general. Because S is finite, the generator will eventually return to a state already visited (i.e., $s_{i+j} = s_i$ for some $i \geq 0$ and $j > 0$). Then, $s_{n+j} = s_n$ and $u_{n+j} = u_n$ for all $n \geq i$. The smallest $j > 0$ and smallest $i \geq 0$ for which this happens are called the *period* length ρ and the *transient* length τ, respectively. If $\tau = 0$, the sequence is called *purely periodic*. Of course, ρ cannot exceed the number of states $|S|$. Well-designed generators have their ρ close to this upper bound.

If the seed is chosen randomly (e.g., uniformly from S), using external randomness such as picking balls from a box or throwing a dice, the generator can be viewed as an *extensor* of randomness, which stretches a short random seed into a longer sequence of random-looking numbers.

To add further "real randomness" to the sequence and mix up its regular mathematical structure, one may combine it with physical noise. For example, Marsaglia (1) has produced a CD-ROM containing 4.8 billion random bits by combining the output of some random number generators with various sources of noise such as music, pictures, or physical devices, via bitwise exclusive-or. This is interesting, but some applications require many more random numbers than provided on this disk, and reading numbers from a CD-ROM or from a file does not match the speed and convenience of a good RNG.

To stimulate random variables from different probability distributions such as the Normal, exponential, binomial, geometric, and so on, or to simulate more complicated random objects, one would transform the output of a RNG in the appropriate way. See, for example, Refs. 4–6. These transformations are not always simple. They usually assume the availability of a uniform RNG.

Henceforth, we assume that the generator's purpose is to *simulate* i.i.d. $U(0, 1)$ random variables (uniform over the interval [0, 1]). The goal is that no user could easily distinguish between the output sequence of our dream generator and a sequence of i.i.d. $U(0, 1)$ random variables, apart from the finite precision. A necessary (but not sufficient) condition is a huge period length, long enough to make sure that no one can ever exhaust it. The RNG must also have good statistical behavior, and in certain contexts such as in cryptography, unpredictability is a major issue as well. From the theoretical viewpoint, unpredictability turns out to be asymptotically equivalent to uniformity and independence. These properties can be tested empirically, but, more importantly, should be supported by theoretical analysis. Efficiency is also an issue. For certain types of applications such as simulations in statistical mechanics, the RNG eats up much of the computing time, which is often hours or days on supercomputers. The amount of memory required can be an issue when several generators are used in parallel, which happens frequently in simulation (6).

Repeating exactly the same sequence of random numbers is needed, for example, for program verification or to compare competing systems via simulation under similar conditions (4,6). Repeatability of the sequences is a major advantage of RNGs over physical devices. Ideally, RNG implementations should be *portable* (i.e., work without change and produce the same sequence across most compilers and computers). A single RNG is often split into several virtual generators simply by partitioning its sequence into long disjoint substreams. One then needs fast algorithms to compute the state s_{n+v} for any large v, given s_n. Efficient methods to do this are known for several types of generators, including most of the linear ones (see, for example, Ref. 3 and the section Jumping Ahead).

The RNGs should be designed on the basis of a sound mathematical analysis of their structural properties. This is sometimes called *theoretical testing*. For example, the parameters of linear congruential or multiple recursive generators are chosen based on a lattice structure analysis called the *spectral test*, which we explain later. Once a generator is constructed, one can apply *empirical statistical tests* to it, to detect significant statistical defects. These theoretical and empirical analyses remain heuristic, in the sense that they can never prove that a given generator is fully reliable for any simulation. The best they can do is improve our confidence in the RNG.

The rest of this article is organized as follows. The next section describes theoretical frameworks and criteria for discriminating among generators, and approximate to some extent the ideal generator. The third section covers the linear congruential methods based on integer arithmetic and the associated lattice properties. The fourth section discusses linear methods based on digital expansions, and some equidistribution properties. The fifth section is devoted to methods based on nonlinear recurrences, such as inversive congruential generators and other methods stemming from cryptology. Statistical testing is discussed in the sixth section, and the last section gives pointers to well-tested implementations.

FRAMEWORKS FOR PSEUDORANDOM SEQUENCES

Unpredictability and Computational Complexity

A first theoretical framework for pseudo-RNGs is based on asymptotic analysis and *computational complexity theory*. Consider a *family* of generators, $\{ \mathcal{G}_k,\ k = 1, 2, \ldots \}$, where $k = \log_2 |S|$, the number of bits to represent the state. Assume that T and G can be computed in polynomial time in k and consider only the family of statistical tests $\mathcal{T}_p$ taking a polynomial time in k [the tests taking $O(|S|)$ time, for example, are excluded]. The family $\{ \mathcal{G}_k \}$ is called *polynomial-time perfect* if for any test in $\mathcal{T}_p$ trying to distinguish the output sequence of the generator from an infinite sequence of i.i.d. $U(0, 1)$ random variables, the probability that the test makes the right guess does not exceed $\frac{1}{2} + e^{-k\varepsilon}$, for some constant $\varepsilon > 0$. It has been shown that the following requirement (among others) is equivalent: No polynomial-time algorithm can predict any given bit of u_n with probability of success larger than $\frac{1}{2} + e^{-k\varepsilon}$, after observing $u_0, \ldots, u_{n-1}$. This framework links unpredictability with statistical uniformity and independence. It is built on the familiar complexity theory assumption that what cannot be computed in polynomial time in k is, for practical purposes, impossible to compute for moderate k. For more precise definitions, proofs, and further results, see Refs. 7–9 and the references given there.

How practical is this framework? Are there efficient polynomial-time perfect generators around? Which k is large enough? These questions have no clear answers at the present time. Some generator families are *conjectured* to be polynomial-time perfect, and among them is the BSS generator discussed in the section Nonlinear Methods, but no one has been able to *prove* even the existence of such a family. The fast generators commonly used for simulation are known not to be polynomial-time perfect. However, the "recommendable ones" seem to have good enough statistical properties.

What Is a Good Periodic Sequence?

Choosing a fixed-size RNG amounts to choosing a deterministic and periodic sequence of (given) period length ρ. How to discriminate among such sequences? One can view the periodic sequence as a giant roulette, with ρ numbers around. Suppose U is a finite set (a discretization of [0, 1]) and that the seed s_0 is chosen randomly, uniformly over the period length (i.e., the initial position on the roulette is chosen randomly). We would like every vector $\mathbf{u} = (u_0, \ldots, u_{t-1}) \in U^t$ to have the same probability, ideally for every t. This is possible only if $|U|^t$ divides ρ. For $t > \log(\rho)/\log(|U|)$, there is not enough positions around the roulette to cover U^t, so some of these vectors must have zero probability [i.e., $\Psi_t = \{ \mathbf{u}_n = (u_n, \ldots, u_{n+t-1}),\ 1 \le n \le \rho \}$ is a strict subset of U^t. In fact, for large t, Ψ_t can cover only a tiny fraction of U^t, and the question arises of how the points of Ψ_t should be spread over U^t. Some want Ψ_t to look like a random set of points, for each t. Others prefer Ψ_t to be very uniformly spread over U^t, based on the rationale that Ψ_t should be viewed as a discretization of U^t, from which a few points are drawn randomly, and that the uniform distribution is better approximated by a regular and uniform discretization than by a random one. This makes sense only if several orders of magnitude less than ρ random numbers are used.

For example, let $U = \{0, 1/1024, 2/1024, \ldots, 1023/1024\}$, so that we look at the 10 most significant bits of each output value, and $\varphi = 2^{200} = 1024^{20}$. In dimensions $t \le 20$, it is possible to have perfect equidistribution, all t-dimensional vectors appearing the same number of times over the entire period. However, for $t = 30$, for example, only one point out of 2^{100} belongs to Ψ_t, in the best case. Theoretical analysis of RNGs is meant to understand the structure well enough to make sure that the points are approximately equidistributed for small t and that Ψ_t is evenly distributed for t up to some large value such as 50, and preferably more. This will be our criterion for constructing "fair" generators. Similar ideas are used in, for example, Refs. 3 and 10–12. Perhaps generators with well-understood structural properties look less random, but the less understood ones may hide important defects.

Discrepancy

Well-established measures of uniformity for finite sequences of numbers are based on the notion of *discrepancy*, which is covered in Ref. 13. Let $P_N = \{\mathbf{u}_n = (u_n, \ldots, u_{n+t-1}), 0 \le n \le N - 1\}$ be a set of N points formed by overlapping vectors of successive values. For any box of the form $R = \prod_{j=1}^{t} [\alpha_j, \beta_j)$, with $0 \le \alpha_j < \beta_j \le 1$, let $I(R)$ be the number of points $\mathbf{u}_n$ falling into R, and $V(R) = \prod_{j=1}^{t} (\beta_j - \alpha_j)$ be the volume of R. If $\mathcal{R}$ is the set of all such regions R, then

$$D_N^{(t)} = \max_{R \in \mathcal{R}} \left| V(R) - \frac{I(R)}{N} \right|$$

is called the *extreme discrepancy* of P_N. If we restrict $\mathcal{R}$ to only the boxes with one corner at the origin, then the corresponding quantity is called the *star discrepancy*. Other variants also exist.

Low discrepancy is linked to superuniformity. So, in line with our previous arguments, one might want to *minimize* the discrepancy for $N = \rho$, the period length. On the other hand, for $N \ll \rho$, the discrepancy, viewed as a random variable, should behave as the discrepancy of a sequence of i.i.d. $U(0,1)$ random variables; for example, be (roughly) in $O(N^{-1/2})$. The linear-type generators discussed in the forthcoming sections enjoy these properties, at least asymptotically (13). Unfortunately, discrepancy is too hard to compute, except for special cases. Only loose bounds on it are available in general.

Point sets with much lower discrepancy than typical i.i.d. uniform random points are called *low-discrepancy* point sets. Infinite sequences for which P_N has low discrepancy for all large enough N are called low-discrepancy sequences. Such point sets and sequences are also called *quasi-random* and are sometimes used for finite-dimensional numerical integration in replacement of (or in combination with) the basic Monte Carlo method (12,13).

LINEAR METHODS BASED ON INTEGER ARITHMETIC

The Multiple Recursive Generator

Define the linear recurrence

$$x_n = (a_1 x_{n-1} + \cdots + a_k x_{n-k}) \mod m, \tag{1}$$

with *order* k, *modulus* m (a positive integer), and integer *coefficients* $a_1, \ldots, a_k$ in the range $\{-(m-1), \ldots, m-1\}$. Let $\mathbb{Z}_m = \{0, 1, \ldots, m-1\}$ with operations performed modulo m. The state at step n is $s_n = (x_{n-k+1}, \ldots, x_n) \in \mathbb{Z}_m^k$ and the output function can be defined simply by $u_n = G(s_n) = x_n/m$, giving a value in [0, 1], or by a more refined transformation if a better resolution than $1/m$ is required. This is the *multiple recursive generator* (MRG) (2,11,13). The special case where $k = 1$ is known as the *linear congruential generator* (LCG). Then, a_1 is denoted by a, and a constant is sometimes added to the recurrence, yielding

$$x_n = (ax_{n-1} + c) \mod m. \qquad [2]$$

When $c = 0$, the LCG is called a *multiplicative* LCG (or MLCG).

The largest possible period for Eq. (1) is $\rho = m^k - 1$, which is reached if and only if m is prime and the characteristic polynomial of the recurrence, defined by $P(z) = z^k - a_1 z^{k-1} - \cdots - a_k$, is a primitive polynomial over $\mathbb{Z}_m$, identified as the finite field with m elements. This means that the smallest positive integer v such that $(z^v \mod P(z)) \mod m = 1$ is $v = m^k - 1$. Equivalent conditions that are more convenient to verify are given in Ref. 11. For $k > 1$, for P to be primitive, it is necessary that a_k and at least another coefficient a_j be nonzero. It is also easy to find primitive polynomials of this form, and they yield the more economic recurrence

$$x_n = (a_r x_{n-r} + a_k x_{n-k}) \mod m. \qquad [3]$$

For faster speed, one may prefer $m = 2^e$, a power of 2, instead of a prime m. The recurrence [1] or [2] is then easier to compute (e.g., if $m = 2^{32}$ on a 32-bit computer), but the period length is much smaller than $m^k - 1$. For $m = 2^e$, the maximum period length is 2^{e-2} if $k = 1$ and $e \geq 4$ [it is reached if $a_1 = 3$ or 5 (mod 8) and x_0 is odd (11, p. 20)], and $(2^k - 1)2^{e-1}$ if $k > 1$. For example, if $k = 7$ and $m = 2^{31} - 1$, the maximal period length is $(2^{31} - 1)^7 - 1 \approx 2^{217}$, whereas if $k = 7$ and $m = 2^{31}$, the upper bound becomes $(2^7 - 1)2^{31-1} < 2^{37}$, which is more than 2^{180} times smaller! Another drawback of power-of-2 moduli is that the low-order bits are typically much too regular. For $k = 1$, an upper bound on the period length of the ith least significant bit of x_n is $\max(1, 2^{i-2})$ (Ref. 4), and if a full cycle is split into 2^d equal segments, then all segments are identical except for their d most significant bits. For $k > 1$, the upper bound on the period length of the ith least significant bit is $(2^k - 1)2^{i-1}$. For $k = 7$ and $m = 2^{31}$, for example, the least significant bit has period length at most $2^7 - 1 = 127$, the second least significant bit has period length at most $2(2^7 - 1) = 254$, and so on.

For $k = 1$ and $m = 2^e$, one can obtain a period length of $\rho = m$ by using Eq. [2] with $c > 0$, c odd, and $a \mod 4 = 1$ (see Ref. 11, p. 16). However, the short periodicity of the low-order bits remains: The ith least significant bit of x_n has period length 2^i. For $k > 1$, adding a constant c in the recurrence [1] is not very helpful. The recurrence then becomes equivalent to a linear recurrence of order $k + 1$ with $c = 0$, so the period length cannot exceed $(2^{k+1} - 1)2^{e-1}$ (see Ref. 2).

Implementation for Prime *m*

For prime m, computing $ax \mod m$ in integer arithmetic can get tricky, because the product ax is often not representable as an ordinary integer on the computer at hand (e.g., if $m = 2^{31} - 1$ on a 32-bit computer). General techniques to compute this product modulo m without overflow, using only integer arithmetic, are compared in Ref. 14. In the case when $a = i$ or $a = \lfloor m/i \rfloor$, for $i < \sqrt{m}$, there is an efficient *approximate factoring* method (15). Another approach is to perform all the arithmetic modulo m in double-precision floating point. For example, if the floating-point numbers are represented over

64 bits and if the computations are performed according to the IEEE standard, all non-negative integers less or equal to 2^{53} are represented exactly in floating point. In this case, if $a_i(m-1) \le 2^{53}$, then each product $a_i x_{n-i}$ will always be represented exactly in floating point. Similarly, if $(|a_1| + \cdots + |a_k|)(m-1) \le 2^{53}$, then $a_1 x_{n-1} + \cdots + a_k x_{n-k}$ is always represented exactly. The following instructions then perform the assignment $x := ax \bmod m$:

$$y := ax; \qquad x := y - \lfloor y/m \rfloor m.$$

Jumping Ahead

To jump directly from x_n to x_{n+v} with an MLCG, for large v, use the relation

$$x_{n+v} = a^v x_n \bmod m = (a^v \bmod m) x_n \bmod m.$$

The constant $a^v \bmod m$ can be precomputed using a divide-to-conquer algorithm (2). For an LCG with $c \ne 0$, one has

$$x_{n+v} = \left(a^v x_n + \frac{c(a^v - 1)}{a - 1} \right) \bmod m.$$

To jump ahead with the MRG, one way is to use the fact that it can be represented as a matrix MLCG: $X_n = AX_{n-1} \bmod m$, where X_n is s_n represented as a column vector and A is a $k \times k$ square matrix (2). Jumping ahead is then achieved in the same way as for the MLCG:

$$X_{n+v} = A^v X_n \bmod m = (A^v \bmod m) X_n \bmod m.$$

Another way is to transform the MRG into its polynomial representation (Ref. 3), in which jumping ahead is achieved by multiplying this polynomial by $z^v \bmod P(z)$, and then apply the inverse transformation to recover the original representation.

Lattice Structure of LCGs and MRGs

The set

$$T_t = \{ \mathbf{u}_n = (u_n, \ldots, u_{n+t-1}) \mid n \ge 0, (x_0, \ldots, x_{k-1}) \in \mathbb{Z}_m^k \} \tag{4}$$

of all t-dimensional vectors of successive values produced by Eq. [1] and $u_n = x_n/m$, from all possible initial seeds, is the intersection of a lattice L_t with the hypercube $[0, 1)^t$ (see, for example, Refs. 11, 15, and 16).

For $t \le k$, L_t contains all vectors in dimension t whose coordinates are multiples of $1/m$. However, for $t > k$, L_t contains only a small fraction of these vectors, namely m^k out of m^t. The lattice structure of T_t means that its points lie on a limited number of equidistant parallel hyperplanes, at a distance, say, d_t apart. Figures 1 and 2 illustrate the lattice structure of two small MLCGs with modulus $m = 251$ (a prime), in dimension 2. They have $a = 78$ and $a = 167$, respectively. The figures show all 250 pairs of successive values (u_n, u_{n+1}) produced by these (full period) generators. In dimension 2, the parallel hyperplanes are lines, and one can see from the figures that d_2 is smaller, and the points are more uniformly distributed, for $a = 78$ than for $a = 167$.

Computing d_t is often called the *spectral test*, for historical reasons (Ref. 11). The available algorithms for doing so are exponential in t in the worst case, but current

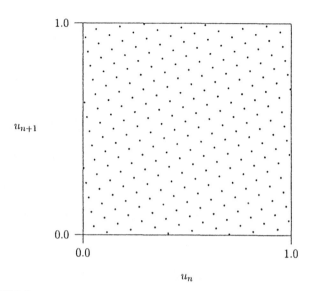

FIGURE 1 All pairs (u_n, u_{n+1}) for the LCG with $m = 251$ and $a = 78$.

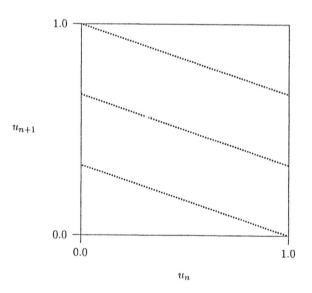

FIGURE 2 All pairs (u_n, u_{n+1}) for the LCG with $m = 251$ and $a = 167$.

implementations permit one to compute d_t up to 40 or more dimensions, for m exceeding 2^{100} (16).

As we saw in the examples, a large d_t is bad, because it means thick empty slices between the hyperplanes. For any lattice, the value of d_t is nondecreasing with respect to t. An absolute lower bound, for any lattice whose intersection with $(0, 1]^t$ has m^k points, is given by

$$d_t \geq d_t^* = \frac{1}{\gamma_t m^{k/t}}, \qquad\qquad\qquad [5]$$

where γ_t constant currently known for $t \leq 8$ (see Ref. 11). For larger t, lower and upper bounds on γ_t are known. For example, an upper bound can be deduced from Rogers bound on the density of sphere packings (17, p. 88; 18). The value of d_t can then be normalized to $S_t = d_t^*/d_t$, where γ_t in the definition of d_t^* is replaced by its upper bound for $t > 8$. Then, for any fixed $T > k$, one can define the figure of merit $M_T = \min_{k < t \leq T} S_t$, which lies between 0 and 1. We seek generators with large values of M_T.

Another lower bound on d_t, for $t > k$, is (see Ref. 19): $d_t^2 \geq 1/(1 + \sum_{j=1}^k a_j^2)$, which implies that an MRG whose sum of squares of coefficients is small is guaranteed to be bad with respect to d_t.

Other figures of merit for random number generators, in terms of their lattice structure, have been introduced as well. For example, one can count the minimal number of hyperplanes that contain all the points, or compute the ratio of lengths of the shortest and longest vector in a Minkowski-reduced basis of the lattice. See, for example, Refs. 16 and 20 and the references given there. These other figures of merit do not tell us much more than d_t.

Values of d_t and S_t for certain MRGs and LCGs can be found, for example, in Refs. 11, 15, 16, 18, and 20. The values of S_t or M_T for different generators can be compared only if these generators have the same period length (i.e., the same lattice density). A generator with period length less than 2^{60}, for example, should not be recommended for serious use, whatever its values of S_t, because such a period length is too short. MRGs with large periods and good figures of merit are given in Ref. 15.

Lacunary Indices

The vectors forming the set T_t do not have to be constructed from successive output values. More generally, one can select a fixed set of *lacunary indices* $I = \{i_1, i_2, \ldots, i_t\}$ and define, for an MRG,

$$T_t(I) = \{(u_{i_1+n}, \ldots, u_{i_t+n}) \mid n \geq 0, (x_0, \ldots, x_{k-1}) \in \mathbb{Z}_m^k\}.$$

Let $L_t(I)$ be the lattice spanned by $T_t(I)$ and $\mathbb{Z}^t$, and let $d_t(I)$ be the distance between the hyperplanes in this lattice. This $d_t(I)$ can be computed as explained in Ref. 16. An easy lower bound on $d_t(I)$ is given as follows (19,21): If $\{i : a_{k-i} \neq 0\} \subseteq I$, then $d_t(I)^2 \geq 1/(1 + \sum_{i=1}^k a_i^2)$. In particular, if $x_n = (a_r x_{n-r} + a_k x_{n-k}) \bmod m$ and $I = \{0, k - r, k\}$, then $d_3(I) \geq (1 + a_r^2 + a_k^2)^{-1/2}$. A further special case is the so-called *lagged-Fibonacci* generator, based on a recurrence with two nonzero coefficients, $a_r = \pm 1$ and $a_k = \pm 1$. In this case, for $I = \{0, k - r, k\}$, $d_3(I) \geq 1/\sqrt{3} \approx 0.577$, and all the vectors (u_n, u_{n+r}, u_{n+k}) produced by this generator lie in only two planes! Specific instances of this generator are the one proposed in Ref. 11 (p. 186), based on the recurrence $x_n = (x_{m-37} + x_{m-100}) \bmod 2^e$ for e equal to the computer's word length, and the "addrans" function in the SUN UNIX library, based on $x_n = (x_{n-5} + x_{n-17}) \bmod 2^{24}$. These generators should be discarded.

Combined LCGs and MRGs

It is often advocated to combine the output of different generators to enlarge the period and improve the statistical properties (2,22). Combination is supported by a large amount of empirical experience. For sequences of independent random variables, certain types of combinations (e.g., addition modulo 1) yield a combined sequence whose distribution is provably closer to the uniform than that of any of its components alone (22,23). However, in the case of *deterministic* sequences, these results are not really meaningful and can only be used as heuristic arguments. One can construct counterexamples where the combined sequence is worse than each of its components. Therefore, to assess its quality, one must study the structural properties of the combined generator itself. This applies not only to MRGs, but more generally.

Two classes of widely used combination methods are as follows:

(i) Shuffling one sequence with another or with itself
(ii) Adding two or more integer sequences modulo some integer m_0, or adding sequences of real numbers in [0, 1] modulo 1, or adding binary fractions bitwise modulo 2

Methods of the first class shuffle (locally) the sequence of a generator with the aid of a second generator. Usually, the first generator fills up a table and then, at each step, the output of the second generator determines a position in the table, the value at that position is returned as the output of the combined generator, and is replaced in the table by the next output value from the first generator. There are several variants of this shuffling scheme. Sometimes, the same generator is used for both fill-up and selection. Shuffling has good empirical support, but its effects are not well understood theoretically and efficient jump-ahead algorithms are not available.

The combination of MRGs by modular addition is better understood and, in that case, jumping ahead is easy, because it suffices to do it with the individual components, independently. Consider the J recurrences:

$$x_{j,n} = (a_{j,1}x_{j,n-1} + \cdots + a_{j,k}x_{j,n-k}) \quad \bmod m_j,$$

for $j = 1, \ldots, J$. Assume that the m_j are pairwise relatively prime and that each recurrence is purely periodic (has zero transient) with period length ρ_j. Let $\delta_1, \ldots, \delta_J$ be arbitrary integers such that for each j, δ_j and m_j have no common factor. Define the combinations:

$$z_n = \left(\sum_{j=1}^{J} \delta_j x_{j,n} \right) \quad \bmod m_1; \qquad u_n = \frac{z_n}{m_1}, \qquad [6]$$

and

$$w_n = \left(\sum_{j=1}^{J} \frac{\delta_j x_{j,n}}{m_j} \right) \quad \bmod 1. \qquad [7]$$

Let $k = \max(k_1, \ldots, k_J)$ and $m = \prod_{j=1}^{J} m_j$. The following is proved in Ref. 24 for the case of MLCG components ($k = 1$) and in Ref. 25 for the more general case:

(i) The sequences $\{u_n\}$ and $\{w_n\}$ have period length $\rho = \text{lcm}(\rho_1, \ldots, \rho_J)$ (the least common multiple of the ρ_j).

(ii) The w_n obey the recurrence

$$x_n = (a_1 x_{n-1} + \cdots + a_k x_{n-k}) \mod m; \qquad w_n = \frac{x_n}{m}, \qquad [8]$$

where the a_i are computed as explained in Ref. 25 and do not depend on the δ_j.

(iii) One has $u_n = w_n + \varepsilon_n$, with $\Delta^- \le \varepsilon_n \le \Delta^+$, where Δ^- and Δ^+ can be computed as explained in Ref. 25 and are very small when the m_j are close to each other.

The combinations [6] and [7] can then be viewed as efficient ways to implement an MRG with large (composite) modulus m. The idea is to choose MRG components that are fast and easy to implement (e.g., only two nonzero coefficients) and for which the MRG [8] has good structural properties. If m_j is prime and $\rho_j = m_j^{k_j} - 1$ for each j, then each ρ_j is even, so $\rho \le (m_1^{k_1} - 1) \cdots (m_J^{k_J} - 1)/2^{J-1}$.

A specific combined MRG with $J = 2$, $k = 3$, and period length $\rho \approx 2^{185}$ is proposed in Ref. 25. It was selected after a computer search for combined MRGs of this size with good lattice structure. An implementation in the C language is given.

Matrix MRGs

A natural extension of Eq. [1] is to define MRGs in matrix form:

$$X_n = (A_1 X_{n-1} + \cdots + A_k X_{n-k}) \mod m, \qquad [9]$$

where $A_1, \ldots, A_k$ are $L \times L$ matrices and each X_n is a L-dimensional vector with components in $\mathbb{Z}_m$. At each step, one can use X_n to produce an output *vector*. Niederreiter (26) studies this generalization and calls it the *multiple recursive matrix method*.

Linear Recurrences with Carry

Consider the recurrence

$$x_n = (a_1 x_{n-1} + \cdots + a_k x_{n-k} + c_{n-1}) \mod b, \qquad [10]$$

$$c_n = (a_1 x_{n-1} + \cdots + a_k x_{n-k} + c_{n-1}) \text{ div } b, \qquad [11]$$

$$u_n = x_n/b,$$

where div mean *integer division*. This is similar to Eq. [1], except for the *carry* c_n, and the state is now $s_n = (x_n, \ldots, x_{n+k-1}, c_n)$. This type of generator, proposed by Marsaglia, is studied in Ref. 27 and is called *Multiply-with-Carry* (MWC). Define $a_0 = -1$, $m = \sum_{l=0}^{k} a_l b^l$, and let a be the inverse of b in arithmetic modulo m, assuming for now that $m > 0$. If we define

$$w_n = \sum_{i=1}^{\infty} x_{n+i-1} b^{-i}, \qquad [12]$$

then the sequence $\{w_n\}$ obeys (see Ref. 27)

$$z_n = a z_{n-1} \mod m; \qquad w_n = \frac{z_n}{m}. \qquad [13]$$

The MWC is then equivalent to this LCG, up to precision $1/b$. A period length of $(m-1)/2$ can be achieved if b is a power of 2, and this is the major advantage over an MRG. For example, one may take $b = 2^{32}$. Note that the MWC has many more states than $(m-1)/2$, some of them being transient. The set of recurrent states is precisely characterized in Ref. 27. In particular, if $a_l \geq 0$ for all $l \geq 1$, then the carry c_n is always smaller than $a_1 + \cdots + a_k$, so if $b-1$ fits into a computer word and $a_1 + \cdots + a_k \leq b$, then each component of the state fits into a computer word.

The lattice structure of the LCG (13) satisfies the following (see Ref. 27). For $t \leq k$, d_t does not depend on $a_1, \ldots, a_k$, but only on b, and for $t = k + 1$, one has

$$d_{k+1} = (1 + a_1^2 + \cdots + a_k^2)^{-1/2}. \qquad [14]$$

To minimize this distance and get a large m, one should choose a_k close to b, with $a_0 + \cdots + a_k \leq b$. Specific parameter sets are proposed in Refs. 27 and 28.

Special cases of the MWC, called the add-with-carry and subtract-with-borrow generators, were proposed in Ref. 29 and analyzed in Refs. 21 and 30. These special cases have $a_r = \pm 1$, $a_k \pm 1$, and the other a_l equal to 0. They resemble the lagged-Fibonacci generators and turn out to have the same defect: $d_{k+1} = 1/\sqrt{3}$ from Eq. (14), and all vectors of the form (w_n, w_{n+r}, w_{n+k}) lie in only two planes in the three- dimensional unit cube (21).

One way to get around this problem is to take only blocks of k successive values of x_n and skip many values in between, so that triplets of the form (w_n, w_{m+r}, w_{n+k}) never appear. Such an approach is proposed in Ref. 31 for a specific generator, with heuristic justification based on Lyapunov exponents, and a Fortran implementation of the generator is given in Ref. 32. A similar one is proposed in Ref. 11.

THE DIGITAL METHOD

Digital Multistep Sequences

To improve the resolution of the output, one can construct each u_n from several successive x_n in Eq. (1), as follows. Redefine

$$u_n = \sum_{j=1}^{L} x_{ns+j-1} m^{-j}, \qquad [15]$$

where s is called the *step size* and L is the *number of digits* in the expansion. The u_n are now multiples of m^{-L} and this sequence $\{u_n\}$ is called a *digital multistep sequence* (3,13). If the MRG sequence has period ρ and if s is relatively prime with ρ, then $\{u_n\}$ also has period ρ.

LFSR or Tausworthe Generators

An important special case is $m = 2$. Then, $\{x_n\}$ becomes a sequence of bits and the corresponding generator is called a Linear Feedback Shift Register (LFSR) or Tausworthe generator (3,13,33) (often with the bits of u_n filled in reverse order to that in Eq. [15]). Specific implementations for recurrences of the form $x_n = (x_{n-r} + x_{n-k}) \bmod 2$, with $s \leq r$ and $2r > k$, are given in Refs. 12, 34, 35. For jump-ahead algorithms, see Ref. 34.

Simple LFSRs with only two nonzero coefficients have bad structural properties (see, for example, Refs. 12, 34, 36, and 37 and references therein), but several of them can be combined, much as for the combined MRGs, yielding fast generators with good properties. Take J LFSR recurrences, the jth one having a primitive characteristic polynomial $P_j(z)$ of degree k_j, and step size s_j relatively prime with the period length $\rho_j = 2^{k_j} - 1$. Assume that the polynomials $P_j(z)$ are pairwise relatively prime, that the ρ_j are also relatively prime, that these LFSRs use a common L, and let u_n be the bitwise addition modulo 2 of the output values of these J LFSR components at step n. Then, this combined sequence $\{u_n\}$ is exactly equivalent to that of a LFSR generator with characteristic polynomial $P(z) = P_1(z) \cdots P_J(z)$, whose period length is $\rho = \Pi_{j=1}^{J} \rho_j$. See Refs. 34, 35, and 38 for more details and specific implementations. For better statistical behavior, it is recommended that $P(z)$ have approximately half of its coefficients equal to one.

Matrix Methods and GFSR Generators

The digital method can be applied also to the matrix version [9] in the following way:

$$u_n = \sum_{j=1}^{L} x_{n,j} m^{-j}, \qquad\qquad [16]$$

where $x_{n,1}, \ldots, x_{n,L}$ are the first L components of X_n. This is studied in Ref. 39. Under specific conditions on the seeds (see Refs. 3 and 40), Eq. [16] gives exactly the same sequence as Eq. [15] with a proper choice of s, so these are then two different implementations of the same generator. The implementation based [9] and [16] needs more memory but may be faster. An important instance of it is the Generalized Feedback Shift Register (GFSR) generator (41–43), for which $m = 2$ and L is the computer's word length, so Eq. [9] can then be computed by a bitwise exclusive-or of the X_{n-j} for which $a_j = 1$. If there are only two nonzero coefficients, say a_k and a_r, we obtain

$$X_n = X_{n-r} \oplus X_{n-k},$$

where $\oplus$ denotes the bitwise exclusive-or. This gives a very fast generator, but our caveat for trinomial-based LFSR generators also applies here.

The GFSR requires kL bits of memory, but its period length is only $2^k - 1$ instead of near 2^{kL}, as we should expect. It then comes to mind to *twist* it slightly, to improve its properties without impairing the speed too much. For example, as a coefficient of X_{n-k}, one can take some binary matrix A_k instead of the identity matrix, and choose A_k so that the period becomes $2^{kL} - 1$ and the implementation remains fast. A specific way of doing this and a concrete implementation are given in Ref. 44.

Equidistribution Properties for the Digital Method

A partition of the hypercube $[0, 1)^l$ into m^{tl} cubic cells of equal size is called a (t, l)-*equidissection in base m*. A set of points is (t, l)-*equidistributed* if each of these cells contains the same number of points. For a set of m^k points, this is possible only for $l \le \lfloor k/t \rfloor$. For a given digital multistep sequence, let

$$T_t = \{ \mathbf{u}_n = (u_n, \ldots, u_{n+t-1}) : \quad n \ge 0, (x_0, \ldots, x_{k-1}) \in \mathbb{Z}_m^k \} \qquad [17]$$

and $l_t = \min(L, \lfloor k/t \rfloor)$. If T_t is (t, l_t)-equidistributed for all $t \le k$, we say that the generator is *maximally equidistributed* (ME). We also call it collision-free (CF) if for all t, for $l_t < l \le L$, no cell contains more than one point. ME–CF generators have their point sets evenly distributed in the hypercube in all dimensions.

The GFSRs are (t, L)-equidistributed for $t = \lfloor k/L \rfloor$ if and only if their initial state satisfies independence conditions given in Ref. 41. One can verify (t, l)-equidistribution rapidly by computing the rank of a binary matrix that expresses the first l bits of $\mathbf{u}_n$ as a linear combination of $(x_0, \ldots, x_{k-1})$. Reference 34 explains this and provides specific ME and ME–CF combined LFSR generators, with an implementation in C.

A stronger notion than (t, l)-equidistribution is that of a (q, k, t)-*net in base m*, where the partition into cubic boxes is replaced by a richer set of partitions into rectangular boxes of equal volume m^{q-k}, with each coordinate of each box corner equal to a multiple of $1/m$. Niederreiter (13) defines a figure of merit $r^{(t)}$ such that for $t > \lfloor k/L \rfloor$, the m^k points of T_l for Eq. [15] form a (q, k, t)-net in base m with $q = k - r^{(t)}$. This $r^{(t)}$ is difficult to compute for medium and large t (say, $t > 8$).

NONLINEAR METHODS

The generators discussed so far have a linear structure, which may be deemed too regular. To get away from it, one can either use a nonlinear transition function T, or keep T linear and use a nonlinear transformation G to produce the output. Several types of nonlinear generators have been proposed and analyzed in the literature; see for example, Refs. 8, 9, 13, and 45–48 and references therein. The sequences produced by these generators, over their entire periods, tend to behave more like truly random sequences than like superuniform ones (e.g., in terms of their discrepancy bounds). A major drawback of nonlinear generators is that they are typically significantly slower than the linear ones. A general class of nonlinear transformations is defined by

$$x_n = T(x_{n-1}) = f(x_{n-1}) \quad \text{mod } m, \quad x_{n-1} \in \mathbb{Z}_m, \tag{18}$$

where m is a positive integer. The output can be produced simply by $u_n = x_n/m$, or by more complicated means if desired.

Inversive Congruential Generators

Some generators use inversion modulo m as their nonlinear transformation. For example, let $\{x_n\}$ be an MRG sequence with prime m and define the output as

$$z_n = (\tilde{x}_{n+1} \tilde{x}_n^{-1}) \quad \text{mod } m \quad \text{and} \quad u_n = \frac{z_n}{m}, \tag{19}$$

where $\tilde{x}_i$ denotes the ith nonzero value in the sequence $\{x_n\}$, and $\tilde{x}_n^{-1} = \tilde{x}_n^{m-2}$ mod m is the inverse of $\tilde{x}_n$ modulo m, which can be computed with $O(\log m)$ multiplications modulo m. The sequence $\{z_n\}$ has period m^{k-1}, under conditions given in Refs. 13 and 45.

Another approach is the *explicit inversive congruential* method: Let $x_n = an + c$ for $n \geq 0$, where $a \neq 0$ and c are in $\mathbb{Z}_m$ and m is prime, and define

$$z_n = x_n^{-1} = (an + c)^{m-2} \quad \text{mod } m \quad \text{and} \quad u_n = \frac{z_n}{m}. \tag{20}$$

This sequence has period $\rho = m$ and, according to Ref. 46, seems to enjoy the most favorable properties among the currently proposed inversive families.

Inversive congruential generators with power-of-two moduli have been studied, but their structural properties are not as good as for the generators with prime moduli (46,49).

Inversive generators can be combined much in the same way as MRGs and LFSRs (e.g., by addition modulo 1).

The BBS and Other Cryptographic Generators

Several types of nonlinear generators, some conjectured to be polynomial-time perfect, have been proposed in the area of cryptology (Refs. 8,9). A well-known example is the BBS generator (Ref. 7), defined as follows. For an instance of size k, the state is a triplet (p, q, x) where p and q are $(k/2)$-bit primes, both congruent to 1 modulo 4, and x is a quadratic residue modulo $m = pq$, relatively prime to m. The initial state is random, but after it is selected, only x changes, according to the recurrence $x_n = x_{n-1}^2 \bmod m$. At each step, the generator outputs the v_k least significant bits of x_n, where $v_k = O(\log k)$. Under the assumption that there is no general polynomial-time (in k) algorithm to find p or q given m, the BBS generator has been proved polynomial-time perfect. Of course, all of this is only asymptotic. In practice, how large should k be and how small should v_k be? This remains unclear. This generator is rather slow compared with the linear ones, but for certain cryptographic applications, it is a good choice.

EMPIRICAL STATISTICAL TESTING

Define the null hypothesis $\mathcal{H}_0$: "u_1, u_2, u_3, . . . are i.i.d. $U(0, 1)$ random variables." Formally, we know that this hypothesis if false, but can we detect it? A test is defined by a statistic T, function of a fixed set of u_i, whose distribution under $\mathcal{H}_0$ is known. Different tests may detect different defects. Ideally, T should resemble the random variable of practical interest, so that a bad interference between the generator's structure and the problem of interest would show up in the test. However, designing specific statistical tests for each problem is not practical. For general-purpose random number generators in software libraries, the best we can do is to apply a large and varied set of tests. Note that no statistical test can prove that a generator is totally foolproof. For better confidence, it is a good idea to rerun important simulations with random number generators of totally different types.

A standard (one-level) test will reject $\mathcal{H}_0$ if T is too far in the tail of its theoretical distribution. A two-level test would compute N "independent" copies of T and compare their empirical distribution with the theoretical distribution of T under $\mathcal{H}_0$, via a goodness-of-fit test such as those of Kolmogorov–Smirnov or Anderson–Darling (11,50). Several statistical tests for random number generators are given in Refs. 3, 11, 22, 49, and 51 and references therein.

Some experience with empirical testing tells us the following: (i) Generators with period shorter than, say 2^{32}, easily fail a lot of tests and should no longer be used; (ii) generators with power-of-two moduli are easier to crack than those with prime moduli, especially when looking at lower-order bits; (iii) LFSRs and GFSRs based on primitive trinomials, or lagged-Fibonacci and AWC/SWB generators are also easy to crack; (iv) combined generators with long period and good lattice structure or good equidistribution do well in the tests. Generators based on more complicated recurrences tend to do better. This favors combined generators.

AVAILABLE IMPLEMENTATIONS

We conclude by giving pointers to available implementations. No generator can be guaranteed against all possible defects, but those that we now mention have fairly good theoretical support, have been extensively tested, and are easy to use. Our list includes the twisted GFSR in Ref. 44, the combined MRG in Ref. 25, the combined LCG in Ref. 52, the combined Tausworthe generator in Ref. 34, the MRG in Ref. 15, and the RANLUX code in Ref. 32.

For some applications (e.g., for implementing certain variance reduction methods in simulation), it is convenient to have several (virtual) generators available, each one having its sequence partitioned into very long segments, and where one can jump rapidly to the beginning of the next segment, or the previous segment, or the first segment, for each generator. One such software package is described in Ref. 52.

RECOMMENDED READINGS FOR FURTHER STUDY

For the readers interested in learning more about the design of pseudorandom number generators, we recommend Refs. 3, 11, and 13. Several articles and other material related to RNGs are available from the web pages:

http://www.iro.umontreal.ca/~lecuyer
http://random.mat.sbg.ac.at

ACKNOWLEDGMENTS

This work has been supported by the National Science and Engineering Research Council of Canada grants Nos. ODGP0110050 and SMF0169893, and FCAR- Québec grant No. 93ER1654.

REFERENCES

1. G. Marsaglia, "The Marsaglia Random Number CDROM," see http://stat.fsu.edu/ ~geo/, 1996.
2. P. L'Ecuyer, "Random Numbers for Simulation," *Commun. ACM, 33*(10), 85–97 (1990).
3. P. L'Ecuyer, "Uniform Random Number Generation," *Ann. Oper. Res., 53,* 77–120 (1994).
4. P. Bratley, B. L. Fox, and L. E. Schrage, *A Guide to Simulation,* 2nd ed., Springer-Verlag, New York, 1987.
5. L. Devroye, *Non-Uniform Random Variate Generation,* Springer-Verlag, New York, 1986.
6. A. M. Law and W. D. Kelton, *Simulation Modeling and Analysis,* 2nd ed., McGraw-Hill, New York, 1991.
7. L. Blum, M. Blum, and M. Schub, "A Simple Unpredictable Pseudo-random Number Generator," *SIAM J. Comput., 15*(2), 364–383 (1986).
8. J. C. Lagarias, "Pseudorandom numbers," *Statist. Sci., 8*(1), 31–39 (1993).
9. P. L'Ecuyer and R. Proulx, "About Polynomial-Time "Unpredictable" Generators," in *Proceedings of the 1989 Winter Simulation Conference,* IEEE Press, New York, 1989, pp. 467–476.
10. A. Compagner, "Operational Conditions for Random Number Generation," *Phys. Rev. E, 52*(5-B), 5634–5645 (1995).

11. D. E. Knuth, *The Art of Computer Programming, Volume 2: Seminumerical Algorithms*, 3rd ed., Addison-Wesley, Reading, MA, 1997.

12. S. Tezuka, *Uniform Random Numbers: Theory and Practice*. Kluwer Academic Publishers, Norwell, MA, 1995.

13. H. Niederreiter, *Random Number Generation and Quasi-Monte Carlo Methods*, SIAM CBMS–NSF Regional Conference Series in Applied Mathematics, Vol. 63, SIAM, Philadelphia, 1992.

14. P. L'Ecuyer and S. Côté, "Implementing a Random Number Package with Splitting Facilities," *ACM Trans. Math. Software*, *17*(1), 98–111 (1991).

15. P. L'Ecuyer, F. Blouin, and R. Couture, "A Search for Good Multiple Recursive Random Number Generators," *ACM Trans. Model. Computer Simul.*, *3*(2), 87–98 (1993).

16. P. L'Ecuyer and R. Couture, "An Implementation of the Lattice and Spectral Tests for Multiple Recursive Linear Random Number Generators," *INFORMS J. Comput.*, *9*(2), 206–217 (1997).

17. J. H. Conway and N. J. A. Sloane, *Sphere Packings, Lattices and Groups*, Grundlehren der Mathematischen Wissenschaften Vol. 290. Springer-Verlag, New York, 1988.

18. P. L'Ecuyer, "A Table of Linear Congruential Generators of Different Sizes and Good Lattice Structure," *Math. of Comput.*, 1998 (to appear).

19. P. L'Ecuyer, "Bad Lattice Structures for Vectors of Non-successive Values Produced by Some Linear Recurrences," *INFORMS J. Comput.*, *9*(1), 57–60 (1997).

20. G. S. Fishman, *Monte Carlo: Concepts, Algorithms, and Applications*, Springer Series in Operations Research. Springer-Verlag, New York, 1996.

21. R. Couture and P. L'Ecuyer, "On the Lattice Structure of Certain Linear Congruential Sequences Related to AWC/SWB Generators," *Math. Comput.*, *62*(206), 798–808 (1994).

22. G. Marsaglia, "A Current View of Random Number Generators," in *Computer Science and Statistics, Sixteenth Symposium on the Interface*, North-Holland Elsevier Science Publishers, Amsterdam, 1985, pp. 3–10.

23. M. Brown and H. Solomon, "On Combining Pseudorandom Number Generators," *Ann. Statist.*, *1*, 691–695 (1979).

24. P. L'Ecuyer and S. Tezuka, "Structural Properties for Two Classes of Combined Random Number Generators," *Math. Comput.*, *57*(196), 735–746 (1991).

25. P. L'Ecuyer, "Combined Multiple Recursive Generators," *Operat. Res.*, *44*(5), 816–822 (1996).

26. H. Niederreiter, "Pseudorandom Vector Generation by the Multiple-Recursive Matrix Method," *Math. Comput.*, *64*(209), 279–294 (1995).

27. R. Couture and P. L'Ecuyer, "Distribution Properties of Multiply-with-Carry Random Number Generators," *Math. Comput.*, *66*(218) 591–607 (1997).

28. G. Marsaglia, "Yet Another rng," posted to the electronic billboard sci.stat.math, August 1, 1994.

29. G. Marsaglia and A. Zaman, "A New Class of Random Number Generators," *Ann. App. Probab.*, *1*, 462–480 (1991).

30. S. Tezuka, P. L'Ecuyer, and R. Couture, "On the Add-with-Carry and Subtract-with-Borrow Random Number Generators," *ACM Trans. Model. Computer Simul.*, *3*(4), 315–331 (1994).

31. M. Lüscher, "A Portable High-Quality Random Number Generator for Lattice Field Theory Simulations," *Computer Phys. Commun.*, *79*, 100–110 (1994).

32. F. James, "RANLUX: A Fortran Implementation of the High-Quality Pseudorandom Number Generator of Lüscher," *Computer Phys. Commun.*, *79*, 111–114 (1994).

33. R. C. Tausworthe, "Random Numbers Generated by Linear Recurrence Modulo Two," *Math. Comput.*, *19*, 201–209 (1965).

34. P. L'Ecuyer, "Maximally Equidistributed Combined Tausworthe Generators," *Math. Comput.*, *65*(213), 203–213 (1996).

35. S. Tezuka and P. L'Ecuyer, "Efficient and Portable Combined Tausworthe Random Number Generators," *ACM Trans. Model. Computer Simul.*, *1*(2), 99–112 (1991).
36. A. Compagner, "The Hierarchy of Correlations in Random Binary Sequences," *J. Statist. Phys.*, *63*, 883–896 (1991).
37. M. Matsumoto and Y. Kurita, "Strong Deviations from Randomness in *m*-Sequences Based on Trinomials," *ACM Trans. Model. Computer Simul.*, *6*(2), 99–106 (1996).
38. D. Wang and A. Compagner, "On the Use of Reducible Polynomials as Random Number Generators," *Math. Comput.*, *60*, 363–374 (1993).
39. H. Niederreiter, "The Multiple-Recursive Matrix Method for Pseudorandom Number Generation," *Finite Fields Applic.*, *1*, 3–30 (1995).
40. M. Fushimi, "An Equivalence Relation Between Tausworthe and GFSR Sequences and Applications," *Appl. Math. Lett.*, *2*(2), 135–137 (1989).
41. M. Fushimi and S. Tezuka, "The *k*-Distribution of Generalized Feedback Shift Register Pseudorandom Numbers," *Commun. ACM*, *26*(7), 516–523 (1983).
42. T. G. Lewis and W. H. Payne, "Generalized Feedback Shift Register Pseudorandom Number Algorithm," *J. ACM*, *20*(3), 456–468 (1973).
43. J. P. R. Tootill, W. D. Robinson, and D. J. Eagle, "An Asymptotically Random Tausworthe Sequence," *J. ACM*, *20*, 469–481 (1973).
44. M. Matsumoto and Y. Kurita, "Twisted GFSR Generators II," *ACM Trans. Model. Computer Simul.*, *4*(3), 254–266 (1994).
45. J. Eichenauer-Herrmann, Inversive Congruential Pseudorandom Numbers: A Tutorial," *Int. Statist. Rev.*, *60*, 167–176 (1992).
46. J. Eichenauer-Herrmann, "Pseudorandom Number Generation by Nonlinear Methods," *Int. Statist. Rev.*, *63*, 247–255 (1995).
47. P. Hellakalek, "Inversive Pseudorandom Number Generators: Concepts, Results, and Links," in *Proceedings of the 1995 Winter Simulation Conference*, edited by C. Alexopoulos, K. Kang, W. R. Lilegdon, and D. Goldsman, IEEE Press, New York, 1995, pp. 255–262.
48. H. Niederreiter, "New Developments in Uniform Pseudorandom Number and Vector Generation," in *Monte Carlo and Quasi-Monte Carlo Methods in Scientific Computing*, edited by H. Niederreiter and P. J.-S. Shiue, Lecture Notes in Statistics No. 106, Springer-Verlag, Berlin, 1995, pp. 87–120.
49. P. L'Ecuyer, A. Compagner, and J.-F. Cordeau, "Entropy-Based Tests for Random Number Generators," unpublished (1996).
50. M. S. Stephens, "Tests Based on EDF Statistics," in *Goodness-of-Fit Techniques*, edited by R. B. D'Agostino and M. S. Stephens, Marcel Dekker, Inc., New York, 1986.
51. P. L'Ecuyer, J.-F. Cordeau, and R. Simard, "Close-Point Spatial Tests for Random Number Generators," unpublished (1997).
52. P. L'Ecuyer and T. Andres, "A Random Number Generator Based on the Combination of Four LCGs," *44*, 98–107 (1997).

PIERRE L'ECUYER

VIRTUAL REALITY IN DRIVING SIMULATION

INTRODUCTION

In the mass media, the concept of virtual reality is sometimes reduced to being a plausible fiction, an excuse for the exhibition of advanced technology, or a resource only useful and available for very specific applications. Our objective in this article is to present the evolution and the current status of driving simulation as an example of the rich set of techniques (e.g., database modeling and management or sensorial feedback) involved in most virtual reality projects. The following discussion regarding these techniques will include some of the solutions to the specific problems found in driving simulation that can be applied to other virtual reality areas.

Historic Profile: The Evolution of Driving Simulation Technology and Its Applications

The birth of driving simulation within the realm of a virtual reality environment, which can be broadly defined as an immersive and real-time interactive environment, can be dated to the early seventies when the Volkswagen company (1) developed the first driving simulator including a mobile platform and synthetic image generation.* During the first two decades of immersive driving simulators, their use and availability were limited to the largest car manufacturers—the only organizations which could afford such expensive equipment and technological investment. During the same period, mobile platforms, three-dimensional (3D) graphics systems, and mechanical simulation techniques were steadily evolving in parallel, frequently as an imitation of the technology widely used in flight simulators and mechanical engineering. The aim of driving simulators was focused on the vehicle itself. The key objective was to test the mechanical designs of vehicles in realistic driving conditions. For this reason, more attention was paid to the physical interaction between the car and the roadway than to behavioral elements.

The constraints of a small industrial and research market together with the high cost of the devices and the human resources required to create and maintain such simulators limited their application and, as a result, the evolution of specific technological solutions. However, two important developments broke this trend. One was the evolution of simulation technology itself which made possible less expensive mobile platforms, high-resolution projection systems, and—especially—the widespread use of 3D graphics, first in workstations and most recently in personal computers.

The second development that influenced the expansion of the field of driving simu-

---

*Other types of driving simulators are based on video recordings and include very simple interaction devices. This kind of simulator is often used in driver testing and evaluation, offering a different set of features and problems, but they cannot be considered as virtual reality applications, even in our weak sense.

lation was the rising interest in other types of applications. Major research institutions in the area of traffic and transport (VTI in Sweden, TRL in the United Kingdom, TRC in The Netherlands, INRETS in France, etc.) became more and more interested in the use of simulators to carry out behavioral research tasks and driver evaluation studies. At the same time, a new market for less expensive but still powerful simulators was opened; they were seen as a tool for training specialized drivers, such as those in the military and those who drive heavy vehicles. As a result, some simulator vendors and government agencies began to respond to this demand. As a consequence to these growing needs, the owners of the main simulation facilities, that is the vehicle manufacturers, were happy to rent or share their installations so they could be used for these new purposes. Since then, close joint development and technology transfer has been maintained between many research institutes, private simulation industries, and vehicle manufacturers (e.g., VTI—Volvo, Renaul—Autosim, or Ford—University of Iowa).

Quite recently, the new graphics hardware for personal computers and the availability of tools for 3D modeling, traffic simulation, and scenario control has made possible the development of PC-based simulators that maintain a quality that is acceptable in the education and training of nonprofessional drivers (2). Today, the variety of driving simulator owners and applications is continuously increasing and a combination of common growth and diversity characterizes the interaction between basic research and industrial approaches. A proof of current interest in this field is the celebration of specific conferences and seminars (for instance, the Driving Simulation Conference '96 in France, or the Workshop on Traffic Generation for Driving Simulation—Scenario '96—in Orlando, Florida), as well as the existence of specialized sessions dedicated to driving simulation in traditional conferences [International Training Equipment Conference (ITEC), Real Time Systems (RTS '96), International Conference on Traffic and Transport Psychology '96].

Present Challenges

In spite of the original similarities that the ground vehicle simulation shared with flight simulation, there have always been marked differences between the two, and it is these differences that represent the key challenges involved in many virtual reality applications. In flight simulation, aerodynamics can be reproduced by quite simple models and the response interval (the time between the pilot's actions and the effect on the plane motion) is measured in seconds or several tenths of a second. On the other hand, in ground vehicles, the physical contact between the tires and the asphalt causes an immediate response to any steering or braking action. In this situation, the driver perceives almost no time lag between his/her steering inputs and the vehicle motion, nor between visual variations in the road surface and its effect in the vehicle dynamics. Also, sound stimuli and scene features are tightly coupled. Thus, the real-time capabilities of the simulator (transport delay, update rate) must be increased. Visual displays must be refreshed at least 30 to 60 times per second, and the total response time should not exceed several miliseconds (3). This requirement not only has strong implications with regard to the graphics subsystem, but is also related to the mechanical dynamics simulation and the control of the system processes, including data acquisition and output of efectors.

The paradigmatic complexity of driving scenes makes it even more difficult to meet this requirement. In flight simulators, the long distance between the landscape objects and the pilot's viewpoint allows many details to be minimized. However, in driving simulation, especially in an urban environment, the visual details and the number of different objects present create a need for special data management techniques. But the complexity is not only in the graphics data describing the graphical properties of the objects but also in their behavior and relationships. A driving scene contains many objects (vehicles, pedestrians, traffic signs, and lights) that interact with the subject and among themselves, offering a good testbed for virtual environment control techniques. In certain applications, such as behavioral research, training, and learning, the simulation of these behavioral dynamics becomes crucial. Today, this has become a very active research field.

In flight simulation, the data structure required for visualization consists primarily of a representation of the terrain and other simple elements of the landscape, and these features can be generated quite easily from aerial and satellite photographs. By contrast, in driving simulation, the visual data structure required for displaying the scene is not the only part of the simulation database. In addition, a high-spatial-resolution surface description is required to compute vehicle dynamics, and path and roadway topology information is necessary to guide traffic simulation. Also, it is essential to include references to meaningful elements which play some behavioral role along with their visual representation (e.g., traffic lights and pedestrian crossways). All these elements and relationships constitute what is usually called a *correlated* data structure (4). The inherent complexity as well as the need to keep these data coherent makes it indispensable to use specific modeling tools capable of generating and managing driving scene data structures. In summary, the experience in driving simulation reveals that coupling visual and behavior-related data and its management procedures is an essential task if we want to build realistic virtual worlds. In the following section, some of the techniques that have been developed in response to these as well as other challenges will be presented in more detail.

DATABASE MODELING

Spatially Correlated Data Layers

The concept of "correlated databases" is the key to understanding both the problem of scene modeling for ground vehicle simulation, as well as the solutions provided. As can be seen in Figure 1, a simulation database must be conceived of as a set of related layers, among which the most commonly considered are the road network topology, the visual data, the path network and associated behavioral objects, and ground surface data. The different elements in each layer are linked by spatial relations, and usually each element is also connected to others at different levels which share the same position in the scene.

In conventional interactive 3D graphics applications, visual objects are organized in a conventional tree structure to optimize rendering costs through visibility checking and detail selection (5). This corresponds to the built-in graphics data structure provided by most of real-time rendering libraries such as IRIS Performer. This fact may lead one to think that the visual layer of the simulation database is not isomorphic to the other network-shaped ones. However, in a driving simulation application developed by the authors to reproduce urban environments (6), it has been shown that a good alternative in such highly sight-occluded scenarios is to group visual objects in a graphlike structure. When the rendering process is run, the location of the viewpoint within this scene graph is used as the starting point of a graph traversal. The graph is spanned, building a display list that can be used in conventional graphics libraries. The advantage of this technique

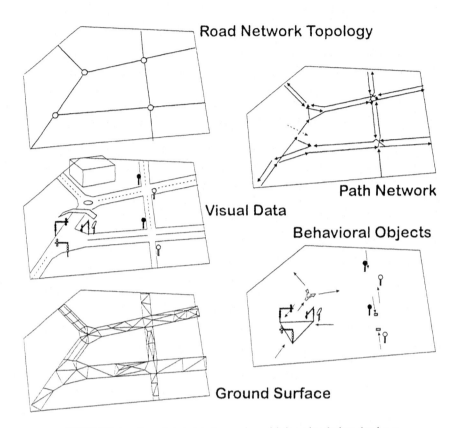

Road Network Topology

Path Network

Visual Data

Behavioral Objects

Ground Surface

FIGURE 1   Correlated data layers in a driving simulation database.

is that the object selection process is improved if it is initiated from the driver's view-point. In addition, this option allows the system to check interobject visibility. This kind of procedure has also been used in virtual environments which include architectural inte-rior visualization, in order to select the objects that would be seen along the line of sight, passing through any number of open doors.

Even if the visual layer is not organized in a graph structure for rendering purposes, the isomorphic relation to the spatial network structure of the other layers is important from the point of view of the modeling process, because the generation and modification of visual objects will be guided by the spatial relations and geometrical properties of logical elements.

The logical network layer is usually formed by two kinds of element, intersections and segments, which are connected in a graph.* The rest of the layers inherit the spatial

*Sometimes, the logical intersections and segments correspond directly to sections of the road surface, but other times, they are used in a more abstract sense to create a higher level of description. In this second sense, an intersection element in the graph could represent a complex road junction which is made up of many smaller sections, each of which—at the same time—may include subintersections and segments. In this way, even an entire city could be seen as an element in a graph representing the junction of several main roads.

connections already present in the road logical network or add new ones. For example, the path or lane graph must preserve the topology of the intersection–segment graph but can also introduce new information, as several consecutive lanes may be present within an intersection. We can see that the same object can be present in several layers of the structure but playing different roles. For instance, a traffic light can be represented at the same time as a visual object, as an entity that affects the vehicles following certain paths—to which the traffic light should be linked—and as a dynamic object whose state is probably related to other ones ruled by a behavior pattern.

Modeling Tools

This complex graph-oriented multilayer data structure can hardly be generated by using general-purpose geometry modeling tools (oriented to computer-aided design or to real-time visualization). Although the visual layer could be generated by means of this kind of software, further costly work would be needed to create the other layers and associate them to the visual data layer. This problem has been solved partially by some new modeling features included in tools that focus on the development of real-time simulation databases, such as the Road Tools module developed by the Multigen Software Company. However, the availability of such tools is still limited, and they lack the behavior-related information (e.g., path structures to guide intersection negotiation, traffic lights, and signs).

Another aim of the specific modeling tools that should meet the driving simulation requirements is to help the designer to reduce the cost of creating or modifying objects in the scene. The polygonal objects corresponding to the road surface must be created* using quality criteria (e.g., the greater the curvature of the surface, the greater the detail in the polygon meshes that are generated) and the tool must take care of computations such as those of texture coordinates. The program must include flexible and powerful algorithms for maintaining certain topology and geometry constraints during the design process. If the designer moves, for instance, the edge of a road segment, all elements attach to that point must be modified coherently (see Fig. 2).

A simulation database can extend through several square kilometers of landscape, including all road details, as well as the surrounding terrain where the road fits, houses, side "decoration," and cultural and natural features. Here, an important issue is the relationship between the road surface and the surrounding terrain. Some tools use external digital terrain data as a base to build a road that fits the ground elevation. A different approach, not as well studied, is the automatic generation of terrain data after the road design, so that the off-road surface may satisfy the previous constraints given by the road shape and other specifications† (see Fig. 3).

The generation of additional objects to complement the simulation environment can be accomplished by using automatic database population procedures. In the road tool developed by the authors, side decoration is added by stochastic processes using average and standard deviation parameters associated with attributes of road segments. For instance (see Fig. 4), blocks of houses are created along road segments of "urban" type

---

*In fact, for each road element, several levels of detail must be generated so that real-time control of the visual system load is possible.

†The designer can force the terrain to reach a certain height at a given point or to pass over a road segment to create a tunnel.

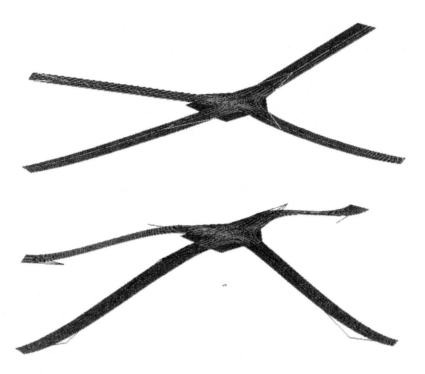

FIGURE 2   Example of automatic coherence maintenance in road design (while changing the height of an intersection).

FIGURE 3   Results of automatic generation of constrained terrain.

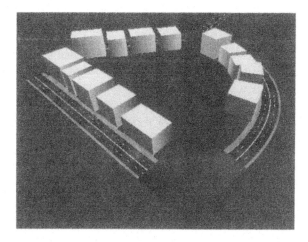

FIGURE 4   Automatic generation of side decoration (buildings).

with different heights, separations, widths, and textures depending on several subtypes. The designer can also control these parameters directly. Parks, trees, fences, and other elements can be created by similar procedures.

Other tools [like VUEMS (7)] permit the designer to build a virtual copy of real environments by introducing different kinds of information, provided by the urban planning or geographical information systems, in the program. In this way, scanned maps can be used as a background to model streets, buildings, and signs.

Segmentation of the Simulation Database

The amount of data required to describe a driving simulation scene is sometimes too large to be fully loaded in the main memory of the host computer. For this reason, it is necessary to be able to load into memory only the parts of the scene, with the appropriate detail representations, that are required at any given moment. To make this possible, we need an update mechanism that continuously checks the necessity and availability of different parts of the database, discarding from the main memory the ones that remain unused and loading from disk some others that are likely to be required and are still not present in the memory. Later in the following section, we will see how such a data management procedure works. In addition to the run-time management system, the modeling tool also has an important role to play here; it has to create a structure* in the database that makes this partition management possible and efficient, a task that would be too costly to be performed by other means. Some simulators use a simple spatial partition and load into memory only the nearest parts of the database (8), but this approach limits the area of the visible scene. A better solution is to have partitions of different granularity within the database, so that nearest parts of the database can be

---

*Some type of spatial partition. "Segmentation" or "pagination" are commonly used terms.

represented by pages containing visual objects with a higher level of detail, whereas the farthest parts require the run-time system to load pages with lower granularity.

The mentioned modeling tool includes such a segmented database generation. The simulation area is divided recursively into smaller and smaller rectangular areas (see Fig. 5). The terrain data and the visual objects—whose level of detail is adapted to the segment granularity—are assigned to those pages. A unique identification mechanism is required for visual objects associated to pages in order to guarantee that each one will be drawn only once although it has different representations attached to several pages.* To improve data reading efficiency in a conventional UNIX file system, it is convenient to store the whole database in a single file. One important feature of this file is that the data must be codified in memory-map mode (i.e., in the same binary form that will be directly recognized by the simulation processes), so that no data transformation is needed each time a new segment is loaded in memory. This means, taking the visual data as an example, that the internal run-time data structures of the graphics library or programmer-supplied code must have an exact correspondence in the file format, something that usually is not true in conventional applications. Another important feature, currently not supported by most visual data structures, is the use of relative references. The conven-

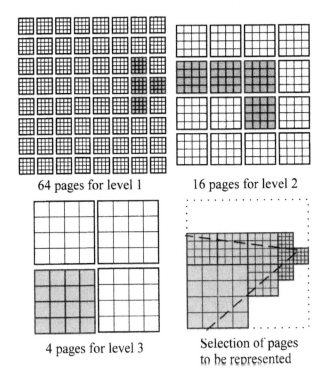

64 pages for level 1   16 pages for level 2

4 pages for level 3   Selection of pages
                             to be represented

FIGURE 5   Visual database segmentation based on area and detail.

---

*Because the same visual object could extend through the area of several database pages, it is included in all their visual trees.

tional use of references through memory addresses ("pointers" or "handlers") would make a transformation process necessary between file data and memory data, because the memory address references lose their meaning once the segment is discarded from memory* and must be recomputed each time the segment is loaded in memory. The use of relative references not only in the file but also in the memory structure avoid those computations.

DATA MANAGEMENT AND VISUALIZATION

Once the segmented database is generated, a run-time management procedure is required to ensure the availability of required data to all processes, especially to the visualization process. Some graphics libraries, like Silicon Graphics' IRIS Performer, provide simple mechanisms to modify data structures in memory while all processes keep running, using a specific process for database updates, but the programmer is still in charge of implementing the whole database management, which is not supported by conventional relational or object-oriented DBMSs. This type of page management system for real-time simulation has been also developed for some architectural visualization applications where the amount of visual data is really huge (9).

The authors devised such a system based on the use of quadtrees to define the pages required at each time step of the simulation (see Fig. 5) (10). An algorithm similar to the one which is used in cache memory management was used to remove unused pages. The algorithm uses several lists of pages that are loaded in memory before they are actually required. This preload is necessary in order to avoid the equivalent to "cache faults," when the system needs to load a new page that is suddenly required and this causes a noticeable decrease in the performance of other subsystems (e.g., the visual one). The different lists of pages correspond to decreasing the likelihood of these data segments to be needed in the near future. This probability is computed for each page depending on its membership in quadtrees that can be defined by points a certain distance away from the present viewpoint (see Fig. 6a), but in the case the vehicle is always moving on a roadway, the points where the observer can be most likely located the next time are downstream on this roadway (see Fig. 6b).

In order to minimize the computation required by this management task during run time, the modeling tool precomputes the quadtrees for a set of discrete areas where the viewpoint can be located and stores them in the scene file. This precomputation phase also allows the application of further optimization by eliminating pages from each quadtree that will not be seen due to the sight occlusion caused by the terrain or other objects.

Specific visualization methods can be required for immersive displays. Panoramic screen systems need to combine the output of at least three graphics channels (see Fig. 7), which sometimes conveys hardware or software border fading. Some manufacturers like SEOS Displays provide complete solutions for panoramic projection, including screens projectors and the necessary corrections and adjustments. Quality stereo view is possible using video projectors or monitors and shutter glasses. Also, more compact collimated projection systems have been commercialized using monitors and a mirror

---

*Of course, it is nonsense to store these pointers in the file because it is not guaranteed that the segment can occupy the same physical memory addresses again.

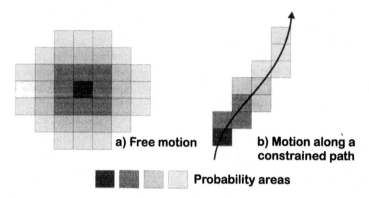

FIGURE 6   Selection of areas where the viewpoint is likely to move, from which required pages
and their probabilities must be computed to allow database page management.

system (Glass Mountain Optics) or large flat-screen retroprojectors (i.e., the ones by
Barco). Cheap solutions can be achieved by using video monitors (see Fig. 8).

In those systems, the views of real mirrors are simulated by additional graphics
channels projected onto properly located screens. If head-mounted displays are used, rear
mirror images must be integrated in the unique 3D synthetic scene view with the cockpit image. Several projecting and masking techniques can be used to perform this integration (6).

However, the use of head-mounted displays in driving simulator applications is up
to now limited. The main disadvantages that these devices convey come from the feeling
that they are still very uncomfortable (it is almost a torture to wear some of them for
more than a few minutes), they do not provide the required high-quality graphics resolu-

FIGURE 7   View of panoramic screen from the vehicle cockpit in the three-projector installation
at TRC in the University of Groningen.

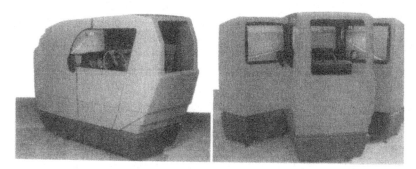

FIGURE 8   The Rousseau Driving Simulator uses video monitors for display.

tion, and the head orientation tracking devices have a significant delay. It is also difficult to make the synthetic view of the vehicle compatible with the real cockpit with which the driver is in physical contact. On the other hand, the cost of those display devices and the required space is clearly smaller than the ones of panoramic screens and high-quality video projectors, providing an inexpensive and compact 360° field-of-view solution. The depth perception that can be also obtained in video projectors systems by using stereo glasses could provide additional realism during the driving task. However, so far, the literature does not mention any experiment devised to test the role of depth perception.

Head-mounted displays have been mainly used in vehicle interior design and ergonomics test applications,* as well as to increase the feeling in accident simulations to show the effectiveness of passive safety systems (e.g., the passive safety demonstration of Volvo). However, some interesting applications have been developed, even using low-cost personal computers (11). The authors believe that helmets can be a good solution (once the technology has progressed to acceptable resolution and comfort) for urban environments, where the surroundings, mostly at intersections, make a special demand on the driver's attention (see Fig. 9). Currently, an integrated system that includes a dual helmet–screen display system with a light mobile electropneumatic platform is being developed.

OTHER SENSORIAL RESTITUTIONS

An important part of the information that the driver receives while driving comes from the perception of forces and vibrations in the steering wheel and inertial forces acting on his/her body. Usually, the forces on the steering wheel are simulated, depending on the driving speed and angle, although real driving situations are much more complex. Something similar happens with vehicle dynamics. The interaction between the road surface of variable roughness and the tires is a very active line of research and some models have been devised for real-time simulation (12). The computation of nonlinear equations

---

*General Motors is using a CAVE system, based on stereo video projection in a room with translucent walls, to visualize and test the car interior design.

FIGURE 9   View of an urban scenario in the head-mounted display version of the SIRCA driving simulator.

deduced from these models that achieve the desired performance is difficult in the case of multibody vehicles, like articulated trucks and military vehicles. The present lines of research include the use of parallel and distributed architectures as well as automatic equation-solving code generation from the specifications of the physical system (13).

After the correct vehicle position, speed, and acceleration are computed, there is still the problem of making the driver perceive them in the virtual reality environment. The acceleration acting on the driver* cannot be simulated by the actual inertial acceleration of the simulator cockpit, as it is usually standing on a platform with very limited lateral displacement.† The usual approach is to simulate the lateral accelerations by inclining the cockpit so the gravitational forces make the driver feel an acceleration toward the desired direction. The problem in driving simulation‡ is that although the driver has no external reference to infer the inclination, if the turning speed is high, then he or she can feel (thanks to the sense of balance) the motion as an actual turn more than as the desired lateral acceleration. This is the reason why the acceleration values are commonly scaled down, so the driver feels a smaller force but the possibility of confusion with a turn is decreased.

Another major advancement in hardware technology related to driving simulation is the emergence of newer motion base systems which provide reliable motion cues with three or six degrees of freedom. These recently developed mobile platforms are smaller, less expensive, and less noisy. Most of them (Fokker Control Systems, Moog Inc.) are based on electrical actuators, so that they do not need hydraulical pumping devices.

---

*Due to inertial forces when the vehicle speeds up, brakes, turns, or suffers the effect of surface irregularities.

†Some of the newest simulators, like the Daimler-Benz one or the projected National Driving Simulator facility in the University of Iowa, include a track on which the mobile platform is mounted so that real lateral accelerations can be reproduced. There are still some other limitations concerning the direction and duration of such an acceleration.

‡Unlike what happens in flight simulators, where the accelerations may be higher but its changes are slower.

These new actuators are cleaner and require simpler maintenance, although the supported payload is usually smaller than conventional hydraulics systems* (see Fig. 10).

Even with reliable dynamics simulation, motion cues and proper coordination with the visual systems, the intrinsic limitations of computer simulation are revealed by the fact that a significant percentage (around 20%) of drivers feel simulation sickness. The factors that produce this effect are difficult to determine and are also related in a complex manner (14). Some experiments have demonstrated that high-fidelity dynamics simulation or high-resolution graphics can either reduce, increase, or maintain the sickness, depending on other (not very well defined) variables.

The last piece of sensorial information that must not be forgotten is sound restitution. The driver obtains additional data regarding the speed of the vehicle from the sounds and vibrations he/she feels, and some information concerning the relative direction and speed of other vehicles is taken from the Doppler shift in their sounds.† Sound provides information about the type of environment (the sound the driver perceives also changes depending on surrounding obstacles). A sampler (a kind of synthetizer) that allows the sound output system to mix and shift the frequency of real base sounds (samples) is commonly used to generate quite realistic stereo sounds. However, conventional stereo does not provide precise directional information. This effect can be achieved by special virtual reality hardware with very limited features. Even more difficult and costly is the simulation of the reflection and dispersion effects that occur in real environments.

EXPERIMENTAL DESIGN AND SCENARIO CONTROL

It was pointed out earlier that the variety of driving simulator uses has been greatly increased recently. Its use in behavioral experiments is one of the most significant new

FIGURE 10 An example of a large payload driving simulator using a hydraulics motion base, the Iowa Driving Simulator (IDS) at the University of Iowa.

---

*However, electric motion systems can now reach payloads as high as 6000 kg.

†This is why some road safety researchers warn against sound isolation and high-volume music in today's cars.

areas of application, producing a rising interest in research and development of new techniques that will aid in the design of these simulation experiments. Experimental design tools must cover a wide variety of situations and aims; an experiment oriented toward the measurement of perception capabilities will have different requirements than another devised to test how the subject learns to overtake correctly. Another important issue that has to be addressed by the designer is the control of the conditions in which the experiment is going to be performed (the change of a traffic light, the sudden appearance of an unexpected vehicle, the change in surface or weather conditions, etc.). These features fall within the concept of scenario control.

Currently, there are no commercial tools which allow the researcher to fully design and execute the experiment without any computer programming. However, there have been several research developments oriented toward solving this problem. At the Traffic Research Centre in Haren, The Netherlands, a specific language called Scenario Specification Language (SSL) (15) has been developed, which permits the researcher to design an experimental environment including traffic characteristics, change of traffic lights, data sampling and storage, and so forth. After the codification of the experiment using this high-level language, an interpreter evaluates and executes the scenario commands in real time. This approach is easier than direct codification in a common programming language, but some programming skills are still needed by the experiment designer to create the scenario.

The authors have developed an automatic traffic generator and a simple scenario control tool (see Fig. 11). The scenario modeling tool not only creates the visual database

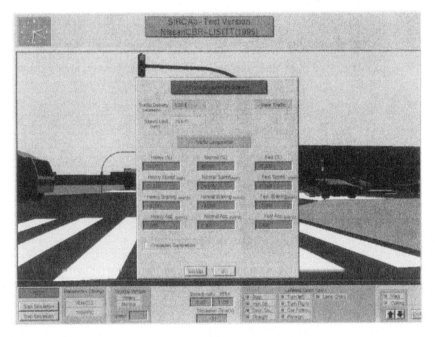

FIGURE 11   Interface of Scenario Control Tool developed by the authors and used at the Nissan CBR laboratory.

but also includes path description and information regarding the dynamics of traffic lights. The experiment designer can use a graphical user interface to specify the parameters for the environment ("ambient") traffic (density, average speed, percentage of heavy vehicles, etc.). The tool also allows the researcher to introduce some special vehicles that can be controlled directly during the experiment run time to force the driver to perform a specific task or to respond to certain situations. This tool is being used at the Nissan Cambridge Basic Research Center in Boston to evaluate new automatic driving devices as well as to perform basic cognitive experiments (16). Figure 12 shows a view of the Nissan CBR simulation cockpit.

Other interesting work in scenario control and authoring tools has been carried out at the University of Iowa. Their approach is based on the use of hierarchical concurrent state machines (HCSM) that provide a natural framework for programming and directing the behavior of synthetic entities in interactive simulation environments (17). In the Iowa Driving Simulator (IDS), an authoring tool allows the researcher to create path information and to associate objects such as passenger vehicles, trucks, bicycles, and pedestrians (18). Each object class includes a set of built-in procedures called behavior modification options (BMOs) (for instance, changing lane or desired speed). These procedures can be instantiated and coordinated by high-level coordination entities that act as a kind of "choreographer" in the scenario.

TRAFFIC MODELS

The generation of both autonomous intelligent traffic and vehicles with predefined behavior has become an important topic in recent years. These are examples of the kinds of problem that need to be solved when defining the dynamics and behavior of interrelated objects in a virtual environment. As we mentioned earlier, the first driving simulators belonged to the large car manufacturers and their main aim was to test vehicle performance, so, generally, the surrounding traffic was not relevant for the purpose of the experiment. In those cases when some other vehicles were included in the simulation, their behavior was very simple; in most examples, the vehicles followed predefined

FIGURE 12   View of the Nissan CBR driving simulator where eye motion can be tracked.

paths. A simple reactive traffic model could be designed by using some control parameters or events (like traffic light changes) to trigger the predefined vehicle (19).

When the use of the simulators was extended to road safety experimentation and learning applications, the complexity of the traffic generation and control grew accordingly. The base for such new traffic models was provided by traffic engineering and robotics. In these areas, work in the field of traffic mobilization had already started in the early 1960's, focused on traffic analysis and autonomous mobile robots. However, these methods must be modified in order to be included in a driving simulator. The new needs come from the requirement of a real-time response and coordination of traffic behavior, as well as from the visual quality and perceived behavior realism demanded by the application.

There are two main approaches to computer traffic generation. On the one hand, it is possible to perform a macroscopic simulation based on state equations of the system, the relations followed by fundamental variables such as speed, flow, and density (20). In this case, we obtain, as a result, the description of the global state of the traffic in the simulated road network. On the other hand, we can use the microscopic approach, based on behavior models for the elementary objects in the traffic system—the vehicles. Vehicle behavior is characterized by motion equations containing quantitative (with different values for each vehicle) and qualitative influence from elements in the environment, such as traffic lights and signals. This system provides a description of the movements of every vehicle in the network. Of course, it is also possible to obtain information about the global state of the network by adding the contribution of each vehicle. The presentation of a microscopic system aimed at traffic engineering can be found in Ref. 21.

Because the output of the macroscopic approach only contains information about the global state of the traffic, it is not useful for the purpose of a realistic visual simulation, in which the position of each vehicle must be defined. For this reason, traffic microsimulation is the methodology used in the creation of traffic models for driving simulation. Nevertheless, in some cases, it is a good idea to combine the two approaches: Macrosimulation can provide a general road network state coherence and microsimulation computes the position of the vehicles in a limited area within the whole network. In this way, the performance of the system, as well as the final visual appearance, is improved. The authors have developed an automatic traffic generation system based on this approach. An image of the latest version of the SIRCA simulator is shown in Figure 13.

In addition to the previous considerations, in the field of psychology and human factors research, the driving task has been understood as consisting of three levels: strategic, tactical, and operational (22). At the highest (strategic) level, a route is planned and goals are determined. At the intermediate (tactical) level, maneuvers are selected to achieve short-term objectives (this includes decisions such as passing a vehicle that is blocking the road). At the lowest level, these maneuvers are translated into steering, throttle, and brake commands. This way of understanding the driving task makes a layer-oriented approach the most appropriate to tackle the problem of simulating realistic traffic behavior in a driving simulator. The most critical levels from the visual simulation point of view are the tactical and the operational ones, as their simulation should provide the required realism in the visual appearance of the traffic surrounding the human driver.

Several models have been used to solve the specific problems of autonomous traffic in driving simulators. However, it is interesting to point out that all of these approaches can be combined to generate higher-quality output and each one presents its own advantages and drawbacks. In the following paragraphs, we will present a short summary of

FIGURE 13   Visual output of traffic simulation in the latest version of the SIRCA simulator.

the most useful ones as a sample of the different techniques that can be used to achieve object behavior in virtual environments.

Rule-Based Systems

This traditional artificial intelligence approach tries to translate human expert knowledge into production or decision rules. The vehicle model is usually implemented in the form of *if–then* clauses. The *if* condition (the "precondition") is a function of the state of the vehicles and the environment, and the *then* part consists of a set of actions performed to change the vehicle parameters (15). These sentences can also be translated into finite-state machines or more advanced hierarchical-state machines (17). The main drawback of the classical ruled-based systems is that the preconditions must match exactly, so the firing of a rule is often sensitive to ad hoc thresholds, producing undesired discontinuity effects in the behavior of the vehicles. A second problem is that the set of rules is very difficult to maintain and modify incrementally. A small change can often have global repercussions.

Fuzzy Logic

This approach is based on the insight that linguistic categories are not absolutely clear-cut (for instance, a car does not become a "slow car" once its speed drops below some magic threshold). The use of linguistic labels as possible values for the variables allows an approximate match between the input data and the precondition of the rules, so the problem of exact matching is avoided. Now, the expression of the rules look almost like natural reasoning. For example, a rule for the car-following behavior may be stated as

> if *my speed* is "slow" and the *car ahead* is "far enough away," then accelerate.

In such systems, knowledge is acquired in a symbolic way, but is computed internally as quantitative values by using the membership functions which assign a numerical correspondence between continuous variables and lingüistic labels. The final action resulting from the fuzzy rules has to be "defuzzified" to give a numerical output. The main problem with this method is the selection of membership functions.

The authors have developed a car-following fuzzy reasoning system (23) and are now involved in the development of an automatic traffic generator based on a whole fuzzy-based reasoning system. Other authors have already proposed fuzzy rules for other manouvers, such as lane changing (24).

Probabilistic and Hidden Markov Models

This approach is based on the fact that vehicle behavior is uncertain. This is because we usually do not have information about each driver's goals and how the vehicles affect each other. It is possible to define a set of states for each vehicle and generate a probabilistic function that provides the next most likely action from an initial state, based on the current traffic context. This type of model is known generically as a Markov model. This approach is quite elegant, but it has the problem of undefined initial assignation of probabilities. A possible solution is to initialize each state transition with a priori values, and, later, these probabilities can be adjusted iteratively by studying its observed actions.

A more powerful approach, based on the analysis of real drivers' behavior, has been developed at the Nissan Cambridge Research Center jointly with the authors. In this approach the driving actions can be modeled as a sequence of internal mental states, each of which has its own characteristic set of interstate transition probabilities (16). The behavior (the output associated with each state) is also determined by probabilistic rules. This variation in the probabilistic model is known as a hidden Markov model (HMM). In this model the driving actions can be broken into a long chain of simpler subactions. A lane change, for instance, may consist of the following steps: a preparatory task to center the car in the current lane, an exploring task to look around to make sure the adjacent lane is clear, a steering task to initiate the lane change, the change itself, a new steering task to complete the lane change, and a final recentering of the car. Once we have represented the sequence of steps within each action statistically, we will be able to generate a driver model based on these basic sequences. The time evolution of the vehicles will be driven by the input parameters, which will produce the change of internal states in each autonomous driver and the corresponding output variables which describe its trajectory.

It is necessary to stress that the generation of traffic by any of the previously described models needs to be compatible with the scenario control system and the experimental designs that were mentioned earlier. This is currently one of the main topics in the field of driving simulation research. Finally, it is also interesting to mention that the final visual appearance of the traffic has to be very carefully managed. In the same way that we have described the use of detail levels in the geometric representation of the visual environment, different levels of accuracy in the description of vehicle behavior can be selected based on the distance from the human-driven vehicle.

CONCLUSIONS

We have seen how the problems associated with driving simulation have generated a set of techniques and solutions to database generation and management, sensorial restitution, and object behavior definition and control. As a consequence, knowledge of most of these techniques is required in order to successfully integrate a useful application in any of the areas where driving simulation is now used. The problems and solutions that we have presented here are examples of those that can be found in many virtual reality applications.

REFERENCES

1. "Ein dynamischer Fahrsimulator zur Untersuchung des Systems Fahrer-Fahrzeug-Strasse," *Zeitschr. Verkehrsich., 22* (1976).
2. M. Kergall, "The Rousseau Simulator, a Tool for Driving Training," in *Proceedings of Driving Simulation Conference in Real Time Systems '94.* January 12, 1994.
3. S. Nordmark, "Driving Simulators, Trends and Experiences," in *Proceedings of Driving Simulation Conference in Real Time Systems '94.* January 12, 1994.
4. D. F. Evans, "Correlated Database Generation for Driving Simulators," in *Proceedings de IMAGE VI Conference,* 1992.
5. J. D. Foley et al., *Computer Graphics: Principles and Practice,* Addison-Wesley, Reading, MA, 1991, Chap. 12.
6. S. Bayarri, M. Fernández, and M. Perez, "Virtual Reality in Driving Simulation," *Communi. ACM, 39*(5) (1996).
7. S. Donikian, "Driving Simulation in Realistic Urban Environments," in *Proceedings of Scenario '96: Workshop on Traffic Generation for Driving Simulation.* December 6–7, 1996.
8. S. Falby et al., "NPSNET: Hierarchical Data Structures for Real-Time Three-Dimensional Visual Simulation," *Computer Graphics, 17*(1), 65–69.
9. T. A. Funkhouser, "Database and Display Algorithms for Interactive Visualization of Architectural Models," Ph.D thesis. Department of Computer Science. University of California, Berkeley (1993).

10. S. Bayarri et al., "Virtual Reality Techniques in Urban Simulation," in *International Training Equipment Conference ITEC '96*, April 16–18, 1996.

11. O. H. Levine and R. R. Mourant, "A Driving Simulator Based on Virtual Environments Technology," *74th Annual Meeting of the Transportation Research Board*, January 1995, Paper No. 950269.

12. D. R. Turpin, "Application of High-Fidelity Surface Tire Force Models in Real-Time Simulation," in *Proceedings of Driving Simulation Conference '95*, Teknea, 1995.

13. S. Detalle et al., "Automatic Equation Generation for Real-Time Dynamic Vehicle Models on SARA Project," in *Proceedings of Driving Simulation Conference '95*, Teknea, 1995.

14. R. S. Kennedy, "Simulator Sickness: Relationship of Different Symptoms to Equipment Configuration and Safety," *Proceedings of Driving Simulation Conference '95*, Teknea, 1995.

15. P. C. van Wolffelaar and W. van Winsum, "A New Driving Simulator Including an Interactive Intelligent Traffic Environment," *3rd International Conference on Vehicle Navigation & Information Systems (VNIS)*. September 1992.

16. A. Pentland and A. Liu, "Towards Augmented Control Systems," in *Proceedings of Intelligent Vehicles '95*, September 1995.

17. M. Cremer, J. Kearney, and P. Willemsen, "A Directable Vehicle Behavior Model for Virtual Driving Environments," in *Proceedings of 1996 Conference on AI, Simulation, and Planning in High Autonomy Systems*, March 1996.

18. Y. Papelis, "Graphical Authoring of Complex Scenarios Using High Level Coordinators," in *Proceedings of Scenario '96: Workshop on Traffic Generation for Driving Simulation*, December 6–7, 1996.

19. M. Kergall, "Traffic Generation in Drive-Learning Context," in *Proceedings of Second Seminar on Traffic Generation for Driving Simulation*, December 13, 1994.

20. F. Toledo et al., "Qualitative Simulation in Urban Traffic Control: Implementation of Temporal Features," in M. G. Singh and L. Travé-Massuyés, *Decision Support Systems and Qualitative Reasoning* edited by Elsevier Science Publishers, Amsterdam, 1991.

21. P. G. Gipps, "MULTSIM: A Model for Simulating Vehicular Traffic on Multilane Arterial Roads," *Math. Computers Simul.*, *28*, 291–295 (1986).

22. J. Michon, "A Critical View of Driver Behaviour Models: What Do We Know, What Should We Do?, in *Human Behaviour and Traffic Safety*, edited by L. Evans and R. Schwing, Plenum Press, New York, 1995.

23. M. Fernández, A. Liu, S. Bayarri, and A. Pentland, "Tuning of Driver Behaviour Models Used in Driving Simulation," *First International Conference on Traffic & Transport Psychology ICTTP '96*, May 22–25, 1996.

24. N. Bourbia and S. Espié, "Modelisation Floue du Dépassement," in *Proceedings of Driving Simulation Conference '95*, Teknea, 1995.

SALVADOR BAYARRI

MARCOS FERNÁNDEZ

INMACULADA COMA